It's
Christmas
Time
at the Movies

Robert Mitchum in *Holiday Affair* (Photofest)

It's
Christmas
Time
at the
Movies

by *Gary J. Svehla and Susan Svehla*

with additional contributions by:
Cindy Ruth Collins, Robert A. Crick, Joe Indusi,
Leonard J. Kohl, Steve Kronenberg, Bob Madison, Lorne Marshall,
Michael H. Price, David H. Smith, Don G. Smith and John Stell

Midnight Marquee Press, Inc.
Baltimore, Maryland

Acknowledgments

This book would not have been possible without the help of many people. Special thanks to everyone who helped locate photographs for the book: Jim Doherty, Joe Indusi, Lenny Kohl, Jerry Ohlinger's Movie Material, Lorne Marshall, Photofest, Steve Sally, Steve Sally, Jr. and especially Eric Caidin (one of the nicest people in the world). Thanks to Eric Hoffman for his help in locating some rare films and to Fred Olen Ray for a copy of his latest film *Secret Santa*. And thank you to our proofreaders: Betty Cavanaugh, Wayne Shipley and Linda J. Walter who always manage to make the impossible deadlines we work under. Special thanks to classic movie cable channels American Movie Classics and Turner Classic Movies. Without their dedication to keeping classic cinema alive, this book wouldn't have been possible.

For more information about Midnight Marquee Press, Inc. titles write to:

Midnight Marquee Press, Inc.

9721 Britinay Lane

Baltimore, MD 21234

or visit our website at www.Midmar.com

Cover Design: A.S. Miller
White Christmas cover photo © Paramount, 1954
Mrs. Santa Claus back cover photo © Hallmark Home Entertainment, 1996
Photographs from Walt Disney, Buena Vista and Touchstone © Walt Disney Productions

ISBN 1-887664-19-X
Library of Congress Catalog Card Number 98-65678
Manufactured in the United States of America
Printed by Kirby Lithographic Company, Arlington, VA
First Printing by Midnight Marquee Press, Inc., October, 1998

Dedication

*For my mother, Aurelia Miller, who made Christmas so special for her rowdy six-pack of children;
to the memory of my father, Melvin Miller, who gave me such inspiration;
to my brothers John and Dan and sisters Jean, Sharon and Becky
for bringing fun and excitement to those happy Christmases of my youth;
to my grandma Erma Palm, and finally,
to my husband Gary, who brought the joy of Christmas back into my life .
—Susan Svehla*

*To three special Christmases—1957-1959—when Christmas meant going to bed early,
waking up at 5 a.m., sneaking quietly out into the living room area to find that, quite magically,
a fully decorated Christmas tree had appeared surrounded by mountains of presents.
Those three Christmases—when I was seven, eight and nine—have lingered with me ever since.
Every other holiday, every other Christmas, is measured by the excitement and joy of those three Christmases.
To my parents, who made all my Christmases magical,
and to my wife Sue, who continues the magic of keeping that little boy alive inside, all my love.
—Gary J. Svehla*

Table of Contents

They're going steady... straight to your heart!

LIBERTY FILMS, Inc. presents

FRANK CAPRA'S wonderfilm...

"It's a Wonderful Life"

starring JAMES STEWART AMERICA'S FAVORITE FELLER...

and DONNA REED

Table of Contents

A Christmas Carol, 1938 (Photofest)

Welcome to It's Christmas Time at the Movies.

Each Christmas we shamelessly wallow in sweet sentiment brought to us courtesy of Hollywood, a glittering Tinsel Town filled with holiday spirit.

It wouldn't seem like Christmas if we didn't spend some quality time with Jimmy Stewart and the folks of Bedford Falls or the March sisters—Jo, Beth, Meg and Amy. Scrooge is always a welcome guest in our home during the festive season, as well as newcomers such as the seemingly cursed but eternally optimistic Clark Griswold in "National Lampoon's Christmas Vacation" and Ralphie and his quest for a BB gun in the seminal "A Christmas Story," a film that has justifiably attained classic Christmas status.

Our love of Christmas movies goes back to our childhood as many of the chapters in this volume relate. Christmas is our favorite time of year, a time people seem a little friendlier, children more closely resemble angels and family ties are a little more important. We decided it was time we share our love of the season and our favorite Christmas movies with other holiday cinema fans. You hold the results in your hands.

When we began this book, we had no idea how many films are centered on Christmas. Unfortunately, due to limited space and the unavailability of obscure titles, we weren't able to include many films in this volume. But like many Christmas movies, there could always be a sequel.

Merry Christmas and may your journey though these pages provide you with many happy returns.
Susan Svehla

I'll Be Home for Christmas...

Few things are more important during the holiday season than the love and support of your family—whether man or beast (in the case of Babe). This chapter delves into the foibles and follies, the love and compassion, and the smiles and tears that bring people closer together, especially during Christmas.

***Little Women*, 1948 (Photofest)**

Meet Me in St. Louis

1944

It's difficult to know where to begin discussing *Meet Me in St. Louis*. Do we start with the stunning sets shown in glorious Technicolor that helped create the richness and beauty of the early 1900s? Or perhaps the Academy Award nominated cinematography by George Folsey as we marvel at his use of light and camera angles. Of course there is the sure direction of MGM wunderkind Vincente Minnelli whose work on *Cabin in the Sky* would lead him to the welcoming streets of St. Louis for this classic film. And then there is a stellar cast consisting of Mary Astor, Leon Ames, Marjorie Main, Lucille Bremer (whom MGM was grooming for stardom), Tom Drake, Harry Davenport and the scene–stealing Margaret O'Brien as Tootie. Let's not forget the outstanding score that featured songs such as the Academy Award nominated "The Trolly Song" as well as The Boy Next Door" and "Under the Bamboo Tree." Or should we begin with the fabulous Judy Garland who was never more beautiful and appealing than in this film?

Each viewing of this filmic wonder leaves one longing for those glorious days when life was polite, elegant and simple, and the biggest worry the loving Smith family had was leaving their beloved St. Louis for the frightening New York.

The film was based on a series of stories by Sally Benson that appeared in *The New Yorker*. Benson was also a talented screenwriter who co-wrote *Anna and the King of Siam, The Farmer Takes a Wife* and *Shadow of a Doubt*.

Arthur Freed and Minnelli were convinced of the charm of the film, but their lead wasn't so sure she wanted to take a step backward by playing another teenager. At 21 Judy Garland was already an old pro. She had just completed *Presenting Lilly Mars,* a role she considered her first grown-up part. Freed prevailed and Judy, however reluctant, was to star.

The story revolves around a year in the life of the Smith family and their misgivings about moving to New York when their father (Leon Ames) is promoted. The family is also in a tizzy over the romantic relationships of oldest daughter Rose (Bremer), 17-year-old Esther (Garland) and brother Lon (Henry Daniels, Jr.).

Meet Me in St. Louis occurs throughout four seasons. The Christmas vignette highlights the family spending their last bittersweet Christmas in St. Louis. As the scene opens the children are outside building a family of snowpeople. Rose and Lon, neither having dates for the big Christmas Eve dance, begin arguing and eventually are convinced to go together. Esther is a bit smug since she has a date with her handsome boy-next-door John (Tom Drake). Little Tootie, an endearing five-year-old with a delightful sense of the macabre, has already dug up her dead dolls from their graves in the backyard and readied them for their trip to New York. The sisters prepare for their dance deciding they must be particularly outstanding for they plan to monopolize all the attractive young men so Lucille Ballard (June Lockhart) and her date Warren Sheffield (Robert Sully) will be suitably jealous. Warren is Rose's beau who has not proposed to her yet and, as Esther notes in the beginning of the film, "she's not getting any younger you know." Meanwhile, Lon is pining for Lucille. As Esther primps, John arrives to announce sorrowfully his tuxedo is locked in the tailors and he can't escort Esther. She sheds unhappy tears until her grandpa (Harry Davenport) comes to the rescue and squires her to the ball.

Garland's wardrobe has never been more suitable to her. The red velvet gown she wears to the dance is a thing of beauty enhancing her girl-next-door loveliness. Rarely has a more Christmasy pair been seen as Esther stands beside Rose, who is wearing an appropriately green gown. In his autobiography *I Remember It Well*, Vincente Minnelli notes how Technicolor advisor Natalie Kalmus kept telling him he couldn't have red and green in a scene. Minnelli notes, "I had enough faith in the technology of the time to assume the camera wouldn't distort the colors, as it picked up the movement of the costumes under the constantly changing lights." Minnelli couldn't have been more correct; the sequence with the sisters in their Christmas finery is a visual delight.

Esther has taken the liberty of filling out Lucille's dance card, managing to find every pathetic bachelor at the dance. But the tables are turned when Lucille announces that Warren would rather be with Rose and she pairs up with Lon—leaving Esther the unpleasant task of changing dance cards and heroically taking the dances she had mischievously lined up for the unsuspecting Lucille.

Grandpa rescues Esther, whirling her behind a huge Christmas tree to the strains of "Auld Lang Syne" and, lo-and-behold, out she dreamily waltzes with John who has managed to get to the ball.

After the festivities John and Esther stand beneath a tree outside her house. Garland has never looked more lovely as a sparkly scarf covers her auburn hair and the camera seems to adore her. John has asked her to marry him to which she tearfully agrees, but the much-too-young couple soon decide that is a mistake and perhaps they can still carry on their relationship even if she is in New York.

As Esther climbs the stairs to her room, she hears music coming from Tootie's bedroom. The little girl is curled up on a window seat playing her music box and waiting for Santa Claus. She asks Esther if Santa has been there yet and how he will find her next year. A light shines through the window and we expect to see Santa, but it is only John in his neighboring room. He slowly pulls down the shade. Shadows fall softly on Esther as she comforts Tootie who tells her she is taking everything to New York, even her dead dolls. She can take everything but her snowpeople Esther replies, "We'd look pretty silly trying to get them on the train!" The tot giggles and then sorrowfully looks out at the snowy creations. The sisters sit before a window staring at the snowpeople as Garland heart-breakingly sings "Have Yourself a Merry Little Christmas" to Tootie. Although the lyrics of the song are not sad, Garland's rendition of this holiday treasure rarely leaves a dry eye in the house. The song and Judy Garland brilliantly manage to compress all the confusing feelings of Christmas into a few short stanzas—the love, happiness, sadness and longing for perfection.

As viewers are sniffling into their hankies, Tootie, sobbing, runs from the house and begins to destroy the snowpeople. Esther runs after her, soothing the hysterical child. From above the camera looks down on the pair, Tootie in her white nightgown almost blending into the landscape and Esther's brilliant red dress flowing over the blanket of snow. Father sees this from the upstairs window, calls the family downstairs and announces they will not be leaving for New York. Instead, they are staying right here in St. Louis. Warren rushes in to propose to Rose, presents are opened and a merry Christmas is had by all.

Mary Astor, Leon Ames and Margaret O'Brien would reunite as a family in 1949's *Little Women*. *Meet Me in St. Louis* would be the film debut of lovely Lucille Bremer who would go on to become one of Fred Astaire's most talented partners in *Yolanda and the Thief* and *Ziegfeld Follies*. However, even with the stellar casting of *Meet Me in St. Louis*, the film belongs to little Margaret O'Brien and Judy Garland.

O'Brien is mesmerizing as little Tootie, who ghoulishly gives her dolls fatal diseases and happily buries them in the backyard. In his autobiography Minnelli relates how Margaret couldn't get worked up enough for the snowpeople scene. Her mother and aunt would whisper to her before her dramatic scenes, but that night she was angry at her mother, who told Minnelli he would have to get Margaret to cry:

"'But how?' I asked. 'She has little dog,' her mother replied. 'You'll have to say someone is going to kill that dog.' ...I could see Margaret sitting inside the house, a blanket wrapped around her shoulders. It was a bitterly cold night. She looked expectantly at me. I braced myself, then walked over to her. 'Margaret... There's this little dog... and somebody is going to take a gun... and shoot it.' Her eyes got even larger. 'Is there going to be lots of blood?' 'Yes,' I answered... and the dog is going to suffer terribly,' I heard my sinister voice saying. 'AND THE DOG IS GOING TO DIE!' 'Oh no,' Margaret said in a tiny voice. Her tears started flowing. I turned to the assistant director. 'Turn them!' She did the scene in one take... mercifully for me... and went skipping happily off the set. I went home feeling like a monster."

In her biography of Judy Garland, Anne Edwards notes that Judy was broke at the beginning of the film and needed to work, although she didn't want to face another lavish musical. Garland, after seeing the performance Minnelli drew from her, grew to trust the director and they were later married in 1945. Their daughter Liza was born in 1946 and would appear at the ripe old age of two in another holiday film, *In the Good Old Summertime*.

Judy Garland faced many personal demons, but they were nowhere to be seen in her magnificent performance as Esther. It is one of the highlights of her film career.

Judy Garland and Tom Drake in *Meet Me in St. Louis*. (Photofest)

In *Meet Me in St. Louis*, Tootie (Margaret O'Brien), sobbing, runs from the house and begins to destroy the snowpeople. Esther (Garland) runs after her, soothing the hysterical child.

The motion picture was nominated for several Academy Awards including Screenplay and Scoring but came up empty-handed. The big winners of 1944 would be *Going My Way* and *Wilson*. However, Margaret O'Brien received a special miniature Oscar for outstanding child actress, joining the ranks of child stars such as Shirley Temple and Judy Garland.

Meet Me in St. Louis was released by MGM in November of 1944. *Variety*'s review read, "*Meet Me in St. Louis* is the answer to any exhibitor's prayer. Perhaps accented in these days as ideal 'escapist' film fare, it would be surefire in any period. It holds everything for the film fan." Or as *The New York Times* noted, "...it is a ginger-peachy show." And so it is.
—SS

Little Women

1918, 1933, 1949, 1978, 1994

In 1868 Louisa May Alcott earned a place in the heart of any young woman who has ever picked up a copy of the endearing novel detailing the four loving March sisters coming of age. That novel was, of course, *Little Women*, whose irresistibly warmhearted Christmas scenes have earned the film versions a place in this volume.

I remember discussing Christmas with my mother, and she sadly remembers a Yuletide when we received only one small present each. While this still caused her a tinge of sorrow many years later, my brothers and sisters and I don't remember any Christmas not overflowing with gifts and love. As we grow older, we realize the spirit and best memories of Christmas don't involve presents under the tree, but the affection and warmth of family and friends. This feeling is wonderfully put forth in the novel and transfers beautifully to the screen.

Alcott was born November 29, 1832 in Germantown, Pennsylvania. Her family later moved to Massachusetts, where her Concord home and her dear sisters were the inspiration for her most famous work. Like Jo in *Little Women*, Louisa May Alcott had three sisters: Anna, Lizzie (who, like Beth in the novel, died at age 22 from scarlet fever) and Aba. Alcott also had a brother who died in infancy. Her family was very progressive for the times and Alcott was an ardent feminist who was very active in the suffrage movement—which makes the political correctness of the 1994 film adaptation seem almost destiny.

Little Women was originally published in two parts. The first, *Meg, Jo, Beth, and Amy* was published in 1868; and the second part, *Good Wives*, saw print the following year. While the novel and film

Katharine Hepburn in 1933's *Little Women* is indeed wonderful as the exuberant Jo and physically fits the character to perfection. (Photofest)

versions cover several years in the girls' lives, the opening Christmas tale is a charming and delightful look at the sisters who, rather than spend their hard-earned money on themselves, buy gifts for their dear mother Marmee. On Christmas morning the girls eagerly sit down to a hot breakfast, only to learn their mother has gone to help a poor family who have no heat nor food. The girls agree to give their Christmas breakfast to the family, although Amy, the youngest, while a tiny bit reluctant at first, soon enters into the spirit of giving and becomes quite proud of herself for being so unselfish.

The first film version of the novel was the 1918 silent feature starring Dorothy Bernard as Jo, Henry Hull as John Brooke and Conrad Nagel as Laurie. Dorothy Bernard was a popular silent film star who worked for D.W. Griffith. She appeared in films such as *The Cricket on the Hearth* and *The Girl and Her Trust*. Henry Hull was a relative newcomer to the silver screen in 1918 (his first film was 1917's *The Volunteer*), although he would go on to have a successful career as a character actor. *Little Women* was the first screen appearance of Conrad Nagel. The handsome matinee idol would go on to make 225 films.

The second film version is the most critically acclaimed. 1933's *Little Women* starred Katharine

Hepburn and was directed by George Cukor, who helmed such classic films as *Camille* with Greta Garbo, *Dinner at Eight* with John Barrymore and Jean Harlow, *Gaslight* with Ingrid Bergman, *The Philadelphia Story* with Katharine Hepburn, Cary Grant and Jimmy Stewart and *A Star is Born* featuring the outstanding Judy Garland in perhaps her finest film performance (1954). The film would garner several Academy Award nominations including Best Picture, Director, and Writing (adaptation). However it would only earn the golden trophy for writers Victor Heerman and Sarah Y. Mason. The Best Picture and Director awards would be won by *Cavalcade,* a film that traces the lives of a British family. While not nominated for her performance as Jo, Katharine Hepburn would nonetheless win the Oscar that year for her performance in *Morning Glory.*

The screen adaptation is delightfully close to the novel, often quoting the girls' dialogue line for line. As the film opens a heavy snow is falling on Concord as Mrs. March (Spring Byington) goes about her work at the Commission House. She helps an old man who is traveling to Washington to visit his son in a war hospital there. He tells her he had four sons; two of his boys were killed and the other is a prisoner. She realizes how lucky she is to have her four girls even though her husband has joined the troops fighting the Civil War. The audience is then introduced to Meg (Frances Dee) as she leaves her job as nursemaid to three children. And then there's Jo. The audience gets its first glimpse of Jo (Hepburn) whose job is as a companion to grouchy old Aunt March (the always amusing Edna Mae Oliver). Jo tiredly reads aloud until the old lady dozes off and then sneaks up the stairs hoping to get out early since it is Christmas Eve. Aunt March is awakened by her parrot and catches Jo, who manages to keep her annoyance under control and meekly accepts a gift of a dollar from Aunt March for each of the sisters. Amy, the youngest (Joan Bennett), is being punished for drawing a picture of the headmaster on her slate. She is made to stand in front of the class, her slate reading "I am ashamed of myself." Amy manages to evade punishment and leaves the room with her head in the air, telling the other girls that her mother would be displeased at the way she is treated. This scene is also used in the 1949 version, although in the novel Amy is a model of decorum and is well-liked by the other students. Another girl did the drawing during class.

Beth (Jean Parker), who stays at home and helps with the housework, is trying to play on the old piano even though several keys don't work. She sings a little song as she awaits the arrival of her sisters. The three girls arrive home, Jo happily giving Beth her present from Aunt March. Their mother, whom they call Marmee, comes into the room as the girls are giggling and discussing their recent Christmas play rehearsal. She reads them a letter from their father, who refers to them as his little women. They decide rather than spending their dollar on themselves, they will buy presents for Marmee. Later that evening they hem a sheet and sing a song before retiring.

The next morning Jo, Beth and Meg sneak down the stairs to place their precious gifts at their mother's place at the table. They hear a door open and quickly stand in front of the gifts, but it is only Amy who, ashamed of the size of the perfume she bought for her mother, had gone out early to exchange it for a larger bottle. Their mother has gone to see a poor mother of six who has just given birth to another baby. She returns home and the girls delightedly show her the gifts. She then asks them to give up their breakfast for the poor children and the entire clan packs up the food and troops over to the woman's home. She calls them "good angels" as they set about feeding the family.

Later that evening the girls put on a play for a rapt audience, but pandemonium reigns when the audience is swallowed up in a cot substituting for chairs and scenery falls about Jo and Amy. Hannah (Mabel Colcord) calls them to supper, and they are delighted to find ice cream and four bouquets of flowers sent from their neighbor, Mr. Laurence, who has heard of their kind deed.

Katharine Hepburn is indeed wonderful as the exuberant Jo and physically fits the character to perfection. Alcott describes Jo as "very tall, thin, and brown, and reminded one of a colt; for she never seemed to know what to do with her long limbs, which were very much in the way. She had a decided mouth, a comical nose, and sharp, gray eyes, which appeared to see everything, and were by turns fierce, funny, or thoughtful." Hepburn deftly manages to capture Jo's tomboyish ways but still gives viewers a glimpse of Jo's depth of feeling and sentiment. Hepburn was 26 when she portrayed Josephine March. Mordaunt Hall of *The New York Times* in his review summarized her performance with: "Miss Hepburn goes darting through this picture without giving one a moment to think of her as other than Jo."

Frances Dee, who played the oldest Meg, was also 26 at the time of filming. *Little Women* would be her most famous film appearance although she is also remembered as Betsy in Val Lewton's *I Walked With a Zombie*. Not only did she appear in *Little Women* in 1933, but she married actor Joel McCrea that same year. They remained married 57 years until his death.

Beth would be played by Jean Parker, whose first screen appearance was in 1932. She would go on to appear in *Bluebeard* with John Carradine, *Beyond Tomorrow* and *The Ghost Goes West* with Robert Donat. As Beth, Parker had a quiet sensitivity that drew viewers to this sweet character.

Joan Bennett was 23 when she played the part of 12-year-old Amy. Bennett would have a long film career but became known for her film noir roles in films such as *Scarlet Street* and *The Secret Beyond the Door*. She drew an even larger cult following as Elizabeth Stoddard, matriarch of the Collins clan, in the TV horror-soap opera *Dark Shadows*. Bennett's best scene as Amy was rehearsing the play with Jo—Amy was a notoriously bad actress and Bennett does a suitably comical turn feigning a pathetic thespian. *The New York Times* noted, "Miss Bennett's interpretation is one of her best."

RKO spared no expense on sets by art directors Hobe Erwin and Van Nest Polglase and costumes by Walter Plunkett. The score was composed by the incomparable Max Steiner, whose work on *The Big Sleep*, *Casablanca*, *Gone With the Wind* and *The Searchers* made him a film legend.

In 1949 MGM released the third interpretation of the tale, which was directed by Mervyn LeRoy and featured an all-star cast including June Allyson as Jo, Janet Leigh as Meg, Elizabeth Taylor as Amy and Margaret O'Brien as Beth. The film also starred Peter Lawford as Laurie, Rossano Brazzi as Professor Bhaer, C. Aubrey Smith as Mr. Laurence, Mary Astor as Marmee (quite a long way from her marvelously

Jo (June Allyson), Amy (Elizabeth Taylor), Meg (Janet Leigh) and Beth (Margaret O'Brien) prepare for Christmas in 1949's *Little Women*. (Photofest)

evil *femme fatale* in *The Maltese Falcon*) and Leon Ames as Mr. March (Ames portrayed the father in another stellar holiday film, *Meet Me in St. Louis*).

Filmed in Technicolor, art directors Cedric Gibbons and Paul Groesse and cinematographers Robert Planck and Charles Schoenbaum made excellent use of color and lighting, particularly in the opening scenes, to portray the snug and loving March home. Marmee, surrounded by the girls, reads a letter from Father as the fire glows warmly dispelling any trace of the family's hard times while enchanting viewers who become emotionally involved in the lives of this devoted family. Planck and Schoenbaum earned an Academy Award nomination for their work while Gibbons and Groesse would actually win the Oscar for Art Direction of *Little Women*.

The Christmas scenes stick closely to the book, although in the film version the girls receive their precious dollar from Aunt March (Lucile Wilson) rather than having earned it working. On Christmas morning they decide to give their breakfast to the poor family on their own; whereas, in the book their mother asks them to be charitable.

June Allyson leaped from the Broadway stage in *Best Foot Forward* directly onto the silver screen in 1943 for the Hollywood version of the play. She was suitably tomboyish and perky as the rambunctious Jo—bounding over fences and dueling fierce opponents in the girls' amateur productions. Allyson was 32 when she played the part of 15-year-old Jo. *Variety* noted in its review of the film: "...June Allyson shows that there is meat in the role for more than one actress. Her thesping dominates the film... On the basis of this pic, Miss Allyson is ready for major dramatic assignments." Allyson would take that step away from musicals to throw her hat into the dramatic ring in films such as *The Glenn Miller Story, The Opposite Sex* and *Strategic Air Command*.

Janet Leigh made her film debut in 1947 at the age of 21, appearing in *The Romance of Rosy Ridge*. She would have six films premiere in 1949 including *Holiday Affair* and *Little Women*. Leigh's work in musicals and comedies would be overshadowed by her Oscar–nominated performance as Norman Bates' infamous shower victim in Alfred Hitchcock's *Psycho*. Leigh brings the right touch of young womanhood to

Jo (Winona Ryder), Meg (Trini Alvarado), Amy (Kirsten Dunst), Marmee (Susan Sarandon) and Beth (Claire Danes) share a Christmas letter from Mr. March in 1994's *Little Women*.

her character of 16-year-old Meg, who is the voice of reason when Jo and Amy indulge in a sisterly squabble.

The youngest but by far the grandest sister (in her mind, at least), Amy (Elizabeth Taylor), sleeps with a clothespin on her nose so the nasty girls at school won't make fun of her and chastises Jo for being so boyish. Taylor, at 17, played the youngest March sister in a curly blonde wig and with a sweetly funny superior air that fit prissy little Amy perfectly. Taylor made her film debut in *There's One Born Every Minute* (1942) with Hugh Herbert, Guy Kibbee and Peggy Moran but gained notice with her role as Velvet in MGM's extremely successful *National Velvet* (1944).

But the most heart-tugging sister in this version was without a doubt Margaret O'Brien as the shy and doomed Beth. Margaret O'Brien began her film career at the ripe old age of four in *Babes on Broadway*. She would steal American's heart with roles in such films as *The Canterville Ghost, Lost Angel, Our Vines Have Tender Grapes, The Secret Garden, Tenth Avenue Angel* and, of course, *Meet Me in St. Louis* in 1944. Margaret O'Brien was 12 when *Little Women* was released. Her character Beth was 13 years old in the novel. O'Brien's uncanny ability to make audiences believe any scene she ever played only made the sad death of Beth all the more poignant.

Of the film *Variety* noted: "Metro mobilized its potent studio resources and combined a star constellation for its unstinting remake of Louisa May Alcott's *Little Women*... The lot has come through with a handsome, tasteful Currier & Ives delineation of those times and mores in personal terms."

Little Women again resurfaced, this time as a television movie in 1978. The cast was filled with television celebrities including Meredith Baxter Birney (*Bridget Loves Bernie*) who starred as Meg, Susan Dey (*Partridge Family*) as Jo, Eve Plumb (*Brady Bunch*) as Beth and Ann Dusenberry as Amy. Dorothy McGuire appeared as Marmee and Mr. March was portrayed by William Schallert (*The Patty Duke Show*). The cast even boasted William Shatner (*Star Trek*) as Professor Bhaer.

In 1994 *Little Women* would again receive the Hollywood treatment. This updated version benefits from the more appropriate casting of the March sisters with actresses closer in age to the girls depicted in the book, as well as opulent costuming (nominated for an Academy Award), and an all-star cast consisting of Susan Sarandon, Winona Ryder, Gabriel Byrne, Claire Danes, Kirsten Dunst and Mary Wickes, who was once again typecast, this time as feisty old curmudgeon, Aunt March.

This modern version treats us to not one but two Christmas scenes, taking liberty with the novel, but adding emotional depth to the story with slight changes.

Little Women opens with a Christmas wreath being hung on a door; while a horse-drawn sleigh glides along a snow-covered road as laughing children pull a Christmas tree down a path. Evergreen garlands decorate the front of the March house as the girls gather. The camera is a Peeping Tom looking through a falling snow into the warm yellow glow at the loving family inside.

On Christmas day the girls exclaim with delight over the feast before them—sausages, baked apples, bread and butter. Hannah (Florence Patterson) sends Jo (Winona Ryder) to fetch Marmee (Susan Sarandon) who has gone to help the Hummels. "May as well take a stick of firewood for they haven't got any, or breakfast either."

Beth (Claire Danes) thinks aloud, "Perhaps we could send the Hummels our bread." "May as well send the butter too. Butter's not much use without bread to put it on," Jo answers. Meg (Trini Alvarado) offers the sausage and apples and little Amy (Kirsten Dunst) reluctantly hands over her precious orange. As the girls carry the breakfast down the snowy path, Jo sees their neighbors Mr. Laurence (John Neville) and his grandson Laurie (Christian Bale) and calls "lovely weather for a picnic." Meg chastises her for speaking improperly, but Laurie seems delighted. The sisters sing "here we come a wassailing" as they laughingly head for the Hummels.

Christmas evening Laurie stares at the March house as shadows of the girls pass the attic window. The sisters, dressed in men's clothes and hats, are having a meeting of the Pickwick Society and reading from their newspaper, *The Pickwick Portfolio*. Jo paces dramatically as she reads her latest story. They begin to discuss Laurie and gather at the window to gaze upon him playing piano, alone on this Christmas evening. They wistfully wish for better times.

Christmas season is still being celebrated when Jo and Meg prepare for a party at the home of Belle Gardiner (Corrie Clark). Jo's dress is scorched so she must keep her back to the wall the entire evening. Meg's shoes are too small and Jo manages to burn off her front curls when she is helping Meg get ready.

At the party Jo, trying to avoid an eager dancing partner, stumbles into an alcove where Laurie is hiding and they quickly become fast friends.

Time passes quickly. Meg has made the acquaintance of John Brooke (Eric Stoltz), Laurie's tutor; Beth has been sick and Mr. Marsh has been wounded in the war. But the family happily prepares for another Christmas. Meg, Jo and Amy, along with Laurie, two of his college friends and Mr. Laurence, laugh and stand in front of a piano, a surprise for Beth from Mr. Laurence. Marmee and Hannah help her downstairs and she tearfully hugs Mr. Laurence for his wonderful gift. She plays "Deck the Halls" and everyone joins in. Meg and Marmee put sugar atop a cake and discuss Meg's proposal from Mr. Brooke. Jo is shocked. "Why can't things stay as they are?" she cries.

But Jo's distress is soon put aside as another surprise awaits the family—John has accompanied Mr. March home for Christmas. The family hugs happily, and the festivities continue as Meg and John romantically kiss against a backdrop of an open door with snow falling in the background.

I really must confess, I think the 1994 version may be my favorite. The film seems to capture the spirit of the novel and delves a little deeper into the story than the other versions. Amy grows from the precocious Kirsten Dunst into an elegant young lady portrayed by Samantha Mathis. Kirsten Dunst steals the show from veterans like Sarandon and Ryder. She is sprightly, cocky and assured as the youngest daughter Amy. Dunst made a splash earlier in the year with her outstanding performance in *Interview With a Vampire*, earning rave reviews for her first screen role.

Winona Ryder is one of today's most talented stars. She made her impressive debut in *Beetlejuice* in 1988. She would be cast as Mina in *Bram Stoker's Dracula* and work with Martin Scorsese in his impressive *The Age of Innocence*, a film that would earn the young actress an Academy Award nomination. Ryder was not physically a match for Jo as Hepburn was, but Ryder brings a naturalness to the role that, in my opinion, makes her character the more believable Jo.

Claire Danes was fresh from her acclaimed teenage angst role in 1994's television show, *My So-Called Life*. Beth was a dramatic turnabout for this talented actress. Danes managed the role with insight, never turning the performance into the sickly sweet parody it could easily have become.

Director Gillian Armstrong manages to bring the bond of love and squabbling between sisters to vivid life, while the cinematography is truly exquisite.

—SS

Christmas Eve

1947

"Christmas Eve, that's the time when families are together!" declares matriarch Aunt Matilda (Ann Harding) near the beginning of *Christmas Eve* an anthology movie that is both heart-warming and eccentric, dramatic and humorous, traditional and outlandish.

Judge Alston (Clarence Kolb) and Dr. Doremus (Carl Harbord) have tea with Aunt Matilda (Ann Harding) and her nephew Phillip (Reginald Denny) in *Christmas Eve*. (Photofest)

The story involves an eccentric older woman, Aunt Matilda, whose despicable nephew Phillip (Reginald Denny) claims that she squanders her fortune on unnecessary things such as charities and helping the poor. Calling Judge Alston (Clarence Kolb) and psychiatrist Dr. Doremus (Carl Harbord) to the family home, Phillip wants to have his spinster aunt name him as the manager of her estate (which she will have no part of). "She's such a lovely old heirloom, despite her eccentricities," Phillip declares.

Suddenly a loud gong sounds, a door opens, and the family butler announces Aunt Matilda: "I always ring that gong to warn people to stop talking about me—behind my back." After she opens the windows and invites the outdoor birds inside for a good feeding, she summons her human companions in to her dining room for tea. Matilda uses her "sons'" toy train set, now placed atop the magnificent dining room table, as a means to transport lemon and cream for tea. "The trains belonged to my sons... too much of an effort to play with them on my hands and knees. It's fun pretending my boys are with me at the big table—is that crazy?"

Whether she is crazy or not becomes the dominant theme of this warm-spirited movie, a theme very popular in the 1940s and 1950s. The aunt's eccentricities keep piling up: She spent $1,675,000 paying for half a million dead rats, according to Phillip.

The entire truth, revealed by Matilda, is that she paid half a million poor children a dollar apiece for capturing rats. "Who would you trust... to handle the estate?" she asks. Phillip, the human leech who connives and schemes to wrestle the family fortune away from Matilda, or one of her three "sons," the boys she adopted at birth and raised as her own?

Phillip informs the Judge that the "sons" left as soon as they were grown, but Matilda corrects him: "They decided to go out in the world and make their own way—I loved them for it." Unfortunately, none of the children has been in touch since. However, Aunt Matilda declares, "They refused to sponge off me." She remembers them saying that if you ever need us, we'll be there!

Aunt Matilda declares that all three of her sons will be present at her house on Christmas Eve so the Judge can meet them himself. Of course, doubting that this reunion will ever occur, the Judge declares he won't follow through with Phillip's demands if the sons show up for the holiday. Thus, in order to hold onto her birthright, the spunky old aunt must use all her resources to round up all three of her strays and get them together for Christmas. Using the power of the press, Matilda invites a slew of reporters to her home (hoping her late father will forgive her) and announces her predicament. Soon headlines are flashed across the screen: "Matilda Reed Fortune in Jeopardy"; "Old Maid's Millions Under Court Fire"; "Spending it Foolishly, says Nephew." One common citizen reading the newspaper declares, "Imagine that, saying the old lady's crazy! The whole world's crazy!!!"

From this point on, intercut with Matilda hiring detectives and household servants to track down her three boys, the movie divides into three segments, each one focusing upon the current whereabouts of her three sons: Michael, Mario and Jonathan.

First we meet the dandy, irresponsible playboy Michael Brooks (George Brent), a man trying to maintain his wealthy persona even though he is deeply in debt and resorting to writing bad checks. The woman who loves him, Ann Nelson (Joan Blondell), is getting the kiss-off as Michael has plans to marry the wealthy Harriett (Molly Lamont), hoping to help his financial status. "I told you yesterday we were through," Michael rants, but the deeply-in-love Ann responds enthusiastically, "I love you! What's she got that I haven't got?" In this comedy of errors, enacted very much in the screwball vein, Michael is trying to get Ann out of the apartment before fiancée Harriett comes up. In fact, Harriett sends up a small gift announcing her imminent appearance, which Ann grabs and throws off the balcony. When Harriett does enter, Michael announces that Ann is his sister, but when the two women spend several moments alone, Harriett gets suspicious. The bellhop appears, returning the discarded gift (which he complains hit a bellman in the head), and Harriett realizes the truth.

Michael's frivolous personality softens slightly when he admits the marriage of two wealthy families has been his goal, but that he still loves Ann. However, Phillip finds Michael and tightens his grip by stating he paid off $75,000 in rubber checks Michael wrote and advises him to blow town. "Aunt Matilda is getting along, but she can't stand another shock," referring to Matilda's obvious disappointment in her son Michael if she found out the truth. Phillip stresses Michael mustn't go to his aunt. He soon realizes the "stranglehold" that Phillip has over him. Michael wants to pay off the debt immediately. "The further away I am, the better it would be for Aunt Matilda," Michael says, but hints he doesn't have the money to stay away. So he hits up Phillip for $10,000 in cash, to which the disappointed Ann Nelson disgustedly yells, "Been nice knowing you Michael." The news of Michael's dire straits gets back to Aunt Matilda, and she is disappointed that he would allow himself to try to marry for money. The word is that Michael has gotten out of town, and Matilda hires people to locate him.

Second son Mario (George Raft) lives in South America and runs the Yank's Club. He fled the United States over an indiscretion that remains a secret from the audience. A 20-year prison sentence awaits him if he ever returns to the States. He meets a beautiful woman at the train station who tells Mario, "I'll never go away again... it's no fun without you!" But FBI agents are hounding him again. "I didn't fly down here to nail you," they assure him, but Mario yells back chisel-faced, "I'm no stooge for the cops."

It seems the beautiful woman from the train station, Claire (Virginia Field), is involved with an important Nazi fugitive, Reichman (Kionstantin Shayne), who escaped from Europe and is now assumed to be hiding in South America. In the midst of all this Mario is made aware of Aunt Matilda's problems back home; while the dutiful son seems concerned, his more pressing problems occupy his attention at the moment. Soon Claire has disappears and Mario feels jilted, but the story is not this simple. It seems that Claire has in her possession 10 million dollars in cash and jewels that belongs to Reichman. Reichman, thinking the romantic duo are in cahoots, kidnaps Mario and takes him aboard his yacht and tortures him: "You can work me over, but how can I tell you something I don't know?"

Claire appears on the boat, looking guilty and declaring, "Darling, I was a fool. I never realized just how rotten they were." She claims she wanted to protect her lover Mario by running off and letting him think she dumped him, while in fact the truth is she loves Mario very much. She makes a deal with Reichman: she will tell him where his money is if he agrees to let Mario go. Reichman agrees immediately. Of course, the evil Nazi has no intentions of freeing the witnesses. "Promises are the counterfeit currency that inferior people exact from each other when unsure of their own strength." This on-the-lam Nazi is filled to the brim with metaphors. But the repentant Claire states she wanted "to get right with myself, to settle my own score" without involving the safety of Mario. "I wanted you to hate me, that's why I left the office."

Soon Mario fights his way free from the Nazi henchman as sparks from the bullets set the boat on fire. Mario uses the fire extinguisher to put the flames out, then sneaks into a small room that is above the area where Reichman is still holding Claire. Mario lifts the metal grate and carefully aims his pistol. He fires the gun and the Nazi falls to the floor but Reichman manages to get off one shot that mortally wounds Claire. "Darling, have I made myself right with you... hold me close... I love you!"

What a plot. *Christmas Eve* segues from a story of a conniving playboy to a refugee American who gets involved with a dangerous dame and Nazis. Then we find an American drunken cowboy, a rodeo cowboy to boot, who gets involved with a baby-snatching outfit. Ho, Ho, Ho... Merry Christmas!

Jonathan (Randolph Scott) is remembered by the family as always hiding alcohol on his breath before kissing Aunt Matilda, and forever making rest stops at punchbowls, saloons, etc. However, he is also the shy and always happily polite guy with the heart of gold. As Matilda's servant Williams meets Jonathan at Grand Central Station on Christmas Eve (he's the only son officially located and sure to attend the party with Aunt Matilda and the Judge), the cowboy immediately wants to head to the nearest saloon for a drink or two. Soon Jonathan is approached by an attractive young woman (next to booze, Jonathan's other weakness is that he is a constant flirt who is a sucker for the ladies), Jean (Dolores Moran), who insists he accompany her to 128 W. Meredith Street so she can pick up her new baby! Jonathan thinks the woman must be pregnant even though she is dressed to the nines in a form-flattering dress that must have come straight from the film noir wardrobe department store. Even Williams warns him, "Be careful, she'll pin more things on you than on the baby!"

It seems Jean is taking Jonathan to a clandestine apartment building where a doctor sells babies for adoption. She realizes that if the good-hearted Jonathan pretends to be her husband, her chances of getting a baby are improved. To further complicate the plot, Jean is an undercover policewoman out to expose the baby-selling operation. However, the amorous Jonathan has his hands and lips all over her while suggesting a more common way of having children. "Don't let being a prospective father go to your head," Jean warns him. When the doctor tells Jean he doesn't like her looks, Jonathan comes to her rescue by pulling out his gun and demanding a child. Soon the pair are led to a small nursery area where three babies are cribbed, and both take an immediate liking to the kids.

But the doctor smells a rat and Jonathan is taken upstairs and clubbed over the head while Jean is bound and thrown into the closet. Waking up and hearing police sirens, Jonathan grabs the three kids and escapes through the back window. Williams is instinctively waiting for him there. "I know three other kids who got out of a joint like this," the cowboy mutters as he carries the children to safety.

Meanwhile, back in the living room of Aunt Matilda, the Judge and Phillips are impatiently waiting, pacing back and forth. Finally the Judge declares, "It's been an hour and a half. My grandchildren will kill me if I don't decorate the tree." However, all is

well when Jonathan arrives with the three children, hands them over to Aunt Matilda, who, delightfully finding herself back in the saddle, so to speak, sends out for formula and bottles. Jonathan excuses himself and heads for the punch bowl. Jean, arriving on the scene, is worried about the children. After finding out that they are safe and in good hands, she settles down. Jonathan puts the make on her by smiling and saying, "If you're that interested in babies, it's time we got acquainted."

Next, unexpectedly, Michael and reunited fiancée Ann Nelson are approaching Aunt Matilda's. Ann is concerned that Michael's presence will cause great trepidation within the household, but Aunt Matilda matter-of-factly declares she is aware of what Phillip has been doing for a long time and Michael is welcomed with open arms. Outside, Matilda hears a Christmas carol and declares it is Mario's favorite and that Mario must be nearby. However, as soon as Mario does in fact knock on the door, FBI agent Joe Bland is two steps behind him. But since it is Christmas Eve, he decides to allow Mario to enjoy the holiday with Matilda—as long as he is allowed to accompany the fugitive. Mario and the agent have to leave for Washington that night. In the midst of the frivolity, Mario takes Phillip aside and tells him, "We're both leaving town, but you're leaving first!" reminding Matilda's nephew that to spare Aunt Matilda pain Mario took the rap for Phillip's crime 10 years ago in New Orleans. But once again the intuitive Matilda announces, "I know you covered for Phillip in New Orleans. But I know everything is going to turn out right."

The family then retires to the dining room, heads bowed in silence. Christmas music reaches a crescendo; and a toast, "A Merry Christmas to All," ends the film, with the entire family united in peace and harmony.

What an interesting Christmas film: Nazis, stolen money, baby-snatchers, a refugee American lying low in South America, an eccentric old lady who runs trains around her elegant dining room table. But somehow, in this wonderful little piece of holiday cheer directed by Edwin L. Marin, it all comes together. The three separate little stories are well-interconnected, the characters are all distinct and interestingly portrayed. They are flawed, but each individual overcomes his/her small failings to restore the faith placed in them by Aunt Matilda. Ann Harding, portraying the wonderful quirky aunt, becomes the glue that holds all these components together. It is her stern determination that her sons will return for Christmas Eve dinner and everything will work out okay that becomes so involving for the audience. Since she believes, we believe. And when she is pressured to turn her estate over to nephew Phillip, she steadfastly declares she might have considered it had he left home to find his way in the world, but in reality she is aware of his criminal escapades and tainted ethics. However, she never reveals everything she knows, not even when she is threatened with losing all she cherishes, because she maintains that faith that her boys will come to her rescue and, together, as families usually manage to do, they work things out themselves, without outside intervention.

It is Aunt Matilda's unwavering faith in family and the bond that is created (not by blood, because her children are adopted) within the family that firmly anchors this movie. Using Christmas as its chief metaphor, that time of year when the family is at its strongest, *Christmas Eve* is a tribute to the power of the family to overcome all obstacles. Wayward son Mario is detached and cut off, living alone in South America, but once he returns to the States, a 20-year jail term staring him square in the face, the family fixes all the wrongs committed against him. The alcoholic and lonely Jonathan, once he returns to his family, is immediately reminded of how he was one of three orphaned children who were raised and supported by an "old maid" aunt, and returning the favor, he himself looks out for three infant orphans. Realizing the power of family, he bonds with Jean and suggests that they start a family by having their own babies to go along with the three babies upstairs. And finally even poor Michael, who momentarily forsakes love for money, surrenders to love and commits to marrying his long-time fiancée Ann (which he proudly announces to the family). Separated from the family, all three sons are fragmented, scared, and lost (spiritually, emotionally, physically), but once they have returned to the "nest," they are whole and functioning healthfully again. Except for Matilda's actual blood relative Phillip, who cuts himself off from and

works against the family and is the outcast at the movie's end. Having lived for years with Aunt Matilda, he is the most fragmented, scared, and wasted family member of them all.

Christmas Eve is a most positive and forceful proponent of the Yuletide essence and its story detailing how the unity of the family can heal all wounds is most specifically indicative of the holiday spirit.
—GJS

Tenth Avenue Angel
1948

Yes *Tenth Avenue Angel* is hokey, and yes it pulls out all the stops in the heart-wrenching category, and yes the characters are stereotypical, but nevertheless several things make this minor little film a holiday keeper.

Margaret O'Brien is her usual effervescent self as Flavia Mills, a little girl who revels in her little world that encompasses the neighborhood of Tenth Avenue. She is adored by all as she scoots about the street on her one roller skate (her family is unable to afford a real pair) calling hello to everyone on her way to help blind newspaper salesman Mac (Rhys Williams) sell his papers. Flavia trusts everyone and truly believes the fairy stories her mother tells her.

But like George Bailey in *It's a Wonderful Life*, Flavia finds her world shaken to the core when she learns family friend Steve (George Murphy), planning to go straight, wants to leave town without her Aunt Susan (Angela Lansbury). Flavia is also disenchanted when, believing the mouse she has caught turns to money, is set straight by the adults she loves. She is crushed to learn the wonderful stories her mother told her are not true and loses her faith. The contented little girl who charmed everyone on Tenth Avenue is no more.

Flavia's family is poor, her father Joseph (Warner Anderson) gives violin lessons, but the couple is happy when Helen (Phyllis Thaxter) learns she is having another child.

On Christmas Eve, as Steve is purchasing roller skates for Flavia, he meets her father who is planning to hock his violin. Steve, knowing that is his only source of income, tells him not to worry, he will lend him the money.

Unfortunately, Steve doesn't have the money either and goes to the man he took the fall for on the botched job that sent him to prison. Steve agrees to take a truck from the garage where he works as well as drive for the job planned that night.

In *Tenth Avenue Angel* Steve (George Murphy) and Flavia (Margaret O'Brien) find a cattle car so Flavia can see the cows kneel on Christmas Eve.

Aunt Susan (Angela Lansbury) and Steve watch Flavia open her roller skates in *Tenth Avenue Angel.*

A heavy snow is falling on Tenth Avenue as the doctor leaves the Mills' apartment. He tells Helen she must rest or she could lose the baby and tells Flavia to run to the drugstore to get her mother a prescription. As Flavia is getting the money, she knocks her little cow bank to the floor. The front legs are broken off, but her mother tries to reassure the little girl.

> "Oh look darling, the little cow isn't broke. She's just kneeling. Getting ready for Christmas. All over the world cows kneel on Christmas Eve. Didn't you know that? They kneel in honor of the Child who was born in the manger. They were the first to worship Him."
> "How do cows know that it's Christmas?" Flavia asks.
> "Because then God is very close and the cows feel his presence as they did on that first night and they fall on their knees for his blessing."
> "What's a blessing?"
> "It's God's love enfolding us darling. It's his way of answering our prayers."
> As her mother hands her the bank Flavia asks, "Mama, did you ever see a cow kneel?"
> Her mother pauses, wondering what to do, but decides truth is the best route. "Why... I... No. Not really darling."
> Flavia is not ready to accept stories yet. "Then it isn't true."

Her mother tries again. "Don't you like to think the Holy Child loves us so much that he comes back on Christmas Eve? Don't you want to believe it Flavia?"
"Yes, mama, but I can't."

On her way to the drugstore for the medicine, Flavia goes to see Steve to see if he is really leaving. She overhears a conversation and learns he wasn't really traveling the world, but was in prison. She feels her entire life has been a lie. She confronts her mother, "Everybody lies to me. Even the ones I love the most." The little girl runs out of the apartment and down the stairs, her mother following the sobbing child. Helen loses her balance and falls. The baby is safely delivered, but the doctor notes, "Only a miracle can save the mother." Flavia, sitting quietly in a corner, hears this information and then looks at the kneeling cow and wipes away her tears. She decides she must find a cow—not an easy thing to do in the big city. Mac tells her she should find someone to take her to the stockyards.

Now it just so happens the stockyards are where Steve has driven the truck to meet those crooks who are pulling a Christmas Eve job. He spies Flavia who desperately asks for his help in finding a cow. Steve realizing Flavia and those he loves are more important than money, walks out on the job—just in time—for the police were waiting for the crooks.

Steve and Flavia find a cattle car and get an attendant to open the door. A policeman watches from a distance. The cow is lying down but when the clock strikes midnight the cow kneels. Flavia folds her hands and, in a tearful voice that Margaret O'Brien managed to do so well, prays:

"I can't see you, but I know you're close. Please listen to me. I've been a very bad girl. I didn't believe. But now I saw. You made the cow kneel to show me. I know you're close listening. Make my mama live. Only you can. It would be only one more miracle. Please, please dear God, make my mama live."

The policeman smiles and walks away as a star shines in the sky. Steve takes Flavia home. The little girl is confident she will find her mother well. But Helen is still unconscious. Flavia strokes her face.

"Mama, mama, oh mama. You've got to get well because everything you said was true. We found the cow and just as it started to turn Christmas the bells started ringing and the cow kneeled. It's true mama. It's really true!"

Joe, unaware anything has happened, returns home announcing he has a job. Helen wakes and Flavia gets to open some Christmas presents. A pair of skates from the Tenth Avenue businessmen, a pair from Steve and a pair from Mac. Carolers sing outside the window as Steve and Susan reconcile. Steve announces he will not leave the city.

Although *Tenth Avenue Angel* was not critically praised, *Variety* chiding, "Hokum plot lays the sob stuff on thick, and without too much interest...," it is still worthwhile Christmas viewing that will warm the cockles of your heart. As Flavia, Margaret O'Brien is her usual effervescent self; we have no trouble believing any neighborhood would fall in love with this little angel, who not only won the hearts of those on Tenth Avenue, but the entire country as well in her debut as a frightened war orphan in *Journey for Margaret* (1942).

George Murphy, who starred as Steve, is a underrated performer whose always dependable work contributed to many excellent films. Murphy could sing and dance with the best of them, holding his own with Judy Garland and Gene Kelly in *For Me and My Gal* (1942). He would also appear in dramas including the war films *Battan* and *Battleground*. In 1950 he received a special Oscar "for his services in interpreting the film industry to the country at large." After that he was elected to the U.S. Senate.

Angela Lansbury, another trooper who always turns in fine performances, gives Susan life, while

Phyllis Thaxter as Helen brings a tear to the eye as a mother who wants to shield her child from the harsh realities of life with fantastic stories of myths and miracles, and what child doesn't need to believe in magic?
—SS

The Holly and the Ivy
1954

Seldom seen today, 1953's *The Holly and The Ivy* is a quaint, quiet British sitting room drama that is very character heavy. The setting occurs mostly in one family's home during the holidays. The film comes off more as a stage play with its dysfunctional family trying to put on airs around its titular leader, the aging parson father, whom they believe they have to shelter from the harsh realities of the world. Fortunately, by Christmas morning, individual members of the family have grown closer together as the Christmas season becomes, once again, a cure for all ills.

Philosophically, this movie is the post WWII era version of *Home for the Holidays*, perfectly capturing the joy and pain caused by the pressures which the Christmas holiday creates amidst members of any family. A British Lion Production filmed in England, the film is largely unseen outside its native shores.

The movie opens to a montage of Christmas music and store fronts decorated festively for the holidays. We see a hand shuffling through and mailing invitations, framed by falling snow, at the Wyndenham Post Office for the annual family Christmas celebration which will bring relatives together from all over the country.

We first meet the delightful 70-year-old Aunt Lydia (Margaret Halstan) speaking to a desk clerk at the hotel at which she lives. Always smiling, a distant look twinkling in her eyes, Aunt Lydia is seemingly well-to-do, having lived in hotels since the death of her husband 30 years earlier. "Will you be here for Christmas?" the clerk asks. Lydia responds that she typically goes to her sister's for the holidays, but "she died in the spring," so this year she is not sure of her plans. She admits, in these last 30 years, "I've never yet spent a hotel Christmas." But the very letter she is opening is an invitation to her brother-in-law's home for Christmas. She merrily announces, "No, I will not be here for Christmas!"

Another invitation reaches the hands of a distinguished, graying gentleman, gathered with his cohorts sharing a few drinks, at his club. When one of them asks Richard (Hugh Williams) to come share the holidays with him and his family, he matter-of-factly announces, "I always do the same thing at Christmas," and that is visit with a cousin. When he is kidded about spending the holidays with a man of the cloth, Richard announces, "I nearly went into the church," (the announcement is met with declarations of "what!" all around). He explains after he left school, his father said, "My boy, it's time you made your mind up. What are you going to do, be a soldier or a clergyman?" Richard answered clergyman "and my father burst out laughing." Thus, Richard joined the service and became a Colonel.

We next are introduced to another invite, Aunt Bridget (Maureen Delany), an old maid and grouch. When her neighbor asks her if she is going away for the holidays, she glares back, "I can't leave!" looking at her cat who is sitting on the sofa. The neighbor kindly offers to care for the pet while Bridget is away. "I'm only next door, and you do so enjoy going to your brother's for Christmas, don't you?" Melting slightly, the hardened old woman is revealed to actually possess a softer interior than the cool exterior she projects. She admits her brother has a "beautiful place" and that she "is very fond of it." Thus, she agrees to go.

Another invite is the young rogue, Michael Gregory (Denholm Elliott), serving time in military service, but who is caught sneaking back into the barracks after hours the night before his 48-hour Christmas leave begins. Since his leave is then immediately taken away, Michael requests a chance to see the Major where he turns on the sob story: His mother recently died last May, his father is a parson, so Christmas is very important, and his sister alone must now care for her father at the family home. Of course his Christmas leave is reinstated.

Next we cut to the Gregory home, and meet daughter Jenny Gregory (Celia Johnson) who is caught between a rock and a hard place. She feels the obligation to care for her elderly father, Parson Martin Gregory (Ralph Richardson), who needs watching over. In her early 30s, she has at long last found love in the person of David Paterson (John Gregson), who is madly in love with her. However, the budding engineer's job requires him to work and live in South America for five years. He wants to marry her so they can move down there together, and she deeply loves him. But there's the obligation and love she feels for her father. "They want me to sail the end of January. I want you to leave with me, as my wife... What is between you and me is what the whole of mankind depends on." With regret David announces that if she waits until he returns five years later, Jenny will be 36 years old, "that's middle-aged!" David thinks Jenny's father must be a nasty, self-possessed old man. But Jenny, with tears in her eyes, announces that her father wouldn't let her stay if he knew about David. "That's why he must never know," she says,

A rather uncomfortable Christmas Eve dinner at the home of the Gregorys in *The Holly and the Ivy*.

as the price of being a martyr lies heavy upon her heart. Unable to fully understand, David asks why doesn't Jenny's single sister watch the old man?

Not a very happy Christmas for all concerned.

As young Michael returns home and helps David decorate the house for the holiday, they each agree to decorate one side of the room with ivy. David opens up and divulges, "It's a strange thing, but I find all these Christmas decorations peculiarly depressing." To which Michael reveals, "I used to like it as a child, but now, I find it, well, as you say, depressing," referring to Christmas. Michael announces his father won't retire because of him, that he still has four more years of military service, and then his father wants him to attend Cambridge "and that costs money. I don't want him to kill himself for me... besides, I'm not sure I want to go to Cambridge."

Aunt Bridget arrives and complains about the ducks she saw in back of the house. "You don't eat duck eggs, do you! They're poison!" To which Jenny smiles and states, "We used them for years."

Next Aunt Lydia arrives, singing the praises of how well Jenny cared for her recently departed sister and now her father. To which David begrudgingly answers, "A bit too wonderful... In my opinion, you can carry self-sacrifice a bit too far." The intuitive Lydia immediately knows that David and Jenny are in love, and she is delighted. "I can see it all over you... This is right, absolutely right. You're cut out for each other!" But Jenny asks the family to keep this secret, as the engagement hasn't been announced yet; besides, she doesn't wish her father to know.

Next Richard arrives and announces that his godchild Margaret (Jenny's sister) will not be attending the festivities this year, because of a case of flu. But all the family appears to be able to read between the lines, for Margaret has a drinking problem.

Soon the parson Martin Gregory enters the living room, voicing concern that his daughter Margaret (Margaret Leighton) will not be attending. When the parson offers to phone her at home, Richard pulls the phone away, declaring she's probably asleep now anyway.

Immediately, the parson is also revealed to be depressed by the Christmas holiday. "You know, since I was ordained, I must have written enough sermons to fill 150 books, and I doubt if anyone has paid the slightest attention to one of them."

The optimist Lydia pipes in with words of encouragement: "I still remember one you preached, soon after my Philip died." To which Martin quickly blows off her comment of heartfelt sentiment by politely rambling on, "I'm glad my dear. I'm glad."

Margaret, finally deciding to attend the family celebration, arrives at the house, looks around, finds a bottle and pours herself a drink. Finishing the glass, she is surprised by members of the family, and the parson himself offers her a whisky, "We got it especially for you." She politely turns him down but, in the spirit of the holidays, he still insists. Now raising her voice and almost shouting, she clearly responds, "Didn't you hear me say *no thank you*!!!"

Lydia, once again a distant, far-away look in her eyes, beams forth, "I always thought Christmas is the best of all the festivals." To which Martin dramatically answers her: "I hate it!!! Ah, the retail traders get ahold of it. It's all eating and drinking and giving each other knickknacks."

But the love-sick Jenny now chimes in. "But Christmas morning, there's something about Christmas morning... Somehow I don't know why I always know it's Christmas morning. It's as though during the night, when you're asleep, something happened. You even expect the world to look as different as it feels... and you realize it's Christmas everywhere."

Martin again pulls the sentiment and good tidings down a rung by declaring: "Of all the sermons during the year, it's the one on Christmas morning I dislike. Nobody wants to hear you, they're all fidgeting in their pews, no time to tell them anything important."

For Britain of 1953, *The Holly and the Ivy* must have felt like the anti-Christmas film of all time, but to the regular movie viewer, they probably saw a lot of the truth in this movie. The family leader past his prime, one daughter not able to live her life because of her responsibility to her father, another sister with a hidden past, now a drunk, two busy-body aunts, one an old grouch, the other living in la-la land. David, the frustrated lover who must leave the country in a matter of weeks, unable to convince his lady to pick up, marry him and leave. This was good soap-opera melodrama before the era of the soaps. But even though every image and sound emitting from the film reeked of Christmas and the holiday spirit (Christmas music, carolers, snow outside, holiday store fronts, holiday decorations, Christmas geese and turkeys, Christmas church services, etc.), all these images were undermined by the dysfunctionality of the human drama unfolding before our eyes. Unlike *A Christmas Carol*, produced in Britain two years earlier, in this more realistic universe the ghosts of Christmas past, present and future were not about to interfere and correct all the wrongs in one long wintry night.

The heart of the family's problems worsen as Margaret and Jenny, doing dishes together, speak of both their problems. "Then it's true, you are fed up (living at home with father)?" Margaret asks Jenny. "Well no, not exactly... it's a bit limiting. It's simple... I want to get married, that's all." Then she reveals how she has to watch over Daddy and couldn't Margaret come home for a while (to relieve her of this responsibility, thus permitting her to marry the man of her dreams). To which Margaret quickly and firmly answers, "No, I'm sorry. That's out of the question." Jenny, taken slightly aback, comments, "You say it so immediately, like it's done with. Life must be very easy for people like you... you have grown hard, haven't you?" To which Margaret matter-of-factly answers, "Life does change people." Jenny digs deeper, "Why must you always crackle like ice? What's happened to make you feel all frozen over inside?"

But tragedy has hit Margaret's life, and now, for the first time, she reveals the very factors which made her so hard. First of all, she fell in love with an American military man who was killed in the war. She was pregnant with his child (out of wedlock), and fearing the wrath of her father, she never told him. The child became sick and died at age four, a second tragedy in less than 10 years. Again, the secret must be held inside, it could not be shared with members of the family. Thus, all these pressures led to her dependency upon alcohol. Margaret reveals the reason she cannot come home again. "Father thinks of me as somebody I no longer am. If I came back to live with father, I would be pretending to be like I used to be."

In fact, the entire family walks on egg shells around the parson, afraid to open up their lives and share their everyday problems with him, in fear that their perception of their father as rigid man of the cloth would never allow him to understand everyday family problems. In a quiet conversation after finishing speaking to Jenny, Margaret speaks to her godfather Richard, discovering that neither one of them even believes in God. Disappointed by her godfather's lack of faith, Margaret cries that if he believes in something, perhaps she could believe in something too! Feeling unable to get closer to her father, she instead

In *The Holly and the Ivy* Ralph Richardson, as the parson, is oblivious to the problems within his own family, including those of his son Michael (Denholm Elliott).

sees her godfather as a father figure and tries to find strength within him for herself. But Richard's callousness and hardness toward the world only reinforces her own feelings.

After Michael and Margaret, supposedly escaping from the pressures of the family by going to the movies on Christmas Eve (but in reality both hitting the nearest pub and drinking themselves silly), return home and are caught by the parson (she fainting dead away in the living room), Martin implores Michael to tell the truth. To which he replies, "The truth! Can't be told the truth, that's the trouble. That's the whole trouble—you can't be told the truth" (by now shouting).

Martin, in a humbling position, attempts to connect with his own son. "Do you think that because I'm a parson I know nothing about life? Why do you think I was ordained in the first place? Do you think it was because I was so easily shocked I couldn't face reality?"

To which Michael tries to explain, "As a parson you have a different attitude to life. You think a thing like this that happened to Margaret is wrong and ex-

pect everyone else to feel the same way... Don't you see, how can parsons be expected to be told the truth if one cannot even talk to them as normal human beings?"

Dumbfounded by this perception, the parson states, "Well, if that's the way I've made you all feel. Well, I've failed. I failed completely." Martin realizes that his children have come to understand him by his religious stereotype and have never known the real man inside of the collar.

Meanwhile, Jenny reveals to Aunt Lydia that she and David will not marry, since Margaret is unable and unwilling to assume the role as keeper of father. "Strange how our lives always seem to have meaning because of somebody else. You understand Jenny, you're in love." She tells Jenny that if she's in love with David, she mustn't let anything stand in her way. Lydia uses Aunt Bridget as a metaphor. "Loneliness is a terrible thing... that's why I am always so sorry for people like Bridget. She did what you're thinking of doing... she stayed at home to look after your grandmother... Ever since your grandmother died, Bridget has been quite alone. If she died tomorrow, it wouldn't make the slightest difference to anyone. That's why it means so much for her to be here with all of you at Christmas."

Emotionally affected by Michael's truth (even if delivered at the height of his drunken state), the parson greets Margaret alone and tries to reconnect in a way he hasn't been able to for years. "I'm sorry. I've been of no use to you at all... Do I seem the type of man who turns away from the sorrows of his own children? It's no wonder my work has so little effect all these years. I've been misrepresenting religion all my life without knowing it. It's too late now." Margaret opens up and speaks of the disappointment of losing her lover during the war and then valiantly trying to raise their infant son Simon. When the baby got sick and died, her faith in life dried up and died too. Speaking of life, she admits, "It's doomed to failure." To which Martin responds, "That's the trouble with your generation. You must see and touch before you believe... Can you touch the wind???" Martin reveals his confusion about the meaning of life originally that led him to be ordained, that he also had difficulty in finding truth and faith in something in which to believe.

On Christmas morning, everyone is dressing and preparing for church. Aunt Bridget, in her typical crusty manner, confronts Martin about Jenny falling in love with David. "So you've woken up to the truth at last... and I hope you've been telling Margaret where her duty lies..." When David enters the house moments later, she says to him: "If you're half a man you'll take Jenny out of this trouble quick." David is confused by all these changing events occurring within the family—but one thing is certain, he wishes to marry Jenny.

A newly lucid Margaret, having helped her father leave for his Christmas sermon (surprisingly, in a very excited and pleased state of mind), now prepares to leave for church herself telling David, "It's Christmas, the family festival. We've all learned a thing or two about each other," and with a smile she announces she's coming back home to live with father. Abruptly, the scene changes as a few members of the family arrive at the church, "The End" superimposed over this entrance.

The Holly and the Ivy is more a character study than pure cinema, but the performances are marvelous. Ralph Richardson as the parson is first viewed doddering and tentative, oblivious to the problems within his own family, but by movie's end, he has grown more compassionate and strong by virtue of connecting feelings of inadequacy as a reverend to his failings as a father. Once the parson can connect one-on-one with members of his family, he feels he can also connect with his parishioners and make those books of sermons meaningful. He grows excited be-

cause he is emotionally able to help heal the pain in his family, something he as a parson should have been able to do for some time. Celia Johnson as Jenny features the proper amount of stiff upper lip, duty to family and burning, internal desire. She also comes off too British stereotyped, but her smoldering desires hidden barely beneath the surface create a subtle intensity. Margaret Halstan as Aunt Lydia is perfect as the other-worldly, eccentric aunt whose sensitivity and empathy for those around her juxtapose to the cold and callous exteriors displayed by the members of her family. She intuitively recognizes the love that exists between Jenny and David, and she is not afraid to express her opinion that such love comes before responsibility (and in this family, service and responsibility always come first: Jenny and her duty to father, Aunt Bridget and her duty to her mother, Michael and his duty to country, Martin and his responsibility to his church) and that love must never be denied. As she delivers her lines, she is usually staring off in space, stating each phrase in slow motion, as if she were speaking directly to the zone between the living and the dead. But her words and feelings always speak the truth and manage to be the right thing to say at the time. In a life of tragedy, she manages to always keep optimistic and hopeful. Finally Margaret Leighton as Margaret is also a delight. Secretive, haunted, and boozy in her initial appearances, she transforms into aloof coldness and detachment, unable to approach her father about all the pain in her life. Only after opening up to Jenny, and then Michael opening up to his father, only then are Margaret and the parson able to come together and understand one another. By movie's end, Margaret has transformed into a woman at peace with herself, excited at the prospect of returning home, everything out in the open at last.

Bittersweet, dysfunctional, and melodramatic, *The Holly and the Ivy* is not great cinema, but it does remind us of both the pain and the passion evoked by the wondrous season of Christmas. Bringing members of the family together, each of whom has some type of burden to bear, the strength of the family and the breaking down of barriers leads to not exactly Christmas bliss but rather to the healing warmth and potential for hope that crackles with every log placed on the Christmas fire.

—GJS

A Dream for Christmas
1973

This television film follows the trials and tribulations of Reverend Will Douglas (Hari Rhodes) and his family as they leave the small town of Sweet Clover, Arkansas for the big city of Los Angeles. Things are tough in Sweet Clover in 1950, and Will has accepted a job as preacher at a Baptist church. The family eagerly looks forward to hearing Will's Christmas sermon in the new church.

Tearful farewells are said—the most heartfelt between Emmarine (Ta-Ronce Allen) and her best friend and between Bradley (Marlin Adams) and his dog Toby, whom he is leaving behind with his cousin.

Finally, after 10 days and numerous car problems, the family arrives at the new church. They think it's wonderful. The attached house seems huge with three bedrooms.

But their joy is tempered by a large sign outside the church announcing a new shopping center being developed by Briggs Construction. Will is told by the church deacons that there is no money to pay him and that the church will be foreclosed on January 1. Little Bradley has his own worries; there is no fireplace for Santa Claus.

The children go off to their new schools, but Emmarine is made fun of and is very quiet that night at dinner. Their first weekend they clean the church and make it ready for Will's first Sunday sermon. Unfortunately, the family is larger than the congregation. Will remarks in his sermon, "Let the Lord see this church jammed packed by Christmas... Make this Christmas dream of mine come true."

Learning of their financial difficulties, Will's wife Sarah (Lynn Hamilton) and mother Bessie (Beah Richards) go to work housecleaning. Older son Joey (George Spell) finds a job washing cars.

Will has a difficult time dealing with the fact that his wife and mother are working to support the family. He tries to find a job, but even with a college education, it is difficult. Meanwhile he tries to see Mr. Briggs (Robert DoQui) to save the church. Mr. Briggs is not a bad man and admits he'll feel sorry about tearing down the church since his father's name is on the cornerstone as one of the founders. But he thinks a shopping center will help his community more than an empty church.

Will is forced to sell his father's car to a junk dealer for $15. He feels unworthy and unhappy with his wife and mother working and insists they quit for he has decided to give up the ministry. Christmas is two weeks away when Emmarine stuns her family by telling them how very unhappy she is. She hates her school and the girls who make fun of her and wants to go back to Arkansas. Her father tells her, "Don't toss in the sponge without a fight." He realizes the truth of his words and decides to fight for his church. He believes that the only way to convince Mr. Briggs is to fill the church with worshippers Christmas morning. He talks to people on the bus and in the market. He goes door to door and puts up a basketball court for the young men of the community hoping that will lead to their attendance at services.

Joe, while getting poles for the basketball court at the junkyard, finds a present for his father that the

In *A Dream for Christmas* the Douglas family does not need to be reminded of "peace on Earth good will toward men" only on December 25. They practice Christmas all year long.

owner agrees to deliver on Christmas Eve. He pays for it with the money he has earned on his job.

Grandma Bessie collapses and Will feels even more anxiety, believing her illness resulted because she went to work. She agrees to rest and prays she is there for Will's Christmas sermon.

On Christmas Eve the family decorates the house with colorful paper chains and strings the tree with popcorn strands and homemade ornaments. Will carries Grandma into the living room as the family contentedly sings Christmas carols. Bradley awakens early this Christmas and is delighted to find Joey has made a ladder for him to climb into and out of the top bunk bed.

On Christmas morning the sound of a bell interrupts the festivities. That was the present Joey bought for his father. A more perfect gift could not have been imagined. The Christmas service is packed and even Mr. Briggs shows up. He sees the overflowing worshippers and approaches the lectern to shake the hand of Will. We know the church will be saved. The congregation sings "O Come All Ye Faithful" as the Douglas family happily realizes they have found a new home and a new beginning.

This television movie doesn't pack the punch of splashier bigger-budgeted Christmas films and at times seems to need a little editing. It also doesn't spend a lot of time focusing on Christmas but rather on the trials of the Douglas family. But it is an important film and one of the earlier Christmas features with an all African-American cast. And an impressive cast it is too. Hari Rhodes appeared in feature films including *Conquest of the Planet of the Apes* and many television shows such as *Matt Helm, Most Wanted* and *Roots*. He died in 1992. His performance as Will is low-key and strikes just the right chord as the man struggles with his love of God and his desire to provide for his family.

Beah Richards as Grandma Bessie appeared in another Christmas film, *A Christmas Without Snow* as well as *Guess Who's Coming to Dinner*. But it was in television she would make her mark starring in *Sanford and Son* as the hilariously crabby Aunt Ethel. Lynn Hamilton, who perfectly matched film husband Rhodes' performance as the soft-spoken but tough-as-nails Sarah, also made television her home with recurring roles on *The Waltons* as Verdie Foster and as Donna on *Sanford and Son*.

The film doesn't seem dated and is actually refreshing in its approach to the Douglases and their troubles. No blame is placed for the family's plight; the tightly knit family just pull closer together and tries to make things better for themselves and their community. The Douglas family does not need to be reminded of "peace on Earth, good will toward men" only on December 25. They practice Christmas all year long by their love and belief in each other and in their commitment to the church and the local citizens. Their moral upbringing is strongly established when Joey shows remarkable courage by returning an item his friend Carter has stolen from a store, not allowing himself to be sucked into a bad lifestyle by peer pressure, and Emmarine, with the wise guidance of her father, refuses to give in to bullies and faces what to a lonely teenager is more terrifying than any monster—a new high school. She pulls herself together and finally makes friends and begins to enjoy her new life. This film is available on videotape and will made a pleasant viewing experience for the entire family.

—SS

Jessica Riggs (Rebecca Harrell) and her father (Sam Elliott) in *Prancer*.

Prancer

1989

Prancer may have flown from theaters before many people had a chance to view this charming little film of a girl, a reindeer and a fierce belief in all things wonderful. But it is available on videotape and should become mandatory holiday viewing for families.

Jessica Riggs (Rebecca Harrell) is a joyful vibrant little girl who dearly loves Christmas—she sings carols all year long and bubbles over with innocent childlike enthusiasm as the holiday approaches. Her teacher wishes her enthusiasm were a little quieter—Jessie manages to drown out the other children as they rehearse carols for their Christmas pageant. Later in the film after a fight with her father (Sam Elliott), Jessie is soon playing her record "We Wish You a Merry Christmas" and hanging reindeer across her window. Aunt Sarah (Rutanya Alda) is visiting and calls Jessie to supper.

Jessie excitedly discusses the approaching holiday: "There's going to be a full moon this Christmas."

"Don't talk with your mouth full," her father corrects.

"Sorry. That means there's bound to be magic things happening." Jessie is so full of life and wide-eyed belief in all things that the audience wants to embrace her and recapture this lovely feeling so many may have lost.

Jessie skips through life with her best friend Carol (Ariana Richards) by her side, but she and Carol have a falling out over Jessie's strong beliefs. Jessie is still wearing her angel costume as she walks home with Carol and is bubbling over with the thought of Santa. Carol doesn't believe in Santa but lets Jessie ramble on. They watch as workmen hang Santa's sleigh and reindeer across the main street. One of the deer falls, the third one—Prancer—and is run over by a car.

Later Jessie and Carol go sledding down a hillside. Jessie's sled is broken and she crashes through the garden of creepy old Mrs. McFarland (Cloris Leachman). With black high heels slipping on the snow, hair and clothes flying wildly, brandishing a shovel, the woman, resembling a nightmarish witch, chases Jessie through the yard. That evening darkness is falling and the woods seem quiet and spooky as Jessie heads home. She hears a twig snap and begins to run but stumbles and falls. She looks up to see a most majestic sight, a huge reindeer. She reaches out to touch him but he runs away.

The next day at lunch she tells Carol about the deer.

"The moon's almost full. It'll be full on Christmas Eve. Don't you see, it all fits together," Jessie excitedly tells her friend. She is sure the deer is Prancer.

Carol is troubled. "The problem is Jessie, I don't believe in Santa Claus anymore."

"What!"
"I mean think about it. How could one man climb down all the chimneys in the world in one night?"
"He's magical, Carol," Jessie answers rolling her eyes at her friend's ridiculous thinking.
"It doesn't make sense."
"Well Carol, not everything in the world can be explained."
"I've never seen Santa Claus and I've done a lot of looking."
"Well, you've never seen God either. Does that mean there's no God?"
"I don't know about that for sure."
Jessie is getting more upset. "Because if there's no God, there's no heaven."
"Well maybe there isn't."
"All right for you Carol Wetherby. You're not my friend anymore.
"What did I say?"
"That there was no heaven."

"So."
"What about my mother then?"

Jessie, like many children who lose a beloved parent, finds some small comfort in the belief that her mother is happily living in heaven. When Carol questions the big picture, Jessie cannot face the thought of her mother not being anywhere.

Jessie, although seemingly cheerful, also seems like a lost little girl. At the pageant, the children sing "Silent Night" as they walk toward the stage, while their proud parents sit in the audience. Jessie is still joyfully singing at the top of her voice. But after the pageant, when the other children run to their parents, she looks with sorrow at the happy families.

Another small but telling scene shows Jessie pouring imaginary tea from a play set and setting the little cup along with a flower before a picture of her mother.

The relationship between father and daughter is loving but strained. Jessie buries her sadness at losing her mother deep, but not as deeply as her tough-talking father John. Sam Elliott as John Riggs portrays the character as a sad, tired man, not sure how to cope with his motherless children and fearful of losing his farm. He clearly loves his two children but hasn't a clue how to deal with them. After the school

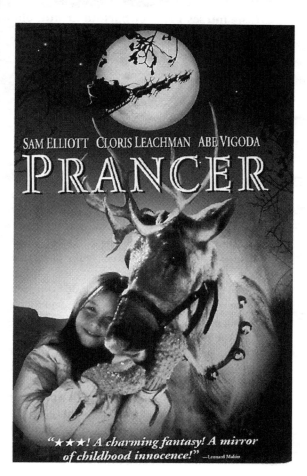

SAM ELLIOTT CLORIS LEACHMAN ABE VIGODA

PRANCER

"★★★! A charming fantasy! A mirror of childhood innocence!" —Leonard Maltin

Jessie nurses Prancer back to health, planning to return him to Santa Claus Dec. 23.

pageant, Jessie arrives home to find John working in his apple orchard. Jessie, her arms waving about, begins to describe the pageant to her preoccupied father.

"Are we going to starve?" Jessie asks.

"Of course not. Stop worrying about these things will ya. We're going to be all right."

Later she hears her father and aunt talking: "Have you told her yet, John? You've got to."

"I know," he replies.

Later Jessie walks home alone after school, once again walking through the woods, even though her father has warned her not to. She follows deer tracks before hearing gunshots. As Jessie continues home along a snow-covered road, a truck pulls alongside and her father yells, "Get in here."

He is very angry and tells her she could have been shot by hunters. Jessie asks him what he and Sarah were talking about.

"You know it's just not right when a little girl's got to grow up without her mom around. We've been talking about you maybe going to live with her [Aunt Sarah]."

Jessie is frantic. "No daddy, please. I don't want to do that. You're what's best for me." This is truly a real, heartbreaking scene and one not uncommon just a few generations ago when parents sent children to relatives who could better care for them.

As the father and daughter argue, Jessie yells, "Dad, look out!" He throws his arm across her and slams on the breaks. Prancer is standing in the middle of the road. Jessie wants to help him but her father takes his rifle to put the shotgun-wounded deer down. "I hate you," Jessie screams. When they look up the deer has vanished.

Jessie finds the deer (which she is convinced is Prancer) in the barn and hides it in a shed. She persuades the local vet to treat the deer and manages to keep it secret from her father.

Jessie has the enviable ability to charm those around her. The crusty old vet (Abe Vigoda) gives in to her pleas and helps Prancer. She hugs him saying, "History's going to love you for this." She also manages to warm the heart of the frightening Mrs. McFarland when she offers to clean any room in her house for five dollars. The sly old woman tries to take advantage of Jessie, but soon melts under the exuberance of the child. Jessie finds a box of Christmas lights in the attic and strings them up yelling "Surprise!" when Mrs. McFarland comes looking for her. She talks the woman into decorating her house—like she used to many years ago. Mrs. McFarland gives Jessie extra money, enough for Jessie to buy a red beribboned bag of oats for Prancer.

Jessie also urgently bullies a department store Santa (Michael Constantine) into delivering a message to the real Santa. "I'm sorry I don't have any time to chitchat. Can you get this letter to him?" Rebecca Harrell is priceless in this scene as she grabs the startled Santa by the beard. "Prancer is in the shed, near my house. I plan to take him to Antler Ridge on December 23, midnight." This is not the usual request and the man reacts with amazement. "Oh, wait a minute. Now is that all you want for Christmas?" Jessie hurriedly answers, "Well, for now, anyway. I really don't want to live with my aunt, but I don't know if Santa can do anything about that."

Santa takes the letter to the local newspaper editor who prints it under the heading "Yes, Santa, there are still Virginias." That Sunday Jessie attends church with her aunt and brother. The preacher reads her letter as she slowly sinks into the pew. Meanwhile, her father is home reading the Sunday paper feeling something is amiss, but he's not quite sure what. John is even more perplexed when cars begin pulling up looking for the reindeer. He finds Prancer wandering through the house wreaking havoc. John grabs a rifle but someone yells, "Don't shoot!" John sells the deer to a local butcher who is going to display him.

Jessie's relationship with her father hits a new low. Sobbing she proclaims, "Mom would have never done this—I wish she were here instead of you!" Words that cut deeply into the soul of the bereaved father.

Jessie and her brother Steve (John Duda) have the typical brother/sister relationship—constant bickering. But as Jessie sets out that night to rescue Prancer, Steve follows, asking why she is taking her clothes with her. Jessie explains about Aunt Sarah. "I didn't think you'd care." "Of course I do," Steve answers.

As any parent of emotional children can attest, Jessie considers herself the ultimate martyr and sorrowfully declares, "With Prancer gone there's nothing left for me in this town. Good-bye Steve."

Steve, as any good brother would, goes along to help. Jessie climbs a tree and tries to remove the wire from the top of the cage. She pulls the wire back and tells Prancer to fly. When he doesn't, Jessie loses her last ounce of faith. Then local constable Burt (a tribute to *It's a Wonderful Life* perhaps?) stops by to check on Prancer; Jessie grabs a tree limb and holds on precariously. Steve begins to climb the tree but Jessie loses her grip and falls to the ground. Her frantic brother runs for help while Prancer breaks down the cage and lays down beside the unconscious girl to keep her warm.

Steve decorates the Christmas tree as John, on the phone, asks the hospital if Jessie was released too early. She won't get out of bed or play her Christmas records. "It's just a deer, Aunt Sarah," she tells her worried aunt.

The finale of the film resembles Disney's *Pollyanna* as neighbors gather outside singing Christmas carols. Even Mrs. McFarland, the vet and Carol are in the crowd. John enters the darkened room.

"Haven't got much to give you this Christmas."
"That's okay, Daddy."
"No, it isn't. I've been thinking maybe we could do some of the things we used to do, you know, before. On other Christmases."
"I'd like that Daddy... I didn't really want to run away. I just wanted you to find me and bring me back here and tell me everything's going to be okay, like it used to be."
"Aw, Jessie. I can't tell you everything's going to be all right... Could be we'll even lose this farm some day. I can bear that. What I can't bear is when you were gone last night, I saw what it would be like around here not to have you around. I love you Jessie."

John has Prancer in the back of his pickup and he and Jessie finish the little girl's quest of returning Prancer to Santa.

John comes to realize the magic of Christmas is within ourselves and our precious loved ones. He and Jessie both regain their shaken faith and look forward to a life lived happily ever after.

Prancer was released in 1989 and filmed on location in Three Oaks, Michigan and Laport, Indiana. The film was directed by John D. Hancock whose first directorial effort was the horror film *Let's Scare Jessica to Death* in 1971. He would follow that film up with baseball tearjerker *Bang the Drum Slowly* in 1973. Sam Elliott has the rugged looks that fit comfortably into cowboy/farmer roles in films such as *Butch Cassidy and the Sundance Kid* and *Gettysburg*. *Prancer* was the first film of Rebecca Harrell, who stole the show from the seasoned veterans. Her exuberance and sparkle drive the film; her disappointment in the harsh realities of the real world devastates the audience as much as Jessie herself.

Roger Ebert in the *Chicago Sun-Times* noted, "The best thing about *Prancer* is that it doesn't insult anyone's intelligence. Smaller kids will identify with Jessica's fierce resolve to get Prancer back into action, and older viewers will appreciate the fact that the movie takes place in an approximation of the real world."

—SS

Babe

1995

"Christmas means dinner. Dinner means death. Death means carnage. Christmas means carnage!" No, I'm not playing the role of Ebenezer Scrooge. I am, instead, quoting from the worldly wise Ferdinand, the duck who almost becomes Christmas dinner in *Babe*. (*Babe* was nominated for seven Oscars. But Ferdinand was robbed of a Best Supporting Actor nod despite delivering one of filmdom's classic comedy performances.) Now, it's no secret what day is a turkey's least favorite holiday of the year. But because I grew up in a part-Italian household which prepared homemade ravioli for the Christmas feast, I never gave much thought to either the eating traditions of other families or the effects such traditions would have on wildlife. Thus *Babe* was something of a message movie for me: While little kids and their kin were running towards the Christmas tree to open their gifts, others (like ducks) were running for cover so they wouldn't be "opened" come dinner time.

Of course, *Babe* isn't really a movie about Christmas. It's a truly marvelous fairy tale "about an unprejudiced heart," namely Babe the pig. Babe is won by Farmer Hoggett (James Cromwell) at a local fair ("Think Christmas day…What a feast!" the barker tells him) and is then brought to the Hoggett farm for fattening up, or so it would seem. In the meantime, Babe gets mothered (he's an orphan) by Fly, the wife of the farm's watchdog, Rex. Babe also meets Maa, a sheep who thinks none too kindly of Fly and her ilk. And then, of course, there's Ferdinand, who lures the "extremely gullible" pig into a prickly plot involving the theft of the Hoggetts' alarm clock. (I suppose it bears mentioning that Ferdinand is attempting to take over the rooster's job of crowing in the morning. The alarm clock threatens the livelihood of both rooster and duck. "The treachery of it!" Ferdinand laments.)

Babe's "I love everyone" attitude comes into play when he's "asked" to help prepare the sheep for clipping. Although he initially tries the dog's tactic of barking and threatening ("Move along there ya… big buttheads!"), he finds that simply being himself ("…a nice little pig") does the trick. Hoggett realizes what a special pig he has and registers him for a sheep herding contest, even though the unofficial rules would indicate only dogs can participate. The film's climax has this wonderful little sow silence the skeptical audience as he flawlessly guides his sheep through the "obstacle course." (How wonderful it is to watch a film designed for children of all ages that doesn't end with small kids being in danger, as in, say, *The Flintstones*.)

Of course, messages of trust, love, tolerance, compassion and acceptance are very appropriate for anytime of the year. And Babe is certainly not a "Christmas film" in the sense that it chooses not to center its actions around the Yuletide. That being said, however, Christmas is the one time of year where most people (hopefully) might try to adopt an unprejudiced heart. Thus *Babe* is certainly in the *spirit* of Christmas movies.

I don't mean to give the impression that the film is some serious, message-driven film which drips over with false sentiment. No, the film is a comedy first, which uses its gentle story and endearing characters to teach the lessons. We just don't realize we're being taught. (My favorite teachers were always the ones whose enthusiasm was so contagious that the class didn't realize they were learning something.)

In attempting to create a fairy tale come to life on the screen, the filmmakers give us a narrator (Roscoe Lee Browne) to guide us through the story; title cards, such as "Crime and Punishment" and "Pork is a Nice Sweet Meat," to alert us to key plot points; and a trio of singing farm mice to open and close several scenes. Director Chris Noonan (who was nominated for an Oscar) continuously gives us the animals' perspective of the world by employing low-angle camera shots and allowing the audience to "eavesdrop" on the livestock's meetings. The non-humans are at the center of *Babe*, and the top-notch special effects team makes us believe in this world where animals can talk, at least to each other.

Basically the animals live in a rigidly structured environment: Cows, horses, dogs, sheep, pigs and ducks all have their place. Before Babe comes along, "Pigs were given no respect," the narrator tells us. When Babe arrives, however, trouble was already afoot thanks to Ferdinand's attempt to take the place of the rooster in an effort to prove himself useful. Babe inadvertently becomes a "sheep pig," which further shakes up the farm.

The funniest sequence in the film takes place when Ferdinand talks Babe into helping him commit the great "crime": the theft of the alarm clock. While Ferdinand watches outside through a window, Babe enters the kitchen via the dog's entrance and slowly makes his way through the living room. Unfortunately he bumps into a table, which causes a ball of yarn to fall off and almost wake up the cat. Then the little porker gets a hoof caught in the yarn and almost knocks over an entire table. Meanwhile Ferdinand is going nuts outside, his wings flapping about, his little eyes getting wider and wider with panic, as he watches the possible catastrophe unfold. Luckily he stops the pig before any real damage is done. However, on the way out, the stolen alarm clock is dropped and goes off, waking the sleeping cat, who then attacks the pig

On Christmas Eve, Babe hums "Jingle Bells" ("La la la, La la la, La la la—la la…").

and duck. Ferdinand becomes an outcast. (Babe's let off the hook since he's but a child.)

Other humorous moments abound. Ferdy cracks up when the cat gets thrown out of the house (during a thunderstorm no less) for scratching Babe. Babe does a couple of cute pratfalls, like when he's looking through the Hoggetts' window trying to learn what goes on inside. The audience for the contest suddenly becomes completely silent, while the commentators fumble for the right words to say. Still, the humor is counterbalanced by some serious moments such as when Fly must give up her puppies, or when some vicious stray dogs attack and kill Maa. But, for the most part, *Babe* is a cheerful film filled with gentle humor.

When Christmas time does arrive, Babe gets so caught up in the festive nature of the season that, on Christmas Eve, he hums a chorus of "Jingle Bells" ("La la la, La la la, La la la—la la…"). Mrs. Hoggett (Magda Szubanski), meanwhile, plans to serve Babe as the Christmas meal. But Mr. Hoggett, by this point, has realized there's something special about Babe and persuades the missus into opting for the duck ("Shame to miss out on the best ham prize at next year's fair.") But, we the audience don't want to see Ferdinand get the ax either. Thus when the farmer enters the barn, as the animals watch on, and we hear a duck's cry of terror, we are a bit saddened. Luckily for us, it turns out it wasn't Ferdinand who got eaten. ("Her name was Rosanna," Ferdy tells us.)

The filmmakers also have some fun with the Hoggetts and their grandchildren, who visit at Christmas. Hoggett's granddaughter cries out in disappointment when she finds out her gift is a homemade doll house, which is not like the factory-made one she's seen on television. (Hoggett had been working on that doll house for quite a while. In one of the film's earliest scenes—when he learns he's won Babe—we see him working on his granddaughter's gift.) Meanwhile the Hoggetts themselves are confused by the gift they receive: a fax machine. What on earth are these simple-living farm types going to do with such a high-tech piece of equipment? (Of course, it does prove beneficial when Farmer Hoggett faxes Babe's application for the sheep contest.) Despite the absence of snowflakes (it *looks* like Christmas in July), carolers and other such traditional trappings, there is something very familiar about these Christmas Day Kodak moments.

Babe and the rest of the farm's non-human residents watch the Christmas proceedings with interest. The holiday's events are capped off with a fireworks display, courtesy of Farmer Hoggett, while some crooning mice sing "Blue Moon."

While the religious nature of Christmas is not directly addressed in *Babe*, the film nonetheless deals with many fundamental issues about life. For example, we all, at one time or another, ask the question, "Why am I here?" In a key scene, a vicious cat named Duchess decides to relate the purpose of the

Babe and friends look on in sorrow as Rosanna the duck is served for Christmas dinner in *Babe*.

various animals (the dogs protect the Master, the cat keeps the Master's wife company, cows provide milk for humans, etc.). "Why are any of us here?" Babe asks. The sole purpose of pigs, it would seem, is to be eaten by humans. From a pig's point of view, this is not a cheery thought.

Another issue addressed has to do with how, er, people relate to one another. The sheep hate the "wolves" (their name for dogs) and think all wolves are irretrievably stupid, while the dogs have nothing but contempt for sheep and think all sheep are dumb. Babe, who sees the good in both, inadvertently brings the two "cliques" to a better understanding of each other by film's end. Both the dogs and the sheep care for Babe, so Rex asks the sheep's help in aiding Babe during the contest. The sheep, in turn, pass on a secret code to Rex, who will pass it to Babe, but not before making Rex promise to treat the sheep better in the future.

Babe, himself, is a child, and thus his perceptions and attitudes capture some of the best attributes of childhood. He trusts completely: He doesn't even realize that Hoggett is about to shoot him (he thinks it's some new way of dispatching food) when the farmer incorrectly believes Babe attacked Maa. He bears no hatred because he hasn't been taught to hate: Babe can't believe the things Maa says about Fly and vice versa. He wants everyone to be happy: He tries to "make up" with Rex even though Rex's initial dislike of Babe has nothing to do with the pig's behavior. Babe, as it turns out, is something of a rebel because he doesn't accept that "the way things are is the way things are." Babe makes all this niceness gar-

bage look so *easy*. He wins the hearts of humans and non-humans before all is said and done: Everyone jumps for joy when the little pig is victorious in the end.

While most of *Babe*'s cast is non-human, James Cromwell does wonderful work as Farmer Hoggett, who perhaps has the least amount of dialogue in the entire picture. He reacts with a mere, "Oh...," when he learns he's won Babe. And most of his discoveries throughout the film must be kept to himself. But his tearful, "That'll do, pig. That'll do," the film's closing line, speaks volumes. And his wonderful jig, which he delivers to save the life of his favorite pig, shows an uncharacteristically buoyant and cheerful Hoggett. Although Cromwell went on to play the chief nasty in *L. A. Confidential* (1997), he'll always be Farmer Hoggett to me.

But it is Babe, himself, that makes this story come to life. He's a reminder of how all of us started out: free of cynicism and prejudice. And since Christmas preaches the feelings of goodwill towards *all* people, I find *Babe*, despite only a brief Christmas scene, is perhaps the only film in recent years to capture the true meaning of Christmas. I doubt the film was ever meant to be taken with such seriousness. Still, if the Ghosts of Christmases Past, Present and Future had just taken old Eb to a screening of *Babe*, they might have saved themselves all that extra effort.
—JS

The following films also focus on or have scenes pertaining to Christmas:

All I Want for Christmas
Cast: Leslie Nielsen, Lauren Bacall, Harley Jane Kozak, Jamey Sheridan, Thora Birch
Credits: Producer: Marykay Powell; Director: Robert Lieberman; Paramount; 1991

Adorable little Hallie O'Fallon (precocious Thora Birch) visits the *real* Santa (a tribute to *Miracle on 34th Street*) at Macy's to ask him to reunite her parents for Christmas. Big brother Ethan (played convincingly by Ethan Randall) warns her not to ask Santa for personal things, not wanting Hallie to be disap-

Hallie O'Fallon (Thora Birch) asks Santa (Leslie Nielsen) to reunite her parents in *All I Want for Christmas*.

pointed when Santa can't deliver. The relationship shown between brother and sister is charming, rather than the typical love/hate scenario in most films. Ethan looks out for his little sister (as do most big brothers in real life), zipping up her jacket when he picks her up outside school to walk her home (granted that no responsible adult would have allowed Hallie to go out into the snow wearing a tutu under that jacket—one of many such scenes in the film that make responsible adults shake their heads).

The kids live with their mom Catherine (Harley Jane Kozak) at their grandmother's luxurious townhouse in Manhattan. Not just an ordinary grandmother either, she's the famous actress Lillian Brooks played by the always stunning Lauren Bacall. At her Christmas party Lillian and Hallie sing a sweet duet to "Baby It's Cold Outside," a delightful Academy Award winning song written by Frank Loesser and first introduced in the Esther Williams/Red Skelton film *Neptune's Daughter*.

Catherine is dating the requisite creepy boyfriend, Tony Boer (Kevin Nealon), whose phony friendliness to the kids literally makes Hallie nauseous. Of course, Catherine and the kids' dad Michael are still in love. Michael even calls Catherine a favorite name, "Slick"—a slight tribute by the screenwriters or merely a coincidence that Bogart's pet name for Bacall was the sound-alike Slim?

Wanting Hallie to have one more Christmas morning with her parents, Ethan hatches a plan to throw his parents together on Christmas Eve.

Hallie sacrifices Snowball, one of the mice she has grown attached to, so they can save their parents' marriage.

They get rid of the boyfriend to clear the way for Catherine to be stood up, but how to get her to Michael's? Hallie pretends to be sick and Catherine rushes to her side. The kids spend the night in the diner while Catherine curls up next to Michael on the sofa. Unfortunately, Hallie and Ethan forget to go back to dad's loft and the frightened parents rush off to Lillian's to see if the kids are there. The family is reunited and Ethan is about to explain when Tony bursts in and tells Catherine her kids are brats and will be dealt with when they are married. Tony is soon history, much to Lillian's delight, and the family is reunited in front of a glorious Christmas tree with snow falling gently outside the living room windows. Suddenly a knock is heard at the front door and, low and behold, there's Santa (the *real* Santa) from Macy's with a gift for Hallie, that's right... Snowball.

The film, like the glorious snowfall it showers on New York City, is pure fluff. While the adult roles in the film could have been portrayed by any competent actors, it's the kids and the idyllic picture of New York at Christmas that shine.

The Best Christmas Pageant Ever
Cast: Fairuza Balk, Jackson Davies, Teri Dean, Beau Heaton, Loretta Swit
Credits: Director: George Schaefer; Television 1983

The town bullies decide to participate in the Christmas pageant with remarkable results.

Bush Christmas
Cast: Chips Rafferty, John Fernside, Stan Tolhurst, Pat Penny
Credits: Producer/Director/Writer: Ralph Smart; Gaumont; 1947

Australian children's film that has a group of kids chasing thieves who stole horses. I haven't been able to find a copy of this film so we have no way of knowing how Christmas relates to the movie.

Bush Christmas
Cast: John Ewart, John Howard, Nicole Kidman, Mark Spain
Credits: Producers: Gilda Baracchi and Paul D. Barron; Director: Henri Safran; Writer: Ted Roberts; Hoyts; 1983

Australian remake of the 1947 film. I'm still not sure what Christmas has to do with it.

The Christmas Box
Cast: Richard Thomas, Maureen O'Hara, Annette O'Toole
Credits: Producer: Erica Fox; Director: Marcus Cole; Writer: Greg Taylor (based on the Richard Paul Evans novel); Television 1995

A widow takes in a young family that changes her life in this popular Christmas story that became a television film.

Christmas Comes to Willow Creek
Cast: John Schneider, Tom Wopat, Kim Delaney, Hoyt Axton
Credits: Producers: Billie Andre, Jeffrey Fischgrunk and Margaret Murphy; Director: Richard Lang; Writers: Michael Norell and Andy Siegel; Television 1987

Two truckers (Wopat and Schneider) are feuding brothers who drive a rig to Willow Creek, Alaska for Axton. He wants to deliver a special Christmas to his old hometown whose residents are jobless since the local cannery closed down.

A Christmas Memory
Cast: Patty Duke, Piper Laurie, Anita Gillette, Eric Lloyd, Esther Scott
Credits: Producers: John Philip Dayton and Glenn Jordan; Director: Glenn Jordan; Writer: Duane Poole (Based on a Story by Truman Capote); Hallmark; 1997

A boy (Eric Lloyd) whose parents have divorced moves in with his Southern relatives and quickly becomes attached to one special person, Sook (Patty Duke).

A Christmas Reunion
Cast: James Coburn, Edward Woodward, Meredith Edwards, Gweirydd Gwyndaf
Credits: Director: David Hemmings; Cinematography: Barry Stone; Peakviewing Productions; 1993

This British television film tells the story of a young boy who runs away from his stern grandfather. He is invited into a shop with a neon light over the door that glares "Santa's." Santa tells the boy a story of a young lad named Tim and his difficult life in Wales. The story is interesting and finely acted but the Christmas story is merely a framing device for the main story of young Tim's adventures. While not necessarily a Christmas film, the family should enjoy this movie throughout the rest of the year.

A Christmas to Remember
Cast: Jason Robards, Eva Marie Saint, Joanne Woodward
Credits: Director: George Englund; Writer: Stewart Stern; Television 1978

Robards is a farmer who brings his grandson to his farm for a holiday visit.

The Christmas Wife
Cast: Jason Robards, Julie Harris, Don Francks
Credits: Producer: Patrick Whitley; Director: David Hugh Jones; Writers: Katherine Ann Jones and Helen Norris; Television 1988

Robards lives a lonely existence in a mountain cabin. He decides to pay a woman (Harris) to be companion over the holidays.

A Christmas Without Snow
Cast: Michael Learned, James Cromwell, John Houseman
Credits: Director: John Korty, 1980 Television film

Michael Learned is a divorced mother who moves to San Francisco to start life anew. Her son stays with her mother in the midwest until she can afford to send for him. She finds a family in her church choir that has a new choirmaster (Houseman) who wants them to perform Handel's *Messiah* on Christmas day. There is very little Christmas seen in the film but we are overloaded with the sad problems of the choir members: Learned's mother is constantly harping at her, a churchmember loses her husband to cancer, the Reverend's son trashes the pipe organ, the stereotypical desperate female turns in a young black choirmember whom she sees leave the church the night the organ is destroyed and he is arrested, an older woman is asked to leave because she can no longer sing the correct notes and Houseman has a stroke.

What a fun movie. The scripters wish us to see how the conflicts of every-day life can be overcome by a love of church and family and a lofty goal, but the film is heavy-going and not the type of holiday viewing most people are looking for in December.

Dondi

Cast: David Janssen, Patti Page, Walter Winchell, Mickey Shaugnessy, David Kory
Credits: Producers: Albert Zugsmith and Gus Edson, Director/Writer: Albert Zugsmith; Allied Artists; 1961

This film, based on the popular comic strip of the same name, begins with Dondi, a war orphan, befriending American GIs on Christmas Eve. Patti Page sings "Jingle Bells." This film is not available on videotape so the only hope of seeing it is on television. We were unable to find a copy to view and had to rely on other sources for the description.

The Gathering

Cast: Edward Asner, Maureen Stapleton, Bruce Davison, Veronica Hamel, Gregory Harrison
Credits: Director: Randal Kleiser; Writer: James Poe; Television 1977

A dying man (Asner) gathers his family together for one final Christmas. Won the Emmy for Outstanding Television Drama in 1978. Unfortunately the videotape of this film has been discontinued and interested movie buffs' only option is to try to catch it on network television during the holidays.

The Gathering Part 2

Cast: Maureen Stapleton, Patricia Conwell, Bruce Davison, Veronica Hamel, Jameson Parker
Credits: Director: Charles S. Dubin; Television 1979

Widow (Stapleton) again gathers the family together, this time to introduce the new man in her life. Follow-up to *The Gathering*.

Hans Brinker

Cast: Robert Askwith, Eleanor Parker, Richard Basehart, Cyril Ritchard, John Gregson
Credits: Director: Robert Scheerer; Walt Disney; 1969

This Disney film has always been a Christmas mainstay in our household. The story concerns Hans Brinker (Robin Askwith) and his family. His father has been comatose since an accident at work and the

Ed Asner and Maureen Stapleton appear in the touching family Christmas drama *The Gathering*. (Photofest)

family has no money. They are barely able to survive with the jobs they can manage while attending school. Hans and his sister Gretel (Roberta Torey) enter a skating contest hoping to pay back a doctor who has helped restore their father to normal. A wonderful family film that will have young and old mesmerized.

Has Anybody Seen My Gal

Cast: Piper Laurie, Rock Hudson, Charles Coburn, Lynn Bari
Credits: Director: Douglas Sirk; Producer: Ted Richmond; Writer: Joseph Hoffman; Based on a Story by Eleanor H. Porter; Universal; 1952

Coburn stars as a millionaire who wants to leave his fortune to the family of the girl who turned him down to marry a bookkeeper. If she hadn't turned him down he wouldn't have made his fortune. He moves in with the family as a boarder and observes how they handle his anonymous gift of $100,000. Of course, the money causes them grief, but things work out during the Christmas season when the family lose all their money and Piper Laurie gets out of her engagement with a spoiled playboy and goes back to her true love, Hudson. The family moves back to their old house, having learned money doesn't buy happiness.

Hobo's Christmas
Cast: Barnard Hughes, Gerald McRaney, Wendy Crewson, William Hickey
Credits: Producer: Paul Freeman; Director: Will Mackenzie; Writers: Joe Byrne and Jeb Rosebrook; Phoenix Entertainment; Television 1987

A man who gave up his family and friends to be a hobo returns home for Christmas 25 years later.

Home of Angels
Cast: Sherman Hemsley, Lance Robinson, Craig Sechler, Abe Vigoda
Credits: Producer: James Oliva; Director: Nick Stagliano; Writer: James Oliva; Cloverlay Productions; 1994

A young boy rescues his Alzheimer-afflicted grandfather (Vigoda) from a nursing home so he can spend the holiday with the family.

The Homecoming: A Christmas Story
Cast: Richard Thomas, Patricia Neal, Edgar Bergan, Ellen Corby, Cleavon Little
Credits: Producer: Robert L. Jacks; Director: Fielder Cook; Writer: Earl Hamner, Jr.; Lorimar; 1971

This made-for-television film was the prelude to the popular *Waltons* series. Regular viewers will find the different actors portraying the familiar family a little disconcerting. It is Christmas Eve and the family is preparing for the arrival of John who has been working 50 miles away. During the Depression, the family living in the Blue Ridge Mountains has little money. The children fight and bicker as siblings are wont to do and mother worriedly waits for the arrival of her husband. A news report announces a bus has overturned and one passenger is dead. She sends John Boy out to find his father but, although he tries his best, things are not going his way. He arrives back home alone.

Finally John makes it home and the family members are delighted with the presents he has brought home, although his story of wrestling the gifts from a frightened Santa Claus may bother younger children. Another Christmas special featuring the Walton family was made in 1978 called *The Waltons: The Children's Carol.*

A House Without a Christmas Tree
Cast: Jason Robards, Mildred Natwick, Lisa Lucas
Credits: Producer: Allen Shayne; Director: Paul Bogart; CBS; 1972

This CBS television production is the story of Addie (Lucas) and her unhappy father (Robards) who live with his mother (Natwick) since he was widowed. He wants nothing in the house that reminds him of his deceased wife, including Addie. During Christmas of 1946 he comes to terms with himself and brings home the Christmas tree Addie so longs for. Touching television film with fine acting. Robards is especially memorable as the strong man who can't face his emotions.

The Kid Who Loved Christmas
Cast: Cicely Tyson, Sammy Davis, Jr., Della Reese, Esther Rolle, Ben Vereen, Vanessa Williams
Credits: Director: Arthur Allan Seidelman; 1990

After his adoptive mother is killed a boy is taken away from the husband. The child writes to Santa Claus for help. We were unable to find a copy of this film to view and had to rely on other sources.

A Lion in Winter
Cast: Peter O'Toole, Katharine Hepburn, Timothy Dalton, Anthony Hopkins, Jane Merrow, Nigel Terry, John Castle
Credits: Producer: Martin Poll; Director: Anthony Harvey; Writer: James Goldman Based on his Play; Cinematographer: Douglas Slocombe; Music: John Barry; Avco Embassy; 1968

"What shall we hang, the holly or each other?"— King Henry II

This film could be listed as a slice-'n'-dice film, but the slicing and dicing is done with the tongue in this historical salute of the ultimate dysfunctional family—King Henry II (O'Toole), his imprisoned wife Eleanor of Aquitaine (Hepburn) and their three conniving, back-stabbing sons: Richard the Lion-Hearted (Hopkins), Geoffrey (Castle) and John (Terry). The family gathers for a Christmas holiday which is also attended by King Philip of France (Dalton) and Henry's mistress (who is also Philip's sister) Alais (Merrow). It is difficult to follow the slings and arrows of outrageous fortune as this dueling family battle for supremacy as Henry prepares to name his successor. Eleanor schemes with Richard, John and Jeffrey plot with Philip, Richard conspires with Philip (his former lover), Jeffrey connives with Eleanor, Henry uses Alais as a bridal pawn for the victor, Eleanor takes perverse pleasure in wounding Henry and on and on.

The writing is of 1940s caliber—witty and biting, while the acting is absolutely superb. If during the holiday season you think you can no longer bear another family event, watch this film—you'll soon appreciate your own family.

A Matter of Principle
Cast: Alan Arkin, Barbara Dana, Alison Jacoby, Virginia Madsen
Credits: Producer: Neal Miller; Director: Gwen Arner; Writers: Nancy Miller and Neal Miller; Rubicon; 1983

Arkin plays a grim man who will not allow extravagances. When his family wants a Christmas tree, he throws it out. The next morning they are gone, but the man comes to his senses in time to regain his family.

Miracle Down Under
Cast: Dee Wallace Stone, John Waters, Charles Tingwell, Bill Kerr
Credits: Director: George Miller; Disney; 1987

A family in 1980s Australia endures hard times but a Christmas miracle brightens their holidays. Miller also directed family favorite *The Man From Snowy River*.

My Side of the Mountain
Cast: Teddy Eccles, Theodore Bikel, Tudi Wiggins, Frank Perry, Peggi Loder
Credits: Producer: Robert B. Radnitz; Director: James B. Clark; Writers: Joanna Crawford, Jean George, Jane Klove and Ted Sherdeman; Paramount; 1969

A young boy leaves home and takes up residence in a hollowed-out tree to conduct experiments. He awakens Christmas day to find himself completely snowed in. He digs out with the help of a friend who talks the boy into returning home.

On Moonlight Bay
Cast: Doris Day, Gordon MacRae, Leon Ames, Rosemary DeCamp, Billy Gray
Credits: Producer: William Jacobs; Director: Roy Del Ruth; Writers: Booth Tarkington, Jack Rose and Melville Shavelson; Warner Bros., 1951

This musical features a Christmas segment where young Wesley has again gotten into mischief and his angry father is searching for him. A group of carolers approach the house, and lo and behold there's Wesley dressed in an angel costume singing sweetly. Doris Day and Gordon MacRae meeting the carolers on the front porch sing "Christmas Story" as the smiling parents look on though the living room window. Wesley offers a tentative wave and smiles with relief when father waves back.

The Railway Children
Cast: Dinah Sheridan, Iain Cuthbertson, Jenny Agutter, Sally Thomsett, Bernard Cribbins
Credits: Producer: Robert Lynn; Director/Writer: Lionel Jeffries (Based on a Novel by E. Nesbit); Universal; 1971

During Christmas an employee of the Foreign Office is sent to prison. His family, who have lost almost everything, must move to a poorer neighborhood. While their mother makes a game of pretending they are poor, the children make friends, one of whom helps them clear their father's name.

A Tree Grows in Brooklyn
Cast: Dorothy McGuire, Peggy Ann Garner, James Dunn, Lloyd Nolan
Credits: Producer: Louis D. Lighton; Director: Elia Kazan; Writers: Frank Davis, Anita Loos, and Tess Slesinger (Based on the Betty Smith Novel); Fox; 1945

A wonderful film that follows Francie Nolan (Peggy Ann Garner) and her family as they struggle to make ends meet. Francie is the apple of her father's eye, but John Nolan can't keep a job and frequents the local bars. He is beloved by everyone but his wife Katie (Dorothy McGuire), who still loves him but can't abide his ways and constantly worries over money. She moves the family to a smaller apartment upstairs when she finds she is pregnant. Christmas Eve, Francie and her younger brother Neeley (Ted Donaldson) anxiously await midnight so they can go to the Christmas tree lot. The owner throws the trees, and if you can catch one, you can keep it. Francie and Neeley have been eyeing a large tree which together they manage to catch. They drag the tree home. Officer McShane (Lloyd Nolan) helps them carry it into the foyer. Katie watches out the window as her sister Sissy (Joan Blondell) tells her, "They're trying to make a Christmas; help them, kid."

Outside snow falls as the Nolan family happily decorates their tree with candy canes and paper chains in *A Tree Grows in Brooklyn*.

John rushes down to help and as they carry the tree up, all the neighbors come out of their apartments and laugh and sing "Silent Night" as the merry family carries the tree. Officer McShane sadly watches and turns away.

Snow is falling heavily outside as the family decorate the tree with candy canes and paper chains. Francie and Neeley open their presents, long underwear, but are happy nonetheless. Officer McShane stops in on his way home and gives the children more candy canes for the tree. They invite him to stay but he declines saying, "This evening's for families."

Katie tells John she is having another baby and Francie will have to stop going to school and get a job. John knows how much Francie loves her school and is distraught. He goes in to see Francie who tells him she is going to be a writer.

"Papa, the people in the hall when we brought up the tree, the look on their faces, all friendly and nice. Why can't people be like that all the time, not just at Christmas?"

Her father doesn't really have an answer. "Well, I don't know. Maybe it's because Christmas is like they really are and the other part ain't true." He kisses Francie goodnight and goes out. "Don't start drinkin', not tonight," Katie tells him as he leaves. "I won't

Katie." He doesn't return and Katie goes looking for him in his favorite bars. But she has no luck. Officer McShane comes to the door and tells her they found him collapsed in the doorway of an employment agency in Manhattan. Francie is devastated by the death of her father and believes her mother doesn't love her, only Neeley. But in the spring the two come to an understanding when Katie needs her help delivering the new baby. Francie can stay in school because a friend of their father's, Mr. McGarrity (James Gleason), offers her and Neeley part time work after school. Officer McShane asks to keep company with Katie and the film ends as Francie and Neeley discuss how the baby will not have the tough life they did and look at the little tree that survived the cold winter, now blooming again.

Peggy Ann Garner would receive a special Oscar for Best Child Actor for her performance as Francie in this film, while James Dunn took home the Best Supporting Actor trophy for his role as John Nolan.

A Tree Grows in Brooklyn does not center on Christmas but on the Nolan family throughout the year. However, this is an always enjoyable and heart-warming film that should be on your top holiday viewing list.

The Brady Bunch was reunited for *A Very Brady Christmas*.

A Very Brady Christmas

Cast: Florence Henderson, Robert Reed, Ann B. Davis, Maureen McCormick, Eve Plumb, Barry Williams, Christopher Knight, Mike Lookinland
Credits: Director: Peter Baldwin; Paramount; 1988

The Brady kids, now grown up and moved away, return home to spend Christmas with the family. Of course they are all unhappy and sit in the kitchen eating pie and being miserable. Marsha's husband is out of work, Jan and her husband are thinking about splitting up, Greg's wife and son can't be with them, Peter is in love with his boss, Bobby is hiding his true career and Cindy wants to be on a skiing trip with her friends. But a family emergency makes them realize what Christmas and family is truly about.

Credits:

Babe

Cast: Christine Cavanaugh, James Cromwell, Roscoe Lee Browne, Miriam Margolyes
Credits: Producers: Bill Miller, George Miller and Doug Mitchell; Director: Chris Noonan; Writers: George Miller and Chris Noonan (Based on the Dick King-Smith Novel *The Sheep Pig*); Universal; 1995

Christmas Eve

Cast: George Raft, George Brent, Randolph Scott, Joan Blondell, Reginald Denny
Credits: Producer: Benedict Bogeaus; Director: Edwin L. Marin; Writer: Laurence Stallings (Based on a Story by Laurence Stallings and Richard H. Landau); UA; 1947

A Dream for Christmas

Cast: Hari Rhodes, Beah Richards, Lynn Hamilton, George Spell, Marlin Adams, Robert DoQui
Credits: Director: Ralph Senensky; Writers: Max Hodge and John McGreevey (Based on a story by McGreevey); Producer: Walter Coblenz, Lorimar Productions; 1973

The Holly and the Ivy

Cast: Ralph Richardson, Celia Johnson, Margaret Leighton, Denhold Elliott
Credits: Producer: Anatole de Grunwalk, Director: George More O'Ferrall; Writers: Wynyard Browne and Anatole de Grunwald; London Films; 1954

Little Women

Cast: Dorothy Bernard, Henry Hull, Conrad Nagel
Credits: Director: Harley Knoles; Producer: William A. Brady; (Based on the novel by Louisa May Alcott); Silent, 1918

Little Women

Cast: Katharine Hepburn, Joan Bennett, Paul Lukas, Edna May Oliver, Jean Parker, Frances Dee
Credits: Producer: Kenneth MacGowan; Director: George Cukor; Writers: Sarah Y. Mason and Victor Heerman (Based on the Louisa May Alcott Novel); RKO; 1933

Little Women

Cast: June Allyson, Peter Lawford, Margaret O'Brien, Elizabeth Taylor, Janet Leigh, Mary Astor
Credits: Producer/Director: Mervyn LeRoy; MGM; Writers: Sarah Y. Mason, Victor Heerman, Andrew Solt (Based on the Louisa May Alcott Novel); 1949

Little Women

Cast: Meredith Baxter Birney, Susan Dey, Eve Plumb, Dorothy McGuire, Robert Young, William Shatner, Greer Garson
Credits: Producer: David Victor; Director: David Lowell Rich; Writer: Suzanne Clauser (Based on the Louisa May Alcott Novel); Universal; 1978

Little Women

Cast: Winona Ryder, Susan Sarandon, Samantha Mathis, Kirsten Dunst, Claire Danes, Mary Wickes
Credits: Producer: Denise DiNovi; Director: Gillian Armstrong; Writer: Robin Swicord (Based on the Louisa May Alcott Novel); Columbia; 1994

Meet Me in St. Louis

Cast: Judy Garland, Margaret O'Brien, Lucille Bremer, Tom Drake, Marjorie Main, Leon Ames, Mary Astor
Credits: Producer: Arthur Freed; Director: Vincente Minnelli; Writers: Irving Brecher and Fred F. Finklehoffe (Based on the Story by Sally Benson); MGM; 1944

Prancer

Cast: Sam Elliott, Rebecca Harrell, Abe Vigoda, Rutanya Alda, Cloris Leachman
Credits: Producers: Raffaella De Laurentiis, Greg Taylor and Mike Petzold; Director: John Hancock; Writer: Greg Taylor; Orion; 1989

Tenth Avenue Angel

Cast: Margaret O'Brien, Angela Lansbury, George Murphy, Phyllis Thaxter, Warner Anderson
Credits: Producer: Ralph Wheelright; Director: Roy Rowland; Writers: Eleanore Griffin and Harry Ruskin (Based on a Story by Angna Enters and Craig Rice); MGM; 1948

Later on We'll Conspire as We Dream by a Fire...

Love stories and Christmas seem a match made in heaven (as indeed it is in "The Bishop's Wife" and "The Preacher's Wife"). In this chapter we look at love stories that occur during Christmas. Some are sweet, some are funny and some are sad, but almost all are guaranteed to delight viewers.

Bachelor Mother

1939

Although *Bachelor Mother* takes place during the Christmas holidays, after the opening sequence little remains to be seen of the season except for a New Year's Eve party. However, the film is a charmer and will appeal to all ages.

Single working girl Polly Parrish (Ginger Rogers) receives her pink slip from J.B. Merlin and Son thanking her for working the holiday season. As Polly visits an employment office on her lunch hour, she finds a baby on the doorstep of a foundling home. The people within assume the baby belongs to Polly. She mentions where she worked and the home not only gets her job back but a $5 raise. David Merlin (David Niven) tells her not only has she received her job and a raise but that night she will receive the greatest gift possible. Polly's confused but doesn't look a gift horse in the mouth.

That evening, as she prepares to leave for a dance contest with obnoxious co-worker Freddie (Frank Albertson), the baby is delivered, complete with gift basket. She insists she is not the mother, but with disgust, the employees of the foundling home leave the adorable bundle with Polly.

She indignantly takes the baby to David Merlin, telling the butler the baby is David's responsibility, he got her into this, now he can get her out! She hops in the car with Freddie—David and butler (E.E. Clive) in hot pursuit. David, baby in arm, enters the dance hall where Polly and Freddie are in the contest, but he manages to get himself ejected. Three hours later, Polly arrives home to find a disheveled David and the baby waiting. He not only assumes she is a loose woman, but also a terrible mother and threatens to blackball her from a job at any department store in the city. Polly quickly decides to give up and play along. Feigning regret, she tells him she had nowhere to turn. She even shows David where the baby's father supposedly hit her on the head with a coffee pot! David gives her the job back and beats a hasty retreat.

Of course David soon falls victim to the charms of Polly. When he is stood up on New Year's Eve, he invites Polly out for a night on the town, arranging to have a complete formal outfit (including fur coat) delivered to her apartment. The romance seems to be blooming until Freddie (who thinks Polly used her influence to get him a better job at the company), mistaking David for a shoplifter, tackles him and is immediately busted back to stockboy. Well, Freddie is basically a heel and writes an anonymous note to

the big guy, David's father, J.B. Merlin (Charles Coburn), telling him he is a grandfather.

J.B. discovers the duo in the park and with a tear in his eye, picks up the baby. "What's his name?" he asks. "John." Merlin looks at David grimly, "Well, thank you for that." David is panic stricken when he realizes what his father is thinking and rushes after him. Polly laughs delightedly. But her delight is short lived when David tells her J.B. wants to take the baby away from her.

Polly talks her landlady's son Jerome (Leonard Penn) into pretending he is the father, and they pay a visit to J.B. He's almost convinced when in bursts David with Freddie proclaiming he's the father. Well, David, thinking Jerome is the father, hits him on the head with a coffee pot. Freddie thinks David is the father. And J.B. thinks he is the grandfather and doesn't care who the father is!

Polly sneaks away from the ruckus and rushes home to pack. She is interrupted by David who proposes and tells J.B. he is the father. They are to be

Polly (Debbie Reynolds, center) gets more than she bargained when she gets her job back at Merlin and Sons in *Bundle of Joy*.

married that very night. As they embrace, Polly gives a little ha, ha, knowing David is in for a big surprise on their wedding night.

Bachelor Mother is another sophisticated farce from Hollywood's golden age. The film was directed by relative newcomer Garson Kanin and written by Felix Jackson, who received an Academy Award nomination for his effort. Kanin directed several films but would forever make his mark on Hollywood with his clever writing skills, often collaborating with his wife at the time, Ruth Gordon. The duo would win an Academy Award for their script for *Adam's Rib*. In 1940 Kanin would direct another hit, *My Favorite Wife,* starring Irene Dunne and Cary Grant.

Jackson's script was risqué for the time and, amazingly, many of his double entendres managed to slip past the censors. The film was based on a Hungarian film from 1935 called *Klein Mutter* which in turn was a version of a 1934 German film called *Klein Mutti* directed by Henry Koster, the director of *The Bishop's Wife*.

Ginger Rogers, always an appealing screen presence, brings her usual charm to the part of Polly. Rogers began her film career in the chorus but soon gained fame as the partner of Fred Astaire. Their big

break would come as supporting characters in RKO's *Flying Down to Rio* in 1933. Rogers would eventually break away from the dance partnership to tackle a solo career. That move paid off in *Bachelor Mother*, a role that garnered her major attention. The next year she would make *Kitty Foyle*, earning an Academy Award for her performance as the title character.

David Niven, the personification of debonair, was, as usual, wonderful as the playboy conquered by the charms of a typical working girl. Niven would appear in over 80 films including *The Bishop's Wife* and *Around the World in 80 Days*.

Variety's review of *Bachelor Mother* stated, "Will play a sweet tune at the summer box offices. It's a broad farce-comedy, decidedly human in texture, and studded with laugh situations and dialog. Carries some rather spicy lines aimed for the adult trade..."

Bachelor Mother was remade in 1956 by RKO as *Bundle of Joy* and starred Hollywood's most adorable couple, Debbie Reynolds and, in his big screen debut, Eddie Fisher. The story remained basically the same. Debbie, portraying Polly, is told she's fired from her job as salesclerk at J.B. Merlin's department store, and by the way, Merry Christmas. While waiting for an employment office to open she finds a cherubic blond baby in front of a foundling home. Once again, the helpful but obtuse employees think she is trying to abandon the baby because she has lost her job. Playing Guardian Angel, one of the administrators of the home visits J.B. Merlin's to get Polly her job back. He sees the younger Mr. Merlin, Dan (Fisher), who not only gives Polly her job back but a $10 raise (a suitable increase since 1939). Poor Polly thinks the store has finally seen the light and realizes what a great employee she is. Her bubble is soon burst when the foundling home delivers the baby to her doorstep later that night.

As in the earlier film, she falls in love with the younger Merlin and complications ensue when J.B. thinks the baby is his grandchild.

Bundle of Joy is really more of a musical than a holiday film. It just happens to occur at Christmas, and with a wink and nudge, we are reminded of a virgin birth since everyone assumes the baby belongs to Polly who the screenwriters make quite clear is not the type of girl to have a baby without benefit of marriage.

Fisher is a fine singer, but the film only lights up when Reynolds is onscreen, and even she can't overcome the rather inept script. The songs, while pleasant enough, especially the Fisher/Reynolds duet "Lullaby in Blue" written by Josef Myrow and Mack Gordon, are not really memorable. The same can be said of the film.

—SS

The Shop Around the Corner

1940

In the Good Old Summertime

1949

Budapest, Hungary
Box 237
Modern girl wishes to correspond on cultural subjects anonymously with intelligently sympathetic young man.
Address Dear Friend.

In direct contrast to the lavishly well-to-do characters of Depression-era films of the 1930s and the film noirs soon to become a mainstay of 1940s Hollywood, comes Ernst Lubitsch's *The Shop Around the*

Corner, a film filled with simple working-class folks who, like the rest of us, are neither all good nor all bad.

Released by MGM in 1940, the film boasted a cast list that was virtually a who's who in Hollywood. Directed by the highly respected Ernst Lubitsch and starring Jimmy Stewart (an Academy Award nominee the previous year for his performance in *Mr. Smith Goes to Washington*), Margaret Sullavan (Academy Award nominee in 1938 for her performance in *Three Comrades*) and the Wizard of Oz himself, Frank Morgan, *The Shop Around the Corner* was bound to do a brisk business.

The story centers on Mr. Matuschek (Frank Morgan) and his happily middle-class group of employees who work in his leather goods shop. Times are tough in Budapest, and the workers live in constant fear of rocking their safe little boat. As the film begins we see the employees arrive for work and indulge in harmless chatter while awaiting the owner. As in any workplace, there is the office snitch, in this case Mr. Vadas (Joseph Schildkraut), who overhears everything and immediately changes the context to fit his own little nefarious schemes. The employees are aware of his intentions and comically stress each point they make as being extremely benign, frantically gaining agreement from their co-workers as to the harmless intent of their words—be it the quality of Mrs. Matuschek's goose liver on which Kralik (Jimmy Stewart) dined the prior evening or whether Matuschek's wife had a face lift.

Later that day, when Mr. Matuschek asks for their honest opinion on an annoying cigarette box he has selected for the shop, the conniving Ferencz Vadas cloyingly agrees it is a wonderful box as Mr. Pirovitch (Felix Bressart) overhears those frightening words and slips away. Only Alfred Kralik, the oldest employee in the store, tells Mr. Matuschek the truth, whether he wants to hear it or not. Into this little mix comes Klara Novak (Margaret Sullavan) looking for a job. Kralik informs her he knows everything Mr. Matuschek thinks and he would never hire her. Matuschek hears this and, thinking the lady is a customer, asks her the problem. He is extremely miffed Kralik didn't save him from the situation, but Kralik stands his ground and tells him it was his own fault. Meanwhile, Klara still hasn't left and, managing to sell a lady the cigarette box at a higher price than Matuschek was going to charge. Matuschek is so happy, he gives Klara a job as clerk.

At work Klara and Kralik are like oil and water—no matter how hard they try to get along they always manage to take each other's words the wrong way. But, after work, well, that's another story. They both have a secret. Box 237. The two have been unknowingly corresponding as "Dear Friend" and each has grown to love the other through their letters—although they don't even know their correspondent's name.

As Christmas approaches Mr. Matuschek becomes increasingly cantankerous, usually taking his wrath out on Kralik. Kralik has problems of his own. He keeps putting off meeting his "Dear Friend" for fear of disappointing her or of being disappointed himself. They finally arrange that all-important first meeting, and both begin their day eagerly awaiting closing time and the long-awaited rendezvous with their unseen lover.

Matuschek arrives at the store in a fouler mood than ever and decides to redo the store windows, ordering everyone to stay late. Klara decides to beguile Kralik into helping her get the evening off. Margaret Sullavan sparkles in this scene as she sits atop a ladder helping Kralik stack boxes while charmingly whittling down his defenses. But Kralik is no dummy and soon realizes the reason she is being nice to him. Klara rushes to Mr. Matuschek and tells him she cannot work that night. He asks Kralik if he can do without Klara but, when Kralik tries to tell him he too needs the evening off, Matuschek flies into a rage and they exchange bitter words.

At closing time the shop curtains are lowered and the staff proceed to redecorate the windows. Kralik and Klara are hanging ornaments on a small Christmas tree when Matuschek calls Kralik into his office. The employees smile encouragement as he walks to the office, thinking he is going to get the raise he had been planning to request. However Matuschek dismisses him, sadly handing him severance pay and a letter of recommendation. Jimmy Stewart brings a tear to the eye as he cleans out his locker and tosses the red carnation he was going to wear to his rendezvous onto the floor. With no position he can't ask his "Dear Friend" to marry him. As Kralik leaves, he places his salesbook onto a cloth-covered counter. Director Lubitsch has the camera focus on that book as two small pencils and the shop key are placed with it. The hopes and dreams of poor Kralik are left behind in that little book.

Meanwhile, Matuschek receives a phone call and sends the rest of the employees home. A visitor arrives, a detective (Charles Halton) who has been following Matuschek's wife. Matuschek had received an anonymous letter informing him his wife was having an affair with one of his employees. Since Kralik was the only employee he ever took home, he naturally assumed he was the villain. But the detective tells him it is Vadas who has been dallying with Matuschek's wife. Frank Morgan turns in a fine performance in this scene as the bitterly disappointed husband. He tells the detective to send him a bill and slowly goes into his office. Fortunately Pepi (William Tracy) the delivery boy opens the office door and stops Matuschek's suicide attempt.

Kralik has asked Pirovitch to deliver a letter to his friend. Outside the restaurant, his curiosity gets the better of him and he asks Pirovitch what she looks like. "She's very pretty," Pirovitch answers. "She looks a little like Klara." Well, this day just keeps getting worse and worse for Kralik when his friend tells him, "it is Klara."

Kralik decides not to send the note and just leave Klara waiting. But his conscience gets the best of him, and he returns to the restaurant where they do verbal battle—he knowing she is "Dear Friend," and she anxiously trying to be rid of the pesky Mr. Kralik so she can finally meet the man of her dreams. He states Klara will turn into an old maid while she meanly replies, "I have to laugh when I think of you calling me an old maid. You, you little insignificant little clerk." A pitiful look of sadness crosses Kralik's face before he slowly departs, leaving Klara alone.

Matuschek has Pepi call Kralik to the hospital where he apologizes for believing Kralik could have had an affair with his wife. He gives him the key to the shop and promotes him to manager. The next morning the employees happily welcome him back, Vadas trying to worm his way into Kralik's good graces. Kralik works himself into an anger and fires the "two-timing back-stabber." Klara has called in

Pepi (William Tracy) and Kralik (Jimmy Stewart) help Vadas (Joseph Schildkraut) leave Matuschek's as Flora (Sara Haden) readies his severance pay in *The Shop Around the Corner*.

sick, but after checking her post office box and finding no letter, she goes to work and asks Kralik if she could see Mr. Matuschek; she refuses to believe him when he tells her he is now in charge and falls into a faint when a phone call confirms Kralik's story.

He visits her at home that evening inquiring about her health. She condescendingly tells him that her problem is psychological but perks up when her aunt brings in a letter, which she anxiously reads. Jimmy Stewart is at his most endearing in this scene as he twitches and rolls his eyes as Klara reads portions of the letter (which, of course, he wrote) to him. She tells him that she will be back to work tomorrow and to save one of the musical cigar boxes. The look of panic that crosses Stewart's face is priceless as he tries to talk her out of the odious box and instead convince her to buy a nice wallet. "A wallet is quite romantic. You see, on one side he has your last letter, on the other side a picture of you, and when he opens it, there you are. And that's all the music he wants."

The next morning, Christmas Eve, the staff is pleased to learn Mr. Matuschek is doing better and they send him a Christmas tree for his hospital room.

Kralik encourages them to make this the best Christmas ever for the store. Pirovitch asks Klara if he could have the music box for his wife's uncle, whom he doesn't like; he can't think of a more annoying gift. He says to Kralik, "You'll get the wallet."

The shop is bursting with customers and the day passes quickly. A heavy snow is falling as Mr. Matuschek pushes through the crowd and glances into the shop window with a smile. He and the staff await Flora's total for the day, "the best since '28!" he enthuses. Matuschek thanks them for the thoughtful gift they sent and then proceeds to hand out Christmas bonuses, Flora shyly taking hers, staring with adoration at Matuschek. (They'll get together eventually, the audience hopes.) He even remembers the new delivery boy Rudy (since Pepi has been promoted to clerk). In this scene with his distinct voice, Frank Morgan as Matuschek reminds us of the Wizard of Oz when he admits to Dorothy and her friends that he is a fraud. Sad and alone, Mr. Matuschek leaves but stands outside in the falling snow with nowhere to go this Christmas Eve. He speaks to each employee leaving and asks their plans. We hope each will invite

Mr. Matuschek (Frank Morgan) and the staff await Flora's total for the day. "The best since '28!" Matuschek enthuses in *The Shop Around the Corner*.

him home with them but none do, all excited to get home to their families. Rudy leaves and stops to thank him quietly for the gift. When asked about his holiday plans, he tells Mr. Matuschek that he has no people in Budapest and the two depart for a lavish dinner with strudel for dessert at an expensive restaurant.

Still in the shop, Klara is wrapping her precious wallet and, since it is Christmas Eve, she buries the hatchet with Kralik, even telling him that when she first started working there she was falling for him! She is flustered but remembers her important date with "Dear Friend" and announces they both may be engaged when they come back to work. Kralik replies that he knows they will. When she asks how he knows, he proclaims that her fiancé came to see him. "Popkin... A very nice fellow." He begins to turn out the lights in the shop. "Don't put him on a diet... a good solid mature citizen... out of a job... he feels both of you can live very nicely on your salary. Let me tell you, mentioning that bonus didn't do you any harm."

Klara is crushed. Her idolized knight-in-shining-armor is a fat, bald, unemployed bum. Kralik tells her it's a shame he didn't know how she felt at the beginning, because then he would say, "Klara, darling, so dearest, sweetest Klara. I can't stand it any longer. Please take your key and open post office box 237 and take me out of my envelope and kiss me."

Kralik puts a carnation in his buttonhole. "Dear Friend," he says. It takes a few moments for this to sink in for Klara who replies, "Psychologically I'm very confused but personally I don't feel bad at all."

The Shop Around the Corner was based on the play *Parfumerie* by Nikolaus Laszlo. The screenplay was adapted by Samson Raphaelson, author of the play *The Jazz Singer* and long-time Lubitsch collaborator on films such as the Academy Award nominated *Heaven Can Wait*, as well as *The Merry Widow*, *One Hour with You* and *That Lady in Ermine*.

Ernst Lubitsch was born and began his acting career in Berlin, which slowly evolved into directing. He arrived in Hollywood in the 1920s bringing with him a European sense of class and style and a light-hearted approach toward sex that was missing from many American directors. His style, which nobody has ever been quite able to imitate or even describe, became known as the Lubitsch touch. He directed *Love Parade* with Maurice Chevalier in 1929 winning his second Academy Award for directing—the first had been for *The Patriot*, 1928 and followed those films up with merry musicals and cheery love stories, including the highly acclaimed *Trouble in Paradise* and *Ninotchka*. In his biography, *Ernst Lubitsch: Laughter in Paradise*, author Scott Eyman asks Lubitsch's niece which of his movies was most like him. *"The Shop Around the Corner.* It's so European; it contains the most of what he was, all the types, the people that were his friends, the people he loved." The film delightfully exudes this loving feeling.

Margaret Sullavan was said to be the great love of Jimmy Stewart's life, although they never managed to get together. They, along with her future husband, Henry Fonda, appeared together with the University Players in Falmouth, Massachusetts. She was at home in comedies but spent most of her film career in melodramas. She quickly grew tired of the Hollywood hubbub and returned to the stage. Margaret Sullavan died at the age of 49. She had also been married to director William Wyler and famed agent Leland Hayward.

Jimmy Stewart needs no introduction to the American public. His charm, endearingly boyish good looks and easygoing manner won him the love of the adoring public. He was a real-life war hero and all-around nice guy. When he passed away in 1997 we felt as though we had lost one of our best friends. Before Jimmy Stewart fell ill, fans would write him requesting he do a drawing of Harvey, his invisible rabbit friend from the film of the same name. He always complied.

The cast was ably supported by Frank Morgan, a Broadway actor who found his rainbow in Hollywood. Morgan began his film career in the silent pictures and would find his niche as an always befuddled but unceasingly friendly gentleman as an MGM contractee. He appeared in over 75 films including *Boom Town, Summer Holiday, Green Dolphin Street, Naughty Marietta* and *Thousands Cheer.* Felix Bressart as Pirovitch fled his homeland when the Nazis came to power. He would work with Ernst Lubitsch in one of his most famous films, *To Be or Not To Be* (1942), a Nazi satire starring Jack Benny at his best in his role of ham actor and Carole Lombard as his flirtatious wife.

In their January 10, 1940 review of *The Shop Around the Corner Variety* noted, "It's smart and clever, but still packaged with easily understandable situations and problems of middle-class folks."

For delightful holiday fare, a visit to *The Shop Around the Corner* could be just what Santa ordered.

The film was remade by MGM 1949 as *In the Good Old Summertime.* Rather than latter day Budapest, the film has gone back in time to Chicago at the turn of the century with art director Cedric Gibbons, along with Randall Duell, turning the Technicolor film into a visual treat. Reportedly the film was originally developed for June Allyson, who didn't have an extremely strong singing voice. Allyson

---

Matuschek's Apple Strudel

1 pound cold butter
2 teaspoons salt
ice water
1 pound flour, sifted

Work 2 tablespoons of the butter into the flour and salt. Mix with the ice water to form a dough. Turn onto a floured board, pat smooth and divide into 2 portions. Roll both to same size. Over one sprinkle a little flour. Take the remaining cold butter, form into a roll and roll thin to match size of rolled out dough. Place the butter between the 2 sheets of dough, then roll as thin as possible without allowing the butter to come through. When thin, fold in the sides until they meet, turn half around and roll out. Fold and roll this way twice then chill for 15 minutes. Repeat the rolling and chilling 3 more times. Then roll out and spread with the apple mixture, pressing it in lightly with a rolling pin.

1 cup fine dry bread crumbs
1/4 cup butter
2 cups finely chopped peeled apples
1/2 cup chopped raisins
1/2 cup chopped almonds
1/2 cup sugar
1 teaspoon cinnamon

Brown the crumbs in the butter, combine with all the remaining ingredients and cook until the apples are soft. Place on dough. Roll up strudel like jelly roll, transfer to a well-greased shallow pan and bake in a 400-450° oven until the crust is golden brown.

---

bowed out because of pregnancy, to be replaced by Judy Garland. Consequently the songs don't do justice to the talent of Garland who only gets to cut loose on "I Don't Care," but the energetic number seems too modern for the film setting.

Often dialogue is word from word from the original, but the adultery theme is tossed into the junk heap. The owner of the shop, Mr. Oberkugen (S.Z. Sakall), has been dating his bookkeeper Nellie (Spring Byington) for years without offering a proposal (he's waiting to become a concert violinist—the poor woman will never see her wedding day; Oberkugen's playing could make a grown man cry). His bad temper is due to Nellie telling him she has a date—with another man. He orders everyone to stay late causing Veronica Fisher (Judy Garland) to miss her rendezvous with her pen pal. As in the original, Veronica's nemesis at work, Andrew Larkin (Van Johnson), is her secret love. Realizing the employees are being kept unreasonably, Nellie apologizes to Oberkugen, who then allows the workers to leave. Rudy Hansen (Clinton Sundberg) helps the nervous Larkin get ready for the big night. As they approach the restaurant he makes Rudy look for the lady and describe her. Finding it is Veronica, Larkin leaves in a huff and goes to hear his neighbor Louise play her violin at another eatery. On his way home, he passes the restaurant only to see Veronica still seated at her table. He enters and the two trade insults.

The next day Veronica calls in sick and, at the urging of Rudy, Larkin goes to see her. The duo begin to get better acquainted as he happily helps take

Van Johnson and Judy Garland in *The Good Old Summertime*. (Photofest)

crushes the instrument. Larkin confesses it wasn't the real Stradivarius, which was at the audition. Veronica, Hickey and Oberkugen wait backstage at the Symphony Hall with a policeman; but when Oberkugen hears Louise play the violin, he cannot have Larkin arrested. He merely fires him. Veronica, feeling a little jealous, thinks Louise is Larkin's girlfriend. The next day, Christmas Eve, Larkin arrives early to let the employees into the shop, and Nellie makes him wait while she gets a letter of recommendation. Oberkugen, praising Larkin in the letter, realizes he has made a mistake and makes him manager. Larkin enters the storeroom to hang up his coat and, while trying to propose to Veronica, only winds up having another argument with her. He tells Rudy the whole thing is off, but then listens as Veronica sings "Merry Christmas" (by Fred Spielman and Janice Torre—a pleasant little song, but it certainly isn't "Have Yourself a Merry Little Christmas") and his bad temper melts away.

As they close the store Oberkugen happily announces that this was their best day ever. Hickey apologizes to Larkin for taking Veronica to the party. He tells him he didn't realize she

care of a baby left in Veronica's charge, when her aunt brings in a new letter. Larkin tells her to bring her boyfriend to the engagement party of Nellie and Mr. Oberkugen.

That afternoon Nellie pulls Larkin aside and begs him to do anything so Mr. Oberkugen can't play his violin at the party. Oberkugen has entrusted his precious Stradivarius to Larkin, who takes it home with him. Louise sees the instrument and assumes Mr. Oberkugen has lent it to her for an audition that night with the symphony.

Poor Larkin arrives late at the party without the violin. Oberkugen insists he get it. Larkin gets Louise's old violin and reluctantly takes it to the party. Oberkugen's clumsy nephew Hickey (Buster Keaton) hurries to the front of the room to give it to his uncle when he trips (as only Buster Keaton can do) and

was in love with Larkin, thus encouraging the new manager to put the moves on Veronica. As in the original, he turns out lights in the shop as he tells Veronica of meeting her fiancé. Disillusioned, she sits beneath a Christmas tree as Larkin strokes her hair and finally tells her he is her "Dear Friend." Garland's reading of the "psychologically I'm very confused, but personally I don't feel bad at all" line is actually more effective than Margaret Sullavan's, as the statement ends with an embrace and the camera pans up the tree.

Judy Garland has matured before our eyes, and in this performance her voice has traces of the caustic wit she was known for. The prior year she had made the musicals *Easter Parade* with Fred Astaire and *The Pirate* with Gene Kelly, turning in two dazzling performances. In 1950 she would make her last film for MGM, *Summer Stock*. Her "Get Happy" number in

that film would be one of the best musical numbers she had ever performed.

One of Van Johnson's first film appearances was as a chorus boy in RKO's *Too Many Girls* with Lucille Ball in 1940. He would have his first starring role in Warner Bros.' *Murder in the Big House* in 1942 and that same year would become an MGM contract player working in many musicals including *Easy to Love* and *Brigadoon*.

In 1963 *The Shop Around the Corner* would be made into a highly acclaimed Broadway musical, *She Loves Me*, by Jerry Bock and Sheldon Harnick.

Another film version, *You've Got Mail*, for release December 1998, is being directed by Nora Ephron and stars Tom Hanks and Meg Ryan. Bringing the film into the nineties, the romance is conducted via e-mail between two bookstore managers; Ryan operates a small independent children's bookstore and Hanks manages a book superstore. With the above-mentioned golden names that helped make *Sleepless in Seattle* such an audience favorite, this updated *Shop Around the Corner* is sure to please.

—SS

Remember the Night
1940

Back in 1940 when Preston Sturges was writing movies, memorable Christmas ones like *Remember the Night*, the term literate script really meant something. Even when working within the restrictive confines of Hollywood's infamous production code era when those who broke the law had to be "punished" for their infractions by movie's end, Sturges was still able to offer a world of moral ambiguities where the good and the bad were never clearly defined. Even though Sturges works with stereotypes—the smug and heartless big city lawyer, the hardened yet beautiful female jewel thief, the hick Justice of the Peace, the spinster

aunt, the outraged farmer—his characters all demonstrate some aspect of surprise in their characterizations, they grow and gain insight. They surprise the audience and force us to change the way we look at them as the movie unreels. Even though Christmas is pivotal to this movie (the movie occurs a few days before Christmas and concludes on January 3)—both in setting and theme—the holiday becomes a mere steppingstone to explore the many divergent themes of home, family, personal morality and falling in love. *Remember the Night*'s tone changes from playfulness to sadness, from hilarity to warmth, from passion to fear, sometimes within the same scene. And under Mitchell Leisen's direction and Ted Tetzlaff's photography, the wonderful Preston Sturges story resonates and somehow manages to reflect the true spirit of Christmas, on adult terms.

The movie begins almost as a crime caper, with a wonderful tight close-up of a black-gloved hand wearing a gold bracelet. "Could I see that one down there, please?" As the salesman bends over, then looks up, the woman, wearing the bracelet, has suddenly disappeared. The panicked salesman starts to yell for his boss. Moments later, the same woman, wearing an expensive fur, still wearing the bracelet, walks down the holiday-decorated New York City streets, passing both people carrying Christmas presents and the Salvation Army Santa ringing his bell for donations, as holiday tunes are heard in the background. She rushes into a pawn shop, shows off the bracelet, and the man behind the counter quickly closes the front door, locking it shut as the woman bangs upon it to be let out.

Even though this is an open and shut case, the District Attorney realizes it is very difficult to get a woman convicted, especially at Christmas, and especially one as beautiful as Lee Leander (Barbara Stanwyck), so the D.A. phones John Sargent (Fred MacMurray), an expert lawyer when it comes to getting female convictions. Houseboy Rufus (Snowflake) answers the phone and covers incompetently for his employer: "If this is the office, he's already left." From the background, the nasty John yells, "I didn't say to say that, you dumb bell." Picking up the phone, John pleads that he was told once he finished the Matthews case, he was free for the holidays—free to begin his seven-hour car ride home, to his mother's farm in Indiana. The D.A. promises the case will be finished by noon tomorrow.

In court John is further dismayed that the woman's lawyer is Francis X. O'Leary (Willard Robertson), "a windbag" who is a former ham actor who loves the sound of his own voice. In a marvelous sequence where O'Leary holds the jury and entire courthouse in the palm of his hand, he creates a fantastic, melodramatic story where Leander is supposedly hypnotized by the gem, steals it being unaware, comes to her senses and returns to the store to return the gem, but panics as she realizes the store is closed. She then supposedly uses the phone book to find the owner's number at home, but she has no money to either make the call or take a train. Thus, the pawn shop idea came into her head. At the end, the lawyer concludes with, "The defense rests," turning around as though expecting a standing ovation. John, who is calm and smiling throughout, is repeatedly asked by his assistant why he doesn't object. Instead, the handsome lawyer sits back and enjoys the show. When he is at last allowed to speak, he does so briefly and effectively: "The hypothesis of hypnotism is a very interesting one, let me be first to admit it. But I am no Svengali. Nor are you, ladies and gentlemen of the jury." The state psychiatrist, an expert on the matter, is unfortunately away for the holiday, but the wily John, realizing getting a conviction against a woman near Christmas is almost impossible, instead asks for a continuance. The court will reconvene Tuesday January 3, and a $5,000 bond is placed on Leander as she is led off to the promise of a turkey dinner in jail. John smiles to himself, very proud, "he fell for that one."

However, John's guilt gets the best of him for putting a lady away for the holiday (besides, the store got its bracelet back); he calls in a favor to bail bondsman "Fat" Mike (Tom Kennedy), who surprisingly drops the grateful girl off at John's apartment (thinking the young lawyer expected the girl to demonstrate her gratitude via hanky panky). When the astonished lawyer eyeballs the attractive woman, she asks, "Well, what do I have to do for it?" The lawyer, composing himself, answers, "Well, for one thing you might say thank you, but if that doesn't fit in with your plans, skip it."

Lee, still not convinced of John's honorable intentions, states, "One of these days one of you boys is going to start one of these scenes differently, and one of us girls will drop dead from surprise... I guess you do this with all of the lady prisoners!" To which John playfully replies, "Oh yes, my life is just one long round of whoopee!" "And I guess if anyone says no, you put them right back in the cooler!" she says. John explains his intention to put her in prison after the holiday, but since she hasn't been convicted yet, she deserves a good holiday like any decent person does. "Then why did that gorilla bring me up here?" To which John honestly reveals, "Because he has a mind like a sewer." When John tells Lee she is free to leave, she decides to stay anyway. "There's nothing as dangerous as a square shooter. If all men were like you there wouldn't be any nice girls left." Since she is giving up a free room and a turkey dinner in jail, John agrees to take her out on the town for a nice turkey dinner.

At the supper club Lee and John have the opportunity to get to know one another better, and before long a mutual attraction appears to be brewing beneath the surface. "You really didn't want me to come up at all then," Lee asks slightly confused and disappointed. Beginning the theme of ambivalent morality, Lee states: "Right or wrong is the same for everybody, but the rights and the wrongs aren't the same... like in China they eat dogs... Try it like this..." Lee sets up a story, you are poor and starving, but you have no money. Loaves of bread are set out in front of a market, and the owner's back is turned. "Would you swipe one," Lee inquires of John. "You bet I would," John smiles back. Surprisingly, Lee says, "That's because you're honest. I'd have a six course dinner... across the street and say I've forgotten my purse. Get the difference?" To which John responds, "Yeah, your way's smarter." Soon the very same judge trying the case ambles past John's table offering a quick, polite hello but his eyes glare disapproval all the same (socializing with the very women he seeks to prosecute). Soon, Lee asks John (who has just requested "My Indiana Home" from the band) to dance and it is revealed they are both Hoosiers, having grown up 50 miles apart in the American heartland. But how differently both turned out. John reveals that his mother (his father having died) still runs a successful farm; Leander states that she ran away from home, that the only time she heard from her mother was the letter she wrote when her father died. John, always the thoughtful one, offers to drive her home to her mother's place and pick her up on his way back.

However, in the changing tone of the story, John is sidetracked by a WPA roadblock and gets thoroughly lost, ending up in a farmer's field after first crashing through his fence. The next morning, after trying to milk one of the cows for breakfast, the duo finds an irate farmer holding a rifle on them. The farmer makes a citizen's arrest taking them (in John's car, no less) to the Justice of the Peace. Taking Lee's advice to not use their real names, Lee becomes Mary Smith, bubble dancer, and John becomes Henry Wadsworth Longfellow, a steamfitter. However, the major concern of both the farmer and the Justice is that they are "not even married" and both "spent the night in my fields," the farmer leers. When John asks the judge, "what will you settle for?" the Justice becomes outraged over the notion, spouting "when you drive girls over the state line." Creating a diversion, Lee sets the trash can on fire, allowing the fugitives to sneak away, vowing that for their return trip that they will have to take the longer route via Canada. Confessing that she started the fire, she adds "I told you my mind works differently than yours." "But that's arson!" John rants and raves, bringing up the morals of the case. To which Lee smiles and answers,

In *Remember the Night*, John (Fred MacMurray), his mother (Beulah Bondi) and Aunt Emma (Elizabeth Patterson) help Lee (Barbara Stanwyck) feel at home.

"What do morals have to do with it... you treated me like a sister!" With lines like these, the duo's romance begins to spark.

They arrive in Eltonville and drive to Lee's home and knock on the door late at night, Lee's stepfather answers the door and calls for Ma. When the bitter old woman appears, she grudgingly invites the young people in, then lowers the boom. "What did you come here for!" Lee mentions "it was Christmas" to which her mother barks, "Good riddance to bad rubbish," reminding her daughter of when she stole mission money. Lee pleads, "I didn't steal it. I told you a thousand times I only borrowed it. I was going to pay you back!" But her mother reminds her she never paid it back. Her only defense: "How could I after you called me thief in front of the whole town. Do you think anyone would let me work for them after that!" Mother stills holds a grudge and damns her daughter for this one act of childhood indiscretion. John, getting Lee out of the house as quickly as possible, indicates that she is spending the holidays at his mother's farm for the next week!

The visit is idyllic for both John and Lee. John demonstrates that the $14 spent on his piano lessons was money well spent as he plays and sings for the family. Presents are shared, gifts are even given to Lee. Lee fits right in, volunteers to do the dishes and help around the house, a loving family home which she envies. At the end of the day, alone in her room, Lee's eyes fill with tears because of her acceptance in the family home. Mrs. Sargent (Beulah Bondi) tells John "I think she's charming—she reminds me of your father's cousin..." But John must be honest with his mother. "She's charming mother, but unfortunately, she's a crook. When I get back to New York, I'm gonna try to put her in jail. In the meantime, she didn't have any place to spend Christmas." Mother finds such a statement hard to swallow: "That girl's as honest as all outdoors... if she did anything, I'm sure it was entirely by mistake... She probably didn't get enough love as a child." Then creating a parallel situation, mother reminds John how he stole her stash of money that she was saving for a new dress, that he had to work to pay it off. John tenderly admits, "You

The Christmas visit is idyllic for both John and Lee in *Remember the Night*.

made me understand," to which mother responds, "No, it was love that made you understand." In other words, Lee steals from her mother and is branded as a thief by the entire town; mother does not forgive her, and she is forced to run away from home (continuing to steal throughout her adult life). John, on the other hand, commits a similar offense but is confronted by the unwavering love of a devoted mother who both forgives her son and allows him the opportunity to work off the debt. Two people the same age, growing up in a similar environment 50 miles apart, but one is disciplined with the family spirit of love, and the other is damned and cursed for the unforgivable crime. One grows up amidst a loving family and becomes a successful big city lawyer, the other has to fend for herself in a loveless environment and becomes an adult thief.

Mother's sister, Aunt Emma (Elizabeth Patterson), a spinster who views the ways of romantic love only as a spectator, states that she can tell John and Lee are in love, a statement which concerns mother, now knowing the sad history of the young house guest. At the old-fashioned New Year's Eve barn dance, it is readily apparent that the young couple are indeed fast falling in love (sharing a long, passionate kiss at the crack of midnight). Returning home,

John invites Lee to his room "for a cigarette." She says she'll come in a few minutes. However, mother wishes to have a few words alone with Lee. "I wanted to tell you how sorry I am that you're in trouble and how much I hope everything will turn out all right." Then she tells Lee John's story, how he worked to put himself through college and law school. "I don't think we should allow anything to spoil it now." Then she confesses, "He's in love with you!" To which Lee responds, "He never had any more interest in me than some panhandler you buy a meal for." Mother reminds her, "But he kissed you tonight!" To which, in an almost shy, retreating way she mumbles, "Well, I'm not exactly... ugly... oh, he might have a little fever for me, but it isn't going any further, and it hasn't been anyplace, either. I wouldn't hurt him or you!" When asked "you do love him though," she responds, "I'm afraid so."

After breakfast and good-byes, John and Lee leave for New York the next morning, John drives through Canada as promised. He reminds Lee that he could not force her to return to New York if she didn't want to return, offering the woman he loves a way out. He confesses the dirty trick he pulled in court, forcing the trial to be continued after the holidays. Lee smiles and says, "So your conscience was bothering you, when all the time I thought it was my legs... you seemed so gentle." John then explains the legal strategy of using kid gloves to get convictions from juries for women, how, if a male lawyer comes on too strong, the case will always be lost. "Part of the technique, I'm a specialist."

Later that night at Niagara Falls, John and Lee confess the love they feel for one another. John mentions he wishes to marry her after the acquittal stating "everything's gonna come out all right" and Lee realizes this means John is purposely throwing the case.

Back in New York City, back in court, John makes his strategy very clear immediately: He comes on like gangbusters. The D.A. is listening to the case from the judge's chambers, and as John becomes more and more aggressive, the D.A. says to himself, "Not so rough, Jack. How many times have I told you when you're working with a woman..." Even the jury members notice his harsh manner. "What's he getting so tough about," to which another jury member responds, "He's just naturally mean!" The first jurist continues, "I sat in on a murder case and they didn't get that rough!" Finally, in the courtroom, tears begin to well up in Lee's eyes as she realizes what John is doing, despondent that such an act will jeopardize his career, she turns to the judge and pleads, "I just want to plead guilty; I am guilty—when you make a mistake, you have to pay for it. Otherwise, you never learn!" Reluctantly the judge sets the sentencing date for January 10 as Lee is led by the matron to her city jail cell.

John, who follows her there, is upset that she pleaded guilty just when he thought her acquittal was in his hand. "You understand—there's no appeal, no retrial, no mistrial... nothing but jail!" he storms at her. She peacefully answers, "I'd never have a chance against you and you'd never have a chance with me... like just now when you were trying to lose the case... aren't you ashamed..." Her tone soon changes as she pleads, "Will you come and see me some time," to which John responds by asking her to call in the judge to marry them right here, right now. She slows up things by stating, "If you still wanted me afterwards. I'd be all square. And you would have had plenty of time to think things over, plenty of things." She then asks John to stand by her and hold her hand during sentencing. They then passionately declare their love for one another, hug, and kiss, as the end credits appear. No happy holiday ending here!

Obviously, the Production Code demanded that Lee Leander pay for her sin of stealing a diamond bracelet during the Christmas season, and pay she did at the end. She could have remained silent and allowed ace John Sargent to skillfully lose the case, both lawyers now working in her corner. But unlike the courtroom sequence at the movie's beginning, Leander was a different woman after the holidays, a woman who wanted to clean the slate of her past indiscretions, to make amends, and to start life afresh. As she swore to John's mother, she would never do anything to harm John or allow him to harm his hard-earned career. As this movie makes clear, love is both the end-all (as John's mother told him, it was love that turned him around after he stole her dress money) and the true test of self-sacrifice: Love prompted Lee to monkey-wrench John's plans and to plead guilty. For once, love made her think of John before herself. Love just wasn't reason enough for her to flee the country by staying in Canada or allowing John to throw the case so both of them would be free to marry. For Lee, love means looking into the mirror and feeling good about yourself and good about your actions and deeds. Once her two-year (as John predicted) or so jail sentence is complete, she would then be able to start a fresh life, allowing her to look ahead, not behind.

Remember the Night is a movie that both embraces the Christmas message (to offer good will toward all men, to help your fellow man, to be kind, to forgive and to love unconditionally) but also transcends and goes beyond it. The movie's moral vision is not that simplistic or easy to achieve. The movie shows the limitations of love, the ability for human beings to return to the past and learn from it—and most importantly—to change. Morality is always convoluted and complex. "Fat" Mike is anxious to help his lawyer friend, but Mike thinks John wants the woman freed for all the wrong reasons. The rube farmer and the power-hungry Justice of the Peace see the law as vindictive; for a relatively minor infraction they want to punish John for bringing a girl across state lines, a morals rap of which John and Lee are innocent (John only wished to unite her with her mother). At the movie's beginning, John plays legal tricks to win a continuance to have a better chance of winning a conviction; by movie's end John again plays legal tricks to get the same woman off the hook, simply because he now knows and loves her. John's mother likes Lee very much and wishes her son to marry, but she realizes all the hard work he has put into his career and doesn't want him to throw his life away over a tainted woman.

A delightful romp that literally will make you laugh and cry, a movie rich in thematic insight by exploring the hard moral decisions all of us have to make sooner or later, *Remember the Night* is a movie too infrequently screened and discussed. It is a Christmas movie that forces us to think about the importance of the past, our home, our family, our careers and of love. *Remember the Night* reminds us that Christmas movies can be both fun and thoughtful, and the performances of MacMurray and Stanwyck drive the point home time and time again.

—GJS

C. Aubrey Smith, Harry Carey and Charles Winninger throw wallets out the window hoping "they'll bring back somebody to have dinner with us," in *Beyond Tomorrow*.

Beyond Tomorrow

1940

"Bah Humbug" could have just as easily been uttered by crusty old George Melton in this RKO Christmas fantasy. Charles Dickens was surely the inspiration for scripters Mildred Cram and Adele Commandini, who wrote this light comedy in which three old gentleman take a young man and woman under their wings and, when the three are tragically killed, come back as ghosts to try to help the estranged lovers.

The beginning of the film stresses there is nothing sadder than being alone on Christmas Eve. George Melton (Harry Carey, Sr.) and Chad Chadwick (C. Aubrey Smith) keep their employees late this Christmas Eve, frantically working on an important engineering project. In bustles partner Michael O'Brien (Charles Winninger), a sparkling elf-like character with more than a touch of the blarney about him. Michael distributes Christmas presents to the staff and dismisses the eager-to-get-home workers. George exclaims, "Christmas. Nothing but a merchant's holiday." The men expect dinner guests, but they cancel at the last minute. George feels they have canceled

because they didn't want to associate with him. In his younger days George lost his wife and children over a loose woman. The experience has made him angry and bitter even though his two best friends have stood beside him. Chad also has no family; he lost his only son to the war and his wife is long dead. Michael never married and he too is alone.

The three form an extended family with their beloved Russian servants Madame Tanya (Maria Ouspenskaya) and Josef (Alex Melesh). Madame Tanya solemnly presents Josef the Order of Stanislav.

"You were a great friend to follow me to America, Josef."

"It was no longer my Russia without you there, excellency."

"Josef, when I had jewels and lands and palaces I was often weary and discontent. When everything was taken away except my life, I learned that the way to be really happy is to serve others, to be needed. So don't be sorry for me or what was lost."

Hardly subtle, but the good intent of the writers wins out as the audience perhaps thinks of the things they are blessed with and for a few moments forget the quest for material possessions.

When the trio of old gentlemen present Madame Tanya with a fur coat as a Christmas present she remarks,

"It's beautiful, but it will keep me no warmer than your kindness has all these years."

At first we expect to find the old men as mean and tight as Scrooge, but this is not the case, they are merely eccentric, using their work to shield them from their loneliness.

Chad looks at a photo of his long gone family and remarks, "It really seemed like Christmas in those days. What we should have, George, is a troop of grandchildren."

Michael and Chad try to bolster George's spirits with a hearty toast. "Confusion to our critics and to us, a merry Christmas."

Deep down George realizes he is lucky to have his friends. He pulls aside the heavy curtain and watches the crowds hurry through the falling snow. "There must be some lonely souls out in that crowd."

Michael gets an idea and takes three leftover Christmas presents, wallets with $10 in each one. The men each insert their card into the three wallets.

"We'll throw them out of the window and maybe they'll bring back somebody to have dinner with us."

Chad is slightly shocked. "What, strangers out of the street?"

Michael replies, "There are no strangers on Christmas Eve. Besides it's better than sitting around hooting at each other!"

George, as usual, takes the negative view, "Bet not a one of them comes back."

"I'll take you up on that... win or lose we dine at seven." The first wallet is found by a rich couple who give it to their chauffeur.

It's close to seven when George announces, "Well, it looks like you pay for the dinner O'Brien."

"Maybe I do [the doorbell rings] and then again, maybe I don't!"

The second wallet is returned by a young cowboy, James Houston (Richard Carlson), who has no overcoat and worn out boots.

The men happily lead him into the cozy room and offer him a drink.

"It really feels like Christmas Eve in here," Jim tells the gentlemen. He came to New York with a rodeo in September and stayed too long. He was now working for the money to return home.

The third wallet is returned by a young woman, Jean Lawrence (Jean Parker). Jean and Jim notice each other immediately and they and the gentlemen spend a charming holiday eve together. After dinner they gather for a sing-a-long where it is discovered Jim has a marvelous singing voice, lending it to "Jeanie with the Light Brown Hair." Even old George cracks a smile. Everyone, including servants, joins in for a truly international "Jingle Bells" with Russian, German and Italian lyrics thrown in. As the young couple prepare to depart, Madame Tanya in-sists Jim forgot his overcoat; grouchy old George has given him his without making it seem charity. As those inside wave good-bye from the window, Michael notes, "Ah, they're grand youngsters." Chad remarks, "That boy reminds me of David."

Jim walks Jean to the children's hospital where she lives and works. She contentedly remarks, "You know I wouldn't be a bit surprised to see Santa Claus' reindeers and all sliding right down the sky any minute. Would you?"

Jim and Jean find it difficult to part company but they force themselves. Christmas day Jim, Madame Tanya, and the gentlemen arrive to entertain the children at the hospital. It's difficult to know who is having the most fun. The little group grows closer throughout the following weeks, as do Jim and Jean. They go with the gentlemen to the airport to see them off on a business trip. But tragedy occurs when the plane crashes and all are lost. Jim and Jean are devastated—they were going to announce their engagement to them when they returned. Madame Tanya can feel their presence in the room, and indeed she does, for the old gentlemen are right there watching over their friends. Jim gets his big break on radio and, in a typical success-spoils-all story, is stolen away from Jean by slinky seductress Helen Vinson (Arlene Terry). The ghosts try their hardest to set things right, but one by one they depart. Chad joins his dear son, George is called to a dark oblivion, and soon Michael is alone; he is called but cannot go, feeling responsible for the troubles of Jim and Jean. Michael watches in horror as Jim is gunned down by Helen's ex-husband and lays dying on the operating room table. Michael appeals to God to save Jim and his faith and goodness are rewarded for Jim is spared and Jean forgives him. Michael walks toward the light as the credits roll.

The film was not critically well-received and does become slow going after the initial Christmas scenes. *Variety*'s Walt noted, "Picture carries initial handicap of no strength for marquee dressing, and its overall content won't help to either get customers in or to provide entertainment during its unfolding. It's one of those pictures that turn up so often to present the question 'Whatisit.'"

Charles Winninger as Michael is as always a charming character. Winninger, a well-known character actor is perhaps best known as Captain Andy in 1936's *Showboat*. Harry Carey, Sr. left the wild West for this role in *Beyond Tomorrow*. He was more comfortable in dusty cowboy duds and a 10 gallon hat. C. Aubrey Smith was another well-known character actor whose refined British accent ensured him steady work in Hollywood. He appeared as the March family's neighbor Mr. Laurence in *Little Women* (1949) and with Shirley Temple in John Ford's *Wee Willie Winkie*

(1937). Jean Parker was another *Little Women* alumna appearing as Beth in the 1933 version. Richard Carlson, who appeared as Jim, was a man of many talents and, in addition to his starring roles in films such as *Too Many Girls* and *The Magnificent Ambersons*, he also wrote and directed.

The only critical praise offered the film was for cinematographer Lester White and producer Lee Garmes for their special effect photography of the spirit scenes.

Although the film has flaws, it is still an important Christmas title with its examples of the extreme value of friendship, loyalty and humble happiness.

—SS

Holiday Inn

1942

"I'm dreaming of a white Christmas..."

Truer words were never written as Irving Berlin turned his well-stocked song trunk into an everlasting piece of film history with his construction of *Holiday Inn.*

Laurence Bergreen, in his biography of Irving Berlin, *As Thousands Cheer,* remarks Berlin had been trying for nearly 20 years to mount a show based on a lazy entertainer who opens a county inn only for the holidays. As war clouds gathered, Berlin felt Americans would once again turn to family holidays for comfort.

When Berlin finished penning "White Christmas" he rushed to his office and told his transcriber, "I want you to take down a song I wrote over the weekend. Not only is it the best song *I* ever wrote, it's the best song *anybody* ever wrote," and who can argue? Bing Crosby introduced the song on his December 25, 1941 Kraft Music Hall radio show on NBC. The film would be released in August of 1942.

Paramount and Berlin agreed to terms and production on the film began.

December 24. A trio is finishing their run at the Midnight Club. Snow is falling as Ted Hanover (Fred Astaire) happily exits a cab and brushes snow from the placard with the trio's faces: Hanover, Hardy and Dixon.

Jim Hardy (Bing Crosby) happily enters the dressing room of Lila Dixon (Virginia Dale), his Christmas Eve bride-to-be. He's planning on their being married and retiring to his newly purchased farm in Connecticut. Unfortunately she doesn't seem happy to see him. Jim leaves and an equally happy Ted enters and kisses Lila asking, "Did you tell him?" Lila

replies, "...he gets a look." "He's always had that look. It doesn't mean anything emotionally. It has something to do with his liver... You don't want to give up your career and live on a farm?" he says. To which Lila, in a neat double entendre replies, "He's already bought the farm."

They decide to break their news to Jim after the show. The opening musical number "I'll Capture Your Heart" will neatly lay out the film's plot in a few short minutes. Ted and Jim both chase Lila who eventually spies a better offer and wanders off stage. Crosby croons "I'll win her heart with my singing," while Astaire woos with taps, "just wait till I go into my dance."

In the dressing room their clueless agent Danny Reid bursts in and tells Ted and Lila he has booked them for 15 weeks. Poor old Jim looks stunned, learning the couple plan to team up on stage as well as in matrimony.

Jim moves to his farm seeking a quiet and lazy life. But each succeeding holiday finds him working harder than ever. Thanksgiving day rolls around, the alarm clock screams its early morning wake up and Jim tosses it to the wall.

It's December 24 once again. One year from the date Jim had been dumped by Lila. He sends a telegram to Ted, who is appearing with Lila at the Club Pierre in New York. "Got great idea while resting up in sanitarium. See you tonight. Merry Christmas. Jim."

The retired farmer enters Ted's dressing room bearing a gift he made himself, peach preserves (which happen to explode, covering the duo in peach slime). Danny, leaving for a trip down South, has forgotten to send orchids to Lila from Ted and rushes from the dressing room announcing he will send them from the airport. The girl in the flower shop, Linda Mason (Marjorie Reynolds), recognizes Danny and, after promising to deliver the flowers herself, tells him she wants to be in show business. He thinks he is giving her the brush off by handing her Jim's card and telling her to go to the audition the next day. She delivers the flowers and unknowingly sits next to Jim during the floor show as Lila and Ted dance to "You're So Easy to Dance With." Jim and Linda introduce themselves doing a little bragging along the way; Linda tells Jim she is in show business and knows Ted quite well. Jim tells her Ted and Lila may not be big enough for his club. Linda flees when Ted and Lila come to the table.

The next day, Christmas Day, a lovely snow is falling as Linda arrives at the inn in a horse-drawn sleigh and asks the man fixing the roof for the owner. Jim looks down, recognizes Linda and promptly falls off the ladder onto Linda, both landing in the snow. They instantly hit it off, and he takes her inside to

In *Holiday Inn* snow is falling as Ted Hanover (Fred Astaire) exits a cab and brushes snow from the placard with the trio's faces: Hanover, Hardy and Dixon. (Photofest)

change and warm up by the fire. The photography is lovely in this film, the cinematographer making the most of falling snow, firelight and Christmas decorations.

Snow falls outside wreath-covered windows as Linda and Jim sit by a roaring fire. They move to the piano facing a lighted Christmas tree and Jim begins to play a song he wrote and promised to sing at the inn for Christmas, "White Christmas." Linda joins Jim singing the song for the first time on film.

What is it about this simple song that brings a flow of tears and an aching in the heart whenever it is heard? Does it remind us of our idyllic childhood Christmases past ("I'm dreaming of a white Christmas, just like the ones I used to know...") or perhaps of a secret longing for the perfect Christmas dreamed of but never achieved ("may your days be merry and bright and may all your Christmases be white").

Bergreen quotes Berlin (as saying when Crosby first went over the song), "When he read the song he just took his pipe out of his mouth and said to me: 'You don't have to worry about this one, Irving.'"

The song wasn't an instant hit in America, but the soldiers overseas kept requesting it from Armed Forces Radio (which most probably influenced the Berlin spin-off film *White Christmas*).

After the emotional impact of Crosby's rendition of "White Christmas" (the *only* one to listen to as far as I'm concerned), the film progresses to New Year's Eve and the opening of Holiday Inn. Newspapers herald the event. In a tribute to one of Berlin's more famous compositions, one announcements states: "Where to go to—Holiday Inn: Opens tonight. Don't ask why! Just go and God Bless America!"

Back in New York Lila has dumped Ted for a Texas millionaire. Ted proceeds to get roaring drunk and head for Connecticut to commiserate with his old buddy Jim. As Ted drunkenly stumbles around the dance floor he bumps into Linda and they dance together—she doing her best to keep the jilted lover on his feet. The crowd loves it thinking it is part of the show. Astaire is incredible dancing as a drunk—his brilliance as a dancer has never shown brighter than in this comical routine.

Danny overhears the crowd raving and decides Ted has found his new partner—unfortunately Ted can't remember what she looked like and Danny only saw her from the back. Jim, who's been burned be-

Jim (Bing Crosby) looks down, recognizes Linda (Marjorie Reynolds) and promptly falls off the ladder onto Linda, both landing in the snow in *Holiday Inn*. (Photofest)

fore by Ted, pretends he doesn't know who they are talking about. The remaining months of the year are taken up with a game of cat and mouse as Ted tries to get Linda to join him and Jim tries to keep her away from the Casanova. February he has her do their act in blackface for Washington's birthday; on Valentine's Day Ted discovers Linda and as they dance they twirl through a huge paper heart which tears—just as we know Jim's heart is tearing; Easter Sunday Ted pretends to give up show business—moving into the inn to "help" Jim with the shows; July 4th finds Jim plotting to waylay Linda so two Hollywood producers won't see her dance with Ted and offer them a contract. The plot backfires and Linda angrily leaves Jim and goes to Hollywood where filming begins on a story based on Jim's dream, Holiday Inn.

Thanksgiving rolls around. Snow is falling and a closed sign hangs over the door of the inn. Jim sits alone at a table writing a letter to Linda, telling her the inn is doing great and offering congratulations on her engagement to Ted. Thankfully Mamie (Louise Beavers) gives Jim a good talking to, telling him to go to Hollywood and get Linda back.

Christmas Eve. Ted is nervously waiting for the final scene to be filmed so he and Linda can catch a plane and be married. A knock is heard at the door as Danny tells him, "Everything is all set and ready. What could possibly happen..." In strolls a smiling Jim.

Ted and Danny realize Jim could ruin all their plans and try to lock him in a closet but Jim turns the tables and manages to lock them in the dressing room. He heads for the set where the final number is being staged. He walks onto a perfectly built reproduction of the inn—complete with snow, fire and Christmas tree. He moves the tree closer to the piano and leaves his pipe on the top of the instrument.

The director leads Linda to an elaborate sleigh. "When you get on the set do your song. Let's see, I think you have the mood. Your Hollywood success was empty. You've lost the only man you love. You know—the usual hokum. Just make me cry and you can get to that wedding."

Linda feels those same sentiments as her character exits the sleigh and enters the inn. She slowly walks about the room before sitting down at the piano to sing "White Christmas" as a tear runs down her cheek. Linda picks up the pipe and taps the bells on the tree—the same way Jim did a year ago. Suddenly she hears whistling and then that unmistakable voice as Jim joins in the song. She runs to him and they embrace.

Ted and Danny arrive too late. "How could he get that far in five minutes?" Danny proclaims. Ted, realizing turnabout is fair play, replies, "The lady must have been willing."

New Year's Eve the inn is reopened, Ted is special guest and the trio sing a new version of "I'll Capture Your Heart." But Ted is not alone for long as Danny pushes Lila onto the stage for a reunion with her old partner. We're sure a happy New Year will be had by one and all.

Holiday Inn is a sweet Christmas confection filled with delightful holiday songs sung by the golden-voiced Crosby and danced to by the suave Astaire. The Christmas scenes are filled with snow, decorated trees, glowing fireplaces and beribboned wreaths.

"White Christmas" would garner an Academy Award for Irving Berlin and become the most popular song of all time. Its record would only be broken this past year by Elton John's Princess Diana tribute "Candle in the Wind." But I have faith "White Christmas" will regain its position as the best selling song of all time.

In true musical tradition, the audience doesn't find the two-timing Ted or the too laid-back Jim annoying; we only appreciate their quirks that help bring us to the happy ending. Bing Crosby and Fred Astaire would once again compete for the same girl in an-

other film based upon the work of Irving Berlin, 1946's *Blue Skies*. Crosby would again sing that old Chestnut "White Christmas" in this Paramount film before going all the way and starring in what is often referred to as a remake of *Holiday Inn*, *White Christmas*.

Marjorie Reynolds had a varied film career beginning in the 1920s. She appeared as a bit player in *Gone With the Wind*, starred in the Fritz Lang classic noir *Ministry of Fear* and portrayed Vincent Price's snobby wife in *His Kind of Woman*. Her last starring role would be in the 1962 police drama *The Silent Witness*. Reynolds' singing was dubbed by Martha Mears, a singer and actress who also provided singing for Rita Hayworth in *Cover Girl* and Veronica Lake in *Star Spangled Rhythm*.

Director Mark Sandrich was an old pro at musicals with directing credits for numerous RKO classics such as *The Gay Divorcee*, *Follow the Fleet*, *Shall We Dance* and *Top Hat* under his belt.

In its June 17, 1942 review *Variety* opined, "It's a standout film. With those Berlin tunes, a strong story content and Bing Crosby and Fred Astaire for the marquee it's an undeniable box-office parlay, a winner all the way." *Holiday Inn* was actually the inspiration for the hotel chain of the same name.

I can't think of a more comforting afternoon than curling up on a chilly December weekend with a bowl of hot popcorn and a double-feature of *Holiday Inn* and *White Christmas*—the perfect prescription for holiday blues.

—SS

Linda, in the finale of *Holiday Inn*, reprises "White Christmas."

Elizabeth (Barbara Stanwyck) and Jefferson (Dennis Morgan) cautiously flirt in *Christmas in Connecticut*.

Christmas in Connecticut

1945

BARBARA STANWYCK, DENNIS MORGAN AND SYNDEY GREENSTREET WISH YOU A MERRY CHRISTMAS IN CONNECTICUT—Title card for *Christmas in Connecticut*

Long before American women were ever intimidated by Martha Stewart, there was *Christmas in Connecticut*'s Elizabeth Lane—super wife, adoring mother and gourmet cook whose idyllic life on a Connecticut farm was nothing less than perfect. Or so her adoring fans and kept-in-the-dark publisher believed.

However, working-girl Elizabeth (Barbara Stanwyck), as it happens, is a great writer but a very bad homemaker; she is neither mother, good cook nor wife. We first meet Elizabeth sitting in her little apartment eating canned sardines for breakfast and typing away on her next column. Her dear friend Felix (S.Z. Sakall) delivers breakfast from his restaurant—Elizabeth had helped him with his business, and now he watches over her like a mother hen. Elizabeth's editor Dudley (Robert Shayne) arrives in a panic. Their publisher, Alexander Yardley (Sydney Greenstreet), has decided it would be good business if Elizabeth would entertain a war hero in her home over the Christmas holiday. Yardley also invites himself along to sample her fabulous Christmas duck and, as a sideline, hopes to convince Elizabeth to have another baby—so they can increase circulation, not to mention the population.

Elizabeth and Dudley commiserate over their soon-to-be-lost jobs when they are joined by Elizabeth's slimy boyfriend John Sloan (Reginald Gardiner), who is constantly proposing marriage to the reluctant writer. This time he hits the jackpot, for although Elizabeth has told him she doesn't love him, her defenses are at an all time low and she agrees to become his wife. When Sloan mentions his farm in Connecticut, the place that inspired many of Elizabeth's stories, a plan is hatched—Elizabeth and John will hastily get married. Felix is convinced to come along to cook, and the trio rush to the farm to welcome the war hero and Mr. Yardley.

Arriving at the farm, they plan to be married immediately; but something keeps popping up, mostly Felix who happens to despise the boring self-absorbed John whose love of architecture and plumbing make him a terribly dull suitor for the lively Elizabeth. Although, to John's credit, he does think of everything as he produces a baby (a child housekeeper Norah [Una O'Connor] baby-sits). Jefferson Jones (Dennis Morgan), a sailor who had been lost at sea for 18 days, arrives early and is shocked to find Elizabeth Lane is not the matronly women he pictured but a real dish. Elizabeth is also surprised to find a handsome hero who puts the foppish John to shame.

Stanwyck shows a flair for comedy as Elizabeth tries to appear knowledgeable in the ways of motherhood, constantly calling the baby "it." Her dislike and squeamishness around the wriggling baby is amusing, and the look of desperation that crosses her face when Jones asks to be allowed to watch her bathe the baby is priceless. Elizabeth slyly turns the tables and allows the hero the honor of washing the little child.

Ooops, she told him it was a boy named Robert. He looks up with confusion. "I mean Roberta," Elizabeth quickly answers. She is definitely a fish out of water in this domestic sea of tranquillity.

Jefferson and Elizabeth are soon mooning over each other, but Jefferson is not the kind of man to kiss a married woman. And Elizabeth constantly seems to forget she is married (or supposed to be). Of course, the gallant soldier is not telling everything either, as, in desperation, he became engaged to his hospital nurse so he could cajole her into providing the steak he had been dreaming of while stranded in the lifeboat.

On Christmas day the self-absorbed group attend a dance where Elizabeth and Jefferson become even friendlier and slip off for a romantic horse-drawn sleigh ride. John, oblivious to the fact that his bride-to-be is being stolen right from under his nose, is obsessed with the fact that Yardley has offered him a job as editor of a new home segment of the magazine.

However, Yardley does notice and tries to follow the couple before he comically falls down a snow-covered hill. He arrives back at the house in time to see the baby's mother pick up the child, and, erroneously thinking it is a kidnapping, calls the police. In the meantime, Jefferson and Elizabeth have been arrested for stealing the sleigh. They arrive home at seven a.m. and confront Yardley who is scandalized by Elizabeth's behavior and her apparent lack of concern over the kidnapping. She explains the whole story, he fires her, Jefferson's lovelorn nurse shows up and things just couldn't get any worse for the lovers.

But it's 1945, and we know there is a happy ending right around the corner. The nurse has married Jefferson's friend Sinkewicz, Felix convinces Yardley that Elizabeth had a better offer and he hires her back at double her salary. John doesn't seem to mind the fact that Elizabeth loves the war hero. He's more interested in his new job, and finally Jefferson and Elizabeth get married.

There are really no moral lessons in the film. Honesty isn't the best policy, if it were Elizabeth would never have gotten her job in the first place, and she would never have found the man of her dreams. *Christmas in Connecticut* is really just pure fluff whose Christmas decorations and romantic sleigh rides only make us want to snuggle closer to the one we love. And who can argue with that? The movie is a perennial holiday favorite full of Christmas ambiance—sleighs gliding over snow-covered roads a huge Christmas tree, cozy roaring fires, Christmas carols and a cheerful ending.

The film was blessed with a talented cast of leads and supporting players. The year prior to the release of *Christmas in Connecticut* Barbara Stanwyck had received an Academy Award nomination for her work as deadly ice queen Phyllis Dietrichson in *Double Indemnity*. As the scheming she-demon who enticed hapless Fred MacMurray into murdering her husband, she set the standard for film noir's most dangerous dames. Stanwyck along with Hollywood's reigning royalty Bette Davis, Greer Garson and Claudette Colbert would lose the Award to Ingrid Bergman for her performance in *Gaslight*. Co-star Dennis Morgan was one of Warner Bros.' highest paid actors who appeared in films such as *Kitty Foyle* with Ginger Rogers and put his singing voice to good use in *My Wild Irish Rose*, the story of composer Chauncey Olcott. As Jefferson Jones he is suitably charming, easily softening up the feisty Elizabeth but with just enough of a hint of scoundrel to keep her interested. "Miss Stanwyck and Dennis Morgan make a delightful team as the writer and the sailor," *Variety* reported.

Sydney Greenstreet was a mainstay of theater before entering films at the young age of 61. His film debut as Kasper Gutman in *The Maltese Falcon* would earn him an Academy Award nomination. Not a bad first effort. Greenstreet would be typecast as a villain but often appeared in other roles such as Alexander Yardley in *Christmas in Connecticut*.

Also helping along the farce would be S.Z. Sakall—known to one and all as Cuddles—who would also be typecast in Hollywood, usually as a lovable uncle, friend or relative. He appeared in many musicals as well as working with Greenstreet in *Casablanca* (as Carl the head waiter) and with Stanwyck in *Ball of Fire* (as one of the absent-minded professors). Una O'Connor, as housekeeper Norah, typically portrayed characters of that sort. Her most famous appearance is probably as the comical maid who meets up with the Monster in *Bride of Frankenstein*. Reginald Gardiner as John Sloan was usually cast as the suave sophisticate and appeared in dozens of films including *Born to Dance* (his American debut), *Sweethearts*, *A Damsel in Distress* and *The Man Who Came to Dinner*.

The film was directed by Peter Godfrey, an actor turned director whose most famous film is perhaps *The Two Mrs. Carrolls*.

The film was released in July of 1945. In its review *Variety* pronounced, "Laugh-paced farce that does an excellent job of entertaining."

Christmas in Connecticut was remade in 1992 for television. The remake, directed by action-hero Arnold Schwarzenegger, starred Dyan Cannon as Elizabeth (now host of a television cooking show), Kris Kristofferson as Jefferson (updated in this version as a heroic park ranger) and Tony Curtis as a sleazier version of Sloan who poses as Elizabeth's husband. When Jefferson is interviewed on TV, he remarks he would love to have a home-cooked meal for Christmas. Before you know it, Curtis has arranged a live Christmas special with Elizabeth and her adoring family and the heroic Jefferson. Things literally fall down about their ears on the live broadcast, but Elizabeth and Jefferson find true love. Dyan Cannon and Kris Kirstofferson are both appealing performers and the film, although not as good as the original, is enjoyable holiday fare. The film was originally shown April 13, 1992 with Schwarzenegger making a cameo appearance à la Alfred Hitchcock.

—SS

The Bishop's Wife
1947

Perhaps the screen's most famous Christmas angel is Clarence from *It's a Wonderful Life*, the Frank Capra classic. However, Henry Koster's *The Bishop's Wife*, with inspired screenplay by Robert E. Sherwood and Leonardo Bereovici (based upon the Robert Nathan novel), features the screen's most debonair and sexy Christmas angel, Dudley, as portrayed by Cary Grant. The story of *The Bishop's Wife* involves the triangle relationship existing between Bishop Henry Broughton (David Niven), a stuffy and aloof man, passionless and obsessed with building a new cathedral, his wife Julia (Loretta Young), a woman deeply devoted to her husband, but a woman extremely neglected and unsatisfied, and their savior, Dudley, an angel who relishes the human experience and is attracted to the woman, Julia, and who knows the se-

cret of creating heaven on Earth. The tale unwinds during the Christmas season, and by its conclusion, when the Bishop delivers his Christmas Eve sermon, every character has undergone some significant change based upon the self-understanding of an inner vision which comes about through setting personal priorities and learning the simple joys of living and being a human being.

The movie shows another idyllic Christmas land: The sounds of Christmas carols, joyous and impassioned, frame the night time cityscape, snow falls gently as choruses on street corners sing, Santa rings his bell and shoppers are attracted to storefronts which feature nativity scenes, toy trains, Santa's reindeer and sleigh and mechanical Santas. A happy-go-lucky gentleman becomes our eyes, appreciating the joy and happiness which Christmas brings. This man volunteers to accompany a blind man across the street, oblivious to cars cruising rapidly down the street. When a mother lets go of her baby carriage to lift her older daughter higher so the child can see a Christmas display, the carriage rolling down the sidewalk in front of a passing truck, this same man appears out of nowhere and stops the carriage. Soon the man sees an enraptured Julia Broughton look longingly at a special hat on display inside a store window, and watches as she moves on to a Christmas tree store and orders a tree to be delivered on Christmas Eve. This inquisitive man listens as Julia meets and greets an old friend, the Professor (Monty Woolley), a broken-down scholar who used to belong to Julia's husband's old parish, a man who has no religion but buys a pathetic, straggly Christmas tree because it reminds him of his childhood. Asked about husband Henry, Julia's eyes sadden and she states that Henry is tired and worried about raising the money for a new cathedral. To brighten up the lovely lady, the Professor gives Julia his lucky coin, a Roman coin he claims is of little value. "We *were* happy back here with old friends," Julia sighs. Soon the observant man approaches the Professor, greets him warmly, saying they met back in Vienna; but the Professor seems confused. Julia thinks the entire encounter amusing, but then the young man leaves, and Julia walks home alone, stopping a moment to look at the old parish.

Julia arrives home late, the meeting Henry is having with Mrs. Hamilton (Gladys Cooper) has already begun. Mrs. Hamilton reminds the Bishop that she was the person responsible for having Broughton named Bishop: "I had every confidence in you when you were a poor little parson of the church in the slums... I confess my confidence has weakened." Hamilton's money is tied to the proposition that this new cathedral have a chapel dedicated to her late husband George and other self-serving items about which the Bishop is none too happy. He calls Mrs. Hamilton

66

Dudley (Cary Grant), the Professor (Monty Woolley) and Julia (Loretta Young) drink a toast to Christmas in *The Bishop's Wife***.**

his "guiding spirit." Coming to the point, Mrs. Hamilton rants, "You will build that cathedral as I want it, or you will not build it at all!"

Henry chides his wife for her lateness, declaring, "What a ghastly afternoon, what a ghastly woman!" Appearing as a beaten and whipped dog before Mrs. Hamilton, the Bishop declares to his wife, "I had no intention of being strangled by her purse strings." And Julia smiles and tells him she is proud of him. Julia further suggests he take a rest from all the stress caused by raising funds for the cathedral until after the upcoming holidays, but the Bishop is wise enough to understand that this is the charitable season when deep-pocket individuals are willing to give for such a cause. Julia is worried about her husband, both his physical and mental health. "Henry, if you could see your poor, harassed face... what's happened to you... to us and our marriage?!" Julia reminds Henry that they used to have fun and were happy and made others happy as well. From seeing Henry in action, the audience probably finds it difficult to visualize that former Henry. As Julia gives Henry the Professor's good luck coin, the bitter Bishop frowns and says,

"Old fool, what did he think I could do with that!" Henry needs four million dollars for his new church and tells Julia he wants a quick dinner (with both of them sitting formally at opposite ends of the table) because he has lots of work remaining. Quickly realizing what a pill he has been, Henry slightly softens and offers to schedule time for just them to go out for lunch tomorrow, to go watch the skaters at the park. However, once Julia leaves, smiling and happy, Mildred (Sara Haden), Henry's secretary, reminds him of a luncheon appointment he made a month ago. In utter frustration, now alone, Henry bows his head into his hands and pleads, "Oh, God, please help me!" as the painting of the new cathedral behind him suddenly begins to brighten and radiate. Soon, the strange young man that we met at the movie's beginning appears before Henry in his chambers. The man declares that Henry's prayers have been heard, and that he, Dudley, is an angel without wings here to help. Henry is more than a little doubtful, asking why can't Dudley create the cathedral with one wave of his hand. Dudley, always pleasant and smiling, says, "You wouldn't want me to do that—how would you explain it!" Dudley

As is made perfectly clear in the *The Bishop's Wife*, Dudley and Julia are soulmates, perfect for one another. (Photofest)

tells Henry he will be his assistant, helping the Bishop in any way he can. Once Henry prays he no longer has need of Dudley, Dudley assures the Bishop he will be "gone and forgotten."

The next morning, Julia and daughter Debby (Karolyn Grimes) go to the park and watch the children playing in the snow, throwing snowballs and having a grand time. "They don't want me! Guess I'm too little," the girl cries. Dudley, who magically appears on the scene, tells the valiant little girl, "We'll show them how wrong they are." The so-called kid leaders say they are playing protect the fort but that Debby can't fight because her father's the Bishop. When Dudley tells Debby to pack and throw a snowball (which he magically guides) to smack the kid at the very top of the hill, Debby is immediately chosen by her peers: "Come on kid, you're in our army!" Soon, Dudley offers to take Julia to lunch at Michel's, the very restaurant that Julia wanted Henry to take her to today. Matilda (Elsa Lanchester), the servant, just happens to be traveling by the park and offers to take Debby home. Henry and Julia were engaged at Michel's, and the restaurant holds plenty of pleasant

memories. However, a table of busy-body old hens, all members of the Cathedral Committee, coldly eye Julia for eating with a handsome young man who's not her husband. Dudley reads her palm and sees a woman "who is adored" and who will live a "rich full life." Dudley tells the fascinated young woman, "The world changes, but two things remain constant: youth and beauty." But Julia reminds Dudley that people grow older. Dudley corrects her: "Not everybody. The only people who grow old were born old to begin with. You were born young, you will remain that way." To silence the gossip, Dudley goes over to the table of old women and invites them to sit with Julia and him. Unbeknownst to Julia, Henry canceled his appointment, coming home early to take Julia to lunch, but when he hears she already left with Dudley, he is angered and slams his office door.

On the way home Dudley and Julia run into the old Professor, who invites them up to his place for sherry. Looking at his twig of a tree with an angel on it (one that Julia gave him), the Professor remarks that it creates the "illusion of peace on Earth." Asking about the manuscript of his 20-years-in-the-making book, one that every winter he promises to his publisher next spring, he regretfully states he hasn't written a word, that he doesn't want to repeat the same old dusty history. Soon Dudley returns to the Professor the same Roman coin he gave Julia, and recounts the coin's history. Only 100 were minted by Caesar, and they were used to pay "the hotel bill" for lover Cleopatra. When Caesar's wife discovered this so-called affair, he ordered all the coins be melted—but one survived. Dudley has planted the seeds for the Professor's book. Strangely, as they drink their glasses of sherry, the bottle magically refills itself.

That evening, watching Julia brush her hair, Henry tries to think of romantic little compliments to show his wife how much he loves her, but all his comments come off as being stiff and too reserved. The words are kind—"you lead a well-ordered life... you're an excellent wife..."—but passion is missing. Julia wishes that Dudley will be able to take some of the burden off her husband's hectic life, but Henry can only feel jealousy that this younger man seems to be able to make Julia happy while he cannot.

The next day Henry plans to give in to all of Mrs. Hamilton's demands and sets up a meeting at five o'clock, again missing another planned meeting with Julia at his old parish to listen to the boys choir. Hoping to get this unpleasant business with Hamilton over with rapidly, Henry plans to join his wife and Dudley at St. Timothy's. Things work out well. Henry apologizes, agrees to the special chapel dedicated to her late husband George, agrees to have his name gilded in marble and his likeness matched to St. George slaying the dragon in stained glass. Henry even cynically asks, "Who do you have in mind as the dragon?" With everything quickly agreed upon, Henry asks to be dismissed, but upon rising, the chair in which he is sitting strangely sticks to his rear end, and he is unable to get free. Meanwhile, at his old parish, Dudley and Julia marvel at the constantly improving choir, comprised of children that Julia saw grow up before her eyes. Apologizing for the absence of her husband, Julia and Dudley leave.

Once outside, Julia is in no hurry to return home, telling Dudley, "You seem to make me feel that everything is going to be all right." Dudley takes her in to purchase the hat she has been eyeing for weeks now, and then catching a cab, driven by the ever-pleasant Sylvester (James Gleason), they take a slow drive through the park, coming upon a frozen lake where ice-skaters swing merrily round and round. Soon, Julia and Dudley join in, later joined by the at first clumsy but soon (under Dudley's guidance) graceful Sylvester. As Julia and mostly Dudley dazzle the crowd, the other skaters stand by the side and watch the couple perform. Returning home in the cab, Sylvester does not charge them a dime. "You and the little lady have

restored my faith in human nature." Julia says this has been her most wonderful evening in years, but Dudley counters with "in centuries." As the happy Julia dances into her home, Henry can only muster "charming" when Julia asks him his opinion of her new hat. Henry, maintaining his calm exterior, tells Dudley that Mrs. Hamilton is willing to finance the cathedral. Dudley replies that was a foregone conclusion "if you were willing to make a slight sacrifice of your principles." The angel goes on, that so many need food and shelter, that the big roof of that cathedral could make so many little roofs. Reminding Dudley that once he got his cathedral the angel was free to go, Henry puts that message in prayer as Dudley demands. However, still present and smiling, Dudley informs Henry, Julia still wants me to stay. His jealousy only causes Henry to tell Julia that Dudley was incompetent and that he fired him, distressing his wife very much.

The next day leaving with Henry to catch a cab to attend a meeting, Sylvester makes a comment about Julia bringing a man of the cloth along to marry Dudley and her, but Julia frowns and tells him that this man is her husband. Since it is now Christmas Eve, Henry has asked secretary Mildred to type up his sermon and make five copies, but it is apparent she wishes to leave early to do some shopping. Dudley just happens to come along, offers to do the typing, and he promptly throws the original sermon into the fireplace, dictating a new one to a typer-less typewriter that works by magic.

Dudley manages to make it to Mrs. Hamilton's house before Julia and Henry arrive, and while waiting for her, just happens to open a jewelry case and sees a piece of hand-written sheet music with the marginal note: "This was composed for you, my darling, and you only—Allan." Whispering to himself that Mrs. Hamilton's husband was named George, he goes to the harp and starts playing the song, immediately attracting the dazed woman. Mrs. Hamilton enters and states Allan would have been a great composer, if he hadn't died young, nearly 40 years ago. "He was the only man I ever loved... but I got frightened. He had nothing and I was afraid of poverty. He ran away, I never saw him again... I never loved George Hamilton. He was very much in love with me. He was very wealthy." Mrs. Hamilton, now crying, tries to compose herself as her two new guests arrive. Changing her attitude to one of sweetness and kindness, she mentions that Dudley just left, and she tells Henry that she changed her mind about the cathedral. "Give my money to the poor, the homeless, the unappreciated people. I want you to direct the spending of the money!"

Going home alone, Henry pauses at St. Timothy's, his old church, and decides to drop in on the Profes-

The Briggs family: Julia (Whitney Houston), the Reverend (Courtney B. Vance) Marguerite (Jenifer Lewis) and sons (Justin Pierre Edmund and Darven Davis, Jr.) in *The Preacher's Wife*.

must go away and never come back" and runs upstairs. Henry almost immediately enters, demanding Dudley put up his dukes and fight for Julia, that Dudley will not steal Julia and Debby away from him. "I'm not going to lose her," Henry makes quite clear. Dudley reminds Henry that when he is gone, all memory of him will be erased. Henry reminds Dudley that when he prayed for the angel to go away after he got his cathedral, Dudley did not vanish. But shrewdly, Dudley reminds him he did not pray for a cathedral but he prayed for guidance, and that has now been granted. So his work is done. "When the immortal finds himself envying the mortal entrusted in his care, there's a danger signal," Dudley admits. "Kiss her for me, you're lucky, Henry." Going upstairs as Julia puts Debby to bed, Henry experiences overwhelming happiness and he kisses Julia. He suddenly wants to go downstairs and drink punch toasts and smash the glasses in the fireplace. Going on to church, Henry reads the sermon that Dudley wrote, thinking he himself composed it, delivering its theme of "peace on Earth" passionately as the smiling Dudley momentarily listens and then walks off.

sor, who isn't amazed to find out that Dudley is an angel, since his sherry bottle is still being used and doesn't get any emptier. However, Henry feels Dudley made his wife despise him. "I already lost the love of Julia and Debby." But the Professor tells the Bishop he has the advantage, that Julia is a creature of the Earth, and "you're a man." He tells Henry to fight for her!

Meanwhile, Dudley announces to Julia that his work here is almost done, and once an angel is done a mission, they are never sent back to the same location out of fear attachments could be formed. After telling Julia that she is one of those rare people who can make heaven here on Earth, he implores her to not send him away, that he is tired of being a wanderer, but with tears in her eyes, she tells the angel, "You

Never has a Christmas movie made such a strong case for two characters, in this case Julia and Dudley, to commit adultery. As is made perfectly clear in the movie, they are soulmates, perfect for one another. In a parallel relationship, the bitter old prune Mrs. Hamilton admits she never married Allan, the love of her life, allowing him to slip away and soon die, but she devotes herself to preserving the memory in marble of her late husband George, a man she married for money. It is easy to imagine Allan as Dudley and George as Henry where the loves of both these woman lie. Both woman remain solidly devoted to their spouses, although both marriages are passionless and business-oriented. The emotions of both women are flamed by men outside of marriage, men whom neither can marry. Thus, in a sense, *The*

Bishop's Wife is a cheat, for it sets the audience up for a romantic liaison that can never be. Of course, conveniently, Julia's memory of Dudley will fade, but even with all the constant reminders through the film of the kind, passionate man that Henry used to be, even with his threat to smash glasses in the fireplace, David Niven's character is dull and emotionless. One cannot imagine, not even for one second, that one minute of bliss with Dudley could equal a lifetime with the Bishop.

But in this sacrifice we have the message of Christmas, of lost souls looking for their direction (the Professor finding a topic worthy enough for his book of a lifetime, and Henry finding a cause greater than helping the poor and unappreciated in his parish in the slums), and of doing the valiant thing through self-sacrifice (Dudley giving up the special love he finds in Julia so she can be reconciled with her passion-infused husband, even if he's a few quarts shy; the Professor giving up his special coin to Julia, who in turn gives it to her husband, which in turn ends up in the hands of the Professor once again). *The Bishop's Wife* makes our lives appear bittersweet and sad; sometimes we strive for the unobtainable, sometimes we have to settle for second best, but through "loving kindness and the out-stretched hand of tolerance" the human condition can hope to find "peace on Earth." That's the message of Henry/Dudley's final sermon, and it remains the message of *The Bishop's Wife.*

The Bishop's Wife was remade in 1996 with a stellar cast featuring Whitney Houston as Julia Briggs and Denzel Washington as Dudley. Again, Julia's marriage to Reverend Briggs (Courtney B. Vance) is lacking passion. Briggs, whose congregation is decreasing, is trying to decide whether to stick it out in the old church which Julia's father built or sell out to mega-developer Joe Hamilton (Gregory Hines). Meanwhile their son Jeremiah (Justin Pierre Edmund) is saddened by the loss of his best friend who was taken away by social workers. Angel Dudley appears, to help the Briggs family and indulge in a little flirtation with Julia. Houston gets to put her immense vocal talents to good use in the choir scenes. The film was directed by Penny Marshall and makes pleasant holiday viewing.

—GJS

Holiday Affair
1949

RKO cashed in on the holiday season with this charming love story featuring a stellar cast consisting of Robert Mitchum, Janet Leigh and Wendell Corey.

Connie Ennis (Janet Leigh) and her young son Timmy (Gordon Gebert) are preparing for Christmas. A war widow, Connie is quite happy living with her memories and raising her young son in his father's image. She is still deeply wounded by her husband's death and, like practical mothers in poorer families, doesn't want Timmy to ask for anything too special for Christmas—wanting him never to be disappointed.

Connie faces the rush of holiday shopping as a comparison shopper, seeking out products, purchasing them for her store and returning them the next day. Her problems begin when she buys an electric train from happy-go-lucky salesclerk Steve Mason (Robert Mitchum) who reluctantly pulls himself away from entertaining a group of children to wait on Connie. She takes the train home and Timmy sneaks a peek, delighted with his soon-to-be Christmas present. But his mother rains on his parade when she tells him it was just for work and the train must go back. She returns the train the next day. Steve had her pegged as a spy and is supposed to call security, but can't bring himself to do so. Instead of Connie getting fired, Steve ends up unemployed. He and

Janet Leigh and Robert Mitchum in *Holiday Affair*. (Photofest)

71

Connie (Janet Leigh), Timmy (Gordon Gebert) and Carl (Wendell Corey) decorate the tree in *Holiday Affair*. **(Photofest)**

Connie wind up having lunch in Central Park where, in typical movie time, they learn all about each in two hours. She learns he takes any job available to buy into a shipbuilding company in California, and he learns she is afraid of changing her life, for better or worse. They spend the rest of the afternoon shopping for Connie's job, but get separated—Steve carrying many of her packages.

Steve shows up at Connie's apartment that evening, which doesn't make her long-suffering boy-friend Carl (Wendell Corey) very happy. Suddenly, after meeting Steve (who proceeds to analyze her), she agrees to marry Carl. Of course we know this isn't going to happen. Christmas morning Timmy finds a wonderful present outside the front door—the marvelous train set. Through a series of romantic misadventures including Connie having to go to the police station Christmas Day and trying to convince a delightfully befuddled Police Lieutenant (Henry Morgan) that Steve is not a crook but really a good guy, Carl realizes he deserves to have a girl who loves him, and Connie realizes she should marry someone she truly loves, not Carl. Things seem like they will all

work out, but Steve is having none of it—he wants a woman who will chase him.

Things end happily on New Year's Eve as Steve and Connie get together and Carl gets on with his life.

The film features fine performances, nicely paced direction and a nice but non-intrusive score by RKO regular Roy Webb. Janet Leigh does a fine job as Connie, a tired, confused single mother. Robert Mitchum displays a charm often absent from his more frightening turns in films such as *Cape Fear* and *Night of the Hunter*. His Steve Mason is a charmer who could melt any woman with those bedroom eyes, his enjoyment of kids and his easygoing attitude. Wendell Corey, as poor old boyfriend Carl, elicits our sympathy without raising our ire. He's a nice guy, and we're happy he finally realizes he deserves someone to love him completely. Gordon Gebert is a cutie as Timmy. One of his best scenes is when he takes his precious train back to the store so he can give Steve, who is still unemployed, his money back.

Variety's November 16, 1949 review noted: "*Holiday Affair* is a warm Christmas offering. It concerns itself charmingly with the antics of humans dur-

Della (Jeanne Crain) and Jim (Farley Granger) window shop and dream of extravagant Christmas gifts in *O. Henry's Full House*—"The Gift of the Magi." (Photofest)

ing the Yuletide, developing a lot of rich comedy drama in doing so." They also note: "Hartman's production guidance is as strong as his direction." Unfortunately Hartman's direction failed to save the picture from a weak reception. *Cinemania* notes: "The picture was a box-office disaster, and as a result RKO canceled director Hartman's contract." Hartman would only direct four films including *Every Girl Should Be Married* (1948), *It Had to Be You* (1947) and *Mr. Imperium* (1951) but had a successful career as a screenwriter penning scripts for Hope and Crosby and Danny Kaye among others.

Holiday Affair captures the spirit of Hollywood's love/hate relationships so popular with audiences. The middle class lifestyle of the Ennis family is easy to relate to for the average viewer. There are no professionally decorated Christmas trees in this film. A much more real holiday is pictured—the hustle and bustle of holiday shoppers, a beautifully scraggly family Christmas tree, lovely falling snow and a happy ending. What more could you ask for?

The film (based on the story "Christmas Gift" by John D. Weaver) was remade for television in 1996 starring Cynthia Gibb.
—SS

O. Henry's Full House "The Gift of the Magi"
1952

When I first read "The Gift of the Magi" in junior high school, I thought the greatest gift of all was to have someone love you so much they would give up their most precious possession. As I grow older, I realize, first, that I wasn't such a dumb kid and second, that a gift just as precious is to love someone so much you would give up your most precious possession for them.

Folk writer O. Henry placed pen to paper and wrote short stories filled with such down-to-Earth wisdom—stories that were populated by average people you would be happy to call friend.

O. Henry was the pen name of William Sydney Porter. Porter was a newspaperman who in his younger days had worked at a bank in Austin, Texas— a bank with a sloppy bookkeeping system which led

Della and Jim realize they have the greatest gift of all in "The Gift of the Magi."

to him being called to face embezzlement charges. He had previously argued nobody could balance the books, but decided to flee the country. When he learned his wife was dying he returned and gave himself up. The authorities saw his leaving as an admission of guilt and he spent three years in prison. When he was released he moved to Pittsburgh and began using the name O. Henry. He then moved to New York and began to write his most famous stories.

O. Henry's Full House is a compilation of five O. Henry stories introduced by celebrated author John Steinbeck. All the stories are charming with "The Ransom of Red Chief" perhaps the most amusing as a pair of bumbling kidnappers (Oscar Levant and Fred Allen) snatch a kid so bad his parents finally make the kidnappers pay them to take him back!

But we shall concern ourselves with the final story, "The Gift of the Magi."

"O. Henry said the Magi were the Wise Men. The wonderfully wise men who brought gifts to the babe in the manger. They invented the art of giving Christmas presents," Steinbeck says to introduce the story.

1905. Times are hard and people cherish their few possessions, items often handed down through generations. A scruffy Santa rings a bell outside an apartment building. His sign says, "It is more blessed to give than to receive." It is Christmas Eve.

Della (Jeanne Crain) and Jim (Farley Granger) are content in their small apartment, expecting their first child and make a game of pretending they are among the idle rich. She happily walks him to work and the couple window shop along the way, taking time to "ooh" and "ah" over the beautiful things in the windows—things they can't afford. Della spies a beautiful watch fob [a holder for a pocket watch] for $22.50 that would be perfect for Jim's watch, one that has been passed down through his family. The couple then spy a set of hair combs that once belonged to a Chinese Empress—a mere $25. Jim priced them yesterday, you see.

Della returns home and carefully pours the milk back into the container and replaces it in the icebox right outside their window. She looks up and sees a sign, "Hair Goods of All Kinds" as "O Come All Ye Faithful" is sung in the background.

"Do you buy hair?"
The owner looks her over. "If it's good. Yes."
Della lets down her exquisite hair as he raves about its beauty but not wanting to overpay, he quickly calms down and says, "Hm, it's not bad."
He offers her $20. "Take it or leave it."
Della realizes it is not enough and almost leaves. "Can you cut it quickly so I won't change my mind?"
"Now it's better if you close your eyes."
The lovely locks fall to the floor.

Meanwhile Jim, a clerk, slaves over his books, anxiously checking his watch. In a scene right out of Dickens he is reprimanded by his boss. "Time is money. Christmas Eve here is just December 24." Jim, who makes the kingly sum of 33 cents an hour, is counting on his Christmas bonus to buy Della a gift. He is crushed when he learns there is no bonus this year. They each will receive three dollars, the money the boss didn't spend on a Christmas party.

Della, a scarf over her shorn head, goes to the jewelers to buy the fob. She tells the jeweler it is the only fob as beautiful as Jim's watch. The kindly man sells her the watch fob for $20. She is so happy she drops a coin into Santa's pail. However, her joy is short-lived as she sees her reflection. The barber didn't spare the scissors, taking every piece of hair possible. She sobs, "Oh dear God. Let him still love me. Please let him still love me."

Della is trying to curl her hair when Jim bounds up the stairs singing "O Little Town of Bethlehem."

At first he is speechless when he sees her. Della nervously gives him the priceless gift. Jim, having sold his watch, gives her the beautiful combs. The couple laugh as carolers below sing "Joy to the World."

I'm sure everyone knows the story of "The Gift of the Magi." It is a cherished piece of Americana.

O. Henry managed to touch the heart of everyone with his tale of a love so deep that nothing is more valuable. We either hope someday to find a love that special, thank the Lord we have found that special someone or mourn the loss of such a beloved. In a few short pages of the O. Henry story or in 21 minutes of the film, we are reminded of what is truly important, not only during Christmas, but all the time.

As the sweet Della, Jeanne Crain would steal audiences' hearts in "The Gift of the Magi." She would charm those same folks with roles in *State Fair* (1946) and as the title character in *Margie*. Farley Granger, so caring as Roger, would make perhaps his most famous appearance as one of the cold-blooded killers in Alfred Hitchcock's *Rope*. Of their performances *Variety* said, "...splendidly trouped by Jeanne Crain and Farley Granger under Henry King's topnotch direction."

Henry King, who had directed Crain in *Margie*, was one of Hollywood's most respected directors. His list of film work includes *Alexander's Ragtime Band, Beloved Infidel, Carousel, In Old Chicago, Jesse James* and *The Song of Bernadette*. He also directed the first version of *State Fair* in 1936 which starred Will Rogers.

I consider "The Gift of the Magi" required holiday viewing and urge readers not to miss this lovely film. Copies of the film are difficult to find on video but the classic movie channels can usually be relied upon to broadcast this treasure during December.
—SS

Susan Slept Here
1954

Before watching *Susan Slept Here*, take a deep breath and clear your head of any traces of political correctness lingering there because if you get mired in reality, this movie plays like a particularly sleazy tabloid television show. The 1954 film follows the courtship of a 35-year-old Academy Award winning writer (Dick Powell) and a 17-year-old juvenile delinquent (Debbie Reynolds) put in his charge by two policemen trying to give the kid a nice Christmas while giving the writer material for his next screenplay.

Of course writer Mark would never take advantage of a young girl; he prefers the mature charms of vamp Isabella (Anne Francis) and is rushing to keep

Mark (Dick Powell) tries to keep Susan (Debbie Reynolds) occupied in *Susan Slept Here*.

a Christmas Eve date with her when the cops drop off the wayward kid.

You see, Mark has become discouraged writing fluff for the studio system and has quit to write something serious. The problem is, he can't find any material. The cops (Horace McMahon and Herbert Vigran) advised him on a previous film and, remembering his quest for new material, drop off Susan for Mark to use as research. Susan is none too happy with this arrangement, making it known she is a good girl and won't put up with any hanky panky. Mark isn't pleased either and tries to put the kid in a hotel for the night, but all give him a you're-a-dirty-old-man stare and won't rent him a room. He ends up taking Susan back to his apartment, and they play cards to see who gets the bedroom. She wins and he spends an uncomfortable night on the couch. Susan explains she convinced her mother to marry and move to South America with her new husband. Susan told her mother she was going marry her high school boyfriend. Of course Susan wasn't going to do any such thing, but she wanted her mother to be happy. Mark feels sorry for Susan and tries to think of a way to keep her out of juvenile hall. The only thing he can think of is to marry her (she has a letter with her mother's permission). Against the wishes of his lawyer Harvey (Les Tremayne) and wiseacre assistant Virgil (Alvy Moore), Mark and Susan drive to Las Vegas to tie the knot. Mark, not wanting to spend the night with the teenager, keeps her dancing through the wee hours of the morning until she falls asleep. They drive back to California and Mark carries the new Mrs. into the bedroom, places her on the bed and promptly takes off for his cabin in the mountains, with secretary Maude (Glenda Farrell) in tow to write the dramatic screenplay. Virgil is left in charge of Susan until Harvey can arrange an annulment. But Susan fell in love-at-first-sight with the writer and, when asked to sign the papers, implies she spent the night with Mark and they must be divorced.

Meanwhile, in a perverted little scenario in the mountains, Isabella sneaks into Mark's bed dressed as the teenaged Susan was on that Christmas Eve. She cries crocodile tears and begins to worm her way back into Mark's affections when Mark receives a panic-stricken call from Harvey informing him Susan is at a lunch counter eating strawberries and pickles! Harvey thinks she's pregnant and Mark is the father, Mark thinks Virgil has been taking advantage of Susan and Susan is oblivious to everything happily munching away on the disgusting combination.

Mark discovers he really loves Susan and punches Virgil for taking advantage of her. He learns Susan has always eaten pickles and strawberries and the movie ends happily as the blissfully married couple heads for the bedroom and their belated honeymoon.

The film, too blatant to be a bedroom farce and too offensive to be a comedic love story, is really only for die-hard Dick Powell and Debbie Reynolds fans. Fans of Dick Powell will be happy to see him trip the light fantastic in a musical number with Reynolds. Powell left his dancing shoes at Warner Bros. and moved on to playing hard-boiled detectives in the 1940s in films such as *Murder, My Sweet* and *Cornered*. In the 1950s he would graduate to producing and directing. Two years after *Susan Slept Here,* Powell would produce and direct *The Conqueror*, which was shot on location in Utah about 130 miles from an atomic test site. The cast included John Wayne, Susan Hayward and Agnes Moorehead who, along with Powell and over 90 other crew members, would all succumb to cancer. Powell was 49 when he played Mark, his last starring film role. He died in 1963 at the age of 58. Powell was married to musical star June Allyson at the time of his death. Debbie Reynolds was 22 when she played Susan. In 1964 she would earn an Academy Award nomination for her role as Molly Brown in *The Unsinkable Molly Brown*.

A welcome addition to the cast of *Susan Slept Here* was Glenda Farrell as Maude. Farrell had a successful career in 1930s and 1940s Hollywood as a wise-cracking blonde most typified by her Torchy Blane series. In 1933's *Mystery of the Wax Museum* Farrell practically stole the film from the always delightfully evil Lionel Atwill.

—SS

White Christmas

1954

Critics often shrug off *White Christmas* as sugary fluff that is not as good as its predecessor, *Holiday Inn*. To which I reply, phooey. Hands down, *White Christmas* now and always will be my favorite Christmas movie. The songs, the love story, the glorious Technicolor, the dance routines, the shameful manipulation of our tears and the appealing leads all added up to a warm, fuzzy and delightful movie experience for audiences everywhere. I am not alone in my praise. Audiences of the time agreed, making *White Christmas* (which brought in over 12 million dollars) the top-grossing movie of 1954.

In the finale of *White Christmas* when General Waverly enters the hall and his troops come to attention, well, just hand me the tissues and allow me to wallow in my tears, soon to be followed by more waterworks as the ensemble cast breaks into "White Christmas." My brothers and sisters and I liked nothing better than watching movies with our parents, es-

Bob Wallace (Bing Crosby) and Phil Davis (Danny Kaye) perform for the troops in *White Christmas*.

pecially our dad who was a Western and war film fan (John Wayne practically attained Godhood status in our house). Our dad had been a Jeep driver for a MASH unit during the Korean War and, although he would never talk about it, we just knew he and all the men fighting wars for our country were heroes. The sight of Dean Jagger as General Waverly responding to seeing his old division gathered before him on Christmas Eve reminds me of those simpler days of watching movies with my war hero, my dad. I'm sure that is one of the reasons this film reduces me to tears every time I watch it and, since I am incapable of taking a realistic view of this film, please allow me to gush syrupy sentiment and no criticism, for though my brain may say the film is flawed, my heart says it's perfection.

As is the case in many movie musicals, the story is a simple one, held together by the glue of wonderful Irving Berlin songs.

The opening credits put us in the holiday spirit as the cast and crew are listed on a brilliant red background surrounded by holly leaves.

Christmas Eve, 1944. A rag-tag entertainment for weary troops is taking place. A scraggly deco-

rated tree, a painted backdrop of a Norman Rockwellesque snow scene and a music box that accompanies Bob Wallace (Bing Crosby) as he sings "White Christmas" bring out the longing, homesickness and sadness in the faces of the men who miss their families and wonder if they will make it home to celebrate next Christmas. General Waverly (Dean Jagger) and his adjutant (Richard Shannon) exit a Jeep, with the new commander who wants to know what's going on. Waverly tells the driver escorting the commander back to base to take the "short-cut." Of course, there is no short-cut, Waverly just wanted the men to have a bit of fun before heading toward the front. He sneaks in and sits down.

Bob ends the show:

"Certainly too bad General Waverly couldn't have been here for this little Yuletide clambake, 'cause we really had a slam-bang finish cooked up for him. I guess you know by now that he's being replaced by a new commanding general fresh out of the Pentagon. That's not a very nice Christmas present, is it, for a division like us that's moving up? The old man's moving to the rear. That's a direction he's never taken in his entire life. All I can say is we owe an awful lot to General Waverly and the way he—"

"ATTENTION!" is yelled. Waverly heads toward stage trying to appear gruff but can't find the words to tell the men how he feels. He looks at Wallace.

"Don't just stand there. How do I get off?"
"Just so happen to have a slam-bang finish, Sir."

The men begin singing "We'll follow the old man wherever he wants to go...," as Waverly walks down the aisle shaking hands with his loyal troops. He reaches the back of the hall, salutes his men and rides off into the dark night. Bombing begins in earnest and the men run for cover. A brick wall falls toward Bob but he is pushed out of the way by a private, Phil Davis (Danny Kaye), who injures his arm. Bob visits Phil in the infirmary to thank him for saving his life. "Any time I can do anything for you..." he says.

Phil pitifully replies, "That's all right Captain. I wouldn't want you to feel any special obligation" (as he holds his wounded arm). Danny Kaye establishes Phil as a nice guy but a roguish character as he gives Bob a look with those big puppy dog eyes.

He just so happens to have a song he's written, one he would like Bob to introduce when he gets back to the States. Bob looks at the song, "This is a duet. I work alone."

Phil manages to convince Bob to take him on as a partner when the war is over. Of course they are a smash hit as a duo, taking on Broadway, then becoming successful producers.

The show is just ending a run in Florida and breaking for the Christmas holidays when Phil tries to set Bob up with a dim-witted chorus girl. Bob tells him neither can go out that night, they have to take a look at a sister act. Phil's not too happy but agrees when Bob tells him it's a favor to Benny "freckle-faced" Haynes. "Let's just say we're doing it for a pal in the Army." Phil replies, "Well, it's not good, but it's a reason."

Bob is annoyed at Phil's constant matchmaking and wants to know why he keeps trying to fix him up. Phil, trying to slow down the workaholic Bob, answers, "I want you to get married. I want you to have nine children. And if you only spend five minutes a day with each kid, that's 45 minutes and I'd at least have time to go out and get a massage or something."

They go to the nightclub to watch the act, certain the sisters of Benny are going to be awful. But they are pleasantly surprised when Betty (Rosemary Clooney) and Judy (Vera-Ellen) perform the number "Sisters." Bob is attracted to blue-eyed Betty and Phil to brown-eyed Judy.

After the number, the girls sit down with Bob and Phil to thank them for com-

Bob shows some moves to Betty (Rosemary Clooney) as Judy (Vera-Ellen) and Phil look on in *White Christmas*.

ing. Phil dances off with Judy allowing Bob and Betty to get to know one another. Betty tells him they were gotten there under false pretenses. Judy wrote the letter. Bob laughs it off saying everyone's got an angle, but this infuriates Betty. Phil and Judy think the duo is getting along fabulously and dance off into the outdoors. Danny Kaye and Vera-Ellen perform one of the most enjoyable numbers in the film, "The Best Things Happen While You're Dancing." The chemistry between the couple is charming (Kaye's smiles at Vera-Ellen seems real and approving) and the singing and dancing in this number is delightful.

Danny Kaye replaced Donald O'Connor who had been slated for the role of Phil Davis but was injured. Fred Astaire (who had starred with Crosby in *Holiday Inn* and *Blue Skies*) had originally been offered the role of Phil, but depending on which history you read, either didn't like the script or hurt himself. Either way, Kaye gives a fine performance and is at his most winning.

The girls are ending their run at the nightclub and leaving the next morning. Phil finds out their landlord is trying to hold them up for $200 for damage so he gives them his and Bob's train tickets and helps them escape out the dressing room window and then manages to convince Bob to go on in their place while the owner keeps the sheriff busy. Bob and Phil do a funny pantomime of "Sisters" complete with feathers, fans and rolled up trousers, before climbing out the window themselves barely making the train. Phil pretends he can't find the tickets and they are forced to sit up all night in the club car. Bob is enraged to find he has given the tickets to the girls and is ready to read them the riot act when they rush into the club car and express their thanks. Clooney and Vera-Ellen as Betty and Judy are an enchanting pair and Bob's anger melts as he invites them to have a sandwich, which leads to Phil (with a little help from his old arm injury) talking him into accompanying the girls to their engagement at a ski lodge in Vermont. This leads to another favorite musical interlude as the group imagines a snow-covered Vermont and harmonizes on the sparkling song "Snow."

They exit the train to 68 degrees and no snow. When they arrive at the empty inn and the girls announce they are the entertainment, Emma (Mary Wickes) tells them the inn is vacant and they will have to cancel. The owner enters, and surprise! It's General Waverly who owns the inn. His granddaughter Susan (Anne Whitfield) lives with him. He insists the girls stay and perform, which they do to a basically empty house.

Bob and Phil decide to bring their show up to the inn to help increase business. They plan to open on Christmas Eve with the Haynes sisters filling in for any acts that can't make it.

The first dress rehearsal is a production number revolving around the song "Mandy" and a minstrel show. Bob, Phil and Betty are dressed to the nines in black with red trimming emphasizing the stunning use of color; *White Christmas* is a brilliant example of the best use of Technicolor.

Vera-Ellen gets to strut her stuff with dancer John Brascia (who appeared as a specialty dancer in *Meet Me in Las Vegas* with Cyd Charisse and Dan Dailey) in the "Mandy" production number. Vera-Ellen was an extremely talented dancer discovered on Broadway before being signed in Hollywood. Her first two musicals were with Danny Kaye (*Wonder Man* and *The Kid from Brooklyn*), which may explain the camaraderie between the two.

Judy and Phil, both meddlers at heart, scheme to get Betty and Bob together. They arrange to have the two meet at night in the empty lodge. They sit by a fire and duet on "Count Your Blessings Instead of Sheep," one of the original songs written for the film. The song would earn Berlin another Academy Award nomination for Best Song although he would lose to the title song from *Three Coins in the Fountain*. The couple manage a chaste kiss before being interrupted by the General. Judy and Phil spy through a window.

The next day Bob brings the mail to the General who has applied for active duty in the Army. He receives a reply pretending the request was a joke, letting him down easy. Meanwhile Phil, Judy and cast are rehearsing the "Choreography" production number, a sly spoof of Broadway pretention as Danny Kaye dons a black avant garde outfit and emotes with plainly dressed chorus girls. The drab group lose the battle of dance styles to Vera-Ellen and John Brascia, whose colorful costumes and good old-fashioned razzle-dazzle tapping steal the show.

Bob and Phil agree to try to get the old division to the inn for a Christmas Eve surprise. Bob places a call to Ed Harris, a friend and fellow soldier under Waverly, and gets an appearance on Harris' television show. Harris tries to talk Bob into televising the whole thing, but Bob doesn't want to exploit the plight of the old man. Of course, things can't run too smoothly. After all this is a movie, so to throw a little trouble into this Vermonty paradise, Emma listens in on the conversation and only hears a short bit, enough to convince her Bob and Phil are only doing this for free publicity. Emma spills the beans to Betty who, instead of discussing it with Bob, goes into a snit and refuses to have anything to do with him.

Judy decides Betty is in love and won't commit to Bob unless Judy is taken care of. She convinces

Phil that they should announce a phony engagement. Phil is not very fond of this plan, but Judy oozes charm and gets him to agree. That evening there is a cast party and things are as cold as ever between Betty and Bob (who has no idea what he's done, but is really sorry for whatever it is). Phil announces the engagement much to the shock of everyone. Rosemary Clooney as Betty has the most difficult part in the film, being forced to play the uptight cold woman who begins to melt under the influence of the charming crooner, but then goes back to her frigid ways at the slightest hint of trouble. Clooney was an immensely popular singer and melds her lovely voice beautifully with duets with Bing Crosby.

The next morning Betty has the General drive her to the train station, for she has booked an engagement in New York leaving a letter for Judy. Judy and Phil shamefully confess their scheme to Bob who is leaving for New York to appear on the Harris show. He chides them for their silly plan, but doesn't stay angry for long and instructs Phil to keep the General away from the television during his appearance.

Bob stops by the Carousel Club where Betty is singing. Her solo number "Love, You Didn't Do Right By Me," is a knock-out. Clooney wears a tightly fitted evening gown that flares out at the bottom, and, she is surrounded by elegantly dressed chorus boys in this simple but stylish number.

Bob tells her the story of the fake engagement and is starting to melt a little of the ice, but Ed Harris interrupts and they leave for the show.

Back in Vermont Phil pretends to hurt his knee and, in a slap-stick bit, forces the General to walk him around until the knee feels better.

Bob makes his emotional pitch for members of the 151st Division under the command of Major-General Tom Waverly to show up at the inn Christmas Eve. Betty is watching the show and realizes how wrong she has been about everything.

Christmas Eve arrives and the train station is buzzing as old soldiers and their families arrive for this impromptu reunion. That evening the men don their old uniforms (some of which seemed to have shrunk) and Bob gives them directions.

Waverly's granddaughter and Emma have hidden his suits and he is forced to wear his uniform. Susan watches with pride as he descends the staircase of the inn and proudly takes his arm. As they enter the lodge "Ten Hut" is yelled, a spotlight hits him and the General is met at the door by his old staff and proceeds to his table.

The curtains open and the strains of "We'll follow the old man" is heard as the troops, once again led by Bob, march off stage singing. As General Waverly, Dean Jagger is at his best in this scene. The look on his face as the men line up betrays a wealth of

The finale of *White Christmas* is a Technicolor delight as the cast reprises "White Christmas."

emotion as this man is deeply touched by the love of his troops. The men line up on both sides of the aisle and Bob announces, "Troops ready for inspection sir."

Waverly walks the line.

> "I am not satisfied with the conduct of this division... Look at the rest of your appearance. You're a disgrace to the outfit. You're soft. You're sloppy. You're unruly. You're undisciplined, and I never saw anything look so wonderful in my whole life. Thank you all."

He walks down the line shaking hands and the men break ranks and join their families for the show. Crosby and Kaye joined by Clooney and Vera-Ellen bring to sparkling life Irving Berlin's "Gee I Wish I Was Back in the Army," harking back to Berlin's patriotic musical *This Is the Army*.

The finale is a burst of dazzling Technicolor as the leads—Phil and Bob clad in Santa suits and Clooney and Vera-Ellen in fabulous Edith Head designed red fur-trimmed gowns—are joined by a boys chorus, red and white clad tiny ballerinas and two young boys also dressed as Santa. The stage is flanked by two large Christmas trees with another tree in the center of the stage. They sing "White Christmas" as the tree is pulled aside, the lodge door is raised and the crowd audibly sighs as they see snow gently falling outside.

And they lived happily ever after. Immigrants Irving Berlin and renowned director Michael Curtiz created an indelible piece of Americana. And we as audience can sit back with our hands folded across our stomachs feeling as full as if we have just indulged in our annual Christmas dinner, free to wallow in sweet sentiment and happy endings.

May all our Christmases be so bright.

—SS

Bell, Book and Candle
1958

"Why don't you give me *him* for Christmas, Pye? Why don't you give me *him*?"

The delightful 1958 motion picture adaptation of John Van Druten's 1950 stage comedy *Bell, Book and Candle*, in which sexy screen witch Kim Novak utters the above line to her purring Siamese "familiar" with such heartfelt pensiveness, probably does not quite merit the "Christmas movie" label so commonly applied to such Yuletide favorites as *White Christmas* and *It's a Wonderful Life*, no matter how exuberantly actor James Stewart's publisher hero whistles a jaunty "Deck the Halls" or how eagerly Ernie Kovacs' liquor-soaked book author treats himself to a little "post-Christmas cheer." Though its story does *begin* on Christmas Eve, after all, with strains of "Jingle Bells" even helping herald the opening credits, the tale *Bell, Book and Candle* presents actually wraps up a few months *later*, well after the generally accepted holiday season is over.

And yet, like most films set on or near the holidays, this simple little wintertime comedy does capture that same sense of warmth, charm and magic—"magic" here being the key word—the holidays so often suggest. Where *The Bishop's Wife* has its angel and *The Santa Clause* its elves, *Bell, Book and Candle* gently tweaks the standard Christmas movie tradition by slipping a witch or two into the mix, recalling countless other tales (*A Christmas Carol, How the Grinch Stole Christmas, The Nightmare Before Christmas*, etc.) spotlighting black cats and jack-o'-lanterns amid all the tinsel and snowmen, serving up witch's brew alongside the Christmas punch, inspiring kisses as much through well-aimed spell-casting as strategically hung doorway mistletoe. Though less holiday-focused than most films of the genre, *Bell, Book and Candle* nevertheless falls rather neatly into its tradition, happily delivering a tender, sophisticated little fantasy-fable about a lovely but lonely New York sorceress who wants just one present for Christmas: a passionate romance (or, at least, since a true witch can't love, a *near*-passionate romance) with the man of her dreams.

The premise of *Bell, Book and Candle* is simple, really. On Christmas Eve in New York City, gorgeous, affection-starved shop clerk Gillian Holroyd, secretly a witch, becomes intrigued with Sheperd Henderson, a handsome publisher living upstairs, and, encouraged by her spinster aunt Queenie, a less gifted witch, plots to win his affection. Learning Shep is getting married in 24 hours to haughty Merle Kittridge, a woman she has disliked since college, Gillian casts a spell causing Shep abruptly to jilt Merle to pursue her, and

all is well until Gillian, having accepted a spellbound Shep's marriage proposal, starts to dread his inevitable discovery of her deception. Complicating matters is an earlier spell cast to inspire an involuntary visit from Sidney Redlitch, a besotted author of books on modern witchcraft whom Shep has expressed interest in meeting. Because her overzealous warlock brother Nicky has told Redlitch of his own powers so he can co-write Redlitch's next book, Gillian fears Nicky's recklessness will awaken Shep to the fact that his recent behavior has been spell-induced. To prevent Shep from feeling duped, Gillian wrecks Nicky's ill-conceived publishing efforts with yet another spell, but then tells Shep the truth anyway before anyone else can. Shep laughs off her claims at first but is soon convinced, and, enraged by Gillian's manipulation—she has cost him both a bride and considerable money to have the love spell removed—Shep bitterly makes it clear he wants nothing to do with her from now on.

As with all romantic comedies, of course, all works out fine in the end, here because *Bell, Book and Candle* concludes with two appealing moments of self-discovery. First, confirming the "old wives' tale" that a witch cannot cry real tears, blush or fall in love, Gillian weeps for the first time ever and loses her powers after her breakup with an angry Shep. Second, Shep finds he too has fallen in love, love based no longer on a witch's sneaky trick but rather on genuine, heartfelt affection for a woman whom, even after freeing himself from her control, he realizes he can no longer live without. In short, after all the deceit, machinations, insults and hurt feelings, both Gillian and Shep discover they have fallen under a "spell" of sorts, even *without* all the Old World hocus-pocus. Love, it seems, has bewitched them both, almost like—dare we say it?—magic.

If all of this sounds a trifle corny—true love being equated with "enchantment," "spells," "witchcraft" and such like in some old Doris Day or Frank Sinatra song—*Bell, Book and Candle* is meant that way, as a gentle, warm-hearted love story, as old-fashioned as flowers, chocolates and dinner by candlelight. Gillian, Shep and the rest may *look* 1950s-era modern—live in upscale apartments, dress well, work as urban shopkeepers, executives, artists, writers and musicians—but, deep down, the movie is as well-mannered and innocent as an installment of TV's *Bewitched* (1964-72), whose stylishly romantic early episodes *Bell, Book and Candle* easily calls to mind.

And besides, when one really stops to think about it, has anyone ever made a so-called "Christmas movie"—or even a love story, for that matter—that *wasn't* just a little bit corny?

Although big-screen versions of stage plays often emerge as pale imitations of the works inspiring

Queenie (Elsa Lanchester), Gillian (Kim Novak) and Nicky (Jack Lemmon) cast a spell on the audience in *Bell, Book and Candle*.

them (think *Mame*, think *Camelot*, think *Don't Drink the Water*), *Bell, Book and Candle* holds up quite well. One might think leaving Van Druten's single set for sidewalks, jazz clubs, rooftops, offices, taxicabs and such would weaken the impact of the Gillian-Shep romance, but for once "opening up" a play works because the new scenes are still about people, not places—love, not locales. Screenwriter Daniel Taradash and former child actor-turned-director Richard Quine don't expand the play so much as take ideas Van Druten could only touch upon—Shep's engagement to a woman Gillian despises; Gillian's purchase of a Mexican witchmask; the popularity with witches of an off-kilter night spot called The Zodiac; Queenie's hex on Shep's telephone; Nicky's fondness for his new records and phonograph, and his sketch of a pretty Zodiac dancer; Shep's visit to sorceress Mrs. de Pass to counteract Gillian's spell; etc.—and really "show" instead of "tell," give them color and substance in ways a one-set play never could.

We actually *meet* fiancée Merle, for instance, which gives actress Janice Rule, when told her rival is a witch, the deliciously wicked line, "Oh, Shep, you've just never learned to spell." The mask becomes an item in a shopful of exotic art Gillian now owns (symbolizing Gillian's "unmasking," it still gets shattered, but here with a broom given her as a cruel joke by an angry Shep). The Zodiac, named in the play but unseen, is shown in all its trumpet-screeching glory, and Shep's bewitched telephone, its mild

peculiarities only described before, now emits weird, gobbledygook we can actually hear. Nicky's love of music allows scenes of Nicky as a Zodiac bongo-player, and the oft-discussed but never seen Mrs. de Pass becomes a full-fledged, quirky character all her own. Where Van Druten, hindered by budget and stage size, could merely *relate* events—could only *tell* us warlock Nicky plays tricks with traffic signals, could only present *one* side of Shep's breakup by having him jilt Merle by phone, could only have Shep *describe* the foul-tasting "cure" from Mrs. de Pass—the movie cheerfully *shows* us a gleeful Nicky darkening street lamps, has Shep jettison Merle in *person*, lets us *see* a trembling Shep drink a hideous witch's brew.

Screenwriter Taradash, an Oscar winner for 1953's *From Here to Eternity*, preserves the play's best elements while adding sparkling new lines likely to have pleased even Van Druten, who himself had reworked Kathryn Forbes' *Mama's Bank Account* as *I Remember Mama* and Christopher Isherwood's *Cabaret*-inspiring *Berlin Stories* as *I Am a Camera* on stage. (Sadly, Van Druten passed away a year before *Bell, Book and Candle*'s release.) In the final scene, for instance, in which Shep realizes Gillian has lost her powers, Taradash wisely keeps Van Druten's absolutely perfect curtain-dropping final line from Gillian—"I'm only human"—but also provides a better lead-in (Shep: "Oh, Gill, don't you want to stop crying now?" Gillian: "I don't think I can."), preceding *that* with a still stronger line, earnestly deliv-

Shep (Jimmy Stewart) looks on as Redlitch (Ernie Kovacs) clowns in *Bell, Book and Candle*.

ered by Stewart with just the right note of tender, lovestruck passion: "Or has it been real all along? Who's to say what magic is?"

Van Druten's play actually includes only five roles (six counting the cat who "plays" Pyewacket)— Gillian, Shep, Queenie, Nicky and Redlitch—and not one of the actors in the film appeared in the initial New York stage production. (It's a bit of a shame, really; the original Shep and Gillian, the always brilliant Rex Harrison and gorgeous real-life second wife Lilli Palmer, must have absolutely sparkled together.) In the end it matters little, though, because the new stars have so much appeal. James Stewart, Kim Novak, Jack Lemmon, Ernie Kovacs, Hermione Gingold, Elsa Lanchester, Janice Rule—how many *modern* romantic comedies can boast a cast this strong?

As bewitched publisher Shep, the ever-reliable James Stewart is particularly good in a film that essentially flip-flops his whimsical, pooka-befriended Elwood P. Dowd persona from *Harvey* and leaves Stewart the fantasy-scoffing, sensible type for a change. One of several forerunners to the magic- and miracle-attracting Everyman types popularized by such stars as Dean Jones, Tom Hanks and Steve Guttenberg, Shep is another logic-minded hero whose world turns upside-down after some comfort-shaking supernatural "truth" hits head-on, and the inimitable Stewart plays the part to perfection. Graying hair not-

withstanding, he still convinces as a romantic lead (as he had opposite Novak in *Vertigo* that same year), looking, even at 50, quite dashing in tux and topcoat and handling his love scenes with the 25-year-old Novak without seeming at all out of place—despite the fact that Novak, at half his age, was young enough to play his own daughter!

Also effective is Kim Novak, who may lack the comic flair of an Elizabeth Montgomery (the best early episodes of whose 1964-72 TV series *Bewitched* Van Druten's romantic comedy often resembles) but nevertheless is quite convincing—and drop-dead gorgeous—as Gillian. Slinky and seductive in her formfitting, feline black, lounging about barefoot with an almost palpable feminine allure, Novak recalls some breathtaking cross between ballet dancer and coffeehouse beat poet, exotic Olympic gymnast and cat burglar-spy. Amazingly, even amid Gillian's vindictive threats and calculated plotting, Novak still wins our sympathy, her hypnotically chilly demeanor a near-perfect complement to Pyewacket, Gillian's sly, silky-whiskered cat, her "familiar." Like her eerie Siamese, whose finicky, claws-at-the-ready flightiness make him as dangerous as he is handsome, so is Novak's Gillian at once both vengefully hot-tempered and mysteriously, hauntingly beautiful.

Jack Lemmon's role is a bit more limited, but his work as solid as ever, giving bongo-beating warlock Nicky just the sort of impish, playful recklessness the part calls for. Like Novak, Lemmon has to tread carefully (we have to sense the foolishness behind Nicky's plan to make a "quick buck" exposing New York's "magic underground," but if he seems traitorous and greedy, we'll dislike him), and he reveals just enough of Nicky's adolescent, prankster side that we hold neither his lapses in loyalty nor good judgment against him. Nicky is a big kid, really, like some 1950s teenager taking chances in his new car, and, wisely, that's exactly how Lemmon plays him.

The legendary Elsa Lanchester delivers another of her daffy old eccentric parts (her work opposite Stewart here isn't much different from that between her and Dean Jones in *Blackbeard's Ghost* 10 years later), but nobody is better at it, and she's always a pleasure to watch. In fact, she's so endearing one half-wishes Taradash had kept Van Druten's scene in which spinster Queenie finds a suitor of sorts in Sidney Redlitch. Even a lonely old snoop merits a happy ending.

TV great Ernie Kovacs provides the film's most unusual bit of casting, but he too is an inspired choice, mainly because he does such a fine job turning "a drunk and a nut" into such a relaxed, satisfying presence. Neatly sidestepping the urge to turn the witty, clever Redlitch into some staggering, booze-soaked buffoon, Kovacs keeps the writer just low-key and clever enough even with a drink in his hand that we take his "expertise" on magic pretty seriously—even, amusingly, when he's addressing witches three at a time without even remotely realizing it.

Casting Janice Rule as Merle proves equally inspired, with the talented actress turning what might well have been an all-out villainess—even unseen, the Merle of the play is spoken of with enough contempt to suggest losing Shep ultimately "serves her right"—into a sophisticated, witty woman who, despite her cool arrogance, seems to deserve better than Gillian's cruel tricks and Shep's out-of-the-blue abandonment. When she flatly rejects Shep late in the film, it's hard to blame her after the way she's been so casually discarded, but her presence actually gives Stewart some of his best scenes, and Rule herself is so good we'd actually like to see more of her.

The smaller roles are equally strong—Hermione Gingold as con-artist witch Mrs. de Pass, Bek Nelson as Shep's at-wit's-end secretary, Howard McNear as Shep's befuddled partner—but what truly amazes is how much creativity went into putting this simple little story on film. Thanks to 10-time Oscar nominee (and two-time winner) James Wong Howe, whose cinematography graced works as varied as *The Thin Man, Yankee Doodle Dandy* and *On the Waterfront, Bell, Book and Candle* is an uncommonly beautiful *looking* film, filled with bright, bold colors atop vivid, razor-sharp images, all given a sleek, crisp elegance well-suited to the sophistication of its performers, whether bow-tied, necklaced or collared. What's more, the film *sounds* just as good as it looks, with a refreshingly offbeat jazz score from George Duning (*From Here to Eternity, Picnic, Houseboat, That Touch of Mink, The World of Suzie Wong, Dear Brigitte*) exuberantly peppy or lushly romantic at just the proper moments—a real musical treat from beginning to end.

Richard Quine, having already directed Novak, Lemmon and Kovaks in previous films, lends ample imagination even to the opening credits, his camera making catlike leaps from one work of art to the next in Gillian's shop—art illustrating the personality or function of the cast or crew members whose names are on screen—until finally making one last pounce to Pyewacket himself, who springs from his perch at just the right moment before the camera at last cuts to his landing atop Gillian's shoulders. Because of Quine, Howe and other behind-the-scenes talents, fans are suddenly treated to distorted, powder blue "cat's eye view" shots of both Shep and New York streets; glorious close-ups of Gillian and Pyewacket (when they bewitch Shep, they glare at him deeply while the cat's loud purring roars like floodwaters); unexpected ceiling shots with great visual appeal; well-executed scenes, entirely without dialogue, of Shep romancing Gillian (and Nicky sharing witch secrets with Redlitch); amusing voice-over sequences letting us "overhear" Shep's thoughts while concocting excuses for jilting Merle and pondering if Gillian truly could be a witch; a truly exhilarating moment in which the camera follows, in one long, playful shot, Shep's hat as it sails from a New York rooftop to the streets below; and a wonderfully eerie final glimpse of Pyewacket, crouched atop a lamppost, practically winking at us from the darkness overhead.

Bell, Book and Candle has never achieved the popularity of James Stewart's most admired films, and with gems like *You Can't Take It With You, It's a Wonderful Life, The Philadelphia Story, Harvey, Destry Rides Again, Rope, Rear Window, The Man Who Knew Too Much, Vertigo, Mr. Smith Goes to Washington* and *Anatomy of a Murder* to his credit, it probably never will. Delightful as they are, after all, Shep Henderson is no George Bailey, and Gillian the witch no Harvey. Yet the movie still ranks as one of its day's most engaging romantic comedies—no masterwork, perhaps, but bright, breezy and far better written than most films today. A very different kind of "Christmas movie," *Bell, Book and Candle* is, if no genuine classic, truly a "class act"—and one brand of magic even the most secretive witch shouldn't mind going public with one bit.

—RAC

While You Were Sleeping

1995

Romantic comedies returned to prominence in the 1990s, and 1995's *While You Were Sleeping*, one of the more successful ones of the decade, was set during the Christmas holidays infecting its cast of characters with an overdose of goodwill toward all men and women. Sandra Bullock, a squeaky-clean actress more cute than sensuous, turns in one of her best performances as a lonely young single out to find the man of her dreams. The movie turns out to be a feel-good movie, but one that perfectly suits the holiday season.

The movie begins and ends with Lucy (Sandra Bullock) supplying a voice-over narration reflecting on her life, past, present and future. It becomes a most effective bookend framing device to the sweet story. Lucy thinks back and remembers her father (who died a year ago) when she was a child, having adventures together, going to the church where he and her mother (dead even when Lucy was a child) were married. "Life doesn't always turn out as you plan," were the words that Lucy remembers most from her father, and she remembers the lighted globe that her father gave her as a child: "He gave me the world!"

Lucy, who gave up college to move to an experimental cancer treatment hospital in Chicago with her father, now works as a token-taker at a train station, where she sees the man of her dreams, even though they have never spoken. He comes by several times every week past her token booth flashing a smile or simply walking by, but for Lucy, this is love at first sight. Her boss Jerry, even though he is recommending Lucy for employee of the month, hits her up to work on Christmas day, citing she is the only single employee without family. "Did I mention the extra holiday pay?"

At home, Lucy purchases a $45 Christmas tree which is left on the ground outside her apartment, so using a rope, she attempts to lift it up to her apartment, ultimately losing her grip and dropping the tree through another neighbor's window, offering to pay for damages while delivering her Christmas present to him.

In her token booth, Lucy, working on Christmas day, has a little Christmas tree for company. When the man of her dreams passes by this time he wishes Lucy "Merry Christmas," and Lucy, distracted, only manages to grunt, as she hits herself in the head for missing a perfect opportunity to speak with him. She sees two men accost him near the tracks and push him

over the side. Rushing out of her booth to offer assistance, Lucy jumps down onto the tracks. "Sir, are you okay... God, you smell good!" While yelling out for help as a commuter train rapidly approaches, Lucy manages to roll him out of the way as the train passes. A large bruise is visible on his forehead.

She accompanies him to the hospital. Since only family is allowed to stay with him, she allows the nurse to think she is his fiancée so she can remain to try to awaken him from his comatose state. Soon this man, Peter (Peter Gallagher), is visited by his entire family, and Lucy is introduced as Peter's fiancée. "Too busy to tell his own father he is getting married," the father Ox (Peter Boyle) says as he smiles at her; the family immediately takes a liking to Lucy. "I always wanted him to find a nice girl. I'm so glad it was you," the mother Elsie (Glynis Johns) announces.

The very wise Saul (Jack Warden), a neighbor, now part of the family and godfather to Peter, tells Lucy, "I think you saved the entire family." Soon everyone is asking how Lucy met Peter and what attracted her to him in the first place. She tries to hide her awkwardness.

Later that night, alone, Lucy goes back to see Peter at the hospital, and speaking aloud, introduces herself and tells him the entire story. She admits as a child she imagined her life when she got older, imagining the perfect apartment and cat, "But nobody I could laugh with... do you believe in love at first sight? Have you ever been so lonely you spoke to a man in a coma?" She falls asleep at his bedside and is awakened the next morning when the family returns. Since the tragedy occurred on Christmas Day, the family is planning to celebrate at their house that evening, and they invite Lucy. Deciding to attend, arriving by cab and bearing a beautiful plant, Lucy is met by Saul taking a smoke break. He tells Lucy this family is great, "They took me in as part of the family, and I wouldn't let anyone hurt them." The evening is just perfect; involving looking at photo albums and eating. The family even has a present for Lucy and a stocking over the fireplace with her name on it. She is totally accepted and loved.

Lucy, who is spending the night sleeping on the couch, is awakened by Peter's brother Jack (Bill Pullman), who has just appeared and welcomes her to the family. However, in the back of his head, Jack realizes that something is askew, that Lucy is not exactly the person she claims to be. Jack comes to see Lucy at her place, and encounters the landlord's son, Joe Junior, who claims he is dating her. Jack later visits Peter's apartment to find Lucy there, who speaks about feeding the cat. Jack says that Peter didn't have a cat, but one appears (actually the cat belongs to Jack's on-off again girlfriend Ashley) and Jack is still unable to prove Lucy is not Peter's fiancée. Leaving, Jack sug-

Lucy (Sandra Bullock) and Jack (Bill Pullman) attend a holiday party, growing closer while Peter recovers in the hospital in *While You Were Sleeping*.

gests they take Peter's car, realizing that Lucy would not recognize it, but using Peter's keys, she is able to activate his car alarm, identifying the car.

Soon Saul comes to visit Lucy and informs her that he was present the night Lucy confessed all to Peter at the hospital, so he knows the truth. Saul implores her to not tell the family, that they need her, for Lucy brings Peter back to life for them. Lucy asks Saul to figure out a way that she can come clean with the family, and Saul tells her not to worry.

As the days stretch on, Jack and Lucy grow closer, Jack admitting he is unhappy carrying on the family business "Callaghan and Son" (formerly "Sons" but Peter left), buyers and sellers of estate furniture. Jack, who makes homemade furniture, would love to do that full-time, but he doesn't want to let the old man down. Finding his furniture truck blocked by two cars, he offers to escort Lucy home, both of them slipping and sliding on the ice and snow, laughing all the way. The next day at work Lucy admits to her boss, "I'm having an affair. I love Jack, Peter's brother!" But how can she tell Jack the truth without losing him?

The story becomes even more complex when Peter opens his eyes and snaps out of his coma on New Year's Eve. However, he has amnesia, so Lucy can still pretend she is his fiancée. In the meanwhile, Jack, who is falling in love with Lucy as well, gives her a pre-wedding present, a snow globe of Florence,

the place that Lucy is most excited to visit (not having been anywhere in her sheltered life). "Can you give me any reason why I shouldn't marry your brother?" offering Jack the opportunity to admit his love. But Jack keeps mum, remaining loyal to Peter.

However, at the wedding, Lucy "objects" to the ceremony even before it begins. "I am in love with your son... *that* one, not *that* one," she says. In a poignant speech, Lucy confesses to falling in love with the entire family, something she never had (considering her mother's early death and her father's recent death) and something so much appreciated (allowing her to assume roles as sister, fiancée and daughter). "You saved my life, allowing me to be part of the family." In shame, she runs out of the church crying.

In a sad sequence, Lucy slowly takes down her Christmas tree at home, realizing her life must change. Going to work for her last day on the job, she is surprised as Jack and the entire family appear at her token booth. Jack plunks down a diamond engagement ring. He asks if he can come inside. She answers no, not unless you have a token (which he naturally does have). Inside, with the entire family lending support, he proposes. She accepts!

Ending the movie with voice-over narration as the train with the newlyweds races away, Lucy remembers her father's line, "Life doesn't always turn out as you plan," telling us that she and Jack will be honeymooning in Florence. And, just as her father gave her the globe when she was a girl, she remarks of Jack that when he gave her the snow globe, "He gave me the world."

Interestingly enough, just like Billy Wilder's *The Apartment*, the entire Christmas holiday, both the days leading up to Christmas and including New Year's Eve, is included in such a way as to develop a blossoming love affair during the total holiday season. Even though Christmas is over a week by the conclusion of *While You Were Sleeping*, one of the last images of the movie is the sequence showing the depressed Lucy taking her Christmas tree down (as a similar sequence showed her hauling the tree up to her apartment and decorating it, at the beginning of the story). Thus, the movie is framed between the day she first puts up her tree and then takes it down, covering lots of ground in little over a week: falling in love with the comatose man of her dreams, being adopted by his family, falling in love with brother Jack, walking out of the chapel on her wedding day and becoming engaged to Jack in her token booth at work. Not to forget her honeymoon to Florence, Italy! As is true with most romantic comedies, the script contains a fair share of holes: the all-too-soon trusting of stranger Lucy by the family, Saul's asking Lucy to continue her lies to the family he loves in order to save it, Peter simply going along and marrying a woman he does not remember nor particularly know, etc. But in spite of such plot holes, Sandra Bullock's lonely desperation and obsession with the concept of finding love, her need to find a new family from the ashes of the one decimated by death, is as miraculous and magical as the spirit of Christmas itself. Just as in fairy tales, all good things happen to those who wait, and for Lucy, her Prince Charming has arrived as her special Christmas present, renewing our faith in the miracle of the season one more time.
—GJS

The following films occur during or have scenes pertaining to Christmas:

The Gift of Love
Cast: Marie Osmond, James Woods, Timothy Bottoms, June Lockhart, David Wayne
Credits: Director: Don Chaffey; 1990
Television remake of O. Henry's *Gift of the Magi*.

Metropolitan
Cast: Carolyn Farina, Edward Clements, Dylan Hundley, Christopher Eigeman
Credits: Producers: Whit Stillman, Brian Greenbaum and Peter Wentworth; Director/Writer: Whit Stillman; New Line; 1990
Wealthy young New Yorkers party through the Christmas season while engaging in weighty after-

Glenn Ford stars in holiday film *Mr. Soft Touch*. (Photofest)

party discussions. This film, more a character study than a holiday fest, would probably put viewers looking for happy holiday cheer to sleep.

A Midwinter's Tale
Cast: Michael Maloney, Richard Briers, Joan Collins, Julia Sawalha, Hetta Charnley, Jennifer Saunders
Credits: Producer: David Barron; Director/Writer: Kenneth Branagh; Castle Rock; 1995
A band of depressed actors join for a slightly radical performance of Hamlet. The play is to open Christmas Eve but chaos reigns when the lead (Maloney) decides to leave for a film career. Happily he returns to take his place in the production which is met with cheers from the village crowd. Families are reunited and love wins out for the lead and his Ophelia (Sawalha). Watch for cameos by Jennifer Saunders and Joan Collins. It's good to see Saunders and Sawalha (her television daughter from *Absolutely Fabulous*) together if only briefly.

Mr. Soft Touch
Cast: Glenn Ford, Evelyn Keyes, John Ireland, Beulah Bondi, Percy Kilbride
Credits: Producer: Milton Holmes; Directors: Henry Levin and Gordon Douglas; Writer: Orin Jannings (Based on a Story by Milton Holmes); Columbia; 1949

Ford plays a gambler seeking shelter in a settlement house during Christmas. Evelyn Keyes, mistaking Ford for a wife abuser, tries to reform him, falling in love with him in the process. This is another rare film and as such was unavailable for screening.

The Nativity
Cast: Madeline Stowe, John Shea, John Rhys-Davies, Freddie Jones, Audrey Totter, Kate O'Mara
Credits: Director: Bernard L. Kowalski; Writer: Millard Kaufman; Television 1978

Television story of the romance between Joseph and Mary and the birth of Jesus.

Bo Hopkins and Dolly Parton star in *A Smokey Mountain Christmas*.

A Smokey Mountain Christmas
Cast: Dolly Parton, Lee Majors, John Ritter, Bo Hopkins, Dan Hedaya
Credits: Director: Henry Winkler; Television 1986

Dolly Parton stars as a celebrity who goes to a mountain cabin to get away from everything and everybody over Christmas. She finds a group of orphans have taken over the cabin. Dolly and the children manage to have a merry Christmas and she even finds the time to fall in love with Majors. Nice little Christmas story.

A Summer Place
Cast: Sandra Dee, Troy Donahue, Dorothy McGuire, Richard Egan, Constance Ford
Credits: Producer/Director/Writer: Delmer Daves; Warner Bros.; 1959

Soap opera of two forbidden pairs of lovers. Dee is the daughter of Constance Ford, a frigid, bitchy woman who worries constantly over the state of her daughter's virginity. They have a fight and Ford throws Dee into a Christmas tree, taking dysfunctional families to a new film height.

Sandra Dee in *A Summer Place*.

Untamed Heart
Cast: Christian Slater, Marisa Tomei, Rosie Perez
Credits: Producers: Tony Bill and Helen Buck Bartlett; Director: Tony Bill; Writer: Tom Sierchio; MGM; 1993

It is the Christmas season and Tomei, a waitress in a small town diner, is saved from a rape by Slater who also works at the diner. He is terribly shy and it takes his love of Tomei to open him up. He sneaks into her house and leaves a decorated Christmas tree at the foot of the bed. Sweet love story, but beware the unhappy ending.

You've Got Mail
Forthcoming (December 1998) holiday film that is a remake of *The Shop Around the Corner*. Stars Tom Hanks and Meg Ryan as feuding bookstore owners (he is a chainstore mogul who is trying to drive independent children's bookstore owner Ryan out of business). They fall in love via e-mail. Also stars Greg Kinnear and Parker Posey and is directed by Nora Ephron.

Credits:

Bachelor Mother
Cast: Ginger Rogers, David Niven, Charles Coburn, Frank Albertson, E.E. Clive
Credits: Producer: B.G. DeSylva and Pandro S. Berman; Director: Garson Kanin; Writer: Norman Krasna (Based on a Story by Felix Jackson) RKO; 1939

Bell, Book and Candle
Cast: James Stewart, Kim Novak, Jack Lemmon, Ernie Kovacs, Hermione Gingold, Elsa Lanchester
Credits: Producer: Julian Blaustein; Director: Richard Quine; Writer: Daniel Taradash; Columbia; 1958

Beyond Tomorrow
Cast: Harry Carey, C. Aubrey Smith, Charles Winninger, Jean Parker; Maria Ouspenskaya, Richard Carlson
Credits: Producer: Lee Garmes; Director: A. Edward Sutherland; Writer: Adele Comandini (Based on a Story by Mildred Cram and Adele Comandini); RKO; 1940

The Bishop's Wife
Cast: Cary Grant, David Niven, Loretta Young, Monty Woolley, Elsa Lanchester
Credits: Producer: Samuel Goldwyn; Director: Henry Koster; Writers: Robert E. Sherwood and Leonardo Bercovici (Based on a Novel by Robert Nathan); RKO; 1947

Bundle of Joy
Cast: Debbie Reynolds, Eddie Fisher, Adolphe Menjou, Tommy Noonan, Nita Talbot, Una Merkel
Credits: Producer: Edmund Grainger; Director: Norman Taurog; Writers: Norman Krasna, Robert Carson and Arthur Sheekman (based on a Story by Felix Jackson); RKO; 1956

Christmas in Connecticut
Cast: Barbara Stanwyck, Dennis Morgan, Sydney Greenstreet, Reginald Gardiner, S.Z. Sakall, Una O'Connor
Credits: Producer: William Jacobs; Director: Peter Godfrey; Writers: Lionel Houser and Adele Comandini (Based on a Story by Aileen Hamilton); Warner Bros.; 1945

Christmas in Connecticut
Cast: Dyan Cannon, Kris Kristofferson, Tony Curtis
Credits: Producer: Cyrus I. Yavneah; Director: Arnold Schwarzenegger; Writers: Janet Brownell, Adele Commandini, Aileen Hamitlon and Lionel Houser; Turner; 1992

Holiday Affair
Cast: Robert Mitchum, Janet Leigh, Griff Barnett, Wendell Corey, Gordon Gebert
Credits: Producer/Director: Don Hartman; Writer: Isobel Lennart (Based on "Christmas Gift" by John D. Weaver); RKO; 1949

Holiday Inn
Cast: Bing Crosby, Fred Astaire, Marjorie Reynolds, Virginia Dale, Walter Abel
Credits: Producer/Director: Mark Sandrich; Writers: Claude Binyon and Elmer Rice (Based on an idea by Irving Berlin); Paramount; 1942

In the Good Old Summertime
Cast: Judy Garland, Van Johnson, S.Z. Sakall, Spring Byington, Buster Keaton
Credits: Producer: Joe Pasternak; Director: Robert Z. Leonard; Writers: Samson Raphaelson, Frances Goodrich, Ivan Tors and Albert Hackett (Based on "The Shop Around the Corner" by Miklos Laszlo); MGM; 1949

O. Henry's Full House (The Gift of the Magi)
Cast: Jeanne Crain, Farley Granger
Credits: Producer: Andre Hakim; Director: Henry King; Writers: Lamar Trotti, Richard Breen, Ben Roberts, Ivan Goff, Walter Bullock, Nunnally Johnson (Based on the Story by O. Henry); 20th Century-Fox; 1952

The Preacher's Wife
Cast: Denzel Washington, Whitney Houston, Courtney B. Vance, Gregory Hines, Cissy Houston, Jenifer Lewis
Credits: Producer: Samuel Goldwyn, Jr.; Director: Penny Marshall; Writers: Nat Mauldin and Allan Scott (Based on *The Bishop's Wife* by Leonardo Bercovici and Robert E. Sherwood); Buena Vista: 1996

Remember the Night
Cast: Barbara Stanwyck, Fred MacMurray, Beulah Bondi, Sterling Holloway
Credits: Producer/Director: Mitchell Leisen; Writer: Preston Sturges; Paramount; 1940

The Shop Around the Corner
Cast: James Stewart, Margaret Sullavan, Frank Morgan, Joseph Schildkraut, Felix Bressart
Credits: Producer/Director: Ernst Lubitsch; Writer: Samson Raphaelson (Based on the Play "Parfumerie" by Nikolaus Laszlo); MGM; 1940

Susan Slept Here
Cast: Dick Powell, Debbie Reynolds, Anne Francis, Alvy Moore, Glenda Farrell
Credits: Producer: Harriet Parsons; Director: Frank Tashlin; Writer: Alex Gottlieb (based on "Susan" by Alex Gottlieb and Steve Fisher); RKO; 1954

While You Were Sleeping
Cast: Sandra Bullock, Bill Pullman, Peter Gallagher, Peter Boyle, Glynis Johns
Credits: Producers: Roger Birnbaum and Joe Roth; Director: Jon Turteltaub; Writers: Daniel G. Sullivan and Fredric LeBow; Buena Vista; 1995

White Christmas
Cast: Bing Crosby, Danny Kaye, Vera-Ellen, Rosemary Clooney, Dean Jagger
Credits: Producer: Robert Emmett Dolan; Director: Michael Curtiz; Writers: Norman Krasna, Norman Panama and Melvin Frank; Paramount, 1954

Have a Holly, Jolly Christmas...

Since Christmas is the time people are usually at their happiest, it stands to reason Hollywood would add to the giddiness with comedies that occur during the jolly season. This chapter covers the entire spectrum of comedy, from the innocent charms of Laurel and Hardy to the witty dialogue in the 1940s and the antics of Bob Hope and the Three Stooges. We also examine modern Christmas films that take a decidedly more cynical view of the holidays, although Bob Clark's "A Christmas Story" harks back to the innocence of the 1930s and has become one of the few modern films to attain classic status.

Stan and Ollie visit Santa Claus (Ferinand Munier) in *Babes in Toyland.* (Photofest)

Babes in Toyland
1934

"'Which one—of all the Laurel and Hardy films—was your favorite?' I asked Stan Laurel one day.

"It was a question he had been asked before and he had a standard answer: He really couldn't pick just any *one* film as his favorite. He loved special bits and pieces from all that he had done, and he could not just honestly single out one as the apex of them all. I persisted in my questioning, but from another angle. Since he was meticulously candid about any lacks or faults in his films, which of them all (I asked) had fewer imperfections, which of them all had more continuing and consistent entertainment values? The answer was prompt: *Babes in Toyland.*

"It was for him an ultimate tribute to the world of childhood, a world both Oliver Hardy and Stan Laurel loved. Stan's only regret was that the film had not been filmed in color."
—John McCabe (from the liner notes of the 1974 Mark 56 soundtrack record album).

It's funny how a film can influence you in a quiet but powerful way, without your really understanding it. It's been nearly 30 years since I saw the 1934 version of *Babes in Toyland*, in edited form and re-titled *March of the Wooden Soldiers*, but I remember it as if it were yesterday. I was 11 or 12 when I saw it in late November or early December of 1969 or 1970 at the local neighborhood theater, the Adelphi, on the far North side of Chicago. The Adelphi had been showing old comedy films, and it was a great time for a kid like me to see them on the big screen. Being a klutzy little kid myself, I seemed to "bond" with the childlike Stan Laurel and Oliver Hardy. Nostalgia was fashionable then, in the late '60s and early '70s. There were posters of Laurel and Hardy or W.C. Fields or

Karloff's Monster and Lugosi's Dracula everywhere, but little was written about these actors, and certainly, nothing we could find out about comedians like the Three Stooges.

As I remember it, my friend Jim Nally, his brother Vince, my brother Jerry and I trudged through the cold, heavy snow to the theater, more, I think, due to my enthusiasm than anything else. Having only vaguely heard about this movie, I was looking forward to seeing *March of the Wooden Soldiers*. I can still remember the "thrill" of seeing it for the first time all these years later. This is remarkable in that I generally didn't (and still don't) like films that have musical numbers that get in the way of all "the funny stuff." I waited patiently for Bo-Peep (Charlotte Henry) and Tom-Tom Piper (Felix Knight) to finish singing to each other so that evil Silas Barnaby (Henry Brandon) could tangle with the *real* heroes of the movie, Ollie Dee (Oliver Hardy) and Stannie Dum (Stan Laurel). The thing I liked best about Stan Laurel and Oliver Hardy was how much like us they behaved. For instance, Stan has borrowed all of Ollie's money to buy "peewees," a kind of flying boomerang that you smack with a stick. When Ollie wants to try it, he can't do it as well as his friend, and that frustrates the heck out of him! This brings to mind Oliver Hardy's wonderful understanding of his character, "the smart, smart guy who's dumber than the dumb guy, only he doesn't know it." Generally, Ollie assumes the role of the "smarter brother" in their friendship, but may do something equally as "dumb" as his slower thinking friend. Yet, there are other times when both Stan Laurel and Oliver Hardy have flashes of brilliance that are perfectly in character.

The plot is slightly based on the Victor Herbert (1859-1924) operetta. Creepy old Silas Barnaby threatens to evict Mother Peep and her children out of the shoe they live in, unless Mother Peep's lovely daughter Bo-Peep consents to become Barnaby's wife. Ollie senses that something is terribly wrong when he looks at Mother Peep, and she tells him her troubles. Ollie unselfishly wants to help Mother Peep by giving her all of his money that he has saved. Of course, he finds Stan's "I.O.U." note in his little chest. Ollie then says that he'll borrow the full amount from their boss, the Master Toymaker, reasoning that once the Toymaker finds out that Barnaby is "up to his old tricks again," he'll lend the boys the money. When Mother Peep questions whether she can depend upon this, Ollie brags, "Why, of course you can. Why, you know the Toymaker and I are just-like—*that*! (Ollie crosses his first two fingers.) Aren't we, Stanley?" Stan is not so sure about this.

When visiting Santa Claus comes in for an inspection, he finds that Stan got the order all wrong. The mechanized wooden soldiers are supposed to be 600 soldiers at one foot high, not 100 soldiers at 6 foot high. Santa thinks this is hilarious, but the Toymaker does not. He fires both of the boys, and they head home to face the triumphant Barnaby and the soon to be disappointed Mother Peep. A sad-eyed Stan tells her that Ollie made a mistake! "He and the Toymaker... are *not* like that! (Stan does the finger gesture, and looks at Ollie.) Are ya?" (Stan doesn't say this spitefully, he's only sadly stating a fact.) Barnaby says that papers will be served immediately, and waving the mortgage deed around, stuffs it in his coat. Ollie carefully tries to snatch it away, but gets his hand caught in a large mousetrap found in Barnaby's coat pocket. "Big bait catches big rat!" says Barnaby, gleefully.

The boys decide that the only thing to do—even though it is technically breaking the law—is to get inside Barnaby's house and steal the mortgage deed. Stannie carts a huge Christmas present (with Ollie inside), and they make it to Barnaby's house without being seen, which delights Ollie. "So far, so good," he says. "It wasn't so far," says Stan. "We just came across the street!" Exasperated, Ollie says, "Ring the bell!" Stan does and then wheels the present into the house. Everything seems to be going well until Stan says good-bye to Barnaby and can't resist saying good-bye to his friend Ollie, who starts to reply, but then realizes what he has done, and is caught by Barnaby. Unable to escape, Ollie, in a wonderful nervous gesture, takes his finger and carefully polishes the edge of the box.

Stan and Ollie are then sentenced to be "dunked" in the ice-cold pond, and then "banished to Bogeyland forever," which is the stiff sentence for burglary. This is too much for Bo-Peep. "Mr. Barnaby! Can't something be done to stop this?" "Why yes!" he says, smiling evilly, "Consent to become my wife, and they will go free!" "All right, Mr. Barnaby," she sniffles, "I consent!" (Bo-Peep is, of course, not only thinking of her friends, but of her family too, and she sees her sad-eyed mother sitting on the steps of her former home.) All does not look well, but Ollie will shortly redeem himself to Mother Peep, Bo-Peep and Tom-Tom when he thinks of a wonderful way to outfox Barnaby.

Mother Peep (played by Florence Roberts) makes one last attempt to plead to Barnaby "for her daughter's happiness," but gets nowhere. "Woman, you're a fool! The bargain's made, and you'll abide by it!" he snaps. Ollie, as "best man," arrives with the modestly veiled Bo-Peep. Or, could that be Stannie in disguise? When Barnaby lustfully cries out, "And now, to kiss the bride!" and Ollie says, "Just a moment, haven't you forgotten something, Mr. Barnaby?" and Barnaby tears up the mortgage; I saw what was coming. "Now," Ollie says, eyes twinkling, "you may

Santa Claus makes sure things run smoothly in *Babes in Toyland*. (Photofest)

says the King. The citizens are angry, except for Barnaby, who is thoroughly enjoying himself.

Meanwhile, Stan and Ollie sadly discuss Tom-Tom's troubles, and Stan asks Ollie about Bogeyland and the fearsome Bogeymen, and Ollie tells him what the horrible creatures are supposed to look like, and that if they catch you, "They'll eat you alive." One of the King's guards tells Stan to watch over part of the evidence—"Exhibit B"—which is the string of the supposed "pig sausage." Hungry Stannie can't help taking a bite out of the sausage link, which would be kind of sickening if we didn't know that Elmer was alive. Stannie tells Ollie that the sausage doesn't taste like "pig," but tastes like pork, and tells Ollie to try it. Ollie does and says that it tastes like beef. Ollie figures that the evil Barnaby is up to no good.

Sure enough, the boys search and find Elmer, and rush to the King, hoping it's not too late. "Just a minute! Just a minute!" Ollie yells, "Mr. Majesty, Tom-Tom is innocent! We found little Elmer in Barnaby's cellar!" Barnaby leaps away from a now angry mob of villagers. This is the only mob scene I've ever enjoyed, for this is one villain that truly deserves what he gets. "I'll give 50,000 guineas for the capture of that scoundrel, dead or alive!" says the King emphatically, and Stan questions him again, and, when the King repeats himself, a confused Stan says: "Cantcha make up your mind which way you want him?" Barnaby sneaks down his back stairs and then through a secret passage way to—uhhh ohhh, Bogeyland! Bo-Peep bravely sets out toward Bogeyland to find her Tom-Tom. While the villagers run toward the front entrance to Barnaby's domain, Stan and Ollie rightly think that Barnaby has sneaked into his home through the basement door. While the boys wait for Barnaby, Bo-Peep finds Tom-Tom in the dreaded Bogeyland, and they try to find their way

kiss the bride!" Barnaby is understandably furious, Mother Peep is delighted and the boys are laughing hysterically. "What is the meaning of this?!" thunders Barnaby. "Big bait," Ollie reminds him, "catches big rat!" Plotting revenge, Barnaby kidnaps one of the Three Little Pigs and places evidence that Tom-Tom is guilty. Tom-Tom is then sentenced to be "banished" to Bogeyland, leaving Bo-Peep without her true love, which suits Barnaby just fine. Barnaby has tied up Elmer Pig down in his cellar, has his servant plant his hat and fiddle in Tom-Tom's house, and, most gruesomely, has him also leave a string of what looks like pork sausage there as well. Confronted with this evidence, Old King Cole (Kewpie Morgan) decides that Tom-Tom must be guilty. Tom-Tom's protestations that he is innocent, along with those of Bo-Peep and her Mom, don't dissuade the King from carrying out his legal duty. "It is with deep regret that I have to enforce the law of our Kingdom. Take him away!"

out, taking time out to sing another dreaded musical number. Meanwhile our heroes are still on duty:

"Did he come up?" asks the sleepy Stan to Ollie.

"Shhhhh! No! Are you coming up?" calls down Ollie to the cavernous cellar.

"You better come up dead or alive!" warns Stan.

"Now, how can he come up dead, when he's alive?" asks Ollie.

"Let's drop a rock on him, then, that will make him 'dead' when he's alive."

"Now, you're talking sense!" says a delighted Ollie. Ollie tosses a fairly large rock down.

"Look out!" warns the good natured Stan.

"Don't tell him to 'look out'!"

"Well, it might have hit him!" reasons Stan.

"That's what I wanted to do!" states Ollie.

Hearing nothing, the boys both go down into Barnaby's cellar, Stan in front, of course. He discovers the secret entrance which leads to Bogeyland. They find Bo-Peep and Tom-Tom, and since they can't find Barnaby, naively think they have scared him and the Bogeymen off. Not so, for Barnaby and his fearsome friends have been eagerly searching for them! "They've escaped me," shrieks Barnaby, "but I'll get them if I have to destroy the whole of Toyland—to the last!" He almost does too, but after firing darts from a cannon and smacking them with his "peewee" stick, Stan gets a brilliant inspiration and both the boys send the wooden soldiers out to defend the town.

This is why I turned into a bona fide fan of Laurel and Hardy, and later loved, for example, *Abbott and Costello Meet Frankenstein* (1948), along with Red Skelton's *Whistling in the Dark* (1941) and sequels, Bob Hope's—rarely seen—*The Cat and the Canary* (1939), *Ghost Breakers* (1940), Danny Kaye's *The Inspector General* (1949) and the two *Ghostbusters* movies (1984 and 1989) with Dan Aykroyd, Bill Murray and company: In these types of comedies with a "horror" or "mystery" element to them, there are some striking similarities. All of these comic heroes find themselves in a deadly confrontation, with the odds totally against them. What do they do? Naturally, at first they panic and run, but, *then* they figure out a way to save the day. It's like the memorable day you finally face up to the bully in grade school. Here, in *Babes in Toyland*—and these other films—the confrontation is not strictly a comic hero (or heroes) against a villain (or villains) on a personal level, for the stakes in this "game" are much higher. The comic hero or heroes in these films are not only fighting the villains for themselves, but they are, in a way, fighting for *us*, too! It is one of our greatest and most cherished wishes as an American citizen, that the unloved, the unwanted, the foreign immigrant, the clown, the buffoon, can redeem him/herself and redeem "society" as well.
—LJK

The Man Who Came to Dinner

1942

Imagine preparing for a lovely family Christmas when your entire life is turned topsy-turvy by the houseguest from Hell. That is the premise of Warner Bros.' *The Man Who Came to Dinner,* a delightful farce starring Monty Woolley and Bette Davis.

The film was based on the stage play by the dynamic Broadway team of Moss Hart and George S. Kaufman, who also penned the highly successful *You Can't Take it With You* (1938), which was turned into a memorable film starring Lionel Barrymore and Jimmy Stewart. The writers wanted a play to feature their friend Alexander Woollcott (infamous curmudgeon who was a theater critic, actor and one of the founders of that vicious circle known as the Algonquin Round Table). The scribes based the lead character of Sheridan Whiteside on Woollcott. Other roles were parodies of Gertrude Lawrence, Noel Coward and Harpo Marx.

As with many plays and films written in the 1940s, the dialogue is sharp, biting and extremely witty. The dialogue, combined with a grand cast, spells grins galore in this holiday entry.

It is November 26 and Sheridan Whiteside, the "First Man in American Letters" is about to descend upon Mesalia, Ohio, but Mesalia is nowhere near ready for the whirlwind known as Sheri. As a train bears the irascible Whiteside (Monty Woolley) and his patient secretary Maggie (Bette Davis) to Mesalia, Whiteside whines, "I simply will not sit down to dinner with mid-Western barbarians. I think too much of my digestive system." Maggie, knowing full well her boss' foibles, listens with a slight smile.

As they meet their hosts Mr. and Mrs. Ernest Stanley (Grant Mitchell and Billie Burke), Mrs. Stanley asks (in that unmistakable Billie Burke voice), "Did you have a pleasant trip?" To which Whiteside replies, "Charming. I killed the woman in the next compartment. She asked me to lunch!"

Things are not boding well for the Stanleys. Ernest never wanted Whiteside there in the first place and his qualms are even stronger after meeting the annoying old coot. As they mount the stairs to the Stanleys' house, Whiteside slips and falls on the ice, making national headlines, "Sheridan Whiteside Famous Author Injured in Fall on Ice!"

Whiteside banishes the Stanleys to their upstairs bedroom while he grandly takes over the downstairs. Cards, letters, telegrams and packages are delivered by the dozens. December 10 arrives and the massive effort of getting the great man out of bed proceeds. When asked by his reluctant hosts the harmless, "I hope you're better?" he replies, "Thank you. I'm suing you for $150,000. Since this corner druggist at my elbow tells me I will be confined to this moldy mortuary for at least another 10 days—due entirely to your stupidity and negligence—I shall have to carry on my activities as best I can."

Whiteside is even harsher (if that is possible) with his poor nurse Miss Preen (Mary Wickes), telling her, "You have the touch of a love-starved cobra."

Mr. Stanley's sister Harriet comes downstairs and drops some holly into Whiteside's lap and hastily departs.

"And what may I ask was that?... Strange, she's right out of the *Hound of the Baskervilles*!"

Whiteside continues to terrify his hosts and nurse Preen, who dumps some pills in his lap and scurries away. He enjoys himself immensely by running up their phone bill, calling his famous friends from around the globe. One such friend is the actress Lorraine Sheldon (Ann Sheridan), a spoiled beauty who is trying to get her claws into dull, old Lord Bottomly. Whiteside calls her "my lotus blossom" to which Maggie cattily replies, "little Miss Stinkweed." Maggie manages to smile while enduring Whiteside's fits but draws the line at the obnoxious Lorraine.

Local newspaper man Bert Jefferson (Richard Travis) arrives to interview the great man. Whiteside is his usual charming self, "There's nobody home. The Stanleys have been arrested for peddling dope—go away." He introduces Maggie to Jefferson, "This aging debutante, Mr. Jefferson, I retain in my employ only because she is the sole support of her two-headed brother."

The doorbell rings admitting Whiteside's luncheon guests, murderers from the nearby penitentiary. Maggie explains to the confused newshound, "You see Mr. Jefferson, the fact that Mr. Whiteside happens to be the nation's foremost authority on murder and murder trials forms a bond between them." Maggie becomes enchanted with small-town America and specifically with Mr. Jefferson.

Christmas Eve arrives and an eagerly awaited broadcast from Whiteside is to take place that evening. Whiteside is not content to prepare his radio show; he decides Maggie cannot be serious about loving Jefferson and devises a plan to stop the romance. He also offers his worldly wisdom to the Stanley children, who desperately need some guidance. Son Richard is an avid photographer whom Whiteside convinces to follow his dream of hopping a ship and photographing the world. Daughter June is in love with a union organizer who is trying to unionize her father's company. Whiteside tells the young couple to run away and be married tonight. While Whiteside meddles with the Stanleys' lives, Bert is giving Maggie a charm bracelet for Christmas.

Now Whiteside has been able to walk for a while (the doctor sheepishly tells him he was looking at the wrong X-rays) but decides to remain in his wheelchair until he devises a plan to keep Maggie working for him.

The once peaceful house now becomes even more riotous as gifts arrive from Winston Churchill, Deanna Durbin, Gypsy Rose Lee, along with four penguins that are from Admiral Byrd! The strange mix is stirred as Lorraine Sheldon breezes in, anxious to see Jefferson's play that Whiteside has informed her has a lead for which she would be perfect.

Maggie is surprised to see Lorraine as the two indulge in a little girl talk. "You know every time I see you I keep thinking your hair could be so lovely. I always want to get my hands on it," Lorraine snips. "You know, I've always wanted to get mine on yours Lorraine," Maggie replies.

Meanwhile, the doctor is trying to get Whiteside to read the massive and boring book he has written: "Dr. Bradley is the greatest living argument for mercy killing," and ham actor Beverly Carlton (Reginald Gardiner) arrives for a quick visit demanding to see his "magpie," his pet name for Maggie. Now men are arriving to begin setting up for the big Christmas Eve broadcast. Confusion reigns supreme.

Maggie knows Bert Jefferson is about to be offered for slaughter to the man-hungry Lorraine and fights sneakiness with sneakiness and gets Beverly to phone Lorraine impersonating Lord Bottomly. Beverly eagerly complies, happy to play the trick on the obnoxious Lorraine and one-upping Whiteside. Things are going swimmingly for Maggie until Jefferson spills the beans telling Whiteside about Beverly's call from a phone booth and the funny faces he was making. Whiteside puts two and two together and comes up with a phony phone call. Lorraine is now even more eager to ruin Maggie's love affair, "If I were you, I'd hang onto that charming little bracelet my dear. It'll be something to remember him by."

Mr. Stanley stalks in, Jefferson innocently brings in drinks, and Maggie runs out sobbing. Stanley finds the notes from his children who have run off, the penguins get loose, choir boys are rushed in and begin singing "Silent Night" with angelic voices.

"This is Whiteside speaking. On this eve of eves when my heart is overflowing with peace and kindness..."

Maggie (Bette Davis) keeps track of the Christmas presents received by Sheridan Whiteside in *The Man Who Came to Dinner.*

This is infamy at its most obnoxious as the revered Whiteside plays fast and loose with the lives of the little people.

Christmas morning dawns. Mr. Stanley is off searching for his children. Mrs. Stanley is crying in her room and Maggie is deeply hurt and about to leave, but not before giving Whiteside a piece of her mind.

"Sheri, you're quite wonderful in a way... I wish I had a laugh left in me. I think you're a selfish petty egomaniac who would just as soon see his mother burning at the stake if that was the only way he had of lighting a cigarette. I think you'd sacrifice your best friend without a moment's notice if he interrupted the sacred ritual of your self-centered paltry little life. I think you are incapable of any emotion higher up than your stomach."

"Well... as long as I live I'll never do anyone a good turn again," he indignantly proclaims.

Jefferson arrives drunk as a skunk declaring everything is wonderful... Miss Sheldon thinks the play

Banjo (Jimmy Durante) torments Lorraine (Ann Sheridan) as Whiteside (Monty Woolley) looks on in *The Man Who Came to Dinner.*

is wonderful but needs a little work. She's taking him away to Lake Placid to "fix" the play. Maggie flees the room and the doctor goes with Jefferson for some breakfast and coffee.

A tornado blows into town in the form of Whiteside's friend Banjo (Jimmy Durante) who stops to visit Whiteside on his way to Nova Scotia. Nurse Preen answers the door and the short Banjo swoops the towering nurse into his arms and demands a kiss. "I can feel the hot blood pumping through your varicose veins," he jests. Whiteside admonishes, "Put that woman down... you mental delinquent." Banjo complies (the sight of Jimmy Durante carrying the tall Mary Wickes into the room is hilarious), "Come to my room in a half hour and bring some rye bread," he tells the now hysterical nurse.

But Whiteside is not all bad, merely self-centered, and realizes he's made a mistake ruining Maggie's romance. He turns to Banjo for help.

"She's turned on me like a viper... I didn't believe for a moment she was in love with him." He explains the situation to Banjo, forgetting to tell him why Lorraine is in town. And Banjo, knowing his friend's devious side, announces, "I smell a rat Sheri— a rat with a beard."

Whiteside admits his error, "I got Lorraine out here, now I've got to get her away." Banjo, always willing to help a friend (and mess with Lorraine) assuredly answers, "We'll get Lorraine out of here if I've got to do it a piece at time!"

Poor old nurse Preen has reached the end of her rope. Playwrights Hart and Kaufman offer some of their most waggish lines to Mary Wickes (here recreating her stage role) in this scene. "I am not only walking out on this case Mr. Whiteside, I am leaving the nursing profession. I became a nurse because all my life... I was filled with the idea of serving a suffering humanity. After one month with you, Mr. Whiteside, I'm going to work in a munitions factory. From now on anything I can do to help exterminate the human race will fill me with the greatest pleasure!"

Stanley arrives home with the unwed June and announces a detective is bringing Richard home. Stanley has a warrant forcing Whiteside to depart and gives him 15 minutes. Banjo comforts Maggie, Lorraine arrives for Christmas breakfast—"better make it a one minute egg," Whiteside tells John, the butler. As Lorraine gloats over her victory over Maggie, a sarcophagus arrives for Whiteside. Lorraine dramatically enacts the life of an Egyptian princess by placing her hands over her chest and stepping into the coffin. Whiteside and Banjo exchange knowing glances and, after a bit of subtle coaxing, manage to shut Lorraine up in the artifact. "I'll let her out as soon as we get on the plane," Banjo announces. Maggie is delighted and forgives Whiteside.

One problem solved, but what to do about Mr. Stanley? Whiteside solves that problem when he recognizes Stanley's sister Harriet as the infamous murderer who hacked up her parents with an ax. Banjo laughs, "She gave her mother 40 whacks... how the Dodgers could've used her!"

Not only does Whiteside blackmail Stanley into allowing his children to pursue their dreams, but he also steals Stanley's cook and butler. Finally, the Stanleys' nightmare is almost over as Whiteside descends the front stairs when Mrs. Stanley excitedly calls him back to take a phone call from Eleanor Roosevelt. Well, you guessed it, he falls again on the ice, now proclaiming he's going to sue for $300,000!

While we all can remember Christmases that didn't quite live up to our expectations, hopefully many aren't as bad as Mr. and Mrs. Stanley's holiday was that year.

A truly versatile cast added to the merriment as Monty Woolley portrayed the blustery Sheridan Whiteside with appropriately annoying pomposity. Woolley was a former Yale professor before turning to acting. He portrayed himself in *Night and Day* (as composer Cole Porter's professor and friend). Of his performance *Variety* noted, "Monty Woolley is even better than he was in the Broadway edition."

Bette Davis had a rare charisma, dominating the silver screen with her presence. Her best moments as Maggie are when she turns on the venom and lets Whiteside and Lorraine feel her wrath. That side of her talent would be put to excellent use in one of the best pictures Hollywood has ever produced, *All About Eve*. Davis occasionally played softer characters, notably in this film and *Dark Victory*, but was at her best as a murderous female. Reportedly, when Jack Warner was asked to define the term movie star he replied, "Bette Davis."

Ann Sheridan as Lorraine Sheldon was proclaimed by Warners to be the "Oomph Girl." Sheridan had a varied film career with roles in *They Drive by Night*, *Angels With Dirty Faces*, *Kings Row* (with Ronald Reagan) and *Shine on Harvest Moon*. *Variety* called her "a pip as the beautiful and hammy actress menace."

Reginald Gardiner makes a too brief appearance as Beverly Carlton (the playwright's tribute to Noel Coward). His appearance in *Christmas in Connecticut* is much more substantial, although his character is not as likable as Beverly.

Jimmy Durante as Banjo (the Harpo Marx spoof) brings his usual frenetic energy to the screen. Durante was a much-loved performer whose mediocre singing and slaughter of the English language only served to endear him to audiences. His last film was *It's a Mad, Mad, Mad, Mad World* in 1963. Thanks to 1993's *Sleepless in Seattle*, Durante's rendition of popular songs such as "Make Someone Happy" enjoyed a new-found popularity when they appeared on the movie soundtracks.

The film was directed by William Keighley, who began his career as an actor before directing films such as *The Adventures of Robin Hood* with Errol Flynn and *George Washington Slept Here* with Jack Benny.

The film is centered in the living room of the Stanley home, and with its grand gestures and over-the-top theatrics, one can easily imagine being seated in a theater while watching it performed on stage.

The Man Who Came to Dinner is a witty farce as well as a biting satire of fame and as such is a welcome addition to any collection of holiday cinema. As an added bonus, the film's dysfunctional characters will make one appreciate his/her down-to-earth friends and family.

—SS

The Miracle of Morgan's Creek

1944

America's obsession with good girls and wartime romances is delightfully skewered in this Preston Sturges comedy that reaches its happy (if incredibly unbelievable) conclusion during the Christmas season.

Betty Hutton stars as Trudy Kockenlocker, a fun-loving small-town girl who lives for military dances. There's just something about a man in uniform. Eddie Bracken is Norval Jones, the love-sick bank clerk who adores the feisty Trudy, but his love is unrequited.

Trudy's grouchy father forbids her from attending a military dance, but Trudy manages to convince Norval to pick her up for a date. She pleads, whines and cries until he agrees to go sit through three movies himself (and lend her his car) while she parties the night away with handsome young soldiers. Unfortunately, Trudy gets snockered and winds up married to someone shipping out. The only thing she can remember is his name sounds like Ratzywatski. I wonder how many soldiers got a little action when they used the old "I'm shipping out and could be dead tomorrow" routine? Well, Trudy falls for it hook, line and sinker. At eight the next morning, Trudy, still a little drunk, finally picks up Norval outside the theater where he spent the night. Norval barely manages

Chaos erupts when Mr. Kockenlocker (William Demarest) takes Norval (Eddie Bracken) in to see Trudy in *Miracle of Morgan's Creek*.

to escape strangulation at the hands of Mr. Kockenlocker when he takes Trudy home.

Trudy tells the whole story to her sister Emmy (Diana Lynn), who is amazed anyone could have been so dumb. Emmy is one mature 14-year-old. Trudy didn't even give her real name when they were married so they have no way to find out if it was legal.

Things are bad but get much worse when Trudy pays a visit to the family doctor. It seems the first time really was a charm. Trudy and Emmy decide she must get married and the most likely candidate is, of course, Norval. He proposes (with a lot of prompting from Trudy) but Norval is so happy that Trudy begins crying and confesses. Norval wants Trudy even more than he wants to be a soldier (he can't get in because of his eyesight) and agrees to a hackneyed plan to make her legitimately Mrs. Ratzywatski. The frightened couple sneak away to be married, he impersonating a soldier so Trudy can protect her reputation. Unfortunately Norval isn't the brightest bulb in the pack and can only find a World War I uniform. The Justice of the Peace smells a rat and calls the police. Trudy is disgraced and Norval is locked up for corrupting the morals of a minor. Trudy, who now realizes she loves Norval, tells all to her father (William Demarest), the town law-enforcer guarding Norval. He allows Trudy and Emmy to conk him on the head enabling Norval to escape. Norval pays a visit to the bank to get his money and declares he won't return until he finds Ratzywatski.

It is now Christmas. Mr. Kockenlocker has been discharged from his policeman's job, the Kockenlocker house is up for sale and the family has quietly moved to the country hoping to keep the whole thing hushed up.

A discouraged Norval returns to town only to find the Kockenlocker house abandoned. He visits his former landlord, the town lawyer, to find out what happened, but is encouraged to turn himself into the authorities. Norval is surprised to learn the charges against him are now legion and include bank robbery and impersonating an officer. He visits a friend of the Kockenlockers who is going to see them that evening. Unfortunately, Norval is spotted by the still angry bank manager who immediately has poor old Norval locked up.

At the Kockenlocker's farm Emmy plays carols on an organ while Trudy sits before a fire. Their father trims a Christmas tree and tries to improve Trudy's spirits. She is distraught to learn Norval has been arrested and vows to go back to town the next day and tell the whole story. Her father and Emmy try to talk her out of it. After all, they have spent the last six months trying to cover it up. But she is adamant.

The town council is having a meeting trying to decide the fate of poor Norval, the banker insisting the book be thrown at him, when Mr. Kockenlocker angrily interrupts and tells them that Trudy wants to speak to them. He tells them she is not feeling too well and they have to come down to the car. The men all exchange knowing looks and raised eyebrows. But Emmy runs in yelling for her father—Trudy is having the baby. Everyone rushes to the hospital. Emmy and Mr. Kockenlocker anxiously wait as nurses rush back and forth. Fingers are held up in excitement. One, two, three—more rushing around by nurses, four—doctors are running through the halls yelling, "yippee!" Five, six! All boys.

A miracle has occurred. Newspaper headlines scream, "Platoon born in Midwest!," "Mussolini resigns," etc. Hitler is enraged. The governor becomes involved in this amazing story circling the globe. He hears the entire story and orders things be made right for Trudy and Norval. The first marriage is annulled, the second marriage to Norval is confirmed and Norval is given an honorary military position and fancy uniform. A Christmas wreath hangs on the hospital door as a very confused Norval is ushered in to see Trudy.

Norval tells her they are really married and he is going to be the papa. When Trudy asks if it was a boy or girl, Norval looks at Emmy questioningly. She crooks her finger and leads him to the nursery where he makes goo-goo faces at the babies before asking, "Which one?" "All of them," Emmy replies. Norval, never one to hold up under stress, panics and runs screaming into Trudy's room before fainting.

The Miracle of Morgan's Creek takes a humorous though poignant look at the length girls in small town America had to go to trying to protect their reputations. Any slip could ruin families, careers and lives. Happily, Trudy's father accepted the inevitable and took care of Trudy while Norval remained true to her.

Although people are at their most forgiving during Christmas, there was no forgiveness for Trudy and Norval until the birth of the babies brought fame and fortune to Morgan's Creek.

Betty Hutton was usually a ball of energy, often almost overwhelming audiences with her presence. She toned down her performance in this role to good advantage, especially in the Christmas scenes. Her most famous roles would be Annie Oakley in *Annie Get Your Gun* and Pearl White in *The Perils of Pauline*.

Eddie Bracken was an up-and-coming comic who would do his most successful film work with scripter Preston Sturges in *The Miracle of Morgan's Creek* and *Hail the Conquering Hero* (1944). He would go on to appear in light comedy and musicals including *Summer Stock* as the fiancé of Judy Garland. Bracken would make an appearance in 1983's *National Lampoon's Vacation* as the owner of Walley World.

Preston Sturges turned his sharp pen to Hollywood, writing and directing some of its best product including *Hail the Conquering Hero*, *The Palm Beach Story* and *Unfaithfully Yours*. He was nominated for the Academy Award for screenwriting *The Miracle of Morgan's Creek* and *Hail the Conquering Hero*.

Christmas for the Kockenlockers in Morgan's Creek reminds us how sad the holiday can be for some people, but it also reminds us how wonderful it can be if you are lucky enough to have the love and support of friends and family.

—SS

The Cheaters

1945

After finally tracking down this rare holiday film, I must say I'm surprised it hasn't become a holiday staple. All the right conditions are there for Christmas immortality: falling snow, warm little cottage, help for those less fortunate, spoiled rich kids learning a much needed lesson, homey Christmas tree, a love story, marvelous performances by a well-known list of character actors, good reviews and a happy ending. But unfortunately this film has remained virtually unknown to modern audiences.

As the film begins, Christmas is almost upon us and J.C. Pidgeon (Eugene Pallette) is lectured by his secretary for being close to bankruptcy due to the extravagant spending of his empty-headed wife Clara (Billie Burke). His good-for-nothing brother-in-law Willie (Raymond Walburn) is waiting outside to hit him up for money as well as a summons server J.C. is trying to avoid. But good news arrives in the form of a letter from his son Reggie (David Holt), who announces Uncle Henry (who's loaded) is close to death. Pidgeon and Willie cheer right up and go out to buy a diamond bracelet for Clara for Christmas. They figure to be in the money soon.

When Pidgeon arrives home, he finds his wife and her large staff busily wrapping gifts for everyone they know. Daughter Therese (Ruth Terry) has arrived home with ideas garnered from the wealthy mother of her boyfriend Stephen (Robert Livingston). They must not display their wealth, and she insists the Christmas tree be in the library rather than in front of the window. Since Stephen is to spend the holidays with them, she also talks her parents into taking in a charity case (and pretending they have always done so) to impress Stephen and his mother. This shallow family can't even select a person to help without thinking of their own comfort—they don't want anyone too depressing. Into this confusion saunters daughter Angela (Ann Gillis), a spoiled brat with a bad attitude and little respect for her family.

A chauffeur is sent to pick up the charity case, Mr. Anthony Marschon (Joseph Schildkraut), a John Barrymore look-alike who's down on his luck since a car hit him and he ended up with a limp. He can no longer find work on the stage and has been without a job since the mattress factory where he worked as nightwatchman burned down.

Mr. M (as he is called in the newspaper where the family picked out his name by chance) happily settles in with the family, charming everyone including butler MacFarland (Robert Greig) who prepares him a special alcohol-filled drink each morning and night (for the pain, you know).

Things are going along quite well until Reggie shows up with the announcement that Uncle Henry has left all his money, five million dollars, to an actress, Florence Watson (Ona Munson), he saw on stage many years ago as Little Eva in *Uncle Tom's Cabin*. Pidgeon calls the lawyer, who is executor of the will, and gets him to agree to only search for the woman for a week, promising him a hefty payday for the favor. If the woman is not found the money will go to Pidgeon. He figures if they find the woman and hide her with them, like Poe's purloined letter, nobody would look for her right under their nose. Marschon has been quietly sitting in a chair, hidden from the family, but makes his presence known by offering to help find the woman. Reggie, another spoiled brat, insults the actor who grandly exits the room. We're a little suspect of Marschon ourselves. Does he really want to help or is he working an angle? Pidgeon insists Reggie apologize to Marschon who listens outside the door. As he walks away Angela, sitting in an armchair, gives him a wink.

The next day Marschon and Willie easily find Florence Watson. Florence, a struggling actress now middle-aged, faces a slew of overdue bills. She thinks the Pidgeons are nuts when Willie tells her she is a cousin and they want her to spend the holidays with them. She recognizes Marschon and is enchanted by meeting this actor she holds in high regard. He makes no bones about being a charity case taken in by the Pidgeons. Florence knows she's not related, but rather than facing bill collectors and eviction, she gladly packs a bag and heads for a warm bed and a life of luxury.

The next morning panic erupts when the newspaper runs a story about Henry Pidgeon and the mysterious showgirl to whom he left his fortune. Pidgeon decides to pack up the family, servants, presents, Christmas dinner and all and move to a country house where there are no radios, newspapers or nosy neighbors. He borrows the keys to a country house owned by one of his clients who now lives overseas, and the entire family and their assorted guests head for Christmas in the country.

We see a beautiful snow-covered house, the perfect place for a holiday gathering. The family is quite enchanted, but their peace is shattered when they find that all the servants have quit and they are left to fend for themselves. Florence convinces them it will be a wonderful Christmas and sends the men out for wood and persuades Clara to help her cook.

The country and Florence's goodwill and charming personality melt the spoiled family, and we begin to see the humanity underneath the Pidgeons. Angela and Reggie good-naturedly argue as they decorate a tree they cut down themselves, comfortably hanging popcorn and cranberry strands. Willie happily pops corn over a fire. Pidgeon dozes by the fire. Therese and Stephen flirt and string popcorn, and Clara proudly enters with a plate of freshly baked cookies. Marschon and Florence watch the family from an outsider's vantage point and realize they quite like the Pidgeons, and so do we.

A detective looking for Florence follows a lead to Pidgeon's office where he tells Pidgeon's secretary Mattie (Norma Varden), "to you it's Christmas Eve, to us it's Tuesday." They follow the trail to the cottage but Pidgeon and Marschon give them a story and they leave, although they are convinced the Pidgeons are hiding something.

Florence finds Marschon in the cellar where he has found a stash of booze and is happily getting soused. She tries to talk him into giving up drinking and to begin to teach acting. He bitterly laughs and Florence leaves.

That evening the quaintness of the isolated setting is wearing thin as the family sits in front of the fire. Carolers singing "Silent Night" soften the faces of everyone and remind them of what the holiday actually means. Marschon turns away from the window. "Nothing will ever be quite the same for any of us after tonight," he says. He launches into a frightening version of A Christmas Carol, pounding home the pathetic reason why Scrooge has no friends and why he was doomed to spend eternity wrapped in the chains of his wrong doings. The actor digs deep into his soul as he brings the Ghost of Christmas Yet To Be to vivid life for the squirming Pidgeon family. Finally reaching the pinnacle of the story, he collapses in a drunken heap. Therese, Angela, Reggie and Clara all insist Pidgeon tell Florence the truth. He does and they earnestly beg her forgiveness. Rather than be annoyed, Florence can't get over her good fortune, and they all happily make a toast with a frothy drink called Tom and Jerrys, which Willie has whipped up.

Christmas day Florence goes in search of Marschon, but all they find is a note telling them he is sorry for the way he acted and of the fondness he feels for Florence. She gets a ride to the nearest bar and finds him there. She tells him everything (including the fact that she and the Pidgeons are splitting the money) and convinces him to leave. They go to pay the check but between the two they have no money and laugh at the irony.

Uncle Willie's Tom and Jerrys

Tom and Jerrys are a traditional American Christmas drink.

6 eggs
2 jiggers rum
powdered sugar
1 large pinch baking soda
1/2 teaspoon allspice

The eggs are separated, beaten, then combined by heating with enough powdered sugar to make a stiff batter. The other ingredients are added and beaten again with more sugar to restiffen the batter. The baking soda is used only as a preservative, if using the batter immediately it may be left out.

Tom and Jerry Serving
1 tablespoon Tom and Jerry batter
1 jigger rum
1/2 jigger brandy

The batter is dissolved in the bottom of a heated mug with a little hot water or hot milk. The rum is added and the mug is filled with hot water or hot milk, the brandy is floated on top and mug is sprinkled with cinnamon.

In *The Cheaters*, Florence's goodwill and charming personality melt the spoiled family and we begin to see the humanity underneath the Pidgeons. Pictured: Raymond Walburn, Joseph Schildkraut, Ona Munson, Ann Gillis, Eugene Pallette, Billie Burke, Ruth Terry and Robert Livingston. (Photofest)

Director Joseph Kane was obviously trying for the zaniness of *You Can't Take it With You* for this film and almost succeeds. The Pidgeons are neither as innocent nor as bizarre as the Sycamores of *You Can't Take it With You*, but do manage to worm their way into your heart as they let their guard down and actually allow the veil of pretention to fall away.

Joseph Schildkraut, first billed, gives a marvelous performance as the down on his luck actor. The Dickens scene is indeed the work of a master craftsman as he mesmerizes the room with the Christmas tale. His character of Mr. Marschon is multi-layered as the broken actor wavers between the dream of a full life with the engaging Florence and the escape of the bottle. He seems to take a perverse delight in being the designated charity case of the Pidgeons. Schildkraut's role is much more sympathetic than his role in *The Shop Around the Corner* where he played the sleazy Mr. Vadas.

Eugene Pallette's name may not be recognizable to the majority of readers but his rotund, gruff personality is. The actor has graced over 100 films in-

cluding appearing as Friar Tuck with his friend Errol Flynn in *The Adventures of Robin Hood*. Pallette always brought a spark to each performance, and his J.C. Pidgeon is no exception. The character, for all his flaws, is really a warm person who only wants the best for his family.

Ona Munson as the down-to-Earth Florence made a name for herself playing shady ladies such as Belle Watling in *Gone With the Wind*. Her performance as Florence is a sheer delight as the poor, under-educated Florence puts the upper-crust Pidgeon family to shame and shows them true class.

Rounding out the cast are fine performances by the always remarkable Billie Burke in another stereotypical scatterbrained role and Ann Gillis as the little girl with a razor tongue, Angela. Gillis appeared as Becky Thatcher in *The Adventures of Tom Sawyer* (1938) and appeared as Gary Lockwood's mother in *2001: A Space Odyssey* (1968).

In its review *Variety* remarked, "Republic should hit the jackpot with this one. Aside from standout performances of Joseph Schildkraut and supporting cast, its story content and nifty direction by Joseph Kane, dualling as producer-director, and with such names as Billie Burke, Ona Munson, Ray Walburn and Eugene Pallette for additional cast hypo, it should bring many happy returns at the b.o."

Right now the only way to see this film is by scanning television listings hoping against hope some well-versed programmer realizes the delights of this little gem. Good luck, it's worth the search.

—SS

The Three Stooges— Malice in the Palace

1949

The humorous shenanigans of The Three Stooges—Moe Howard, Larry Fine, Curly Howard and sometimes Shemp Howard—is anything but subtle, being based upon physical violence and abuse, pratfalls and other forms of visual/physical humor. Although unsubtle, The Three Stooges are still accomplished, well-rehearsed craftsman, perhaps even artists, whose recurring comedic antics reveal an unvarnished and

rough-around-the-edges style. Such a style would not easily lend itself to the Christmas movie sentiment, although The Stooges' short, *Malice in the Palace*, while technically not a Christmas story, allows the boys to wear Santa Claus outfits for half the short's running time and to poke some fun at the holiday season. With a screenplay by Felix Adler and produced/directed by Jules White, *Malice in the Palace* becomes an above-average exercise in costume comedy with all the Christmas fringes.

The title card tells us the setting is the Stooge-run Cafe Casbahbah, the meeting place of Black Sheep—Bah-Bah-Bah! Sinister Middle Eastern stereotypes make an entrance into the Cafe: one heavy-set man with a turban and full beard, Hassan Ben Sober, and his skinnier accomplice who wears a fez and a thick mustache. The two men are soon joined by a third man who carries the map of the tomb of King Rootin' Tootin'. However, he informs his partners a duplicate map exists and then he disappears. The goal is to acquire the rare gem to be found within the sacred tomb, but a curse falls on anyone who touches the gem: That person is doomed to 1,000 deaths. After the Stooges first break china over the heavier man and then spill pasta over the head of the skinnier one, these fools still order dinner. In a protracted sight

Larry, Moe and Shemp create havoc in "Malice in the Palace."

gag, the men order hot dogs, and when a cat steals a hot dog from the kitchen, Larry, armed with a meat cleaver, chases the cat out into the restaurant. Capturing the cat, Larry forces it back into the kitchen where the people in the restaurant hear Larry hack away with the cleaver while the cat wails (in actuality, Larry is stepping on the cat's tail). A few minutes later Larry is now chasing a dog around the restaurant, and after capturing the dog, the patrons again hear a chopping sound and a dog's frantic howling (in actuality, the window fell on its tail). Outside in the restaurant, our friends from the Middle East have lost their appetite and force the equally repulsed Moe and Shemp to eat Larry's cooking.

Soon a note, delivered at knife-point by messenger, announces that the Emir of Shmow has gotten the diamond and that these gentlemen "got the gate." Hassan Ben Sober cries, "Ruined, defeated, that murderous cutthroat has the famous 100 carat diamond... the map is useless... I could have quit my job as doorman at the Oasis." Shemp, distressed that this impressive appearing man is only a doorman, tells him, "There's the door, man!" and kicks him out. The other man, pulling out his knife, asks if the Stooges would give him five for it, but Moe offers, "No, but I'll give you two," poking the man in the eyes and twirling him around before shoving him out the door. The Stooges then decide to find the valuable gem and return it to the government to collect a reward.

Approaching the Palace is a horse-drawn sleigh manned by Larry, Moe and Shemp all disguised as Santa Claus. Stopped by a guard who demands, "Halt, who goes there?" To which, in unison, the Stooges respond, "Santa Claus." The guard replies, "There ain't no Santa Claus." Then as the Stooges open up their white Santa bag, they claim, "Oh yes there is, and we have a present for you," knocking the guard unconscious and stuffing his body in the bag.

Inside, still wearing full Santa Claus get-up, a large Nubian with a sword approaches the Stooges who engage him in a game of leap frog, using his own sword to knock him unconscious while he bends down and waits for the next man to leap over him. The Emir of Shmow enters the room wearing the diamond on his turban. Hoping to frighten him, the Stooges stand on each other's shoulders, Shemp on top, still wearing his Santa outfit, yelling, "Fe, Fi, Fo, Fum. I'm the evil spirit that guards the Rootin' Tootin' diamond." With four arms waving, Shemp demands, "Give it to me!" The Emir, after handing over the gem, is then commanded to stand on his head in his Lily pond, and within the next few minutes, he swallows all the water, still standing on his head.

While passing through a low entranceway, the Stooge beast is knocked on its behind as all three men fall, quickly losing their beards but still wearing their Santa suits. Soon the revived Nubian is in full pursuit screaming, "I will kill you!" as the Stooges bombard him with fruit. The counterfeit Santas run out of the Palace, screaming all the way.

Even though this Palace slapstick really has nothing to do with Christmas, the sight of seeing Moe, Larry and Shemp running around doing the typical manic things they do, dressed as Santa Claus, is a treat. The Stooges as Santa create a visual that is not easily dismissed from the mind.
—GJS

The Lemon Drop Kid

1951

The Lemon Drop Kid, much like Damon Runyon's fictional realm, is populated by charming scoundrels, showgirls with hearts-of-gold and tough-talking mugs who get teary-eyed with the mention of their mother. Add to the charming story a delectable mix of Hollywood veteran character actors (adding weight to the "they had faces then" theory) and the personable schnoz of funnyman Bob Hope and you have a delightfully silly holiday farce that tickles the funnybone and managed to introduce a classic Christmas song at the same time ("Silver Bells" by Jay Livingston and Ray Evans).

Hope stars as the Lemon Drop Kid, a small-time crook who constantly pops lemon drops. He's working the Florida tracks touting races (the Kid covers the entire race by convincing gullible bettors he somehow knows who the winner is going to be and the happy bettors agree to split their win with the Kid. He does this for each horse running—he can't lose). But lose he does when he pulls the con on a dumb doll who just so happens to be the girlfriend of Moose Moran (Fred Clark), a big-time gangster who doesn't like being laughed at. Of course the horse the Kid talked the girl out of betting on wins and the Kid now owes Moose 10 grand by Christmas Eve.

The Kid goes to New York to put the touch on his friends, but they are few and far between. The Kid, still attired in his spiffy white Palm Beach suit, battles the blustery wind and snow of New York City. Hope puts his unique brand of physical humor to good use in these scenes, one of which has the wind blow him around a corner and two little girls have to help him forward, and another as he mugs a little dachshund, Fifi, for its dog coat. The Kid runs into old friend Nellie Thursday (Jane Darwell) and tries to put the touch on her, but she has troubles of her own. The landlord is threatening to throw her out into the street and, when her dear husband Henry is released from prison Christmas Eve, they will have nowhere to go.

The Kid (Bob Hope) supervises his squadron of sad-sack Santas as they prepare to begin their collection in *The Lemon Drop Kid*. (Photofest)

Having no luck with Nellie, the Kid goes to see girlfriend Brainy Baxter (Marilyn Maxwell). The last time she saw him he pawned her fur coat and headed for Florida without her. But she's still a sucker for the Kid and he manages to get 10 bucks from her for a marriage license: "I'd do anything to be worthy of you. I'd even get a job!" the Kid pleads; Brainy doesn't realize she's been tricked until the Kid is out the door. The Kid next tries to tap Oxford Charlie (Lloyd Nolan), who has problems of his own with the IRS.

Fresh out of luck and with Christmas rapidly approaching, the Kid sees a bell-ringing Santa and gets an idea. Soon he's attired in a pathetic Santa suit and scraggly beard ringing for dear life beside a kettle with the words, "Save a Life" above it. A cop hauls him before a judge for collecting money without a license. The judge gives him 10 days or $50. Meanwhile the Kid runs into Nellie who's been arrested for trying to get her possessions from her apartment. He manages to convince Brainy to bail him out (she has to borrow the money from Oxford Charlie) and, while waiting in jail, is visited by Sam the Surgeon (Harry Bellaver), a henchman of Moose Moran. The Kid has now hatched a surefire scheme to get the money. He explains to the Surgeon that he's going to get a license

and collect money for the Nellie Thursday Home for Old Dolls, but the home will be in Moose's closed-down casino. Even Sam the Surgeon is shocked, "This is the most legal double-cross I've ever heard. You gonna dump all those nice old ladies out on the street at Christmas time?"

But the Kid is trying to save his own neck and has no qualms about throwing those nice old dolls into the street. He manages to convince all the riff-raff that Nellie has helped to pose as Santas and collect for the home. Kid takes Nellie and some other unfortunate old ladies to the casino and tucks them into their nice warm beds—well, nice warm crap tables that have wrestling mats on top of them. The room is wired for raids: When you push a button all the gambling equipment slides into walls and quickly disappears.

The Kid supervises his squadron of sad-sack Santas as they prepare to begin their collection. Characters with names like Straight Flush (Jay C. Flippen), Gloomy Willie (William Frawley) and the Super Swedish Angel (Tor Johnson) hit the streets for Nellie. When a little girl tosses a coin into the kettle of Gloomy Willie, she asks him, "Are you going to bring a doll?" Willie answers, "No, my doll's working Christmas Eve."

The Lemon Drop Kid **introduced a classic Christmas song sung by Hope and Marilyn Maxwell ("Silver Bells" by Jay Livingston and Ray Evans). (Photofest)**

The Kid is pleased with his scheme and he and Brainy stroll the snow-covered streets of New York collecting the money (Brainy thinks this is on the level). They duet on "Silver Bells," one of the few non-Irving Berlin Christmas songs to be introduced in a film that went on to become a holiday standard. The direction in this scene is truly impressive. Helmer Sidney Lanfield manages lovingly to illustrate the brotherhood and goodwill among men and women that occurs during the Christmas season, as his camera focuses on people of all backgrounds sharing the special glow that the holiday brings.

Brainy, who works for Oxford Charlie, quits the show to manage the old ladies and the home. She tells Charlie how much the Kid has managed to make in just two days. Charlie decides to muscle in on the action and kidnaps the old dolls and Brainy, and he takes the money the Kid had hidden in a statue. Willie and the Kid find a footprint in the snow which leads them to the conclusion Charlie is up to no good.

They high-tail it to Charlie's where Nellie and the old ladies plead for the Kid's help. "Kid, save us, we're prisoners. Mrs. Feeney tried to call the police and they hid her false teeth!"

But Charlie tells Willie that the Kid has been playing them and Brainy for suckers and convinces them to work with him. The Kid sneaks out the door. Later Nellie tries to pawn her wedding ring, but a hand reaches out and stops her. The Kid has a plan. "Look Nellie, a bunch of swell guys collected a lot of money for you. I'm not going to let a cheat, chiseler and crook gum up the works."

He has Nellie round up the boys and take them to the courthouse, and he infiltrates the home disguised as an old lady. His theft of the dress is another funny bit that uses Hope's comedy ability to good advantage. He sneaks into the home and manages to steal the money back while knocking out Charlie.

The Kid meets Moose at the casino on Christmas Eve and hands over the money. Oxford Charlie arrives and claims the money. Things look bad for the Kid but he hits the switch and the casino comes to life, stocked by Nellie, the old dolls and the hoods, all gambling with glee. The cops bust in and arrest Moose and Charlie.

Things end happily as Henry, Nellie's husband, arrives home and Brainy and the Kid kiss. Ice cream and cake cap off the Christmas Eve celebration.

Bob Hope plays true to his screen persona as a wise-cracking hustler whose turnaround at the end of the film is just a little questionable. Did he realize how much Nellie and the other ladies needed a home, or did he just manage to figure out a way to get out of his predicament and keep everyone happy?

Hope, still at the peak of his popularity, had the year before completed *Fancy Pants* (1950) with Lucille Ball and the following year would continue the *Road* series with Bing Crosby and Dorothy Lamour in *Road to Bali* (1952). Bob Hope's overseas tours during the wars often overshadowed his film work in the public's eye, which is too bad, for Bob Hope helped to create many classic Hollywood comedies including *The Ghost Breakers* (1940) and *My Favorite Brunette* (1947). Hope would also capitalize on the sparkling chemistry between himself and Bing Crosby in their seven *Road* pictures, as well as turn in a stunning performance as Eddie Foy in *The Seven Little Foys* (1955).

Marilyn Maxwell, who appeared with Hope in two other films (*Off Limits* and *Critic's Choice*), also entertained troops overseas during WWII and the Korean War.

William Frawley, who would become known far and wide as Fred Mertz on *I Love Lucy,* had been in the first film adaptation of this Damon Runyon story in 1934 appearing as The Professor with Baby LeRoy and Lee Tracy.

The March 7, 1951 *Variety* review of the film was rather harsh noting, "Although it has a number of entertaining and amusing qualities, *The Lemon Drop Kid* is a disappointing picture. It is neither true Damon Runyon, from whose short story of the same title it was adapted, nor is it very funny Bob Hope."

While the film is lacking in true sentimentality found in other Runyonesqe films such as *Lady for a Day* and *Sorrowful Jones* (remade as *Little Miss Marker*), chuckles still abound and the staging of the "Silver Bells" number alone makes the film worthwhile holiday viewing.

—SS

A Christmas Story

1983

Jean Shepard's America was brilliantly realized in 1983's *A Christmas Story*, Bob Clark's film version of Shepard's *In God We Trust, All Others Pay Cash.*

Shepard is addicted to America, and most of his work reflects the sensibilities of his hometown of Hammond, Indiana. (He was born there on July 26, 1921.) His is a distinctly American literary voice, filled with color and hyperbole. In his book *A Fistful of Fig Newtons*, he describes the local football hero as: "wedge-shaped; pure sinew, gristle, and covered with a thick, bristly mat of primitive fur. Numerous broken noses had reduced his nostrils to blow-holes."

Shepard himself admits that he would probably still be in Hammond, perhaps retired now from the steel mill, if it hadn't been for World War II. The Signal Corps snatched him out of the mills at age 17, and infected him with the radio bug. He tried to avoid a life before the mike several times, working as a Volkswagen dealer and a sportscar racer, but without long-term success.

He came to New York's WOR after doing a show from Shuller's Wigwam in Cincinnati. His nightly show on KYW in Philadelphia led him to New York. Regular listeners would be treated to openings like: "Okay, gang are you ready to play radio?" Then, Shepard would get down to the real business at hand: telling a story.

There are few pleasures more satisfying than a master storyteller at the top of his form. This was the secret of Shepard's success. Reading from the newspaper or relating a current piece of news, Shepard would be reminded of his old pals Flick and Schwartz, and soon spin a tale as intricate, but as beautifully constructed and gossamer as a spider's web. Marshall McLuhan put it best when he called Shepard "the first radio novelist."

Shepard's tales of his boyhood were not mere exercises in nostalgia. Shepard does not simply remember the good, allowing the bad to slip by unnoticed. Bittersweet is perhaps the best way to classify Shepard's memoirs, for the boyish sense of wonder he remembers so well is often tempered by recollections of disappointment or loss.

Shepard's perspective was wonderfully realized on the screen in 1983's delightful *A Christmas Story*. Directed by Bob Clark, the film earned a disappointing $19 million in the box office, but went on to become a television perennial. In some television markets, *A Christmas Story* is outdistancing *It's A Wonderful Life* as the medium's showcase Christmas film.

The initial failure of the film, Clark believes, can be attributed to the film's ad campaign. Marketed as a children's movie, complete with Norman Rockwellesque poster art and Peter Billingsley in a rabbit suit, the film never found the adult audience it deserved.

In a 1997 article on the incredible television popularity of the film, Clark told the *Chicago Daily Southtown* that he argued with studio brass about the film's child-directed publicity campaign. "This story is on another level," he argued. "This movie has a sardonic, different twist on the idea of Christmas."

Set in the American Midwest in the 1940s, *A Christmas Story* details the Herculean efforts of nine-

Ralphie (Peter Billingsley) receives his Orphan Annie decoder in *A Christmas Story*.

year-old Ralphie Parker (wonderfully played by Peter Billingsley) to get a Genuine Red Ryder Carbine Action 200-Shot Lightning Loader Range Model Air Rifle with a Shock-Proof High Adventure Combination Trail Compass and Sundial Set Right in the Stock.

In pursuit of his personal Holy Grail, Ralphie turns to his mother, teacher, and, in one of the film's most memorable moments, a department store Santa Claus. The response from all of them is identical: "You'll shoot your eye out."

Along the way there are several delicious diversions. Ralphie's continuing feud with green-eyed school bully Scott Farkus (and his toady, Grover Dill); the Double Dog Dare incident, where Ralphie's friend Flick gets his tongue stuck to a frozen pole; the saga of his Old Man (Darren McGavin) and his "major award," a woman's leg lamp; and, perhaps most affectingly, the Little Orphan Annie decoder badge disappointment.

In the end, Christmas presents opened, the Old Man reveals one last package. Inside, Ralphie finds the gift of his dreams: his Red Ryder BB rifle. Throwing a coat over his pajamas, Ralphie runs out back for a little target practice. His first shot out of the gun ricochets, nearly taking out his eye.

Adding insult to injury, the pack of dogs owned by the hillbillies next door herd through the house, stealing the Christmas turkey and breaking the kitchen table. That night, the family has Christmas dinner in a Chinese restaurant, the waiters serenading them with "Deck The Halls."

Perhaps the real core of the film is the way Shepard and Clark (who co-wrote the screenplay) deal with the myth of boyhood. Shepard's voice-over narration of the film is written and delivered in a wonderfully mock-epic manner. It is a voice filled in equal parts with satire and affection; an adult looking backward but still in touch with the child's skewed and exaggerated view of the world.

Amazingly, the narration was one of the first things the studio wanted to cut. Director Clark said: "They were telling me, no one has done narration in 10 years. The form is dead." Clark credits the success of the device with later filmic reflections on childhood, including *The Wonder Years*. Many still feel that the television series borrowed heavily from Shepard's style.

Whatever. The style is especially significant to men and their memories of boyhood. Except for Ralphie's mother (Melinda Dillon), girls and women play almost no part in the story at all. This isn't surprising remembering the boy's mind set of the 1940s: Girls were sissy stuff.

But what Shepard and company have gotten down so right was the way boyhood really was (and perhaps still is). Ralphie Parker is an endless dreamer,

In pursuit of his personal Holy Grail, Ralphie, in one of the film's most memorable moments, turns to a department store Santa Claus (Jeff Gillen) in _A Christmas Story_.

and his fantasies have a peculiar reality for him. His mouth washed out with soup for using "the Queen Mother of all swear words" in front of the Old Man, Ralphie dreams of returning home blind, complete with dark glasses and cane, a victim of soap poisoning. Reflecting on his uses for a Red Ryder gun, Ralphie imagines his home overrun with bandits led by the villainous Black Bart, whom only he, resplendent in a sequined cowboy suit, can repel.

Shepard also realizes how potent adventure tales are to boys this age. Family drama and BB gun dreams take a back seat whenever the _Little Orphan Annie_ radio adventure serial is on the air. It is a world that Ralphie desperately wants to be a part of, and he pines endlessly for his Orphan Annie decoder badge, a talisman that will draw him closer to this adventurous realm. Once he receives his decoder, he feels part of a secret society, as if, at only nine years old, he has already made it.

The difference between the boyish fantasy and the more crass, commercial reality is underscored when Ralphie first gets to use his decoder. Feverishly taking down the evening's code, he locks himself in the bathroom (the only place of privacy in the house), and frantically decodes the message. "What," he wondered desperately, "was Little Orphan Annie trying to tell me?!" The message, it turns out, was a plug for the program's sponsor: BE SURE TO DRINK YOUR OVALTINE.

"Son of a bitch," Ralphie says. "It's a crummy commercial."

It doesn't matter. Quickly past the disappointment, Ralphie, like any other boy, moves on to the next prize. He writes a school essay on the perfect Christmas gift. In his imaginings, he sees his exasperated teacher going through a slush pile of truly awful essays, only to stop at his in music-swelling rapture. (A+++ she writes on the blackboard.) When he finally does get his essay paper back (a C-), the red scrawl at the bottom reads: "You'll shoot your eye out." In his mind's eye, his teacher becomes a green-faced witch.

That this cross-cutting between boyish fantasy and reality is true to the experience of growing up is something to which I can personally attest. (In fact, many would say I haven't grown out of it at all.) Every boy inhabits reality only part time, the rest of the time is spent in boy's pursuits, and aggressive fantasizing is chief among them. It is impossible to watch _A Christmas Story_ without harking back to childhood

Ralphie and Schuartz (R.D. Robb) are amazed when Flick (Scott Schwartz) gets his tongue stuck to a flagpole in *A Christmas Story*.

fantasies of your own, either with warm nostalgia or a feeling of loss, depending on where you fall in the matter. Despite its snowy skies and all-American milieu, I cannot watch *A Christmas Story* without thoughts of dense, impenetrable jungles and my own boyhood dreams of world exploration and exotic travel. It is this frisson between fantasy and reality that *A Christmas Story* best realizes: The ability of our dream lives to help make the real, everyday world more bearable.

For though Ralphie's parents love him, and he seems comfortable enough in his working class milieu, the reality of this boy's life is somewhat bleak. Shepard's memory is perfect in this respect: Children are powerless in the real world, and it is only in the realm of dreams and fantasy that they can wield any power all. If *A Christmas Story* is about anything, it's about the triumph of fantasy.

Ralphie is dominated by his gruff Old Man (despite the love his father feels for him), squirms under the thumb of his mother and is even burdened with looking after his little brother. Thoughts that his teacher may be an ally are quickly squashed with the reality that she feels no particular allegiance with him, and the scruffy backyard bully Scott Farkus openly

beats up Ralphie through most of the film. Growing up is very hard work indeed.

Under the circumstances, of course, Ralphie would retreat into the wish-fulfillment world of Red Ryder and his "peacemaker." It is only in his alternate reality that Ralphie has any independence or volition over his own destiny. Most boys have a secret fantasy world (or worlds) to which they regularly retreat; it is often the only viable defense mechanism during those hard-to-navigate formative years.

It is also a rich vein of expression for men remembering the boys that they were. Weaving dreams of Red Ryder into the tapestry of *A Christmas Story*, Jean Shepard draws upon a time-honored theme in the literature about boys, ranging from Mark Twain's Tom Sawyer and Huckleberry Finn and their pirate fantasies, onto Windsor MaCay's Little Nemo and his Slumberland and continuing recently with Bill Watterson's Calvin and his stuffed tiger Hobbes. Boys first flex their muscles in the company of their pop-culture heroes, making the very existence of such characters as Sherlock Holmes, Tarzan, Superman and all the rest not only a pleasure, but a *necessity*.

It is the movie's genius in never allowing these fantasies to become too sugary, or to allow the dream world of Ralphie to completely sponge away the many challenges of his real, daily life. Even closer to "reality," Shepard never allows Ralphie's Red Ryder fantasies to become such a part of the boy's psyche that they are responsible for some kind of cowboy resolution to the film. In less expert hands, *A Christmas Story* would have ended with Ralphie saving the day with his rifle, becoming, in some symbolic way, the Red Ryder of his dreams. Instead, the authority figures that so oppress Ralphie are totally right: He nearly *does* shoot his eye out.

A Christmas Story is a modern holiday classic, and the audience it eventually found on television and video attest to its enduring appeal. There are several Web sites devoted to *A Christmas Story*, complete with sound bites and still photos, and in 1997 alone, the film aired more than a dozen straight times on the Turner Broadcast network in 24 hours!

The universal appeal of the story transcends the fantasies and rituals of a boy's life: Jean Shepard's story is about the lives we live and the times in which we live them. Although set in a long-lost 1940s, *A Christmas Story* is fresh and contemporary today because it touches on the basic truths about people, outlining genuine emotions rather than Hollywood confections.

While promoting the movie during its initial release, Shepard said: "I set a lot of my stories around rituals—Christmas, Easter, the prom. Times may change, but the rituals don't. I think that's why my books are still popular with kids today. It doesn't matter if I write about sending in for a Little Orphan Annie secret decoder ring. The kids today identify with the ritual of sending in for something, anything. It's the same with a BB gun. Nowadays, it might be a video game that a kid wants for Christmas."

Though Shepard's script and narration provide the essential framework of the film, it is Bob Clark's direction and the excellent cast that bring the piece to life. Peter Billingsley does a wonderful job as Ralphie. Both intelligent and adrift behind his thick-framed glasses, the young actor delivers a richly comic and deeply affecting performance. Clark smartly allows Billingsley to be a kid, and not a paragon, resulting in a performance that has range, depth and humanity.

Melinda Dillon is almost equally good as Ralphie's Mom, but it is a thankless role. (Much like real motherhood.) With her drab wardrobe and hangdog look, the viewer can well believe that she has to make do with two kids and an irascible husband.

The movie's chief joy is Darren McGavin as the Old Man. Although he is nearly a generation too old for the part (maybe two generations too old—he looks more like Billingsley's grandfather than his father), McGavin delivers a performance of boundless energy and invention. Watching McGavin play against

Shepard's voice-over narration, it almost seems as if the part were written for the actor.

Shepard was equally taken with McGavin's performance. "I always pictured the Old Man as Kolchak," Shepard said in 1983, referring to McGavin's star turn in the *Night Stalker* television series. "But this time something really terrible has happened to him—he's married and has two kids."

Not every film becomes a classic—even most Christmas films fall into an often well-deserved obscurity. However, director Bob Clark knew he had something special with *A Christmas Story*. "When I was making the movie," he said, "I fully intended to make a classic. Whether I did or not, well, I'm not making that claim."

Clark doesn't have to make the claim, the millions of fans who have embraced *A Christmas Story* do it for him. The characters and incidents are real enough for Shepard's memories to almost feel as if they were our own memories. It's this appeal to the Everyman (or the boy inside of every man, gone but not nearly forgotten) that is the true core of *A Christmas Story*.

—BM

Trading Places
1983

John Landis is commonly thought of as a director for the masses, a director who is not afraid to appeal to lovers of low art and pop culture. The title of Landis' debuting film as director, *Schlock*, sums it all up. He is most known for *Animal House*, *American Werewolf in London* and *The Blues Brothers*, common denominator films that entertain the great unwashed masses of American movie viewers. However, one of Landis' best films, *Trading Places*, aims a tad higher, offering thoughtful insights about human nature, while at the same time making its audience laugh. It just happens to be one of the most inventive Christmas movies of the last two decades.

Trading Places is a movie of extremes, contrasting the haves and the have-nots, as the opening credit sequences reveal. On the one hand we have images of the poor: A man sleeps in a stairway, several poor folks warm their hands over a fire in a steel drum, people swarm to a welfare/unemployment office, inner city children play basketball. On the other hand we have images of the very affluent: well-dressed servants preparing complex breakfast meals, expensive homes with fancy cars in front populated by nattily dressed businessmen.

Into this prosperous world steps Louis Winthorpe (Dan Aykroyd), the golden boy of Duke and Duke, commodity stock brokers who do not always play by the rules, but always win. The Duke brothers Randolph (Ralph Bellamy) and Mortimer (Don Ameche) like to wager bets (one dollar goes to the winner), and their latest concern is the controversy surrounding heredity vs. environment (what really makes the man, his gene pool or where he is raised and brought up?). Randolph and Mortimer are petty, greedy, unfeeling people who are only concerned about one thing: making money. "You are about to make millions of dollars in frozen orange juice and you talk about human nature," Mortimer warns. "Mother always said you were greedy," Randolph retorts. "But she meant it as a compliment," Mortimer adds. Meanwhile, the black servant serving them drinks is given a Christmas bonus by the brothers, five dollars. Sarcastically the servant offers, "Oh, five dollars, maybe I can go to the movies—by myself!" Mortimer chimes in, "Half of it is from me!" Meanwhile Winthorpe, stiffly walking through the office as the employees offer mechanical good-mornings, offers checks for the Duke brothers to sign. One check for $50,000 to a Clarence Beeks is suspect, and when Winthorpe questions it, the Dukes act suspiciously and tell him not to worry. After he leaves they both express how lucky they are to have a manager like Winthorpe, one brother claiming he's the product of good environment, the other claiming he's the product of good breeding. "Like race horses, it's in the blood," Mortimer declares.

Billy Ray Valentine (Eddie Murphy) tries to hustle Mortimer Duke (Don Ameche) in *Trading Places*.

Meanwhile Billy Ray Valentine (Eddie Murphy) is a black street hustler, a man pretending to be a Vietnam veteran getting around on a platform because he supposedly lost both legs. "Merry Christmas," he shouts and smiles, asking for donations. When people ignore him he pops off little asides, such as "you got lots of soul, I appreciate it!" Eyeing a beautiful woman scurrying past, his eyes light up and he beams, "Once you have a man with no legs, you never go back, baby... we can make it baby, me and you!" By now he has latched on to her coat, but she pulls away. "You bitch!" Soon the two policeman come upon the scene and figure out his angle. Pretending also to be blind, his head bobbing and weaving like Stevie Wonder, he mentions stepping on land mines in Nam, losing both legs. He says his inside name was Agent Orange. However, as both policeman lift him up by each arm, Valentine's legs drop down to the ground and Valentine turns on the act, screaming, "I can see! I have legs! I can walk! Jesus! Praise, Jesus! This is beautiful!" Slowly backing off down the street, Valentine

keeps smiling telling the policemen they are beautiful as he disappears farther and farther down the street. While keeping a watchful eye on his pursuers, Valentine bumps into Winthorpe, knocking him over. Valentine smiles and picks up his briefcase to hand it back, but Valentine thinks this black man is robbing him and he screams for help and tells Valentine to take his case. Soon police are chasing the misunderstood Valentine through the exclusive Heritage Club where he is cornered. Winthorpe wants to press full charges. However, the crafty Randolph immediately asks Valentine if he's from a broken home ("We was broke I guess," he answers), if he had a history of juvenile arrests, spent time in reform school, had any drug arrests. Randolph immediately declares he is a product of a poor environment. Mortimer claims that since he is a "Negro" he probably stole since he could crawl; thus, a product of bad genetics. Soon they strike a wager, betting that they will ruin Winthorpe, making him lose his job, his money, his fiancée, his friends and that he will resort to a life of crime (a product of bad environment). By taking Valentine and putting him into Winthorpe's environment, Randolph claims he will become just as good a worker as Winthorpe was.

113

Winthorpe (Dan Aykroyd), the sorriest looking Santa imaginable, tries to invade the Duke's office Christmas party in *Trading Places*.

Using the Dukes' dirty-dealings man Beeks, Winthorpe is framed for stealing money from the Heritage Club and is immediately fired by the Dukes. Arrested and taken downtown to police headquarters, he is forced to strip. Another man working for the Dukes hides a bag of Angel Dust in Winthorpe's jacket, which causes his very exclusive bank to freeze his accounts and take back his credit cards. Thinking he is a drug dealer, his fiancée Penelope is about to forgive him when Beeks hires prostitute Ophelia (Jamie Lee Curtis) to kiss and caress Winthorpe and beg him for more drugs, claiming she will do "all the things you like!" Penelope slaps him and leaves him there on the spot. However, the prostitute with the heart-of-gold honestly tells Winthorpe that some man paid her $100 to pull off that stunt as a joke, but realizing she caused real damage, she takes the broken man home to her place to offer him help.

Meanwhile. the Dukes bail Billy Ray Valentine out of jail, citing their privately funded program to rehabilitate culturally disadvantaged people. They offer to provide Valentine with a car, a home, a generous bank account and a job starting at $80,000 per year. The charges against Valentine have been dropped, so he can leave a free man if he chooses, or accept their offer. Of course Valentine is offered

Winthorpe's house and his servant Coleman (Denholm Elliott). The first order of business is for Valentine to revisit one of his old haunts, a bar filled with people ready to party. He invites the entire crowd back to his home. However, within the hour, Valentine is upset that people spill drinks on "his" Persian rug and drop cigarette butts on his floor. Soon the women are taking off their tops and going wild, and Valentine even finds a naked girl in his bed waiting for him. Immediately realizing that these people don't belong here, he orders them "to get...out!" He tells Coleman that they are a bunch of freeloaders who treat his home like a zoo. Already he has become alienated from the people he used to hang out with.

Nervous about starting his new job, Valentine is told by Coleman, "Just be yourself; whatever happens, they can't take that away from you!" But the street-smart Valentine takes well to the commodity broker market. As the Dukes explain, "We broker commodities (coffee, wheat, pork bellies, frozen orange juice concentrate, gold, etc.); we are speculators. We buy or sell such commodities for our clients who empower us to use their money for this purpose." The Dukes smile and say we make a commission whether they make or lose money. Valentine, becoming savvy fast, says they are like bookies. However, using common sense, Valentine catches on quickly and becomes an ace predicting at what price the Dukes should buy or sell.

Back at Ophelia's place, she lays down the law. She claims she is 24 years old, has saved $42,000 and in three more years of working "on her back" she will be able to retire. She doesn't use a pimp and she doesn't do drugs. Hearing and believing Winthorpe's tragic story, she tells him she will help him get back on his feet and carry him temporarily if he pays her "five figures" when and if he gets his past life back. But she truly cares for Winthorpe, and uses her body heat to warm him when he catches cold and develops a fever of 103 degrees. In one comic sequence, getting drunk dressed in a Santa Claus outfit, Winthorpe invades the annual Duke and Duke Christmas party, shoving huge pieces of fish and meat down the front of his Santa outfit, stocking up food for later. Soon he breaks into his old office, now Valentine's, looking for papers to vindicate him. However, he is caught by Valentine, and pulling a gun on the entire office staff, he threatens "you will all be very, very sorry," before leaving. When Randolph and Mortimer voice sympathy for their old employee Winthorpe, Billy Ray says, "But he has money to buy drugs. You can't be soft on people like that, I know!" In other words, the characters of Valentine and Winthorpe have flip-flopped, each becoming the man the other used to be. With this realization, Randolph turns to Mortimer and smiles.

Billy Ray is hiding in a bathroom stall, sneaking a quick buzz (the drugs Winthorpe found in Valentine's office were Valentine's, not a "plant" as Billy Ray claimed), when he overhears Randolph and Mortimer reveal their entire scheme and plan to return Valentine to the ghetto. Mortimer remarks the idea of having Billy Ray run the business is ridiculous.

However, in a very complex scheme, Billy Ray gets back together with Winthorpe, and with the aid of Coleman and Ophelia, they pull all their money to concoct a plan using orange juice stock to make a fortune for themselves and drive the Dukes into bankruptcy, By movie's end, all of them are living in a tropical paradise, while the Dukes are facing their worst nightmare—becoming financially ruined.

Interestingly, amidst a Christmas (and New Year's) framing story, the true message of Christmas is illustrated through American capitalism and greedy money-makers. In the best illustration yet of "the first will be last and the last will be first," Winthorpe learns that all his status and money are transient and can vanish in an instance, that his friends are not his friends but only like his status and wealth. Learning humility once his wealth vanishes and the meaning of friendship, something Ophelia extends to Winthorpe simply because she cares about people, Winthorpe learns

what an empty life he had and what an interesting life lies ahead. By flushing his life of all excess and insignificance, he can retire to a tropical island where money is needed only for the basics of living and not to impress because of his breeding. True, Ophelia wants Winthorpe to take care of her needs, but she still brings him into her home realizing that the chances of him paying her back are next to none. And Billy Ray Valentine, a shrewd, sharp operator, does the right thing and helps Winthorpe get his revenge when Valentine realizes that he is being set up by the Dukes. He also needs Winthorpe's experience of the business world to insure their scheme's success. By movie's end the greedy and the uncaring have been vanquished, and the meek have surely inherited the Earth, or at least a little corner of it.

—GJS

National Lampoon's Christmas Vacation

1989

One of the major problems facing today's Christmas movie makers is how to set the tone: Do today's productions seek out that warm and fuzzy sentiment of old; do they try for the bittersweet and harsh reality of today's complex world; do they attempt to go for a mocking or satirical tone; or do they create a tone of absolute insanity by going for the broadly humorous with plenty of slapstick? In the instance of *National Lampoon's Christmas Vacation* (with the emphasis on *National Lampoon*'s reputation as a magazine of broad farce and biting satire), the John Hughes Production machine (with a script written by Hughes) decided to blend all these elements together to create a movie that from moment to moment can be humorous in a physical sense, emotional and touching the next and then can become a bitter travesty of what is wrong with today's society. Such a movie, changing tone so frequently, can be a jarring, over-the-top mess, or it can masterfully transform itself into being all these things at once. *Christmas Vacation* falls somewhere in-between these two extremes, becoming a hit and miss operation that is, thankfully, most often consistent and sometimes hilarious, and sometimes emotionally involving.

The Griswold family, out in the wilds of the open road, are caroling their way to find a Christmas tree farm to cut down their own tree. The wacky Clark (Chevy Chase), his down-to-earth wife Ellen (Beverly D'Angelo) and the Griswold children Audrey (Juliette Lewis) and Rusty (Johnny Galecki) represent the typical modern family—well, up to a point. After a tedious slapsticky road-hog game of "chicken," the Griswolds' car literally flies into the tree farm, Clark finding the tree of his dreams draped in celestial light. Unfortunately, the tree is almost as big as a house, and since Clark forgot his saw, he has to literally dig the tree up by its roots and sling it over the family station wagon. At home, garbed in his Jason hockey mask, armed with a chain saw, Clark begins the pruning process to get the humongous tree to fit into the living room. Once it's tied securely and placed in its holder, Clark uses hedge clippers to cut the cord releasing the branches that then swing free breaking windows and displacing furniture. This clever sight gag is typical of the physical slapstick which this film regularly employs. Telling husband Clark that he "sets standards no family can live up to," Ellen knows Clark's plans of inviting both their parents and families to the Griswold home for the holidays is a bad idea.

At work Clark tells his co-worker that he is really counting on the annual Christmas bonus this year, as he has already put a downpayment on a swimming pool for the family this summer. Clark is told he is an excellent choice to be named designer of the year, and his boss hopes to mention his work in a trade show speech coming up, but the bonus is not guaranteed and Clark is worried.

In the next over-the-top sequence, Clark goes to the department store to buy his wife a present, but he is immediately awe-struck by a salesgirl, Mary, whose chief aspects are literally busting out all over. Of course she happens to be selling lingerie. Giggling and walking her to her counter, Clark is sweating and makes an adolescent comment about it couldn't be any "hooter" than it is. Then, after commenting on the heat, he mentions how nippy it is, but he says "nipley," referring to the objects of his attention. She smiles and not-so-innocently asks, "Can I take something out for you," and this sends him over the top. He tells her he wants something for his wife, "God rest her soul," but when she expresses condolences, he explains "She's history," meaning divorced. Then more nonsense blurts out, "Of course she doesn't wear underwear... plenty of shopping days left until adultery." Then he mentions his big Yule log. Soon his son Rusty happens by just as the salesgirl Mary raises her skirt to show Clark that the underwear she is wearing does not show any lines. Juvenile and silly, *Christmas Vacation* has a few too many of these kinds of moments.

To the chorus of "this is what Christmas is all about" from Clark, both families arrive at the same time, descending upon the happy household like ants at a picnic. Clark is merrily outside with Rusty decorating the house with Christmas lights, literally stapling strands of lights over every square inch of the

house. After climbing up the side of the house on a ladder, of course the ladder collapses. The second time Clark climbs back up, he staples his shirt cuff to the house, and pulling himself free, thrusts the ladder backwards, happily stopping on a huge tree branch. Pushing himself off, he lands back on the side of the house with enough force that he almost falls off. He slides down the shingled roof, catching the rain spout at the edge, dangling off the side. Immediately one end of the spout comes free thrusting outward, propelling a shaft of ice through the nosy neighbor's window, shattering their home stereo unit. Clark loses his grip and falls off the roof, luckily landing atop a large evergreen. Some nice, well-timed slapstick here.

Inside, teenager Audrey is bemoaning the fact that she has to sleep with her adolescent brother in the same bed—"Do you know how twisted that is," she rants. She then says the thoughts of what he might be doing when he's alone in that bed give her nightmares. Mother Ellen shakes her head in agreement, "I sleep with your father." But as survivor Helen reminds her daughter, "This is Christmas and we are all in misery."

That evening, called out of bed, all wearing night clothes out in the cold, Clark wants the entire family assembled while he turns on the lights, 250 strands of lights, 25,000 individual bulbs. After asking for a drum roll, and getting one from the family, Clark breaks out into a carol before plugging in the connection. But no lights! Everyone is disappointed and angry about being forced out of their warm beds, but sympathetic daughter Audrey tells her complaining grandmother that Dad worked really hard on these lights and tells her father, "Looks good even if they're not lit, Daddy."

The next night, in utter frustration, Clark dutifully tests every single bulb and works again to light up his house. When his wife mentions that perhaps the extension cord may not be plugged in, Clark goes to the back of the house to check. Surprisingly, everything is properly plugged in, using a maze of power strips. However, the gag is that a light switch that gives power to the receptacle is not turned on, and a whole slew of gags involve people at first innocently turning on and off that switch, which in turn causes the already over-stressed Clark to totally spazz out as lights glow and then stop glowing. He resorts to punching and kicking the front lawn Santa and sleigh. Ellen finally figures out the problem and turns on the switch at the exact instant Clark puts in the plug in. The initial illumination looks like something out of *Close Encounters* with blinding lights flooding the neighbor's bedroom just as they are getting romantic. Closing in on a tight shot of the electric meter going haywire, we next see a hand at the power station activate a level marked auxiliary power.

The relatives all gather for Christmas Eve dinner at the Griswolds. Clark (Chevy Chase) attempts to carve the turkey in *National Lampoon's Christmas Vacation*.

The latest batch of relatives, Eddie (Randy Quaid) and Catherine, arrive in their rust-bucket RV, which Clark refers to as "the tenement on wheels." They arrive with two kids and a huge dog named Snots. The redneck family manages to destroy Christmas decorations simply by passing through.

One night while the family is asleep upstairs, Clark wistfully looks out the backyard window and imagines the pool upon which he has already overextended himself financially (and no Christmas bonus in sight). He envisions all his relatives wearing their swim suits splashing around. Soon the family vanishes and the salesgirl of his dreams, Mary, does a slow strip on the diving board, finally splashing into the pool. Eddie's youngest daughter comes down, sad that Santa Claus never came to their RV last Christmas, realizing that this year will be no different. Of course, the always optimistic Clark tells the child that he knows for a fact that Santa will be coming here this year. The next morning, Clark catches Eddie pumping raw sewage from his RV into the sidewalk sewer in front of the house, an act against the law because of the buildup of gases this can cause. But Clark still goes to Eddie and offers to help him out financially by buying presents for the kids and wife—

the always ready Eddie slaps out an alphabetical listing of what everyone wants at a moment's notice.

It is Christmas Eve, and the final relatives, the oblivious Uncle Lewis (William Hickey) and nearly senile Aunt Bethany arrive for dinner and celebration. The presents they bring include the family cat accidentally wrapped up in a box and a drippy Jell-O mold. Sitting down at the table for turkey dinner, Clark asks Bethany to say grace, but she mutters that Grace died 30 years ago. Finally, Lewis explains what is needed of her, and she starts to dramatically recite the Pledge of Allegiance, which Clark ends with a respectful "Amen." However, when Clark cuts the turkey, the overcooked dried-out bird falls apart. Soon Snots disrupts the trash cans and chokes on a bone, and the now liberated cat chews on the Christmas tree lights, pulling out the plug. When Clark plugs it back in, sparks fly, the cat shrieks and Clark moves the terribly burned living room chair to reveal the outline of a supercharged kitty burned into the rug. Now, that's funny! Putting the chair out immediately by the curb, Clark smells gas created by Eddie's raw sewage pump job. Inside Uncle Lewis lights his cigar near the tree which he incinerates, catching the back of his sports jacket on fire, still unaware of what he's done.

Clark's string of bad luck is driving him to the breaking point in *National Lampoon's* *Christmas Vacation.*

One horrible event occurs after another. Next the Speed Ball Messenger Service delivers the belated Christmas bonus from work, a year's membership to the Jell-O of the month club. However, after tearfully confessing his plans to buy a pool and fly the entire family in for the pool's christening, the formerly pleasant Clark rattles off every conceivable curse/obscenity/insult he can think of regarding his boss Mr. Shirley. He even mutters something to the effect that he wishes Mr. Shirley could be brought here to his home so he can see the results of his cheapness. Of course Eddie takes Clark at his word, and goes right out in the RV and kidnaps Shirley from his home, with his frantic wife phoning the police.

Soon the totally stressed-out Clark cuts down an evergreen from outside, sets it up and decorates it as a Christmas tree, and then finds out a squirrel is lurking on a branch when it breaks free, running throughout the house, being chased by Snots, destroying everything in their wake. By this point the visiting families want to leave, but Clark won't have it. The crazed homeowner declares, "No one's leaving, we are pressing on. We will have the best Christmas since Bing Crosby tap-danced with Danny...Kaye. And when Santa squeezes his jolly white ass down the chimney tonight, he's gonna find the jolliest bunch of assholes this side of the nuthouse." Turning around and looking in disbelief, he states, "Look around you Helen, we're at the threshold of Hell!"

However, in a tender scene, Clark's father has a heart-to-heart talk with his son. "I love you, we all love you... you're too good a father to act like this." When he asks his father how he got through the holidays, the father smiles, "I had a little help from Jack Daniels." His father tells Clark, "This is your house, your Christmas, so I am retiring." He lets Clark read "The Night Before Christmas" to the family.

Once Mr. Shirley (Brian Doyle Murray) is brought back to the house, he understands just how important Christmas bonuses are to Clark and his other employees, realizing he made a mistake by discontinuing them, especially when he can see the looks of hatred/disappointment in the staring eyes of all the assembled family members. Mr. Shirley tells Clark, whatever your bonus was last Christmas, add another 20 percent for this year! Almost immediately, this feeling of victory, of absolute family harmony and happiness, is ruined by the arrival of the SWAT team who breaks through windows knocking over the Christmas tree and holding everyone frozen at gun point. However, Shirley explains everything and states he will not press any charges. But damage has been done.

Peaceful at last, the family goes outside to watch the Christmas sky, full moon and stars. Uncle Lewis lights up another cigar and throws his match into the gutter, instantly blowing up the car. Aunt Bethany breaks into a solemn chorus of *The Star-Spangled*

Banner, with the Griswolds all standing at attention. In a quick image, Santa's sleigh silhouetted against the full moon appears to be on fire. Finally standing alone outside his family's house, Clark smiles and declares "I did it," as the movie ends.

National Lampoon's Christmas Vacation tries to do too many things scatter-gun. The dominant thrust of the movie is the sometimes inspired slapstick humor, the physical gags, the sight gags: The cat gets electrocuted, the uncle blows up the tree and car, Clark falls off the roof, a squirrel wreaks havoc in the home, etc. However, we have far too many poignant moments which jar with these more comic events: the heart-to-heart between Clark and his father, Clark speaking to Eddie about financially giving them a good Christmas, Clark's impassioned speech to his family about what they mean to him and his plans to fly them in to break in the new pool. And, finally, we have the more sophisticated, biting satire that mocks the Christmas spirit in suburban America: everyone accepting the fact that too many families under one roof will kill one another, the over-emphasis on the material to celebrate the holidays, especially depending upon the "gift" of a Christmas bonus, etc. All these conflicting "tones" never come together quite smoothly enough. Instead, the film feels segmented and sometimes works against itself, almost as though different sequences were directed by different directors. Perhaps the film was saved in the editing room by a crafty crew of experts who felt they could hold the entire thing together by framing the film in hilarious sequences of pratfalling insanity. Funny thing is, they almost pull it off, as *Christmas Vacation* is hilarious in sections, touching in others and, while not everything works consistently well, the film is finally more hit than miss and becomes overall quite entertaining.
—GJS

Home Alone

1990

By the 1990s, Christmas movies of every sort had been depicted, so producer/writer John Hughes decided to combine several different plot elements to create a Christmas film for the current age. Take a child star with extreme cuteness (just like Shirley Temple was in *Heidi*), add two lovable criminals who are expert at pratfalls and physical humor (an outlaw Laurel and Hardy), add in the subplot of the misunderstood and feared neighbor who needs to be reconciled with his son, add the frivolity and hijinks that occur with an extended family of 15 taking a holiday trip to Paris and mix together all these elements in a frantic pace

and we have *Home Alone*, the major Christmas movie of 1990.

As the movie opens, a household of 15 (mostly children) are preparing their long-awaited Christmas trip to Paris, as a strange-looking police officer happens to enter the house just to assure the owners that "it's in safe hands" when leaving on the trip. In a matter of minutes, we are introduced to child megastar Macaulay Culkin as Kevin, the eight-year-old that everyone, from siblings to cousins to uncles to mother, cracks on. Kevin screams announcing, when he grows up, "I'm living alone," which seems to make sense amidst a household of unlimited anxiety and anticipation. The kids warn Kevin of strange old neighbor Old Man Marley (Roberts Blossom) who supposedly, according to the neighborhood urban legend, murdered his family and half of the neighborhood back in 1958. Soon the pizza delivery man arrives, asking for $122.50, so the relatives pass the buck for a few minutes while the kids dig in to eat. Kevin, who is threatened with the promise that he will share a bed with Fuller, an avowed bed-wetter, overhears adults warn Fuller, "Go easy on the Pepsi," as Fuller smiles and turns to Kevin. Big brother and chief tormentor Buzz says he ate Kevin's plain cheese pizza, but he offers to barf it up for the kid. Kevin is pushed too far, so he runs and attacks Buzz, knocking over food and drink and causing a major mess. Kevin, as punishment, is sent up to the third floor bedroom by mom, who promptly forgets he's up there. Kevin says his family "sucks," but his mother (Catherine O'Hara) reminds her son, "You'd feel pretty sad if you woke up tomorrow morning and you didn't have a family." The angry Kevin declares, "No I wouldn't. I hope I don't see any of you jerks again." Thus, the premise of the movie is laid out on a platter.

Next morning, a few contrivances occur—power lines fall causing a blackout which will disrupt all the neighborhood telephone lines for several days—causing the extended family to oversleep and then hurriedly prepare to board the two airport vans parked in front of the house. Coincidentally, a young neighbor boy from across the street just happens to come on by as the family is about to leave, being included in the final "head count" before the vans depart. Of course, Kevin is alone upstairs sleeping.

Just as family members arrive at the airport terminal and board their plane in the nick of time, a sleepy-eyed and wild-haired Kevin awakens and calls for his family as he comes down from upstairs. Looking very solemn, Kevin declares, "I've made my family disappear," but within seconds he shouts, "I'm free" and takes advantage of every kid's wildest dreams—jumping up and down on the beds while eating junk food, running down the stairs at full throttle, riding a sled down the living room stairs to the outside and

Kevin (Macauley Culkin) prepares to celebrate Christmas alone as inept burglar Harry (Joe Pesci) spies on him in *Home Alone*.

down the front steps, going through your brother's private things and finding wondrous, taboo things such as firecrackers and copies of *Playboy*. For the first hour, unbridled happiness ensues. But soon Kevin yells out loud, "Guys, you better come out and stop me," but no one does. Aboard the plane, now in flight, mother is irked that she forgot something, until in a panic she remembers and screams, "Kevin!!!" They arrive in Paris and phone home, but the phones are still out and the only choice is for the family to catch the fastest possible return flight to Chicago, which isn't easy the day before Christmas.

Harry (Joe Pesci) and Marv (Daniel Stern), two pathetic cat burglars, have the entire neighborhood scoped out, down to the exact minute that departed travelers have their timers turn outside Christmas lights on. Harry, whom we recognize as the policeman who entered Kevin's home, wants to rob that house most of all, because of all the great material he saw that he can fence. However, when the duo sneaks around the back to try to break in, Kevin turns on some lights, frightening them off for the moment. In mortal fear, Kevin runs upstairs and hides under the bed. Quickly coming to his senses, Kevin declares, "Only a wimp would be hiding under the bed... I'm the man of the house." He declares he's not afraid anymore, but when he ventures outside, he sees the dreaded figure of Old Man Marley, armed with his shovel he uses to throw salt on the sidewalks, clearing the path for his neighbors. Kevin screams bloody murder, run-

ning back inside. When his parents, still in Paris, finally get the police to send a patrolman over to the house to check on Kevin, Kevin instead thinks the robbers are back, so he hides and the policeman leaves.

The robbers, very stupid but lovable saps, call themselves "the wet bandits" because Marv feels they need a trademark by which to be remembered, so when they finish heisting a house, Marv leaves the water running.

Kevin survives quite admirably, remembering to shower and use deodorant, though he cannot find his toothbrush. He goes to the store to buy supplies, is spooked once again by Marley, this time nursing a bloody, bandaged hand. He orders pizza for food, using clever editing from an old videotaped movie to provide adult dialogue to respond to questions asked by the delivery man. Even when going grocery shopping, he reminds the clerk that he has a coupon for one item purchased.

While the main family awaits a return flight to Chicago, mother decides she must act so she takes the first available flight to the U.S. and then tries to get a connecting flight to Chicago. She hooks up with a polka band who are renting a Budget truck to Milwaukee, but they offer to leave her off in Chicago, the entire band tooting away in the back of the truck, making a bad situation worse.

In one touching sequence, on Christmas Eve night, Kevin walks around the neighborhood after seeing a pretty pathetic Santa Claus, telling the man of the hour that he doesn't want any presents, just his family to return. Walking home, he sees relatives gather as households hold Christmas Eve parties, hug and exchange gifts. Spotting a brightly decorated church, Kevin wanders in and sits in the empty pews as the church chorus rehearses. Sitting alone, on the other side, is Old Man Marley, who comes over, introduces himself and asks if he could sit next to Kevin. Marley recognizes Kevin as one of the children who lives next door to him. "Merry Christmas," he wishes Kevin, turning to a young girl in the chorus about Kevin's age. "She's my granddaughter." Marley explains he's not welcome in his son's home and hasn't spoken to his son in years. Marley is afraid to phone his son, in fear that he would still be rejected. Kevin, in a wonderful sequence, advises Marley to try, "Give it a shot for your granddaughter." Old man and young boy, both very much alone, smile at one another.

Of course, the movie is building up to the acclaimed slapstick sequence where Kevin defends his home from the easily outwitted outlaws who have at last figured out that Kevin is home alone (in one clever sequence, Kevin fools the saps by playing loud Christmas music, turning on all the lights, and creating silhouettes of people partying and walking around the living room, in reality dummies and cardboard posters on train tracks filling in for the actual missing people). "This is my house, I have to defend it," Kevin declares, making preparations for his visitors. When Harry and Marv arrive, they are indeed in store for many surprises. First, the duo knocks on the door, but Kevin uses his air rifle to shoot Harry in the leg and Marv in the forehead. The walkways have been iced up, and the robbers continually fall on their backs and behinds as they attempt to enter the home. When Marv finally gets his balance on the cellar stairs, he finds his crowbar wasn't necessary as the door is unlocked. However, as soon as he pulls on the light chain, a hot iron from above falls and brands his forehead. When Harry touches the front doorknob which is red-hot, he falls down the stairs with his hand sizzling in the snow. Marv, trying to mount the cellar steps, covered in oozing tar, steps in his bare feet on Kevin's well-placed nail. Attempting to enter from another door, Harry slowly sticks his head through the entranceway activating a blow-torch which singes both his cap and his hair. Gradually working their way upstairs, Harry is now covered in feathers while Marv, still barefooted, steps onto broken Christmas tree ornaments. "I'm up here you morons," Kevin chimes. By the time the robbers reach the first floor level, they are bombarded by swinging paint cans on rope, knocking both of them momentarily unconscious. Working even higher, the men trip over wires while running at breakneck speed. Kevin even throws a spider on the terrified Marv, which he throws on the flattened Harry. Telling the

In *Home Alone 2*, Kevin's mother (Catherine O'Hara) finally finds him in New York City.

semi-conscious Harry to remain perfectly still, Marv uses his crowbar to try to squash the spider but misses and hits Harry directly in the gut. Kevin cleverly swings on his rope (using bicycle handles for balance) to get to his tree house, but when Harry and Marv attempt to hand-walk across, Kevin uses his clippers to cause the bozos to crash head first into a brick wall. Once Kevin is finally captured and hung on a door hook, hero Old Man Marley sneaks up behind the pair of thugs and whacks them over the head with his shovel.

The police tell the bungling burglars thanks for leaving the water running once again, an act that links this crime to all the others. As Marv proudly exclaims, "We're the wet bandits," Harry begins hitting his stupid friend with his cap. As they are driven off in the squad car, they look back and catch a smile from Kevin.

The next morning, Christmas morning, mother is reunited with Kevin, the rest of the family arriving soon afterwards. Even brother Buzz is kind: "It's cool that you didn't burn down the house!" Everyone is happy to see Kevin, who amazes his family with his shopping spree antics whereby he bought much needed items such as milk, eggs and fabric softener. Glancing outside in the snow, Kevin sees Mr. Marley reconciling with his son, everyone hugging and slowly walking inside. Seeing the smile on Kevin's face, the old man smiles and waves.

Home Alone, as concocted by the John Hughes marketability production machine, and crisply directed by Chris Columbus, is not great art, but it is competent Hollywood movie-making in the best sense. It focuses upon a charismatic child star who plays terrified and, in a change of pace, terrifier quite adeptly. The two goons (an energized Joe Pesci and Daniel Stern, whose physical interaction and reaction to one another is priceless) complement Culkin. What could have become the horror film of the 1990s—Home Invasion—quickly becomes ridiculous fun, straight out of the annals of Laurel and Hardy. The Three Stooges live in this demented slapstick farce based upon burning heads, crowbars to the stomach and hot irons on the face. The violence and threats are so over-the-top that no one could really get outraged, and besides, Hughes/Columbus have the tugging-the-heartstrings subplot whereby the so-called neighborhood serial killer turns out to be a kind, lonely man who only wishes to find the courage to phone his son. *Home Alone* is perhaps too manipulative and contrived, but ultimately, the only thing that matters is that the movie works.

In 1992 John Hughes would again revive the Home Alone characters in *Home Alone 2: Lost in New York*. As in the first film, young Kevin is separated from his family, this time he is alone in New York City during the Christmas holidays. Bumbling crooks Harry and Marv have escaped from jail and guess what—they're in New York too! Kevin makes friends with a homeless woman (Brenda Fricker), makes the life of a hotel manager (Tim Curry) miserable, and makes mincemeat out of poor old Harry and Marv.
—GJS

Mixed Nuts

1994

Sometimes Christmas films can be so totally outrageous that one wonders why the plot has been linked to the Christmas season at all. *Mixed Nuts*, a remake of the 1982 French film *Le Pere Noel est une ordure*, rewritten by Nora and Delia Ephron and directed by Nora Ephron, is the quirkiest mainstream Hollywood movie included in this book. By the film's conclusion, the Yuletide spirit has enveloped its cast of oddball characters, but, mostly, *Mixed Nuts* is more an excuse to offer black comedy and demented visual gags amid a Christmas Eve setting. Fortunately, in sections, the film is hilarious and truly inspired; however, overall, the jaded Christmas film misfires more often than hitting the bullseye.

More than creating a plot, *Mixed Nuts* establishes distinct characters who interact in numerous comic situations, at first separately in small groups, but by the movie's end, all these dementos are brought together to interact as one large ensemble of goofy people.

The movie begins on a rather traditional note, as visual images of Christmas (two rollerbladers carrying a Christmas tree, a person wearing a Frosty the Snowman outfit on skates, visions of Christmas trees, a large group of children dressed as angels, etc.) are pictured amidst the musical background of "White Christmas."

Then the mood is disrupted by a young man wearing a Santa Claus outfit, running out of a store, as his young pregnant lover screams at him: "You don't deserve to be the father of my child." Charging out of the store, the young man, Felix (Anthony La Paglia), rams into two rollerbladers carrying a Christmas tree, knocking it to the ground. "You jerk, you ruined our tree. It was perfectly symmetrical!" Coming onto the scene is good Samaritan Phillip (Steve Martin), who operates a telephone crisis hot-line called Lifesavers, and who tries to be peacemaker. "It's Christmas, it was an accident. Why can't we all show a little Christmas spirit here." With that a fight breaks out with the rollerbladers fleeing, leaving their tree behind. Phillip picks up the tree to help decorate the Lifesavers office, in actuality, his own personal apart-

Adam Sandler, Liev Schreiber, Madeline Kahn, Steve Martin, Rita Wilson, Juliette Lewis and Anthony LaPaglia star in *Mixed Nuts*.

ment. On the way up to the "office," the landlord Stanley (Gary Shandling) serves Phillip with an eviction notice for first of the year. He owes $5,000 rent.

To keep the bad news from his two employees Mrs. Munchnik (Madeline Kahn) and Catherine (Rita Wilson), Phillip tries to wear a happy face. Mrs. Munchnik takes her telephone counselor skills very seriously and her self-absorbed attitude only annoys the others. Catherine, a mousy woman who lives at home with her mother, is depressed that she will never find true love, and seems more like the person who would make the phone call to Lifesavers than the counselor on the other end. Catherine is terrified of becoming a victim of the Seaside Strangler, a local serial killer who murders women by choking them with fishing line.

Back at the little shop, very pregnant and gun-toting Gracie (Juliette Lewis) opens up the front door to find her ex-boyfriend Felix still wearing the Santa suit. She explains she uses the gun as protection from the Seaside Strangler. Gracie is still angry at Felix, who she tells could have sold his Santa suit for a car seat for the baby, but Felix reminds her he doesn't own a car! Then Felix counters by complaining that if Gracie hadn't cut up all his clothes, he could afford to sell his Santa suit. Her excuse—she was angry at

Felix. Claiming she wants to meet a businessman and not "a loser," Gracie wants to break up once and for all; Felix protests he is not a loser but a wall painter (as in graffiti artist) who will make good.

On Christmas Eve, the Lifesavers don't seem very sympathetic. They complain that on such an emotional holiday, the phone lines shouldn't be so quiet, that they should be hearing from people thinking of jumping out of windows or slitting their wrists. The most unsympathetic is Mrs. Munchnik. When a desperate caller states, "I'm at the end of my rope and I want to die," Munchnik replies she hears too much static, then proceeds to click on the receiver button, disconnecting an unpleasant call. But Phillip chimes in, "If they're really upset, they'll phone back," but after staring at the phone, which never rings, they move on.

Later, Lifesavers gets a call from a deep-voiced man, actually a transsexual, who wants their address so he can stop by. Citing the rules, that they are not allowed to give out an address, Phillip momentarily slips and blurts out the street address, regretting the action immediately. At home, the poor transsexual, Chris (Liev Schreiber), is being taunted by his family, who are all standing around the living room decorating the tree. The family refers to Chris as Arnold

Schwarzenegger; the depressed young man yells he hates being called that, so his entire family joins in a chorus of "Arnold! Arnold!" as the dejected Chris runs out of his home.

Catherine, secretly in love with Phillip, describes her loneliness in symbolic terms. She says she went to the supermarket, where everyone was buying turkeys, and as she stood in the "10 items and under" line (apparently, single people do not buy much food), she noticed that she was the only one buying a chicken breast. She is depressed that for the tenth year in a row she has nothing to do for New Year's Eve. But as the always optimistic Phillip reminds her, "In every pothole there is hope," something his father told him a day or so before walking out the front door and being run over by a truck selling mixed nuts.

As these vignettes continue, Chris the transsexual arrives at Lifesavers. The phone rings and the daily pervert calls asking, as always, to speak to a woman, always ready to bombard Catherine or Mrs. Munchnik with vivid obscenities. This time Chris answers, "You are speaking to a woman," and the pervert immediately clicks off. When Phillip returns, shocked that his mystery voice on the phone turns out to be a man dressed in woman's clothing, he listens patiently, as trained, to what he/she has to say. Chris finally admits, "I bore everyone!" when Phillip chimes back, "I personally find you very entertaining and informative—perhaps you could come back after the New Year..." Finally, Phillip tells Chris that he didn't have confidence in himself until he entered a mambo contest in 1968 and won, thinking this would be the perfect way to get Chris to leave, but instead the man beams, "Do you have music?" Pretty soon the two are dancing around the apartment, with Mrs. Munchnik coming to after fainting, observing the insanity, and simply stating, "I'm suing you!" Chris rubs Phillip's butt which causes the shocked but polite therapist to extend his rear as far back as possible. However, when Chris lifts and tosses Phillip up in the air, this becomes the final straw. Phillip blurts out, pointing his finger, "This is insane. This is all I do all day is deal with nuts like you!" Demoralizing the suddenly happy dancer, Phillip tries to apologize and says, "In person I'm a disaster." Chris, trying to regain his dignity, exits.

During the climax, the entire family of mixed nuts all converge at Lifesavers, with the exception of Mrs. Munchnik who is attempting to drive away from Phillip, first calling Triple A to fix her car, which won't start, and then getting her windshield smashed when Phillip unknowingly throws a can of fruitcake out his office window, making a direct hit. However, things look up for the woman when a neighbor with three dogs, Mr. Lobel (Robert Klein), comes to her aid and she seduces the willing gentleman on the beach. Back inside, the feuding Gracie and Felix enter, he pointing a gun at everyone. Chris also returns saying, "The crazy person is back," claiming he forget his cape. Chris bravely stands up to Felix, hitting him over the head with his pillow, which explodes everywhere. They both struggle over the gun, but the pistol discharges and Chris is nicked in the foot, although his screams seem to indicate a slow, painful, bloody death. The irate Gracie grabs the gun, stating they have to get rid of all the bullets, which she does by firing the gun haphazardly, afterwards noting that someone is leaning on the door bell buzzer with two distinct bullet holes fired through the front door. Slowly approaching the door, the buzzer still sounding, Phillip finds that landlord Stanley has been shot in the head, and he falls forward, inside the apartment, dead.

Catherine starts to hyperventilate and Phillip runs bath water for her, propping her up on the edge of the tub. The sexually charged woman seductively asks Phillip to undress her for the bath as both of them admit their passion to one another and fall to the cold bathroom floor, alongside the toilet.

The group wonders what to do with Stanley's corpse. They decide to put the body in a burlap bag and use Super Glue to disguise him as a Christmas tree, and plan to carry him out to the boardwalk, set him up and leave, just another neglected holiday decoration. Phillip, in disgust, says that in the six years that Lifesavers has been operating, they have nothing to show for it except one dead body. The entire group carries the tree outside, all acting cheerful and singing "tis the season to be jolly." However, Mrs. Munchnik and Lobel have finished on the beach, and his dogs begin sniffing the human Christmas tree out in the middle of the boardwalk. Now the same rollerbladers from the beginning of the movie return shouting, "Your tree is history." The rollerbladers strike the tree, sending it up into the air, branches flying everywhere. A crowd of people, including the police, gather as the tree hits ground, now looking more like a corpse than the spirit of Christmas. Felix, now with the gun, admits to the crime, and climbs up the side of the building near a neon sign of Santa and his sleigh. Still wearing his Santa Claus outfit, Felix points a gun to his head stating he will blow his brains out. Children begin to gather. Everyone yells up that the murder was an accident and that Felix should not worry, but he states he served time in prison and "I don't have faith in the criminal justice system."

Then in a faith-renewing experience, the downtrodden Phillip, using his best Lifesavers training, successfully talks Felix down asking, "Don't you wish to spend Christmas with your baby?" Speaking from the heart, Phillip tells Felix that today started out to be the worst day of his life, with the eviction notice and $5,000 bill, "But then something wonderful happened... there's magic in Christmas... if you come down, you'll find that out." Gracie yells, "I love you Felix," and when the pistol-packin' Santa does in turn come down, Phillip realizes he is not always a disaster in person. Finally, checking Stanley's bag, the police come over to congratulate the group, "You have killed the Seaside Strangler," claiming all the fish net paraphernalia was located there. Gracie will get the $250,000 reward, enough to give Phillip the $5,000 he needs. The magic of Christmas. The pregnant woman, jumping up and down from joy, finds her water breaks and she goes into labor, delivering her child under a Christmas tree in the town square. Midnight strikes, Phillip wishes everyone Merry Christmas and Felix proposes marriage to Gracie. "This is the miracle," he smiles. Soon Felix is ringing his Santa bell, as the movie ends with all the characters appearing as a wall painting signed "By Felix" as the credits roll up.

This last sequence certainly does attest to the healing and renewing powers of Christmas, demonstrating the movie's late theme that there's magic in Christmas. The fact that an accidental murder is turned into congratulatory slaps on the back and $250,000 reward money travels far beyond reason and believability, but it does illustrate how everything can turn out when filtered through the spirit of Christmas. This huggy-feely change in fortune seems to be the only excuse for making *Mixed Nuts* a Christmas movie. It is dark and even mean-spirited especially in scenes where trained therapists hang up the phone on desperate people with life-or-death needs. Even Phillip early-on seems slightly callous, burned out and sick of trying to help people. Of course, he too is renewed and finds his life's work can be successful and that he is not bound to be a failure counseling people. However, not all the characters seem properly motivated nor even real in this black comedy that only seems to spring to life within the final half hour where the joy of Christmas heals all the ugly wounds inflicted upon the audience during the first hour. It is wonderful to know that Felix and Gracie declare their love for one another before the reward money is mentioned, and it is nice to know that Felix can be successful as an artist by the movie's end, but this sudden transformation from being one of the most dysfunctional couples ever to fall in love seems momentary and tentative, as if the entire relationship could ex-

plode within seconds. Besides, with Gracie giving birth to his son in the public square, how could Felix act any differently. *Mixed Nuts* tries to show how dysfunctional people can come together and help heal one another, all in the spirit of "peace on Earth" and "Ho! Ho!! Ho!!!" Too bad the first hour wasn't as emotionally engaging as the final 30 minutes!
—GJS

The Ref
1994

Like *Mixed Nuts*, 1994's *The Ref* is another twisted Christmas tale, one where the spirit of the Christmas log does not warm the cockles of the heart as much as suggest a means of burning it to a cinder. Director Ted Demme, working with a screenplay by Richard La Gravenese and Marie Weiss, takes a reality-based approach to the holidays, and the tone is anything but "ho, ho, ho." Presenting a bevy of grating, dysfunctional characters that come at us from different directions (the central family, the incoming visiting family, the Baybrook police, Santa Claus-garbed neighbor George, etc.), Demme seems to think that all these ugly interactions can meld into the warm spirit of Christmas if everything is worked out in a tidy fashion in the final minutes of the movie. But ultimately, the mean-spirited and ugly proceedings cannot be erased by a few minutes of warmth and understanding.

Once again the scene is set for an ideal Christmas in small-town America. Framed by a Christmas wreath, we have a high angle shot of the main street of Baybrook, bathed in the warm glow of Christmas lights. The camera pans revealing a manger scene, a

Lloyd (Kevin Spacey) and Caroline (Judy Davis) are held Christmas hostages by Denis Leary in *The Ref*.

Caroline serves a traditional Scandinavian Christmas feast, requiring family members to wear a wreath of lighted candles on their heads in _The Ref_.

chorus singing in front of a church, the Salvation Army collecting money, store fronts showing toy trains and ice skaters, and children running up and down the street. We slowly zoom to the office of Dr. Wong, Marriage Counselor, above the Village Books shop. But this ends the traditional season of peace on Earth.

Inside Wong's office, Lloyd (Kevin Spacey) and Caroline (Judy Davis), the fragmenting married couple, are attempting to talk out their problems. Caroline shares a recurrent dream she has of Lloyd's head sitting on a salad. Lloyd seems offended by such an image, so Wong asks about sexual problems. Lloyd complains that they haven't had sex in a long time, and Caroline adds the same routine and the too fast conclusion led to sexual monotony. Caroline admits to an affair, but seems annoyed that Lloyd expects her to wear the scarlet "A" on her chest. "It didn't mean anything to me so it doesn't matter," Caroline pleads. Lloyd turns to Wong and snaps back, "I think we need a ruling here!" Their problem child Jesse (Robert Steinmiller, Jr.) is mentioned as being a strain on the marriage. Caroline confesses she is not happy in the marriage, while Lloyd states he is very content with things as they are now. She confesses she is disappointed that Lloyd gave up the excitement of running their own restaurant to work for his mother and manage her antiques shop, taking out a loan from "Satan Mom" for 18 percent. The session ends with concurrent obscenities being directed at Dr. Wong.

Elsewhere, a masked bandit is breaking into the safe of a rich neighbor in the community. At first, after opening the safe, the thief is bombarded with a spray of animal urine, but he continues onward. Next, moving another gem, an alarm system goes off, a trap door opens and the criminal falls to the floor below, where he is bitten in the leg by a huge dog, but still manages to escape.

The session is over but Lloyd and Caroline are bickering in the car driving home. "You can divorce me, say I was unfaithful," Caroline states matter of factly. Lloyd, angered, says, "Say you were unfaithful, no, you _were_ unfaithful!" He refuses to grant her a divorce. Halting their bitching long enough to stop in a convenience store, Caroline goes inside shopping, but the very same criminal who attempted to rob the house in the earlier scene holds a gun on Caroline and demands they go out to her car. Forcing Lloyd to drive, the gunman, Gus (Denis Leary), tells Lloyd to drive him to their home. Lloyd and Caroline are still bickering and Gus comments in disgust, "I hijacked my... parents!"

Meanwhile, the incompetence of the Baybrook police department comes into play, as their police chief confesses that nothing ever happens in this town and they lack experience to handle any type of real crime. Starting the on-scene criminal investigation, the Baybrook Police are called off as the State Police are on the way.

Getting home, Caroline tells Gus that their son is due back from military school at any time, and that Lloyd's family is due by nine for Christmas Eve dinner. Of course, Lloyd's very same family is stuffing their faces at some roadside restaurant claiming they all hate Caroline's cooking.

Back at the home, Gus ties up the married couple with bungee cord that Caroline tells him where to find. But even when tied up, the married couple continue to yell accusations at one another, to the extent that Gus has to knock their chairs backwards and startle them into submission. Only when Caroline and Lloyd are tied together, face to face, and Caroline detects her husband's excitement, does she playfully comment she should have tied him up more often.

Gus contacts his older drunken partne, Murray, in a local bar. Murray abandoned Gus, citing the excuse, "I was scared." Not knowing exactly where to go, Gus orders Murray to go to the boatyard and steal them a boat, to escape.

Gus wants a cigarette, and while Lloyd sneers, "I've never smoked," Caroline more softly offers that she quit. Gus then immediately asks Caroline where she keeps them hidden, realizing that the woman is lying. When she confesses where her stockpile is, this gives Lloyd more reason to yell at his wife, but Gus quickly proves that Lloyd is also a liar. When Caroline sees Gus' leg bleeding, she tells him where to find the band-aids, but "use the Ouchless in the green container." Lloyd comments that she will use this trama as her excuse to have her next affair.

Soon neighbor George, dressed as Santa Claus, rings the bell, and the too-jolly man declares, "Bet you thought Margaret forgot you on the fruitcake list," as he delivers his annual present (that in a few moments Gus will spit out when he attempts to eat a slice). Before leaving, George reminds Lloyd to ask Jesse if he saw his baby Jesus lawn decoration which was missing from last year. Of course Caroline is offended that the neighbor would hint that their son stole something, but minutes later, Gus, searching through Jesse's room, finds it hidden in his chest.

Gus mocks the couple, stating "at least I have a skill," that he can break into any house in 10 minutes, leave no prints and get away. The criminal hates the rich. "What do you do?" Gus asks Lloyd, and then Caroline reveals he works for his mother. But Lloyd proudly admits, "Someone has to take responsibility!"

The local police department (trying to solve the case before the state boys arrive) manage to record a copy of *It's a Wonderful Life* over a videotape of Gus in action, literally stealing gems from the vault, identifying him as the burglar. Also, Murray befriends a woman who lives on a boat in the harbor who agrees to take the criminals away, but that the boat needs a little work, and Gus gives them an hour to fix it.

Jesse comes home and is tied up, causing even more headaches for the burglar who declares that the family is ready for *Oprah* and he screams, "I am in Hell. It is the fifth ring of hell!" Continuing, he explains that the robbing of the Willard mansion was going to be his final job. "It sucks when you're 35, have no family, no house, a partner 55 who can't figure out why they took *Happy Days* off the air." He tells the depressed Jesse that he has "opportunities up the ass... everything goes your way." Before the relatives arrive, the local police arrive to check every house for the burglar; but, of course, their incompetence allows Gus to remain undetected.

The family rolls in and all hell breaks loose, with Caroline serving a traditional Scandinavian Christmas feast, requiring family members to wear a wreath of lighted candles on their heads. This is in honor of a female saint who was burned at the stake by the Romans, but when she would not burn, they stabbed her to death. Mother yells, "My head is blistering." Before the main course is finished, mother manages to bring up Caroline's adultery, making everyone feel uncomfortable. Gus turns to Lloyd and, referring to Lloyd's mother, says, "She's a... bitch."

The animosity that threatens to consume Lloyd and Caroline is fueled by his mother, who declares that Caroline is "a selfish woman who thinks only of herself." And Caroline retorts, "Why don't you sleep with him and let all of us off the hook!" But soon the arguing leads the married couple back to the truth. Caroline always felt Lloyd gave up on himself, on them, when he allowed their restaurant to fail. But Lloyd defends his actions by saying, "When the Restaurant Guide Book recommends you to Hindus looking for a fun night out fasting, I closed." Further damning him for accepting the loan from his mother, Lloyd says I refused mother at first, but you were confused and felt we should consider it. Lloyd accuses her of not being able to make a decision, but he made the one he felt was best for them at the time. Lloyd finally stands up to his mother, telling her, "Mother, is it possible for you to shut... up," offering to give her a wooden cross next year, so she can nail herself to it whenever she likes. Gus then sums up his first impression of Lloyd's mother. "I know loan sharks nicer than you!"

Neighbor George returns briefly to complain that their family gives Lloyd and Caroline a fruitcake every Christmas, "and you don't give us a god-damned thing." Charging into the living room, Santa meets Gus' fist and winds up unconscious. Gus convinces Jesse to face up to his problems, "that once you start running, you never stop." Caroline and Lloyd, starting to warm up to each other again, allow Gus to escape to the boat, guided by Jesse. Gus, disguised in George's Santa suit, isn't recognized by the police who call him George. Gus' final words before escaping are, "Christ, I'm never having kids!" And back at home, Caroline and Lloyd give conflicting stories about where Gus has fled, pretending they were tied up by the criminal. As the boat speeds off to safety, a Christmas tree shines from the back of the boat.

True, Lloyd and Caroline are reconciled by movie's end, and Jesse agrees to stay at home and clean up his act. All ends well. Lloyd stands up to his mother and defends his wife in front of her. But somehow, after 90 minutes of Tennessee Williams filtered by way of *Who's Afraid of Virginia Woolf*, this pat, warm little ending just does not work. Too much animosity has been fueled for everything to be tidied up in a cinematic speech or two. Too much nastiness and insensitivity to be so neatly settled after Christmas Eve dinner. Perhaps reality-based humor is a characteristic of the 1990s, but *The Ref* is ultimately hollow and unconvincing, containing several funny gags and comic situations, but overall, films like this one give Christmas a bad name.

—GJS

Jingle All the Way

1996

What do you mean, "No room at the inn"—?! Reckon Arnold Schwarzenegger could've strong-armed some decent lodgings out of that snooty bell captain.

That is, anyhow, if Schwarzenegger were playing Joseph in an Ivan Reitman or John Hughes remake of the Christmas Story.

The *original* Christmas Story, I mean. Heck, hire Sigourney Weaver or maybe Kathy Bates to impersonate the Virgin Mary, and her entourage would wind up occupying the Penthouse Suite at the Four Seasons. Might even get valet parking for the donkey.

"Donkey," indeed! Any Hollywood account of the Nativity, these days, would have to outfit Mary and Joseph with a chauffeured limousine. You know, like the one Macaulay Culkin commandeers for decidedly unsanctified purposes in that No. 2 *Home Alone* Christmas parable. Even the Culkin kid finagles his way into posh lodgings during a cram-packed Yuletide season, and he hasn't any pregnant lady in tow to appeal to those snooty hoteliers' kindlier sensibilities. Pure resourceful deceit—now, that's the ticket. Not to mention the ticket-seller.

If you remember your Gospel According to Luke—and isn't that the whole point of keeping Christmas?—then you'll be hip to the sense of desperate adventure that lurks at the heart of any Christmas worth its mistletoe and holly, by golly. But desperation in those last few days B.C. was an entirely different crock of frankincense from what the motion picture industry has made of Christmas in these last few years before the Millennium.

Joseph and Mary were scrambling for a safe haven to administer the First Coming, and comfort be darned. They took what they could get and made do, on account of it just wouldn't be the godly thing for the Christ Child to be born into the sort of comfort that was taken for granted by the fat-cat Caesar Augustuses and King Herods, who were browbeating the masses with taxation and genocide in those tormented days.

These days, the masses—or the *mass audience*, to use a term more dear to the movies' corporate soul—get their holiday desperation with precious little life-or-death urgency. Arnold Schwarzenegger has, after all, starred in a Christmas movie, one called *Jingle All the Way* (1996), and in it he even has the vaguely Joseph-like role of a father-figure on an urgent quest. Call it a career strategy, a reinvention of one's stardom as one's 50th birthday approaches, but you can't help wondering: Is Christmas dignifying Schwarzenegger, or is Schwarzenegger demeaning Christmas?

The elusive room at the inn? It gets transmogrified in *Jingle All the Way* into a selfishly cherished impulse-purchase gizmo, like one of those queasy reproduction-anxiety Cabbage Patch dolls or some Power Rangers knockoff. And lo, the ex-Terminator finds himself in the undignified position of having to locate this artifact of a passing fad among a dwindling inventory at the eleventh hour—or else. The kid, a figure crucial to any Christmas story, is no holy infant waiting to be born for the salvation of a suffering world. It is a spoiled (albeit somewhat neglected) brat waiting to be placated, lest a hissy-fit be pitched smack-dab in the middle of the season to be jolly.

In the most hype-worthy scene from *Jingle*—an image reproduced larger-than-life on lobby standees and video-store banners—Schwarzenegger looks genuinely terrified of the temperamental consequences as he takes a mad flying leap to grab the last specimen of the cherished plaything, a toy that no doubt will lie busted and forgotten by New Year's Day. Only in the trend-maddened high-concept world of Hollywood would the distinction between Savior and oppressor become so blurred.

But such blurring has been a gradual process of corruption, and it is unfair to blame a miserable little (albeit big-budgeted) movie like *Jingle All the Way* for the misrepresentation that afflicts Christmas on the big screen. Sensationalism sells tickets, and in the cutthroat marketplace of Hollywood's Christmas season—a month-and-a-quarter span that accounts for about 20 percent of a year's ticket sales—*louder* and *schmaltzier* translate to *better*.

Arnold Schwarzenegger desperately seeks a Christmas present for his son but runs afoul of grumpy Santa Claus impersonators (Jim Belushi in center) in *Jingle All the Way.*

Twenty-five major-studio pictures reached the theaters, as direct competition for *Jingle All the Way*, during November and December of 1996, with another 25 from the independent studios jockeying for screens. The situation was practically a replay of the 1995 season, when the earliest and most promising Thanksgiving-to-New Year's contender, Jodie Foster's heartfelt satire *Home for the Holidays*, sank with scarcely a trace. Such overkill has established a pattern that shows no sign of letting up; it is compounded by the studios' habit of loading the final months of any year with pictures that might garner nominations for the next spring's Academy Awards.

Even if a glut makes economic sense, it still takes a toll on the human spirit, which Christmas time is popularly supposed to nourish. "It's a dehumanizingly nerve-wracking season," the comedian/filmmaker Albert Brooks told me on the eve of his Christmas-of-'96 production of *Mother*, a non-season-specific, low-key entry that hung on against formidable odds. Sometimes, quality *does* prevail.

But oftener, it is quantity that prevails. Back in the 1980s, the *National Lampoon* satirist-turned-feelgood-filmmaker John Hughes discovered that ticket sales would escalate in direct proportion to the quantity of mayhem inflicted upon a picture's characters. This revelation was passed along in its turn to Hughes protégé Chris Columbus, who helmed producer Hughes' Yuletide perennials-to-be, *Home Alone* and *Home Alone 2: Lost in New York*. It is here that the template was struck for *Jingle All the Way*.

You know the formula: Macaulay Culkin, playing a child, Kevin, alienated from his own household, winds up unsupervised in both instances. (*Home Alone 2* is more an elaboration than a sequel.) Culkin incurs the enmity of two nincompoop burglars, played by Daniel Stern and Joe Pesci, and then proceeds to bait and bash them with elaborate Rube Goldberg traps.

Now, various parents' groups have registered formal protests about the violence of these *Home Alone* things, but the adults in whose company I've viewed the pictures have seemed merely to waver between amusement and annoyance. It is the children who grow the more impatient, after a while. During one showing, Macaulay Culkin had just visited an appalling show of brutality on one of the bad guys, whose accomplice then stumbled across the screen, calling his pal's name in vain. A little girl in the audience, visibly put-out with these escalating atrocities, shouted at the screen: "He's *dead*, you idiot!"

And a very merry Christmas to John Hughes, too.

Jingle All the Way finds Columbus in the role of producer, with *Happy Days'* veteran producer/scenarist, Brian Levant, in the director's chair. Screenwriter Randy Kornfield's name fits him something beauti-

Howard Langston realizes the only way to square himself with his wife and son is to find the Turbo Man action figure in *Jingle All the Way*.

ful, given the unbearably cornball sentimentality that undermines all the rough-and-tumble silliness on parade here. As with his directorial efforts on the dog movie *Beethoven* and the live-action *Flintstones* feature, Levant brings an insipid sitcom sensibility to bear, with even broader characterizations than Columbus and Hughes usually employ and a tendency to wrap up his set-pieces hastily as if making way for a laugh-track or a commercial interruption.

Schwarzenegger plays Howard Langston, an overworked family man who never quite manages to "prioritize" his own household. The last straw is his unexcused absence from his son's athletic awards ceremony. Langston realizes the only way to square himself with the "fam" is to make certain his impatient kid (Jake Lloyd, who seemed such a charmer in the same year's *Unhook the Stars*) receives for Christmas a coveted Turbo Man "action figure" (read: *doll*, a perfectly okay term that has become curiously under-used despite the prevailing social climate of gender disorientation). Langston looks especially wretched by comparison with a single-dad neighbor (Phil Hartman), who bought *his* kid a Turbo Man months ago—and who pays way too much attention to Langston's wife (Rita Wilson).

The turmoil comes to a head, naturally, on Christmas Eve. All legitimate inventories of Turbo Man are

long since sold out. Langston is lurching from store to store, growing more desperate by the moment, when he encounters Myron Larabee (played by the stand-up comic known as Sinbad), a similarly motivated father. Larabee is an overwrought U.S. Postal Service worker, which should be reason in itself for Langston to give the guy a wide berth. The emotionally stable majority of postal workers should start up an anti-defamation league of their own.

As Langston and Larabee pursue their competitive quests, with each encounter becoming more violent and futile than the last, Langston also runs afoul of a shady Santa Claus impersonator (played by James Belushi), who is hawking factory-reject Turbo Man dolls; a radio personality (Martin Mull) who purports to be about to give away a Turbo Man doll; and an ill-tempered police officer (Robert Conrad) who keeps sidetracking the search and stepping into the combat zone between Langston and Larabee. The central idea of *Jingle*, that "so-what-else-is-new?" notion that a guy just really ought to devote more time to his loved ones, plays itself out during the first 20 minutes, leaving an hour and change to fill with hollow mayhem and sappy philosophizing.

(Violent slapstick, of course, is nothing new in Christmas movies. Edgar Kennedy's 1934 short subject, "Poisoned Ivory"—shown often but randomly nowadays on cable television's Nostalgia Channel—is one of those pioneering cases of putting the *fun* in *dysfunctional* at Christmas time, a loud and even morbid shaggy-dog story.)

To Schwarzenegger's credit, his recent re-definition of himself has brought forth a winning comical presence that cries out for a more substantial story, retaining the one-liner deadpan wisecracks that distinguished his early days as an action-adventure star. Sinbad holds his own, proving himself more than one of Schwarzenegger's stock-in-trade straight-man second bananas, despite the wretched writing of his character. Rita Wilson, Robert Conrad, Phil Hartman and the others register neither as actors nor as particularly memorable "types," defeated by the screenplay's reliance on convenient quick-sketch characterizations.

Where *Jingle All the Way* does deliver the goods is in its energetic consistency with all those early Schwarzenegger actioners of the middle '80s, from *Raw Deal* to *Commando* to *Predator*: The stunt players outnumber the principals six-to-one, and the actionful segments are staged with sufficient inventiveness to help obscure the vacuum at the heart of the story. Vivid location work, including elaborate mob scenes in Minneapolis' massive Mall of America, keeps things interesting on a purely visual level. Another saving grace is the film's wealth of standard "found-object" Christmas blues/pop tunes and newly recorded seasonal gems, including Chuck Berry's "Run, Rudolph, Run" and Charles Brown's "Merry Christmas, Baby," as well as a Lou Rawls track, "So They Say It's Christmas." The soundtrack album (TVT Soundtrax CD 8070-2) comes with high recommendations, assuming that it achieves the "perennial" status that 20th Century-Fox has accorded the film's video edition.

It proved scarcely enough for Columbus and 20th-Fox to mutilate and trivialize the scriptural Christmas Story into the all-but-ultimate commercialization of *Jingle All the Way*. Meanwhile in the real world, the big studio seized upon the inspiration of peddling a Turbo Man "action figure," as if hoping to provoke such consumer desperation as Schwarzenegger and Sinbad experience in the movie. To the credit of the massed public, the toy-store marketing scam fizzled. —MHP

The following films also occur at or have scenes pertaining to Christmas:

Babes in Toyland

Cast: Ray Bolger, Tommy Sands, Annette Funicello, Ed Wynn, Tommy Kirk
Credits: Producer: Walt Disney; Director: Jack Donohue; Writers: Lowell S. Hawley, Ward Kimball, Joe Rinaldi (Based on the Victor Herbert and Glen

Annette Funicello posed for this Christmas publicity portrait for *Babes in Toyland*.

MacDonough Operetta); Walt Disney Productions; 1961

Disney version of the Victor Herbert and Glenn MacDonough operetta upon which the Laurel and Hardy version had been based. Ray Bolger portrays the evil Barnaby, which most critics agree was a bad idea. Bolger is most loved for his Scarecrow from *The Wizard of Oz* and doesn't fit the villain mold.

Although critically blasted, many babyboomers, myself included, remember this Annette Funicello film as wonderfully entertaining and, even if today we watch it with the jaded eyes of adulthood, there is still that little kid in there having the time of his life.

Babes in Toyland

Cast: Drew Barrymore, Eileen Brennan, Keanu Reeves, Jill Schoelen, Pat Morita, Richard Mulligan
Credits: Producers: Tony Ford and Neil T. Maffeo; Director: Clive Donner; Writer: Paul Zindel (Based on the Victor Herbert and Glen MacDonough Operetta); Orion; 1986

Lisa (Barrymore) takes responsibility for her family when her single mom (Brennan) works. On Christmas Eve she goes to the store where her sister works, and while on the way home in a blizzard, is knocked unconscious and lands in Toyland where Mary and Jack Be Nimble love each other, but the evil Barnaby (Mulligan) has other plans for Mary.

Christmas in July

Cast: Dick Powell, Ellen Drew, Raymond Walburn, Alexander Carr, William Demarest

Credits: Producer: Paul Jones; Director/Writer: Preston Sturges; Paramount; 1940

Dick Powell thinks he has won a coffee slogan contest and gleefully spends the money on family, friends and neighbors, making it a real Christmas in July! Trouble erupts when he finds he didn't really win, he was just the victim of a joke. Wonderful Preston Sturges film that is sure to please the entire family.

The Christmas Tree

Cast: William Burleigh, Anthony Honour, Kate Nicholls, Anthony Baird

Credits: Producer: Ed Harper; Director: James Clark; Writers: James Clark and Michael Barnes (Based on a Story by Edward Harper); Augusta; 1966

British film which concerns three youngsters and the adventures they have while taking a Christmas tree to a hospital. We were unable to find a screening copy of this film and had to rely on a description from other sources.

Crooks Anonymous

Cast: Leslie Phillips, Stanley Baxter, Wilfrid Hyde-White, Julie Christie

Credits: Producers: Julian Wintle and Leslie Parkyn, Director: Ken Annakin; Writers: Jack Davis and Henry Blyth; Independent Artists; 1962

British comedy has criminal Phillips join an organization that helps bad guys reform—Crooks Anonymous. He does quite well and ends up with a job as a department store Santa. Things begin to go awry when he is locked in the store overnight and gives in to temptation. This film is unavailable for viewing and we had to rely on other sources for the description.

Dear God

Cast: Greg Kinnear, Laurie Metcalf, Tim Conway, Roscoe Lee Browne

Credits: Producer: Steve Tisch; Director: Garry Marshall; Writers: Ed Kaplan and Warren Leight; Paramount; 1996

Greg Kinnear is a small-time con man who is sentenced by a judge to find a job, which he does in the

Lauire Metcalf, Tim Conway and Greg Kinnear pose with cast members of *Dear God*.

Post Office dead letter department. He is about to rip off some jewelry when his supervisor walks by. Kinnear hurriedly addresses an envelope using a return address he spies on a letter to God, stuffs in the jewelry and accidentally puts in his freshly cashed paycheck. He goes to get the money back, but can't when he finds the woman so desperately in need. He begins to leave when co-worker Metcalf spies him. She is a former lawyer who went off the deep end and ended up working at the Post Office. She still uses her knowledge of law by doing charity work

The workers begin to read the mail addressed to God and select letters of those they can help. A joyful holiday spirit infests the city as people begin to place their faith in God. Everyone that is except the Post Office, who arrest Kinnear and puts him on trial. Metcalf defends him and gets him off after hundreds of postal workers and the Post Master (Garry Marshall) himself show up to speak up for Kinnear.

Critically lambasted, but this is a sweet little film that sends a message of faith and hope.

Diner

Cast: Steve Guttenberg, Daniel Stern, Mickey Rourke, Kevin Bacon, Timothy Daly, Ellen Barkin, Paul Reiser

Credits: Producer: Jerry Weintraub; Director/Writer: Barry Levinson; MGM-UA; 1982

Lelani (Jacqueline Malouf), Amelia Dedham (Elizabeth Allen) and "Guns" Donovan (John Wayne) cut down a Christmas tree in *Donovan's Reef*. (Photofest)

Levinson received an Academy Award nomination for Screenplay for this film that is close to the hearts of everyone in Baltimore as well as anyone who ever spent hours on end sitting in a diner with their friends. The film takes place over Christmas but mostly focuses on a close group of friends and the problems they are having. Guttenberg, about to be married, is such a devout Colts fan that he is preparing to give his fiancée the ultimate Colts trivia test, which she must pass before the nuptials can take place.

Donovan's Reef

Cast: John Wayne, Lee Marvin, Elizabeth Allen, Jack Warden, Cesar Romero, Dorothy Lamour
Credits: Producer/Director: John Ford; Writers: Frank S. Nugent and James Edward Grant; Paramount; 1963

Three old army buddies have settled in French Polynesia where Wayne owns a shipping company and saloon; Marvin sort of hangs around and Warden is beloved Dr. Dedham to the islanders. His grown Boston daughter arrives trying to cheat him out of shares in a prominent shipping company. Wayne, Romero and Marvin, along with Father Cluzeot (Marcel Dalio) trying not to offend the proper Miss Dedham (Allen), pretend Warden's three children are Wayne's.

Christmas is getting closer as Wayne, Allen and the children chop down an island Christmas tree. Christmas Eve they attend services at the local church where a Christmas pageant is presented. The oldest daughter Lelani (Jacqueline Malouf) plays the organ, Lamour sings "Silent Night" and younger children are adorable angels who lead the three kings solemnly down the aisle—the King of Polynesia, the Emperor of China and the King of the United States (Marvin). A rain storm erupts and worshippers casually put up umbrellas and continue the service until the rains become too fierce and poor Father Cluzeot sits on the stage, the leaky roof once again getting the best of him.

Although the film takes place entirely during December, Christmas actually has very little to do with the story. After the Christmas Eve rainstorm, the day dawns bright and clear and Lelani is carried to a beautiful celebration where the island inhabitants are presented to her, including her sister Allen who has forced Father Cluzeot to spill the beans. She embraces the young girl much to the happiness of her father. But it's uncertain whether this is a Christmas tradition or an island tradition. There is also a Christmas day brawl between Wayne, Marvin and British sailors but the fight has more to do with John Ford's love of a good manly fistfight than anything having to do with Christmas.

Ford had seen better days, Wayne and Marvin seemed a little too old to be engaging in roughhousing and there is a definite sexist bent to the film; however, it's still the two Johns, Wayne and Ford, and with that combination the audience is pretty much guaranteed a good time.

Female Trouble
Cast: Divine, David Lochary, Mink Stole, Edith Massey
Credits: Director/Writer: John Waters; New Line; 1975

John Waters pays his own sort of bizarre homage to the Christmas scene in *A Summer Place* when Dawn Davenport (Divine) doesn't get the cha-cha heels she wants for Christmas and throws a tantrum. Over goes the Christmas tree and Dawn begins a life of crime. Warning: View only if you are familiar with (and enjoy in a perverse sort of way) the films of John Waters!

I'll Be Home for Christmas
Forthcoming holiday film (November 1998) that stars Jonathan Taylor Thomas as a spoiled rich kid who hitchhikes cross-country dressed in a Santa suit. He is hurrying home to get a Porsche his father promised him. Along the way he learns the meaning of Christmas and family.

It Happened on Fifth Avenue
Cast: Don DeFore, Ann Harding, Charlie Ruggles, Victor Moore, Gale Storm, Grant Mitchell
Credits: Producer/Director: Roy Del Ruth; Writers: Everett Freeman and Vick Knight (Based on a Story by Herbert Clyde Lewis and Frederick Stephani); Nominated for an Academy Award for Best Original Screenplay; Allied Artists, 1947

Each November third, Aloysuis T. McKeever moves into the vacated mansion of Michael O'Connor (Charlie Ruggles) for the winter while O'Connor resides in Virginia. McKeever's idyllic home life is shaken up when he invites Jim Bullock (Don DeFore) to stay with him. Jim is an ex-serviceman who can't find housing. He has just been evicted by minions of O'Connor, who is tearing down Bullock's apartment building to build offices. They soon take in Trudy (Gale Storm) a girl they think is poor and all alone in New York. Trudy is really the daughter of O'Connor, who has run away. Into this mix comes two service buddies of Jim's and their families. Christmas is ap-

Christmas is celebrated in the O'Connor home by an assortment of houseguests in *It Happened on Fifth Avenue.* (Photofest)

proaching and O'Connor has found Trudy working in a music store. She tells him everything and convinces him to pretend to be poor and out of work so he can meet the man Trudy has fallen in love with—Jim. Jim and his buddies plan to buy an abandoned Army base and turn it into ex-soldier housing. O'Connor is unknowingly bidding against them. O'Connor, tired of doing dishes and following the orders of McKeever in his own house, tells Trudy they must all be out of there the next day. Trudy calls in reinforcements in the form of her mother, Mary (Ann Harding). She pretends to be a cook and keeps O'Connor in line. McKeever recognizes the two still love each other and encourages them to get married. They do still love each other but Mary thinks O'Connor hasn't changed and still loves his money best.

On Christmas Eve, the extended family spends a merry holiday together. Mike and Mary realize how important the little things in life are. Trudy and Jim plan to be married as soon as the deal goes through. Jim is downcast to find they have been outbid by O'Connor and decides to take a job in Bolivia. But O'Connor, whom they all know as Mike, tells him he has managed to get him an appointment with O'Connor. Jim and his buddies are speechless when they find their old friend Mike is actually O'Connor. He signs over the base to them, and the film ends happily as everyone gets what they truly desired.

Like *The Cheaters*, *It Happened on Fifth Avenue* preaches the rich are really miserable and cannot be truly happy until they go back to their poorer roots and join the ranks of the average person.

This film is a Christmas treat that everyone will enjoy. It is not available on video, so you have to scan the television listings hoping it will show up for the holidays.

Jack Frost
Forthcoming holiday film (Fall 1998) that stars Michael Keaton as a father who dies in a Christmas car crash. He comes back in the form of a snowman.

Look Who's Talking Now
Cast: John Travolta, Kirstie Alley, David Gallagher, Danny DeVito, Diane Keaton
Credits: Producer: Jonathan D. Krane; Director: Tom Ropelewski; Writers: Tom Ropelewski and Leslie Dixon (from characters created by Amy Heckerling) TriStar; 1993

The third film in the *Look Who's Talking* series is a charm as Travolta and Alley deal with her unemployment from cutbacks and his new job as a pilot for a sexy executive during the Christmas season. The chemistry between Alley and Travolta still works, now even more than ever, especially in a dream sequence where the couple have dreams of the other fooling around, Travolta with his new boss and Alley with her old lover from the first film, George Segal. The dreams merge and the couple do a "Fred and Ginger" dance routine.

In another funny sequence, Alley has taken a job as a Santa's elf complete with dorky costume and pointy ears. She must deal with rather obnoxious children waiting in line. "Santa doesn't want you to be a naughty girl," Alley tells her. The little girl, hands on hips replies, "Who are you, his mother?" To which Alley replies, "No, I'm a Vulcan, How would you like a little death grip?" This, of course, is an inside joke since Alley portrayed Lt. Saavik in *Star Trek II: The Wrath of Khan*.

Another funny scene has Travolta, Alley and their daughter Julie (Tabitha Lupien) try to cheer up Mikey

John Travolta, Kirstie Alley, Tabitha Lupien and David Gallagher pose for a Christmas family portrait in *Look Who's Talking Now*.

(David Gallagher) who has discovered the department store Santa isn't real. They enter his bedroom pantomiming "The Chipmunk Song."

The talking this time around is done by two dogs, voiced by Danny DeVito and Diane Keaton. The dogs are really secondary to the story; it really could stand alone as a sweet Christmas film.

Travolta's boss is trying to put the make on him and on Christmas Eve makes up a story about having to attend a business meeting in a cabin in upstate New York or 3,000 people will lose their jobs. Of course there is no meeting. Alley discovers this and packs the kids and dogs in the taxi (they still own) and heads off to spend Christmas with James. While yelling at the dogs, she narrowly avoids a tree blocking the road and the car zooms through the snow deeper into the woods. Rocks, the DeVito-voiced dog, saves her from a wolf and then he sends Daphne, the Keaton-voiced dog, for help while he goes to find Travolta. By now

Errol Flynn is threatened by another Santa (Donald Woods) as Lucile Watson, Eleanor Parker and Patti Brady look on in *Never Say Goodbye*. **(Photofest)**

Travolta has finally figured out his boss' motives and, hearing Rocks barking outside, leaves the cabin fired but much happier. The family is reunited at a park ranger's cabin and spend Christmas Eve together. Kids will like the talking dogs, and adults will enjoy the antics of Alley and Travolta.

Love Finds Andy Hardy

Cast: Lewis Stone, Mickey Rooney, Judy Garland, Ann Rutherford, Lana Turner
Credits: Producer: Carey Wilson; Director: George B. Seitz; Writer: William Ludwig; MGM; 1938

Poor old Andy has a problem: two dates for the Christmas dance—Lana Turner and Ann Rutherford. Every boy should have such a problem. Typically enjoyable Andy Hardy film that marks Judy Garland's first appearance as Betsy Booth.

Never Say Goodbye

Cast: Errol Flynn, Eleanor Parker, S.Z. Sakall, Forrest
Credits: Producer: William Jacobs; Director: James V. Kern; Writers: I.A.L. Diamond, James V. Kern and Lewis R. Foster (Based on *Don't Ever Leave Me* by Ben and Norma Barzman); Warner Bros., 1946

Patti Brady is the precocious Flip, an adorable youngster who is trying to get her divorced parents Phil and Ellen (Flynn and Parker) back together. On Christmas Eve, Flynn, wanting to see Flip, locks an earnest friend playing Santa (Donald Woods) in the bathroom, steals his pants and cheerily poses as Santa Claus for Flip. He hands presents to daughter Flip and ex-wife Ellen, and, when it is time to give one to Ellen's mother (Lucile Watson), he says now for the "old bag." Woods has managed to climb down the outside of the house and bursts into the room where he and Phil engage in a rout, as Woods falls right into the Christmas tree, much to the delight of Flip and Phil. On Christmas Day Ellen goes to see Phil hoping to get back together, but leaves when she finds he was planning to go away for a weekend with another woman. Meanwhile, a solider Flip has been writing to arrives (Tucker) to visit, and Ellen decides to use him to make Phil jealous. Flynn has several funny moments; in one scene he tells Flip he is neither Sir Lancelot nor Robin Hood, and, in another, he does a funny Bogart impersonation (Bogart actually dubbed the lines). Of course all ends well as Flip runs away to force her parents together.

Tony Franciosa and Jane Fonda star in *Period of Adjustment*. (Photofest)

Period of Adjustment

Cast: Jim Hutton, Jane Fonda, Anthony Franciosa, Lois Nettleton

Credits: Producer: Lawrence Weingarten; Director: George Roy Hill; Writer: Isobel Lennart (Based on the Tennessee Williams Play); MGM; 1962

During Christmas, Korean vet Hutton marries a nurse (Fonda) who helped him recover from a breakdown. The marriage gets off to a bad start when they have their wedding dinner in a low-class diner and spend the night in an even lower-class motel. Hutton wants to become a partner in a cattle business with his friend from the service (Franciosa), so they travel to his house. But he is having difficulties himself. He got drunk at the company Christmas party and told his wife's father (his boss) exactly what he thought of him. His wife (Nettleton) takes their young son and moves in with her parents. Franciosa comes to realize that even though he married Nettleton for the job, he has come to love her.

Franciosa and the in-laws, along with Hutton and Fonda, are hauled down to the police station when they cause a commotion. Nettleton goes down to settle the dispute and meets Hutton and Fonda. They go back to the house to discuss Christmas for their son. When Nettleton finds a fur coat Franciosa has bought her for Christmas, she forgives him, and they plan to move West to a cattle ranch. Hutton confesses his fears of inadequacy to Fonda, who tells him they have the rest of their life to discover each other, and Christmas Eve ends happily for all involved. It always disturbs me that they all forgot the kid, who was still at the in-law's house. Based on a play by Tennessee Williams.

Pocketful of Miracles

Cast: Glenn Ford, Bette Davis, Hope Lange, Arthur O'Connell, Peter Falk, Edward Everett Horton

Credits: Producer/Director: Frank Capra; Writers: Hal Kanter, Harry Tugend, Jimmy Cannon (Based on the Damon Runyon Story "Madame"); Franton; 1961

Glenn Ford stars as Dave the Dude who believes his good luck is brought on by his purchase of apples from old Apple Annie (Bette Davis). Dude is about to make a deal with Chicago gangster Darcey (Sheldon Leonard) when Annie learns that her daughter (Ann-

Margret), who has been educated in a Spanish nunnery, is coming to New York to visit Annie. She believes Annie is an important socialite and is bringing her fiancé and his father Count Romero to meet her mother. Queenie (Hope Lange) forces Dude to help Annie pull off the charade of the century in this film based on Damon Runyon characters. The film takes place in December, but actually little of the holiday is seen. The film would be the final one for Frank Capra.

This Man is Mine
Cast: Tom Walls, Glynis Johns, Hugh McDermott, Barry Morse
Credits: Producer/Director: Marcel Varnel; Writers: Doreen Montgomery, Norman Lee, Nicholas Phipps, Reginald Beckwith, Mable Constanduros, Val Valentine and David Evans (Based on *A Soldier for Christmas* by Reginald Beckwith); Columbia British; 1946

This British-made comedy is unavailable for screening but *Variety* notes, "Christmas of 1946 finds Bill Mackenzie [Hugh McDermott], ex-Canadian soldier enjoying his holiday in Saskatoon. Greetings cable signed "The Fergusons" is excuse to flashback across the Atlantic to an English village in 1942 where soldier was Christmas guest of the Fergusons. Home is in a pleasant state of turmoil. Brenda has left her husband because he couldn't supply a turkey, second daughter Phoebe can't make up her mind about boyfriend Ronald, ex-maid Millie (Glynis Johns), now in uniform, arrives as a billette and MacKenzie, primed by his Colonel about Anglo-American relations, comes in time to sweep Millie and Phoebe off their feet. Both girls make a bee line for him, having decided that the gloves are off... Final shot shows Millie preparing Christmas for her Canadian husband Mackenzie."

Trapped in Paradise
Cast: Nicholas Cage, Jon Lovitz, Dana Carvey, Madchen Amick
Credits: Director/Writer/Producer: George Gallo; 20th Century-Fox; 1994

With such a talented cast it would be difficult to make a bad film, but not impossible as the creators of *Trapped in Paradise* prove. Cage, Lovitz and Carvey portray bumbling brothers who rob a bank in the peaceful town of Paradise, PA. They manage to crash their car while fleeing and the people, especially the bank president and his wife, are so nice to them they have second thoughts and return the money. Before this occurs however they must escape the clutches of

Jon Lovitz, Nicholas Cage and Dana Carvey are *Trapped in Paradise*.

the FBI, two moronic store clerks and an escaped con who's annoyed they pulled the gravy bank job he had been planning for years. His daughter (Amick), who is a bank teller in Paradise, realizes the trio are the robbers but, rather than turn them in, tries to get them to leave town. The ex-con holds everyone hostage but the slow-witted town deputy saves them as Cage tries to persuade the con to let the innocent people go.

The FBI hauls everyone to the police station but the local townspeople cover up for the trio. Cage stays with Amick while the other two head home with their mother (Florence Stanley).

There are some truly lovely Christmas scenes in this film, and kudos must be given to the art department and set designers for the Norman Rockwellish flavor of the movie. But the film seems to last forever and offers very few laughs amid the misery it puts the audience through.

Turkey Time
Cast: Tom Walls, Ralph Lynn, Dorothy Hyson, Robertson Hare
Credits: Producer: Michael Balcon; Director: Tom Walls; Writer: Ben Travers; Gaumont; 1933

This film is not available for screening. *Cinebooks* remarks, "A durable comedy about two pals, Walls and Lynn, who spend Christmas at the seaside home of Walls' fiancée. Walls soon falls for another girl, Hyson, but is restored to his first love when Lynn also falls for Hyson."

We're No Angels
Cast: Humphrey Bogart, Aldo Ray, Peter Ustinov, Joan Bennett, Basil Rathbone
Credits: Producer: Pat Duggan; Director: Michael Curtiz; Writer: Ranald MacDougall (Based on the Play

Peter Ustinov, Humphrey Bogart and Aldo Ray celebrate Christmas in *We're No Angels*.

La Cuisine des Agnes by Albert Husson); Paramount; 1955

Bogart, Ray and Ustinov are lifers who escape from Devil's Island on Christmas Eve. They intend to rob a store owned by a sweet family, but become so charmed by them that they stay for Christmas and begin to help the father get the store back into shape and make a profit. When all has been set in order, the three decide that rather than face the unknown world, they should go back to prison.

Credits:

Babes in Toyland
Cast: Stan Laurel, Oliver Hardy, Henry Brandon, Charlotte Henry
Credits: Producer: Hal Roach; Director: Gus Meins and Charles Rogers; Writers: Nick Grinde and Frank Butler (Based on the Operetta by Victor Herbert); MGM; 1934

Cheaters, The
Cast: Joseph Schildkraut, Billie Burke, Eugene Pallette, Ona Munson, Raymond Walburn
Credits: Producer/Director: Joseph Kane; Writer: Frances Hyland; Republic; 1945

A Christmas Story
Cast: Melinda Dillon, Darren McGavin, Peter Billingsley, Ian Petrella, Scott Schwartz
Credits: Producers: Rene Dupont and Bob Clark; Director: Bob Clark; Writers: Jean Shepherd, Leigh Brown and Bob Clark; MGM; 1983

Home Alone
Cast: Macaulay Culkin, Joe Pesci, Daniel Stern, John Heard, Catherine O'Hara
Credits: Producer/Writer: John Hughes; Director: Chris Columbus; Fox; 1990

Home Alone 2: Lost in New York
Cast: Macaulay Culkin, Joe Pesci, Daniel Stern, Catherine O'Hara, John Heard, Tim Curry, Brenda Fricker

Credits: Producer/Writer: John Hughes; Director: Chris Columbus; Fox, 1992

Jingle All the Way
Cast: Arnold Schwarzenegger, Sinbad, Phil Hartman, Rita Wilson, Robert Conrad, James Belushi
Credits: Producers: Michael Barnathan, Chris Columbus and Mark Radcliffe; Director: Brian Levant; Writer: Randy Kornfield; 20th Century Fox; 1996

The Lemon Drop Kid
Cast: Bob Hope, Marilyn Maxwell, Lloyd Nolan, Jane Darwell, William Frawley
Credits: Producer: Robert L. Welch; Director: Sidney Lanfield; Writers: Edmund Hartmann, Frank Tashlin and Robert O'Brien (Based on a Story by Edmund Beloin and Damon Runyon); Paramount; 1951

Malice in the Palace
Cast: Moe Howard, Larry Fine, Shemp Howard, George J. Lewis, Frank Lackteen, Vernon Dent
Credits: Director: Jules White; Writer: Felix Adler; 1949

The Man Who Came to Dinner
Cast: Bette Davis, Ann Sheridan, Monty Woolley, Richard Travis, Jimmy Durante, Billie Burke
Credits: Producers: Jerry Wald and Jack Saper; Director: William Keighley; Writers: Julius J. Epstein and Philip G. Epstein (Based on the Play by George S. Kaufman and Moss Hart); Warner Bros.; 1942

The Miracle of Morgan's Creek
Cast: Eddie Bracken, Betty Hutton, Diana Lynn, William Demarest, Brian Donlevy
Credits: Director, Writer, Producer: Preston Sturges; Paramount; 1944

Mixed Nuts
Cast: Steve Martin, Madeline Kahn, Adam Sandler, Rita Wilson, Robert Klein
Credits: Producers: Tony Thomas, Paul Junger Witt and Joseph Hartwick; Director/Writer: Nora Ephron; TriStar; 1994

National Lampoon's Christmas Vacation
Cast: Chevy Chase, Beverly D'Angelo, Randy Quaid, Juliette Lewis, Diane Ladd, E.G. Marshall
Credits: Producers: John Hughes and Tom Jacobson; Director: Jeremiah S. Chechik; Writer: John Hughes; Warner Bros.; 1989

The Ref
Cast: Denis Leary, Judy Davis, Kevin Spacey, Glynis Johns
Credits: Producers: Ron Bozman, Richard LaGravenese and Jeff Weiss; Director: Ted Demme; Writers: Richard LaGravenese and Marie Weiss; Buena Vista; 1994

Trading Places
Cast: Dan Ackroyd, Eddie Murphy, Jamie Lee Curtis, Ralph Bellamy, Don Ameche
Credits: Producer: Aaron Russo; Director: John Landis; Writers: Timothy Harris and Herschel Weingrod; Paramount; 1983

I'll Have a Blue Christmas...

Christmas is a time of great joy, but for many it can also be a time of great sorrow—sorrow that often leads to personal redemption. The films covered in this chapter never fail to bring a tear to the eye and an ache to the heart. As we wipe our eyes, we realize we wouldn't miss these films for the world.

Meet John Doe

1941

In 1941 the world was changing rapidly and the "New Deal" era was envisioned much as the world of today is envisioned: The world was going to Hell in a handbasket. All the apple pie American values that built our country were being reexamined as the modern world created even more political corruption, big corporations squeezed out the little guy, the media's increasing power controlled people's opinions and votes, and the average Joe felt naked and alone. Director Frank Capra created *Meet John Doe* as his tribute to the great working class masses, the increasingly forgotten average guy or gal, the very people who made America the great nation it had become. Those same people who now felt neglected and victimized.

And by placing the plot during the Christmas season, with the climax itself occurring on Christmas Eve, that spirit of brotherly love and the unity of the common people could be symbolized by Christmas itself. Also, though slightly awkward by movie's end, John Doe is recast as a Christ figure, whose rebirth on Christmas Day drives that unsubtle point home.

The movie begins with images of scary changes: "*The New Bulletin*—a streamlined newspaper for a streamlined era" replaces *The Bulletin* when it is purchased by a larger corporation and "40 heads are chopped off" as new Managing Editor Connell (James Gleason) is installed. He tells the startled columnist Ann Mitchell (Barbara Stanwyck), "Sorry sister, I was sent down here to clean house." The feisty Mitchell receives these words as a slap on the face: "I cannot afford to be without work, not even for a day." Espousing the new philosophy the newspaper is projecting, Connell states "people who can hit with sledgehammers" are the type of writers they will maintain. Cold-heartedly Connell demands, "Turn in your last column before collecting your check."

Such a sequence seems more fitting to today's decade of the 1990s with hostile corporate takeovers, downsizing, dedicated workers callously given their walking papers/pink slips. But this was Capra's vision of America at the start of the new decade of the '40s.

American ingenuity takes over as "never say die" reporter Mitchell writes a bogus letter to the paper, her attempt to create sledgehammer journalism. "...but looking around it seems the whole world's gone to pot, so in protest, I'm going to commit suicide by jumping off the City Hall roof, signed a disgusted American Citizen, John Doe. Editor's Note: If you ask this column, the wrong people are jumping off the roofs."

The governor, reading the published letter, thinks the newspaper's new owner, D.B. Norton (Edward Arnold), is out for his scalp. The mayor, in disgust, sighs, "Why did he have to pick on my building," referring to the negative publicity involving City Hall. The mayor is advised to "pull down his blinds," as if out-of-sight-out-of-mind is an effective answer to the problem.

Revealing the truth to Connell, that no such John Doe exists, Ann Mitchell states "you say you wanted fireworks" to which she is told—"Don't you know there are nine jobs waiting for this guy, 22 families want to board him free, five women want to marry him, the mayor's practically ready to adopt him." To which Mitchell shrewdly responds, "There's enough circulation in that name to start a shortage in the ink world." Her gimmick is to have "John Doe" write a column—"I Protest"—everyday in *The New Bulletin* until Christmas Eve, when he is supposed to commit suicide at City Hall. While Mitchell will write the daily column (once she is rehired and given a $1,000 bonus to keep her mouth shut), she suggests they hire an out-of-luck hobo to become John Doe to give visual impetus to the column.

Enter Gary Cooper, America's Everyman, who as John Doe delivers one of the definitive characters of his career. The down and out baseball player (always in bush leagues, never the majors—out of luck

You don't have to die to keep the John Doe movement alive, Ann (Barbara Stanwyck) tells John (Gary Cooper) in *Meet John Doe*.

because of a chipped bone in his elbow which ruined his pitching career), ruggedly handsome but a tad rough and dirty, reduced to riding the rails, cleans up perfectly to fit his proper media-controlled image. His best friend and moral conscience, the "Colonel" (Walter Brennan), becomes that little voice in the back of John's mind that encourages him to do the right thing. Long John Willoughby, "desperate for money," agrees to accept money to say he wrote the letter (rewriting the original in his own handwriting) and is told he will be given a railroad ticket to get out of town on Christmas Eve, his job done.

While the newly christened John Doe thinks his actions are being motivated by practicality, his old buddy the Colonel tells him his soul is now owned by the corporation. "You're gonna get used to all that stuff that will wreck you." Doe stresses that "$50 won't ruin me." But the Colonel digs in deeper: "When you become a man with a bank account, they got you... and when they got you, you have no more chance than a road rabbit." To the Colonel the enemy is the "helots," referring to lots of heals.

Soon the columns begin spinning out daily: "I Protest!"; "Against Collapse of Decency in World"; "Against Corrupt Local Politics"; "Against Graft in State Relief"; "Against County Hospitals Shutting Doors to Needy." And the newspaper's daily circulation increases as the weeks continue.

The governor realizes that John Doe is a myth, but he feels his political adversary (and newspaper owner) D.B. Norton is behind this entire campaign.

And the conniving Norton does indeed have a scheme: to put John Doe on the radio to reach 130 million listeners around the nation. He requests that Mitchell write the radio speeches, to be delivered live in the studio by Doe, and that she answer directly to him and not Connell any longer. But Mitchell cannot come to grips with the subject matter of the radio programs, as her newspaper columns have already tapped into the negativity of big city corruption. But Mitchell's mother (Spring Byington) comes up with a solution: "People are tired of hearing doom and despair on the radio... let him say something simple and real... with hope in it." Her source of inspiration is the personal diary kept by her late husband... "enough in here for 100 speeches," she says, quietly stating that the diary keeps his memory alive for her.

Meanwhile, preparing for the first radio broadcast, the Colonel is working on his friend John. "When John Doe is revealed as a fake, you'll be washed up in baseball [his plan for accepting money is to finance surgery on his elbow to return to baseball]. What about the kids who idolize you?" The owner of the rival newspaper *The Chronicle* offers John $5,000 for getting on the radio and reading one of their speeches, stating the whole thing's a fake, to embarrass *The New Bulletin* and especially D.B. Norton. John's actual speech, prepared by Ann Mitchell, is delivered to him at the station where he can read the speech cold (his preferred choice so his performance seems unrehearsed).

When push comes to shove, even when *The Chronicle* plants a heckler in the studio audience, John Doe reads Mitchell's speech. "I'm gonna talk about us, the average Joes. He's simple and wise... we're the people and we're tough... the little punks who have always counted... we all have to get in there and pitch, to get together with your teammates. It's no miracle. I see it happen once every year at Christmas time—to see what it does to people, all kinds of people. Now why can't that spirit, that same warm Christmas spirit, last the whole year round? If each and every John Doe would make that spirit last 365 days out of the year... we would create such a tidal wave of good will that no human force could stand against it."

Soon grass roots organizations spring up all over the country, so-called "John Doe Clubs," whose members, the common Joes, try to keep the philosophy of the radio broadcasts alive at the neighborhood level. When D.B. Norton observes the power of such clubs, he decides to organize a national John Doe Convention at which time Doe will announce the formation of the John Doe political party, for which D.B. Norton will be their candidate for President of the United States. But Doe, who is falling in love with Mitchell, is afraid that she is in love with "another man, the one she made up, John Doe." And Doe wants her mother to help break the ice to help them get together. But when Doe finds out she is willing to write the speech putting forth the name of Norton for political office, he is disappointed in his foolishness in believing she was decent and pure. Doe is insistent, "They can't use the John Doe Clubs for politics!" Connell, getting drunk at the local watering hole, prepares John for the corruption generated by Norton, showing himself to be imbued with the American spirit and everything that Doe stands for in his speeches.

But Norton tries to remind Doe of the truth: "Get off that righteous horse... and come to your senses. You're the fake, the one who was paid 30 pieces of silver. You're a fake John Doe, and I can prove it." In utter disillusionment, John Doe sputters back to Norton, "You mean to tell me you'll kill the John Doe movement if you can't use it to get what you want... like dogs, if you can't eat something, you bury it!"

At the Convention, Norton, with his money and power, calls all the shots. The newspaper runs a headline revealing John Doe as a fake, Norton pays people to disrupt the proceedings, and he himself appears live to confront Doe with the facts directly. When Doe tries to respond, his mike is turned off and nobody can hear him. The mob grows ugly and starts pelting Doe with trash and fruit. The worm has turned, and John Doe has disgraced the very movement he helped create.

There's only one thing left for Doe to do to prove his honesty and commitment to his cause: commit suicide by jumping off the roof of City Hall on Christmas Eve. Amidst the joyous celebrations of the season, as choruses sing of "Silent Night, Holy Night," as servants wish their employers "Merry Christmas," Norton and his men rush to City Hall to search out Doe. On the other side, a bedridden Ann Mitchell and the Colonel rush to City Hall to try to find Doe before he takes his own life. Ann has finally come around and turns against Norton realizing her love for John.

Of course John Doe manages to sneak up to the 14th floor, the rooftop, and is preparing to jump, but is soon confronted by Norton and his men; he

is told that if he jumps the mayor has orders to remove any identifying articles from his clothing and see that he is buried immediately in Potter's Field, so nobody will know that he even jumped.

John replies, "You killed a John Doe movement— now you're going to see it born all over again... now take a good look, Mr. Norton!" People from the disbanded John Doe Clubs are assembled, having had second thoughts about their too-quick dismissal of a wonderful idea. By now, Ann Mitchell has arrived, pleading, tears streaming down her face. "It's not too late, the John Doe movement is not dead yet. See John, it isn't dead or they wouldn't be here... We can start clean. It can grow big. If it's worth dying for, it's worth living for... You don't have to die to keep the John Doe movement alive. Someone already died for that one, the first John Doe, and he's kept that idea alive for 2,000 years... They're calling to us to keep on fighting... this is no time to give up."

Capra, unfortunately, stretches too far by creating both a metaphor for the common spirit of middle class America and of Jesus Christ in the John Doe character. The fact that Capra links the American spirit

Ann manages to convince John not to commit suicide and then faints from illness in *Meet John Doe*.

and the spirit of Jesus (sort of in the spirit of God is on our side) becomes a little too pat and sugary to drive home the realistic message that the film's harsher tone seems to support. In a sense, *Meet John Doe* seems to echo the spirit of John Steinbeck's *Of Mice and Men*, most explicitly in the line "we're the people and we're tough." The concept of strength from the unity of the Middle Class spirit, all people and their neighbors bonding, comes directly from the Steinbeck classic. But while *Of Mice and Men* (both the novel and the classic Lewis Milestone movie) are serious, solemn, and gritty, *Meet John Doe* seems set to attack all the evils of modern society, so brilliantly illustrating the corruption of corporate America in the film's first minutes, that by the time the John Doe Clubs are formed, and we hear the story of how one grumpy neighbor Sourpuss is revealed to be partially deaf and not ignorant of his neighbors' needs after all, well, the good spirits, humor and warmth seem too simplistic in such a subtle satire of modern society. It's almost as if Capra took the easy way out instead of investigating the hard, brutal problems head on.

However, the idea of using the Christmas holiday as both a metaphor for the message of Christ and of the bonded spirit of working class people across America seems satisfying. The despondency and suicidal urges, which contrast most greatly to the spirit of Yuletide, would be revisited in the superior *It's A Wonderful Life* (also directed by Frank Capra) several years later. But once again, it is the spirit of the people, the solidarity of the working class, that saves a desperate, lost soul. Since John Doe embodies that spirit, when the spirit thrives so does John Doe, but when the spirit strikes out against itself, John Doe himself withers and dies.

Interesting enough, the movie flees to the rural riverside twice, escaping the ravages of the corrupt city, with John Doe and the Colonel seeking the sanctuary of nature's respite to rethink and energize. "Glad we're out of that mess," the Colonel declares sitting near the river bank. And Long John, seeing his surgery within his reach, cries out, "What was I doing up there doing that speech... $5,000 bucks, had it in my hand!" referring to the offer made by *The Chronicle* to expose himself on national radio as a faker. The image fades to the duo playing harmonica duets on the midnight train, poor but satisfied. The song played out? "Hi Diddly-Dee, An Actor's Life for Me!"

Ultimately, Gary Cooper's portrayal of John Doe is so startling because, like all of us, he can be tempted by greed, money, sex and power, but like the best of us, he can rise above these flaws and become someone truly great by looking deep inside and remembering all the values that are part of his spirit and soul. John Doe becomes so much more than a flesh and blood character: he becomes the barometer of the American spirit. The cohesion of people working in harmony keeps him thriving; the corruptive influences that force men to turn against their brother momentarily weaken him. Fortunately, in the optimistic world view of Frank Capra, there's very little chance that John Doe will belly-flop off City Hall. Capra simply bursts with too much faith in the human community to allow that to happen.

But in the spirit of Christmas and the American spirit, would we want it any other way?

—GJS

Roger (Cary Grant) and Julie (Irene Dunne) decide to be married before he leaves for Japan in *Penny Serenade*. (Photofest)

Penny Serenade
1941

Christmas time is the season of both the greatest joy and greatest tragedy in the life of Julie and Roger Adams (Irene Dunne and Cary Grant) in this tear-filled offering from Columbia. The film begins in the present where Julie is preparing to leave Roger. She sadly listens to records she and Roger have collected though the years—records that bring back precious memories.

Newspaperman Roger Adams meets Julie, the girl of his dreams, at a record store where he buys an armful of records (even though he has no record player). They fall in love and, when Roger gets a promotion

Trina (Eve Lee Kuney) sings a reply to the angels in her school Christmas pageant in the heartbreaking *Penny Serenade*.

which means moving to Japan, he and Julie quickly decide to be married. When Julie arrives in Japan, she tells Roger he is to be a father. Roger is a happy-go-lucky sort who takes things as they come. When he receives a small inheritance, he quits his job and tells Julie they are going to see the world before the baby arrives. Julie, thinking of the future, is angry with him and heads upstairs when an earthquake hits. She is pinned under rubble and, when she awakes in the hospital, she has lost the baby and can never have another child.

Roger buys a small-town newspaper, and Julie tries to make a home but her heart isn't in it. Family friend Apple Jack (Edgar Buchanan) engages in a little white lie telling Julie that Roger wants to adopt but is afraid to suggest it. Julie is delighted, and Roger is relieved something has brought her back to her old self. The couple arrive at the adoption home expecting to pick out a baby like they would a head of lettuce. They are crushed when they find they may have to wait a year or more.

Luckily, Miss Oliver (Beulah Bondi) soon has a little girl for them. Roger isn't sure he wants a girl, he had his heart set on a boy, but he melts when the tiny baby grabs his finger. A year passes, and it is time for a hearing for final adoption. The newspaper has

temporarily closed and the couple has no income. The judge is going to place Trina in a foster home when Roger makes an impassioned plea for his daughter. Grant heartbreakingly delivers this speech as a tearful Miss Oliver (not to mention viewers) looks on. The judge relents, and the little family is once again united.

The years pass happily and little Trina (Eve Lee Kuney), a freckle-faced sweetheart, is the apple of her daddy's eye. She is anxiously awaiting Christmas and her first Christmas play. She is too little to be on stage, but happily tells her parents she needs a pair of sneakers because she is to be the voice of the angels. She will push a cloud into the sky and sing a reply to the song sung below.

The big day arrives, and she can hardly sit still as they drive to the school. "I hope we're not late," she worries. The audience is filled with proud parents, not the least of which are Roger and Julie. Apple Jack sneaks in just in time to hear Trina, in a sweet voice, sing her reply to "Silent Night." She starts to move down the ramp when she slips and slides down, offering a sorry smile to her surprised teacher. In the car she is in tears as they drive home. Julie tells her the teacher said she did fine and next year she will be an angel.

145

Truer words were never spoken. The next year, three weeks before Christmas, Trina comes down with an illness and dies. Thankfully we are not subjected to this, merely the convincing sadness of Roger and Julie—which may actually be even more heart-wrenching. Rather than turning to each other in their grief, Roger and Julie can no longer communicate. We ache for them to take each other in their arms and comfort each other, but they cannot get past their own grief, especially Roger. It is pouring rain when a knock is heard at the door. It is a little boy and a soaked mother whose car broke down. They ask to use the phone. The boy is in the school Christmas play. Julie tells them she will drive them, but Roger says the car will have to be cranked and drives Julie and the mother and son. The little boy jumps out of the car (we see his little sneakers) saying, "I hope we're not late."

Roger stops the car in front of a bar and tells Julie to take it home. He tells her he won't be back. He never wants to see anything that reminds him of his prior happiness. Julie can no longer take the strain and decides to leave. Roger does come home and proclaims he doesn't blame her for leaving. He never gave her anything he promised. They are about to leave when the phone rings. Miss Oliver just happens to have a little boy who needs a home.

Watching this film is actually physically draining. Even those who manage to make it though the earthquake, miscarriage and court scene will never be able to hold back the tears against the tide of Cary Grant's grief. His performance was so strong he was nominated for an Academy Award. Irene Dunne also turns in an excellent performance. While Dunne was a huge star in her day, today the average person rarely places her name up there with those of Hepburn and Davis. But Dunne did some absolutely wonderful work in films such as *Show Boat* (1936), *Love Affair* (1939) and her tour de force performance in 1948's *I Remember Mama* for which she was nominated for an Academy Award. In 1937 Grant and Dunne had appeared together in the highly successful *The Awful Truth* and in 1940 they again starred in *My Favorite Wife*—both classic screwball comedies much adored by audiences. Irene Dunne died at age 91, by all accounts a wonderful person onscreen and off.

Edgar Buchanan, perhaps best known as Uncle Joe on TV's *Petticoat Junction*, turns in a fine performance as Apple Jack. When Julie cries under the strain of trying to bathe the squirming baby, he nonchalantly steps in and proceeds to take charge—a wonderful scene that shows the strength of this versatile character actor.

The film was based on a story by Martha Cheavens from *McCall's* magazine and directed by veteran George Stevens, whose work would include *Alice Adams, The Diary of Anne Frank, I Remember Mama, A Place in the Sun, Giant, Woman of the Year,* and *Shane.*

Variety advised, "Exhibitors would be smart to furnish handkerchiefs at the box-office. Incidentally, they had better lay in a big supply. This is the best tear-jerker that has come to the screen..."
—SS

It's a Wonderful Life
1946

A television character sees angels in times of danger and in sadness hears a bell ring, and blurts out "Oh, great, another damned angel just got its wings."

Two nights later, on *The Simpsons*, Homer bellows at daughter Lisa to stop banging out "Hark the Herald Angels Sing" on piano, while the whole town makes monetary contributions to replace the Simpsons' "stolen" gifts.

Yes, it's Christmas time! That's when *It's a Wonderful Life* parodies come out in full force—and they can come out because nearly everybody is in on the joke. After all, in the half-century since its disappointing first release, *It's a Wonderful Life* has become more than just a Christmas classic. It has become central to the American Christmas celebration.

As the story goes—or as George's Guardian Angel hears the story in heaven—George Bailey, our hero, has wanted to get out of Bedford Falls ever since he was a boy. He needs to explore, see the world, build things, make a difference. He wants to play out his life on a grander stage than the one his tiny home-town offers; to do "something big and something important," as he tells his father in their final conversation. Unlike his father, he has never seen Bedford Falls as a place where he can do anything important.

Of course, George never leaves town. While his childhood friends, and even his brother, all carve out successful lives for themselves elsewhere, George can't seem to get away, not even for his honeymoon or the war. External circumstances (and a 4-F rating) keep him in town. And even though many people would still have set out on their own, George just simply has too good a heart to shake the "dust of this crummy little town off" his feet… and let his father's business fold, or the miser Potter destroy the hopes and dreams of the working people of Bedford Falls. Instead he chains himself to the Bailey Building and Loan during the 17 years between his father's sudden death and the Christmas Eve on which he desperately considers suicide; yet despite his hard work and compassion, he still comes face to face with imminent bankruptcy, scandal and jail.

To prevent George Bailey's suicide, heaven sends him the Guardian

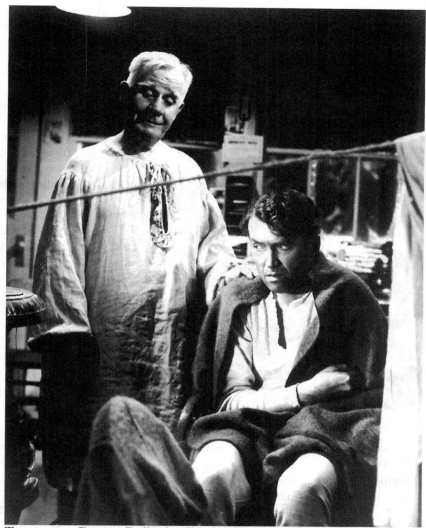

To prevent George Bailey's (Jimmy Stewart) suicide, heaven sends him the Guardian Angel, Clarence Oddbody (Henry Travers), in *It's a Wonderful Life*.

Angel, Clarence Oddbody. Clarence, a "failed" angel, has yet to win his wings (a possible tribute to actor Stewart, who won far more than just his wings as a WWII pilot). But when George announces that he wishes he'd never been born, a suddenly insightful Clarence grants the wish—and George sees for himself the nightmare resulting from his nonexistence.

In this alternate reality, Potter wins. Without George there to stop him, he takes over the town, which becomes "Pottersville." Bars line the downtown. Mr. Martini's nice Italian restaurant is now Nick's hard-drinking joint. Mr. Gower's drugstore turns into a pawnshop. And the Bailey Building and Loan houses a "dime a dance" joint, a hangout for prostitutes and target for the vice squad.

In the hard and mean streets of Pottersville, most citizens devote themselves to self-destructive escapes, having already turned into joyless shells, living on the lowest rung of their potential. Mr. Gower,

George's childhood boss, disintegrates into dereliction; his mother into harshness and suspicion; his uncle into lunacy; his friend Ernie into bitterness and abandonment; and Violet, the "bad girl" with a crush on him, into full-blown prostitution. As Pottersville, Bedford Falls degenerates into a village of the damned. Yet hope still remains that it can return to itself—if George returns to life.

George never learns that the reason his business has fallen $8,000 short in its books is that Mr. Potter willfully failed to return the money to absent-minded Uncle Billy, but he does learn how much his wife and kids and all the people in Bedford Falls mean to him— and even more importantly, he does discover that (regardless of the consequences) he wants "to live again," and bring Bedford Falls back to life. Heaven, of course, gladly grants this wish.

In the end, the "little people" of Bedford Falls (all of whom are deeply indebted to George's kind-

ZUZU BAILEY'S
IT'S A WONDERFUL LIFE COOKBOOK

Recipes and Anecdotes Inspired by America's Favorite Movie

KAROLYN GRIMES as "ZUZU" & FRANKLIN DOHANYOS

Fans of *It's a Wonderful Life* will not want to miss Zuzu Bailey's cookbook by Karolyn Grimes. The book is filled with recipes such as Zuzu's Strawberry Rose Petal Pie and Nick the Bartender's Rum Cake.

ness) pour into the Bailey home on this Christmas Eve to repay their debt… in cash. Dollar by dollar, they bring George the money he needs to avoid financial bankruptcy. But Clarence has already given George an even greater gift: the chance to see the difference his life has made. In helping George, Clarence, of course, finally receives his wings. And the audience finishes the film moved deeply, weeping tears of joy.

And so it should be. *It's a Wonderful Life* carries tremendous power. Producer/Director/Co-writer Frank Capra and his writers took a flat and lifeless story ("The Greatest Gift" by Philip Van Doren Stern) and made it live and breathe. In the original story, small-town bank clerk George Pratt seeks to commit suicide merely because his life is boring. There's no evil miser to combat, no zeal for working folks, not even a bankruptcy looming over his head. These changes are typical Capra, who had built his career on these themes—on vindicating the underdog while showing the power and worth of common people.

The Capra themes, combined with the added resonance of a Christmas setting, give us a film which stands out even in the Capra catalogue. *It's a Wonderful Life*, obviously, is set partly during the Christmas preparation (complete with decorating the Christmas tree). But it also gives us an underdog hero whose life reflects the Christmas spirit. George Bailey lives a life of giving and "goodwill toward men," but that goodwill is sorely tested by Mr. Potter's ill will, and by the growing frustration and bitterness that George feels. In showing the difference George Bailey's life has made, the film invites us to reflect on our own lives, and to hope that we too have made such a positive difference in the world.

The story, then, touches us on many different levels. But the film's power comes not just from the story it tells but from the way it tells that story. *It's a Wonderful Life* was made by one of the greatest filmmakers of his time, using one of the greatest casts anybody could have assembled.

When WWII broke out, Frank Capra had been on one heckuva roll. He had won three Best Director Oscars in a period of four years with *It Happened One Night* (1934), *Mr. Deeds Goes To Town* (1936) and *You Can't Take It With You* (1938). And during his "off years," he directed such classics as *Lost Horizon* (1937) and *Mr. Smith Goes to Washington* (1939). Nevertheless, Capra's optimism and success had also made him a whipping boy for intellectuals, who labeled his work "sentimental" and full of what they termed "capracorn."

When WWII came, Capra served by making propaganda films, and after the war, he and some other filmmaking friends formed their own production company, Liberty Films, and set *It's a Wonderful Life* to be the company's inaugural project, as well as Capra's first cinematic effort following the war. Needless to say, he painstakingly made it a memorable one.

On a four-acre set, he had his production crew "build" Bedford Falls in minute detail. And he selected (*hand*-selected) a cast that could make even the smallest character "live" onscreen. This cast boasted four previous Oscar winners—James Stewart (George Bailey), Lionel Barrymore (Mr. Potter), Thomas Mitchell (Uncle Billy) and Henry Travers (Clarence); two previous Oscar nominees—Beulah Bondi (Ma Bailey), and H.B. Warner (Mr. Gower); and two top character actors who had appeared in Oscar-winning films (including *Gone with the Wind*)—Frank Faylen (Ernie Bishop) and Ward Bond (Bert the Cop). In fact, as Bim (the male nurse in the drunk ward), Faylen had given one of the most memorable character performances in the previous year's Best Picture, *The Lost Weekend*.

Even the youngsters in the main cast, Donna Reed (Mary Hatch Bailey) and Gloria Grahame (our bad

George can't suppress his anger with Peter (Larry Simms) and Mary (Donna Reed) when he goes home to his family after finding the money missing in *It's a Wonderful Life*.

girl, Violet Bick), would carry on the tradition—with Reed winning an Oscar for her supporting role in 1953's Best Picture, *From Here to Eternity*, and Grahame winning 1952's Best Supporting Actress Oscar. Not surprisingly, cast members lower on the bill had been involved—or later would be involved—in excellent films, from *The Maltese Falcon* to *The Invisible Man*, from *Psycho* to *Saboteur*, from *Shadow of a Doubt* to *The Bishop's Wife*, from *Casablanca* or *Best Years of Our Lives* to *Road to Rio*.

Heck, even some of the kids were seasoned pros!

Capra took great care in picking his cast because he wanted his characters to come alive. Though some critics seek to reduce Capra's characters to bloodless abstractions (representing principles of capitalism or socialism or what have you), for Capra "films were novels filled with living people." In his autobiography, he writes that he "cast actors that [he] believed could be those living people… James Stewart *was* Jefferson Smith and George Bailey."

Is it any surprise, then, that George and his world come so vividly to life?—that we laugh and cry at his encounters with Mary and Mr. Potter and Uncle Billy

and Mr. Gower?—that we palpably feel his mounting frustration, or cringe and weep when he finally explodes? That, no matter how many times we have seen it unfold onscreen, we find ourselves so caught up in, and ultimately moved by, his final triumph?

Considering our response to this film, we would naturally assume that *It's a Wonderful Life* became an immediate and glorious success. But legend has it that when this well-loved film first went into release, it received bad reviews, bombed at the box-office and was saved only by the advent of television, where it hit its stride as a classic many years after its theatrical release, following an endless stream of holiday season showings.

This legend crops up in the published film script, which claims that "initial reviews were mixed to poor; *The New York Times* said [the film] was 'so mincing as to border on baby talk'" (a quote actually coming from the *New Yorker*), and that "Audiences took the hint, and ultimately the film barely broke even. It was snubbed at the Oscars."

Is it true? Did the original critics and audiences fail to recognize that *It's a Wonderful Life* is not merely

It's a Wonderful Life **cast photo.**

one of the finest Christmas movies ever made, but one of the greatest movies of all time? Partly. Yes, the film was not the smash hit anticipated (and needed) by fledgling Liberty Films, and yes, television gave the film its status as a Christmas classic; but *It's a Wonderful Life* was not the poorly reviewed, box office horror that the legend indicates.

It's a Wonderful Life first appeared in theaters during the Christmas 1946 season. Even back then, Hollywood moguls were saving their Oscar contenders for year's end, and so within weeks of each other, *The Best Years of Our Lives* (Goldwyn), *The Razor's Edge* (Zanuck), *Duel in the Sun* (Selznick), *The Yearling* (MGM) and *It's a Wonderful Life* all entered release.

In New York City, it had the bad luck of opening in the middle of one of the most astounding box office feats of its time, as *The Razor's Edge* repeatedly hit "all-time highs for any house in the world," and drew in more dough per week than anybody had ever seen. In fact, as luck would have it, *It's a Wonderful Life* competed throughout the country with no fewer than seven of the top 25 box office draws of 1947,

several of which have also become indisputable classics.

The film, though, did receive positive press from most mainstream publications—despite some negative reviews in the more snobbish mags which always hated the director's "capracorn." *Life* considered it a strong Oscar contender, despite the extremely stiff competition. *Variety* noted that "the recounting of this life is just about flawless in its tender and natural treatment," while the reviewer for *Commonweal* defied the reader "not to be moved by" the film. Perhaps the greatest praise came from *The New York Daily News*, whose reviewer proclaimed that *It's a Wonderful Life* "momentarily restored this reporter's faith in human nature."

Movie-going audiences did respond to the positive press. The film played nine weeks in New York, and opened very strongly in Los Angeles and Chicago. Soon afterwards, reports indicated that San Francisco and Minneapolis adored the film, that it was performing well in Providence and Boston, "boff" in Cincinnati, "sock" in Washington, D.C. and "smasho" in Baltimore—where it opened at the Town Theater and packed the new house throughout its first week in operation.

Still, it needed to do better.

After opening well (and what immediate postwar film directed by the hottest director of the 1930s and starring the hottest leading man in prewar America wouldn't open well?), attendance tended to drop off by about 20 percent in the second week, and kept on dropping in increments. At the end of 1947, this 2.8 to 3 million dollar film had hauled in only 3.3 million dollars, and took 27th place among the top draws of 1947. *It's a Wonderful Life* may not have bombed. But it was hardly the megahit that Liberty Films needed—and that its own budget required. And so the "bomb" legend was born.

Nevertheless, it did receive five Oscar nominations—including nominations for Best Picture, Best Director and Best Actor (James Stewart). Some of those same films it had already competed with at the box-office competed against it again for Best Picture: *The Razor's Edge, The Best Years of Our Lives, The Yearling* and *Henry V*. And though most publications favored *Best Years* or *The Yearling*, the *Hollywood Citizen News* bet on *It's a Wonderful Life*, "a definite Academy Award dark horse."

It didn't win, of course. The 1946 Oscars became a virtual *Best Years of Our Lives* juggernaut, running down even Best Actor front-runner James Stewart. But to say that *It's a Wonderful Life* was "snubbed at the Oscars" is a bit like saying that *Mr. Smith Goes to Washington* (or *Wuthering Heights*) was snubbed during the *Gone with the Wind* sweep of 1939.

Regardless of how audiences first received it, though, one thing remains certain: History has vindicated *It's a Wonderful Life*. It is no accident of Christmas programming that new generations give this film their unrestrained adulation.

Capra's brilliant direction and casting, combined with the power of this story, have gained *It's a Wonderful Life*, and its beloved star, a multigenerational following. We, the generations who made this film a Christmas tradition, feel passionately about George: about his warmth and kindness, his suffocating frustration and ultimately his discovery that the same strategically bad luck and painful good choices which have kept him in Bedford Falls all these years have ironically worked behind the scenes to save that "crummy little town" from the hellish nightmare of despair and hopelessness that he finds in the alternate universe of Pottersville.

He, it turns out—George Bailey—had been needed to "fight the battle of Bedford Falls" long before the war. And bad luck (or perhaps Divine Providence) had seen to it that he *was* there to fight it, in wartime and out.

—CRC

It's a Wonderful Life **has inspired many fans to begin collections featuring memorabilia such as dolls of Mary and George Bailey and Clarence (from Target), books, games and Christmas tree ornaments—which happen to make a great fireplace mantel display for the holidays.**

All Mine to Give

1957

While Christmas is a happy and joyful holiday for many people, for others it is a dark and depressing season. Whether through loneliness or sadness, often the days leading up to that special time are gloomy indeed.

Therefore, those wishing to have a good cry or badly in need of a severe lesson on how truly blessed their lives are, should take time to view *All Mine to Give,* a five-hanky film if I ever saw one.

Produced by RKO in 1956, the film was based on a true story first published in *Cosmopolitan* by Dale Eunson and titled "The Day They Gave Babies Away." The story was adapted by Eunson and his wife Katherine for the cinema version.

Starring as Scottish immigrants who come to America are Cameron Mitchell as Robert and Glynis Johns as Jo (most credit lists list Glynis Johns' character name as Mamie, but I swear I heard Robert call her Jo, so that's what we'll go with), often referred to as the Missus or Lassie. Johns and Mitchell turn in outstanding performances as a truly loving husband and wife in this touching dramatization. Mitchell is especially poignant as the proud papa of an ever-increasing brood. Glynis Johns has had a varied film career but is probably most remembered for her role as Mrs. Banks, crusading mother of Jane and Michael, in the award-winning 1964 Disney film *Mary Poppins.* Cameron Mitchell was fresh from a sensitive performance as Johnny Alderman, the one true love of singer Ruth Etting (Doris Day), in 1955's *Love Me or Leave Me.*

The young couple, against the advice of their families, pin all their hopes and dreams on an invitation from an uncle to the New World. As they arrive in the small town of Eureka, they are crushed to discover the uncle has been killed in a house fire just three weeks earlier. As they sit desolate on the charred remains of the cabin, the town doctor Dr. Delbert (Ernest Truex) and his wife (Sylvia Field) arrive and insist the couple stay with them. Robert and Jo decide to stay in Eureka, have their baby, start a new life and rebuild the cabin.

As they battle to rebuild the cabin, desperately struggling to finish before winter and the arrival of the baby, their neighbors arrive to help construct the home. Time to pull out that first handkerchief. The film reminds us of the spirit and kindness of the early pioneers as well as how strong and decent our forefathers were.

Immediately after Robbie is born, Robert travels all night to his new job in a logging camp. The tough Irish boss (Alan Hale, a long way from *Gilligan's Island*) and Robert are destined to come to blows, which they do in a good old-fashioned John Ford–style fistfight whose outcome (like that of Ford's *The Quiet Man*) results in newfound respect between the two.

Robert does manage to return home occasionally, which results in the birth of Jimmie, followed soon after by Kirk. The family continues to grow and Robert quits the logging camp and begins a boat-building business. Mother, desperate to learn to read, starts school alongside Robbie. Kirk is soon followed by Annabelle, Elizabeth and Jane.

Life was difficult for families back then, and the rapidly growing children are whisked away by Robert when the doctor places a green quarantine cloth on the front door of the little home—Kirk has come down with diphtheria. Robbie (Rex Thompson), approaching his teenage years, realizes Kirk could die. He watches as his father learns Kirk is getting well, and they can soon return home. Later, Robert, alone on the porch, breaks into tears. Time for the second hanky, but don't put it away just yet. The family reunion is not the joyful one imagined. Robert and Jo, both tired and overwrought, have words because the children are so dirty, and Robert storms out of the house. Robbie explains their pa did the best he could and Jo, realizing she has been too rough on her husband, hurries to find him. She finds Robert in the barn, coughing violently. While Kirk has recovered, Robert is not so lucky.

The funeral is held in the pouring rain. The six children sit together, the rain mixing with their tears. This scene is especially difficult to watch for anyone who vividly remembers burying a truly loved father. The feelings of loss and rage are almost unbearable, long-buried emotions that immediately resurface while viewing *All Mine to Give.*

Jo begins sewing to help support the family, and Robbie begins sweeping up at the lumber mill, but soon Jo too is overcome by typhoid fever. The children try to take care of her; but, with Christmas fast approaching, she asks Robbie to bring the family to her. He frantically sends Annabelle to fetch Jimmie and Kirk, who are two of the wise men in the town Christmas pageant. The children gather around their dying mother, who mistakes them for her own brothers and sisters after whom her children were named. Robbie angrily pushes them from the room.

She regains her senses and speaks to Robbie:

"Your brothers and sisters have to have homes, good homes, where they're wanted and loved. I want you to decide where they're to be offered. Place them with families that have children of their own. So they won't be so lonesome for each other. Robbie, I don't know

Jimmy (Stephen Wootton) and Kirk (Butch Bernard) are fetched from the church Christmas pageant to the side of their dying mother in *All Mine to Give*.

what I would have done without you. You've truly been a man of the house and find a good place for yourself."

Jo is buried on Christmas Eve as the church bells toll mournfully in the background, and the children convince the town adults to allow them to stay together one last Christmas. Could this film get any sadder?

It is at this point the filmmakers pulled in the reins and rapidly brought about the conclusion, perhaps thinking the audience could not take much more emotional onslaught. Unfortunately, this hasty conclusion is where the film begins to break down. We have come to care for Robbie (played competently by Rex Thompson, who had appeared with Jean Simmons in 1953's *Young Bess* as young King Edward and as Anna's son in *The King and I* [1956 with Deborah Kerr and Yul Brynner]) and the rest of the children. *All Mine to Give* would be Thompson's last film appearance as well as the last film role of Stephen Wootton. Wootton played the freckled-faced Jimmie, who brought smiles to viewers as he tried to avoid the attentions of little blonde twins who constantly fol-

lowed him around telling him he was cute, the kiss of death to young boys.

The children return home and Robbie reads them "The Night Before Christmas" until they have all fallen asleep, all except for Jimmie. As "Silent Night" is heard in the background, Robbie fetches the slate from his mother's room and, with Jimmie sitting alongside, begins to make a list of families that would take the children.

> "Tomorrow's the best day for me to do what mama told me."
> "But tomorrow's Christmas," Jimmie responds.
> "That's just it. On Christmas we ought to get just about anybody we want to take any of us in, you see."

Robbie takes Annabelle to the Tylers who have two sons but no girls. They are just saying grace over their Christmas dinner when Robbie knocks. Annabelle was played by Patty McCormack, who had been nominated for a Best Supporting Actress Academy Award the previous year for her performance as

Robbie (Rex Thompson) finds a home for baby Jane in *All Mine to Give*.

the demented Rhoda Penmark in *The Bad Seed*. He tells the Tylers she is a hard worker and knows her ABCs, which she annoyingly begins to recite. The Tylers gladly accept, as Mr. Tyler thanks the Lord for this unexpected blessing and Annabelle nonchalantly removes her coat and gloves. She doesn't even glance up as Robbie leaves. Robbie takes their old cow to Dr. Delbert in payment of his care of Kirk, father and mother. Dr. and Mrs. Delbert tell him they would be happy to take any of the children, but he politely implies they are too old.

He meets Jimmie, who is pulling Elizabeth on a sled. The family they had chosen for her was not home. They see a couple, the schoolmaster and his wife approaching in a sleigh, and stop and ask them if they would like to take Elizabeth. The woman happily bundles up the child, and they drive away. Jimmie notes, "She didn't even wave."

They go back to the cabin where Kirk is frantic as the town busybody, Mrs. Runyon (Reta Shaw), has decided to take baby Jane away. The three boys line up in front of the door and block her way until she angrily departs. They must hurry since she will cre-

ate trouble, causing Robbie to be unable to fulfill his mother's dying wish.

Since Kirk has a talent for music, Robbie orders Jimmie to take Kirk (Butch Bernard) to the only couple in town who have a piano. Kirk sobs saying he doesn't want to go, but Robbie yells at him and forces them to leave. When Jimmie returns, Robbie has finished dressing baby Jane and tells Jimmie he is taking her to a town 10 miles away and then he will be going to work at the lumber mill. Jimmie is to ask the family with the annoying twins to take him. They part in the snow as Jimmie asks Robbie to come to see him. Robbie answers that he will, but we don't really believe him. He pulls the baby 10 miles through the falling snow until he spies a homely little cabin with the sound of children's laughter. He knocks on the door and asks the strangers if they want the baby.

This is the part of the film I find most difficult to accept; and, after wallowing through a box of tissues, I was a little annoyed with the ending. While my brothers and sisters and I fought like cats and dogs when we were kids, the bond between siblings is a strong one, and I can't accept children who just lost

154

their mother and then are plopped down in new homes showing such little emotion. Also, I don't think Robbie would just drop off the baby at a house that looked happy. While we were growing up, our baby sister was our pride and joy, and we would have fought like tigers to protect her. Finally, Robbie knew his mother wanted nothing more than for him to return to school. Since he struggled so hard to fulfill her last wish, I don't think he would have ruined it by working in a logging camp, an idea she detested. A more satisfactory ending would have had Robbie give the baby to a family in town and live with Dr. Delbert. The children could have kept that special family bond, and we would have had a somewhat happy ending rather than Robbie walking alone in the falling snow pulling that sad little sled on Christmas Day.

—SS

The Apartment

1960

The Apartment, winner of the Academy Award for Best Picture (1960), is a classic adult comedy conceived and executed by the exceptional Billy Wilder (director and co-writer, with I.A.L. Diamond). Ushering in what became known as the swinging 1960s, The Apartment has the look of a hip 1950s comedy with 1960s sensibilities and mores. Surprisingly, most audiences forget that at least 50 percent of the movie occurs during the Christmas holidays, specifically on Christmas Eve and Christmas Day. And while The Apartment is not Christmas-oriented in either sentiment nor attitude, the holiday still plays a pivotal part in the story's development.

The movie begins on November 1, 1959, in New York City, on the 19th floor, desk 861, of the Consolidated Life Insurance Company, where chief focus C.C. "Bud" Baxter (Jack Lemmon) works for $94.70 week. However, the three-year-employed rising star often stays an hour or so working overtime at the office, not because he is dedicated, but because he "loans" out his apartment to his "higher-ups" since he finds it difficult to say no, and maybe, just maybe, these types of favors may lead to promotion at the firm. Baxter is specific that Mr. Kirkeby (David Lewis, III) and switchboard operator Sylvia (Joan Shawlee) must be out of his place by 8, but at 8:45 Kirkeby is just pulling up her dress zipper, trying to push her along. Asking whose apartment this is, Kirkeby states, "Some snook who works in the office." Getting Sylvia outside, Kirkeby offers to drive her to the subway, but she snaps back, "Like Hell you will, you will buy me a cab!" Asked if he brings other girls up here, he says, "Certainly not. I'm a happily married man!"

The neighbors in the apartment house, especially next door snoops Doctor Dreyfuss (Jack Kruschen) and wife (Naomi Stevens), think Baxter is a playboy with an insatiable appetite for sex. "From what I hear through the walls, you got something going for you every night—and sometimes there's a twilight double-header... Slow down, kid," the Doc advises, enviously.

Turning in for the night, taking a sleeping pill, after a quick TV dinner and a flip of the television dial, Baxter is again disturbed by another office superior Mr. Dobisch (Ray Walston) who phones to say he just got lucky with a Marilyn Monroe look-alike in a joint on 61st Street, and he needs to use the apartment for about 45 minutes. After he pauses his phone conversation to say a few words with the buxom sexpot, he yells back into the phone, "Make that 30 minutes!" He says his monthly efficiency-rating report puts Baxter into the top 10, and that could mean a promotion. Baxter dresses quickly and exits the apartment, falling asleep on a nearby park bench. Doc comes home, hears commotion in Baxter's apartment, and yells to the wife, "Mildred, he's at it again!"

However, the next day at work Baxter has a cold, having been locked out of his apartment because Dobisch forgot to place the right key under the front door mat, causing Baxter to awaken his landlord at 4 a.m. after staying outside for most of the night. As he flirts with attractive elevator operator Fran Kubelik (Shirley MacLaine) whom Baxter has the eye for, she advises, "You should have stayed in bed this morning." While he counters with, "I should have stayed in bed last night."

Baxter, expecting his hoped-for-raise, is summoned to come up to the 27th floor to meet with Director of Personnel, J.D. Sheldrake (Fred MacMurray). Very excited and energized, Baxter asks elevator operator Fran if he looks okay, and she compliments him, putting a carnation in his lapel. Going into Sheldrake's office turns out to be a different experience than anticipated. "What makes you so popular... look, I'm not stupid!?" Sheldrake inquires, recounting a story of a former office employee as popular as Baxter who was found out to be doing a bookie operation and was immediately fired. Baxter smiles and tries to play this off. "There's a certain key to a certain apartment— do you know who this key belongs to—loyal, resourceful, cooperative C.C. Baxter!" Volunteering to explain how his "loaning" out of his apartment originally begun, Baxter states that over a year ago, when he was attending night school, one of the employees was attending a banquet and needed a place to change into a tux. Pretty soon, Baxter recounts, everyone was attending banquets, and he couldn't say yes to one without saying yes to everyone. "The whole thing got out of hand," but Baxter sputters, "Never again, I can promise you that!" Sheldrake, over the phone, tells his wife he won't be home until late, that the branch manager from Kansas City is in town, and he is taking him out to see the latest hot play, *The Music Man*. However, smiling after the phone conversation, Sheldrake offers Baxter two tickets as a swap in order for him to use the apartment tonight, keeping all this hush-hush, of course. "I see a shift in personnel next month; I see you as executive material."

Hoping to share his good fortune with another, Baxter goes to Fran and asks her to join him tonight to see *The Music Man*; but she states she has to meet a man tonight, but that she will meet him in the theater lobby by 8:30. Surprisingly, when Fran journeys to the bar to meet her man, it turns out to be Mr. Sheldrake himself, the man with whom she is having an extra-marital affair. It seems last summer, when his wife and kids were away, Fran and Sheldrake had a fling which lost momentum when the family returned. It's been a month since they last met, and Fran is anxious to end the relationship. "It's over," she pleads, but Sheldrake says, "I never said goodbye." Sheldrake confesses he spoke to his lawyer, but Fran cuts in, "Jeff, I never asked you to leave your wife, if you just tell me you love me." Immediately he responds, "You know I do." Turning on the charm, Sheldrake convinces Fran to continue things and to forget about her date tonight and take a cab with him. Leaving as a new crowd of people enter, Sheldrake is unaware that his secretary sees the two of them together. Lingering and lonely outside the theater, Baxter waits for the date that never arrives, unaware that she is with his boss in Baxter's own apartment.

The next day, Baxter gets a new office and a promotion and Sheldrake comes in to congratulate him and thank him for the use of the apartment. Baxter returns a compact with a broken mirror that Sheldrake's lady friend left at his place, Sheldrake laughing that she threw it at him. "You see a girl a couple times a week, just for laughs, and right away they think you're gonna divorce your wife... is that fair!" Sheldrake explains.

But what does all of this have to do with Christmas, you ask!

All the switchboard operators are wishing customers "Merry Christmas" as a Christmas party is in full swing on the 19th floor with workers singing "Jingle Bells," dancing on desk-tops, making out in side offices, drinking and eating. Baxter offers Fran a seat. She notes that Baxter has been avoiding her elevator. He tells her he was very much hurt when she stood him up on their theater date. He says she is tops decency wise, but she counters that just because she wears a uniform doesn't make her a Girl Scout. Soon Miss Olson, Sheldrake's secretary, takes Fran aside and tells her she was Sheldrake's "ring-a-ding-ding" four years ago, and she lists the women who came both before and after her. Baxter soon escorts Fran into his new office, asks her if she likes his new junior executive derby hat—which she does—and asks her out for a date. But Fran tells him she's having a bad day, and Baxter understands that the Christmas holiday means family, but perhaps some other time. Opening her compact to show him how he looks in his derby, Baxter notices the cracked mirror and instantly realizes who Sheldrake's date was, although he never lets on he knows anything; but he appears confused and hurt. Referring to the cracked mirror, Fran says, "It makes me look how I feel."

As Baxter, feeling pretty low, leaves the office party, now featuring a young lady stripping on an office desk, he goes to a crowded bar, alone in his thoughts, as a fairly drunk and rugged Santa rings his bell, disrupting Baxter's mood. Soon a party-girl looking for a wild time approaches Baxter. She tells him that her husband Mickey, a jockey, is being held prisoner in Castro's Cuba, and she is depressed and wants to celebrate to forget. "No action, dullsville," Margie MacDougall (Hope Holiday) complains. Suggesting sexual companionship, she states a night like this spooks you when you walk into an empty apartment. Baxter counters, "I said I had no family. I didn't say I had an empty apartment."

Meanwhile, Sheldrake and Fran are back at Baxter's apartment. She tells him what Olson told her, and he tells her that after 12 years of marriage it is difficult to ask his wife for a divorce, that she must be patient. "It's Christmas Eve. Let's not fight," Sheldrake implores her. Instead of giving her a present, he reaches into his wallet and hands her $100, telling her to get something she wants. Then he reminds himself, it's quarter to seven, time to go home and decorate the Christmas tree with the family. Slipping her coat back on, she frowns and says, "Okay, I just thought as long as it was paid for," referring to the cash offered and his leaving without having sex. "Don't make yourself out to be cheap," Sheldrake admonishes. Wishing her a Merry Christmas, he pops out the door. She puts on a record, washes her face in the bathroom, and finds a bottle of sleeping pills, which she stares at longingly.

Back at the bar, everyone has gone home, but Baxter and his floozy are still dancing, until the manager kicks them and Santa Claus out. "Your place or mine," Mrs. MacDougall asks. Baxter decides on his, since everyone else goes there. Once there MacDougall and Baxter get drinks, start to dance, but when Baxter finds Fran unconscious on his bed with the bottle of pills nearby, he throws MacDougall out and gets the doctor, who knows how to treat such overdose victims. "If you came home half an hour later, you would have had quite a Christmas present," the doctor reveals. However, the crisis passes after they

C.C. Baxter (Jack Lemmon) nurses Fran (Shirley MacClaine) back to health on Christmas Day in *The Apartment*. (Photofest)

force her to throw up, drink coffee and walk. The doctor tells Baxter to allow Fran to sleep for the next 24 hours or so. Baxter phones Sheldrake to tell him about the suicide attempt, but Sheldrake is with his family and could not care less about Fran, telling Baxter to take care of things himself. When she wakes up Christmas morning, Baxter tells her, "It's always nice to have company for Christmas," rattling off a string of dull, lonely Christmases of the past. Confessing she still loves Sheldrake, she just wants Baxter to return his $100 to him, telling Baxter, "I think I'm going to give it all up... why do people have to love each other anyway?" She bemoans her talent for falling in love with the wrong guys. She wonders aloud why she can't fall in love with somebody nice like Baxter. He wonders the same thing.

Soon Fran begins to understand that there are two types of people, the "takers" and "those being took" and those being took cannot help it. She says that Sheldrake is a taker, realizing this after she speaks to him on the phone when he brushes off her life-threatening pill overdose. Baxter states he once bought a pistol to kill himself over a girl, accidentally shooting himself in the knee instead. He confesses he couldn't

bend the knee for a year, but "I forgot the girl in three weeks."

Back at the office the day after Christmas, Sheldrake fires the loose-mouthed Miss Olson, but she goes right to Sheldrake's wife and spills the beans. The wife immediately leaves Sheldrake. However, he tells Fran he left his wife for her. Fran, being tentative and cautious, tells him that nothing can happen until after his six-week quickie Reno divorce. Sheldrake approaches Baxter about using his apartment with Fran for New Year's Eve, but he flat out refuses: "Sorry, you're not going to bring anyone to my apartment, *especially* Miss Kubelik." In anger, Sheldrake tells Baxter that he could be on the street again in 30 seconds, and Baxter hands him his newly earned executive washroom key, saying, "I'm all washed up around here," quitting his position, going home and packing.

Dressed up and partying with Sheldrake on New Year's Eve, Fran hears the story about Baxter and his loyalty to her, and she disappears from his table moments after the clock strikes midnight. Running at full speed down the street with a smile on her face, Fran runs up to Baxter's apartment, but seconds from knocking on his door, she hears a loud bang, as if a pistol discharged. As she knocks frantically on the door, Baxter opens it holding a fresh bottle of champagne. Telling Fran that he absolutely adores her, she smiles and tells him to shut up and deal the cards.

Christmas, occupying about half of *The Apartment*'s running time, becomes pivotal for contrasting the new-founded morality of the 1960s (unemotional sex, extra-marital affairs, prostituting oneself to get ahead in business or a career, lonely singles living without the comfort of families) to the traditional morality which the Christmas season embraces (love and commitment, the family, love before career, the importance of self-esteem). Pivotal movements in this movie involve the Christmas season. When Sheldrake gives Fran $100 in cash as a Christmas present, this pay-off makes Fran feel dirty, and she sees herself as Sheldrake sees her, as a night of cheap diversion. Meanwhile, Baxter, alone and drinking in a bar on Christmas Eve, accepts the drunken comfort of Mrs. MacDougall more out of loneliness and the fear of being alone on Christmas than because he needs or wants the cheap sex. In fact, the relationship between Fran Kubelik and C.C. Baxter matures and grows over Christmas Eve night and Christmas Day, after Baxter first saves her life and then gets to really know her from their quiet little chats and card-playing episodes. The Christmas spirit shakes both of these singles out of their stagnated, morally depressing modern existence and reminds them of the relationship that might be if only they take the chance.
—GJS

The Christmas Tree
1969

"Pascal, I'll go to any length—I'll go to *great* lengths—to make you happy..."

Terence Young's *The Christmas Tree* (1969), in which, with the above line, movie father William Holden acknowledges far more than he knows in reluctantly agreeing to an ill-fated beach outing with his young son, features one of the most unlikely premises for a Christmas film ever—which, amid the likes of *Silent Night, Deadly Night* and *Santa Claus Conquers the Martians*, is saying a great deal. Though ostensibly a film for children, or at least families, it's hard to imagine many youngsters counting this downbeat little melodrama on their list of Yuletide favorites, and it comes as no surprise that so few adults recall it with the same enthusiasm reserved for such timeless hits as *A Christmas Story* and *It's a Wonderful Life*. Holiday films typically leave one smiling, not sitting in stunned silence, yet *The Christmas Tree* practically aims for outright tragedy, evidently on the theory that watching a once healthy schoolboy sink

slowly toward death has the power, if not to lift the viewer's spirits exactly, then at least to touch him, move him, stir his senses a little.

And, in fact, *The Christmas Tree* (a.k.a. *When Wolves Cry*), based on the novel by Michel Bataille, *is* remarkably affecting in its own way, with a final image—stolen zoo wolves howling from within a wintry French chateau upon a small boy's death, the lad's huntsman-like, crimson-costumed body discovered by his father under the Christmas tree—so exquisitely heart-rending it's almost guaranteed to reduce even the most unsympathetic viewer to tears. It's the sort of film that sneaks up on a person; no sooner has he decided its quiet, leisurely pace simply isn't working, then those extraordinary closing five minutes arrive and, shattered, he's left sobbing with despair.

The Christmas Tree is also, despite our learning the boy's disease is incurable early on, one of the most unpredictable holiday films ever, largely because it squeezes in so many elements far too odd to ever anticipate: beaches, wolves, horses, dying children, exploding aircraft, scout troops, mineral water, tractors, hospitals—even atomic radiation. In theory, such spontaneity should make for a great film (and even here it makes a good film), but its very out-of-nowhere strangeness also can't help sending *The Christmas Tree* a tad off course, makes it too puzzling to succeed completely. Replace the word women with such unlikely match-ups as tractors, airplanes and A-bombs, and perhaps its young hero says it best: "Women and wolves don't mix."

Indeed, it takes only about 10 minutes before one starts to realize how unconventional *The Christmas Tree* really is. After a relatively traditional opening in which 10-year-old Pascal (Brook Fuller), welcomed home at a French depot by his millionaire father (William Holden) and the man's beautiful girlfriend Catherine (Virna Lisi), happily plans a fun father-and-son summer away from boarding school while the three dine out; the film suddenly obliterates all expectations and—to our utter amazement—takes an abrupt left turn into near-science fiction. Pascal and his father cheerfully are next seen swimming and sunbathing in sunny Corsica when, alone briefly, Pascal absorbs an invisible wave of lethal radiation when an atomic bomb-carrying military plane explodes nearby. The strange juxtaposition of two so vastly dissimilar situations is at once aesthetically awkward and undeniably startling, and the viewer, flung headlong into *Fail Safe* territory, is suddenly left feeling he's watching another film entirely, dropped into some sort of atomic tragedy *Love Story*-type tearjerker whose focus is on how Pascal's father devotes time and money making his leukemia-laden, doomed child's last six months carefree, blissful and fun.

Unique as it sounds, of course, *The Christmas Tree* isn't the only film ever to combine atomic imperilment and childhood death into a single story (remember 1983's *Testament*?), but put together, the two motifs still make quite an uneasy mix. Indeed, *The Christmas Tree* relates its unhappy tale by way of so many incompatible ideas it never adds up to a smooth, fully satisfying whole. Sort of half *The Amazing Colossal Man*, half *Lorenzo's Oil*, the film delivers ever-weirder material at every turn (in one scene, Pascal is attacked by a terror-maddened horse, a beast then shot to death after a pair of wolves, yes, wolves, charge in and attack the horse in turn), and while such disparate images are woven together better than one might expect, even the most deep-thinking symbol-hunter may still find his or herself hard-pressed to figure out just what this all means.

The Christmas Tree aims for outright tragedy as we watch once healthy schoolboy Pascal (Brook Fuller) sink slowly toward death.

What it all means, apparently, has something to do with the grim cruelties of blind chance ("People need good luck, don't they?" observes Pascal. "They sure do," his father agrees). It also looks at the civilian risks of a worldwide arms race (in the film's closing seconds, and earlier, the screech of overhead jets reminds us that weapons of mass destruction may casually crisscross our skies even now); and the instinctual, "call of the wild"-type courage of childhood (while the adults curse his pitiable fate, Pascal, brave beyond his years, lives for now). Despite the best intentions of writer-director Terence Young, however (yes, the Terence Young, of *Dr. No, From Russia With Love* and *Thunderball* fame), even if we do "get" what the film is trying to say, it ultimately says too much for all of it to really gel. In what other film would a little French boy die from a parachute-harnessed A-bomb while vacationing with his millionaire father at a Corsican seashore—and spend his remaining six months coddled with farm tractors and stolen zoo animals? Unfortunately, for all the movie's emotional impact and potent subject matter, all its different pieces never quite fit.

One reason *The Christmas Tree* fails to fully satisfy is that, unless we have some degree of familiarity with its settings and dialects, a single viewing likely isn't enough for us to grasp what's going on. Perhaps a European will know right away the tale opens in Paris, knows where Corsica is, recognizes by sight and name the resort area where lovable humbug Verdun (Andre Bourvil), the father's World War II pal, helps an entrepreneur friend with staff problems, but anyone else may have to watch (and, especially, listen) two, three, four or even five times to grasp who everyone is, where and why. For the non-European, ears unaccustomed to accents and locales foreign to

William Holden stars as the father of the dying Pascal in *The Christmas Tree*. (Photofest)

his own, it may instantly sink in, that Verdun is also a chateau employee (as we know from his racket-filled phone call with Pascal), but then again we may not take a firm hold on this until he is actually at the chateau. We may notice the running gag about cook Marinette's (Madeleine Damien) poor hearing right off, or we may be straining so hard to follow who's who, what's what, and where's where that this, her religious mannerisms, and other defining character traits go unnoticed.

It doesn't help that nearly all the film's exposition is delivered at the precise moment our attention has been diverted, keeping us so busy trying to get our bearings ("Wait a minute! Who *is* that? Where are we now?"), that we miss dialogue clearing matters up. It's quite possible to hear Pascal's father identify the man pressured for facts by phone as a cabinet minister without really absorbing it because we're only now realizing Pascal's health may be in danger; to hear Pascal's father tell Catherine he was born in France, left, then returned without taking in any of it because we're trying to learn why she has been brought to the chateau; to hear Catherine describe her Paris magazine job without concentrating on it because, even with Pascal away, we're so shocked to see his father and her in the same bedroom; to hear the unusual advice an aging doctor (Mario Feliciani) gives Pascal's father without zeroing in on it because we're so taken aback by his prognosis and his unexpected censure of government spending; to hear the tale behind a wolf's tooth adorning a horse of elderly neighbor Vernet (Friedrich Ledebur) without assimilating it because we're trying to examine the tooth, not to mention figure out who the old man is and why he has dropped by the chateau at all. We're listening, sort of—we try to, anyway, want to—but we can't really focus because both Young's script and scene shifts keep throwing us curves.

Making matters worse, the accents in the film further fragment our attention. Holden and Fuller enunciate clearly enough for non-European audiences, but whenever either speaks to nearly anyone else— Lisi, Bourvil, Damien, Ledebur, Feliciani—the back-and-forth between crisp, no-frills precision to cadenced, European exoticism is so jarring we're more likely to wonder how all these different-sounding people could know one another than follow what's being said. What's more, even when the performances are quite good, some of the accents, especially Lisi's and Bourvil's, are so naturally heavy it's occasionally all the non-European can do to make out all the words.

Further distracting us, the film's unintended message—that, because Pascal is incurably ill, his rich father is right to indulge his every whim—seems ill-advised; "Money can buy happiness" and "Presents equal love" aren't the best life lessons one could teach a child, no matter how noble the intent. Worse, the tale comes perilously close to condoning theft, provided the thief feels it's for "a good cause," and while Pascal won't live to adopt this philosophy, one wonders if everyone seeing the film—child or adult—is level-headed enough to reject its slightly off-center moral view.

And yet, given all this, *The Christmas Tree* remains an interesting, if curious, nonsuccess. True, Young is a better director than writer, but that stunning ending (anyone unmoved by the farewell left on Pascal's Christmas gift for his father must be made of stone); the lush locales, so exquisitely photographed; the ongoing "luck" motif; and even the dazzling use of color almost—*almost*—lift the tale above its dying schoolboy doldrums. A scene in which a hard-to-

frighten Pascal, having wet his bed, quietly appears before his father with an embarrassed, half-whispered "I thought we might get up now" strikes just the right note of frail childhood shock, and there's a splendid moment wherein huge close-ups of a wolf's eyes and then Pascal's, framed and pulled away from exactly the same way, suggest natural kinship between boy and beast. In addition, two action sequences with the wolves (their zoo capture and horse attack) feature such truly terrific rat-a-tat-tat cutting to create a sense of frenzied fury that—well, let's just say it's easy to tell this is the same Terence Young behind the classic train fight in 1963's *From Russia With Love*.

As for the actors, most of the secondary performers—gorgeous Italian star Virna Lisi as Catherine; Andre Bourvil as fun-loving servant Verdun; Mario Feliciani as the doctor delivering the bad news; Madeleine Damien as chateau cook Marinette; Friedrich Ledebur as horse-raising neighbor Vernet— handle their limited roles with all the soft-spoken sadness appropriate in a tale of a dying child. The legendary William Holden, meanwhile, whose all-American look and manner usually help, not hinder, his projects, seems oddly out of place for once (when his character calls Pascal "Little One," it rings false coming from an American), but he does fare better as mournful father than one might expect considering he seems to have blindly wandered into the wrong film.

The tale's real focus, however, is child actor Brook Fuller, turning in an eager, confident performance that, if hardly star-making, at least makes us genuinely regret Pascal's passing. If Pascal's behavior—his refusal to grieve openly, the way he often seems healthier than perhaps he should—seems unrealistic, the fault is more script-than actor-related. Asked to play a despairing, death-fearing Pascal, Fuller likely could have obliged, but logic isn't what the film is after; like Young's Bond movies, *The Christmas Tree* depends heavily on willing suspension of disbelief.

The difference is, in a Bond film, where quirkiness is practically the whole point, it would work better, and if *The Christmas Tree* comes tantalizingly close to succeeding despite all this, the fact only makes its failure still more disappointing. One can't help admiring the film—it's quite an impressive near-miss—but *Miracle on 34th Street* it isn't, and the way it overcomplicates a simple story with zoo thefts, A-bombs and tractor rides is almost as tragic as what befalls poor Pascal.

Sadly, given the missed opportunity, his wolves have more to cry about than they know.
—RAC

The cast of *One Magic Christmas*: **Arthur Hill, Elizabeth Harnois, Robbie Magwood, Gary Basaraba and Mary Steenburgen.**

One Magic Christmas

1985

When I watch this movie, and I've seen it quite a few times, the ache it causes deep in my heart is actually a physical pain that comes back each time I watch or even think about the film.

One Magic Christmas is sometimes compared to the story of *A Christmas Carol* as Ginnie Grainger (Mary Steenburgen) comes to terms with her derisive attitude toward Christmas. But Ginnie really is more closely related to George Bailey of *It's a Wonderful Life,* for Ginnie is not the ogre Mr. Scrooge was, but a loving wife and mother who cannot bring herself to enjoy the spirit of the holiday or to even say "Merry Christmas." George loses his faith in one brief moment, but we're never sure why Ginnie is so anti-Christmas. It could be the death of her father the previous year, but we don't think so, for this emotion seems to have built up in her over a period of time.

Of course, Ginnie does have reason to be depressed. Her husband Jack (Gary Basaraba) has been out of work since June, and they must be out of the house they are living in by January first (in one scene Ginnie must stand by while her husband's former employer brings new tenants to look at the house. The woman cuttingly insults Ginnie's choice of paint color for the kitchen). She's stuck in a dead-end job as a grocery store clerk (when she goes to the bank to stop Jack from taking out money, Ginnie tells manager Herbie [Timothy Webber] she has to go across the street. "That's it. You're fired, Ginnie." "Go jump in the lake Herbie," she replies). Finally there is no money for Christmas this year. When Ginnie comes home from work one night, she shows Jack the presents she bought for the kids, an Etch-a-Sketch for Cal and a tea set for Abbie. Jack adds they'll get the rest of the gifts later; Ginnie agrees, adding they will only be small items. Jack wants to take a couple of hundred dollars from savings to give the kids a wonderful Christmas, but Ginnie argues with him. "Jack, that money's all we've got between us and the poorhouse."

The film opens with angel Gideon (Harry Dean Stanton) sitting in a tree top. Nicholas (could this be Saint Nicholas?), a heavenly voice, gives him his Christmas assignment. "I have a very difficult case for you this year... Ginnie Granger... she never even says Merry Christmas."

Gideon arrives at the local mall in time to hear Ginnie tell daughter Abbie (Elizabeth Harnois) she can't afford to let her see Santa. Back at home Jack wants to work on bicycles that he is putting together for the neighborhood kids, but Ginnie wants him to help her pack. He is also making a bike for Molly Monaghan (Sarah Polley), a little girl in the neighborhood whose family is very poor.

Parents not having money during the holidays is always painful to them. In one scene, Molly's mother is at Ginnie's checkout; but she has too many items for the number of food stamps left. Ginnie doesn't know what to do but offers to lend her the money. Even with all her problems, we know Ginnie is a good person.

Ginnie good-naturedly tells Jack to go work on the bikes. Jack and his friend are also collecting money to help light the community Christmas tree. In the few short moments we meet Jack, we know he is a good man who loves his family and community and can't understand his wife's loathing of Christmas.

Abbie and her brother Cal (Robbie Magwood) also don't understand why Christmas brings out the worst in their mother. They sit outside with Molly watching the older kids play ice hockey when Abbie asks Molly what she's getting for Christmas. "Nothin' I guess." "What would you like?" Abbie asks. "A bike I guess." Abbie and Cal exchange knowing smiles. "Does your mom like Christmas? My mom doesn't... wish she did," Abbie tells her little friend.

We know Ginnie's not the Grinch we may think, for she begins to smile and sing in the shower before being interrupted by a ringing phone and the kids, who have to use the bathroom. She waits outside since Abbie is in the bathroom. "Why don't you ever say

Gideon (Harry Dean Stanton) looks toward the home of Ginnie in *One Magic Christmas*.

Merry Christmas, Mom?" Abbie yells through the door. "Well, nobody ever really means it when they say it anyway," Ginnie sighs.

That night as Jack tucks Abbie into bed, she asks him, "Dad is there such a thing as an angel? Mom says there isn't."

"Oh, well, I believe that there is. I believe that whenever anybody who's really good dies they go up to heaven and become an angel. A Guardian angel or a Christmas angel, all kinds of angels." *One Magic Christmas* explains angels and Santa's elves as kindly people who lead good lives and have died. When Abbie runs outside to mail her letter to Santa, she meets Gideon who tells Abbie he's an angel and explains he was a cowhand out west, and one Christmas he saved a child from drowning but drowned himself. The next thing he knew he was a Christmas angel. Later, when Abbie goes to Santa for help, he takes Abbie through his workshop. She recognizes a janitor from school who died. Santa tells her, "Most people think it's elves, but it's just nice ordinary people, young and old, who work here." This is a refreshing idea and a comforting one for people who have lost loved ones.

Gideon tells Abbie to let her mom mail the letter to Santa, but Ginnie thinks it is nonsense. The next evening Gideon appears in Abbie's room. He tells her they are going to help Ginnie. "We're gonna give her a Christmas present that only angels and children can give, and I want you to listen real careful now. No matter what happens between now and tomorrow night, I don't want you to be afraid."

That same evening Jack discusses his dream of owning a bike shop, but Ginnie insists he be realistic and get a regular job. Jack angrily walks out the door, and Ginnie follows him into the snowy street. "Just seems like nothin's going right for you and me, just nothing and now Christmas. I don't know one thing we've got to be joyful about," Ginnie says in a softly resigned voice. In her own way Ginnie is trying to justify her feelings about Christmas.

Jack continues his walk around the block while Ginnie goes to the mailbox to mail some bills—but not Abbie's letter to Santa. Gideon is waiting there.

"You don't sound like you got much Christmas spirit."
"No, I don't have much Christmas spirit."
"But you should you know. That's sad."
"Why?" Ginnie asks.
"You've got to find out Ginnie. I want you to find out."

She turns to ask Gideon how he knew her name, but the angel is gone. As Ginnie walks back to the house all the Christmas lights on the street go out. Ginnie will soon face an even greater darkness in her own life.

Santa Claus (Jan Rubes) gives Abbie a letter for Ginnie in *One Magic Christmas*.

The next morning, Christmas Eve, Ginnie leaves to work a double shift. She rides to work with her neighbor Betty (Michelle Meyrink), who stops at a gas station. Harry (Wayne Robson), a rude man Ginnie had a problem with in the grocery line, tries to sell the owner his old car. The owner doesn't want it; and Harry, in desperation, tells his son, "I'm gonna drop you off at the bus station for a coupla hours. There's something I got to do."

Harry goes into the bank just as Jack, a Christmas tree atop the car and the kids in the backseat, double parks and enters the building. Abbie disobeys her father and climbs out of the car and goes to see her mother at work. Ginnie fumes as she storms across the street just in time to see Harry rob the bank and take a girl hostage. She watches in desperation as Jack tries to talk him out of taking the girl, but Harry panics and shoots Jack. "He's killed him!" Ginnie

cries. But the worst is to come, for Harry has taken Jack's car with the kids in the backseat.

Ginnie frantically finds Harry's car and follows over the icy roads until the car stops running. A police car picks her up, and they continue to where another police car has blocked the road. Harry tries to avoid the car and crashes through the side of a bridge into the frigid water. Ginnie stumbles down the hillside seeking signs of the children, but the car has vanished.

Our hearts ache for this woman, who now really has no reason to celebrate Christmas. She sits alone in the bathroom sobbing. Great-granddad tells her the police have found the children, and they deliver them safely home.

There are friends and relatives at the house as Ginnie sits with the children and tries to tell them about their dad and how sometimes bad things happen to good people. "What bad things mom?" the children want to know. "He's not coming back ever. Your dad died."

Abbie tries to find Gideon, so she can ask him to bring her dad back. He can't but takes her to see Santa Claus at the North Pole. In the truly wonderful acceptance of little children, Abbie doesn't bat an eye as they travel to see Santa, who tells her he can't bring her dad back, only her mother can. He takes Abbie to the mailroom and gives her a letter that her mother wrote when she was a young girl. He tells her to give it to Ginnie.

Ginnie, thankful for Abbie's safe return, gets her ready for bed, gently scolding her for running away and for fibbing about visiting the North Pole. Abbie, almost asleep, tells her about the letter in her pocket. Ginnie reads the childish scrawl in amazement and can only say, "Oh my." Ginnie's deepest beliefs are shaken to the core as she comes to terms with the yellowed envelope.

Gideon waits by the mailbox as she finally mails Abbie's letter to Santa. "Goodnight Ginnie. Merry Christmas." The Christmas lights come back on and Jack is returning from his walk around the block. Ginnie rushes to him and sobbing, throws her arms around him.

It has been a tough but much-needed lesson as Ginnie finally realizes the importance of her family and the blessings they have.

The next morning she tells them she is not going to work. They are spending the day together. The kids look shocked at this sudden change. Ginnie goes to the gas station and buys a camp stove from Harry for $50. "Thanks a lot lady. Merry Christmas." The family then drops off the bike at Molly's yelling "Merry Christmas" as Molly runs out to the porch in delight. They then attend the tree-lighting ceremony as Jack does the honors and lights up the treetop angel.

Later that evening Ginnie places a check for $5,000 on the tree for Jack's bicycle shop as Cal and Abbie wait in the attic to hear Santa. The children hear the reindeer's hoofbeats on the roof. Cal is astonished and has to rethink this whole Santa thing. Ginnie hears noises too and goes downstairs to find Santa putting presents under the tree. "Merry Christmas, Ginnie." "Merry Christmas," Ginnie replies.

Gideon, the Christmas angel, smiles from a nearby treetop.

I could tell you all sorts of facts about this film, how it was filmed in Canada during February and March but because of warm weather they had to truck in all the snow, or how the agreeable residents took down Valentine decorations to redecorate their houses with Christmas lights. Or I could rave about how the writers and directors wisely stayed within middle-class

roots as the Grangers dealt with struggles achingly familiar to most of the audience. Or we could discuss the wonderful performances by Mary Steenburgen, so strong and touching as Ginnie, Harry Dean Stanton as the kindly Gideon and Gary Basaraba as the loving father and husband. Of course let's not forget little Elizabeth Harnois and Robbie Magwood as Abbie and Cal, who are two of the most precious of movie tots and help make the movie all the more touching.

But let me explain why this film affects me so deeply and why it seems the writers were gazing down at my home one not-so-magic Christmas.

On my 17th birthday my dear dad was admitted to the hospital with another heart attack. Becky, the six-year-old baby of the family, asked our mom if we would still have Christmas even if daddy wasn't home. A week later, December 12, 1972, my mom had to come home from the hospital and tell her six kids, ages 6 through 17, that their 42-year-old dad had died of a massive heart attack. I can still remember my mom trying to be strong, much like Steenburgen tried as Ginnie, when she told us our dad would never be coming home. Christmas would never be the same for any of us. I'm sure there were many presents under the tree that Christmas, the local churches and friends of the family saw to that; but not one of us could tell you what those presents were. We would have given them all back in a heartbeat to have our dad with us. As I watch this film, those memories and feelings rush back as though they happened yesterday.

At the time we didn't have a Christmas angel like Gideon looking after us, but eventually we did have Christmas angels help bring joy back to our holiday. For me it was my wonderful husband Gary, who returned the Christmas spirit to my life. His love of the season is contagious, and we spend delightful Christmases together sharing moments in front of a gaily decorated fireplace and tree. The presents are purely a formality; we don't need them to appreciate our precious time together. My brothers John and Dan and sisters Jean, Sharon, and Becky found their Christmas spirit in their children's joy of the holiday and my mother found her happiness in her grandchildren. Which, when you come to think of it, is what *One Magic Christmas* is telling us—Christmas is the joy in everyday life and the love of our family and friends. If we remember that, then Christmas is every day of the year.

—SS

Bing Crosby and Ingrid Bergman watch the children rehearse a Christmas pageant in *The Bells of St. Mary's*. **(Photofest)**

The following films occur during or have scenes pertaining to Christmas:

An Affair to Remember
Cast: Cary Grant, Deborah Kerr, Richard Denning
Credits: Producer: Jerry Wald, Director: Leo McCarey, Cinematographer: Milton Krasner; Writers: Delmer Daves and Leo McCarey (Based on a Story by McCarey and Mildred Cram)

Grant and Kerr fall in love aboard a cruise ship and vow to meet in New York at the Empire State Building. Kerr is hit by a car on the way to the rendezvous and never makes the meeting. She is now handicapped and doesn't want to see Grant again. He sees her at the theater but doesn't realize she uses a wheelchair. Grant tracks her down and Christmas Day he arrives at her apartment where she is resting on a couch. He almost leaves before realizing the truth, leading to a most satisfying ending for this tearjerker.

The Bells of St. Mary's
Cast: Bing Crosby, Ingrid Bergman, Henry Travers, Ruth Donnelly
Credits: Producer/Director: Leo McCarey; Writer: Dudley Nichols (Based on a Story by Leo McCarey); RKO; 1945

This sequel to *Going My Way* has one truly adorable Christmas scene as a school room of children rehearses their Christmas pageant and sing "Happy Birthday" to baby Jesus.

Blossoms in the Dust
Cast: Greer Garson, Walter Pidgeon, Felix Bressart, Marsha Hunt
Credits: Producer: Irving Asher; Director: Mervyn LeRoy; Writer: Anita Loos; MGM; 1941

This story is based on the life of Edna Gladney, a woman who devoted her life to helping adopted children and having the word illegitimate stricken from their birth certificates. Garson and Pidgeon play husband and wife whose little son is killed on Christmas Day.

The Christmas Coal Mine Miracle
Cast: Mitchell Ryan, Kurt Russell, Andrew Prine, John Carradine, Barbara Babcock, Melissa Gilbert
Credits: Director: Judson Taylor; Writer: Darlene Young; Producer: Lin Bolen; also known as *Christ-*

Greer Garson stars in the tragic *Blossoms in the Dust*.

mas Miracle in Caulfield, USA; 20th Century-Fox; 1977

1977 television movie from 20th Century-Fox featuring Ryan and Russell as coal miners trapped along with 50 other men on Christmas Eve. Gilbert plays Ryan's feisty daughter. The film is standard TV fare but does strike a chord when the men rescue a co-worker by crawling through a small tunnel. The feeling of claustrophobia and the realization of the danger coal miners faced before unions brought new safety standards is quite powerful. The final Christmas dinner scene is also touching.

The Crowded Day

Cast: John Gregson, Joan Rice, Freda Jackson, Patricia Marmont

Credits: Producer: David Dent; Director: John Guillermin; Writer: Talbot Rothwell (Based on a Story by John Paddy Carstairs and Moie Charles); Advance; 1954

The drama concerns the lives of five women working in a London department store over the Christmas holiday. This rare British film was unavailable for screening; we are relying on other sources for the description.

The Devil Makes Three

Cast: Gene Kelly, Pier Angeli, Richard Rober, Richard Egan

Credits: Producer: Richard Goldstone, Director: Andrew Marton; Writer: Jerry Davis (Based on a Story by Lawrence P. Bachmann); MGM, 1952

Kelly is an American war veteran who returns to Germany to spend Christmas with a family who saved his life during the war. Most of the family had been killed during an allied air raid with Angeli the only survivor. Kelly becomes involved with her and a spy plot. Most Kelly fans would rather see him sing and dance than emote in this dark film.

Gene Kelly stars in *The Devil Makes Three*.

Ginger Rogers and Joseph Cotten star in *I'll Be Seeing You*. (Photofest)

Goodbye Mr. Chips

Cast: Robert Donat, Greer Garson, Terry Kilburn, John Mills, Paul Henreid

Credits: Director: Sam Wood; Producer: Victor Saville; Writers R.C. Sherriff, Caludien West, Eric Maschwitz, Sidney Franklin (Based on the Novella by James Hilton); MGM, 1939

While not really a holiday film, *Goodbye Mr. Chips* does feature a lovely Christmas scene between Charles Chipping (Robert Donat, who won the Academy Award for this performance, beating out the popular favorite Clark Gable for *Gone With the Wind*) and his beautiful wife Katherine (Greer Garson in an Academy Award-nominated performance) when Mr. Chipping (or Chips as his beloved Katherine calls him) has been promoted to housemaster. This classic film is a treasure in any season.

Home for Christmas

Cast: Mickey Rooney, Simon Richards, Lesley Kelly, Chantellese Kent

Credits: Producers: Waldemar Blokovski and Beverly Shenken; Director: Peter McCubbin; Writers: Peter Ferri and Peter McCubbin; New World Pictures; 1990

"I've heard it said that Christmas is a time for children. A time I'm told, for magic. But who's to say. Is it magic or coincidence? Is it chance or something else? And sometimes, once in a long while, it is a time not just for children but for everyone. I remember a Christmas not long ago just like that when something wonderful happened."—Opening narration of *Home for Christmas*

Mickey Rooney stars as a homeless man who is taken in by a family to work off a car phone he has stolen from Reg's (Simon Richard) car. Daughter Mandy (Chantellese Kent) decides Rooney is the perfect grandfather. He works at their home and even Reg is starting to melt a little when Rooney spies a picture on the mantel. It is Reg's mother, Rooney's long dead wife. He leaves while the family is attending a neighbor's Christmas party, but Mandy and her brother Justin (Noah Plener) follow him. He saves them from a mugger and takes the children home. Reg is so angry that he orders him from the house never to return. Rooney goes back to his homeless friends, who are his only family, and tells them how Reg's mother was from a wealthy family who forced her to have their marriage annulled. He never knew about Reg. One of the homeless goes to see Reg, who has tears in his eyes when he learns he really has a father.

He enlists Rooney's homeless friends to help find him. The father and son meet in a snow-covered park where they lay their differences to rest.

I'll Be Seeing You

Cast: Ginger Rogers, Joseph Cotten, Shirley Temple, Spring Byington, Chill Wills

William Griffis, Mickey Rooney and Scott Grimes in *It Came Upon a Midnight Clear*.

Credits: Producer: Dore Schary; Director: William Dieterle; Writer: Marion Parsonnet (Based on the Radio Play "Double Furlough" by Charles Martin); Vanguard; 1944

We were unable to find this film anywhere and are relying on the *Variety* review for a description. "...a timely story about Christmas and a shell-shocked war vet. It ties up the immediate problem of the soldier psychiatric finding himself in civilian life with the perennial problem of a convict readjusting herself to society after paying her debt. A poignant, romantic drama, done with taste and honesty, and acted superbly, it is sure box-office.

"A quietly moving, sensitive story about two misfits adapting themselves to the world and each other... The story covers a girl on Christmas furlough from the state penitentiary, where she is serving a term for manslaughter, and an Army sergeant on furlough from the hospital where he is being treated as a neuro case. The sergeant got his shellshock after a bayonet wound in the South Pacific: the girl accidentally caused the death of her employer when she resisted his unsolicited advances.

"They meet on a train, the girl going to visit relatives for the Xmas holiday, the soldier going anywhere... The girl invites the solider to her aunt's home and, in the 10-day leave both have, the soldier strives successfully to shake off his nervous ailment while falling in love with the girl. The latter, also in love with him, and trying to help the soldier in his rehabilitation, keeps her prison secret from him. When he finds out, there is a crisis, but it settles as the two renew their love again for the future when both will be free... There are many memorable moments, as the Christmas scene when the plum pudding is served and the family sings carols."

This film is not available on videotape, but perhaps by searching the television movie listings we may one day be able to view what seems to be a charming Christmas film.

It Came Upon a Midnight Clear
Cast: Mickey Rooney, Scott Grimes, Barrie Youngfellow, George Gaynes
Credits: Director: Peter H. Hunt; Writers: Frank Cardea and George Schenk; HGV; 1984

Rooney turns in a fine performance as Mike Halligan, a retired police detective, who, on the eve of a trip to New York City to show his beloved grandson the grandeur of a real New York Christmas, dies and is sent to heaven. But he begs to return to make the trip and the archangel agrees if he helps find a missing angel who is sent to New York each Christmas to spread holiday cheer. Halligan's daughter and son-in-law follow them to New York, the son-in-law vowing to place Halligan in a rest home.

Although the filmmakers' intentions were good, *It Came Upon a Midnight Clear* ultimately rings a hollow note as we are expected to believe an impassioned plea by Halligan on a Christmas Eve newscast will save the city from a mean-spirited holiday.

As an audience we can relate to Halligan's memories of the charm of a New York Christmas (even if we have never been there, we can vicariously enjoy the city's charm via *Home Alone 2* which shows the city in all its decorated glory). But the decorations are missing (the city council voted to ban them this year), the Santas all look like North Pole rejects and we know it would take more than one speech to turn these New Yorkers into merrymakers. The change in the son-in-law also seems too abrupt and ultimately unbelievable. As for a happy ending, well the Christmas spirit is brought to the city and Halligan's family, but as he and grandson Robbie take a carriage ride through the park, he dies. The End.

Not a terrible film and enjoyable to a certain extent, but if you have limited viewing time, there are other films that rate higher in holiday cheer.

It Happened One Christmas
Cast: Richard Dysart, Christopher Guest, C. Thomas Howell, Cloris Leachman, Wayne Rogers, Marlo Thomas, Orson Welles

Marlo Thomas, Wayne Rogers, Cloris Leachman and Orson Welles from *It Happened One Christmas.*

Credits: Director: Donald Wrye, Writer: Lionel Chetwynd (Based on the Screenplay *It's a Wonderful Life* and the Story *The Greatest Gift*); Television 1977

Television remake of *It's A Wonderful Life* with Marlo Thomas as Mary Bailey Hatch and Orson Welles as Henry Potter. Wayne Rogers plays her loving husband George Hatch. Can't compare to the original but curious nonetheless.

Mercy Mission: The Rescue of Flight 771
Cast: Robert Loggia, Scott Bakula, Rebecca Rigg, Alan Fletcher
Credits: Producer: Derek Kavanagh; Director: Roger Young; Writers: Robert Benedetti and George Rubino; Television 1993

On a Christmas Eve flight from San Francisco to Sydney, a pilot (Bakula) gets lost, and his only hope is an Air New Zealand commercial flight.

Merry Christmas Mr. Lawrence
Cast: David Bowie, Tom Conti, Ryuichi Sakamoto, Jack Thompson
Credits: Producer: Jeremy Thomas; Director: Nagisa Oshima; Writers: Nagisa Oshima and Paul Mayersberg (based *The Seed and the Sower* by Laurens Van Der Post); Universal; 1983

Critically respected prisoner of war film is not something you'd look to for jolly holiday viewing.

A Midnight Clear
Cast: Gary Sinise, Peter Berg, Arye Gross, Ethan Hawke, Kevin Dillon
Credits: Producers: Bill Borden and Dale Pollock; Director/Writer: Keith Gordon (from the Novel by William Wharton); A&M films; 1992

A depressing war film that takes place during Christmas. A group of American soldiers and their commander (who is suffering a breakdown) are to report German troop movements during WWII. They encounter German soldiers who only want to surrender but must put up a fight so their families will not be harmed. The soldiers have a snowball fight and exchange gifts around a Christmas tree. They stage a phony battle, but the commander thinks the fighting is genuine with horrifying results.

A Miracle on Main Street
Cast: Lyle Talbot, Walter Abel, Jane Darwell, Margo
Credits: Producer: Jack H. Skirball; Director: Steve Sekely; Writer: Frederick Jackson (Based on a Story by Samuel Ornitz and Boris Ingster); Columbia; 1940

This film was unavailable for viewing so we are relying on other sources for the brief description. A dancer finds an abandoned baby during Christmas in Los Angeles.

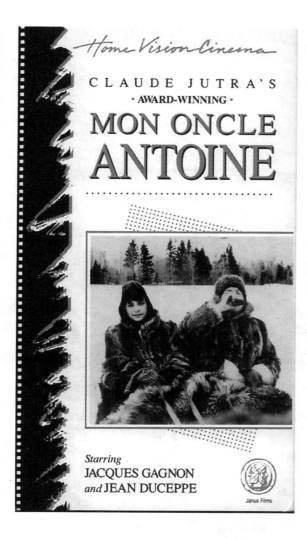

Home Vision Cinema

CLAUDE JUTRA'S
· AWARD-WINNING ·
MON ONCLE
ANTOINE

....

Starring
JACQUES GAGNON
and JEAN DUCEPPE

Janus Films

My Uncle Antoine (Original title: *Mon Oncle Antoine*)

Cast: Jean Duceppe, Olivette Thibault, Claude Jutra, Jacques Gagnon

Credits: Producer: Marc Beaudet; Director: Claude Jutra; Writers: Cladue Jutra and Clement Perrone (Based on a Story by Perrone); Natl. Film Board of Canada, 1971

This multi-Canadian Academy Award winning film has got to be one of the most depressing films ever made. The photography focusing on the stark poverty of a mining town is grim, the direction disjointed and the story disturbing. The film follows a day in the life of Benoit, a young boy working in his uncle Antoine's dry goods store. On Christmas Eve they decorate the store, exchange goodwill with the local townspeople and are forced to pick up the body of a 15-year-old boy who has died. Antoine gets drunk and Benoit, driving the sleigh at a fast speed, loses the body. He leaves the pine box with the child's body in it in the middle of the snow-covered road and drives his uncle home, where he finds his aunt fooling around

with a store clerk. The father of the dead boy finds the body and the film closes as Benoit gazes into the window of the farmhouse as the family grieves. Unless you have a masochistic streak in you, don't bother tracking this film down.

Roots: The Gift
Cast: Avery Brooks, LeVar Burton, Shaun Cassidy, Louis Gossett, Jr., Michael Learned
Credits: Director: Kevin Hooks; Writer: Alex Haley Television 1988

Kunte Kinte (Burton) tries to escape slavery via the underground railroad during Christmas 1770. We were unable to find the film to screen and had to rely on other sources for the description.

Credits:

All Mine to Give
Cast: Glynis Johns, Cameron Mitchell, Rex Thompson, Patty McCormack, Ernest Truex, Alan Hale, Jr., Hope Emerson
Credits: Director: Allen Reisner; Producer: Sam Wiesenthal; Writer: Dale Eunson, Katherine Eunson (Based on the Story "The Day They Gave the Babies Away" by Katherine Eunson); Universal; 1957

The Apartment
Cast: Jack Lemmon, Shirley MacLaine, Fred MacMurray, Ray Walston
Credits: Producer/Director/: Billy Wilder; Writers: Billy Wilder and I.A.L. Diamond; UA; 1960

The Christmas Tree
Cast: William Holden, Virna Lisi, Andre Bourvil, Brook Fuller, Madeleine Damien
Credits: Producer: Robert Dorfmann; Director/Writer: Terence Young; Continental; 1969

It's a Wonderful Life
Cast: James Stewart, Donna Reed, Lionel Barrymore, Thomas Mitchell, Henry Travers, Beulah Bondi, Ward Bond, Gloria Grahame
Credits: Producer/Director: Frank Capra; Writers: Frances Goodrich, Albert Hackett, Frank Capra and Jo Swerling (Based on *The Greatest Gift* by Philip Van Doren Stern); Liberty; 1946

Meet John Doe
Cast: Gary Cooper, Barbara Stanwyck, Edward Arnold, Walter Brennan, Spring Byington
Credits: Producer/Director: Frank Capra; Writer: Robert Riskin (Based on *The Life and Death of John Doe* by Robert Presnell and Richard Connell); Warner Bros.; 1941

Penny Serenade
Cast: Irene Dunn, Cary Grant, Beulah Bondi, Edgar Buchanan
Credits: Producer/Director: George Stevens; Writer: Morrie Ryskind (Based on a Story by Martha Cheavens); Columbia; 1941

God Bless Us Everyone...

It wouldn't be Christmas without a visit from old Ebenezer Scrooge, Bob Cratchit and Tiny Tim. "A Christmas Carol" has been immortalized by brilliant performances, tackled by animated animals and made into musicals. But whichever version you chose, it will remind you to keep Christmas in your heart all year long.

Reginald Owen

Alastair Sim

Fredric March

Albert Finney

Henry Winkler

Scrooge McDuck (Alan Young)

George C. Scott

Michael Caine

Scrooge (Tim Curry)

A Christmas Carol
1938

I will readily admit it: At Christmas time, for me, what was on TV was just as important as what was under the tree. The holiday season would be a poorer one without the classic small screen specials and films that mark the Yuletide. Boris Karloff's Grinch, Jimmy Stewart's George Bailey, and Fred Astaire dancing up a (snow) storm at the *Holiday Inn* (1942) were as much a part of the season as glittering trees, colored lights and beautifully wrapped gifts.

But for me, since childhood, no Christmas was complete without at least one helping of the film adaptation of Charles Dickens' *A Christmas Carol*. No, I am not speaking of the splendid 1951 British version featuring Alastair Sim's memorable Scrooge. My favorite Christmas viewing event has always been MGM's 1938 version of the Dickens classic, with Reginald Owen as Scrooge and Gene Lockhart as Bob Cratchit. As a child, I vividly recall staying up until midnight every Christmas Eve to view this golden age treasure on WCBS-TV's Late Show in New York.

MGM's adaptation, like the Dickens original, is a magnificent missive on the true Christmas spirit. It is also, to me, the most heartwarming and heart*felt* of Christmas films. The film is marked by the high gloss and perfectionism which MGM lavished on all its 1930s classic literary adaptations, such as *David Copperfield* (1935), *A Tale of Two Cities* (1935) and *Captains Courageous* (1937). But the production is also distinguished by a sterling, underrated cast and some magnificent performances.

The film's key player is, of course, Reginald Owen as Ebenezer Scrooge. London's most famous miser was originally to be played by MGM's professor emeritus, Lionel Barrymore. But when Barrymore's crippling arthritis prevented him from playing the part, he suggested that his friend Owen be substituted. MGM acceded, and both Barrymore's and the studio's decision was a wise one. Owen is wonderful as Scrooge, delivering what is arguably the best performance of his underrated career.

Our first glimpse of Owen's Scrooge is almost frightening. He looks ancient, wrinkled, dissolute—with a consistently protruding, pouting lower lip. And his hunched shoulders and stooped walk suggest a desiccated, degenerate Groucho Marx! Owen's superb body language and mouth movements give us a Scrooge that looks downright evil, not just curmudgeonly. And Owen's look of fiery rage when accidentally hit by a Bob Cratchit snowball is positively blood curdling!

Owen's performance is also distinguished by his eyes, which mirror a mix of Scrooge's loneliness, despair, fear and guilt. We look into those eyes and feel a pang of sympathy as we see him consume a solitary Christmas Eve dinner, while a background chorus of Christmas carolers wafts through the night. We see those same eyes convey fear and guilt as they dart and roll when Marley's Ghost (Leo G. Carroll) appears amidst a din of clanging chains and chiming clocks. And Owen's eyes widen with terror and disbelief when he is forced to acknowledge Marley's Ghost as real—and not just "an undigested piece of meat or blot of mustard."

Owen also displays a comedic sparkle in several scenes. His expressive eyes turn squinty and cold as he admonishes Bob Cratchit: "Don't work overtime... you might make something of yourself!" Later, when Marley's Ghost tells Scrooge that three different spirits will visit him separately on Christmas Eve, the miser entreats Marley: "Couldn't I take all three spirits at once and get it over?" And keep your eye out for the scene in which Owen's eyes dart around the room of his "sweat shop," before he sneakily snatches a bottle of port from the wastebasket and hides it in his back pocket!

Owen's broad range continues as he conveys both intimidation and befuddlement at meeting the Spirit

Bob Cratchit (Gene Lockhart) buys a Christmas feast in *A Chrsitmas Carol* (1938). (Photofest)

Scrooge (Reginald Owen) brings presents to the Cratchit children in 1938's *A Christmas Carol*. (Photofest)

Bob tells his children. There are few scenes in any Christmas film more touching than Owen childishly begging the Spirit of Christmas Present to let him stay and hear the rest of Bob's story: "Please let me stay... it's about Aladdin and the Magic Lamp!" Yet, Owen's facial expressions revert to fear and solemnity as the Spirit of Christmas Future confronts him with his tragic and miserable fate.

Owen's astonishing rage as Scrooge culminates in the film's concluding scenes. After his sobering confrontation with the Spirit of Christmas Future, Owen's eyes are wide with hope as he finally resolves to keep the Christmas Spirit always alive in his heart. And Owen's ability to convey childlike wonder is again seen as he awakens on Christmas morning, jumping with delight as he pokes his arm, his bed and his bed sheets to be sure he is awake and alive. Owen's facial expressions convey both joy and love—the touchstones of the Christmas Season. They also denote the desire to be loved— seen especially when Owen's Scrooge encounters the two men whose earlier request for a charity pledge was rejected by him. On Christmas morning, the two men encounter a far different Scrooge, one who asks permission to make a donation and who implores them: "Will you come and see me?" Owen's concluding memorable Christmas visits to his nephew Fred and

of Christmas Past (the beautiful and beatific Ann Rutherford). When Rutherford's Spirit whisks Scrooge away to his old school, Owen's teary-eyed look of joy is heartbreaking. But no scene—in any version of the Dickens classic—conveys Scrooge's despair better than when Owen spies himself as a boy at school, looks up at Rutherford's Spirit, and admits: "I *was* that boy." With this scene, Owen permanently captures our sympathy and our hearts—and holds them both tightly through the remainder of the film.

That scene is also a turning point in Scrooge's late night Christmas Eve lesson. It is from that point that Owen's Scrooge begins to change for the better. We see the transformation in Owen's despairing eyes as he hears the Spirit of Christmas Present predict Tiny Tim's death. We see Owen's facial expression softening with endearment as he spies his nephew Fred (Barry Mackay) and Fred's fiancée Bess (Lynne Carver) gazing lovingly at each other during a Christmas church service. And we share Owen's joyous, ear-to-ear smile as he peeps in at the Cratchits' Christmas Eve dinner, then delightedly listens in on the story

to the Cratchit family are a testament to the actor's range and talent. He has, before our eyes, slowly and skillfully transformed a decrepit, wizened and, yes, frightening creature into the soul of benevolence and childlike joy. In my opinion, Owen's work as Scrooge marks one of the great performances of 1930s cinema.

But the film does not belong to Owen alone. Gene Lockhart is perfect—and perfectly wonderful—as Bob Cratchit. The twinkle rarely leaves Lockhart's eye during the film. When Fred tells Bob that Scrooge's shop is too cold, Bob avoids putting more coal on the fire, for fear of upsetting his skinflint boss. But Lockhart's worrisome frown turns to a delighted smile as he changes his mind and exclaims: "We will... have more coal!" But the film is also a showcase for Lockhart's superb emotional range. Later in the film, Lockhart's Bob touchingly tries to hide the fact that he has been fired from his oldest daughter, fabricating a story about how Scrooge always refers to him as "Cratchit, m'lad." Seconds later, we know from Lockhart's eyes and facial expressions that he is unable to maintain the fib, as he shamefully admits the lie to his daughter—and captures our hearts more than ever.

At work, Lockhart's Cratchit is an eye-rolling, befuddled, nervous wreck, as he slaves under Scrooge's watchful eye. At home, Bob exemplifies the kindly, loving father as he delightedly spends his last few shillings on his family's Christmas Eve dinner—after getting fired by Scrooge for throwing that errant snowball. And Lockhart's penchant for comedy is amply displayed in his shock over Scrooge's miraculous transformation, with the panicky Lockhart convinced that the mean miser has gone mad!

The various supporting players contribute equally to the film's heartwarming and heartrending qualities. Gene Lockhart's wife Kathleen is luminous as Mrs. Cratchit. She exudes sweetness and goodness each time the

Tiny Tim (Terry Kilburn) opens gifts as Scrooge looks on in 1938s *A Christmas Carol*.

camera puts her in view, and her love for her family is almost palpable. Terry Kilburn's Tiny Tim is far less cloying and annoying than most 1930s child actors, playing his part with honesty and warmth. The same can be said of Ronald Sinclair as Young Scrooge, whose stoic exterior barely belies the heart of a little boy delighted with the idea of spending Christmas with his father and sister, and receiving a generous Christmas bonus from his kindly employer, Fezziwig. Leo G. Carroll's Marley adds just the right touch of spookery; his face a ghostly pallor, his diction perfectly conveying his hellish despair. Carroll's entrance in the film is a chilling moment, as we see his cadaverous countenance superimposed over Scrooge's eerie front door knocker. And Barry Mackay as Scrooge's nephew Fred is appropriately handsome, kind and strong, unlike so many of the wimpy and dull leading men of the '30s. Indeed, Mackay's touching speech to Owen's crotchety Scrooge about the true meaning of Christmas, spoken over Franz Waxman's soaring, worshipful music score, is one of the film's highlights. Memorable, too, is the heartwarming Cratchit Christmas Eve dinner, and the church scene, which depicts Fred, Bess, Bob and Tiny Tim singing a heartfelt "O Come All Ye Faithful," as the camera lingers longingly and lovingly on each of their faces.

Finally, Cedric Gibbons' art direction, as always, cannot be over-estimated. Gibbons' foggy, realistic London street settings, replete with brightly lit shop windows, define the excitement and ambiance of Christmas. Conversely, his dank and minimalist sets for Scrooge's "sweat shop" and mansion embody the dark, cold persona of the film's lead character. Gibbons' talent for creating chilling tableaux is displayed as Scrooge meets the Spirit of Christmas Future on a desolate hill dotted with gnarled trees and swept by a raging wind. The lonely, Gothic graveyard to which Scrooge is taken by the Spirit of Christmas Future showcases Gibbons' talent for creating atmosphere and tone with the most minimal materials. And watch for the shot of Gibbons' miniature London rooftops as Scrooge and the Spirit of Christmas Present soar over the city—a memorable example of Gibbons' eye for detail, scale and architectural beauty. In the film, Gibbons was ably assisted by John Detlie and, most importantly, Edwin L. Willis, who worked with Gibbons on such Golden Age horror classics as *Mark of the Vampire* (1935) and *Mad Love* (1935).

It has always appeared to me that MGM's *A Christmas Carol* has lingered in the shadow of the more acclaimed 1951 British adaptation. Alastair Sim, to be sure, made a fine Scrooge, conveying a world-weary pathos which differs in style from Owen's stony-faced, cold-hearted miser. And the British film is darker and more Gothic in tone than the glossier MGM version. But Christmas is all about bright lights, kind hearts and warm smiles—traits best conveyed by old Hollywood. Early in the 1938 film, Barry Mackay's Fred shares a bottle of port with Gene Lockhart's Bob Cratchit (the same one filched by Scrooge only seconds later!). Fred calls the port "the essence of Christmas." I beg to differ. For me, for always, the essence of Christmas is embodied in MGM's *A Christmas Carol*.

—SK

Marley (Michael Hordern) mutters to Scrooge (Alastair Sim), "while there's still time... Wrong, we're wrong... Save yourself!" and then dies in 1951's *A Christmas Carol.*

A Christmas Carol

1951

When it comes to the greatest Christmas movies of all time, Producer/director's Brian Desmond-Hurst's 1951 production of *A Christmas Carol* starring Alastair Sim deserves to be placed right at the top of artistic contenders for several reasons: Its insightful translation of a literary classic (by Charles Dickens) for the screen, its wonderful attention to set decoration and the recreation of Dickens' world, its stellar cast that shines from the starring roles (Sim as Scrooge, Mervyn Johns as Bob Cratchit) to its supporting cast (Ernest Thesiger as the Undertaker, Carol Marsh as sister Fan) and its letter-perfect manner by which it captures the Christmas spirit better than any other film ever made, period.

Primarily Dickens' *A Christmas Carol* is a novel that attempts to recapture the spirit of the past in the evolving industrial world of the present; interesting that Dickens' world-gone-mad world is essentially the very same world that viewers/readers of today's world consider the blissful past, an era itself to be recaptured. But even then, for Charles Dickens, he sensed that his world had lost its spiritual soul; and he needed to remind his contemporary age what Christmas was

all about. Perhaps each generation panics as it realizes this loss of spirit by witnessing its dependency on materialism, and decides that change must come now, it's later than we think!

First and foremost, *A Christmas Carol* establishes its lead character as a man of business, pragmatic and logical. As he tells the two gentleman at the movie's beginning: "I am not in the habit of keeping Christmas, sir... Because Christmas is the habit, sir, of keeping men from doing business... and Christmas is a humbug!" In other words, anything that prevents Scrooge from conducting his business is a major nuisance and must be avoided.

Scrooge then enters his place of business and we see his clerk, Bob, secretly warm his hands using the candle on his desk. In the background, waiting, are two men inquiring whether Scrooge will donate money to the poor and destitute during the holiday season. Scrooge matter-of-factly, inquires, "Are there no prisons? And the union work houses, are they still in operation...? From what you said at first, I thought something had stopped them in their *useful* course." A sly, arrogant smile slowly creeps onto his lips. The two men then ask Scrooge for an exact dollar commitment.. And his answer is simple and to the point, "Nothing... I wish to be left alone!" He states he supports those institutions he asked about before. The two gents counter by stating that many people would rather die than allow themselves to be sentenced to such institutions. And Scrooge, insensitive and seemingly uncaring, announces, "If they would rather die, they'd better do it and decrease the surplus population. Besides, it's not *my* business! It's enough for a man to understand his own business without interfering with other people's. Mine occupies me constantly." And such obsession about one's work proves detrimental to Scrooge's spirit.

To Scrooge, the making of money and living independently is the mark of a successful man. Any person who is poor or unable to work is a curse upon mankind and must be quickly removed, for a man's very moral code and personal identity, to Scrooge, is based upon amassing money and conducting successful business dealings. Those who can compete are worthwhile and may continue, those who cannot compete are a blight and must be removed. To Scrooge, a man's worth is based primarily upon how effectively he conducts his business—nothing more, nothing less.

Scrooge's nephew Fred (Brian Worth) merrily enters the office, inflicting upon the somber surroundings a healthy dose of good will and enthusiasm that falls on Scrooge's deaf ears. Fred states he is here "not to borrow money nor beg a mortgage. Simply to wish you a Merry Christmas." Scrooge, who has never been happy with Fred's marriage, listens as Fred states, "My marriage was the making of me!" To which Scrooge answers, "The ruin of you, you mean!" "Come and see for yourself," Fred counters by inviting his uncle to his annual holiday party tomorrow evening, Christmas night. To which Scrooge asks, "Why did you marry against my wishes!" When Fred answers that he fell in love, Scrooge grumbles and sputters forth, "Fell in love... with a woman as penniless as yourself." In other words, the act of matrimony is itself a business deal, and one should only marry to better one's business positions. A poor man must marry a rich or socially prominent woman; marrying for love is worthless because it cannot better one's professional status in life.

Finally, Bob Cratchit asks his employer, Scrooge, for Christmas off, and the same round of arguments ensue year after year. Cleverly, Scrooge, before always acquiescing, casts himself as the victim, the one who is being taken advantage of by his employee. To Bob he states, "You will want the entire day off tomorrow!" And Bob always gives the same answer, "If quite convenient." And Scrooge retorts with, "It's not convenient—unfair, pay a day's wages for no work!" Bob of course reminds his boss that it's only one day per year. Then Scrooge refers to that one day as "putting one's hands into my pockets," creating the analogy of Bob as a pickpocket, and finally gives in: "I suppose—but be back earlier the next day." This is

an argument that Scrooge realizes he will most certainly lose, but he seems to enjoy the fear and power he wields over the totally dedicated family-man Bob and seems to enjoy this game of cat and mouse. Smiling back at Bob, who is now happy as a lark, Scrooge reminds Bob (and himself): "15 shillings a week. You'll retire to Bedlam!"

The solitary Scrooge, settling down at the local pub for his evening meal before returning home, asks the waiter for some extra bread, to which the servant quietly mentions, more bread will cost extra. Realizing the common sense of business, he mutters back firmly, "No more bread!" Ask for no quarter, get none. But he does understand business and appreciates his own discipline of life is at work when he receives this small rejection in his request for more food at his meal. But he will not pay extra, and he accepts the fact that he will have no bread (though he could afford several loaves each night).

On his way home, Scrooge manages to scare off some innocent young carolers and the resident blind beggar and generally demonstrates that he is recognized by all as an unloved, nasty old man. And Scrooge seems most content in his clearly earned identity.

After a few minutes of sitting in his chair near the fireplace, strange sounds echo through the house, doors fly open by their own will, and the ghost of his dead business partner, Jacob Marley (Michael Hordern), the closest thing in his life to a friend, appears wearing the shackles and chains that he created for himself during a lifetime of making money. Scrooge, who is startled, quickly tries to compose himself by explaining away this supernatural insanity. Scrooge assumes Marley must be "an undigested bit of beef, a piece of cheese, a fragment of an underdone potato... there's more gravy than the grave in you." However, when Scrooge tells Marley that his presence is nothing but a humbug, Marley rattles and wails away, literally shaking the walls, causing Scrooge to accept the inevitable: "I do, I do, I do believe!"

And Marley's lesson, unfortunately not learned in life, is shared with Scrooge in hopes that Scrooge can change before his death condemns him to the ghostly, haunted existence of his former colleague. Marley states that the spirit of all men should walk forward among his fellow man. "If it goes not forth in life, it is condemned to do so after death... to wander forth in death... I am doomed to wander without rest or peace." Marley then refers to his binding chains, each link he created in his life, by his own free will, something he now regrets. To which Scrooge declares, "You were a good man of business, Jacob!" Again we hear Scrooge's morality, that a man is to be judged as good or bad by virtue of his business sense.

To which Marley then delivers the moral of the story: "Mankind was my business. Their common welfare was my business... and it is this time of year I suffer most." The business of serving humanity vs. the business of accumulating wealth. Christmas time, the seasonal symbol of man loving his fellow man, is the season stressing the spiritual over the materialistic. Marley then tells his friend that three spirits will visit him over the course of Christmas Eve night and will offer "the chance of hope."

Cleverly, the character of Scrooge has been firmly etched so clearly and so early in the movie. However, the appearance of the first spirit, the Ghost of Christmas Past (Michael Dolan), explains all the tragic situations that occurred in Scrooge's life that molded him into the cold-hearted businessman that he has become. The purpose of this first Ghost is to make the audience's present loathing of Scrooge fade to pity, so we can feel some compassion for the despicable old fool. Not surprisingly, Scrooge asks of the Ghost, "What is your *business* here with me?" Fearing that he, as mortal, will be dashed on the streets below if he steps outside his window as the spirit requests, the Ghost states, "One touch of my hand and you'd be upheld in more than this."

Revisiting significant incidents from Scrooge's distant and not-so-distant past, the tragedy of his life is interestingly patched together.

Visit A: his old boyhood school. There, all the other children have left for the Christmas holiday except Ebenezer, who is saved from solitary confinement by the arrival of his dear, younger sister Fan (Carol Marsh), the only person he loves and who loves him. She has come to fetch Ebenezer home to celebrate Christmas. Fan's message is now one of reconciliation, to please come home, "that father is kinder."

Visit B: a Christmas dance, jolly and festive. There he has warm memories of his first boss Fezziwig (Roddy Hughes), "never a kinder man."

Visit C: Scrooge proposes marriage to the only soul mate he found in life, Alice (Rona Anderson). Alice, who also loves Scrooge, is afraid the very young man will have a change of heart, that he will come to realize that she is poor, not proud and foolish. However, as long as he remains the man he now is, she accepts his ring.

Visit D: Good-natured boss Fezziwig is offered a business buyout by shrewd Mr. Jorkins (Jack Warner), which he refuses. Fezziwig states that to him a business is "to preserve a way of life that one knew and loved." The wizened old man claims he must remain loyal to the old ways (another theme of the story). "There's more in life than money."

Visit E: Scrooge's sister Fan is near death, having just given birth to her son. In her semi-conscious state, she mumbles on about a promise. However, Ebenezer leaves the room, distraught, and fails to hear her request which he now hears for the first time: "Promise me you'll take care of my boy." This is the same nephew Fred that Scrooge blames for the death of his beloved sister much in the same way that his own father blamed him for the death of his mother.

Visit F: The same businessman, Mr. Jorkins, who attempted to buy out Fezziwig's business, now hires Scrooge away, blinded by the promise of more money. Here Scrooge is introduced to his friend for life Marley. Scrooge mutters, "I think the world is becoming a very hard and cruel place. One must steel oneself to survive it. Not to be crushed under with the weak and infirm." Marley smiles and responds, "I think we have many things in common, Mr. Scrooge."

Visit G: Fezziwig's business sign is lowered, his way of life symbolically having passed. A young clerk who worked for Fezziwig for five shillings a week asks Mr. Scrooge for a position. He is hired for four shillings a week. But Scrooge's avoidance of his former employer signals a sense of profound shame.

Visit H: The dissolution of Scrooge's relationship with Alice is bitter and sparks the spiritual downfall of the formerly kind and salvageable materialist. The Ghost tells Scrooge, "She is not changed by the harshness of the world, but you are!" Alice tells Scrooge that he no longer loves her, that another idol has replaced her in his heart, a golden idol. "You fear the world too much," she protests. Realizing that money means everything to the corrupted young businessman, she wishes him happiness in the life he has chosen.

Visit I: Mr. Jorkins, an embezzler now bankrupt, smiles at the men who are charging him with illegally squandering the business' funds. Jorkins declares if the shareholders find out the bad news, panic will spread and "everyone loses money." Slyly and quietly, Marley and Scrooge offer to use their private resources to return all the misspent funds, with the option of buying 51% of the shares in the business, meaning they will control the business.

Visit J: Marley, now in old age, is ready to die. Scrooge's house servant rushes to his office to implore Scrooge to see Marley at once. Scrooge, very coldly, reminds her that it is "quarter to five" and "the business of the office is not yet finished." He will come at seven. The servant makes a snide remark that Mr. Marley will try to hold on until then.

Luckily for all concerned, Marley is still alive at seven, even though the too-eager undertaker (Ernest Thesiger) waits quietly outside his bedroom door. Rushing in and rotely saying the proper things to his best friend, Scrooge asks and seemingly answers his own question: "There's nothing I can do!!!?" Pull-

The Ghost of Christmas Past (Michael Dolan) explains all the tragic situations that occurred in Scrooge's life in *A Chrsitmas Carol* (1951).

ing Scrooge's ear near his mouth, Marley mutters "while there's still time... Wrong, we're wrong... Save yourself!" and then dies.

Amazingly, in such short snippets, the complex life of Scrooge has been revealed quite dramatically yet compactly by focusing upon all those pivotal events occurring throughout Scrooge's lifetime. Interestingly, the audience sees Scrooge's reactions to what he sees and hears, and we feel his fear and hesitation at being forced to relive painful and tragic events from his past.

Next, the Spirit of Christmas Present (Francis de Wolfe) appears in Scrooge's bedroom, a robust and hearty man with long Santa Claus robes and a wild, dark beard. The Spirit laughs lustfully and freely, a sense of playfulness evident in this most serious lesson.

First the Spirit of Christmas Present shows Scrooge a joyous barroom holiday party, the patrons all singing Christmas carols.

Second, Scrooge is allowed to watch the Christmas dinner and holiday treat occurring at the Bob Cratchit household. All the children are gathered, anxious to surprise their weary father. The family shares the financial bonuses of the holiday, with a holiday roast and two rounds of gin punch. And Bob is able to announce that eldest son Peter will be qualified to start a full-time job earning 4 to 5 sixpence a week, as starting salary. At the Cratchit house, there are many reasons to celebrate the holiday, and Scrooge observes the family in all its joy and happiness.

Third, Scrooge gets to observe his nephew's Christmas party with all the love and joy evident erupting from Fred's happy heart and home. When his wife complains of nasty Mr. Scrooge, Fred corrects her by pointing out that Uncle Scrooge "cheated himself" out of a wonderful dinner and evening of merriment.

Scrooge is next transported to the present day Alice, Scrooge's neglected lost love, who now cares for the sick, the lame and the poor. Alice, who never married, seems to exude contentment as she tends to the needs of those less fortunate. And for the first time in recent memory, bombarded with visions of the woman who once stole his heart, Scrooge feels regret for allowing this wonderful woman to have slipped away.

Finally, becoming momentarily less cheerful, the Spirit parts his huge coat to reveal two shivering and

Scrooge meets the Ghost of Christmas Present (Francis de Wolfe) in 1951's *A Christmas Carol*.

dirty children huddled together at his feet, one a boy and one a girl. The Spirit refers to the boy's ignorance and the girl's want and mocks Scrooge for his earlier apathy.

The final ghost of the evening, the Spirit of Christmas Yet To Come (C. Konarski), is totally silent and wears a black shroud which completely covers his face and features. This is a vision of the Grim Reaper, a Christmas ghost who symbolizes death and displaced opportunity.

The Spirit shows the not-so-festive Cratchit household shortly after Tiny Tim's death, the father returning home after visiting the young lad's grave, a visit that brought him a feeling of peace.

Next Marley's undertaker and Scrooge's housekeeper speak of someone who died as they attempt to sell artifacts from his estate for personal profit. The audience can immediately suspect who this dead person may be.

The scene changes to a hall of businessmen, with Scrooge noticeably missing. The businessmen speak of the fact that they will only attend their colleague's funeral if a luncheon is served.

The Spirit shows Scrooge his own grave stone in the cemetery, as Scrooge wails out and cries. "Are these the shadows of things that must be, or shadows of things that *might* be?" Of course, Scrooge receives no answer. "Spirit, believe me, I'm not the man I was. Why show me all this if I'm beyond all hope! Pity me. I do repent. I'm not the man I was." As if wakened from a dream, Scrooge snaps to life on Christmas morning.

Sensing his life has been salvaged and renewed, that the potential for change lies before him, Scrooge becomes giddy, cackling and dancing like a young schoolboy across his bedroom. His housekeeper screams for her life, believing her nasty old employer has lost his senses. He increases her pay from two to 10 shillings a week. He hires a boy to purchase the prize-winning turkey to send to the Cratchits for Christmas dinner. As the day wears on, he ends up at nephew Fred's home, apologizing to his wife (Olga Edwardes), asking, "Can you forgive a pigheaded old fool!" They dance together with gusto to the cheers of the friends and relatives in attendance.

The next morning, barely beating Bob Cratchit to the office, Scrooge pretends to be upset, as usual, with Bob's tardiness the morning after the holiday. As Bob runs and rushes down the street to arrive as fast as he can, Scrooge, after toying with his employee, says, "I haven't taken leave of my senses, Bob, I've come to them." Scrooge then announces that Bob will receive a raise in salary, but he also wishes to help raise his family by offering financial and other assistance. As for now, he orders Bob to put more coal in the fire. "I don't deserve to be so happy. I just can't help it!" Scrooge mutters.

That night, Scrooge even stops to put money into the can of the same blind beggar who used to flee in fright, "and it was said, he knew how to keep Christmas well."

A lifetime of lessons learned in one night's sleep: damnation, fear, regret and salvation. How wonderful if each of us had the opportunity to confront our regrets and failings in life, if we had the chance to learn from our mistakes and really turn our lives around.

For Ebenezer Scrooge, the harsh realities of life that hardened him into an uncaring, bitter old man, these same realities that had frightened him so in the days of his youth, can be erased and rectified all in a night's rest. The audience pulls for Scrooge's vindication and spiritual renewal because we witnessed the victimized youth, a solitary boy left alone, trying to survive his childhood. We saw his goodness as a youth, but we also witnessed his corruption, turning toward the material, losing the one woman who loved him and turning to a life making money. We care for Scrooge because we knew him before he was cor-

rupted and tarnished and we wish for his spiritual cleansing as we wish for the same within ourselves. This universal quest for spiritual renewal transcends holidays, cultures and time periods: It is simply universal, and both the novel and the movie capture this inner journey with all the passion possible.

For Alastair Sim, his characterization of Scrooge became a landmark performance in all of cinema. His character's former ruthlessness and cruelty, echoed by his dull and cold eyes, transform to schoolboy giddiness and overwhelming joy in a performance that is as textured and as complex as any that has ever appeared on the screen. Sim becomes the definitive Scrooge, and his interpretation has never been topped.

A Christmas Carol 's success lies in the exhilaration it creates in displaying the spiritual redemption that Christmas symbolizes. Not spiritual necessarily in a religious sense, but spiritual as in rebirth of the soul and the hope of an evolution of joy to be found within the flawed human condition. No matter how many times this movie is seen, and no matter what time of year it is viewed, *A Christmas Carol* is a movie that simply transcends the traditional Yuletide message to create something heartfelt and emotionally moving. It remains a true classic of the movies, and it never fails to touch our collective hearts.

—GJS

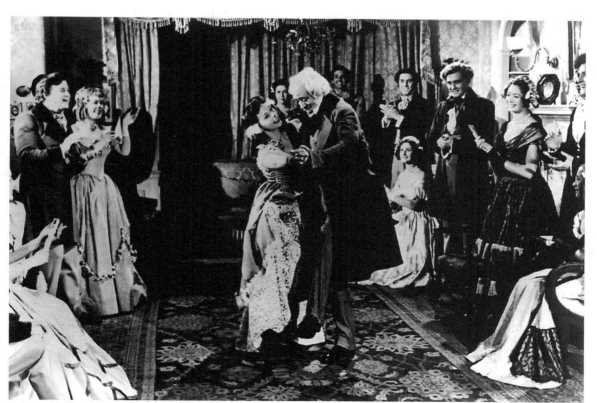

"Can you forgive a pigheaded old fool!" Scrooge asks Fred's wife (Olga Edwardes) and then they dance together with gusto to the cheers of the friends and relatives in attendance in 1951's *A Christmas Carol*.

A Christmas Carol
1954

Charles Dickens' *A Christmas Carol* has not only been developed for the movies but also for television as well, and the 1954 CBS-Desilu TV Production, produced for the *Shower of Stars* TV show, starring Fredric March as Scrooge, Basil Rathbone as Marley's Ghost, with musical score written and conducted by Bernard Herrmann, has a great deal to recommend it. Following closely to the Dickens text, this hour production does truncate the original story, but it also adds an entire musical subtext, featuring the Roger Wagner Chorale and several operatic-styled songs sung by members of the cast. The Bernard Herrmann score, a real coup for television, is wonderful when it is used to underscore the dramatic action, but far too often the ill-placed songs intrude into the story, destroying any mounting momentum.

The setting is masterfully established with the Roger Wagner Chorale singing their hearts out in the London streets at Christmas time, and a man journeys into a shop and looks through a copy of *A Christmas Carol* by Charles Dickens. As the man turns each page, the show's credits appear, and after he makes his purchase and exits the shop, he is approached by the charity solicitors asking for donations, and the book buyer gives generously. Then the two solicitors walk further down the street and enter Scrooge's business, asking him for money with the typical negative results. Interestingly, since the drama is a period piece, it is very odd and not very logical that characters within the story itself see and purchase a copy of the very story that is being produced.

In the initial scenes at Scrooge's office, the dialogue is fairly faithful to Dickens' original. What is outstanding is Fredric March's interpretation as Scrooge, wearing a frizzy white-haired wig, hair receding, and sporting a hawkish beak of a nose. March tackles Scrooge as a one-dimensional (here in these initial scenes) intense businessman who won't allow anything to disrupt him from his work. March projects a quiet intensity and focus which helps to establish the character not so much as being evil or nasty but as being narrowly focused and self-centered. His one-note grumpy disposition and sour face are consistent. Bob Sweeney, portraying Bob Cratchit, is the least developed Cratchit of any live-action version covered in this volume. His character is so tentative as to become almost sneaky and wimpy, appearing to be afraid of his own shadow. Sweeney's Cratchit lacks an innate sense of jolliness, missing that special love of family/mankind that allows him to overlook Scrooge's rudeness and insensitivity. Instead, Cratchit comes

off as any other disgruntled underling who loves to put down his boss, whether he has reason or not. And last, Ray Middleton's performance as Fred is too broad and over the top. First of all, he appears too old to be Scrooge's nephew, and every line is delivered with the actor's artifice showing, almost as if he is posing his body whenever he delivers dialogue. He bulges and rolls his eyes, smiles too long and broadly and never seems to be a human being. Even Scrooge notes that Fred is a good speaker and "is ready for Parliament!"

In one of March's best scenes, after Cratchit has left the office on Christmas Eve, having left the office window open to better hear the songs sung by the chorale outside, Scrooge is distracted by the music. His irritated face scowls from the office window as he comments on how the songs of Christmas even invade his own office and he slams the window shut. Yelling out in disgust the required "hum-bug, humbug!" Scrooge then creates a wonderful little rhyme that expresses his disposition so well, delivered in sputtering grumpiness. "Kris Kringle, old St. Hypocrite... handout for everybody... calculated lists for things to give away... where can you make a profit on Christmas day!"

The sequence with Marley's Ghost, as portrayed by Basil Rathbone, has never been better. Most actors either overplay the role as a howling banshee or underplay the role with morbid internal quiet, almost as if the outfitted chains wear down the spirit to the point that the role is underplayed as a quiet whisper. Rathbone finds a happy medium between these extremes, and truly makes Marley his own. Wearing the necessary bandage around his head and tons of chains and shackles and iron weights, Rathbone appears as a transparent image, delivering all the familiar Dickens lines but with a quiet intensity. "I am nothing to you?" the spirit questions Scrooge. Then Marley reveals his purpose in haunting his former partner: "To undo the evil we have done, to witness happiness we cannot share... happiness that might have been... wearing chains of useless things." In order to really communicate his message to Scrooge, during the middle of his speech, Marley reaches out his ghostly hand and places it firmly on Scrooge's arm, at this point becoming a solid figure, no longer transparent. Thus, Rathbone is fully present when delivering his most essential lines. Picking up their ledger book, Marley speaks of the injustices done by the firm of Scrooge and Marley, "thousands of them." Before leaving, Marley slams the same book to the floor, in utter disgust. From guilt and fear, Scrooge asks, "What can I do, speak some comfort to me!" But Marley can offer none, only the announcement about the three spirits to visit him this night. Slowly fading away, Marley's ghost, evoking pity and shame, mutters, "Oh

Basil Rathbone appears as Jacob Marley in 1954's television version of *A Christmas Carol*.

God, there is so little help for me... oh God!" As a follow-up to such an intense sequence, Bernard Herrmann's score, in the form of haunting choral music similar to the score of *Invaders from Mars*, echoes in the background as Scrooge circles around the room staring and thinking. Here Herrmann's music complements perfectly the dramatics and March's acting in a production where the overuse of music generally is artistically harmful.

The Spirit of Christmas Past appears, played by the very beautiful Sally Fraser, who also portrays Scrooge's love Belle in the Fezziwig sequence which follows (the only sequence to be shown Scrooge by the Spirit of Christmas Past). Featuring the usual party festivities, the blossoming love affair between the young Ebenezer and Belle is shown, and then, in a flash, their emotional break-up. However, the entire sequence is undermined by the duet which the lovers sing, very operatic in tone, containing the lyrics, "What shall I give my love/my girl for Christmas." It brings the festivities down to a crawl. As the Spirit states to Scrooge, "You've forgotten what the world is like for children," and after musical numbers such as this duet, Scrooge might well be better off as a nasty, lonely old man.

Even more annoying is the appearance of the Spirit of Christmas Present, aka Fred (Ray Middletown), here even more of a nuisance than he was at the beginning of the film. Scrooge, sleeping

soundly in his bed, is awakened by the Spirit singing "A Merry, Merry Christmas." Trying to steal the spotlight and over-emoting, Middleton even places mistletoe over Scrooge's head and kisses him on the cheek. As Middleton sings on and on and on, March is left to either stare and look miserable or, worse yet, begin to melt to Middleton's charms by cracking several large smiles and swaying to the music. In other words, after working so hard to establish a consistent, intense character, March is here undermined by being forced to respond to the music's charms. By the song's end, Middleton has grabbed onto March's arms and the two of them begin to dance and spin around the room. Coming to his senses, Scrooge as disbeliever crawls into bed and pulls the covers over his head. Peeking out from under the covers, Scrooge asks, "Fred?" but Middleton now only answers to the Spirit of Christmas Present: "You don't give many of them, do you?" the Spirit, referring to presents, asks. But Scrooge is already lost when he pleads, "If you have anything to teach me, I am ready to learn." And the pair are transported to the Bob Cratchit family as they prepare for their Christmas dinner, each family member carrying out a specific task. Bob Cratchit continues in his nasty mode by asking the family a riddle: "Lives in London... an animal, growls (some debate here), eats everything... people, real estate." Of course the answer is Scrooge. No toast to the Founder of the Feast here. After the Christmas tree is decorated, Bob lifts Tiny

What is outstanding is Fredric March's interpretation as Scrooge, wearing a frizzy white-haired wig, hair receding, and sporting a hawkish beak of a nose in 1954's *A Christmas Carol.*

Tim to place the star on top, unfortunately, this provides an excuse for the young actor to sing a song. Asking the Spirit if Tim will live, the Spirit states: He sees an empty seat and a crutch in the corner next year, but the Spirit of Christmas Future can change this shadow. "Look inside yourself, the answer is there before you," the Spirit cautions.

Utilizing the "look inside yourself" vision, Scrooge never encounters the grim reaper as Spirit of the Future. Instead, he finds himself wandering within a fog-shrouded graveyard and immediately comes across a tombstone bearing his name. In shock he falls to the ground and looks up and sees another tombstone bearing the name Tiny Tim. With that second shock, Scrooge awakens in his own bed on Christmas morning. From here on, the plot develops according to the novel and other film versions, becoming marred by the Christmas song that Tiny Tim sings at the Cratchit Christmas dinner where close-ups focus on Scrooge's face as he longingly drifts into his private thoughts, smiling, being visibly moved by the lyrics. At song's end Tim delivers his "God bless us, everyone!" line and up come the credits.

Surprisingly, this 1954 CBS television version of *A Christmas Carol* has a great deal to recommend it: a superb performance by Fredric March and Basil Rathbone, some clever lines of dialogue, some effective use of Herrmann's music early on, etc. However, the production is undermined by its needless, intrusive, operatic song-fest which destroys the mood rather than enhances it. And Ray Middleton's and Bob Sweeney's performances are either too broad or misinterpret the character as written. Until the Spirit of Christmas Past breaks into her duet, the production is outstanding, but by Christmas dinner at the Cratchits', the film has lost both steam and enthusiasm and becomes something less than it might have been.

—GJS

Bob Cratchit's Christmas Punch

1 large orange
12 cloves
1 quart white wine or claret
sugar to taste

Put cloves in orange and then roast in a hot oven (400) until it is dark brown. Cut it in half and remove the seeds. Place it in a saucepan and add the wine. Sweeten to taste and simmer until a white foam appears on the surface. Do not allow it to boil. Remove from fire and serve.

Children follow Scrooge (Albert Finney) through the streets singing "Father Christmas" in *Scrooge* **(1970). (Photofest)**

Scrooge

1970

Would Charles Dickens be spinning in his grave at the thought of his stories becoming musicals? I don't think so, for *Scrooge* is a delightful romp through Victorian London filled with hummable tunes and energetic dance routines and enough fire and brimstone to make old Charles himself happy.

Fans of Dickens and Scrooge in particular know the story; much dialogue is taken directly from the novel. Where this version differs is in the musical sequences, which lighten up the old tale for a whole new generation.

The first number is after poor Bob Cratchit (David Collings) has received his meager wages of 15 shillings from Scrooge. He happily meets two of his children, and they visit the street merchants buying goodies for a Christmas feast. The director weaves a tap-estry separating the haves from the have-nots as the camera focuses on rich people buying lush products from the shops while the poorer people happily shop among the friendly outside vendors.

While singing "Christmas is for children young and old," Bob makes his way home to wife and children. As they light the candles on the small tree, the scene fades into Scrooge blowing out his one stingy candle in his office.

Albert Finney is a wonderfully mean-spirited Scrooge. As he starts home he warbles, "I Hate People" with a superior sneer on his sour face. He stalks through the streets of merrymaker-filled London repulsed by their joy. The miser collects from the poor street vendors who dread the approach of the legendary skinflint. Out of the kindness of his heart he allows them another week to pay—for a horrendous amount of interest. He even enters the booth of a puppeteer who is delighting the children with Punch and Judy. Nothing is off limits for Scrooge when money is concerned.

Unlike the fearful adults, the children do not quake at the sight of old Ebenezer. They follow him through the streets singing: "Father Christmas—he's the rottenest man in the universe, but no one wants to tell him!"

After a day spent wearing down Bob Cratchit and badgering the downtrodden, Scrooge arrives home to find an image of Jacob Marley (Alec Guinness) on his doorknocker. A ghostly carriage thunders through the dingy front hallway, while the cadaverous driver tips his hat to Scrooge, "Merry Christmas, Governor."

Scrooge disbelieves his eyes and goes about eating his paltry broth dinner, his mean little mouth almost chewing the liquid making sure not to miss a drop.

The film makes use of the (at the time) state-of-the-art special effects. One such example is when Marley's ghost rises into the air, his chains flowing around him. The ghost moans loudly convincing Scrooge he is indeed real. A new twist to the old legend follows as Marley wraps a chain around Scrooge's wrist and the two fly among ghostly inhabitants of hell.

Scrooge's hands covers his face, his fingernails chipped and dirty, when back in his rooms he convinces himself it was a nightmare—but Marley is still present and warns him of the coming of the three ghosts.

Scrooge goes to his cold gray room to climb into bed. He walks hunched over and shuffles as though all that meanness has withered him inside and out.

The clock strikes one and the first spirit arrives, an elegantly dressed older lady (Edith Evans) who takes him on a tour of Christmases past. We see sleighfuls of costumed children singing "A Christmas Carol" as they drive past the school where a lonely young Ebenezer sits alone. Later, we see his sister bring him home for the holidays and, later still, as an apprentice to Mr. Fezziwig (Laurence Naismith), Scrooge romances Fezziwig's daughter Isabel (Suzanne Neve).

The Christmas Eve party at Fezziwig's provides another opportunity for a musical number as the celebrating crowd sings and dances to "December the 25th." Isabel is dressed in a light blue gown which immediately sets her apart from the gathering. Her kindness and loveliness even gets a smile out of the serious young Mr. Scrooge. In flashback scenes of their courtship she sings "Happiness" and we see him place a small engagement ring on her finger.

But the ghost also shows him their breakup as Isabel tells him he has found another love, that of money. She tosses the ring onto a scale and two coins onto the other side. The scale tips in favor of the coins and Isabel walks out of Scrooge's life. "You fool!" Scrooge yells to his younger self.

He is next visited by the Ghost of Christmas Present (Kenneth More), a jolly spirit who is surrounded by the warmth and sparkle of a huge Christmas feast, even an animal roasting on a spit. "Come over here you weird little man," his voice bellows.

Scrooge flies up to sit on the mantel next to the giant. The ghost presents him with a large golden goblet which Scrooge drinks from greedily—it is the milk of human kindness. The ghost sings, "I Like Life" to contrast with the earlier musical number by Scrooge of "I Hate People."

The old man, now drunk on life, soars out the window with the spirit and they fall into a snowbank which sobers up Scrooge. They visit the home of Bob Cratchit.

"I want to look in the window," Scrooge whines.

"It will cost you nothing, which I'm sure will be good news for you," the spirit replies.

"Will they be able to see me?"

"No, which I feel sure will be good news for them."

The Cratchit family is busily preparing for their holiday feast. They are making stuffing for the scrawny goose they so delightedly bought at the market, and Bob is working on his special Christmas punch. Bob proposes a toast to Mr. Scrooge, an idea his wife heartily disagrees with, but she only agrees out of love for Bob. Bob says, "God bless us," and Tiny Tim (Richard Beaumont) answers, "God bless us, everyone." This film version of Tiny Tim is one of the less annoying and his "God bless us, everyone" dialogue is by far the least cloying.

Tiny Tim sings a song for the family, "The Beautiful Day," as Scrooge and the spirit leave the materially poor but spiritually rich family. Their next visit is to the home of Fred, Scrooge's nephew where the celebrants play a game called "The Minister's Cat" with Scrooge delightfully joining in the fun. But his time is soon up with the spirit and, although he begs him not to leave, Scrooge is soon alone in his room, awaiting the most frightening ghost of all.

The terrified old man falls to his knees before the Ghost of Christmas Yet to Be. The spirit shows him a joyous crowd gathered before the office of Scrooge. Scrooge believes the cheers are for him, maybe he wasn't such a bad person after all, he thinks. The crowd led by Tom Jenkins (Anton Rodgers) sings "Thank You Very Much," a song about the "rare and beautiful thing" Scrooge has done. As they dance down the street, Tom does a happy jig atop a coffin. Scrooge never does realize the full import of what is happening and merrily joins in the song and dance. But the spirit pulls him away from the happy crowd to a place of true mourning, the home of Bob Cratchit. Tiny Tim has died and the family waits for Bob to come home. The spirit leads Scrooge to the snow-covered graveyard where Bob visits Tony Tim's grave.

"What is to become of me?" he asks the spirit. A skeletal face peers at him as he falls backward into a grave and plummets to Hell. It is here the film takes a different turn from other filmed versions as the miser finds himself in a place many people wished him. Marley meets Scrooge and shows him to his new quarters: "Nobody else wanted to," he adds. "I rather hoped I'd end up in heaven," Scrooge notes as he looks around at his fierce surroundings. "Your activities in life were so pleasing to Lucifer that he has appointed you to be his personal clerk. A singular honor. You will be to him so to speak what Bob Cratchit was to you." Marley opens the door into an ice-covered hellish version of an office. "You'll be the only man in Hell who's chilly," Marley remarks. Giant hooded men carry in a huge chain and wrap it around Scrooge. "Help me," he cries.

"Bah, humbug. Merry Christmas," Marley answers as he leaves Scrooge to his misery. He has truly been paid back for the misery he caused to others. We may live comfortably on Earth while trampling on the poor

The Ghost of Christmas Present (Kenneth More) gives Scrooge a drink of Human Kindness in 1970's *Scrooge*.

and downtrodden, but who knows what the payback will be in the great beyond? Scrooge finds out in time to save himself.

He awakens to find his bedclothes wrapped around his neck. "I will take the time I have left to live and I will give it all that I have left to give," Scrooge sings as he breaks into the song "I'll Begin Again." He throws open the bedroom door, shouts "Merry Christmas" and slides down the banister. Scrooge goes on a joyful spending spree, stopping at the butcher's for the prize turkey, the toy store for armloads of toys for the Cratchit children and the wine store. He pays those same young lads who taunted

him earlier to help him carry his load. Scrooge sings "I Like Life" as he and the boys parade down the street. More people join in until it is a happy parade on Christmas morning. He meets Fred and his wife, gives them presents and sheepishly accepts their invitation to Christmas lunch at 3:00 p.m. The parade continues as Scrooge spies a red Santa Claus outfit in a window and dons the costume. The crowd sings "Father Christmas," but this time it is as a tribute to the man who has finally found his heart.

When the crowd reaches the Cratchit home, Scrooge shoves the turkey into Bob's arms and gives gifts to all the children. Tiny Tim receives an

Scrooge, dressed as Father Christmas, visits Bob Cratchit (David Collings) and his family in *Scrooge* **(1970). (Photofest)**

enchanting carousel. Scrooge pulls down his beard to show Bob who their benefactor is and promises to raise his salary and help find a good doctor for Tiny Tim.

Outside Scrooge tells Tom Jenkins to forget his debt and tears up all the other debts the poor owe him. Another reprise of "Thank You Very Much" is sung, but this time the crowd is thanking Scrooge for his generosity rather than his departure from the Earth.

The film ends as Scrooge enters his house and pauses by the doorknocker that started it all. "I'm going to have Christmas dinner with my family."

This film is a marvelous version of *A Christmas Carol,* and Albert Finney does a fine job as Scrooge. His turnabout from a withered old man into a life-loving old gentleman is neither overdone or over-the-top. I often thought the Santa suit was going a little overboard, but upon another viewing, I feel the film is delightful and has very few slow moments.

Words and music to "Thank You Very Much" were provided by *Scrooge* screenwriter Leslie Bricusse. The song was nominated for an Academy Award and a Golden Globe but Bricusse was beaten out by the Beatles' "Let It Be."

The film received numerous Academy Award nominations including Art Direction, Costume Design and Musical Score; although it picked up no Oscars, in the words of many losers, "it was an honor to be nominated."

Albert Finney won the Golden Globe for Best Motion Picture Actor in the Musical/Comedy category for his performance, indeed a much-deserved trophy. This is where the Golden Globes outshine the Academy Awards by breaking performances and films into two categories, Drama and Musical/Comedy, giving many musical and comedy performers their often overlooked due.

Scrooge is a visual and tuneful feast not to be missed when planning your holiday viewing.

—SS

An American Christmas Carol

1979

The problem with redoing Dickens' *A Christmas Carol*, no matter how good the leading actor's portrayal of Scrooge may be or how good the dialogue continues to be, is simply this: the story has been told and retold so many times that audiences become bored. Thus, in 1979 a rethinking of the traditional Dickens classic melded into *An American Christmas Carol*, a made-for-TV movie that while not successful in all areas, at least attempted to create a variation to the traditional Christmas story. The immensely popular TV star, Henry Winkler, Fonzie on *Happy Days*, attempted to stretch his creative muscles by portraying the American version of Scrooge, Benedict Slade, as both an elderly man and as he appeared in middle age. And just as *A Christmas Carol* taught a moral lesson to its readers, so does *An American Christmas Carol* attempt to do the same to its viewers.

The story opens in a small town in New Hampshire, December 24, 1933, during the Depression. The Alden Granite Corporation, the quarry that economically supports the community, providing jobs for most citizens, has been closed for several years now, and the workers elect Mr. Thatcher (R.H. Thomson), a man who works for Slade, to speak to his boss about using his resources to reopen the company: "Mr. Thatcher, it means life or death to us!"

Meanwhile, back at Slade's place of business (he sells furniture and home appliances "on time" and becomes the repo man if people cannot keep up the payments), the children from the local orphanage are collecting money. Instead of offering much-needed cash, he offers a personal present he had printed at his own expense: a card bearing the message "You Can Do It!" Telling the children that he and his late partner were self-made men who never asked for anything, Slade encourages the children to work hard and to pay their bills on time. "He really believes he's doing us a favor," one orphan notes, "let's show appreciation to him."

Bob Thatcher and Benedict Slade make their Christmas Eve rounds with their truck, stopping off and repossessing furniture and the stove from the Reeves, black farmers who ask for an extension— "I think we could make the payment!" Shouting "You think," Slade reads aloud the repossession court order and has Thatcher begin to carry out the furniture and stove.

Next, returning to The Children's Shelter, the county orphanage where Slade lived for one year as a child, he repossesses their new piano, purchased because after 42 years the old one fell apart. Stopping next at the University Book Shop, Slade begins to throw books into a pile, ripping out the binding and stating at least he will be able to sell scrap paper for a penny a pound. Telling the proprietor Merrivale (David Wayne) that a University shop should be selling sweaters and bow ties, the owner states he used the loan given him by Slade to purchase wisdom— the books. Merrivale only asks that Slade doesn't take a very special book, an original edition of *A Christmas Carol* by Charles Dickens handed down by his father. But Slade takes that book as well.

At the end of their Christmas Eve journeys, Thatcher does speak to Slade about reopening the quarry, giving the community a second lease on life. Thatcher speaks of "hope for the future" and tells Slade, "These men have nothing left... everyone would benefit," including Slade. Slade thinks that Thatcher must hate him and tells him, "A man who is as soft as an old shoe is generally of little worth," and Slade fires Thatcher on the spot.

Slade returns all the books to his dark and forbidding warehouse where he reads aloud a section of *A Christmas Carol*, then starts to rip out its pages, calling it "claptrap." The lights out go and a thunderstorm rages outside (on Christmas Eve in New Hampshire?). Soon Slade's late partner returns to warn Slade of his present course in life, but Slade thinks that six pounds of powder and paint can make somebody look like his old partner, drawing an analogy to the Frankenstein monster. But this ghost knows intimate secrets of Slade's business dealings: "Like telling Reverend Williams his antique deacon desk was only a cheap reproduction so you could snatch it up as collateral and make a profit... should I go on?" Slade is convinced. "Hell is not what you think it is... it's worse... living in your past all the time, forever," the partner warns. Slade reminds him that he was simply a good businessman, that he never did anything evil. But his partner adds, "Evil is not just what you do, it's what you don't do!" He tells Slade that every day man has a thousand new opportunities but "they're missed forever when you're put in the ground."

Going to bed, Slade fiddles with his radio; and he hears broadcasts from 1927, the past, when Merrivale appears before him, the so-called Spirit of Christmas Past. Back at the orphanage, Slade is again a child, his two parents having died and the boy passed around from uncles and aunts, but Slade is an outcast, a troublesome child who remains isolated from the other children. Enter one kindly businessman Mr. Brewster, looking for a young apprentice. He picks Slade because he'd "rather do something for somebody who needs rather than wants." Taking Slade to the Brewster Furniture Company, the father-figure tells

Bob Thatcher (R.H. Thompson) and his son Jonathan (Chris Crabb) visit Benedict Slade (Henry Winkler) in *An American Christmas Carol.*

the boy he will sweep and clean up, clean the machinery, and most importantly, watch the craftsman do their job and learn. Brewster tells Slade he sympathizes with him, that it has been rough being jostled around from one family to another, but "you never have to leave here, until you want!" Brewster hands the boy a stick of wood, asking him what it is. Slade just stares at the useless wood, but Brewster tells him it can be whatever you want it to be, and the elder hands the apprentice a knife and shows him how to whittle wood.

Slade grows up with and falls in love with Brewster's daughter Helen (Susan Hogan), but Slade won't marry her until he is established in life. He warns of the new technology in making furniture on the assembly line (not as well made but cheaper) and even though he tells Brewster of the changes to come, the proud craftsman won't change his methods. "When the day of quality ends in this country, we'll all be in trouble," Brewster declares. Slade does love this man and tells him, "When you came into the orphanage, you saved my life... I will never forget that!" However, sensing the future, Slade accepts a job with Brewster's rival, a man who manufactures assembly-line furniture, and Slade establishes himself in business, leaving Helen behind.

Several years pass, and Helen and Slade meet each other again. She is now selling war bonds. Slade has established his own company, having left Stapleton because only relatives could advance. His latest gimmick is selling furniture "on time," allowing people to pay 10 percent down of the purchase price, but charging interest. Thus, Slade and his partner can collect as much as 150-200 percent of the purchase price when the object is finally paid in full. And if the customer cannot pay, they can repossess the article and resell it to someone else.

Brewster's furniture factory accidentally burns down; and, in declining health after a series of heart attacks, the old man soon dies.

Next, the current-day orphans appear to Slade, the children becoming the Spirit of Christmas Present. They smile and tell Slade, "You can't block out the Christmas spirit, it's everywhere!" Slade visits the home of former love Helen, who celebrates her Christmas with a grown daughter, having lived a happily married life. Slade sadly notes, "I could have had a child like that." Then Slade goes to the home of Thatcher and sees the distress he caused by firing his most dedicated worker during the holidays, as the family was secretly saving up money to send their child who is lame to a special medical clinic in Australia.

Finally, the black farmer, now a disco-dude dressed in the best late-1970s pimp outfit, becomes the Spirit of Christmas Future. Slade finds his personal articles being sold off and his furniture being burned. An oil portrait of his is sold for $100 and then gleefully burned as well. He finds that Thatcher's young son Jonathan has died, and finally he confronts his own tombstone.

Of course, waking in his own bed in his own time, Slade, like Scrooge, has been granted a second lease on life. Driving first to Thatcher's house, he drops off food, presents and pre-paid tickets for Jonathan to travel to Australia to be treated and hopefully cured. Since the holiday bird will cook for four hours, he asks Thatcher to accompany him as he returns all the repossessed goods to the same people he visited yesterday. He is even paying to have all the books rebound and restored to mint condition, including the original Dickens volume.

However, the last stop is the orphanage, where the children cheer as Slade returns the piano. As the children gather and sing Christmas carols, Slade sees a boy in back, Harry, who reminds him of himself when Mr. Brewster made Slade his apprentice. "I understand that boy," Slade says, and offers to take the boy for a ride, to the burned-out Brewster Furniture Company, telling the boy he wants to get this place humming again, and he can if Harry will become his apprentice. Slade picks up a burned piece of wood and throws it to the boy while asking him, "do you know what this is?" Harry just stares at the wood, but Slade tells him it could be so many things: a baseball bat, the spoke of a ship's wheel. Then offering the boy a wrapped Christmas present, a knife, both the boy and Slade begin to whittle, the elder telling Harry he will be very much like a foster son to him, the potential of the future being limitless.

An American Christmas Carol succeeds mostly in the first third, through the detailed account of the past life of Slade, Helen and Mr. Brewster told via the Spirit of Christmas Past. The tender scene where Brewster asks Slade to be his apprentice, giving him the piece of wood to mold into anything he can dream is touching. And the movie's end, when Slade offers a similar piece of wood to another potential apprentice in the ruins of the very same factory, decades later, is very emotional and such parallel sequences flow together nicely. However, when the movie veers too closely to the Dickens story, it suffers by comparison. Thatcher is no Bob Cratchit, and Jonathan is no Tiny Tim, and the plight of the family here never seems as desperate nor as touching as the similar worries of the Cratchit family of the original. The uses of the spirits seem overtly gimmicky, especially the dated disco-dude Spirit of Christmas Future. He is downright embarrassing, and the futuristic visions of moviemakers back in 1979 were absolutely short-sighted and silly.

Henry Winkler, mostly working under age makeup created by Greg Cannom, always seems like a young man portraying old age. Even though Winkler's performance contains low-key subtlety never to be found in the Fonz, his supposed joy after his transformation is never played as joy, for Winkler is almost the same person, played at one tone, one level, from beginning to end. Winkler acts mean in the beginning and acts nice at the end, but he never changes that inner soul of his character that is so essential when portraying Scrooge/Slade.

Credit must be given to the screenplay by Jerome Coopersmith who faced the creative challenge of both updating the time and place of Dickens' classic, but it must also be noted that only half a great story was developed. Instead of trying to redo the same old Dickens dialogue, at least director Eric Till attempted to make Dickens palpable to a modern TV audience and redefine the classic for the then current generation. While not quite the success it might have been, *An American Christmas Carol* certainly deserves a look-see.

—GJS

Mickey's Christmas Carol

1983

With six credited screenwriters, including producer/director Burny Mattinson and starring voice (as Scrooge) Alan Young, Walt Disney's *Mickey's Christmas Carol* only runs 25 minutes, but unlike the overpadded and listless *The Muppet Christmas Carol*, this animated short recreates all the dramatic high points of the Charles Dickens original story but re-creates them as marvelous cartoon animation starring all the great Disney cartoon characters: Mickey Mouse as Bob Cratchit, Jiminy Cricket as The Ghost of Christmas Past, Scrooge McDuck as Ebenezer Scrooge, the Giant from *Jack and the Beanstalk* as The Ghost of Christmas Present, Goofy as Marley, Donald Duck as nephew Fred, etc.

Beautifully rendered sepia drawings from the story, lurking beneath the opening credits, bloom into full-textured Technicolor brilliance as the story begins in the snowy London streets as we approach the office of Mr. Ebenezer Scrooge, the "Marley" under his name scratched off his hanging sign. Telling us Marley was dead for seven years, the voice of Scrooge states "in his will he left enough money for his tombstone, and I had him buried at sea!" Opening his office door, Scrooge catches clerk Bob Cratchit about to pop a piece of coal into the fire, but the old miser tells Cratchit that "you used a piece last week," so he kicks the coal back into the bin using his cane. Cratchit immediately reminds Scrooge that tomorrow is Christmas day and he needs to have off; the employer agrees immediately, but mentions docking him half a day's salary. Scrooge mumbles half of two shillings, but Cratchit immediately reminds his boss of his raise granted three years ago, when he agreed to start doing his boss' laundry. Scrooge, counting piles of gold coins on his desk and hugging bags of money, is interrupted when his nephew Fred appears to offer his uncle a Christmas wreath and to invite him to his annual Christmas party. Once again, Scrooge refuses, giving the wreath back, but the spirited Fred hangs it on Scrooge's office door blurting out, "Merry Christmas!"

The two gentleman collecting for charity appear, but this Scrooge has a different way to refuse to contribute. "You realize, if you give money to the poor they won't be poor anymore... then you won't have to raise money for them anymore... and you would be out of a job!" Scrooge says he cannot put people out of work on Christmas Eve, hands them the wreath and tells them to share this with the poor. After slamming the door on the gents, Scrooge shakes his head and says, "What's this world coming to, Cratchit! You work all your life to get money, and people want you to give it away!" But the clock strikes seven, and even though Scrooge echoes "two minutes fast" when checking his own watch, he still allows Cratchit to leave. Excited about the holiday, Bob wishes his boss a "Bah-humbug, er, Merry Christmas to you!"

Leaving the office at nine, Scrooge returns home, is haunted by the face of Marley/Goofy as his doorknocker, and once inside hears the haunting tones of Marley chanting his name. The eerie presence of Marley appears, wearing his chains, but his spooky demeanor is broken when the transparent Spirit trips over the cane lying on the floor. Scrooge is happy to see his former partner. "You robbed the widows and swindled the poor... all in the same day. You had class, Jacob!" But Marley corrects Ebenezer, "No, I was wrong... I carry these chains through eternity, maybe longer... same as will happen to you." Telling of the coming of the three Spirits, Marley's ghostly presence disappears beyond the wall, but as Scrooge yells out, "Watch out for that first step," we hear the Spirit stumble and fall.

When Jiminy Cricket arrives at the crack of one, announcing himself as the Ghost of Christmas Past, Scrooge remarks, "I'd thought you'd be taller!" The Spirit lectures about kindness, but Scrooge rambles off, "Kindness is of little use in this world." Scrooge is apprehensive about flying over the rooftops of the city, but giving his hand to the Spirit, both take off into space, Scrooge screaming all the way. "I thought you enjoyed looking down on the world," the Ghost states. After the usual visits at Fezziwig's party and the meeting/parting with true love Isabel (the marriage is off when Ebenezer forecloses on Isabel's cottage when her payment is a mere one hour late), Scrooge winds up in his bed asking, "Why was I so foolish?"

The rumblings of "Fe, Fi, Fo Fum, I smell the blood..." can be detected as the giant from *Jack and the Beanstalk* appears as The Ghost of Christmas Present, wearing kingly robes surrounded by a virtual feast: turkeys, pigs and pies. The surprising thing the Spirit tells Scrooge is that, despite the way he treats people, "many still have warmth in their hearts for the likes of you." The only place that Scrooge visits this time is Bob Cratchit's house for Christmas, where the Spirit comments that Cratchit is poor and underpaid. Scrooge states there's an entire pot of food on the fireplace, but the Spirit corrects him, "That's your laundry!" When Tiny Tim makes a comment about all the wonderful things to eat, he asks that we give thanks to Mr. Scrooge.

Scrooge is back at the graveyard, with billowing clouds of smoke pouring in, as the black-cloaked presence of the grim reaper, The Ghost of Christmas Yet to Come, is causing the "fog" by huffing and puffing on a cigar. Interestingly, all the sequences presented by the Ghost of Christmas Yet to Come occur here in the graveyard, compressing all the action to one setting which works marvelously. When Scrooge asks what happened to Tiny Tim, he points his bony finger to another section of the graveyard, and we see the solemn figure of Cratchit, kneeling at a tombstone, Tim's crutch leaning against the marker. Almost immediately we focus on two grave diggers finishing their newly dug hole in the ground, and when Scrooge inquires whose grave it is, the Spirit flashes a light on the tombstone bearing the name Ebenezer Scrooge, and finally the spirit, speaking and showing his dog face, declares Scrooge to be the richest man in the cemetery. Then amidst throngs of laughter, Scrooge falls into his grave which continues further down to a fiery Hell when he declares, "I'll change!" and awakens in his own bed Christmas morning. This sequence works perfectly in its compactness and truly registers the horrors of Scrooge's future with hardly a touch of humor.

Of course, on Christmas day, Scrooge has reinvented himself as the most generous man alive, giving 100 gold coins (which he wears on the inside of his coat) to the two gentlemen collecting for charities who were formerly refused, wishing strangers on the street a Merry Christmas, stopping Fred's carriage and reminding his nephew that he will be attending his

The Disney characters are so well defined that they seem naturals to fill in for their literary counterparts in *Mickey's Christmas Carol*. © Walt Disney Productions

Christmas dinner party, until he finally arrives at Bob Cratchit's house, with a big bundle on his back. The bag is filled with toys for all the children, and he announces to Bob that he is giving his clerk a raise and making him a partner in the business. With this, Tiny Tim chimes in with, "God bless us everyone," as the story ends.

This short film, nominated for an Academy Award, succeeds on two entirely different levels. The first is the marvelous marriage of familiar Disney animated characters to well-loved characters in the Dickens story. Mickey Mouse is wonderful as Bob Cratchit, the always sincere but generally put-upon valiant mouse. Goofy makes for a clumsy and pitiful Marley's Ghost, but at times is an eerily threatening presence who quickly sinks to pratfalls and stumbles, never making him too fearful to young children. Scrooge McDuck was inspired by the character Scrooge, and his miserly demeanor perfectly fits the character here. Jiminy Cricket's relationship to Scrooge, becoming a wizened voyager whose job is to teach the nasty old Scrooge some humanity, is not that different from his similar relationship to Pinnochio. Amazingly, the Disney characters are so well defined that they seem naturals to fill in for their literary counterparts, and instead of the final film appearing too gimmicky by being populated by Disney cartoon characters, their usage blends in seamlessly.

The second major area of success is the manner in which Dickens' masterpiece has been truncated down to its vital essence without losing too much of the message or subtlety. True, we have no relationship between Scrooge, his father and sister Fan, no childhood birth/death trauma. Yet for a children's audience, the story still hammers home its message that love comes before money, that we bear some responsibility to our fellow man and that the Christmas message renews the spirit and the soul. The manner by which the final Ghost demonstrates so many ideas, mostly told visually (the silent Mickey at Tim's grave, the falling down the shaft of the unmarked grave, the thick clouds of fog rolling into the graveyard, etc.), compressing so many complex morals into simple visuals that are stark and easily understood, only attests to how good the movie becomes. For once the screenwriters are not afraid to change or embellish Dickens lines, and the changes always remain true to the Dickens spirit. Thus, just because we are seeing the same old story, we are not hearing it told in the same exact way. And for once, besides the opening and closing theme song, "Oh What a Merry Christmas Day," the feature is not stopped dead in its tracks by too many listless songs.

Even when cut down to 25 fast-paced minutes, *Mickey's Christmas Carol* seems whole and complete, its message inventively told in a fresh, entertaining way.

—GJS

A Christmas Carol

1984

Granted, Alastair Sim's 1951 *A Christmas Carol* has become the cinematic masterpiece for bringing Charles Dickens' literary classic to the screen. However, since Dickens' novel was very short, and since most screen adaptations use extended passages from the literary work in the screenplay, we must ask how could one movie version be better or worse than the other?

This 1984 adaptation, starring the renowned George C. Scott as Ebenezer Scrooge and directed by Clive Donner (the film editor of the 1951 production), answers the question.

Let's start by covering the film's virtues. Interestingly, the film's screenplay, again sticking closely to Dickens' dialogue and the text from the 1951 film, does embellish certain sequences, adding a nuance of meaning. For instance, at the film's beginning, Bob Cratchit (David Warner, looking a tad young for the role) and Scrooge (Scott) share some juicy dialogue which helps establish Scrooge's aloof tone. Cratchit mentions the fire has grown cold and reaches for more coal. Scrooge coughs and stops his clerk dead in his tracks. "What is this?" Scrooge asks pointing to his shirt and coat. Cratchit rattles off the correct, easy answers. Then Scrooge makes his point: "These are garments, Mr. Cratchit. Garments were invented by the human race as protection against the cold. Once purchased, they may be used indefinitely for the purpose for which they were intended. Coal burns. Coal is momentary and coal is costly... There will be no more coal burnt in this office today."

Another interesting speech delivered by George C. Scott as Scrooge defines his view of the season of Christmas. Speaking to his nephew Fred (Roger Rees), Scrooge declares: "What is Christmas. But a time for buying things which we have no need, no money, finding yourself a year older, not an hour richer. If I could work my will, every idiot who goes around with 'Merry Christmas' on his lips should be boiled in his own pudding and buried with a stake of holly through his heart."

In these early interchanges, the character of Scrooge, as enacted by Scott, seems to borrow heavily from Sydney Greenstreet's "Fat Man" film noir performances (most especially *The Maltese Falcon*) where Scott mumbles his dialogue, spitting it out amongst guttural giggles and little asides. The performance is effective but seems more mannered and rehearsed, showing off its craft, compared to the superior Alastair Sim performance which seems more natural and heartfelt.

Instead of rushing off from the office on Christmas Eve to the local pub for dinner, the Donner version has Scott momentarily return to The Exchange to meet with businessmen who offered to buy corn from him. He named a price yesterday which was not accepted. The shrewd negotiators expect Scrooge to accept an even lower price today, in fear that he might be stuck with corn which will rot if not sold in time. Instead he surprises his colleagues by stating the price has risen 5% since yesterday, and if they do not accept his deal, the price will rise 5% tomorrow. One of the interested parties cries, "It's not fair!" And with a smirk on his face, Scrooge counters with, "No, but it's business!" This sequence is far more successful in demonstrating Scrooge's business sense than the sequence in the pub in the earlier version.

In one of Donner's more innovative visual touches, as Scrooge walks home, a horse-drawn hearse approaches him from beyond, and as he moves over to the side of the snow-covered street to allow it to pass, one lone casket as its cargo, Scrooge believes he hears a voice call out to him, and as he watches the hearse pass by, it disappears into thin air farther down the street. A very eerie and spooky sequence that foreshadows ghostly events to follow.

Even though Michael Hordern made a marvelous, over-the-top Jacob Marley in the 1951 Desmond-Hurst version, the equally gifted Frank Finlay one-ups his performance. Hordern loves to almost sing his dialogue and accent pivotal phrases with wails and screams, almost creating a caricature of the ghostly human spirit returning to Earth as penance. However, Frank Finlay is obsessive and intense: He delivers his warning to Ebenezer as though the souls of all Purgatory depended upon the redemption of Scrooge. Interestingly enough, in this colorful adaptation, the makeup department worked wonders by coloring Finlay in tones of blue-gray making his ghostly spirit a monochrome man in a world of full color. Finlay, referring to his chains and shackles (in the 1951 version Hordern remains superimposed during his entire speech; here, in the 1984 version, Finlay enters the scene superimposed but quickly morphs into a solid presence where each link can be plainly viewed), Finlay states, "mine [the chains] were invisible until the day of my death..." Becoming more menacing and foreboding, Finlay delivers his lines with grim determination: "My... spirit... never walked beyond our counting house... of our money changing *hole*." Finlay's inflections and caesuras, creating dramatic pauses in all the right spots, make his Marley one of the high points of the production. In another ghostly touch, before the ghost enters the room, Scrooge bolt-locks all the doors; but the door flies open when the spirit enters nonetheless. Surprisingly, after the spirit departs, the bolt-locks on the door remain undisturbed!

A few interesting changes occur on his journey when Scrooge is visited by the Ghost of Christmas Past (Angela Pleasence), here played by a female, with blonde hair and white robe, framed by flowers and a bright glow of truth. The first change is the sequence where Scrooge sees himself as a young schoolboy sitting alone at school during Christmas break. While the 1951 version has sister Fan enter now, here Scott (as in the novel) delivers a sensitive sequence speaking of the books he read as a child and how those literary characters came to vivid life, becoming his solitary friends. This pattern of being deserted and left alone at school during holiday break continues for years, thus making the grudge his father holds take on more dramatic meaning. Now, much older, sister Fan rescues him one Christmas season and states father has changed, that he wants him home. However, Silas Scrooge (Nigel Davenport) awaits brother and sister outside the

George C. Scott appears in 1984's *A Christmas Carol*, directed by Clive Donner.

school and it becomes apparent that father only intends to have Scrooge spend three days at home before Scrooge will accept an apprentice position working for Mr. Fezziwig. The gruff manner of the father makes clear that he still holds the grudge and that his son will be welcomed home for only a brief visit.

From here, things go downhill for this production.

Too much in this 1984 version of *A Christmas Carol* is too similar to earlier versions and it offers little that is visionary or innovative. George C. Scott delivers an effective performance, as already stated, but his transformation after the visit from the Three Ghosts is too restrained and subtle for its own good. Scott smiles and giddily laughs occasionally, but his eyes lack that sparkle that the inebriated Sim bellowed forth. Scott plays his performance too safely and fails to make Scrooge his own.

The screenplay is one of the major reasons that Scott's performance seems flat, as much of the subtlety inherent in the short sequences observed by the Ghost of Christmas Past are here truncated or omitted. We see the blossoming romance between the youthful Ebenezer and his beloved Belle (Lucy Gutteridge), but this version never makes clear the changes in Scrooge as a new golden idol controlled his life. We do not see those initial sequences with Mr. Jorkins slowly seducing Ebenezer away from Mr. Fezziwig, nor do we see Fezziwig's business fail. We do not see the initial introduction of Scrooge and Marley, nor do we see how they bailout/buyout out their former employer Jorkins as greed overcomes his formerly kind-hearted manner. In order for Scrooge's redemption at the end to work, we must see his initial corruption from his early life. But most of that seduction to the dark side is omitted here, becoming the film's chief

The Ghost of Christmas Present (Edward Woodward) shows Scrooge the joy of Christmas in 1984's *A Christmas Carol*.

Cratchit house for the sequence where Tiny Tim is now dead and Bob returns home late having stopped to visit the grave. With this "tenderness and depth of feeling," Scrooge states he has seen enough and wishes to return home. But first, the Spirit makes its required stop by the graveyard and Scrooge's face to face encounter with his own gravemarker. Again, working against the grain, Scott plays the scene much more calm and controlled than in earlier versions, almost as if Scrooge knew what his ultimate future visit would be. When he wakes in his own bed, he emotionally thanks the Spirits and states "I will keep my promise... I say this on my knees Jacob Marley, on my knees." This one little sequence fulfills the need of a dramatic climax that seemed missing in the sequence where he sees his own grave.

The remainder of the film is almost verbatim from the 1951 production, except for the already mentioned fact that Scott fails to create the utter schoolboy giddiness required

flaw. And without that earlier transformation, it becomes even more difficult for Scott to create more than a one-dimensional portrayal. Too much plot is wasted for trivialities, such as the lame word game played at nephew Fred's during Christmas celebration as seen by the Ghost of Christmas Present.

The sequences with the Ghost of Christmas Yet To Be elevate the film slightly with a fog-shrouded initial appearance of the Grim Reaper with bony, pointy finger. In this 1984 version, Scrooge is allowed to go to his home and see the corpse of its owner covered by a white sheet. Tempted to remove the sheet, Scrooge stands in mortal terror unable to do what he wishes. In a novel touch, Scrooge demands of the Spirit to see one person who feels any emotion over this man's death, and then he is transported to the foul part of town, where his housekeeper sells his personal artifacts (including his pocket watch) and other household items such as curtains, etc. "Greed and avarice" are the only emotions he is offered. Then, in anger, he desires to see any depth of feeling concerning this man's death. Then he is transported to the somber

for the role at the end. Even in the short sequence where Scott jumps up slightly into the air and flops onto his bed, the man seems more ridiculous than reborn. Scott never seems as utterly evil as Sim, nor does he seem as redeemed. Think of the difference between the Fredric March and Spencer Tracy interpretation of Mr. Hyde from *Dr. Jekyll and Mr. Hyde* to best visualize the analogy. Sim devolves and evolves from radical extremes, while Scott sticks closer to the center point between corrupted businessman and redeemed human being. Scott seems as though he is performing, while Sim appears to be having one hell of an epiphany.

A Christmas Carol ultimately depends upon its characterization of Ebenezer Scrooge. While Scott's performance shines in parts, it is bland in far too many others. However, the film as a whole is respectable and works well enough. It may not be the classic movie the 1951 production has become, but it certainly is a pleasant way to spend 90 minutes during the Christmas season.

—GJS

A Muppet Christmas Carol

1992

Of all the major feature versions of Charles Dickens' *A Christmas Carol* covered in this volume, *A Muppet Christmas Carol* is the weakest. Again the puppetry and Muppet-populated London cityscape is a marvel to behold, and the human actors are integrated quite seamlessly, but the spirit of the story never intensifies nor generates sparks. Most of the blame for the film's failures should be placed squarely on the shoulder of Michael Caine, who portrays Ebenezer Scrooge, one of the most lethargic portrayals the screen has ever seen. Since the story rises or falls based upon the strength of the interpretation of the Scrooge character, this Muppet feature is doomed.

Another failing of the movie is the insistence on the silly banter and physical slapstick occurring between narrators Rizzo the Rat and Charles Dickens (The Great Gonzo), often creating a tone that undermines the mood of the dominant action on screen. Even though this feature is geared toward youngsters, its acting and songs (written by Paul Williams, who here submits a slew of generic, forgettable lyrics and melodies) are so mediocre that the film doesn't stand a chance. Too many long, boring stretches of songs dominate.

The opening setpiece, featuring all the Muppet citizens preparing for Christmas with Rizzo and Dickens selling apples on a street corner, is quite splashy and sets just the right tone. As the narrators tell us, we meet Mr. Scrooge as he comes around the street corner, of course introduced with a song. "When a cold wind blows, it chills you to the bone," the song cautions. Telling us Scrooge is "solitary like an oyster," the man is further described as "he loves his money because he believes it gives him power." Disappearing into his office building, Dickens uses Rizzo to wipe the dirty window clean so we too can peep inside.

There we learn that Scrooge is a moneylender and that his chief job is collecting mortgage payments and evicting those who fail to pay on time. Poor Mr. Applegate implores, "But it's Christmas," but he is quite literally thrown out of the office. Scrooge, working with Bob Cratchit (Kermit the Frog) and an entire office of bookkeepers, tells Cratchit, "Let's deal with eviction notices for tomorrow." Cratchit, surprised, reminds his employer that it's Christmas. Scrooge yells, "You may gift wrap them!" Scrooge, as it turns out, loves the month of December because people waste money on frivolities so foreclosures are up. Of course, when the office workers, using Cratchit as their spokesperson, ask for more coal, they are threatened with the unemployment line. Fred enters and goes through the regular routine trying to instill some holiday cheer into his uncle, but fails. Telling his uncle he married because he fell in love, Scrooge laughs and says, "That's the only thing sillier than wishing someone a Merry Christmas!" Of course the two gentlemen collecting for charity are turned down in typical fashion. When Cratchit mentions about tomorrow being Christmas Day, Scrooge tells him to report by 8:30 instead of 8, but when Cratchit reminds the miser that all businesses are closed tomorrow, that he won't have anyone to do business with, Scrooge begrudgingly allows him the entire day off.

Surprisingly, in this version of the story, Scrooge is the first person to leave the office, leaving Cratchit in charge of having everyone close up, of course to a generic song. "Faith is in our hearts today, shining like the sun... there's only one more sleep 'til Christmas." Leaving the office, Cratchit notices the Penguin Christmas Skating Party and takes a long slide on the ice.

Scrooge returns home and eats his meal by the fire. Soon the fire dies down as the servant bell starts to ring, for no apparent reason. Instead of just one ghost, we have the Statler and Waldorf Muppets portraying Jacob and Robert Marley, wearing their usual matching set of chains, floating in air. Interestingly, as Scrooge enters his line about this vision being "more gravy than of the grave," the Marley brothers note the pun advising Scrooge to "leave the humor alone." They too get their message across via song: "We're avarice and greed... freedom comes from killing love, prison comes with hate." And they are delighted when they remind one another of the time they evicted the entire orphanage. They warn Scrooge, who momentarily wears a set of chains himself, "Your future is a horror story written by your crimes."

The Ghost of Christmas Past, a wondrous, angelic Muppet child dressed in white, her face also glowing, awakens Scrooge from his sound sleep with a sudden burst of blazing light. Cleverly, as the Spirit and Scrooge make their voyage, Rizzo ties a rope to Scrooge so they get carried along too, Rizzo yelling, "Good-bye lunch!" as they are spirited away. However, as the Spirit opens up the gateway to the past, with Scrooge flying above a forest of snow-covered trees, we hear the "oohs" and "aaaahs" of the Muppet narrators being banged and bruised while hitting trees underneath. Such an overly slapstick moment ruins the nostalgic remembrance which the scene is obviously attempting to create. "This was the worst trip of my life," Rizzo comments, until he comes to a stop on solid ground and is chased by a cat. Scrooge re-

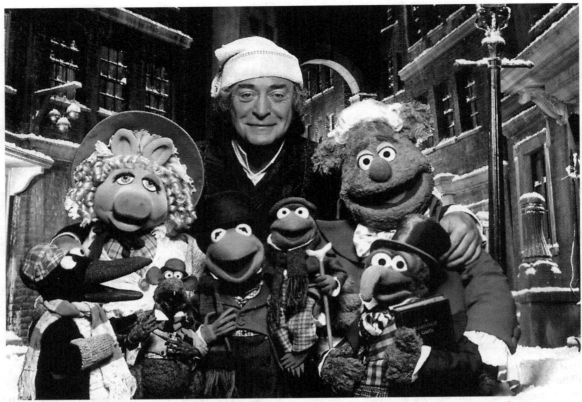

Michael Caine and his muppet co-stars in the *Muppet Christmas Carol*.

flects upon his old school, his old friends who left him alone during Christmas holiday, and his attempt to read and study while stranded at school. Several years pass, and we see a slighter older Scrooge still alone in the classroom, now being advised to enter the world of business by his Headmaster. "It's the American way," the Headmaster rants until Rizzo whispers in his ear and he corrects himself, "It's the British way!"

The next stop is the annual Fozziwig (Fozzie Bear) office Christmas party, a very festive sight to see. Scrooge describes his first boss as being "hard and ruthless as a rose petal." A young Master Scrooge interrupts the festivities to remind Fozziwig that too much money is spent for the party. As a Dixieland Muppet Band (?) performs, Scrooge meets Belle at the party, and meets her again years later, as the blooming relationship wilts on the vine. Belle wishes Scrooge to marry her, but he tells her business hasn't been good, investments haven't turned out as well as planned. He says he loves her, but she corrects him, "You loved me once." Then she sings a bland song: "When love is gone... the love is gone... the sweetest dream that we have known... I wish you well."

No mention is made of the bitter father who refuses to allow his son to visit, nor are the sequences with younger sister Fan shown, creating a parallel relationship.

The second Spirit is a huge Muppet mountain of a man, with cheery round face and wild red hair. The jolly man goes outside with Scrooge, showing him the city and how it celebrates Christmas. In song, "Whenever you find love, it feels like Christmas." By the song's end Scrooge is actually starting to smile, his transformation coming much too early, as snow begins to fall. "Spirit, I had no idea... show me family and friends." Then off they go to Fred's house for his Christmas celebration, people playing the game of "Yes or No." Fred's secret name is Scrooge, described as an "unwanted creature" not a "rat, leech or cockroach." Then onto Bob Cratchit's house where he leads the family in a toast to the "founder of the feast." Several songs create an overt maudlin relationship between Tiny Tim and father Bob and the joy of family life at home. "No place on Earth compares with home... let us always love each another." This second Spirit almost finished, his face now aging and his hair turning white, Scrooge confesses, "You've meant so much to me, you changed me..." but the Spirit vanishes. Once again, Scrooge has never been more than a tad grumpy, so his epiphany is not dramatically feasible.

The third Spirit, the Ghost of Christmas Yet To Be, is another fabulous grim reaper Muppet, his face obscured in dark shadow, introduced by way of billowing fog creepily moving in upon the scene.

Dickens and Rizzo feel this visit is too scary so they tell us they will join us later, "Folks, you're on your own." Of course we have the expected visits to the men of business, who mention they won't go to the funeral unless lunch is served. The servants still try to sell the dead man's curtains and blanket—"still warm." They travel to Bob Cratchit's house, a dead silence lingering, Mrs. Cratchit (Miss Piggy) making excuses to the children for her tears. The grieving but peaceful Bob Cratchit comes home and speaks of the dead Tiny Tim. Without doubt, this sequence is perhaps the shining moment of the film because both the mood and the acting are honest and played without humor or song. This sequence touches the heart because Kermit and Miss Piggy play the scene as pure emotion, never winking or sliding out of character. For one brief moment, director Brian Henson understands and has enough confidence that the children can take it. The sequence ends with a long, lingering shot of the side chair holding the fallen Tim's cap, the little crutch leaning alongside. Returning to the graveyard, Scrooge confronts his own grave marker, clutching at the robe of the Spirit, but he wakens to find himself pulling on his own bed curtain.

Michael Caine's failure at portraying Scrooge convincingly is now brought to the forefront. In the sequence when he awakens and registers the absolute joy that only a life's renewal and turning-around could create, Scrooge merely tells us he is happy, but he fails to show it. No dive-bombing the bed as George C. Scott did, no bouncing and hopping across the room as Alastair Sim did. In fact, the reborn Scrooge is almost the same man as the nasty "bah humbug" Scrooge. There is little sense of a formerly decent man who descends into materialistic hell by loving money more than humanity and who, confronting his mistake, miraculously gets a second lease on life coming through here.

The film ends with Scrooge walking the city streets, stopping at houses such as nephew Fred's, to wish people a Merry Christmas and give them presents. Scrooge finally arrives at the Cratchit house with the prize-winning turkey. Sitting around the dinner table, all the Muppets and Caine sing with lines of people reaching out into the streets, where it seems the entire London society joins them in song. Fittingly at the end, Rizzo tells Dickens, "good story." But Mr. Dickens' answer is brutally honest, "If you like this, you should read the book," because the novel serves up a banquet of literary delights while this movie only offers a light snack.

—GJS

A Christmas Carol

1997

One of the most recent re-interpretations of Charles Dickens' *A Christmas Carol* is the 1997 animated version, starring the voices of Tim Curry (as Scrooge), Whoopi Goldberg, Michael York, and Ed Asner. While the animation is bland, perhaps a step above the typical TV Saturday morning cartoon standards, it does a nice job of capturing the mood of the story. The screenplay adaptation by Jymn Magon borrows heavily, as have the other versions, from the Dickens novel, and only in some cases has the dialogue been simplified or modernized to communicate to children. Much of the juicy dialogue from former screen versions has been kept intact.

A brief pre-credit teaser begins the movie with a piece of interesting dialogue: "Some say life is a song—to some a ditty, to others a dirge—but, for the holiday season, we all sing a carol, a Christmas carol." Nice beginning.

However, the lack of imagination from the animators (most likely just as limited by budget as by imagination) makes this latest version of the Dickens classic seem redundant.

As is expected for animated features, interminable songs fill out the running time, and the ditties/dirges, co-written by Megan Cavallari and David Goldsmith, are soon forgotten as their final notes fade away. "Sing a Song of Christmas..." begins the movie, as the viewer discovers one new character has been added to the cast, most likely to appeal to the youngsters: Scrooge has a pet bull dog named Debit. Bob Cratchit, who is trying to warm his hand by his desk candle, sees Scrooge pick up a handful of coal and throw it at a

Scrooge (voiced by Tim Curry) comforts Tiny Tim in the animated *A Chrsitmas Carol* (1997).

young boy who knocks upon his door. Then the old coot asks Cratchit to hunt through the snow to retrieve all the pieces. Upon Bob's return, Scrooge grouses, "Five lumps, where's the sixth?" The initial plot and speeches closely follow the earlier versions, but instead of using the word "idiot" in one speech, we find the modern slang "numskull" substituted instead.

Interestingly enough, while Scrooge's dog is as nasty and loud as its master, Debit gets along famously with Tiny Tim who finds his face licked, and in return, Tim tickles the dog's belly.

After leaving the office, in this version, Scrooge goes to the local pub for his meal. "Hash for me, scraps for my dog!" The barmaid notes that Scrooge orders the cheapest meal on the menu. Then, the barmaid breaks into typical bland song... "It's Christmas time at last." She dances around serving patrons food and drink, and in a typical reversal that children love, she serves Debit Scrooge's meal and the old codger gets the dog's bones. Leaving, Scrooge says the only tip he would ever offer up is "find a new chief... your hash is not fit for a dog!"

The sequence with Marley's ghost is not played as much for its horrific jolts, but Marley himself resembles a cartoon caricature of Thorley Walters from Hammer's *Frankenstein Created Woman*, although slightly heftier. The ghost first appears, as usual, as a face superimposed over Scrooge's doorknocker, but his face again becomes visible etched as a stone relief on Scrooge's fireplace. When the spirit finally appears, the bedroom door is radiated, from behind, with an eerie green glow, similar to sequences in *Close Encounters of the Third Kind*. Humorously, this Marley floats like a fat balloon and his shackles and chains serve as an anchor for this wayward ship in the night. This ghostly hot air bag bounces and flops all over the room spouting out its warning for Scrooge.

Interestingly, the Ghost of Christmas Past is here portrayed as a young, rascally boy who shows Scrooge his past. Debit, who accompanies Scrooge on his journey, becomes the old man's scapegoat. "Why didn't you think of that, you twit," he screams at his loyal dog. During the sequence where the abandoned boy reads *Robinson Crusoe* during Christmas holiday, characters come to life in the shadows of the fireplace. Time to break into another song, "No friends at all when shadows fall."

The only musical number that works is the duet sung by Scrooge and Belle, as she breaks off their relationship because of changes in Ebenezer's character. He sings, "It's our wealth which will endure," while the sad Belle sings, "I'll cross this bridge with you if you show me the man I once knew... where's your passion, where's your heart?" He asks, "Can we cross this bridge together?" and her answer—"I'll cross this bridge alone." Very touching and a very

imaginative musical number which portrays inner turmoil in a way that a young child can understand.

Politically correct is the Ghost of Christmas Present, now recast as a black woman wearing green Christmas robes with flowers in her hair. After the toast at the Cratchit household, where Bob wishes his family to raise their glasses to Mr. Scrooge, Bob breaks into another very P.C. number, "Random Acts of Kindness, he could use some kindness." Most cleverly, Tiny Tim sits and reads a book, *Robinson Crusoe*, casting Tiny Tim as a younger version of Ebenezer Scrooge. At Fred's house the party gets rolling with a silly song, "Never caught a Santa sight as Santa's sooty suit."

While this animated version of *A Christmas Carol* borrows freely from other movie versions of the literary classic, it follows the George C. Scott version most closely, even including the towering presence of the Grim Reaper whose gigantic proportions make Ebenezer appear small and cowering.

Coming back to present day reality, Scrooge wakes and shows his joy by dancing with his pet Debit. The finale of the story makes a few changes to the plot, as Scrooge sends a message for nephew Fred and his wife to come to the Cratchit home, so both holiday sequences may be combined into one. Scrooge makes a mention of the festive household, comparing it to Mr. Fezziwig's parties of old, and Bob Cratchit repeats his toast, now universally applauded, "I give you Mr. Scrooge, the founder of the feast!"

A Christmas Carol (1997) could benefit from better songs and a more imaginative use of animation and visual imagery. Simply by throwing in a cute old dog and a seemingly helium-inflated excuse for Marley's Ghost does not a classic make. But for kids who might not be ready for the more realistic horrors of the Alastair Sim version, this might be a good first step.
—GJS

The following films are also based on Dickens' *A Christmas Carol* or are works of Dickens that include Christmas scenes:

Blackadder's Christmas Carol
Cast: Rowan Atkinson, Tony Robinson, David Barber, Jim Broadbent, Stephen Fry, Robbie Coltrane
Credits: Director: Richard Boden; Writers: Richard Curtis and Ben Elton; BBC; 1988

Renowned British comic Rowan Atkinson (Mr. Bean) takes a turn as Ebenezer Blackadder in this British comedy series. However, in this version Ebenezer goes to bed as the "nicest man in England" and the spirits manage convince how wrong he is so he wakes and vows to become "the horridest man in the world." This backward view of *A Christmas Carol* is most comparable to the comedy of Monty Python and fans of British comedy will not want to miss this adaptation of the classic.

Bugs Bunny and cartoon mates in the Warner Bros. version of *A Christmas Carol.*

Bugs Bunny's Christmas Carol (Looney Toons Christmas)

Cast: (voices) Mel Blanc, June Foray

Bugs helps give Mr. Scrooge (Yosemite Sam) a dose of the Christmas spirit. Tweety is Tiny Tim and Porky Pig is Bob Cratchit. When Scrooge has seen the light, Bugs says, "Ain't I a little Dickens?"

Carol for Another Christmas

Cast: Sterling Hayden, Peter Fonda, Richard Harris, Ben Gazzara, Steve Lawrence, Peter Sellers
Credits: Producer/Director: Joseph L. Mankiewicz; Writer: Rod Serling; ABC; 1964

Another television special based on *A Christmas Carol*. In this version, a man cannot get over the death of his son during WWII. The visit of three spirits helps him come to terms with his grief.

A Christmas Carol

Cast: (voices) Alastair Sim, Michael Hordern Melvyn Hayes, Michael Redgrave
Credits: Producer/Director: Chuck Jones; ABC; 1972
Television animated special of *A Christmas Carol*.

Ebbie

Cast: Susan Lucci, Wendy Crewson, Molly Parker, Lorena Gale, Nicole Parker, Taran Noah Smith
Credits: Producer: Jayme Pfahl; Director: George Kaczender; Writers: Paul Redford and Ed Redlich; ABC; 1995

Television version with Lucci as Elizabeth "Ebbie" Scrooge, a hard-nosed businesswoman who needs a visit from the Christmas ghosts to realize the joy of living.

Ebenezer

Cast: Jack Palance, Rick Schroder, Amy Locane
Credits: Producers: Douglas Berquist and Michael Frislev; Director: Ken Jubenville; Writer: Donald Martin; Nomadic; Television 1997

Jack Palance plays Scrooge in this Canadian version of *A Christmas Carol* that takes place in the 1870s old West.

Mr. Magoo's Christmas Carol

Cast: (voice) Jim Backus
Credits: Director: Abe Levitow; Television; 1962

Mr. Magoo appears as himself and stars in a stage version of *A Christmas Carol*. This format allows Mr. Magoo to engage in his famous pratfalls before and after performing the play, but keeps the story of *A Christmas Carol* intact with no comic interruptions.

Mr. Magoo (voiced by Jim Backus) as Ebenezer Scrooge.

Mystery of Edwin Drood

Cast: Claude Rains, David Manners, Heather Angel, Valerie Hobson, E.E. Clive, Douglass Montgomery
Credits: Producer: Edmund Grainger; Director: Stuart Walker; Writers: Leopold Atlas, John L. Balderston, Bradley King and Gladys Unger; Universal; 1935

Dark tale based on the Charles Dickens uncompleted novel has Rains murdering his nephew on Christmas Eve.

Scrooge

Cast: Seymour Hicks, Donald Calthrop, Robert Cochran, Mary Glynne, Oscar Asche, Marie Ney, C.V. France
Credits: Producers: Julius Hagen and John Brahm; Director: Henry Edwards; Writer: H. Fowler Mear; Paramount; 1935

This British production is by far the lesser known of the Dickens film adaptations but *Variety* notes, "...unqualifiedly has captured the spirit of the Dickens classic. It has been acted with fidelity to character, directed with consummate skill and intelligence... Heaviest duties are assigned to Sir Seymour Hicks, as Scrooge. His interpretation of this story-book character probably will be approved by most ardent Dickens fans. It is a topnotch performance throughout." Seymour Hicks also co-wrote the script with H. Fowler Mear based on the Dickens story.

Bill Murray and Carol Kane in *Scrooged*.

Scrooged

Cast: Bill Murray, Karen Allen, David Johansen, Bobcat Goldthwait, John Glover, Carol Kane
Credits: Producers: Richard Donner, Art Linson and Ray Hartwick; Director: Richard Donner; Writers: Michael O'Donoghue and Mitch Glazer; Paramount; 1988

This updated version of *A Christmas Carol* is neither funny nor heartwarming. Murray portrays television executive Frank Cross who is staging a historic live Christmas Eve broadcast of the Dickens classic complete with half-naked dancing girls and tiny mice with antlers stapled to their heads (at least that is what Cross orders a technician to do). Cross is visited by four spirits who try to remind him of the joy of Christmas. Johansen portrays a frighteningly grim ghost of Christmas Past who shows Cross his boyhood Christmases when their father returned home to an undecorated house to give him a package of meat for Christmas. If this doesn't sound funny, you're right. Kane is the ghost of Christmas Present and, while knocking the crap out of Cross, shows him his secretary's home on Christmas Eve (her son doesn't speak since experiencing a trauma) and the home of his brother. The spirit of Christmas Yet to Be is a fierce special effect who shows Cross his pathetic funeral that only his brother and sister-in-law attend. Also hovering in the background is fired employee Goldthwait who hits the skids and decides to seek his revenge on Cross. Karen Allen is the love interest, and we are shown their romance as they live in a small apartment and smoke dope. The film may be hip and may display a cynicism common today, but it's not my idea of a Christmas film.

Credits:

An American Christmas Carol
Cast: Henry Winkler, David Wayne, Dorian Harewood, Michael Wincott
Credits: Director: Eric Till; ABC, 1979

A Christmas Carol
Cast: Reginald Owen, Gene Lockhart, Kathleen Lockhart, Terry Kilburn, Leo G. Carroll, Ann Rutherford
Credits: Producer: Joseph L. Mankiewicz; Director: Edwin L. Marin; Writer; Hugo Butler; MGM; 1938

A Christmas Carol
Cast: Alastair Sim, Kathleen Harrison, Jack Warner, Mervyn Johns, Michael Hordern
Credits: Producer: George Minter; Director: Brian Desmond-Hurst; Writer: Noel Langley; UA; 1951

A Christmas Carol
Cast: Fredric March, Basil Rathbone, Ray Middleton, Bob Sweeney, Christopher Cook
Credits: Director: Ralph Levy; Writer: Maxwell Anderson; Television 1954

A Christmas Carol
Cast: George C. Scott, Frank Finlay, Edward Woodward, David Warner, Susannah York
Credits: Director: Clive Donner; Writer: Roger O. Hirson; Television 1984

A Christmas Carol
Cast: Tim Curry, Whoopi Goldberg, Michael York, Ed Asner
Credits: Writer: Louis Gassin; 1997

Mickey's Christmas Carol
Cast: (voices) Alan Young, Wayne Allwine, Clarence Nash
Credits: Producer/Director: Burny Mattinson; Writers: Alan Dinehart, Ed Gombert, Don Griffith, Tony L. Marino, Burny Mattinson and Alan Young; Buena Vista: 1983

The Muppet Christmas Carol
Cast: Michael Caine, Frank Oz, Jerry Nelson, Dave Goelz, Steve Whitmire
Credits; Producers: Brian Henson and Martin G. Baker; Director: Brian Henson; Writer: Jerry Juhl; Buena Vista; 1992

Scrooge
Cast: Albert Finney, Alec Guinness, Edith Evans, Kenneth More, David Collings, Anton Rodgers
Credits: Producer: Robert H. Solo; Director: Ronald Neame; Writer: Leslie Bricusse (Based on the Novel); National General; 1970

Here Comes Santa Claus...

Remember the excitement as you tried to stay awake and see Santa Claus? Remember leaving cookies and milk out for him? Remember the feeling of shock and emptiness you felt when you began to believe maybe, just maybe he wasn't real? In this chapter we examine Hollywood's portrayals of the jolly old elf himself—and we're sure you'll agree with us—there really is a Santa Claus

Discover
the
Miracle.

MIRACLE
ON 34TH STREET

Richard Attenborough

Jose Elias Moreno

Edmund Gwenn

John Call

David Huddleston

Tim Allen

Charles Durning

Miracle on 34th Street

1947 and 1994

One of the classic Christmas movies of all time, *Miracle on 34th Street* is one of the first movies to address the commercialism of Christmas, having been made a few years after the end of World War II, with Americans free to spend their hard-earned dollars without the fear of rationing or guilt. The theme of trying to value intangibles in a very materialistic, realistic world was a theme very important back in 1947, and it continues to be a major theme today at the end of the 1990s.

The story is simple and familiar. An old man who resembles Santa Claus and calls himself Kris Kringle (Edmund Gwenn) is outraged when he sees the Macy's Thanksgiving Day Parade Santa drunk and reports the singing/snoozing Santa to "the person in charge," Doris Walker (Marueen O'Hara). Kris is hired to replace the unconscious Santa, and he attracts hordes of kids to the store. Mr. Shellhammer (Philip Tonge), the toy department manager, tells Kris to always push the names of overstocked toys to children who do not know what they want for Christmas, but Kris, always thinking of the children, tears up the list. He even goes further and tells children and their parents to purchase toys at other department stores, including Gimbel's, Macy's chief competitor. However, parents flood Mr. Shellhammer's office congratulating him and the store "for this wonderful new stunt you're pulling. Imagine sending people to other stores. Imagine a big outfit like Macy's putting the spirit of Christmas ahead of the commercial." Interestingly enough, Mr. Macy himself applauds this sales strategy and stresses it must continue.

In the meantime, Doris Walker, divorced and bitter that her Prince Charming broke her heart, becomes a realist and teaches this philosophy to young daughter Susan (Natalie Wood); thus, Susan does not believe in giants, fairy tales nor Santa Claus. Apartment neighbor and lawyer Fred Gailey befriends Susan to meet her mother, but finds it very sad that the young child is unable to exercise her fantasy life. Even though Fred is a lawyer, he chooses to defend the underdogs—the only "fun" part of law. He seems to truly relish imagination and keeping the little boy alive inside the man.

Soon, Kris befriends a young sweeper at work, a 17-year-old boy, Albert (Alvin Greenman), who takes delight in dressing up as Santa Claus at his local "Y" for the kids in the neighborhood. However, the second-rate store psychiatrist, Mr. Sawyer (Porter Hall), a man hired to give psychological tests to employees, tries to convince the boy that his need to become Santa Claus is a "guilt complex" that results from having done bad things as a child. Kris is outraged that such a good-hearted person can be made to doubt his good intentions, and decides to report such unprofessional consultations to Mr. Macy himself; but before Kris can see the boss, Sawyer has Kris carted off to Bellevue Hospital, where he is committed.

Gailey comes to Kringle's defense requesting a formal sanity hearing before politically motivated (and running for re-election) Judge Henry X. Harper (Gene Lockhart). Gailey's goal is to convince the Judge that indeed Santa Claus does actually exist and that one Mr. Kris Kringle is, in fact, the actual Santa Claus. The Post Office hearing of the trial on the front page of the newspaper feels this would be the perfect opportunity to deliver the 50,000 pieces of mail being stored in the Dead Letter Office to Kris Kringle at the courthouse. Gailey uses the fact that the U.S. Post Office, a branch of the federal government, recognizes Mr. Kris Kringle as Santa Claus, and it is a federal crime to misdirect or intentionally mis-deliver mail. Thus, the government recognizes this man as the actual Santa Claus. Case dismissed.

Finally being won over by Kringle's charm, Doris Walker and daughter Susan both send him a letter of support admitting their belief that Kris is actually Santa

Natalie Wood stars as Susan in *Miracle on 34th Street* (1947).

Miracle on 34th Street attempts to create Christmas magic in the real world of 1947 America, and not just anywhere U.S.A., but cold and aloof New York City, the center of evil commercialism with its rivalry between all the major department stores. The film attempts to further three major ideas: 1) imagination and fantasy and faith are vital elements in everyone's life, 2) insanity is not so easily defined, and 3) kindness and good will toward man can be compatible with the harsh realities of modern life.

The first theme—Imagination and fantasy and faith are vital elements in everyone's lives—can be illustrated by the triangle relationship existing between the bitter Doris Walker, her daughter Susan and new, intended boyfriend Fred Gailey. Walker, returning home from coordinating the Macy's Parade, finds her daughter sitting in Gailey's apartment, watching the parade. Gailey says to Susan, as one balloon approaches, "He's certainly a giant." To which Susan matter-of-factly responds, "There are no giants, Mr. Gailey!" Gailey compromises his position by stating, "Maybe not now, Suzie, but in olden days." But Susan shakes her all-knowing head—no. When Gailey mentions that old fairy tale "Jack and the Beanstalk," Susan asks "Jack—Jack who... I never heard of that." She then announces she doesn't know any fairy tales. "My mother thinks they're silly," Susan explains. She doesn't know what her father thinks because her mother was divorced when she was only an infant. Using Susan as bait, when Doris finally arrives, Gailey has the child pester her mother to invite him to Thanksgiving dinner. But first Fred comments, "I see she doesn't believe in Santa Claus either. No Santa Claus, no fairy tales, no fantasies of any kind, is that it?" To which Doris responds, "That's right. I believe we should be realistic and completely truthful with our children and not having them growing up believing in a lot of legends and myths..." However, Doris does relent and invites Gailey to dinner.

Later in the movie, Gailey quits his law firm to defend Kris Kringle in court, the impracticality of such a move disturbing to Doris. "You don't have faith in me! Faith is believing in things when common sense

Claus. However, come Christmas morning Susan is disappointed and disillusioned that Kris has not delivered her dreamed-for present, a full-size house of which she gave Kris a picture. Gailey and mom, asking Susan to keep faith even if she doesn't get what she wants, are given directions from Kris on how to drive home to avoid traffic. As fate would have it, Susan cries out to Gailey to stop when she sees her dream house with a "For Sale" sign in front of it. Rushing inside, she runs upstairs, finds her room exactly as she dreamed it would be, spots the swing on the tree out back, and declares that Mr. Kringle is indeed Santa Claus. When Fred discovers that Doris told Susan to have faith in Kringle, he kisses her and suggests they purchase the house: a hidden marriage proposal. Both are stopped dead in their tracks when they see Kringle's cane leaning against the wall of the living room.

Edmund Gwenn gets our vote as favorite Santa Claus for his performance in *Miracle on 34th Street* **(1947).**

tells you not to... it's not Kris who's on trial, but everything he stands for—kindness and joy and love and all the other intangibles." To which Doris responds, "Those lovely intangibles of yours are attractive but not worth very much. You don't get ahead that way!" But Gailey, firmly believing in his actions passionately, tells her, "Some day, Doris, you'll find your way of facing this realistic world just doesn't work, and when you do, don't overlook those intangibles. You'll discover they are the only things that are worthwhile." It is only when Doris delivers this same message to daughter Susan that Gailey realizes that Doris has come over to his way of thinking, leading to the marriage proposal and house-buying suggestion.

The second theme—insanity is not so easily defined—is revealed in the raging wars between the two doctors: Dr. Pierce (James Seay) of the Brooks Memorial Home for the Aged and Mr. Sawyer of Macy's. Sawyer (even though Kringle passed his mental exam with flying colors having memorized it from the countless times already taken) believes Kringle will become violent when his delusion of being Santa Claus is challenged. But this is the conclusion from a man that Kringle noticed appears nervous, jittery and bites his

fingernails. Dr. Pierce from the Home calmly disagrees: "People are only institutionalized to prevent them from hurting themselves or other people. Mr. Kringle is incapable of either. He has a delusion for good." But the doctor does suggest that the commute from Brooks Home might be too far for Kris to make every day, that it might be better if Kris roomed with one of the Macy's employees so he could be brought back and forth to work every day during the holiday season. Of course Gailey invites him to share his room, suggesting that Doris could drive him to work every day. The point is this; even if Kris is delusional, he is always kind and helpful and does the right thing for people. Sometimes though, Kris does doubt his sanity. "Then there's Mr. Sawyer. He's contemptible, dishonest, selfish, deceitful, vicious—yet he's out there, and I'm in here (committed to Bellevue). He's called normal and I'm not. If that's normal, I don't want it!"

While Gailey is unable to convince little Susan of the merits of fairy tales, Kris is better able to connect with the child. He asks Susan what types of games she plays with the other children in the apartment building? She responds, "I don't play much with

Fred Gailey (John Payne), Doris Walker (Maureen O'Hara), Susan and Santa enjoy Christmas in *Miracle on 34th Street* (1947).

them. They play silly games... like today... all of them were playing animals. I told them I wasn't an animal, but a little girl." Of course, Kris says it sounds like a wonderful game to him. But, in order to play, Kris warns, "you got to have an imagination." Kris asks Susan if she knows what an imagination is. She says, "When you see things and they're not really there." Then Kris, in his vivid style, explains the imagination. "To me the imagination is a place all by itself. A separate country. Now, you heard of the French nation, the British nation. Well, this is the imagination; it's a wonderful place." Before long, Kris tells her next time the game is played, that she should become a monkey, and he teaches her how to pretend to be one. Insanity, delusion, imagination are all concepts that become blurred and difficult to define in this movie. The line that bests sums up this concept appears right after Doris tells Mr. Shellhammer that she fired Kris Kringle because "he's crazy; he thinks he is Santa Claus.' Mr. Shellhammer responds, "But maybe he's only a little crazy... like painters or composers or some of those men in Washington."

The third theme—kindness and good will toward man can be compatible with the harsh realities of modern life—becomes evident as Kris demonstrates thinking of children first, rather than thinking of commercialism, as he has been instructed by Mr. Shellhammer. "Imagine making a child think something it doesn't want, just because *he* bought too many of the same toys. That's exactly what I've been fighting against for years, the way they commercialize Christmas!"

When Kris asks little Peter what he wants for Christmas, he answers, very specifically, a fire engine. Mom, a few feet back, tries to tip off Santa that nobody, including Macy's, sells such a toy. To which Kris responds, "Well, Peter, you'll get your fire engine!" Mom pushes Peter ahead to "thank" Santa herself. "Macy's don't got any," she pouts. However, Kris immediately checks his notes and tells her the name of the store that carries such a toy for $8.50. "The only important thing is to make the children happy." Peter's mom is only the first of many mothers who personally visit Mr. Shellhammer to thank Macy's for having such a friendly policy in their store.

Peter's mother states she has never been a regular customer at Macy's before, but because of the new policy, she will be one now.

When word of this new "promotion" makes its way to Mr. Macy (Harry Antrim), the owner is delighted. "I want every sales person in this store to do precisely the same thing. If we haven't exactly what the customer wants, we'll send them where they can get it... We'll be known as the store with a heart, the store that places public service ahead of profit. Consequently, we'll make *more* profit that ever before!"

Albert, the sweeper who enjoys dressing as Santa for his YMCA is asked by Kris, "do you enjoy impersonating me?" He responds, "Oh yeah, I don't know, when I give the packages to the little kids, I like to watch their faces get that Christmas look all of a sudden. It makes me feel kinda good and important." Both bemoaning the commercialization of the holiday, Albert gripes, "Make a buck, make a buck. Even in Brooklyn, it's the same thing. Don't care for what Christmas stands for—just make a buck!"

Symbolically, this theme is driven home by one brief sequence where both rivals, Mr. Gimbel and Mr. Macy, pose with Kris Kringle between them, for a publicity photo shoot. Gimbel, realizing that he would appear to be the Christmas ogre, states, "This is the greatest good will policy I ever heard of... From now on, if we haven't got what the customer wants, send him back to Macy's." During the good will photo shoot, Mr. Macy hands Kris a check and asks what he intends to do with the money. Kris wishes to buy a new X-ray machine for his dear friend Dr. Pierce, but Macy admits the check won't cover the cost. Gimbel immediately chimes in, "I'll make up the difference." Macy then counters by offering Kris a 10 percent discount if he purchases the machine through Macy's. Gimbel strikes back with, "I'll sell it at cost!" All three then break out into chuckles and laughter as they shake hands and pose for the photographers. The world of commerce and good intentions/good will toward all men has symbolically come together.

Just as Dickens did a century earlier, screenplay writer/director George Seaton brought humanity and the spirit of Christmas to a compassionless urban center that was more concerned with making money than caring about people. In a wonderful speech delivered by Edmund Gwenn as Kris Kringle, such sentiment is aptly summed up: "For the past 50 years or so, I was getting more and more worried about Christmas. Seems we're all so busy in beating the other fellow in making things go faster and look shinier and cost less. Christmas and I are being lost in the shuffle... Christmas is not just a day, it's a frame of mind, and that's what's been changing. You two [Doris and Susan] are a test case for me. If I can win you over, there's still hope. If not, then I guess I'm through."

Luckily for all of us, Kris Kringle is far from being through.

Though it was neither critically loved nor broke the box-office coffers, the remake of *Miracle on 34th Street*, produced by John Hughes [who adapted the original George Seaton screenplay] and directed by Les Mayfield, shines in its own delightful way, once again bringing a tear to even the most jaded hearts.

First, to get the basics out of the way, Richard Attenborough's portrayal of Kriss (here an "s" is added) Kringle is nowhere near as classic as Edmund Gwenn's, and Elizabeth Perkins as Mrs. Walker is nowhere as effective as Maureen O'Hara's performance. However, Dylan McDermott brings a hound-dog sensitivity that was sorely lacking in John Payne's counterpart performance, and dare I say it, but Mara Wilson (*Matilda*) tops Natalie Wood's performance with a more multi-layered interpretation which brings depths of emotion to the part.

Dorey Walker (Elizabeth Perkins) seeks the help of Kriss Kringle (Richard Attenborough) in *Miracle on 34th Street* (1994).

Mara Wilson as Susan immediately wins over the audience in 1994's *Miracle on 34th Street*.

Wisely sticking to the original script, the major changes made by Hughes generally improve the plot flow and dramatic structure of the story. Instead of Macy's and Gimbel's, we have Cole's (the traditional, Gothic department store that maintains both eloquence and higher prices, but a store in deep financial troubles with the banks) and the nouveau Shopper's Express (cheaper prices and convenience) whose owner hopes to buy out the struggling Cole's once they fall even further on their financial faces. Unlike the good-natured rivalry in the original, here Victor Lambert (of Express) will never pose in the same shot with C.F. Cole (William Windom). Lambert is a corporate cutthroat.

Gone from the new screenplay are dime-store psychiatrist Mr. Sawyer (so there's no need to have the battle of the dueling psychiatrists) and the youthful Alvin.

Even though Dorey Walker (Perkins) and Bryan Bedford (Dylan McDermott) get together almost immediately, their relationship takes longer to solidify into love. In fact, Walker flat out rejects Bedford's romantic marriage proposal by not accepting his diamond ring. Bryan states, "I put my faith in you," to which Dorey responds coldly, "If that's true, then you're a fool!" However, the viewer knows that by picture's end love will win out. Susan makes the scenario clear at Thanksgiving dinner where she tells Dorey and Bryan that "this is just like television." She then pictures Bryan as the dad, Dorey as the mom

and "then we'd need a kind old fat person to be the cook..." She also envisions a little brother as well to complete her idyllic household. However, all is not well in the household: Dorey has been abandoned by her husband since the birth of Susan, and she again makes very sure that Susan is not distracted by confusing childhood myths. As sad-faced Susan tells Bryan, "Santa Claus... I've known for a long time... he's not real!"

However, Natalie Wood's character was convinced and totally believed everything her mother told her in the 1947 original, here Mara Wilson, obedient to her mom, still retains objectivity toward the subject, and her mother supports her by telling her she has the right to believe in anything she wishes. Susan pleads, "Is it okay to think about this a little more?" And her mother says yes and encourages her to ask Mr. Kringle for a very special Christmas present that the child would never ask her mother for, as a test.

While the Macy's drunken Santa Claus is never seen again after he is replaced by Edmund Gwenn in the original, the drunken Santa in the remake plays a larger and much more significant role. A few days before Christmas all the dime-store Santas are lined up at the local bar, including former Cole's Santa Tony (Jack McGee). Jack Duff (James Remar), second in command at Shopper's Express, hires Tony to first taunt Kringle at Cole's, trying to expose him as a phony to the children, and finally, hires Tony for the ultimate setup. After hours as Kriss Kringle leaves

Cole's for his walk home, Tony sneaks up behind him and verbally abuses the old man by calling him a mental case, a savvy old cripple, and worst of all, accuses him of having "a thing for the little ones." With that barb, Kringle turns and smacks Tony with a cane, the washed-up Santa falling to the ground, as instructed. Immediately entering the scene is Jack Duff, his assistant and a photographer who snaps a picture. Of course they loudly shout to Kriss, aren't you Cole's Santa, and the eyes of the crowd draw inward with disappointment. Kriss, taken off by the police to Bellevue Hospital, again purposely fails his mental exam, stating he has disgraced himself. The plot contrivance here is dramatically much more sound and believable than the original.

At the sanity hearing, the trial proceeds in pretty much the same way, with Judge Harper (Robert Prosky) still a political animal who wants to get out of this case unscathed. The prosecutor Ed Collins (J.T. Walsh) once again faces his wife on the stand who reveals that Collins teaches his children to believe that Kriss Kringle is indeed Santa. Instead of all the cards and letters being delivered to the courtroom at picture's end (which was a dramatic strength of the original), here the judge is able to declare Kriss Kringle as Santa because of a Christmas card personally delivered to the judge in court by Susan. Inside the card is a one dollar bill with "In God We Trust" circled. Harper quickly states that since the people are behind the government, and since government currency trusts in God without any actual proof of his existence, then, well, the people's will also stands behind Santa Claus. Case dismissed. Truthfully, this resolution lacks the punch and power of the original, and, to be honest, isn't even that convincing.

As with the original, the film ends with Kriss Kringle delivering his present to young Susan. Susan's wish was that she would get a daddy and baby brother and live in the dream home which Cole's uses as a backdrop for its Christmas catalogue. First, thanks to Dorey's insistence that Cole's stand behind Kriss during his sanity hearing, and now winning the case, having their Santa Claus vindicated, Dorey is rewarded with a substantial Christmas bonus, allowing her to put money down on the house (which is conveniently for sale). Kringle, using trickery, invites both Dorey and Bryan to St. Francis Church after Christmas Eve services with the priest prepared to marry them on the spot. This time Dorey cannot say no. Finally, as the proud parents announce this news to Dorey, Susan is all smiles and quietly declares, "Guess there's no doubt about it—he's real!" To which the confused parents then ask, "What else did you ask Mr. Kringle for?" When she sputters out a little brother, both parents look at each other in great concern, then melt into smiles as the film fades to the credits.

This *Miracle on 34th Street* is no classic, as cookie-cutter remakes seldom are. And the film is weakened by a listless Attenborough performance as Kriss Kringle which lacks the heart and passion of Gwenn's original, but McDermott's and Wilson's performances, and their emotional connections, spark the movie into rising above the standard movie retread. Mara Wilson is simply so cute, and the perky, enthusiastic little kid lurking beneath the polite and well-mannered six-year-old who "talks like she's 64" really wins the audience's sensibilities over quickly. Some of the plot changes actually work to the betterment of the movie, especially those sequences depicting the increased friction between rival department stores and the added scenes showing the revenge of the drunken Santa. The way in which the young child at first quietly doubts her mother's statement that Santa Claus does not really exist and the manner in which she is systematically convinced simply works better here.

Miracle on 34th Street (1947) is the real deal, and while the 1994 remake is doomed to be forgotten in remake Purgatory, it still has enough merits to make it worth viewing and enjoying.

—GJS

Santa Claus

1960

"Away up in the heavens, far out in space, in a beautiful golden crystal palace right above the North Pole lives a kind and jolly old gentleman..."

In 1960, Miami-based motion picture distributor K. Gordon Murray (the K stands for Ken) released

Jose Elias Moreno stars in *Santa Claus*.

Santa Claus's **Toyland is a vast factory in the clouds with candy cane trees and a giant heavenly door.**

the first of what would be a string of kiddie movies that kept theater matinees filled throughout the decade. Acquiring the rights from its Mexican producers, Murray financed the dubbing of the movie's original Spanish dialogue into English for American release. The picture was entitled simply *Santa Claus*. It was helmed by—of all people—grade Z horror filmmaker Rene Cardona, who directed the production with an eye for the macabre. It's no surprise, as a quick look at Cardona's resume reveals weird titles like *Wrestling Women vs. The Aztec Mummy* and *Night of the Bloody Apes* which is also known as *Gomar: the Human Gorilla* (featuring Santa Claus himself, actor Jose Elias Moreno).

Billed as being shot in Eastman Colorscope—which was actually a sales moniker made up by the enterprising Murray—the film today seems to exist only in faded hues. The acting is for the most part juvenile, the scenery seems to be made of cardboard and the dubbing is exceedingly inaccurate. This flick ain't no *Citizen Kane*. Yet for some reason, it would go on to play kiddie matinees into the 1970s and endure as one of the most bizarre and eccentric versions of the Santa legend.

Posters for the movie promised youngsters "An Enchanting World of Make-Believe." For the most part, that is what they got. The movie starts with fes-

tive red titles over a faux wrapping paper background as *Jingle Bells* is performed by the National Symphony Orchestra of Mexico. We see a gleaming Styrofoam castle balanced on a bed of cotton, perched over a starry backdrop. This, we are told, is Santa's crystal palace. Inside, the jolly one is arranging religious articles on a ceremonial crèche. He even talks to the statues of Mary and Joseph, asking the inanimate figures to excuse him so that he can "finish the toys" for Christmas. Of course, the plaster statues don't utter a single complaint.

So it's off to Toyland, a vast factory in the clouds with candy cane trees and a giant heavenly door. In keeping with the shoddy production values to which we've already grown accustomed in this low-budget effort, the clouds are rolls of cotton thrown on the sound stage floor, and the candy cane trees are obviously wooden flats. But who's complaining? The magic here is that it's snowing! And by the way, this factory has no elves (hiring all those midget actors would be too expensive, not to mention the green makeup and all those pointy shoes), so this Santa has assembled an international coalition of boys and girls, each segregated by culture, to toil away in his factory assembling the toys. And from the look of things, either these kids have a serious case of stage fright, or they're miserable! Not to mention the fact that Santa has under-dressed the majority of them in short sleeves—certainly not appropriate for the snowy North Pole. Hmm... shades of Kathie Lee Gifford.

And what is Santa's role in all this hard work? Well, old St. Nick sits up in his warm castle and plays the organ! That's right, he orchestrates the slave labor to tunes from around the world. In fact, we, the audience, are treated to a little song from each of the countries, performed by the child representatives themselves. First, the children from Africa—dressed as tribal primitives, complete with bones in their hair and ooga booga dancing. Shockingly politically incorrect! Then the Spanish kids sing to us with the verve and energy of two-day-old road kill. Next up is China where Santa Claus doesn't even exist (but that doesn't stop Santa from indenturing their children in his factory). The kids from England sing us the festive holiday song *London Bridge is Falling Down*, while Japan's kids look zonked out on Prozac; the kids from "The Orient" show us an underage belly dancer. Russia follows, and Santa is really getting worked up on the organ; his frequent demonic leers classify him as the creepiest Santa Claus ever. The girl from France is so drained of energy that she actually begins to yawn before the film editor quickly cuts away. The sequence

comes to a boil with a Carmen Miranda impersonator from South America, and a couple of kids dressed as Roy Rogers and Dale Evans singing that Yuletide classic *Mary Had a Little Lamb*. The big finale is from Mexico where the kids have those balloon-shaped heads and dead-eyed stares of the puppets in Disneyland's Small World ride. WHEW! A whopping six minutes of screen time that translates into an eternity of syrupy sweetness capable, no doubt, of putting a diabetic in the hospital. Then Santa laughs and laughs and laughs. Why? We can only speculate.

If getting through this mammoth sequence of joy wasn't hellish enough, the next stop on this holiday tour is HELL. No kidding. Hell—that burning fire-filled place of demons and eternal suffering. HUH? Well, every tale needs a villain, and in this one, Santa's adversary is the Devil himself! The horned minions of evil, all costumed in cheap, bright red Devil costumes, perform a ballet of evil around a roaring fire. Satanic priests in ceremonial robes circle around them (yes, this is supposed to be a Christmas movie). Lucifer's voice summons the chief of the demons, a wiry little devil named Pitch, and instructs him to go to Earth and foil Santa's quest to bring joy to the children. His punishment for failure: Instead of red hot

Santa Claus's enemy is the Devil, who sends Pitch to try to get children to do bad things by whispering in their ears.

coals for dinner he will be forced to eat chocolate ice cream. "Not that," cries out the demon, "Frozen foods are very bad for me, especially chocolate, it's very bad for my digestion which is very delicate!" But Lucifer's threat of punishment stands, and Pitch sets out to corrupt the children of Earth.

From here, the story shifts to Mexico and focuses on a little rich boy, a poor girl named Lupita and a group of mischievous boys. The demon can mystically appear to them, unseen by the mortal eye, but apparently visible in Eastman Colorscope. He whispers into their ears, trying to convince them to do naughty things. Santa gets wind of this through a Mexican boy (we know this because he's wearing a sombrero). Santa knows exactly what to do—find the kids and check up on their behavior. So it's off to Santa's Magic Observatory, which is conveniently only a few sound-stage steps away. Here the marvels of a modern age are at Santa's disposal—an array of science fictional gadgets designed to invade a child's privacy. He has the Ear-O-Scope, the Tele-Talker, the Cosmic Telescope and The Master Eye. All are mega spying devices that look like an unholy union of *Man from U.N.C.L.E* gadgetry and Pee-Wee Herman play stuff.

The little sombreroed kid activates the machine with the magic words, "By thy magic powers look for the child we're speaking, whether in a cave or behind a million mountains." At this, the Tele-Talker's giant pouty lips say, "All ready." Then the Master Eye—a vacuum cleaner hose with an oversized glass eyeball on the end—snakes its way outside a view portal. It scopes in on the curly-haired rich boy as he soundly sleeps in his well-appointed bedroom. Not much action here so Santa uses his Dream Scope to get a peek at the boy's dream. In the dream, the boy gets two gigantic boxes under the Christmas tree. They could easily hold a bicycle or a go-cart, maybe even a camping tent. Every boy and girl in the audience salivates over the prospects. Yet out of the boxes emerge his father and mother, both curiously dressed in formal attire, eager to greet their son with hugs and kisses. The boy is filled with glee; his wish has come true. YUK! As if this weren't enough, Santa continues his dream snooping, this time on Lupita. Her dream involves life-sized rag dolls that circle around her in an awkward dance. Whether this scene is supposed to depict a happy dream or a nightmare is anybody's guess. I do know that it gives ME the creeps!

Thus, the stage is set for a final showdown between good and evil—Santa and Satan—to take place on Christmas Eve. Santa first visits Merlin, the resident magician, who supplies him with the proper mind-altering drugs and mystical flower needed to keep his anonymity. Then it's off to Earth on his mechanical clockwork sleigh. His first stop is Mexico City (of course). Here, Santa uses Merlin's magic flower of invisibility and powdery sleep drugs to pull fast ones on the boys and girls who try to catch a glimpse of him. The Devil sets various traps, and even has Santa chased up a tree by a vicious dog named Dante (as in Inferno). But the portly present-giver comes up victorious every time, either shooting razor-sharp darts into the demon's backside, or humiliating him with chimney soot. Santa even unintentionally spits on the demon while clearing his throat (Santa spits!).

Santa does all the expected stuff; he slides down chimneys and leaves wrapped boxes under decorated trees. But perhaps the greatest wish-granting of all takes place in a swank Mexico city nightclub where the rich boy's parents are living it up. Santa mysteriously shows up and appeals to the lush in them by offering them martini glasses filled with his special "cocktail of remembrance." According to Santa, who is disguised as a cocktail waiter, "Those without love could not drink this cocktail as it would burn their throats." Not one to turn down a new form of getting soused, the parents drink up. Well, the sight of screaming parents with burned throats just wouldn't ring true in a holiday picture, so within moments the parents are racing off to hug their little son who had been left home alone. Actually, for the sake of novelty, I was kind of hoping for the throat-burning sequence.

The movie ends on an inspirational note when Lupita is granted her wish with a big, beautiful doll. Her mother is awestruck, and, as she watches Santa fly away in his rocket-like sleigh, gesticulates the holy sign of the cross. From cultural icon to religious deity—Santa is now God.

So as you can see, the K. Gordon Murray *Santa Claus* is a really bizarre piece of filmmaking. It's also full of contradictions. Is it artistically surreal or just cheap? Are parallels between the Santa and Jesus legends brilliant or simplistic? Were the filmmaker's intentions to produce a classic tale or a cash-in enterprise? Well, who cares? It is what it is. But one thing is sure: As far as entertainment value goes *Santa Claus* is a hoot... holding its ground as a goofy Christmas party movie, perfect for background entertainment while guests mingle and get tipsy on spiked eggnog. A party I will surely attend.

—JI

Santa (John Call) doesn't realize he is about to be kidnapped by Martians in *Santa Claus Conquers the Martians*. (Photofest)

Santa Claus Conquers the Martians

1964

Santa Claus Conquers the Martians is like the fat boy on the school playground. Tormenting him is so much fun that nobody can resist. Everybody knows it is unfair and cruel to push him around, but the pleasure of it is too delightful for even the most humane schoolboy to forgo.

Victims are necessary in schoolyards to satisfy the nastier Hydes among the youthful Jekylls. Victims in film circles fulfill similarly shameful needs; but a movie, once draped in the trappings of victimhood, cannot hope for adolescence or exercise or Jenny Craig to help it outgrow the problem.

What is about *Santa Claus Conquers the Martians* that creates a sense of victimhood? Is it its terrible earnestness? Earnestness always invites mali-

cious wit. And in researching *Santa Claus Conquers the Martians*, there is no shortage of that.

The popular image of Santa Claus comes largely from political cartoonist Thomas Nast, who designed a new illustration of him every year for *Harper's Weekly* from the 1860s to the 1880s. The definitive characterization of Santa Claus grew largely out of advertising images produced for the Coca-Cola Company. Beginning in 1931, and for over three decades following, it was illustrator Haddon Sundblom's interpretations of Santa on the back covers of *The Saturday Evening Post* and *National Geographic* that became etched in the American mind.

In the movies, actors both famous and unknown have all donned the familiar galoshes and quilted red suit to play "the right jolly old elf." The movies have run the gamut from overblown spectacles to the most cut-rate fantasy. But, save for an imported Mexican oddity and treacly 1940s fare (and remakes of same), the character of Santa Claus has enjoyed precious little big screen success over the years.

In fact, the greatest successes Santa can lay claim to on the screen have all come in a format that is the

Santa and Billy (Victor Stiles) and Betty (Donna Conforti) are held captive on Mars in *Santa Claus Conquers the Martians.*

antithesis of the nature of the myth. Horror movies embraced the idea of an ax-wielding psychopath dressed as Santa Claus with a fervor in the 1980s, a theme derived from "All Through The House," a 1953 story in *The Vault of Horror* #35. And, just as that issue and others in the classic E.C. Comics line inspired all sorts of psychological mumbo jumbo (and even a Senate investigation), so too did the "Santa-as-slasher" movies cause no end of hand-wringing debate on talk shows and in newsmagazines about parental responsibility and filmmakers' greed. Ho, ho, horrors!

For most of us who grew up in the 1960s, however, Christmas TV specials sufficed as our passports to Yuletide magic. Simply by turning a knob on the old Zenith, we could step from our humble homes into a world of dazzling holiday color, bustling with misfit toys and cartoon snowmen, none of whom had the slightest difficulty breaking into an enchanting song or fabulous dance.

With these annual Christmas telecasts, the three networks made sure, long before retailers and the 1980s glut of shopping malls (16,000 built in just that decade!) beat us over the head with it, we knew Christmas was on its way.

Strangely, only one man recognized the market then for a big screen adventure of Santa Claus. Paul L. Jacobson was a onetime unit manager for *The Howdy Doody Show* who saw the demand for a holiday movie made especially for the youngest consumers. "There is a great void when it comes to a Christmas film for children," he related in the pressbook. "Except for the Disneys, there's very little in film houses during the season that kids can recognize and claim as their own."

Thus inspired, producer Jacobson recruited production personnel from local New York television and, renting The Michael Myerberg Studios (a converted airport hangar at Roosevelt Field on Long Island), set about producing a Christmas movie targeted exclusively at an audience of children.

Jacobson decided to incorporate some very rudimentary aspects of science fiction into his Yule confection, exploiting a favorite selling point for young moviegoers. Thus was born the legendary *Santa Claus Conquers the Martians*.

Budgeted at only $200,000, Jacobson was obliged to cast his film with local talent. In the lead role of Santa Claus, John Call was recruited from the Broadway production of *Oliver!* where he played the relatively minor part of the doctor. Call had been cast in very minor parts in a few films in the 1950s, but the stage was apparently his forte.

Also plucked from the *Oliver!* cast was young Victor Stiles, who played a pickpocket there, to play the Earth child Billy Foster. Similarly cast was Donna Conforti as Billy's sister Betty, who was playing a Dutch child in a minor holiday-themed musical called *Here's Love*, also on Broadway, when Jacobson enlisted her talents.

Two familiar faces to television viewers and moviegoers (in the sense of "Hey, didn't I see him someplace before?") first saw exposure in *Santa Claus Conquers the Martians*. Brawny Vincent Beck, cast as the Martian villain Voldar, would soon pop up regularly on TV, and find work on the big screen in *One Spy Too Many* (1966) and *The Bamboo Saucer* (1967), both minor science fiction offerings. Bill McCutcheon, cast as comic relief Martian Dropo, later showed up in several mainstream movie hits, including *Steel Magnolias*, *Family Business* (both 1989) and *Mr. Destiny* (1990).

The most famous cast member of *Santa Claus Conquers the Martians* is inarguably Pia Zadora, for which the movie receives no little notoriety today. She was born Pia Schipani in Hoboken, New Jersey in 1954. Because she was painfully shy, the nuns at Our Lady Queen of Martyrs school suggested she take drama classes to help her overcome it.

Burgess Meredith took the girl from the American Academy of Dramatic Arts and put her in a Broadway play starring Tallulah Bankhead that he was directing. *Santa Claus Conquers the Martians* producer Jacobson found her there, slathered on some green greasepaint and cast her as Girmar, the daughter of the Martian leader.

Jacobson returned to Broadway for key behind-the-scenes personnel as well. He enlisted Nicholas Webster to direct the proceedings. Up until then, Webster had only one film to his credit, *Gone Are the Days* (1963), a screen version of Ossie Davis' Broadway *Purlie Victorious*. Co-starring Godfrey Cambridge and a young Alan Alda, the movie had earned high marks for its topicality and energetic acting, qualities Jacobson no doubt hoped could be bestowed on *Santa Claus Conquers the Martians*.

With the first telescopes, astronomers saw in Mars a planet most like Earth. It has four seasons, white polar caps that wax and wane and a day only a little longer than 24 hours long. In the 18th century, the astronomer William Herschel felt justified in concluding that the inhabitants of Mars "probably enjoy a situation in many respects similar to our own." For *Santa Claus Conquers the Martians*, however, deprived of Earthly holidays, the Martian civilization is falling on hard times.

Monitoring a newscast beamed from Earth, the children of Mars get their first exposure to Santa Claus (John Call) as he leads a correspondent (Ned Wertimer) on a tour of his North Pole home and workshop. The Martian children have become difficult (refusing their buttered asparagus food pills and unable to rest unless doused with "sleep spray"), and Kimar (Leonard Hicks), their leader, consults with an ancient Martian sage (Carl Don) deep in a forest of Christmastime spun glass ("Angel hair") and dry ice fog.

The wise old Martian determines it is early December on Earth, and reckons the deprivation of such innocent childhood joys as Earthlings have has made the Martian children so listless. Kimar, together with his council, sees Santa Claus as the solution to raise their children from their doldrums. They decide to kidnap the jolly fat man and bring him back to the red planet.

But, upon arriving on Earth, the aliens are baffled by the proliferation of street-corner Santas. Landing, they force (nicely) a pair of Earth children (Victor Stiles and Donna Conforti) to lead them to the genuine article. They blast off again for the North Pole.

Billy and Betty escape when they arrive in the frozen wilderness, hoping to warn Santa. They encounter a polar bear (Gene Lindsey), and are eventually recaptured by the Martians via their boxy robot sentry Torg (Joe Elic).

Invading his Arctic workshop, Santa thinks the clanking Torg is only an elaborate toy, but agrees to accompany the Martians after they temporarily put Mrs. Claus (Doris Rich) and his elves in suspended animation. Voldar (Vincent Beck), a dissenting council member, decides that the two children have to accompany them back to Mars to prevent the Earth people from learning of Santa's cosmic fate and retaliating. (The very next scene has a whirlwind of newspaper headlines from around the world trumpeting Santa's fate, as Mrs. Claus calls the media as soon as she thaws.)

The UN security council convenes, and plans are implemented to launch a rescue effort. This provides the opportunity for stock footage, this time of a Gemini rocket launch, back when NASA was all crewcuts and horn-rimmed glasses; but the mission is seemingly never completed.

Voldar is against the idea of Santa's benign influence over future Martian generations. "Mars used to be the planet of war," he grouses. His efforts to expel the Earth trio out of an airlock en route are thwarted. After arriving on Mars, Voldar escapes imprisonment and plots revenge while sitting in a remote cave.

Santa (whose very appearance inspires giggles from the Martian children) sets up an automated workshop, and the production of toys immediately lifts the Martian children out of their doldrums. When Voldar attempts to kidnap Santa, he mistakenly snatches Dropo (Bill McCutcheon), a goofy Martian dressed up as the jolly fat man.

When the villain learns he has an impostor, he creeps into the workshop. Jumping up from behind the assembly line, the rejuvenated Martian children, together with their Earthling counterparts, attack Voldar. They pelt him with rubber balls and foam tennis rackets, showering him in soap bubbles and confetti. Tears streaming down his cheeks, Voldar is taken into custody.

Santa Claus and the two Earth children are returned home. The Martian people are grateful for their help and inspiration. A sing-along called "Hooray for Santa Claus" (pronounced "Santy" Claus) brings down the curtain, complete with onscreen lyrics so audiences could join in before scampering out the exits.

Despite its intended juvenilia, the script for *Santa Claus Conquers the Martians* has a couple of strangely accurate predictions of future technology and the short attention span of the up and coming generation. The glimpse of a realistic Martian doll (what would be called an "action figure" nowadays) made by one of Santa's elves certainly anticipated the run on "G.I. Joe," "Captain Action" and "Major Matt Mason" lines of boys' toys later in the decade. But the forecast of the up-and-coming generation's short attention span certainly deserves note:

"They are bored," the wise old Martian croaks in his counsel. The dialogue anticipating the reliance modern parents have on TV and computers to broaden their children's minds. He continues, "Our electronic teaching machines are attached to their brain while they are in their cradles, information is fed into their minds in a constant stream and by the time they can walk they are adults." One can almost imagine the Sony PlayStations and Nintendo machines tucked away in the Martian bedroom corner.

Even for children's science fiction, the U.S. military suffers from that ubiquitous Cold War paranoia pervasive of the era, though there's a delightful bit of non sequitur logic when the approaching Martians' spaceship vanishes from radar screens. "[The armed forces] believe the object has either disintegrated in space, or it may be a spaceship from some other planet which has the ability to nullify our radar beams," a straight-faced newscaster (Don Blair) intones.

He continues, "Because of the ominous situation, the President has ordered the Strategic Air Command into action," which permits the ample use of government-approved stock footage of fighter planes scrambling, radar dishes pivoting on their axis and long range bombers refueling in midair.

Over the years, John Call has taken a lot of flak for his performance as Santa Claus, with critics going so far as to question his sobriety during filming. But the criticism is unjustified; Call is everything the part demands. He is alternately jovial and consoling, always working to brighten the kidnapped children's spirits, upbeat and, well, jolly. While a good deal of padding seems to have been used to fill him out for the part (his visible wrists and hands don't look particularly thick), Call is still every inch the Santa Claus idealized by a 1960s child.

Director Nicholas Webster has a sure hand in the proceedings, and it's a shame he was never given a film project (or the finances) he could prove his mettle with. He returned to the science fiction genre in 1968 with *Mission Mars*.

There is some terrific low-budget ingenuity in evidence in *Santa Claus Conquers the Martians*. For the sound effect of the spaceship's retro-rockets firing, someone merely discharges a CO_2 fire extinguisher off-camera each time. The long levers used to lower the spaceship's landing gear really look as if they manipulate something hugely mechanical. Keeping the lights dim—the low-budget filmmaker's oldest trick to disguise set imperfections—probably hides a multitude of sins (it's remarkably dark for a cheery children's movie), but it's forgivable. The shots of the miniature spaceship are well done, belching fiery exhaust against a starry black backdrop.

For all her notoriety in *Santa Claus Conquers the Martians*, Pia Zadora neither proved herself nor embarrassed herself as the little Martian girl. She continued to appear on- and off-Broadway through her late teens but received little critical acclaim. At what must have been her lowest ebb, Zadora was cast in the lead role in a version of *The Diary of Anne Frank*, the 1955 play by Frances Goodrich and Albert Hackett. When the Nazis show up, looking for hidden Jews, the audience started shouting, "She's upstairs! She's upstairs!"

Undeterred, Zadora turned her attention to singing old standards, eventually playing nightclubs and Las Vegas. Here Zadora finally found her niche.

When asked about *Santa Claus Conquers the Martians*, Zadora only laughs and says, "Well, my husband's five grandchildren love it."

Santa Claus Conquers the Martians was picked up by Joseph E. Levine's Embassy Pictures and premiered in some 100 theaters in the Chicago and Milwaukee areas in November 1964. As a general rule, the release of any children's movie was a time for critics to make sure the brickbats were handy and in

Santa Claus is saved by Martian children in *Santa Claus Conquers the Martians*.

good supply. But moviegoers made sure it was their wallets that were ready year after year.

With ads saturating the newspaper and television, Embassy made *Santa Claus Conquers the Martians* an annual hit throughout the mid- and late-1960s.

Leaving no potential marketing stone unturned, a comic book adaptation was published by Dell under the banner of its Movie Classics line in March 1966 with a photo cover; another version was given away with a Golden Record of the soundtrack.

Capitalizing on the box-office success of James Cameron's *Aliens*, Valley Star Productions re-released the movie on video in 1986 as *Santa Claus Defeats the Aliens*. One can imagine the disappointment of seasonal renters plopping down their two bucks who expected slavering, H.R. Giger-designed monsters bursting from the chest of an elf and chowing down on some terry cloth stop-motion reindeer.

It may be difficult for today's jaded readers to believe that, during its initial release, *Santa Claus Conquers the Martians* garnered some pretty good reviews. *The New York Herald-Tribune* found "the children in the film... quite appealing"; across town, Kathleen Carroll of *The New York Daily News* found it "a gay, imaginative Christmas gift for children."

It wasn't until the late 1970s that *Santa Claus Conquers the Martians* began to acquire its dubious notoriety. True, there had been a nasty (and oft-cited) dig at the movie in the 30th issue of *The Monster Times* several years before, wherein Jason Thomas and future "Phantom of the Movies" (of *The New York Daily News*) Joe Kane described it as "absolutely the worst science-fiction flick ever made, bar none!"

This naive assessment anticipated (and may have even prompted) authors Harry Medved and Randy Dreyfuss to include *Santa Claus Conquers the Martians* among *The Fifty Worst Films of All Time*, first published in 1978, and paving the way for a slew of mean-spirited imitators. Why indulge in tilting at windmills and shooting barreled fish like cult favorite *Plan 9 From Outer Space* (ooh!) and big-budget flop *Heaven's Gate* (aah!) when defenseless and inoffensive fare like *Santa Claus Conquers the Martians* exists?

More recently, the tide has started to turn. Audacious film director (and self-proclaimed "Prince of Puke") John Waters, loathing those cheery Christmas movies Hollywood was wont to produce, conceded to *The San Francisco Chronicle* (12/12/96) that he liked *Santa Claus Conquers the Martians*. Perhaps the greatest devotee of kitsch to work behind a camera, Waters fulfilled a long-held ambition and cast Zadora as a beatnik in his 1988 mainstream breakthrough film *Hairspray*.

The distinctive energy of Hollywood Christmas movies petered out in the 1960s. Various reasons can be cited. The people running the studios became more interested in bottom lines than in art. Musicals were very expensive. Tastes change, times change A few bloated tries in the 1980s (*Popeye*, *Annie*) and '90s (*Newsies*, *Evita*) failed to rekindle the flame.

But *Santa Claus Conquers the Martians* is a splendid reminder that not all that long ago, the country and its movies could link arms and, bursting into song and dance, celebrate Christmas with each other. —DHS

Santa's Favorite Christmas Treats

Mrs. Claus's Sugar Cookies
2 1/4 cup flour
2 teaspoon baking powder
1/2 teaspoon salt
1/2 cup butter
1 cup sugar
1 egg, beaten
1/4 teaspoon lemon extract
1/2 teaspoon vanilla
1/4 cup milk

Sift flour with baking powder and salt. Cream butter and sugar, add egg, and beat until smooth and fluffy. Stir in flavorings. Add dry ingredients alternately with milk, ending with flour. Beat well after each addition. Chill dough. Roll 1/4 inch thick on well floured board. Sprinkle with granulated sugar and cut with cookie cutters. Place on greased baking sheet and bake at 375° for 8 to 10 minutes.

Elf Judy's Christmas Cocoa

4 tablespoons sugar
2 tablespoons Hershey's cocoa
1/4 cup water
3/4 cup milk
3/4 cup half and half
1/2 teaspoon vanilla

In a saucepan combine 4 tablespoons of sugar, 2 tablespoons of Hershey's cocoa and 1/4 cup water. Cook on medium heat, stirring constantly until mixture boils. Add 3/4 cup milk and 3/4 cup half and half. Heat but do not bring to a boil. Remove from heat and add 1/2 teaspoon of vanilla or other flavorings. Top with marshmallows or whipped cream for the ultimate in cocoa decadence. Amounts of sugar can be changed to taste and reduced fat milk can be substituted for the regular milk and the half and half.

Elves Delectable Chocolate Chip Cookies

3/4 cup brown sugar
1/2 cup granulated sugar
1 cup butter
2 eggs
1 teaspoon baking soda
(dissolved in 1 tablespoon of hot water)
1 teaspoon vanilla
1 teaspoon salt
2 1/2 cups flour
2 packages chocolate chips

Cream butter, sugar and eggs. Add the rest of the ingredients. Chill dough. Bake 375° for 8-10 minutes on an ungreased cookie sheet.

Frosty's Peanut Butter Cookies

1 cup butter
1 cup peanut butter
1 cup sugar
1 cup brown sugar
2 eggs
2 1/2 cups flour
2 teaspoons baking soda

Cream butter, sugar and eggs. Add the rest of the ingredients. Mix well. Chill dough. Roll into one inch balls. Smash down with fork. Place two inches apart on an ungreased cookie sheet. Bake 375° for 10-12 minutes.

Future Santa Claus (Tim Allen) has cocoa with elf Judy (Paige Tamada) in *The Santa Clause*.

Santa Claus (David Huddleston) makes friends with Joe (Christian Fitzpatrick) in *Santa Claus: The Movie.*

Santa Claus: The Movie

1985

Sometimes the big-budget expectations of Hollywood producers go awry, and such films as *Santa Claus: The Movie* result, a feature that was sold as the ultimate Christmas movie, but a picture that fails on almost every level. The story itself features situations that even the youngest children would find difficult to swallow. The characters are often obnoxious; performances, especially John Lithgow's, sometimes go way over the top. But the bottom line in any Christmas movie is the emotion it instills in the audience; and, while most decent Christmas films leave a lump in the throat or a tear in the eye, *Santa Claus* only leaves a sense of relief that it is over. Even David Huddleston's performance as Santa Claus is listless and generic, doing very little with a characterization that could be developed in so many different directions.

The movie's beginning, occurring centuries ago, recounting the reality and the myth of Santa Claus, is perhaps the most interesting part of the screenplay, and it suggests a dark-toned movie that could have been at least interesting. Under the twinkling stars of the night, and the layer of fluffy clouds underneath, lies the snowy cottage at the top of the world where an older woman is telling her younger kids that Uncle Claus might not be able to make it through the heavy snow this year. But, an older boy doesn't seem to worry; that this was the same story she told last year. However, within moments Uncle Claus in his sleigh arrives at the household with his bag of presents. The children are all focused on his or her presents; but Uncle Claus asks, "Don't I hear something first?" Then in unison, they all chant, "Merry Christmas, Uncle!" The relatives wonder aloud where Claus finds the time to make all the toys for the children every year. However, these same relatives warn Claus to not try to go through the forest tonight; because the storm is simply too dangerous. Claus answers, "Other children need their toys on the other side of the forest," and all the people assembled note the happy expression on Claus' face when he gives the children their toys. But, out in the forest, the snow is getting heavier and the weather is turning colder; and, before long, the reindeer drop in their tracks from exhaustion. Santa tries to rouse them by telling them food and warmth is just a little further ahead. But the ani-

Patch (Dudley Moore) goes to work for B.Z. (John Lithgow) in *Santa Claus: The Movie.*

mals do not respond. Anya (Judy Cornwell), Claus' wife, sits alongside him, slowly freezing to death, her husband trying to warm her. Soon, both Claus and his wife are lulled into a deep, freezing sleep, as the reindeer remain motionless before them. Failing to heed the warnings of the relatives, the reindeer and their human cargo are dead, or close to it, as the snow continues to pound the countryside.

Soon, the stars begin to twinkle again, and the snow stops, the reindeer magically awaken, as do Claus and his wife, and the stars grow brighter. A triangle of vibrant light from the heavens transport an army of elves closer and closer to the sleigh, each elf holding one candle. An elder elf, Dooley, states, "We've been expecting you for a long, long time." Another younger elf, Patch (Dudley Moore), tells them they are home, "This is your home now." Magically, a huge home in the white wilderness appears; and, once inside, Claus and Anya see a wonderland of hardworking elves making toys, toys to be given to the children of the world. Dooley tells the humans that they will live forever, just like the elves. New reindeer are introduced, and soon the elves are working on a new uniform for Claus to wear, at first attempting one colored green. "Green's not his color," Anya protests; but after brown is also rejected, they all agree upon the color red. Eventually the entire household is alive and marching in-step to the Christmas music, as they work on toys methodically and efficiently. All the elves laugh and giggle as they work, totally at peace. Finally the suit, reindeer and sleigh are ready for the Christmas Eve visit, and the wizened elder elf (Burgess Meredith) makes his pronouncement concerning Claus. "Prophecy has come to pass that there would come to us a chosen one. That he,

having no child of his own, would love all children everywhere, and that he himself would be an artisan, a craftsman, a skilled maker of toys... come forth. From this day on, now and forever, you will bring our gifts to all the children in all the world... all this to be done on Christmas Eve... an endless night for you, until all your work is done... you will be called Santa Claus!" The reindeer team are fed sparkling, twinkling food which gives them the gift of flight. And then Santa and the team are off to complete their Christmas Eve duties. In a tale rich with myth, silly performances and noninvolved screenwriting quickly sink the project from this point onward.

Now, the sense of myth, ritual and legend, which returns a kindly old uncle from the dead, reborn and given immortality as the cherished Christmas icon Santa Claus, is quite ambitious and dramatic. True, the special effects cannot quite deliver the illusion; Uncle Claus is not the most endearing or expressive actor and the army of elves is sometimes silly, especially the appearance of devilish Dudley Moore. But, simply put, this is the best the film has to offer.

First, the centuries slip away; and we end up in modern times.

Two elves, Patch and Puffy (Anthony O'Donnell), compete to be Santa's assistant by embarking in a contest to see who can make the most toys in a specified amount of time. The ambitious Patch wants to modernize and use the assembly line method, while Puff prefers the older, traditional method of toy making. Of course, Patch wins the contest and is appointed chief assistant; but his mass-produced toys (failing to undergo any quality control check) fall apart immediately after Christmas leaving children crying. Patch, disgraced, leaves the North Pole for good.

Down in the world of reality, the United States, Patch, at first depressed, wants to find a way to impress Santa Claus that he is the world's best maker of toys; but, first, the audience encounters one B.Z. (John Lithgow), one of the largest manufacturers of toys here in the United States, who at the moment is appearing before a Senate subcommittee investigating parental complaints against his toys. Performing B.Z. totally over the top, Lithgow shouts his lines, rolls back the skin on his forehead and pops out his eyes and he twitches in obnoxious overplay. One toy is shown to easily catch on fire, while another toy is shown to be stuffed with nails. His underlings tell him, department stores are pulling all their toys from the shelves in a mass exodus. B.Z. is at his wit's end.

But soon the naive Patch appears in B.Z.'s office, identifying himself as an elf and manufacturer of toys. Admitting he doesn't know much about money, Patch tells B.Z. to throw out all his old toys. Patch will be able to make something fantastic. What he creates turns out to be called the "Puce Pop," which allows children who eat the lollipop to float into the sky. Of course B.Z. captures the imagination and attention of the children at Christmas, and Santa's old-fashioned toys are forgotten, making Santa feel rejected and worthless. B.Z.'s goal is to replace the image of Santa Claus at Christmas time with his own.

Santa befriends a totally cute runaway boy, Joe (Christian Fitzpatrick), whose cynical, street-smart attitude is too easily won over by the magic of Santa Claus. As written the part is ridiculous, but as enacted by Fitzpatrick, the performance is embarrassing. Joe befriends B.Z.'s parentless niece Cornelia (Carrie Kei Heim), again a very cute little girl, but at least she's an adequate actress. And these two children are here simply to create audience identification with the younger viewing audience; but they fail to ignite a spark with each other or with Santa Claus, who simply goes through the motions with them.

But greed turns out to be the downfall of B.Z., who orders Patch to "juice up the formula" and create a new childhood toy sensation in time for his artificially created Christmas II to hit March 25. Meanwhile, Santa seems ready to throw in the Christmas towel and seems most in need of professional counseling, his inner spirit of "ho, ho, ho" totally dimmed. "The world is a different place. People don't seem to care about giving a gift just to see the light of happiness in a friend's eye. Just doesn't feel like Christmas anymore. Maybe this fellow B.Z. is smarter than I am. Maybe I'm just an old fool," the old elf muses. Elsewhere, B.Z. is enthusing with the old Christmas spirit, which used to belong to Santa Claus. "I'm taking over Christmas. By next Christmas, kids will be writing to me, B.Z.!"

However, the new Christmas II presents, candy canes coated with the new formula, are volatile when exposed to heat and will explode. Soon Patch, in his own super-powered flying auto, heads out with Joey, whom he has rescued from B.Z.'s clutches, unaware that a supply of the candy canes is in the back of his car is getting hotter and hotter as the car flies through the sky. Santa, warned of the peril by Cornelia, is in hot pursuit in his sleigh; but Santa is down two reindeer because of flu, and only by performing the often-tried-but-never-completed "super-duper-looper"

The scenes at the North Pole are the best *Santa Claus: The Movie* has to offer.

can Santa manage to save Patch and Joe after the car explodes throwing its occupants into free-falling space. But all ends up well as the children are rescued, Patch and Santa become friends again and B.Z. eats one of his own candy canes and floats out into the vastness of space, literally destined to orbit the Earth forever. Joe and Cornelia, both parentless, are allowed to live at the North Pole, to be tutored by the elves so their education will not be ignored.

Santa Claus: The Movie tries to touch all the bases necessary for a Christmas movie, but it forgets the essentials: good acting, an imaginative script and a sense of real human emotion. Even though the budget was rather large, this 1985 production, directed by Jeannot Szwarc, is passionless and bland. Trying to sell the movie on Dudley Moore's name was effective marketing at the time, but Dudley Moore simply sleepwalks through the movie playing the neglected elf who unfortunately aligns himself with sleazy B.Z. John Lithgow, rather than sleepwalk through the movie, yells in his performance, projecting every line of dialogue with the volume cranked up to 10, lacking all nuance and subtlety required to make his satiric villain come to life. In a children's movie where the leading child actors are forgettable, the movie's in a great deal of trouble. And what could be worse than featuring a listless actor portraying Santa Claus? This is easily the most forgettable mainstream Christmas movie released in the last 30 years.

—GJS

Ernest Saves Christmas

1988

Today's children lack a comedian that they can call their own. The last generation had Jerry Lewis, and before him Abbott and Costello, Laurel and Hardy and Charlie Chaplin appealed to audiences of the 1920s to the 1940s. If a career misfire hadn't occurred to comedian Paul Reubens (Pee-Wee Herman), he might have been this generation's torch-bearer. But it seems the mantle of this generation's comic fool has fallen to wacky Jim Varney who has starred in a series of feature films based upon his Ernest P. Worrell character. One of the most entertaining certainly has to be *Ernest Saves Christmas* (1988), a movie that like *The Santa Clause*, deals with passing the torch from an older Santa to a new one, done in such a way that the cynical children of today can still accept the magic of Christmas and of Santa Claus.

The movie opens in Orlando, Florida on December 23, as a well-dressed gentleman who looks like Santa Claus exits a plane engaging in small talk with another businessman. When asked if this was his first time in Orlando, Santa Claus (Douglas Seale) says, "I fly in once a year... but in a different way!" When asked where he's from, he answers, "Up north." Next asked about his line of work, he states, "Toys." When asked how long has he been in this line of work, Santa smiles and says, "Longer than you can imagine." Asked if he is here on business, Santa responds that he is here "to select a replacement, someone to take over my duties." However, as this conversation occurs, younger children at the airport point and smile at the kind old man, who twinkles his eyes and smiles back. "Don't think I quite have the magic for another Christmas," Santa tells his companion. ""Now I have trouble recalling who was naughty, who was nice... who asked for a toy truck." The concerned businessman rattles back, "Sounds like a database problem."

Enter our hero, Ernest, who is driving a cab and is told by his lone customer to get him to the airport pronto. Immediately, Ernest goes into overdrive driving aggressively, switching lanes and rocking his passenger back and forth in his seat until the poor man falls out the side door. "I told him about that seat belt," Ernest complains, pulling onto the side of the road, picking up the unconscious man and carrying him back to the cab. "Mister, you can't get out here." The man, lying on his side with a frozen look of shock on his face, is dropped off at the airport and deposited on the luggage rack conveyer belt. It is here that Ernest picks up his next fare, Santa Claus, who is leaving the airport.

Ernest immediately recognizes his passenger as Santa Claus and the old man smiles and states, "I am him!" Soon a lone Christmas tree falls off a truck carrying a shipment of trees, and Ernest reflects on the importance of trees as "a symbol of brotherly love," and almost crashes his cab, stopping on the freeway, backing his car up, to shove the tree in the back seat (which breaks out the side glass) so his friend Vern will have a tree this Christmas. "Christmas is just about my favorite time, ever since I was a little kid. I always felt like it was my own personal holiday... I'm as one with the Yuletide," he declares to Santa. Santa asks Ernest if he knows a Joe Carruthers (Oliver Clark), the man he is seeking out. Ernest sputters out that's the guy from the Uncle Joe show that was canceled only weeks ago. Ernest assumes the man must be rich, but Santa informs him that a man who does a children's show on local television once a week doesn't do it for money. Obviously, Santa has his new replacement all picked out.

Meanwhile, a teenage runaway (but in this sanitized world, she is clean and wears trendy clothes with her hair done up just right), who skips out of paying for her meal at a corner restaurant, runs right into the path of Ernest's cab, jumping in the front seat. Pointing, she cries, "That's my mean uncle! He makes me

Santa (Douglas Seale) tries to pay Ernest (Jim Varney) with play money in *Ernest Saves Christmas*.

work in the restaurant like a slave... don't let him get me!" She introduces herself as Harmony Star (Noelle Parker), a name the world will remember, but we later find out she is really Pamela. Arriving at Santa's destination, the Orlando Children's Museum, Santa is unable to pay his $32.00 fare because all he has is play money, having forgotten that he put real money in a child's game last Christmas. "What we have here is a failure... to accumulate," Ernest states angrily. But thinking and calming down, Ernest tells the old man the drive is on the house and to have a Merry Christmas.

Santa Claus sees prime candidate Joe Carruthers present a dinosaur puppet show to the gathered children, always ending his shows with the magic words, "Please and thank-you!" As Santa introduces himself to Joe and begins to explain why Joe is the chosen one, Joe's sleazy manager interrupts, telling Joe of an audition for a new Christmas movie. But before he auditions, the manager Marty tells him he must shave off his full beard and dye the gray out of his hair. Not wanting to desert the old man, Joe tells Marty to take care of him, but the only thing the agent does is call the police and have Santa Claus arrested, lined up for a mug shot, fingerprinted (he has snowflake prints) and thrown into a cell with hardcore undesirables. But Santa has them all singing "The 12 Days of Christmas" in no time flat.

When Ernest turns his cab in and reports he gave Santa a lift for free, his boss explodes and fires him on the spot, throwing the contents of the trunk at him— Santa Claus' forgotten Christmas sack. Delivering

the free tree to Vern's house, practically destroying the unseen man's living room by tearing the wiring out of the wall, Ernest goes to his truck and remembers the red sack and decides to look inside. When he does, a light radiates from the bag as he hears high-pitched wails of laughter and commotion inside. With shock written all over his hounddog face, Ernest mutters, "He's him," realizing he has the responsibility to get that sack to Santa or Christmas is over before it begins. But when he returns to the Children's Museum, the friendly and helpful clerk Mary (Billie Bird) refers Ernest to the police station and jail. "You mean he got busted," Ernest rants.

Harmony, giving younger audiences someone with whom to identify, becomes the typical young teenager who believes that Christmas and Santa Claus are hum-bug! She rudely asks Ernest how Santa travels around the world and visits all the children in just one night. She asks why he travels by airplane and taxi—"Where's his sleigh... his reindeer?"

Just at that moment at the airport, two Laurel and Hardy-esque maintenance workers are unloading several large wooden crates, hearing strange sounds from inside. Soon a hoofed leg breaks through, and the animals are free in the storage area, reindeer one and all. Some of the reindeer decide to defy gravity and walk across the ceiling. One shipper remarks, "Alien goats" before realizing that he is dealing with magic reindeer.

Ernest, speaking to Harmony, wonders aloud how Santa got into his childhood home, since they never had a chimney (these same questions are asked in *The*

225

Ernest delivers Santa's sleigh to Joe (Oliver Clark) in *Ernest Saves Christmas*.

Santa Clause some years later). Ernest, who is proud he has things figured out, claims Santa must have gotten into the house through the forced air heating system, imagining Santa turning into a gooey blob and oozing through the vent covers. Harmony, always the cynic, utters, "You talk like you believe all this stuff!" And Ernest's eyes become deadly solemn as he answers, "Of course I do! Christmas is a known fact; millions of people all over the world celebrate Christmas every year." In disgust, Harmony states, "You're a sick man, Ernest."

Harmony, even though she does not believe in Christmas magic, is transfixed by Santa's red sack; and she is always reaching in and pulling out a present; but, when it turns out to be a present for little children, she becomes disheartened. "What I really want for Christmas is one million dollars in small, unmarked bills," but when she looks into the sack she never finds anything she wants. Soon Harmony and Ernest (slicked up and disguised as a state official) go to the police to get Santa out of the slammer, telling the officials there that they are making a surprise inspection for the governor; and when they find a man who claims he is Santa Claus (in reality, our Santa Claus) in a cell with regular prisoners, the Ernest inspector hits the roof. When the criminals defend Santa Claus, the inspector calls it "infectious insanity" that has spread to the so-called normal criminals. Somehow the prison authorities release Santa Claus to Ernest and all three get away. However, Harmony still

doesn't believe in the power of Santa Claus, and Santa says, "She's been this way since that Christmas I brought her a doll instead of a baseball mitt... isn't it true, Pamela!" Santa pleads to Ernest that they must convince Joe by 7 p.m. Christmas Eve to become the new man in red. The current Santa took possession of the red suit in 1889 from the former German Santa. "With the passing of time the magic fails. It is recharged with the passing of the torch from one Santa to the next."

However, back on location of Joe's first film, Joe is upset when the script requires him to use objectionable language when he confronts an alien monster. "I sorta can't say that!" he gripes. He is told by the movie makers that this film is called *Christmas Slay* not *Sleigh*, and when Joe is told that it is the story of a space alien who terrorizes children during Christmas vacation, he becomes angered.

Soon a plan is concocted. Santa and his bag will take the bus to the Children's Museum at 7 o'clock Christmas Eve. Ernest will go to the airport to fetch Santa's reindeer and sleigh and bring them downtown by seven. And Joe, who must be convinced, will be at the Children's Museum also by seven.

However, Harmony gets greedy and steals Santa's actual magical sack, replacing it with an identical one filled with feathers. She plans to use what little money she has to buy a ticket out of town—Miami is the farthest she can afford. But she departs at 6:40 and has a long time to wait.

Santa sees Joe (who by this time has dyed his hair and trimmed off his beard) committing himself to a life in the movies. "I don't know how to deal with something like this," Joe pleads. And when Santa shows him the magic of his sack, all he sees is feathers. Not depressed, Santa has absolute faith that the real bag will be returned; and he implores, "Joe, search your heart. There must be something that can convince you of the truth!"

Two elves arrive on Eastern Airlines from Toronto, each disguised in trenchcoats and hats with dark sunglasses. They are in town to rendezvous with Santa's reindeer and sleigh. By now Ernest is at the airport storage room seeking out reindeer when the elves arrive, take off their hats and show their pointy ears. After an aborted attempt to sneak the elves, reindeer and sleigh to the museum as the cargo of a Ryder truck, Ernest and the elves have to pilot the sleigh downtown—with lead-footed Ernest in the driver's seat. Calling out the reindeer's names, the sleigh gains power, glows and takes off into the sky at supersonic speed, Ernest screaming all the way up and down and across the heavens, finally ending up in outer space.

At the same time, Joe is making demands for changes in his contract before continuing with the film; and when he is told he is a nobody and has no right to make any changes in the movie, he walks out after first looking outside the window and seeing Santa's kinetic sleigh prance all over the night sky.

Feeling guilty as she sits and waits at the depot, Harmony hears a big brother tell his younger sister that she is stupid to still be believing in Santa Claus; but Harmony tells him to leave his sister alone, that there is a Santa Claus. But she asks Harmony, "Then why do you have the sack?" And, with that thought, Harmony picks up the sack and storms out of the station, running at full speed toward the Children's Museum.

Soon, everyone converges at the museum, Joe asking Santa if the job offer is still open; and Santa responds, "For the right man!" Shaking hands (which begin to glow), Joe is instantly transformed into Santa Claus, suit, beard and all. Asking where the sleigh is, Ernest from outer space starts the sleigh in a nosedive descent which ends about 20 feet from the ground when he manages to stop the sleigh on a dime, "air brakes" Ernest explains. Trying out his powers, Santa (Joe) is told by the former Santa that he promised a fine gentleman he met on the plane that Santa Claus would make it snow, and within seconds, in hot Orlando, snow is falling. Joe invites Ernest and Harmony (who has phoned her mother and is returning home) to accompany him on his rounds this year.

All alone, the former Santa Claus, again returning to being Seth Applegate, is asked by kindly and interested Mary if he is doing anything tonight. Applegate answers, "Not a thing." Then devilishly, Mary suggests, "We'll think of something," as Santa's sleigh disappears into the night.

Once again, the love of the Ernest character is an acquired taste, and it is a taste most appreciated by younger audiences who enjoy visual gags and broad, physical humor. Jim Varney is only as good as his material, and while he is master of his character Ernest, *Ernest Saves Christmas* succeeds by virtue of its clever script, interesting characterizations and sentimental tone. The film addresses many of the themes to be explored in later films such as *The Santa Clause*, as already mentioned. But Douglas Seal presents a sensitive portrayal of an old-fashioned Santa in a modern world who never once doubts that the spirit of Santa Claus might be becoming passé. Since he never doubts himself, neither do we. Ernest's childlike simplicity and goodness embracing the total holiday package make it easier for children to also accept that old Red Magic. Yes, yes, yes, moments occur in *Earnest Saves Christmas* that are groaners, so infantile that we wonder how anyone could find them humorous. But, somehow, Jim Varney makes believers of us all, charming his audience to laugh at all the stupidity and shed a tear at the more poignant moments (many of which occur). *Ernest Saves Christmas* becomes entertaining for both the young and the young at heart, succeeding all too well in keeping the traditional Christmas spirit alive.

—GJS

The Santa Clause
1994

In today's reality based society, it becomes harder and harder to make children believe all the wonderful myths and fantasies that feed a child's world of imagination. Santa Claus, that wise old elf, is becoming increasingly more difficult for today's children to believe in; and this film, written by Leo Benvenuti and Steve Rudnick and directed by John Pasquin, attempts to make Santa Claus acceptable for our modern world. *The Santa Clause*, whose screenplay borrows from the "Santa '85" episode of *Amazing Stories* covered in the TV chapter (in which Santa Claus sets off alarms while visiting a home on Christmas Eve, Santa is arrested and thrown into a paddy wagon, Santa is broken out of prison and Santa's chief disbeliever has his faith renewed when Santa Claus finally delivers a long overdue present whose absence alienated him from the jolly old elf in the first place), is another fantasy film that renews our fading Christmas spirit with both laughs and tears.

Another fractured 1990s family—divorced father Scott Calvin (Tim Allen), mother Laura (Wendy Crewson), new husband and psychologist Neal (Judge Reinhold) and young son Charlie (Eric Lloyd)—struggles to function harmoniously as, on Christmas Eve, father Scott comes to his former wife's house to take their son Charlie away for Christmas. Scott, who works as a marketing and distribution manager for a company that produces toys, believes in the spirit of Christmas, even if somewhat jadedly. Step-father Neal does not believe in Santa Claus and hasn't since age three (when Santa never delivered his Oscar Meyer Wiener Whistle), so the modern parents explain Santa to their child as a "state of mind." Charlie himself tells his dad, "It's kinda baby to believe in that stuff."

However, Scott's planned Christmas dinner turns to disaster with the turkey and kitchen catching on fire as Scott uses a fire extinguisher on the bird, declaring it's done. Heading out on Christmas Eve to find an open restaurant, Scott, trying to be diplomatic, says there's something about Neal—and he stumbles to find the words. Charlie finishes the thought: "...that wants you to lash out irrationally!" But the sad-eyed boy declares, "He listens to me." Finally finding a Denny's, a fact that excites Scott and depresses Charlie, they go inside to find one side of the restaurant filled with Asian-Americans, but the other half is for turkey eaters and is populated by a sea of single dads and disgusted kids; one father has his hand bandaged, since he also failed in the kitchen arena. At home, Scott reads "The Night Before Christmas" to get Charlie to go to sleep, but the inquiring child wants lines such as "there a rose such a clatter" explained. Then Charlie asks the questions that all maturing children ask their parents: If Santa's so fat, how does he get down the chimney; what about homes that do not have chimneys, how does he get in??? Soon the sleeping child is awakened by loud thuds on the floor, and he runs for his dad stating, there's clatter up on the roof. Going outside in his underwear to explore, Scott startles Santa Claus who loses his balance and falls off the roof crashing into a pile of snow. The jolly old elf is dead. Finding a card with "Santa Claus" printed on one side, the other side advises: "If something should happen to me, put on my suit, the reindeer will know what to do." Looking back to the roof, Scott and Charlie now see a majestic sleigh fronted by a team of reindeer. In an instant, Santa's body is gone, but his suit remains, picked up carefully by Scott; a large metal ladder appears leaning against the top of the house. The ladder, as engraved, states it was made by "The Rose Suchax Ladder Company," and Charlie climbs up immediately. When Charlie and Scott plop themselves down inside the sleigh, the sleigh seems to take off into overdrive; and it quickly lands on another home's rooftop. Charlie wants his

father to go down the chimney, but Scott is hesitant about descending into a strange home in his underwear, so the boy tells him to put on the Santa suit. Immediately thereafter, when lifting the Santa bag, Scott becomes airborne and gravitates toward the chimney, where he magically morphs in size and gets sucked down. Putting the presents contained within the bag around the tree, Scott is confronted by both a dog and an elaborate alarm system, but still manages to escape back up the chimney. Even at houses that do not have fireplaces, Scott is mysteriously sucked down any vent that sticks up from the roof and a fireplace mysteriously appears for him to both enter and exit the house. At one house, a sleeping little girl is awakened and is upset that Scott is too thin and hasn't consumed his glass of milk; but Scott pleads lactose intolerance and leaves.

Finishing his nocturnal duties, Scott orders the reindeer to return home, but surprisingly, home turns out to be the North Pole where his sleigh is mechanically lowered beneath the surface of the ice down into a huge elf toy factory. No adults are present, even though the child-like elves claim to be sometimes 1,000 years old. All the elves answer to Scott/Santa, but one elf, Bernard (David Krumholtz), appears to be the bossy elf manager. Everyone addresses Scott as Santa, to which he chimes, "I'm not Santa," telling the story about the real Santa falling off his roof: "I have homeowner's insurance and a good lawyer!" But the forceful Bernard tells Scott, you put on the suit and accepted the Santa clause. If he would have only read the fine print on the card that he picked up from Santa's corpse, Scott would have realized that by putting on the suit, he accepts all the duties and responsibilities of being the new Santa Claus. In other words, the frozen baton has been passed. Bernard tells Scott to leave, that he has 11 months to get his life in order, that he has to report at Thanksgiving next year. However, he will be forwarded "the list" of all children's behavior, and he will be required to check over the list twice and mark each child as being good or bad. "Suppose I choose not to believe it," Scott asserts to Bernard. With these words the entire factory shuts down, everyone remaining silent. Bernard shouts, "You don't want to be responsible for killing the spirit of Christmas, do ya!" Scott has no answer for that.

A cute child-like elf, who announces she has been perfecting her cocoa for 1,200 years, serves a cup to both Scott and Charlie. Scott tells the elf that she looks good for her age, but she says, "Sorry, I'm seeing someone in wrapping!" The elf, trying to convince Scott of his responsibility, states, "Grownups can't believe in magic—it just, sorta, grows out of them." Correcting the commonly held axiom that seeing is believing, she tells Scott, "Believing is seeing," meaning kids don't need to see something to know

Scott Calvin (Tim Allen) fills in for Santa Claus in *The Santa Clause*.

that a place exists... "they just know." Going to sleep, both Scott and Charlie wake up in their own beds at home. However, he is wearing the red pajamas that he was giving up at the North Pole, monogrammed with the initials "S.C." (Santa Claus or Scott Calvin?).

Neal and Laura are upset that the generally sensible Charlie now unquestionably believes that not only is there a Santa Claus, but that Santa is his father and that they both were with the elves at the toy factory at the North Pole. Even at school Career Day, Charlie proudly introduces his father as the new Santa Claus. When alone in his room, Charlie sets up rows of chairs and pretends they are reindeer and he is Santa leading them. Neal even arranges for a psychiatrist to speak to Charlie, but no one can change the lad's mind. Step-father Neal has a long talk asking how can one man visit all the children of the world in one night, and Charlie immediately answers that not all children celebrate the holiday and then he mentions the term "time continuum," matter of factly. When Neal is disturbed that Charlie states he saw reindeer fly and because Neal never did, Charlie reassures him by saying that he never saw a million dollars. "Just because you haven't seen it doesn't mean it doesn't exist."

Things are getting pretty weird for Scott also. He now grows a full beard by midday even though he shaves every morning, and his hair is starting to grow grayer and grayer almost overnight. Soon he is sporting a full white beard and hair. Also, he develops a huge 45-pound gut within a week.

Pretty soon large boxes are delivered by Federal Express, enough red boxes to fill up a living room. Inside is "the list" of children's names, but Scott focuses upon one name that stands out—Armand Assante! Soon little children corner Scott in the park and tell him, "I want some ballet slippers." However, because of Charlie's delusion encouraged by his father, Neal and his wife go to court to have Scott's visitation rights canceled, the mother more reluctant than Neal to push for this. Even Scott momentarily tries to deny the truth, but Charlie knocks some sense into his dad by telling him, "Of course you're Santa. You can't let them down. They believe in you!" Charlie then throws Scott the snow globe they got up at the North Pole, the father smiling and remembering. Magically, elf Bernard appears in the living room, stating it's okay for Santa to take son Charlie along with him for his Yuletide rounds. In an instant, both father and son are gone, and Neal is phoning the police. Up at the North Pole, Charlie dutifully phones his mother letting her know everything is all right, while the elves reveal a major modification to the sleigh allowing it to make vertical take-offs. Also Santa's suit has been improved to make it completely fire resistant for those drops down fully lit fireplaces. But Scott keeps asking, "But suppose I fall off the roof?" The elves still have no protection for that mis-

Now really Santa Claus, Scott takes son Charlie (Eric Lloyd) with him Christmas Eve in *The Santa Clause*.

hap. Meanwhile, mom is back home facing a line-up of incompetent Santas that have been picked up by the police.

Christmas Eve is upon us, and the elves give Santa a festive sendoff as he begins to make his rounds, more experienced this second time around. He even returns to the house of the sleeping little girl from last year, but this year she happily notes that Santa is fatter and she has soy milk for him, remembering he was lactose intolerant. But soon, visiting Charlie's home, he is surrounded and captured by the police. The Elf Squad goes into action, freeing Santa from his prison cell. Speaking to the police, the elves threaten, "We're your worst nightmare... elves with attitudes!" Using tinsel to cut the bars, Santa is freed. However, stopping his sleigh overhead, Santa returns Charlie to his mother, telling his son, "I can't be with you all the time." And father tells his son, "You believed in me when nobody else did... I love you son!" Mom, finally convinced, admits, "You really are Santa Claus," to which Scott responds, "Pretty cool, isn't it!" Mom burns the custody papers telling Scott he can visit anytime. Bernard tells Charlie that by looking in the snow globe, he can see his father whenever he needs to see him. But Charlie is lonely minutes after his father leaves, so Santa returns and asks mom if he can take his son with him on the rest of his rounds. With the warning "not to fly over any ocean," she tells her men to get out of here. The police force tries to descend upon the house, but the sleigh flies away in seconds. Presents are dropped for Neal and Laura, his wiener whistle and her Mystery Date game, which they never received as children.

The Santa Clause, while not a great movie by any standards, is the perfect family movie for the 1990s. For any cynical kids who question how Santa can live for so long, how he can fit into smaller chimneys and how he can get around the world all in one night, the movie does a credible job of making the fantastic believable. The rapport between all the individuals in the extended family is carefully drawn—Neal is never a total villain, he's just a man drawn by psychological reality, but by movie's end, even he believes. Mom is fair-minded, always mindful of the love that Scott feels for Charlie, and even when she signs the denial of visitation rights papers, the viewer can tell she is not entirely in agreement with that decision. Yet she is also loyal to Neal and understands his side. Charlie is well adjusted and loves both fathers in his life, wanting to spend time with each. He only gets upset when his mother and Scott fight. The film explores both the mystery and the business of conducting the Christmas Eve run, for the North Pole toy factory is set up and run like any other efficient corporation, always trying to better the product and product delivery for the next year. Scott becomes Santa by entering into a legal contract, and his duty to the children of the world makes him honor the contract. *The Santa Clause* takes myth and fairy tale and attempts to make it palpable for the children of today's generation; and, while it is never better than good, by movie's end, viewers cannot help feeling the emotion of continuing Christmas for all the kids of the world.

—GJS

Mrs. Santa Claus

1997

If ever a movie had Christmas written all over it, it is *Mrs. Santa Claus*. After a long dry spell for musical fans, Hallmark debuted a truly old-fashioned confection complete with hummable songs by Jerry Herman, sparkling choreography by Rob Marshall, stylish costumes by Bob Mackie and sprightly performances by a cast of talented newcomers as well as movie veterans. The film is filled with snow-covered streets, evergreen-draped mantels and enough Christmas spirit to choke Scrooge. Even the names during the opening title sequence have sprigs of holly underneath.

Angela Lansbury stars as the title character, a feisty Mrs. Claus who's a little down in the dumps because Santa (Charles Durning) is so preoccupied with the fast approaching Christmas Eve. She wants to help read the mail, but Santa refuses saying it is addressed to him. She lovingly wraps a scarf around his neck and says, "Well, if you don't need me..." Since Santa barely hears her when she tells him she has worked out a faster route, she decides to try it herself. Mrs. Claus has head elf Arvo (Michael Jeter) hitch up the reindeer and with eager anticipation takes off.

Santa (Charles Durning) and Mrs. Claus (Angela Lansbury) in the charming *Mrs. Santa Claus*.

Unfortunately bad weather grounds them in 1910 New York and Cupid hurts his leg on the landing. She finds a stable and with the help of Marcello (David Norona) boards the deer so Cupid can rest. Like Dorothy opening the door of her house into the colorful land of Oz, Marcello throws open the large stable doors and allows Mrs. Claus (or Mrs. North as she introduces herself) to enter the bustling world of Avenue A.

The Avenue is a virtual melting pot and a musical number, "Avenue A," uses this multiculturism to good advantage as the audience is led though a dazzling musical interlude worthy of the Broadway stage. We begin with a young boy tap dancing on a crate then on to saloon girls kicking up their heels on a bar. A Jewish celebration is the next stop and finally an exuberant wedding party dancing in the street is visited. All join together for the toe-tapping finale.

Marcello is taking Mrs. Claus to Mrs. Lowenstein's boarding house and confesses her daughter Sadie (Debra Wiseman) is the apple of her eye. Sadie is a crusading suffragette who has little time to notice things, especially Marcello.

Mrs. Claus explains to the kindly Mrs. Lowenstein that she can't pay; but the sweet woman tells her, "A fine lady like you. You'll get a job, you'll pay me when you can."

They are interrupted by Officer Doyle (Brian Murphy) chasing hellion Nora Kelly (Lynsey Bartilson). Officer Doyle asks Mrs. Lowenstein to tell Nora's father to keep her under control. Mrs. Lowenstein has a deep fear of authority and is afraid the police are going to throw them out of the country because of Sadie. She keeps a suitcase full of her precious mementos, including a single candlestick from her mother, packed just in case.

Mrs. Claus hides Nora from Officer Doyle and the grateful girl explains that her mother and baby brother are in Ireland. Her father works double shifts so he can make enough money to bring them over. Nora has a job too, at the Tavish Toy Company. She offers to get Mrs. Claus a job there. A toy factory! The perfect place for Mrs. Santa Claus to find a job. But this is not a perfect place. It's a children's sweat

Mrs. Claus and Santa prepare to deliver presents Christmas Eve in *Mrs. Santa Claus*.

shop, a hellhole run by Mr. Tavish (Terrence Mann) whose motto is, "It only has to last until Christmas."

He introduces Mrs. Claus (as Mrs. North) and says, "Now my little elves, I do not want a repeat of what happened to the last supervisor." It seems the last supervisor took a little trip, courtesy of one young worker's foot.

The children are from all cultures and look with suspicion upon the newcomer. Mrs. Claus reassures the children with a song "I'm Almost Young" charmingly sung and danced by Lansbury with the children.

She tells Mr. Tavish the children need heat and the toys are defective. She holds out a teddy bear to him and he recoils in horror, refusing her requests.

Meanwhile, Arvo makes Santa his cocoa and has to face Santa when he realizes Mrs. Claus is gone. Arvo bravely speaks up, "You didn't even notice she was gone!" She has been gone for two days and Santa just noticed. The poor man feels terribly guilty and worries about Mrs. Claus being helpless and alone. But Mrs. Claus is having the time of her life. She visits a thrift shop and picks up some stylish new clothes and goes about making friends and nudging relationships along on Avenue A.

Sadie gives her advice about helping the children via a work slowdown, and she counsels Sadie (known as Soapbox Sadie) on how to win over the local women

to her cause. Mrs. Claus helps her convince the women they deserve the vote as well as their husbands do and the two are joined by the local women, Marcello and Nora, as they march to a rally. They sing as they march down the street. Mrs. Claus notes, "But beyond the vote men must acknowledge what we do in little ways every day."

It is three days until Christmas Eve. Marcello gathers the courage to ask Sadie to the Policeman's Christmas Eve dance. They duet on a song called "We Don't Go Together at All," an irresistible teaming that only adds depth of character to the two likable youngsters.

Nora sneaks Mrs. Claus into a vaudeville show. The two are tossed out into the back alley and find trunks and racks of costumes. They sing and dance to "Whistle" frolicking about with various frills taken from the racks and trunks. Lynsey Bartilson holds her own with Broadway vet Lansbury, and the two make an engaging pair.

Mrs. Claus buys two tickets for the dance and asks Officer Doyle to personally deliver one to Mrs. Lowenstein. Officer Doyle turns out to be quite charming, and the once frightened Mrs. Lowenstein decides to attend the dance.

The children at the factory join Mrs. Claus in the work slowdown; but, when Tavish threatens them with work on Christmas day, they rat on Mrs. Claus and both she and Nora are fired. But Mrs. Claus goes down the chimney of the factory, lets Nora in; and they organize the children in a strike. They cover the city with signs telling everyone not to buy Tavish toys because they are poorly constructed and made by suffering little children. Even the mayor gets involved; and the story makes front page news, much to the chagrin of Mr. Tavish.

Christmas Eve is finally here. Mrs. Lowenstein, realizing she is safe, unpacks her precious bag. She gives Mrs. Claus a beautiful red dress that she has made for a customer who changed her mind. At the dance Marcello tells her Cupid is healed and can travel.

Sadie toasts Mrs. Claus who has helped with the suffrage movement and child labor laws. "What you've really been is our Santa Claus." "Mrs. Santa Claus," Nora adds.

Mrs. Claus sadly watches couples dance and misses Santa very much. She goes onto a balcony, a brilliant red stole covers her hair and shoulders as she sings "He Needs Me." Mrs. Claus says good-bye to Nora and heads to the stable for the sleigh and reindeer. But they are gone!

Tavish steps from behind the sleigh. "Missing something Mrs. North? Or should I say Mrs. Claus?" he asks in a gleefully sinister tone.

Tavish realized she really is Mrs. Claus and he had hidden the reindeer to ruin everyone's Christmas. But Mrs. Claus remembers 1872 and a young Augie Tavish getting a special teddy bear. He tells her his step-brother stole his bear; and, ever since, he wants to ruin Christmas for everyone just as his was ruined those many years ago. Mrs. Claus gives him a duplicate of that teddy bear telling him, "It's not the gift, it's the love behind it." The old grump is now as happy as a little boy and leads Mrs. Claus to the reindeer.

Santa is dressed and anxiously awaiting Mrs. Claus' return. She finally arrives and he tells her to close her eyes. She is astonished to find he has a beautifully red fur-trimmed coat ready for her, and he's even going to use her new route.

"Merry Christmas Anna."

"Merry Christmas, Nicky."

Together they set off to deliver Christmas presents to children all over the world.

Mrs. Lowenstein finds a matching candlestick in her stocking; and Nora answers a knock at the door to find her father, mother and baby brother there. It truly is a merry Christmas for everyone.

This film is absolutely one of the nicest surprises of the 1996 television season. After the musical film had pretty much disappeared into oblivion, only occasionally popping up in darker forms such as *Cabaret* and *All That Jazz,* it is wonderful to find a musical that manages to tackle social issues but still remain light-hearted fun. Much of this is due to the score by Jerry Herman, whose work includes the catchy tunes of *Mame, Hello, Dolly!* and *La Cage Aux Folles.* Also, much credit should go to screenwriter Mark Saltzman who wrote the screenplay to the family film *The Adventures of Milo and Otis.* The outstanding costumes were provided by renowned designer Bob Mackie, whose clothes adorned Cher and Carol Burnett during their television heyday.

Director Terry Hughes follows a film musical tradition by shooting the film as a stage play, leaving the audience to feel they are actually watching a Broadway production.

Angela Lansbury as Mrs. Claus has never been more likable, and that's saying something considering her beloved Jessica Fletcher character from *Murder, She Wrote.* Lansbury is a versatile performer whose career has spanned films, Broadway and television. In her younger days, she was often cast as the bitter ex-wife or old girlfriend; she overcame that stereotyping to become one of today's most beloved stars.

Newcomers Norona, Wiseman and Bartilson are destined for big careers on Broadway if their performances in *Mrs. Santa Claus* are any indication. Their characters have a sweet charisma and pleasing singing voices. Terrence Mann, a Tim Curry look-alike who appeared as Tavish, played Larry in the film version of *A Chorus Line.* Charles Durning makes a wonderful Santa and, as usual with all his screen roles, tackles the part with a twinkle in his eye. Durning is also a veteran of musicals and had many sparkling moments as the Governor in *Best Little Whorehouse in Texas* with Dolly Parton and Burt Reynolds. He should be quite familiar with the jolly old elf, having portrayed him in quite a few television holiday movies.

Mrs. Santa Claus can proudly take its place in the small list of truly classic Christmas films alongside movies such as *A Christmas Story, It's A Wonderful Life* and *White Christmas.* The only people who might not enjoy it are those who go about saying "Bah Humbug" during the holidays.
—SS

The following films also occur during or have scenes pertaining to Santa Claus:

The Christmas That Almost Wasn't

Cast: Rossano Brazzi, Paul Tripp, Alberto Rabagliati, Lydia Brazzi
Credits: Producer: Barry B. Yellen; Director: Rossano Brazzi; Writer: Paul Tripp; Childhood; 1966

This Italian film features international film star Rossano Brazzi as the evil Phineas T. Prune who evicts Santa and Mrs. Claus. The children of the world unite

Santa takes Simon and Elodie with him Christmas Eve in *Here Comes Santa Claus.*

to save the day. Not one of the better holiday features and most kids will find it dull.

Here Comes Santa Claus

Cast: Karen Cheryl, Armand Meffre, Emeric Chapuis, Little Alexia, Jeanne Hervlale
Credits: Produced/Directed/Written/Photographed by Christian Gion; Lapaca Productions, 1984

This French film is tough going. Little Simon only wants his parents to be home for Christmas, but they are being held captive in Africa. He and his little friend Elodie manage to get on a plane and find Santa in Lapland. Santa settles them in and with a good fairy goes to rescue Simon's parents. Santa and the fairy are captured, but the local children release them.

They arrive back home to find Simon and Elodie have been snared by a child-eating ogre. Santa and the fairy again come to the rescue and return the children safely home. Lovely scenery, but often the shots are used for filler in this rather dull film. The producers obviously had some budget, for scenes were shot in Finland and Senegal as well as France. This dubbed film will probably be of little interest to most audiences.

It Nearly Wasn't Christmas

Cast: Charles Durning, Risa Schiffman, Wayne Osmond, Beverly Rowland, Bruce Vilanch
Credits: Producers: Harvey Bibicoff, Irwin Meyer and Jimmy Osmond; Director: Burt Brinckerhoff; Writer: Golda David, Alan Jay Glueckman and Stanley Isaacs; Television, 1989

Santa (Durning) decides children don't need him anymore. His wife (Rowland) sends him out to the city to find the truth. He helps a little girl travel to California to find her father and, by reuniting the family, realizes children do still need Santa Claus.

Life and Adventures of Santa Claus

Cast: (voices) Earl Hammond, Earle Hyman, Larry Kenney
Credits: Directors: Jules Bass and Arthur Rankin, Jr.; Writer: Julian P. Gardner; Rankin-Bass; 1985

This animated television special tells the story of the origin of Santa Claus. Based on the L. Frank Baum story.

The Magic Christmas Tree

Cast: Chris Kroesen, Valerie Hobbs, Dick Parish, Charles Nix
Credits: Producers: Diane Johnson and Chris Kroesen; Director: Richard C. Parish; Writer: Harold Vaughn Taylor; Holiday; 1964

This film is unavailable for viewing, but sources describe it "as a boy is knocked unconscious while trying to save a cat. He dreams of adventures including saving Santa who has been kidnapped."

Santa is ready to fly in *Life and Adventures of Santa Claus*.

The Man in the Santa Claus Suit

Cast: Fred Astaire, Gary Burghoff, John Byner, Burt Convy, Nanette Fabray, Harold Gould
Credits: Producer: Lee Miller; Director: Corey Allen; Writers: Leonard Gershe and George Kirgo; Dick Clark Productions; 1978

While it is wonderful seeing Fred Astaire in just about anything, he is really the only reason to watch *The Man in the Santa Claus Suit.* Overall the acting is fairly bad and the stories pedestrian. Astaire is Nick, a man who helps people by renting them Santa Claus suits. He helps John Byner find the man he once was, Gary Burghoff propose to a fashion model and Burt Convy discover the importance of his neglected family. Of course, Astaire is really Santa Claus.

Miracle on 34th Street

Cast: Jane Alexander, David Hartman, Roddy McDowall, Sebastian Cabot, Suzanne Davidson
Credits: Producer: Norman Rosenmont; Director: Fielder Cook; Writer: Jeb Rosebrook; 20th Century-Fox; 1973

Television remake of the 1947 classic. You're much better off renting the original or 1994 remake.

Nearly No Christmas

Gibson Film Productions, 1982
Cast: Michael Haigh, Mildred Woods, Daniel Simpson, Amy Bordsley, Lucy McGrath, Kate Lane
Credits: Producer: Dave Gibson: Director: Yvonne MacKay; Writer: John Banas

Santa's boiler needs a new valve, so Santa goes looking for a job in the city while the elves and Mrs. Claus enlist the help of penguins to help complete the toys. Today's special-effects-savvy kids will probably not take kindly to this amateur-looking production, although younger kids may like the children dressed as elves and penguins.

The Night They Saved Christmas

Cast: Jaclyn Smith, Art Carney, Paul Le Mat, Mason Adams, June Lockhart, Paul Williams, R.J. Williams
Credits: Director: Jackie Cooper; Writer: Jim Moloney; 1984

Art Carney steals the show as an endearing Santa who is worried about oil drillers destroying North Pole City. The drillers led by Le Mat are set to begin blasting at a new site Christmas Eve. Boss Adams greedily urges them on. When Le Mat's wife and children disappear, they are believed to be kidnapped by a rival company but are really with Santa and elf Ed (Paul Williams) who try to convince Smith to talk her husband out of setting off dynamite. Later, the two oldest children go off to warn Santa of the danger, and Smith follows. They are saved by Santa and stay at the North Pole until a dangerous ice fog goes away.

Art Carney, Paul Williams and Jaclyn Smith in *The Night They Saved Christmas.*

Le Mat strikes oil on the old site, and the blast is halted moments before it would have destroyed Santa. The family is reunited Christmas Eve and Santa has a special present for youngest child, C.B.

Nice effects and set decoration in Santa's workshop, but overall standard holiday fare. The actors cannot rise above the stock script, and only Carney strikes a chord as Santa.

Santa Claus is Comin' to Town

Cast: (voices) Fred Astaire, Mickey Rooney, Keenan Wynn, Paul Frees, Joan Gardner
Credits: Producers/Directors: Jules Bass and Arthur Rankin, Jr.; Writer: Romeo Muller; Rankin-Bass; 1970

Animated television special tells the story of how Santa Claus was born, found his wife, delivered toys to all the children and came to live at the North Pole. A traditional holiday viewing necessity.

Secret Santa

Cast: D.L. Green, Debra Rich, Harrison Myers, Richard Gabai, Tena Fanning, Robert Connell
Credits: Producers: Ashok Amritraj and Andrew Stevens; Director: Fred Olen Ray; Writer: Hamilton Underwood; Royal Oaks; 1998

Used car salesman (Green) caves in to his slimy boss (Connell) and agrees to work 12-hour days until Christmas, breaking a promise of a Christmas vacation to his family. An elf appears telling Green he has been selected one of Santa's Secret Santas and he bet-

ter get in the Christmas mood or else. Green turns into Santa and when his boss tries to evict a children's recreation center, he cannot sign. His boss kidnaps him, but Green is soon popped to the North Pole and proceeds to help Santa deliver gifts. On Christmas day he convinces his wife he that has changed and the family reunites.

The Year Without Santa Claus

Cast: (voices) Shirley Booth, Mickey Rooney, Dick Shawn, George S. Irving
Credits: Producers/Directors: Jules Bass and Arthur Rankin, Jr.; Rankin-Bass; 1974

Santa has a cold and decides to take a vacation from Christmas. Mrs. Claus sends elves to find children to convince Santa how important he is.

Santa is under the weather in *The Year Without Santa Claus*.

Yes, Virginia, There is a Santa Claus

Cast: Richard Thomas, Edward Asner, Charles Bronson, Katherine Isobel
Credits: Producer: Bob Banner; Director: Charles Jarrot; Writers: Val De Crowl and Andrew J. Fenady; Television, 1991

Christmas story of little Virginia O'Hanlon (Isobel) and her family, who are having rough times since father (Thomas) has no job. She writes a letter to a newspaper to ask if Santa Claus is real. Bronson

as Edward P. Mitchell is given the job of answering the letter. He is in a deep depression since the death of his wife and has turned to alcohol to ease his pain. His reply to Virginia is now a famous part of the holiday season. Fictionalized story of true events.

Credits:

Ernest Saves Christmas
Cast: Jim Varney, Douglas Seale, Oliver Clark, Noelle Parker, Robert Lesser
Credits: Producers: Stacy Williams and Doug Claybourne; Director: John Cherry; Writer: B. Kline and Ed Turner; Touchstone; 1988

Miracle on 34th Street
Cast: Maureen O'Hara, Natalie Wood, Edmund Gwenn, John Payne
Credits: Producer: William Perlberg; Director/Writer: George Seaton (Based on a Story by Valentine Davies); Fox; 1947

Miracle on 34th Street
Cast: Richard Attenborough, Mara Wilson, Elizabeth Perkins, Dylan McDermott
Credits: Producer: John Hughes; Director: Les Mayfield; Writer: John Hughes (Based on the Screenplay by George Seaton from a Story by Valentine Davies); Fox; 1994

Mrs. Santa Claus
Cast: Angela Lansbury, Charles Durning, Lynsey Bartilson, Terrence Mann, Rosalind Harris
Credits: Producer: J. Boyce Harman, Jr.; Director: Terry Hughes; Writer: Mark Saltzman; Hallmark Home Entertainment; 1996

Santa Claus
Cast: Jose Elias Moreno, Ken Smith
Credits: Producer: William Calderon; Director/Writer: Rene Cardona; Walter Calderon; 1960

Santa Claus Conquers the Martians
Cast: John Call, Leonard Hicks, Vincent Beck, Victor Stiles, Pia Zadora
Credits: Producer: Paul L. Jacobson; Director: Nicholas Webster; Writer: Glenville Mareth (Based on a Story by Paul Jacobson); Embassy; 1964

Santa Claus: The Movie
Cast: Dudley Moore, John Lithgow, David Huddleston, Burgess Meredith, Judy Cornwall
Credits: Producers: Ilya Salkind and Pierre Spengler; Director: Jeannot Szwarc; Writer: David Newman; TriStar; 1985

The Santa Clause
Cast: Tim Allen, Judge Reinhold, Wendy Crewson, Peter Boyle, Eric Lloyd
Credits: Producers: Brian Reilly, Jeffrey Silver and Robert Newmyer; Director: John Pasquin; Writers: Steve Rudnick and Leo Benvenuti; Buena Vista; 1994

Merry Xmas and a Happy New Year

While Visions of Sugar Plums Danced in Their Heads...

As adults we realize the religious significance as well as the importance of family and friends, especially during the holiday season. But basically, Christmas is for children. Children brighten our lives and help us relive the excitement and joy leading up to this wondrous time. This chapter includes films that help children understand the meaning of Christmas. We consider the following films excellent for family viewing, and all are highly recommended.

The Management

Movie theater Christmas poster circa 1934 featuring Shirley Temple.

Charlie Brown and Linus save the little tree in the classic holiday special *A Charlie Brown Christmas*.

A Charlie Brown Christmas

1965

In 1965 the Sunday comics came to television with the classic *A Charlie Brown Christmas* featuring the entire cast of the *Peanuts* comic strip. As written and drawn by Charles M. Schultz, the genius of *Peanuts* was in Schultz' close attention to human nature, having his pre-adolescent cast of characters sometimes speak as children and at other times speak as adults, never knowing for sure which type of insight would be shared when. By the mid-1960s the commercialism of Christmas was a major sin, and in this show, that phrase is repeated a few more times than necessary, making it the dominant theme. However, to me, the smaller, less vocalized themes that run throughout this emotional half-hour animated cartoon strike deeper to the heart and create a far more profound meaning. Seldom has so much passion come from a simple animated short, but *A Charlie Brown Christmas* is one of the most important cinematic explorations of the meaning of Christmas featured in this volume.

The short opens with our cast of characters, children one and all, skating on the local pond, snow falling and covering the surrounding trees and greenery. Charlie Brown, Schultz' alter-ego, leaves his home with friend Linus to join the others. "There must be something wrong with me, Linus. Christmas is coming; I'm not happy. I don't feel the way I'm supposed to feel," Charlie Brown complains, leaning on a wall. Charlie Brown admits he loves to get presents, send and receive cards, decorate trees—"but I'm still not happy, and I always wind up feeling depressed." Linus tries to talk some sense into his friend: "Charlie Brown, you're the only person I know who can take a wonderful season like Christmas and turn it into a problem." But a problem it is for Charlie Brown.

The next day Charlie Brown checks his mailbox to find not a single Christmas card has been sent him, making him even more depressed. "I know nobody likes me, but why do we have to have a holiday season to emphasize it!" Passing Violet on the street, Charlie Brown says, "Thanks for the Christmas card you sent me." The young girl sticks up her nose at Charlie and declares, "I didn't send you a Christmas card, Charlie Brown!" To which Charlie responds, "Don't you know sarcasm when you hear it!"

Even by 1965 it has come to light that the Christmas season is a very depressing time for many people, that the holidays fail to live up to expectations, or the joy they induced when we were children. Charlie Brown embodies this type of thinking—nothing is lonelier than enthusiastically checking the mailbox, hoping to receive a card or two, and finding nothing there. Not being included, not getting any cards, not being invited to holiday activities only seems to validate the fact that the individual is unloved or that he/she is truly alone. Being a child, Charlie Brown cannot verbalize nor fully understand what is wrong. All he understands is that he is supposed to be happy at Christmas time, and he is not.

Lucy, the bane of Charlie's existence, is also the girl who runs the neighborhood psychiatric help booth—five cents a session. Unable to figure out his problem, Charlie goes to Lucy for help. Turning her sign from "Out" to "The Doctor is Real In," Charlie Brown mutters, "I am in sad shape." Lucy, always the professional, asks for payment in advance before they begin. After plunking his nickel into the can, Lucy gets ecstatic: "Oh how I love that beautiful sound of cold hard cash... that beautiful sound... that beautiful sound!!!" Charlie Brown reminds her he is feeling depressed. Smiling and looking for the easy answer, Lucy tells Charlie Brown: "As they say on TV, the mere fact that you realize you need help indicates that you're not too far gone." Lucy tells Charlie they must find the root of his fear, and when she mentions the term meaning fear of everything, Charlie screams, "That's it!" Soon Lucy confesses she herself feels Christmas depression. "I never get what I want. I always get a bunch of stupid toys or a bike or clothes..." Charlie asks her what he really wants for Christmas; and, without missing a beat Lucy whispers, "Real estate!" Interestingly, Lucy and Charlie are depressed for vastly different reasons. Charlie wants to connect with people and feel the joy that he sees in others. Lucy, on the other hand, is selfishly concerned about the presents she gets versus the presents she wants, her depression being based upon materialistic deprivation. But both children feel disappointed and let down. Lucy, wiser than expected, suggests "involvement" as a cure for Charlie Brown, asking him to be the director of the children's Christmas play (of course she plants the idea that Charlie cast her as Christmas Queen). Charlie, immediately excited, accepts the important position.

However, Charlie is still depressed by the commercialism of Christmas he sees all around him. Even his dog Snoopy has his dog house decorated with garish lights and tinsel, entering it in a Christmas Decorating Contest. Charlie's sister Sally asks the older Charlie to write her letter to Santa Claus as she dictates what she wants. "Please note the size and color and send as many items as possible. Don't make it too complicated on yourself—just send money, tens and twenties!" Seeing that his baby sister has gone commercial makes Charlie even sadder.

Traveling to the auditorium for the Christmas play's first rehearsal, Charlie sees the entire cast of kids playing music and dancing on the stage, each child in his/her own world. When Lucy announces Charlie Brown as the new director, the kids don't seem enthused: "We're doomed!" and "It will be the worst Christmas play ever" are heard. However, when Charlie enters, he receives a round of applause, except for Snoopy who boos him (at least he's being honest): "Man's best friend," Charlie utters in disgust. When Charlie introduces himself and gives his cast basic directions, he finds none of the cast are paying attention, instead each has gone back to dancing and playing music, each child lost within his/her own selfish universe. Soon all the children are fighting over their parts, whether their curly hair will turn straight, worrying about memorizing their lines. When Linus asks Lucy to give him a reason why he has to memorize his lines, she makes a fist and says, "I'll give you five reasons why!" Linus then concludes that Christmas is not becoming too commercial, only too dangerous. Lucy then reminds Charlie of making her the Christmas Queen. "You won't let all this beauty go to waste." But Charlie is concerned with having the play express the true meaning of Christmas. But Lucy interrupts. "We all know that Christmas is a big commercial racket. It's all run by a big Eastern Syndicate, you know." Charlie Brown concludes this play needs a tree to set the mood. Lucy tells Charlie to get the biggest aluminum tree and then paint it pink. The cast yells to Charlie, "Do something right for a change."

Linus and Charlie go to the Christmas tree lot, scanning the grounds for the perfect tree. Literally trees of every color and size can be found, all except basic green. Soon Charlie sees a dwarf twig of a tree, an evergreen, one that is non-gimmicky. "Seems to need a home," Charlie declares picking it up with pride. Linus warns him, "It does not seem to fit the modern spirit," as needles immediately begin to fall whenever the tree is touched. "Besides, I think it needs me," Charlie declares, making up his mind to keep it.

As Charlie proudly places the new tree on the piano, the cast and crew are not impressed: "Boy, are you stupid, Charlie Brown," "What kind of tree is that," "I told you he'd goof it up," etc. "Rats," Charlie Brown responds, walking away as the entire cast and crew points and laughs at him for being such a bonehead and getting such a disappointing tree. "I guess I really don't know what Christmas is all about. Isn't there *anyone* who knows what Christmas is all about," he screams in utter frustration. Then, quietly,

Charlie Brown celebrates with his friends, who have discovered the real meaning of Christmas in *A Charlie Brown Christmas*.

friend Linus speaks up, "Sure Charlie Brown, I can tell you what Christmas is all about... lights, please!" Then in his quivering little voice, the blanket-toting dignified child speaks up and recites the story of the birth of Jesus on the original Christmas day, ending with "Glory to God in the highest, and on Earth, peace and good will toward all men. That's what Christmas is about Charlie Brown!"

Without saying a word, Charlie Brown, smiling, picks up his pathetic little tree and walks out into the snowy night and quietly looks up at the shiny stars, hearing the words of Linus echo in his head. The other children are following close behind. "Linus is right. I won't let all this commercialism ruin my Christmas... I'll take this little tree home and decorate it. I'll show them it will work in our play." Grabbing one red Christmas bulb from Snoopy's "First Place" winning dog house, the bulb bends the tree's main branch and it touches the ground. "I killed it! Everything I touch gets ruined!" Charlie screams and walks off. The other kids look at the sorry tree and declare all it needs is a little love; and using the decorations from Snoopy's dog house, they have Charlie's

tree beautifully decorated in a flash. When Charlie Brown returns, all the children smile at him and shout, "Merry Christmas, Charlie Brown," as he also joins in to sing "Hark the Herald Angels Sing," a tribute to the glory of Christmas.

In just 25 minutes, *A Charlie Brown Christmas* has reminded us of what Christmas is really all about, cutting through the selfish commercialism of receiving presents and the dime-store psychology involving depression which still focuses on "me." Instead, it takes an impassioned, unrehearsed recital from Linus to remind everyone of the glory of Christmas and the beauty to be found in even the most pathetic and barren Christmas tree. As the children now understand and accept Charlie Brown into their fold, they all join in to sing the praises of the Christ child and of the wish of good will toward all men. For this rare moment, all the inhabitants of the world of Charles Schultz speak in harmony with one voice, and if that isn't a Christmas miracle, then nothing is.

—GJS

Dr. Seuss' How the Grinch Stole Christmas!

1966

"Someone said, 'If Bacon didn't write Shakespeare's plays, he missed the opportunity of a lifetime.' I didn't miss the opportunity of my lifetime. I worked with Dr. Seuss."—Chuck Jones (from *Dr. Seuss and Mr. Giesel: A Biography* by Judith and Neil Morgan.

Of all the holiday times of the year, Christmas is a time in which you can get very nostalgic. When I think of *How the Grinch Stole Christmas!,* I consider that film, made for television and touted as one of the most expensive Christmas "specials" ever made, to be a "classic," a production worthy enough to stand with any film or TV version of *A Christmas Carol, It's A Wonderful Life* or any other favorite Christmas movie or television show. To explain why, I have to go way back in my childhood, more than 30 years ago. On a cold, snowy December night in Chicago—just a week before Christmas, 1966—an eight-year-old boy's life was suddenly changed, transformed, as if by magic. The youngster's life was changed—not in a dramatic way, nor in a tremendously powerful way; but it was changed in a subtle way the boy did not yet realize. His life was changed by a gentle, yet mesmerizing voice of one of the world's most beloved actors, who was just about a year shy of his 80th birthday. The voice belonged to Boris Karloff, and the little boy was me.

We were told that this was "A CAT IN THE HAT PRESENTATION" with the words around a ring with a blinking and smiling Cat looking at us. After the titles, the commercial announcement, as in "brought to you by...." we heard a bit of the Whos' "Christmas Song," and then we were shown the weird-looking but friendly Whos preparing the large Christmas tree in the center of the town, and then singing. As the song faded, the camera swooped up a huge snow-covered mountain that didn't look quite as cheery as those below. The camera panned to a cave, to show us the Grinch! Then, we heard

a soft voice, almost like a grandfather reading us a story:

> "Every Who down in Who-ville liked Christmas a lot...
> But the Grinch,who lived just north of Who-ville,
> DID NOT!..."—Boris Karloff (as the kindly, grandfatherly Narrator)

and then we heard the voice of the Grinch, a voice that had a strange, hollow kind of sound to it, that sounded, to quote Dr. Seuss, "most unpleasant":

> "Why, for 53 years I've put up with it now!
> I MUST stop this Christmas from coming!
> ...But HOW?"
> —Boris Karloff (as the chilling, evil voice of the Grinch)

Dr. Seuss' *How the Grinch Stole Christmas!* invaded many living rooms on Sunday, December 18, 1966, which was, as I've said, just exactly a week before Christmas. It was run at 7:00 p.m., bumping *Lassie* off the CBS lineup just for this night. Rabid *Lassie* fans might have been initially disappointed,

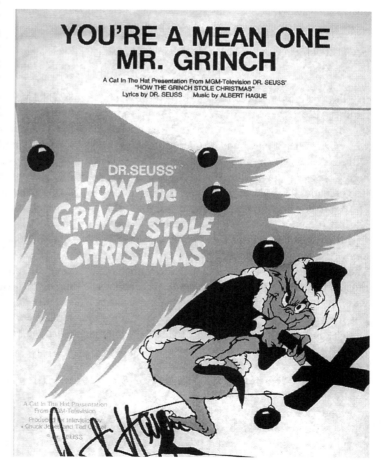

Boris Karloff was the narrator and the voice of the Grinch in *How the Grinch Stole Christmas!* Dr. Seuss and Dr. Seuss characters are ® of Dr. Seuss Enterprises, L.P. Any sketches, etc. from the T.V. production "Dr. Seuss' 'How the Grinch Stole Chirstmas!'" is ©1966, Turner Entertainment Co. All rights reserved.

but most of them wouldn't be, especially after the story began. If my memory is correct, I was sitting on a couch with my brother Jerry and my cousin Joey (who lived downstairs with his family) in what my grandparents called "the television room." As I remember it, we were all set to enjoy ourselves. The apartment was warm. I had a new baby brother Matthew to play with. Everyone was in good health, and we were happy. It was a magic time for an eight-year-old boy like me; and, through the "magic" of television, *How the Grinch Stole Christmas!* introduced me to Boris Karloff (or more accurately, his voice) for the very first time. I had not yet seen *Frankenstein* (1931) or any of Boris Karloff's other horror pictures on TV. The name didn't mean much to me at the time. What most of the younger kids I knew were concerned with was *how* the Grinch would move and talk. As hard as it is for a cartoon fanatic like me to believe, the name Chuck Jones didn't mean anything to me either, at the time. As for the name of Dr. Seuss (aka Theodor Geisel), that's a different story, and what stories he wrote and drew, like *Thidwick, the Big-Hearted Moose* and *Green Eggs and Ham*. Through his stories and his wonderful artwork, Ted Geisel contributed so much to America and the world. They were and are wonderful stories, and *The Grinch Who Stole Christmas!*

was an instant classic. The animated version soon became one too.

"There was never any doubt in my mind that there was only one person to narrate this story and to be the voice of the Grinch: Boris Karloff. The recordings he had done of the Kipling stories and many others had established him not only as the ideal actor but, in my mind and Ted's, as the only one."
—Chuck Jones, *Chuck Jones—Chuck Reducks: Drawing From the Fun Side of Life*

I wasn't really aware of just who Boris Karloff was until just a little over two years later. It was probably the morning after Feb. 2, 1969—the day he died—that the actor's image burned itself onto my memory. One of the nuns in St. Margaret Mary's grade school had let us watch a few minutes of the CBS Morning News. I remember the news commentator stating that Boris Karloff had just died, and I saw a clip of him as the Frankenstein Monster trapped under a beam in a burning windmill, screaming in terror. What the *heck* was *that*? Like the first time a boy gets a home run playing softball, or rides a bike without training wheels or gets kissed by a girl, it was a moment frozen in time. After that, I wanted to know all I could about the actor Boris Karloff. Fortunately for me, it wasn't too long before WGN TV (Channel 9 in Chicago) started showing a bunch of mostly old Universal and Columbia horror films (under the old *Shock Theater* syndication package), which they called "Creature Features." The ads for the films used a bit of Henry Mancini's music for *An Experiment in Terror* (1962), over clips of Dracula, the Frankenstein Monster, the Wolf Man, the Mummy, prowling the landscape, with a staff announcer (Marty McNeely or Carl Grayson) reading a wonderfully ghoulish poem, with a weird whispery echo effect.

I discovered *Famous Monsters of Filmland* magazine, the Aurora model kits and paperback horror movie histories or biographies. Armed with slow but steadily increasing knowledge about Boris Karloff, I looked forward to watching *How the Grinch Stole Christmas!* as the years rolled by, and fruitlessly searched for a supposed soundtrack of the "Grinch" for which Boris Karloff had won a Grammy. Many years later, I was surprised to find out that *How the Grinch Stole Christmas!* almost never got made!

"...What we do shamefully recognize, of course, is that we are all a bit like the Grinch,

for we all hate Christmas a little. Or a lot...
Ted Geisel had no children, and he shared the
Grinch's grumpiness about Christmas—all
those kids running around making a noise."
—Chuck Jones, *Chuck Jones—Chuck
Reducks: Drawing From the Fun Side of Life*

In the spring of 1957, author Ted Geisel (1904-
1991) began work on a new book to protest the commercialization of Christmas, which became a wonderful and wacky variation of Charles Dickens' *A
Christmas Carol*. Geisel's version of Ebenezer
Scrooge was the Grinch, who, like Scrooge, was a
bitter character who hated the Christmas season, and
was bound and determined to do away with the holiday once and for all. Also, like Scrooge, the Grinch
prefers to be left alone, and has no one but a small
dog, Max, to keep him company. The joyous excitement, the noise and especially the singing of Christmas carols, by the Who-ville residents down below,
drive the Grinch crazy. The Grinch plots a scheme to
rid himself of Christmas, and in the process, learns
something good about himself and the holiday he has
hated for so many years. Writing and illustrating the
book did not come easy to Geisel, and so, years later,
when Chuck Jones approached him about producing
an animated version of the book for television, Geisel
was reluctant. The costs of an animated production
made sponsors reluctant to buy the air time as well.

The Grinch has fun burglarizing the Whos' houses
until his sleigh is filled with bursting sacks of decorations, food and presents. Only one young resident of
Who-ville spotted the fake "Grinchy Claus" getting
rid of the Christmas tree, but the nasty villain "thought
up a lie, and he thought it up quick!" He turns to trusting Cindy-Lou Who with as nice a fake smile as he
can, and in the animated version, Boris Karloff's voice
has almost a "Cockney" accent to it, bringing those
audience members with long and sharp memories,
visions of certain old Karloffian villains:

"'Why, my sweet little tot,' the fake Santy
Claus lied,
'There's a light on this tree that won't light on
one side.
So I'm taking it home to my workshop, my
dear.
I'll fix it up *there*. Then I'll bring it back *here*.'
And his fib fooled the child.
Then he patted her head.
And he got her a drink and he sent her to bed.
And when Cindy-Lou Who went to bed with
her cup,
HE crept to the chimney and stuffed the tree
up!"
—Boris Karloff

Karloff emphasizes the word "stuffed" in such a way
that you can actually visualize the Grinch stuffing the
huge tree into the small chimney up to the roof, although Dr. Seuss (I'm just going to call the late Ted
Geisel that from now on) didn't in his text. The book
is written as Dr. Seuss wants the reader to read it aloud
to others, which I've always thought was a wonderful
technique. With wonderful animation of the Grinch
rigging the Whos' toys and other things to fit into his
sacks (later re-used in clever montages to show time
elapsing as the Grinch goes from house to house), the
"icing on the cake" is the clever song, expertly sung
by voice artist Thurl Ravenscroft (sounds like a name
for a Karloff character, doesn't it?), singing "You're
A Mean One, Mr. Grinch," with lyrics that could only
come from the mind of Dr. Seuss, and music by Albert
Hague.

While the reader can imagine poor Max, the dog,
struggling in his makeshift reindeer garb to get the
overloaded sleigh to the top of Mount Crumpit, we
actually see him struggling, plowing the best he can
over snow high over his head, with the Grinch stub-
bornly whipping the poor animal with the reins. It is
now the morning of the next day. The Grinch is all set
to dump his load of stolen Who presents and Christmas time possessions, but pauses to hear the crying
and wailing when the Whos are "finding out now that
no Christmas is coming!" He is simply delighted that
he has finally found a way to stop all the noise and
commotion that comes every 25th of December. The
Grinch has triumphed! Or has he? Even with nothing in their homes, the Whos are still celebrating
Christmas, which staggers the Grinch for quite awhile
and makes his "puzzler" sore:

"*Then* the Grinch thought of something he
hadn't before!
'Maybe Christmas,' he thought, '*doesn't*
come from a store.
Maybe Christmas... perhaps...means a little
bit more!'
And what happened then...? [Softly, and with
all of Karloff's skill!]
Well...in Who-ville they say
That the Grinch's small heart
Grew three sizes that day!"
—Boris Karloff

So, instead of dumping his huge load of Christmas presents and goodies, the Grinch understands the
true meaning of Christmas at last, and in one of my
favorite lines from the TV version, "and the Grinch
found the strength of 10 Grinches—plus two!," the
repentant and joyous Grinch returns everything to the
town. In gratitude, the town bestows on the Grinch
the supreme honor of carving food he had earlier de-

tested, the rare and tasty "roast beast" for the Who-ville Christmas dinner! And so, *Dr. Seuss' How the Grinch Stole Christmas!* all too quickly came to an end. While at least one reviewer considered the expensive accomplishment of Chuck Jones and Dr. Seuss to be excessive, I don't think CBS, which ran it for years, or MGM/UA—which owns it now, would begrudge the production one "red cent," considering the successful profits it made. It has certainly pleased television audiences for more than 30 years now, and it pleased, I think, its creators as well.

—LJK

Annabelle's Wish

1997

Country singer Randy Travis lends his voice to this charming animated Christmas film. A young boy, Billy (voiced by Hari Oziol), has lost not only his beloved parents but his voice when he is trapped in a barn fire. His grandpa Charlie (Jerry Van Dyke) saves him, and together the two live a happy life on the farm. Billy's best friend is a girl named Emily; and together the two defend each other from the mean Holder boys, Bucky and Buster. The only problem in this idyllic life is Billy's nasty old Aunt Agnes (Cloris Leachman), a cold-hearted rich woman who only wants custody of Billy so she doesn't have to spend her Christmas alone.

On Christmas Eve a calf named Annabelle is born. Travis, as the narrator, tells us every Christmas Eve Santa brings the animals a special gift, the gift of speech for a day. Santa places a gift wrapped box on the tree for Billy, ties a red ribbon around Annabelle and is off to finish his rounds. Annabelle is delighted with her special gift of speech and decides to ask Santa if she can fly with him next year.

The next morning Billy opens the box. which tells him to look outside where he sees Annabelle. He even forgets his fear of the barn as he happily runs after the calf. Annabelle forgets Santa's warning and speaks in front of Billy. He is amazed when the other animals join in. They know Billy will not give their secret away. Agnes shows up at the farm on Christmas morning to give Billy presents and to try to talk his grandpa into giving up custody, but the old man won't give in; he knows what is best for Billy.

Annabelle tells Billy about her wish to fly, so he ties two small branches on her head for antlers and Billy and Emily tie Annabelle to a sled; and off they go playing Santa Claus. But the sleigh goes too fast, and they crash through the fence of mean Mr. Holder

Santa comes to the aid of Annabelle in *Annabelle's Wish*.

(Jim Varney) who gets the sheriff (Clancy Brown) and goes to see Grandpa. He doesn't want money, only Annabelle. The sheriff tells Grandpa he must do it, but gives him 24 hours to come up with the money. Grandpa sells a cherished music box that belonged to Billy's mother and gets Annabelle back.

The year passes quickly and Billy, Emily and Annabelle become the best of friends. When Annabelle charges Bucky and Buster, who have been taunting Billy, Mr. Holder calls the sheriff and demands he take action. But the sheriff knows Holder's boys and heard the true story from the bus driver. He tells Holder how Grandpa got the money to buy back Annabelle. "You of all people should know what it's like to lose a loved one."

Christmas Eve rolls around again. Agnes shows up with a court order giving her custody of Billy until he can speak. Grandpa is devastated but goes inside to help Billy pack. The animals tow Agnes' car into the pond, and she is forced to spend the night. Billy and Grandpa can spend one last Christmas together.

Santa arrives to bring his annual gift to the animals and Annabelle whispers her special wish into his ear. On Christmas morning, Billy opens the box on the Christmas tree and says, "There's nothing in here!" Grandpa is joyous and Agnes annoyed. Billy rushes to the barn to tell Annabelle the good news, but she can only moo. Annabelle gave Billy her Christmas voice; she would never speak again.

Gus Holder and Buster and Bucky show up at Grandpa's all decked out in their best clothes. Gus gives the music box back to Grandpa and tells him how sorry he is. Gus and old Anges hit it off, and all are invited to stay for Christmas dinner.

Ah, but this is not our happy ending. Gus marries Agnes and as we are told, "Buster and Bucky got what they deserved." Billy and Emily were married and still live on the farm. Billy never forgot the gift Annabelle gave him. Another Christmas Eve has arrived and Billy is worried about Annabelle who is now old and sick. He goes to the barn to check on her and finds footprints leading away from the farm. He follows the tracks and finds Annabelle fallen in the snow. But Santa has also found Annabelle. He ties a red bow around her neck and she magically becomes a reindeer who not only gets her voice back but will lead Santa's sleigh this Christmas Eve.

This simple little cartoon brings a tear to the eye as Annabelle finally gets her special wish. Randy Travis, Alison Krauss and Beth Nielsen Chapman sing original songs written for the film. While the animation is not in the same category as Disney's best, it is a lovely story that will delight the entire family.

—SS

Beauty and the Beast: The Enchanted Christmas

1997

Disney, hoping to capture some of the magic of the original *Beauty and the Beast*, released this direct-to-video title during the 1997 holiday season.

The animated film finds the now human servants preparing for a festive Christmas. Chip asks to be told the story of Christmas the year before.

The action picks up previously when Beast has saved Belle from the wolves in the original film. She and the Beast are becoming friends and the servants (in the form of talking household items) happily encourage the budding romance—all that is except for the evil pipe organ, Forte (voiced by Tim Curry). Forte thrives on the dependence his master has upon the dark and gloomy music that Forte spews forth. Helping Forte in his quest to ruin the romance is Fife (Paul Reubens), a timid instrument who, although he adores Belle, follows the orders of Forte.

On Christmas Eve, Belle (Paige O'Hara) and the servants decide to have Christmas and surprise the Beast (Robby Benson). Belle carefully wraps a story she has written and sneaks it into the room of Beast. Angelique (Bernadette Peters), the former castle decorator, at first argues with Cogsworth (David Ogden Stiers) and Lumiere (Jerry Orbach) but grudgingly gives in and follows the other decorations downstairs. The hall is festively decorated with wreaths and ribbons, Christmas bulbs and candles. A delectable banquet is supervised by Mrs. Potts (Angela Lansbury) and Belle and Chip (Haley Joel Osmet) go in search of a Christmas tree.

None of the evergreens will do, and they are about to give up when a beautiful music draws them to the hall of Forte. He convinces them that a Christmas tree is just what the Beast needs to cheer him up and suggests they go to the Black Forest. Belle protests. She has promised never to leave the grounds, but Forte turns her words around and makes her seem selfish.

Belle and Chip take a sleigh and head for the frightening forest.

Meanwhile, Forte tells Beast where Belle has gone. Beast is enraged and destroys the decorated hall before heading out after Belle. Beast hates Christmas because it was on that Christmas Day many years ago the spoiled and cold-hearted Prince cruelly turned away an old woman who sought shelter from the cold. The woman put a curse upon the Prince and his household. Beast cannot stand the thought of the holiday.

Belle tries to find a pretty Christmas tree to cheer up Beast in *Beauty and the Beast: The Enchanted Christmas.* © **Walt Disney Productions**

Belle and Chip find the perfect tree, cut it down, and tie it to the sleigh. They start to return to the castle across a frozen lake, but Fife (sent by Forte to make sure they never return) startles the horse who rears and breaks the ice. Chip falls into the water and Belle, trying to rescue him, falls also. The rope from the tree wraps around her leg and pulls her under.

Beast arrives in time to save her but throws her into the dungeon. At midnight, Belle's friends visit her and convince her that Beast cannot cancel Christmas. Christmas is hope and that is never gone. Belle cheers up.

Beast, seeking the solace of the melancholy tunes of Forte, listens as the evil pipe organ tries to convince Beast to destroy the rose that keeps alove Beast's hope of becoming human. Beast, his emotions controlling him, goes to the rose but sees the present from Belle. The story, about a girl and a Beast who discover the joy of Christmas, warms his heart, and he goes to Belle for forgiveness. A festive holiday is planned by all but Forte decides to destroy Beast and Belle so he will live forever as the pipe organ. He plays shattering notes as the walls begin to crumble around Belle and Beast. Beast, with help from little Fife, grabs the keyboard and destroys it, destroying Forte and saving the entire household. Treetop angel

Angelique oversees the decorations and a joyous Christmas takes place in the dark castle.

Mrs. Potts finishes the story for Chip as Belle and her now human prince enter the great hall. Christmas this year is even more grand since everyone is now back to their human forms. Fife leads the orchestra for a Christmas dance.

Beauty and the Beast: The Enchanted Christmas will charm adults as well as children who have grown to love the original movie. The songs are not the quality of the Ashman/Menken originals, but they are sweet. The CGI animation of Forte is quite remarkable and makes him one of the more frightening Disney villains. The animation is heads and tails above Saturday morning cartoons, and the colors are bright and cheerful. The castle glows with warmth and happiness at the end of the film.

Highly recommended for children's holiday viewing.

The following Christmas films are also recommended holiday viewing for children:

Case of the Christmas Caper
Ashley Olsen and Mary-Kate Olsen star in this direct-to-video release featuring a Christmas mystery.

The Christmas Toy

Cast: (voices) Jim Henson, Dave Goelz, Steve Whitmire, Jerry Nelson, Kathryn Mullen

Credits: Director: Eric Till; Writer: Laura Phillips; Henson Associates; 1990

When people aren't in the room, the toys come to life, but if they are caught, they will be frozen forever. Rugby wants to be opened again for Christmas, and the other toys must get him back in place before being discovered.

Elmo Saves Christmas

Cast: Charles Durning, Harvey Fierstein, Kevin Clash

Credits: Producer: Karin Young Shiel; Director: Emily Squires; Writers: Christine Ferraro and Tony Geiss; Children's Television Workshop; 1996

Sesame Street's beloved Elmo (Kevin Clash) meets Santa (Durning) and the Easter Bunny (Harvey Fierstein) in this sweet children's direct-to-video film.

George Balanchine's The Nutcracker

Cast: Jessica Lynn Cohen, Macaulay Culkin, Kevin Kline, Darci Kistler

Credits: Producers: Robert A. Krasnow and Robert Hurwitz; Director: Emile Ardolino; Choreography; George Balanchine; Warner Bros.; 1983

To those who do not follow ballet and rarely know what is going on, this film is for you. Narrator Kevin Kline helps explain the sequences and leads the viewers through this visual candy treat.

The story involves Marie (Cohen) who dreams of her Nutcracker Prince (Culkin) and their adventures in the land of the Sugar Plum Fairy (Darci Kistler). The costumes and set design are splendid and the dancing delightful. The dances of the snowflakes and, later, the Christmas tree angels are especially charming.

Heidi

Cast: Shirley Temple, Jean Hersholt, Arthur Treacher, Helen Westley, Pauline Moore

Credits: Producer: Raymond Griffith; Director: Allan Dwan; Writers: Walter Ferris and Julien Josephson (Based on the Novel by Johanna Spyri); Fox; 1937

Our favorite version of the classic children's story is, without a doubt, the Shirley Temple version. Shirley stars as Heidi, who is forced to live with her reclusive grandfather (Hersholt) in the Swiss Alps. She begins to crack his gruff exterior when she is taken away by a mean aunt, who sells her as a servant. Heidi goes to live with a wealthy family whose daughter Klara (Maracia Mae Jones) can't walk. During Christmas Grandfather walks to the town to find Heidi. He misses her coming out of church and is picked up by the local police. Eventually, the two are reunited. A warm and touching film that will enchant children of all ages.

Heidi has been filmed several times including a 1954 Swiss version starring Elsbeth Sigmund and Heinrich Gretler, and a 1968 Austrian version starring Eva Maria Singhammer, Gustav Knuth and Gertraud Mittermayr. Another 1968 version, written by Earl Hamner, Jr., starred Jennifer Edwards, Michael Redgrave, Maximilian Schell and Jean Simmons. In 1993 a Walt Disney Productions version starred Jason Robards, Jane Seymour, and Patricia Neal with Noley Thornton as Heidi.

The Lion, the Witch and the Wardrobe

There are two versions of this classic tale. One was done by British television (Director: Marilyn Fox; BBC 1988; Cast: Richard Dempsey, Sophie Cook, Jonathan Scott, Sophie Wilcox) and ran in the U.S. on PBS; it is available on video. The other is an animated feature (1979, directed by Bill Melendez), also available on video.

The story concerns the adventures of four children who visit the magical land of Narnia where an evil queen has made it forever winter, but *never* Christmas.

The Little Drummer Boy

Cast: (voices) Jose Ferrer, Paul Frees, June Foray, Ted Eccles, Greer Garson
Credits: Producers/Directors: Jules Bass and Arthur Rankin, Jr.; Writer: Romeo Muller (Based on the Song by Katherine Davis, Henry Onorati and Harry Simeone); Rankin-Bass Productions; 1968

The television special based upon the popular Christmas song. The little drummer hates all people and only finds comfort in his drum and his animal friends. The special tells the story of how he overcame his hatred and gave his own special gift to the Christ child.

The animated *The Nutcracker Prince*.

Mr. Willowby's Christmas Tree

Cast: Robert Downey, Jr., Leslie Nielsen, Stockard Channing
Credits: Producer: Ritamarie Peruggi; Director: Jon Stone; Writer: Mitchell Kriegman (Based on the Book by Robert Barry); Jim Henson Productions; 1995

Sweet Christmas special with adorable muppets, especially a mouse family celebrating Christmas and their quest for a Christmas tree.

The Nutcracker Prince

Cast: (voices) Peter O'Toole, Kiefer Sutherland, Megan Follows, Michael MacDonald
Credits: Producer: Kevin Gillis; Director: Paul Schibli; Writers: Patricia Watson and E.T.A. Hoffman; Warner Bros.; 1990

Animated version of the ballet.

Nutcracker Fantasy

Cast: (voices) Michele Lee, Melissa Gilbert, Christopher Lee, Jo Anne Worley, Roddy McDowall
Credits: Producers: Walt deFaria, Mark L. Rosen and Arthur Tomioka; Director: Takeo Nakamura; Writers; Thomas Joachim and Eugene Fornier); Sanrio; 1979

Animated version of the *Nutcracker and the Mouse King*.

Nutcracker: The Motion Picture

Cast: Hugh Bigney, Vanessa Sharp, Patricia Barker, Wade Walthall
Credits: Producers: Willard Carroll, Donald Kushner, Peter Locke and Thomas L. Wilhite; Writers: Kent Stowell and Maruice Sendak; Director: Carroll Ballard; Atlantic; 1986

Live action ballet of the Nutcracker by the Northwest Ballet.

Rudolph, the Red-Nosed Reindeer

Cast: (voices) Burl Ives, Larry D. Mann, Billie Mae Richards
Credits: Producers: Jules Bass and Arthur Rankin, Jr.; Directors: Kizo Nagashima and Larry Roemer; Rankin-Bass Productions; 1964

Wonderful holiday television special that has Sam the Snowman (Ives) relate the tale of how Rudolph overcame the reindeer who used to laugh and call him names and never let poor Rudolph play in any reindeer games. Rudolph's adventures with another little outcast elf who wants to be a dentist and the Abominable Snowman are the surrounding story as Rudolph saves the reindeer from the Snowman and becomes the lead reindeer for Santa.

Burl Ives was the narrator in *Rudolph the Red-Nosed Reindeer*.

Sandra Dee poses for a publicity shot for the animated *The Snow Queen*.

Rudolph the Red-Nosed Reindeer: The Movie

Forthcoming animated holiday film (Fall 1998) that uses the vocal talents of Paul McCartney and Whoopi Goldberg.

The Small One

Cast: Voices of Sean Marshall, William Woodson, Olan Sovle, Hal Smith, Joe Higgins, Gordon Jump
Credits: Producer/Director: Don Bluth; Music: Robert F. Brunner; Disney; 1978

The animated story of a young boy who must sell his beloved donkey Small One because he is too old and can no longer carry a large load. The boy takes the donkey to the nearest town and has all sorts of adventures as he tries to find a kind person to buy Small One. He finally finds that person, a kindly man who buys the donkey to carry his wife to Bethlehem. A sweet film that will capture your heart.

The Snow Queen

Cast: (voices) Sandra Dee, Tommy Kirk, Patty McCormack, Paul Frees
Credits: Producer: Robert Faber; Directors: Alan Lipscott, Bob Fisher and Phil Patton; Universal; 1959

This Russian animated film was dubbed with a U.S. cast of voices for its release. The story is based on the Hans Christian Andersen fairy tale of the Snow Queen.

Stowaway

Cast: Shirley Temple, Robert Young, Alice Faye
Credits: Producer: B.G. DeSylva; Director: William A. Seiter; Writers: William Conselman, Arthur Sheekman and Nat Perrin (Based on a Story by Samuel Engel); Fox; 1936

Temple stars as orphan Ching-Ching who stows away on a ship to be with Young. In the end Faye and Young marry and adopt Ching-Ching. The final sequence has the happy family around the Christmas tree opening gifts. Temple also sings "That's What I Want for Christmas."

To Grandmother's House We Go

Cast: Ashley Olsen, Mary-Kate Olsen, Rhea Perlman, Jerry Van Dyke, Stuart Margolin, Cynthia Geary
Credits: Director: Jeff Franklin; 1992

The Olsen twins wind up kidnapped by a pair of bumbling crooks while trying to get to their grandmother's house because they think it would be easier for their single mother if they were gone.

Credits:

Annabelle's Wish

Cast: (voices) Clancy Brown, Jim Varney, Randy Travis, Cloris Leachman, Jerry Van Dyke
Credits: Producers: Barbara Dunn-Leonard; Writer: Dan Henderson; Ralph Edwards Films; 1997

Beauty and the Beast: The Enchanted Christmas

Cast: (voices) Paige O'Hara, Robby Benson, Jerry Orbach, David Ogden Stiers, Bernadette Peters, Tim Curry, Angela Lansbury
Credits: Director: Andy Knight; Writers: Flip Kobler, Cindy Marcus, Bill Motz and Bob Roth; Walt Disney Home Video; 1997

A Charlie Brown Christmas

Cast: (voices) Peter Robbins, Tracy Stratford, Christopher Shea, Chris Doran, Bill Melendez
Credits: Producers: Bill Melendez and Lee Mendelson; Writer: Charles M. Schulz; United Features Syndicate; 1965

How the Grinch Stole Christmas

Cast: (voices) Boris Karloff, Thurl Ravenscroft
Credits: Director: Chuck Jones, Writer: Dr. Seuss; MGM; 1966

Then One Foggy Christmas Eve...

In this chapter we look at mystery and action films that take place during the holidays. The cheerfulness of Christmas is used as a bright background for the filmmaker's darkly suspense-laden films.

Christmas Holiday

1944

Imagine not including a film entitled *Christmas Holiday* for our book *It's Christmas Time at the Movies*, a film starring Universal sweetheart Deanna Durbin and natural good-guy Gene Kelly. But facades are sometimes deceiving, and *Christmas Holiday* is perhaps the most un-Christmas-like of all the Christmas films covered in this book (added to the fact that Deanna Durbin plays a tainted lady and that future musical/dancing star Gene Kelly plays perhaps the most evil character in his entire career). Universal Pictures, in 1944, was jumping on the film noir bandwagon, and their emerging star director, Robert Siodmak (fresh from directing the noir-influenced *Son of Dracula* starring Lon Chaney in 1943), was on the rise.

Christmas Holiday begins quite innocently as a huge Christmas tree in the army barracks becomes a centerpiece for the troops eager to take their holiday leave before being shipped out to parts unknown. Lt. Charles Mason (Dean Harens), the squeaky-clean young kid, is preparing to fly out Christmas Eve to San Francisco to marry his sweetheart. "Merry Christmas, Charlie! If I don't see you again..." one of his friends proclaims. Charlie's friend Jerry waits as the anxious lieutenant reads a telegram just handed him,

never a good sign. It seems his girl Mona went off and married a Frank Fabina, wishing the heartbroken young man a happy life. Jerry, seeing that Charlie is shattered, invites his friend to spend the holidays with him in New York; but the outraged Charlie swears he will still fly to San Francisco. Unfortunately, bad weather on the flight diverts the airplane to New Orleans where the mostly military crew are offered free hotel accommodations until the weather clears, and the flight may continue.

Depressed and sitting in the bar, the generally taciturn Mason is interrupted by the obnoxiously bantering Simon Fenimore (Richard Whorf), a reporter who notices that "Christmas is kinda getting you down," thinking the downtrodden Mason needs a friend. Fenimore continues, "Christmas is for kids, not for us." To help cheer the both of them up, Simon suggests they hit a "joint" on Christmas Eve that he knows very well. Of course a gigantic Christmas tree sits near the main entrance, but inside, the mood is anything but Yuletide cheer. Taking a table, Simon leaves to find Valerie, the hostess, as Charlie sits and listens to the swinging jazz combo and sultry torch singer belt out the lyrics "Spring will be a little late this year." Finding Valerie, the hostess tells Simon, "A few drinks and you gotta play the good Samaritan," referring to Simon's request to help his friend get an earlier flight out, but Valerie is willing yet unable to help. Simon does request of Valerie that she ask Jackie (Deanna Durbin) to join them, a sort of

Mason (Dean Harens) and Fenimore (Richard Whorf) try to cheer themselves up in *Christmas Holiday*.

Gale Sondergaard as Mrs. Manette, Gene Kelly as Robert Manette and Deanna Durbin as Jackie give new meaning to dysfunctional family in *Christmas Holiday*.

escort-on-call, a young woman with a bad past and the blank expression that mirrors it all. The type of girl who will sit with a soldier and create nonstop small-talk, offer to dance, just for a few drinks. As Simon smiles, "You won't find Jackie hard to talk to." Jackie, as enacted by Durbin, never seems as sleazy nor as haunted as the role requires. Referring to friend Simon, Jackie blurts out, "He's been drinking himself into the gutter for a long time—they're running out of gutters." Before passing out in Valerie's office, Simon offers Charlie two tickets for midnight mass at St. Louis' Cathedral, and strangely, Jackie implores him "to take me with you... I want to go—please!" Valerie, taking Charlie aside, tells him that Jackie's a "good kid, she deserves a break."

Strangely, during mass, the formerly pleasant Jackie becomes solemn and sad, soon tears begin rolling down her cheeks as she sobs violently, drowning out the background music of joyous Christmas carols being sung by the church choir. Remaining after the mass, sitting within empty pews and total solitude, Jackie asks Charlie to get her something to eat before taking her "home."

Going to a little coffee shop, Jackie begins to open up, trusting the clean-cut military man who seems so decent. "I thought if I went to mass with you, I'd become part of it, share something with all these people. Feelings, praying, forgetting. I've been alone as long as I can remember... You sure Simon didn't tell you anything [about me]." She goes on to reveal that she's not really Jackie. That's her "bar" name,

that she is really Abigail Martin, but she changed her name "after the trial." She explains, "I'm the wife of Robert Manette" (spelled "Mannette" in a newspaper headline but "Manette" in the closing credits). Three years ago Manette murdered a bookie and was sentenced to death, his sentence only recently changed to life in prison. Abigail admits they were only married six months before the murder occured, but these were the happiest months of her life. Not giving in to pressure to now divorce her murderous husband, she admits, "I would keep on loving him."

Stylistically, the film noir conventions were in their formative stages in 1944, and films such as *Christmas Holiday* helped to shape these genre icons. For instance, by the second half of the movie the dominant character has shifted from being Charles Mason (the innocent young man) to Jackie/Abigail who soon narrates the story (in typical voice-over film noir style). Another film noir characteristic, the use of repeated flashbacks and an interrupted narrative, becomes the norm as Jackie now tells Charlie her life story for the past three years. Interestingly enough, the first flashback details the events that occurred immediately after the murder, and the second flashback details how Robert Manette (Gene Kelly) and Abigail first met. By the end of the movie, the viewer is back in the present dealing with the consequences of all these convoluted flashback sequences.

The first flashback creates an Alfred Hitchcock-style *Shadow of a Doubt* "should I trust him or not" style of suspense; however, the audience is already aware that Manette is a murderer (which Abigail does not yet realize in the flashback). Manette, keeping late hours, returns home after wife Abigail is asleep in bed. "I do keep terrible hours, don't I... I keep taking advantage of [her] trusting nature... I'll never ever do it again," he playfully tells his concerned wife. The next morning, the viewer is introduced to "Mother," Mrs. Manette (Gale Sondergaard), the over-protective mother who is more aware of her son's nefarious activities than Abigail would ever admit. Spotting a stain on Robert's pants, Mother grows very attentive and concerned, and when she goes through the trouser pockets and finds a roll of bills, Robert becomes very upset and screams, "You're not to go through my pockets." Thinking quickly, Robert puts the blame on his vice, gambling, which he promised to stop. Later, Abigail secretly oversees Mother burning Robert's pants in the incinerator. Confronting the always cool and calculating matriarch, Abigail asks, "Mother, what's it all about?" To which she responds, "What's *what* all about?" Abigail continues, "This morning, about nothing being in the paper... and Robert's trousers—you burned them..." To which Mother slightly smiles and rambles on, "Remember that old blue velvet dress of mine—I just couldn't stand to look at it another minute... ooohh, Robert's trousers [she giggles]." However, the police soon arrive at the door and politely request that Robert contact the 3rd Precinct. "Routine thing, don't let it worry you." But worried the young wife is.

That evening, when Robert returns home late and Abigail tells him of the events of the day, he tries to calm her down, "Please Abigail, it's nothing." But she pleads with him to open up and tell her everything. "Shut up," he shouts, the rage finally revealing the monster underneath the surface, as he pulls the bed covering to the floor and storms out. The next morning Robert tries to smooth things over. "If it's about last night, I don't have to tell you how sorry I am, do I? You know there isn't anybody [thinking his young wife suspects an affair]—please say you'll forgive me." Robert then makes up a story when confronted about the roll of money Mother found. "You know how silly Mother is about banks and all that cash she keeps in her room. Well, I got into a jam... and there was no other way to get out of it." Abigail very solemnly states, "I don't believe you—what about that policeman, what about those trousers.' Getting very serious and sinister, Robert slowly states, "If anybody asks, I got those trousers dirty cleaning a car for a friend. Mother gave them away to a tramp... that's what she's going to say. About the money, if anybody asks you, *anybody*, you never saw me with that money... my life might depend upon it. Abigail, if you ever loved me..." To which she honestly replies, "I'll always love you."

But unlike Hitchcock, the emphasis here is not on suspense because the narrative structure makes clear from the beginning that Manette is serving life in prison for the murder of a bookie. We never doubt the guilt of Manette. Instead, director Siodmak is dealing with psychological-based character studies and a woman's commitment to love a man she slowly suspects is a murderer. The bond, the passion that connects them, her innocence, her refusal to accept or even see the obvious, his conniving evil—*what* keeps them together? That's the focus of this film.

To contrast this relationship of denial and deceit, the second flashback concerns the original meeting of Abigail and Robert, at a symphonic orchestra concert, where both parties are transfixed by the magic of the music. Both sit emotionally affected by the music's power at concert's end; Robert states, "Unfortunately, you can't make a living from being absorbed in music. You know, sometimes when I listen to it, I feel there's nothing man is capable of that I can't do. Then it stops, and it's over." To which Abigail contrasts, "Not for me. I feel as if something's been added to my life that wasn't there before." These simple lines help to establish the character (and character flaws) of both individuals. Robert is swept away by the mysticism of the music, but when the music stops, its magic is over too. But for Abigail, the magic spell lasts even after "it's over." Robert later asks Abigail, "Which do you like better, the person I pretend to be or..." to which Abigail completes his sentence, not missing a beat, "The person you are." But the truth is she constantly denies the person Robert truly is and, instead, believes in only the person he pretends to be. That complements her fantasy, as much as the concert.

For 1944 Hollywood, Robert's relationship with Mother is most bizarre. It appears the hold she has over her son is unnatural (Mother must approve of Abigail before Robert consents to marry her), and even after the wedding, all three live together. As Mrs. Manette tells Abigail upon their first meeting, "There are certain traits in Robert, they're nothing evil; he sometimes just forgets his sense of responsibility. Between us, we will make him strong." Less subtle, in one curious line of narrative voice-over delivered by Abigail; she admits that she was later told "Robert's relationship with his mother was pathological." No fooling.

However, Mother's approval of Abigail soon dissipates as the young bride gets even more caught up in a world of denial. "He needed your strength—that's why I let him marry you, and all you gave him back was his weakness." Mother continues, "I love him... I am willing to know all about him and keep on loving him... I tried to make him strong myself, but I couldn't alone, so I relied on you—you have failed."

After both women hear the verdict of guilty, outside the courtroom, Mother tells Abigail "you killed him" and slaps Abigail hard.

Returning to the present, Charlie Mason's flight is rescheduled for 11:30 that evening, since the stormy weather has cleared, but he heads back to the nightclub after reading the headlines that Manette has escaped from prison and probably will try to find his wife. Risking missing his flight, he reveals, "I've learned a hundred years worth of life in the last 24 hours. The important thing is being honest with yourself, whatever you feel, whatever you are." He has decided not to fly on to Frisco, but to return directly to his base and face the future, not dwell on the damnable past.

Sneaking into a sideroom along with reporter Simon Fenimore, the gritty fugitive Manette is soon joined by wife Abigail, who kisses and embraces her husband. He suspects during his two-and-a-half year prison sentence that his wife has been less than faithful. To which she solemnly admits, "I love you Robert." Registering his doubt, Robert counters with, "The way you say it I can almost believe it." Soon Lt. Charles Mason has joined the gathering.

Next, the heart of the conflict unfolds, its complexity simply and clearly delivered. Abigail, looking haggard and spiritually drained, confesses, "I had to live like you, suffer like you. The people I met here all had nothing but contempt for me. That's what I *wanted*. This is my prison, Robert, but I'm not as strong as you. I can't break out without you. I need you... I love you! That's why I had to live like you, to suffer like you. I wanted to die, but you were alive, so I had to live."

The cherub-faced Durbin lacked the emotional depth and despair to truly pull off this dramatic moment, but she still does a fine, convincing job. Within seconds the police arrive, and Manette is shot dead. Before he is hit, Manette states, "Anyone who loves as much as you do is entitled to a reward, that's what I think!" After he is mortally wounded, Manette declares, "You can let go now, Abigail." Tears stream down her face as Abigail looks up at the night sky, the clouds quickly separating to reveal the bright stars shining.

What a wonderful role cast against type for the wholesome and goody-goody Deanna Durbin, but an adult role that allowed her character to stretch and deal with the demons that possessed her. Feeling guilty for denying her husband's flaws and her inability to help him by forcing him to confront his problems, Abigail becomes a bar-girl without a home who spends nights sitting up at a coffee shop with the regulars—all this to punish herself for her husband's crime and incarceration, accepting Mother's claim that "you killed him" and now paying the price by squandering

her soul. Only at the end, with Manette's release via death, is Abigail released from her emotional hell with the symbolic parting of the clouds to reveal the shining stars. Gene Kelly, also working against type, reveals the savage villain he was capable of playing and it is unfortunate that his movie roles never allowed him to play such a scoundrel again.

Director Robert Siodmak's film noir universe is one of internal torture and cruel, cold fate. Never has a more anti-Christmas themed movie carried the term "Christmas" in its title. However, the redemption of the damned at movie's end might reflect the Christmas spirit that any individual who sinks to the depths of perversity may still find in his or her spiritual soul once freed from such an emotional albatross. Perhaps this is the spirit of salvation and hope which ends *Christmas Holiday*.

—GJS

Lady in the Lake
1947

Christmas films and film noir seemingly go together like oil and water: Christmas celebrates the birth of a morality and spirit of love that permeates the universe, a universe of hope and redemption. Film noir, on the opposite end of the cosmic scale, celebrates the ambiguity and breakdown of morals and ethics in an unfeeling, uncaring universe. Christmas praises the potential for good residing in every person; film noir projects the evil pit into which even the good can fall.

Lady in the Lake came oozing like a puddle of dirty oil into theaters in 1946, right after the end of World War II. The MGM film starred Robert Montgomery (*Night Must Fall, Here Comes Mr. Jordan*) as existential detective Phillip Marlowe with Audrey Totter (*The Set-Up, The Postman Always Rings Twice*) portraying the crafty leading lady (and potential *femme fatale*). Produced during the Hollywood golden noir era of *The Maltese Falcon, The Big Sleep* and *Murder, My Sweet, Lady in the Lake* becomes an experimental film noir in more than one way. Directed by star Robert Montgomery, the film stylistically reminds the viewer of the slasher horror movies of the 1970s and '80s, with the entire film photographed subjectively showing Marlowe's (Montgomery's) point of view throughout the entire movie. The only time we see Marlowe's face is when it is reflected in a mirror, and the viewing audience sees (first-hand) all the nuances and deceptions recorded in the cast's face as Marlowe confronts each character with sarcastic and cynical questioning and comments. The cinematic gimmick is interesting, but ultimately it grows limiting and tiresome, mainly because good acting involves

Adriene Fromsett (Audrey Totter) and her boss Mr. Kingsley (Leon Ames) host their company Christmas party, soon to be interrupted by Marlowe in *Lady in the Lake*.

interaction between characters, and while we hear Montgomery's clever lines, we usually see only one other actor visually and verbally react to such dialogue; we seldom see actors interact with each other (instead ensemble groups, such as the boys at the police station, react to Marlowe and not each other).

The Christmas theme (to provide visual and moral contrast to the noir world of desperation, hopelessness, and defeat) envelops the film from the very beginning. Above the MGM logo we hear Christmas bells chime and the standby "Jingle Bells" sound. The movie credits are cleverly conceived as a pile of Christmas cards slowly being revealed; after the last credit is finished, the card is lifted to reveal a black pistol. Even "The End" credit at the finale features the Three Wise Men following the Christmas Star. In typical film noir fashion, the opening narration, establishing the deadpan vocal delivery of Phillip Marlowe, reminds the viewer that it is only three days before Christmas. Marlowe, speaking directly to the audience, offers "maybe you'll solve it quick, and maybe you won't... Let me give you a tip... you have to watch them all the time." The movie reaches its dramatic climax on Christmas Day, when the case is finally solved.

The plot unfolds in complicated fashion, revealing that Marlowe has decided to write about murder because "it's safer" and has submitted a short story, "If I Should Die Before I Live," to Kingsly Publications when chief assistant Adriene Fromsett (Audrey Totter) asks Marlowe to visit her at the office to talk contract. There on the glass office door are the names of the pulp fiction magazines that Kingsly's publishes: *Lurid Detective, Crime Monthly, Monster Stories, Murder Masterpieces, True Horror Tales, Midnight Novelettes*. The first view Marlowe (and we the audience) sees of Fromsett is her ranting "not nearly enough gore... take it out and put more blood in." Then the classic noir dialogue starts when Marlowe tells Fromsett that the story is based upon authentic cases. "We get hundreds of authentic cases submitted to us every week." Marlowe matter-of-factly replies: "Why don't you print a few?" As the sexy blonde receptionist enters the office from the far side door, a tracking shot of Marlowe's eyes follow the blonde ignoring the always babbling Fromsett. "Oh... Mr. Marlowe. Have you been marooned on a desert island, or do you find it hard to concentrate... I must be losing my touch!" Getting back on track, Fromsett offers a generous $200 for the story after asking flir-

Marlowe (Robert Montgomery) checks out a Christmas bathrobe given to him by Adriene Fromsett in *Lady in the Lake*.

tatiously: "Are there really detectives like the one in your story who never lie, cheat or double-cross a client, who are loyal, honest, never betray a confidence?"

"Yes," Marlowe responds, "there are a couple of dopes like that."

But Marlowe, always a few steps ahead, has figured out that Fromsett is only plying him with compliments and offering to buy his story because she needs a "dumb, brave, cheap" private detective for her own interests. Having the eye for money, she wants to marry boss Derace Kingsly, whose wife suddenly vanished one month earlier, supposedly running off with gigolo Southerner Chris Lavery. Hoping that Marlowe can get the goods on Mrs. Kingsly; then the old boy might be ripe to marry his executive assistant. As Fromsett states, "I handle all of Mr. Kingsly's affairs." Figuring out her motives, Marlowe refuses her offer and states he would never let her publish his story. However, when Mr. Kingsly (Leon Ames) enters the office, she suddenly increases her offer to $500, which Marlowe is not able to resist (later she tells him it's $200 for the story and a $300 retainer for his taking the case). When asked what the story is full of, he answers "short sentences."

"Every man has his price," Fromsett confidentially smirks. To celebrate the deal, Fromsett invites Marlowe to her apartment for drinks "over a few ice cubes." Marlowe chuckles and offers the dig, "Imag-ine *you* needing ice cubes."

The entire movie contains such clever dialogue, with Totter's wide-eyed reactions subjectively viewed catching conniving, ruthless characters off guard. But after less than a split second of being off guard, the always prepared Fromsett jumps back to her ice princess status. However, by the film's end, more than a few ice cubes have melted.

The intriguing case leads Marlowe to Chris Lavery's home (a Christmas wreath on the door) and back to Fromsett's apartment's where another Christmas wreath adorns her abode. At first politely tolerated by the oily Lavery ("I like your tan, Mr. Lavery, very Christmassy"), the detective's too-clever tongue gets the private investigator punched out cold; his unconscious body is then placed in his car which Lavery makes run a curb. Lavery then pours a bottle of booze over him and the police are called to arrest the drunk. Sgt. DeGarmot (Lloyd Nolan) and Captain Kane (Tom Tully) read Marlowe the Bay City riot act threatening him if he ever starts trouble in their quaint community where only respectable citizens dwell. Marlowe proclaims, "At least he [Lavery] had the decency to hit me *above* the Mason-Dixon line," referring to his shiner.

The case gets more complex. Up at Kingsly's private lake, the body of the wife of the caretaker has been found in the lake, but after 30 days, "[there's] not much left of her." The drowning victim, Muriel Chess, had her name changed from Mildred Havelin because she was hiding out from a mysterious policeman stalker who is after her. Fromsett reveals that Crystal Kingsly hated Muriel and thus tries to plant a motive for murder in Marlowe's mind. After Fromsett specifically tells Marlowe to go up to the lake to investigate and *not* to ever visit Lavery again, Marlowe goes directly to Lavery's house and there finds a mysterious woman with a gun, the so-called landlady, who is trying to find Lavery for her rent money. She claims she needs the money for Christmas presents. She is wielding a small handgun, which she claims she found lying on the steps. Quick-thinking Marlowe tells her he is from the finance company trying to get back payments for Lavery's car. After the so-called landlady leaves, Marlowe investigates further to find bullet holes in the bathroom shower stall with the slumped over corpse of Lavery dripping wet, under running water.

Next, Marlowe interrupts the jolly festivities at the Kingsly office party on Christmas Eve. At the precise moment that Kingsly is distributing presents to his workers, Marlowe enters and the party immediately comes to a screeching halt. Kingsly instructs Fromsett and Marlowe to use the side office, which they enter. The office is well decorated with hanging wreaths and a small Christmas tree. Marlowe obviously thinks that Fromsett is behind all these crimes. "It's Christmas time so tell the truth," he demands. Marlowe hands Fromsett her hanky with the embroidered "A.F." which he found on Lavery's nightstand (Marlowe earlier accused Fromsett of throwing herself at Kingsly only after Lavery jilted her). When the curious Kingsly enters, Fromsett is forced to tell her boss that she hired Marlowe to find Crystal, an admission which outrages her boss. After Kingsly specifically tells Fromsett that he holds no romantic feelings for her, he abruptly leaves. "You lost me my million dollars," the gold-digging executive admits. But in the spirit of the moment she retaliates with: "There's more than one Kingsly on the Christmas tree. I'll shake one loose yet!" As Marlowe is fired by Fromsett and leaves the office, he walks through a merry chorus of workers singing "Jingle Bells," all wishing him a Merry Christmas. Before he exits, Kingsly takes him aside and hires the detective to find out what happened to his wife.

The convoluted plot is finally figured out on Christmas Day. The landlady at Lavery's house turns out to be Mildred Havelin/Muriel Chess, who switched clothes with friend Crystal Kingsly before Crystal "drowns" in the lake. Mildred had formerly worked as a nurse for a doctor, and murdered the doctor's wife, making her killing appear a suicide, so she could marry the doctor herself. Why such a wealthy and attractive women has to resort to murder to snare a man is never adequately answered. That's the pathology of the film noir universe. The same Sergeant DeGarmot (of the proud Bay City police force) played the sap for her and helped her cover up the crime. Promising him her love, she cuts out on him at her earliest opportunity. Since that day, DeGarmot has been trying to find her to even the score. Havelin now pretends to be Kingsly's wife who wants Kingsly to give her a large sum of money because she's in big trouble. Since Kingsly is now being trailed by police detectives, he wants Marlowe to be the money-runner. Marlowe

agrees, but tells Fromsett to give him enough time before she brings Captain Kane to his rescue.

However, the plot takes another twist when DeGarmot first appears at the apartment to surprise Marlowe, with the crazed Havelin (Jayne Meadows) screaming "kill him, kill him!" Plotting to first kill Havelin, then to use Havelin's gun to kill Marlowe, DeGarmot can concoct the story that Havelin killed Marlowe and that he, the hero, killed her. Fortunately, after Havelin is shot to death, Kane and the boys appear on the scene to rescue Marlowe and leave Marlowe and melting ice princess Fromsett to fall in love.

The pivotal Christmas scene occurs at the police station, when Kane is arresting Marlowe for having punched DeGarmot in the face. Kane comes off as a tough-as-nails police captain, threatening to put Marlowe away for good. Suddenly he receives a phone call at his desk, which is overheard by all. It is his baby daughter Elaine: "I know it's the night before Christmas... yes, I'll be home to help you fill up your stocking... By heart! Yes, say it for me, it goes 'the stockings were hung by the chimney with care'... St. Nicholas... that's Santy Claus."

After his tender phone call, Kane returns to his gruff exterior hard-balling the equally tough guy detective. But another phone call interrupts again. "Yes, I know what night it is." Now the wife phones to remind Kane to dress up as Santa Claus for his daughter Elaine. "Don't think we'll need the pillow this year." This soft side of Kane leads him to drop all the charges against Marlowe, and in his toughest police stance he mutters, "Will you get out of here, Marlowe!"

The magic of Christmas polishes and softens all the harsh film noir exteriors. Spending a quiet Christmas together, sitting in the living room, listening to a radio broadcast of "A Christmas Carol," Fromsett contentedly purrs, "I wanna be your girl... that's what I want for Christmas," after both admitted to celebrating Christmas in bars (him) or nightclubs (her). "Don't frighten me—not on Christmas morning, not today. Let's give ourselves today!"

In this ruthless and hard-boiled world of deception, lust, murder, mistaken identities, foul play and bruised faces, the spirit of Christmas and all its goodness transforms an embittered, aggressive piece of female work who is out to snare her man into a woman willing to give up her life as a business woman to support her love, Phillip Marlowe, while he writes detective stories for a living. And Marlowe, smoking away on the couch, peacefully sits and watches Adriene recline on the living room sofa. Two noir prototypes are tamed by the joyous spirit of Christmas.

—GJS

Die Hard
1988
Die Hard 2
1989

Many claim, and quite rightfully so, that the modern action/adventure genre was invented by films like *Die Hard* (1988, directed by John McTiernan) and *Die Hard 2* (1990, directed by Renny Harlin), movies that put Bruce Willis' face on the cinematic map. However, most people soon forget that both of these thrill-a-minute special effects bonanzas are Christmas movies, occurring during the holiday season and incorporating the Yuletide spirit into major plot developments. For at the heart of both movies is the love between that renegade cowboy policeman John McClane and his wife Holly, each film demonstrating just how hard McClane will fight to win his wife back and keep her, as their marriage has lately been rocky. Disguised underneath terrorists' raids, exploding heads, burning buildings, airplanes on fire and ricocheting gun battles is a love story, straight and simple, a love story that is framed by the warmth and humanity of the Christmas holiday.

Die Hard begins with John McClane (Bruce Willis), L.A. bound, obsessing as the plane lands, his co-passenger explaining how to reduce his stress by making fists with your feet while barefoot. However, when McClane gets up and the other man sees his holstered gun, the other guy's apprehension increases, as McClane explains, "Don't worry, I'm only a cop." Meanwhile, McClane's wife, who works for the Nakatomi Corporation, is enjoying the business Christmas party on the 30th floor of Nakatomi Plaza, a state-of-the-art high-rise. As a small string ensemble plays relaxing music, the CEO speaks to the assembly, telling all that this was one of the most successful years for the corporation, ending with wishing everyone a Merry Christmas and a Happy New Year. Holly (Bonnie Bedelia) returns to her office, telling her assistant to get out there and party, apologizing "you are making me feel like Ebenezer Scrooge!" A co-worker hits on Holly, asking her for a date, but she politely turns him down stating this is Christmas Eve, the time for "families, stockings, chestnuts, Rudolph and Frosty." Phoning home, Holly speaks to her kids who ask when she is coming home, and whether Daddy will be joining them. Just in case, Holly asks her housekeeper to prepare the guest bedroom.

Back at the airport, McClane longingly watches families reunite, little children hug and kiss their parents, as he makes the rounds alone, in the snow, carrying a big teddy bear with a red Christmas bow on it. An energetic young limo driver, holding up a sign, approaches McClane, telling the New York policeman that he is his driver (and it's his first job to boot, after driving a cab in the city). The affable driver, Argyle (De' Voreaux White), speaks a mile a minute to the generally nonverbal McClane. Asking questions about his wife and family, why he is a New York cop while his wife works in L.A., McClane at first tells the driver to shut up. Argyle puts all the pieces together: McClane, a New York policeman, is not happy that wife Holly accepted a corporate job in Los Angeles; but, since he has a backlog of six months' work in New York, he just cannot pick up and leave. McClane secretly hopes that Holly's job won't work out and that she'll return to the East Coast before his six months are up. Asking Argyle to put some Christmas music on the car radio, the middle-aged McClane is unaware that "Christmas in Hollis" by rap group RUN-D.M.C. is playing. As the limo pulls up to Nakatomi Plaza, Argyle says he'll hang by waiting for a call on the car phone, since McClane's not sure if Holly will allow him to stay at her place. The cop becomes even more depressed when he discovers that Holly is registered and works under her maiden name Gennaro, but off he goes to the 30th floor for the party. Almost immediately, a stranger comes up to the rough-edged McClane, wishes him a Merry Christmas and kisses him on the cheek. "I can tell I'm in California," the cop mutters aloud.

John is recognized by CEO Mr. Takagi (James Shigeta), who invites McClane into a private office while they wait for his wife. However, another executive is surprised when Takagi opens the door, quickly finishing up a line of cocaine. McClane tells Takagi that he didn't realize that the Japanese celebrated Christmas, to which Takagi answers smiling, "We're flexible. Pearl Harbor didn't work out so we got you with tape decks." Takagi says the celebration is two-fold, first the Christmas holidays, and secondly, today a big deal was closed and Holly was instrumental in closing the deal. Two reasons for which to celebrate. Holly enters and is happy to see her husband, but remains reserved and standoffish. She shyly shows off her bonus: a Rolex watch. When John mentions staying with a retired policeman, Holly immediately invites him to spend the holiday in the guest room. "I missed you," she states longingly, but John interrupts, "but not my name," referring to her use of her maiden name. Without missing a beat, Holly explains that this is a Japanese corporation and that they assume a married woman—with this, her assistant interrupts and states Holly must give her prepared speech to the

Another Christmas is ruined for John McClane (Bruce Willis) in *Die Hard 2*.

troops. Hearing that she will return in a few minutes, McClane remains alone in the room, chiding himself for being immature. It is quite apparent he wants his wife back, but he fears she has given her soul to her job.

Outside, approaching the corporate building is one lone car and a large Pacific Courier van. The car pulls up in front of the buliding. Two men enter, talking a mile a minute about nothing and approach the security man, pull out a pistol and kill him before he knows what hit him. The one man, a computer guru, goes immediately to work on the high-rise's computer/security system. Meanwhile, a van arrives unloading 11 men including terrorist leader Hans Gruber (Alan Rickman). Their intention is to disarm the security system at the building and seek revenge against the "greedy" Nakatomi Corporation. The terrorist band invades the party on the 30th floor, firing automatic weapons while rounding everyone up, but not hurting anyone.

Meanwhile, McClane has taken off his shoes and socks, making his feet into fists, sighing, "Son of a bitch, it works," as he looks at photos of his family in his wallet. But the sound of automatic weapons and people screaming alert him that danger is afoot. Drawing his weapon, he hopes that driver Argyle (the phone lines have been cut) hears commotion and is phoning the police, but the oblivious driver is cranking up the sounds and bopping away inside his limo.

The CEO is escorted to his private office, and Gruber makes his plans clear. He knows that 40 million dollars of bonds are kept in the corporation safe, which is computer controlled. Gruber demands that the businessman give him the code to open the vault to get the bonds. Giving the executive three seconds to speak, the calm Takagi says he does not know the code, and Gruber shoots him through the head, turning to his computer guru to break the code.

By the movie's end, McClane is shirtless, barefoot and bloody, becoming the fly in Gruber's ointment, managing to alert the outside world of the terrorist attack within. However, the high-rise is literally trashed, burned, flooded or exploded by the film's end. Finally, the battered McClane, armed with one pistol in front of him and one hidden pistol taped to his back, confronts Gruber who holds a gun to Holly's head. McClane tells Gruber it was stupid to destroy the entire building just for a robbery. But Gruber demands McClane throw down his gun or guess who gets it. Thinking of McClane as a cowboy, Gruber states that this time John Wayne does not walk into the sunset with Grace Kelly, but McClane interrupts, "Gary Cooper, asshole," referring to the end of *High Noon*. Then quickly pulling out the hidden gun in back, McClane kills one gunman and seriously wounds Gruber, "Happy trials, Hans," who falls through the office plate glass but still manages to dangle by holding on to Holly's hand. By loosening her bracelet, Gruber's hand slips and he falls to a slow, agonizing death.

With fire trucks, police and emergency vehicles surrounding the building, McClane and Holly exit the building and meet the officer, his unknown outside contact, who helped McClane through the ordeal. Introducing his wife to the cop as "Miss Gennaro," she corrects him and says, "No, Mrs. McClane." From the underground parking garage, the battered but working limo with Argyle driving pulls up. McClane smiles, "Merry Christmas Argyle," and the super-charged driver declares, "If this is their idea of Christmas, I gotta be here for New Year's!" Then to the seasonal sounds of "Let It Snow! Let It Snow!" they drive off into the city streets, peaceful and calm at last.

Two years later, *Die Hard 2* appeared, again occurring at Christmas time, the setting changing from a high-rise to a major airport. John McClane is outraged that his borrowed car is being ticketed and towed because he parked in a an 8 a.m.-4 p.m. zone, and it is now past four. He says that since he is a Los Angeles police officer (a compromise to wife Holly) who used to be a New York police officer, he deserves a break. However, the jubilant cop seems to enjoy tormenting the outraged policeman. McClane's beeper goes off, and John enters the mobbed airport, festively decorated for the Christmas holidays, looking for a phone. Waiting rather impatiently in a long line, McClane dials the phone number and, surprisingly, reaches his wife aboard her plane who tells her husband the flight will be half an hour late. The frisky husband pleads, when she gets in, can they leave the children with her parents and get a hotel room, get room service, champagne and have a romantic night together. Holly is anxious to comply.

Meanwhile, over the airport TV monitors, the news is carrying a special report. A deposed military general/dictator is being flown into the United States to stand trial for his drug lord activities. The report mentions the fact that the U.S. Pentagon formerly had supported this same general with weapons and money because he fought to overthrow the Communist government in his own country. However, when the United States cut off this money, the general made it up by conducting an illegal drug trade, the reason for his overthrow and trial here in the States.

Soon weird things are occurring around the airport, with scattered individuals momentarily meeting at a cafe table and coordinating plans, one such man carrying and clutching strange luggage very close to his body. The watchman at a little church is disturbed by two strange uniformed city maintenance men who claim they need to check a line out back. The poor old watchman bemoans the fact that a piece of him is dying along with this church, and one of the workers smiles and says, "You're right about that," pulling out a pistol and shooting him in the chest three times. Using a walkie-talkie, the killer reports, "The clubhouse is open."

Back at the airport, the men at the cafe table get word that everything's in position, and one man, clutching that strange piece of luggage, is followed by McClane. However, when the man vanishes behind a locked door, McClane orders an airport maintenance man to open it, flashing his L.A.P.D. badge, ordering the worker to notify the airport police.

McClane goes inside and finds he is underneath conveyor belts carrying passenger luggage to and from the airplanes. Seeing two men in the distance, he again flashes his badge, and they smile and pull weapons and start firing. Within the next five minutes McClane faces both of the men in a wondrous drop-dead fight sequence atop luggage, on the conveyor belts, using golf clubs and aerosol cans as props. Ultimately, one man is crushed underneath one of the belts and the other escapes. The airport police charge McClane instead of the bad guy who gets away.

McClane is outraged that airport supervisor Lorenzo (Dennis Franz) does not close portions of the airport to conduct a proper investigation of the crime scene, but the totally power-hungry and stressed-out supervisor snaps back at McClane that this is Christmas week: he has the Shriner's Convention, the Boy Scouts and animals from the petting zoo in the airport and that under no circumstance will he be responsible for closing the airport during the holidays. Lorenzo has even sent for two security officers to escort McClane from the premises.

Of course, by the film's end, the renegade U.S. military officers, who support the deposed dictator, have taken over the entire airport and are hijacking a plane to return dictator/general and themselves to the tropics and a well-deserved vacation. Unfortunately, Holly McClane's plane (and many others) is continuing to circle the airport waiting for clearance to land as their fuel runs dangerously low. McClane, having to play cowboy again, boards a broadcast helicopter that tries to prevent the hijacked airplane from taking off. The plane is out of the hanger and racing down the air field; McClane has the copter fly over the speeding plane so he can drop onto the plane's wing. Once down, McClane uses his jacket to jam the mechanism in the wing that allows the plane to take off. The policeman is joined by two tough terrorists, who kick the stuffing out of him. One of them is killed when he is sucked into the jet propulsion engine and ground into mincemeat. The second terrorist manages to kick

McClane off the wing onto the ground below, but the wily cop manages to pull the cap off the fuel tank, watching as gallons of fuel gush out on the airfield below. McClane, bruised but safe, smiles as he takes out his wife's lighter and sets the trail of spilled fuel on fire, the fire racing upward to the departing airplane, at first setting its fuel tank on fire; finally the entire airplane explodes in flame.

The debris from the disintegrated airplane, and the fiery trail of flame on the runway, directs all the circling airplanes in for safe landings. Yelling out to find his wife, McClane spots Holly as she slides down the inflatable emergency exit ramp and he hugs her tightly. "Why does this keep happening to us?" Holly questions. Soon, Lorenzo appears asking, "Did you get this parking ticket in front of my airport?" McClane waves yes. Smiling and tearing the ticket up, the crusty Lorenzo yells, "What the hell, it's Christmas." Then as the familiar strains of "Let It Snow! Let It Snow!" return to flood the soundtrack, Holly and McClane walk off together as the snow begins to fall more intensely.

What makes these *Die Hard* movies successful is the use of juxtaposing extreme images and moods. First, we have the contrast between human relationships. On the one hand, we have the struggling marriage and on-going love affair between John and Holly McClane (McClane sitting alone in the office looking at photos of his children). Contrasted to this we have terrorist acts of violence predicated upon greed, failed politics and power, where relationships between individuals are never sacred and the death of one man can never disrupt "the overall operation." Second, we have the contrast of settings. We have the image of McClane rushing through an airport carrying a huge teddy bear with a red bow contrasted to terrorists firing machine guns and threatening people invading an elaborate office party held in a high-rise. We have the contrast of having John and Holly hug each other tightly standing out on the air field after her plane safely lands with the image of the terrorist plane catching fire and exploding in midair. As too many screenwriters and directors have forgotten, action-adventure works best when it takes time to develop relations between people we care about and we get to see these individuals solve interpersonal problems as we also see them save the world. And what better holiday than Christmas to contrast the traditional season of peace on Earth and good will toward men with all these random acts of violence, explosions, bullets in the head and chaos.

—GJS

The following mystery/action films occur during or have scenes pertaining to Christmas:

Inside Story

Cast: Michael Whalen, Jean Rogers, Chick Chandler, Douglas Fowley
Credits: Producer: Howard J. Green; Director: Ricardo Cortez; Writer: Jerry Cady (Based on *A Very Practical Joke* by Ben Ames Williams); Fox; 1939

This film is not available on videotape and we are relying on a review from *The Motion Picture Guide*. "Whalen is a reporter with a heart. He wants to find the loneliest woman in New York and show her an old-fashioned Christmas on a farm. He meets Rogers, whom he believes to be a stenographer. Actually she's a tough nightclub owner, but her toughness wears down with the Christmas spirit, and she learns to enjoy the simpler things life offers."

Deanna Durbin and Allen Jenkins star in *Lady on a Train*.

Lady on a Train

Cast: Deanna Durbin, Ralph Bellamy, Edward Everett Horton, George Coulouris, Allen Jenkins
Credits: Producer: Felix Jackson; Director: Charles David; Writers: Edmund Beloin and Robert O'Brien (Based on a Story by Leslie Charteris); Universal; 1945

Deanna Durbin was one of the favorite stars during the 1940s. She uses her full charms in this mystery movie when she sees a murder committed and, with the help of a mystery writer, tries to solve the murder. Durbin sings "Silent Night" in this film set during the holiday season in New York.

The Night of the Hunter

Cast: Robert Mitchum, Shelley Winters, Lillian Gish, Peter Graves, Billy Chapin, Sally Jane Bruce
Credits: Producer: Paul Gregory; Director: Charles Laughton; Writer: James Agee (Based on the Novel by Davis Grubb); UA; 1955

Lillian Gish and Billy Chapin celebrate Christmas in *Night of the Hunter*.

Chapin and Bruce are being pursued by their psychotic step-father (Mitchum) who has murdered their mother (Winters) and now seeks money their father had hidden in the house. They are taken in by Gish, a kind woman who has taken in many homeless children. She saves them from Mitchum by shooting him and trapping him in the barn.

It is now nearly Christmas and the children are forced to go to town to testify against Mitchum. Gish gathers the children and hurries them out of town as a religious mob heads toward the courthouse with a rope. Deputies escort Mitchum out the back as Gish and the children pass. On Christmas Day, Gish and the children exchange simple gifts. The children are delighted with their small gifts. Chapin has nothing so he wraps an apple in a doily and presents it to Gish who couldn't be happier. As the children run happily upstairs, Gish looks directly at the camera and says, "Lord save little children. You think the world would be ashamed to name such a day as Christmas for one of them and then go on in the same old way. My soul is humble when I see the way little ones accept their lot. Lord save little children... They abide and they endure."

The Suspect

Cast: Charles Laughton, Ella Raines, Dick Harens, Henry Daniell
Credits: Producer: Islin Auster; Director: Robert Siodmak; Writers: Bertram Millhauser and Arthur T. Horman (Based on *This Way Out* by James Ronald); Universal; 1944

Charles Laughton murders his shrewish wife on Christmas Eve when she threatens to expose his mistress.

The Thin Man

Cast: William Powell, Myrna Loy, Maureen O'Sullivan, Henry Wadsworth
Credits: Producer: Hunt Stromberg; Director: W.S. Van Dyke II; Writers: Albert Hackett and Frances Goodrich (Based on the Novel by Dashiell Hammett); MGM; 1934

The sophisticated comedy sparring of Powell and Loy makes this first in *The Thin Man* series by far the best. Nick and Nora Charles (Powell and Loy) are spending Christmas in New York doing some serious shopping and drinking while schmoozing with Nick's old hoodlum cronies. They have a riotous Christmas party attended equally by reporters, police, detectives and Damon Runyonesque criminals; but they take it in stride only worrying about the supply of booze on hand. During the party, Dorothy Wynant (O'Sullivan), the daughter of an old friend, shows up asking Nick's help in finding her father, who has mysteriously disappeared. Her bimbo mother (Minna Gombell) and egghead brother (William Henry) also show up adding to the confusion.

Nick only wants to retire from the detective racket, but Nora is anxious for a little excitement, and together they solve the disappearance and murder. There is little mention of Christmas except for the party scene, but this film is classic viewing any time of the year.

The Three Wise Guys

Cast: Robert Young, Betty Furness, Raymond Walburn, Thurston Hall, Bruce Cabot, Donald Meek
Credits: Producer: Harry Rapf; Director: George B. Seitz; Writer: Elmer Harris (Based on the Story by Damon Runyon); MGM; 1936

Nick (William Powell) and Nora (Myrna Loy) celebrate Christmas in *The Thin Man*.

This film is not available for review, but *Variety*'s review reads, "Film opens Christmas Eve on a train, with a bogus hard luck story racket [by Cabot and Furness] that cues into a hat-passing among the passengers... the girl marries the rich boy [Young] abruptly and with every indication that it's for coin, yet she immediately claims to her accomplice that she really loves the boy... the father tosses the son out on his own... the couple... are picked up on a farm in Pennsylvania, broke... Not until the end does the spurned accomplice catch up with the dame who has, in his opinion, two-timed him. Again it is Christmas Eve (there are three Christmas Eves in the story) and the girl is alone in a barn with only a kerosene lamp. It's snowing and there's money hidden in the barn. One of the crooks is an ex-doctor and he officiates as obstetrician at the birth of the girl's child. Then the revenge-eager tough guy goes Santa Claus and returns $20,000 in bonds in order that the rich man's son, jailed under an alias, can be cleared. It's all on the Santa Claus motif and the pretty little tongue-in-cheek-fadeout has one of the crooks going wistful about 'Peace on Earth—good will to men' and winding up asking 'what town are we in, anyhow?' Camera then picks up sign: You are now leaving Bethlehem.'"

Variety didn't care for the film, noting, "This one gets pretty boresome as one improbable sequence leads to another."

Credits:

Christmas Holiday
Cast: Gene Kelly, Deanna Durbin, Richard Whorf, Gale Sondergaard
Credits: Producer: Felix Jackson; Director: Robert Siodmak; Writer: Herman J. Mankiewicz (Based on the Novel by W. Somerset Maugham); Universal; 1944

Die Hard
Cast: Bruce Willis, Bonnie Bedelia, Reginald Vel Johnson, Paul Gleason
Credits: Producers: Lawrence Gordon and Joel Silver; Director: John McTiernan; Writers: Jeb Stuart and Steven E. de Souza (Based on the Novel by Roderick Thorp); Fox; 1988

Die Hard 2
Cast: Bruce Willis, Bonnie Bedelia, William Atherton, Reginald Vel Johnson, Franco Nero
Credits: Producers: Lawrence Gordon, Joel Silver and Charles Gordon, Director: Renny Harlin; Writers: Steven E. de Souza and Doug Richardson (Based on *58 Minutes* by Walter Wagner and on original characters by Roderick Thorp); Fox, 1990

Lady in the Lake
Cast: Robert Montgomery, Lloyd Nolan, Audrey Totter, Leon Ames
Credits: Producer: George Haight; Director: Robert Montgomery; Writers: Steve Fisher and Raymond Chandler; MGM; 1947

Every Day is Christmas in the West...

We don't usually associate Christmas with cowboys or the old West. However, Hollywood dusted off their 10 gallon hats, rounded up the horses and created some memorable Western Christmas films.

Hell's Heroes
1929
Three Godfathers
1936
3 Godfathers
1948

While most Christmas films revolve around cheerful characters, Santa Claus and homes filled with presents, not many touch upon the religious significance of the holiday. A notable exception is *Three Godfathers*, a touching story of three outlaws and their quest to save a tiny baby. Drawing upon the story of the Three Wise Men, the film's scripters created an emotional tribute to baby Jesus and the holiest of Christian holidays.

Three Godfathers, based on a story by Peter B. Kyne, was first filmed as a silent by Universal in 1916 and starred Harry Carey, Sr. The story would again be adapted in 1919 by Universal with the title of *Marked Men*, once more starring Carey. That version would be directed by up-and-coming director John Ford (billed as Jack Ford in the credits). Another rendition, *Hell's Heroes,* would follow in 1929. Again from Universal, this version starred Charles Bickford as cold-hearted outlaw Bob Sangster and was directed by William Wyler—another up-and-coming director who would go on to helm such cinematic masterpieces as *Mrs. Miniver, Jezebel, The Best Years of Our Lives* and *Roman Holiday*. With a running time of 65 minutes, the film wastes little time on niceties. The three outlaws in this version are mean, dirty and unattractive. Bob enters the saloon in New Jerusalem and flirts with saloon girl Carmelita (Maria Alba), asking her to sing. She is only too happy to oblige; but, when he grabs another girl, Carmelita is enraged and engages the girl in a catfight as the men all cheer heartily

and Bob laughs out loud. Bob uses this diversion to meet up with his partners to rob the bank. After robbing the bank and killing the cashier, they evade the posse by riding through a dust storm. They survive but their horses are gone. Water is getting low, and they confidently head toward the next waterhole after finding the first one filled with poisoned water. As the outlaws proceed on foot, they hear moans ahead. Bob investigates and finds a covered wagon with a woman (Fritzi Ridgeway) inside. He and Bill (Fred Kohler) argue over the woman, Bob telling him, "I seen her first." It is quite obvious he plans to rape the woman, but after crawling into the wagon, he finds she is pregnant and gives her some water. Meanwhile Bill and Barbwire (Raymond Hatton) find the waterhole next to the wagon has gone dry. Bill in disgust notes, "She'll stay dry till I get religion."

Bob convinces Bill to help deliver the baby while he and Barbwire wait outside. Bill approaches and tells them the woman wants to see all three of them. "Will you three good men save my baby?" They all agree, but only Bill and Barbwire plan to keep the promise. "Take him to his daddy in New Jerusalem. Frank Edwards. You'll find him at the bank. He's cashier." The three men look at each other guiltily; they know he is the man they gunned down. The tiny baby is held up so his mother can have a last look at him. A dirty hand covers most of the infant. "You'll be in New Jerusalem for Christmas with your daddy and three godfathers." The woman then dies.

Bob agrees to accompany them to the outskirts of town. The three struggle onward through the cruel

Barbwire (Raymond Hatton) dies at the base of a cross-shaped cactus in *Hell's Heroes*.

desert. Barbwire, shot in the arm during the hold-up, is the first to go. He refuses to take any water from the child and orders the men to leave him. He shoots himself lying at the base of a cactus which is shaped like a giant cross. When they stop for the night, Bill gives the baby the last of the milk they had found in the wagon. He forms a little shelter for the child by putting a blanket over two upright rifles. The little shelter bears a striking resemblance to the manger of the Christ child. When Bob wakes the next morning, he finds a note on the baby.

"Dear Bob Im makin you a Xmas present. Thar ain't enuf water for the 3 of us so Im goin out in the desert to see a feller. So long Bill."

At this point we feel that old waterhole by the wagon has surely burst forth, for the hardened Bill has found God.

Bob tries to leave the little boy, but can't. He staggers toward New Jerusalem with the child in his arms. When they come to the contaminated waterhole, he drinks deeply, hoping he will have enough time to reach the town. "Com on little falla, we got to drift fast if we're gonna make it."

It is Christmas morning and the good people of New Jerusalem attend church services. A large tree adorns the church and the congregation lifts their voices to "Silent Night." The song can be heard as Bob stumbles toward the church, passing the bank where the baby's father was killed and Bob's fateful journey began. As the words, "With the dawn of redeeming grace" are heard, Bob stumbles toward the church and enters. He gets halfway up the aisle before falling to his knees and then to his side, the baby safe in his arms. The child is removed as "Amen" is sung. The three godfathers have indeed redeemed themselves. This rendering is often overshadowed by the other remade versions with bigger name casts, but unlike other films remade many times over, it is difficult to find a clunker in any version of *Three Godfathers*.

In 1936, MGM would remake the film with an impressive cast consisting of Chester Morris, Lewis Stone, Walter Brennan and Sidney Toler.

As the film open four hardened outlaws gather outside of town to rob New Jerusalem, hometown of Bob (Chester Morris), who holds the devout citizens in high contempt.

Doc (Lewis Stone), the philosophizing elder of the group, notes to Gus (Walter Brennan again type-cast as an old codger with a heart of gold), "Wonderful air, Gus. You can almost smell Christmas." Right off the bat the audience feels an affinity for Doc and

Bob (Chester Morris) takes aim at the Santa-suited Frank (Robert Livingston) as Doc (Lewis Stone) looks on in *Three Godfathers*.

Gus. But the abrasive Bob is another matter. We hope he will be the "deep down he's really a good guy" type bad guy, but our optimism is dashed by the violent robbery soon to occur.

The foursome separate and enter the town. Gus helps an immigrant win a hand of poker against a cardshark while Doc gets a drink. Since they are strangers in town, they are welcomed at the Christmas social. The bandits attend the social where the entertainment consists of a lecture from the comical town dentist (Sidney Toler). The lecture room quickly empties when the band begins to play the "Virginia Reel." The festivities come to a screeching halt when the dressed-in-black Bob enters the room. He tries his best with his old girlfriend Molly (Irene Hervey), who almost succumbs to his dangerous charms before coming to her senses, realizing she truly belongs with her fiancé Frank (Robert Livingston), the town banker. Bob turns his eyes toward the more willing saloon girl Blackie (Dorothy Tree), the typical Western mainstay, a hooker-with-a-heart-of-gold.

The next morning the entire town is at the saloon for a pie sale to benefit the town's Christmas fund. Frank drops Molly off and heads toward the bank where he delightedly tries on a newly arrived Santa suit. But the joy is short-lived as Bob, Doc and Gus hold up the bank. When Frank makes a sudden move, Bob cold-heartedly shoots him. "There ain't no Santa Claus," he announces.

As the outlaws flee, Doc is shot in the arm and the fourth robber, Pedro (Joseph Marievsky), is killed nonchalantly by the dentist. They ride out into the desert looking for the closest waterhole, but when they come upon it, they find a warning sign—it is poison. The next watering spot is not too much farther, so they confidently move on.

Soon the trio come across the body of George Marshall, a tenderfoot who shot himself. They travel a little farther and find a sad-looking little wagon sitting alone in the desert. A woman who is very ill is lying inside.

Gus and Doc give the dying woman a drink from a canteen as a tiny baby peeks his head out. The adorable baby is the image of a live Kewpie doll. The dying woman tells them her husband, George Marhsall, went for help and will be back soon. Doc shakes his head as the woman tells them she knows it is too late for her. She dies with her arm around the baby. Audiences, especially women, are suckers for dangerous men falling prey to the charms of a toddler—this film will tear their hearts out as Doc and Gus immediately submit to the adorable baby's charm.

Doc picks up the child and cradles him in his arms. Always a softie, Bob says, "If it was up to me, I'd put him out of his misery." He intends to leave for the next waterhole in the morning.

That morning, the horses are gone and buzzards circle overhead—the horses found a poisoned water hole and have died. The settlers had three precious cans of milk which the outlaws gather. Bob is about to have one for breakfast when Doc buys it from him for Doc's share of the loot and gives it to the babe. With the horses dead they have no option but to head back to New Jerusalem on foot. Doc takes the child first, knowing his shoulder won't hold out forever—he wants to carry the child as long as possible. Cinematographer Joseph Ruttenberg uses the barren scenery as an effective backdrop when Doc, holding the baby, pays his respects at the mother's grave before starting off.

Doc is forced to drop his books as they continue on under the cruel sun. At sundown Gus, obviously worried about the future, asks Doc to help him make a will. He leaves all his possessions to Bob and scrawls an "X" beside Doc's name as witness. The two outlaws fall asleep with their arms around the baby.

Doc, knowing he cannot go on any longer, tells them to leave him. As they prepare to go, Gus squeezes Doc's arm who grabs his hand in a sad farewell. Lewis Stone is impressive in this last scene as the educated outlaw who faces death knowing he did one last good deed. Doc quotes *Macbeth* as Bob and Gus walk away, Gus carrying the little infant. A shot is heard as the duo continues on.

There are only a few drops of water left in the canteen. When they take a rest Gus pulls his gun out. Is he thinking that if he can't go on, Bob wouldn't take care of the child, and that killing the little baby would be the only way to insure he doesn't suffer?

"Bob, if I give out what will you do?"
"I won't hold him up. If he can crawl to New Jerusalem, it's all right with me."

Gus puts the gun away. The baby is crying because it is teething. Gus looks beseechingly at Bob who gives Gus his most precious possession, his mother's watch, for the baby to chew on.

As they settle down for the night Gus listens to see how much water is left. He cradles the baby and lays him down along with his share of the loot and the will Doc wrote for him. He recites,

"Gentle Jesus, meek and mild. Look upon this little child. Pity my simplicity. Suffer me to come to thee."

He walks off into the desert with the cherished book Doc had given him.

Bob sits beside the baby and reads the will.

"Bob. If you get this will it means that Gus is

Bob dies beneath a crown of thorns at the Christmas Eve services in New Jerusalem in *Three Godfathers*.

dead too. If you never did anything human before—give the kid an even break. James Underwood, Doc."

He begins to gather coins from around the baby who cries. Bob commences to walk away and we see a rattlesnake crawl toward the unprotected tot. Bob turns around and fires his gun. We think it is to hush the child, but he kills the snake.

Bob, his cold heart melting in the desert heat, picks up the baby and gives him a drink of water. "Desert must be getting to me. I'm acting crazy."

Later he gives the child the last drop of water as buzzards circle overhead. They are nine miles from town. He drops the stolen money, his gunbelt and bedroll as he struggles onward.

"Nothing human can help us now." He looks toward the sky.

"Listen, it ain't for me I'm asking. I don't rate nothin. But I always heard you was good to babies... Our father... I can't pray—I don't know how to pray."

Bob sheds tears, possibly the first in his life and looks up and sees water. But it is the poisoned waterhole. The sign says "New Jerusalem, 5 1/2 miles."

He remembers Doc saying that the poison wouldn't affect a person for an hour. He decides he may make it to the town in that time and he smiles at the baby, "Here's to you kid" bending down to drink deeply of contaminated water.

Finally stumbling into town he hears singing from the church and enters. He slowly finds Molly seated in the first row and hands her the baby. Bob leans against a post that holds a crown of thorns. The film makes it clear Bob has become a Christ figure—giving his life to save the baby as Jesus gave his life to save mankind. He lurches into the aisle, a lighted stained glass window behind him as he collapses and dies.

The performances are excellent throughout. Walter Brennan as Gus made a career of character roles, winning the Academy Award for Supporting Actor three times (William Wyler's *Come and Get It* [also in 1936] as Swan Bostrom, *Kentucky* [1938] where he appeared as Peter Goodwin in this Romeo-and-Juliet-at-the-racetrack tale and as the legendary Judge Roy Bean again for director William Wyler in *The Westerner* [1940] with Gary Cooper). Brennan was only 42 at the time of his heart-breaking turn as the elderly Gus. With this character Brennan adds another fine performance to his outstanding career.

Lewis Stone as Doc is perhaps better known to audiences as Andy Hardy's father, Judge Hardy, in that popular film series from MGM. He began his distinguished Hollywood career in silent films and went on to make over 90 pictures including *Grand Hotel, Angels in the Outfield, Key to the City* and *The Mask of Fu Manchu.*

Chester Morris as Bob was also a familiar face to movie audiences. He came to renown as Boston Blackie in the 1940s sleuth films, the first of which was *Meet Boston Blackie* in 1941. He would return to the stage when the series ended, later returning to Hollywood as a character actor in several films.

In its March 11, 1936 review *Variety* noted, "This is a case of the cast surmounting uneven direction and meandering plot development."

Director Richard Boleslawski was trained at the Moscow Art Theatre before turning to Hollywood where he directed films such as *Theodora Goes Wild* with Irene Dunne and *Rasputin and The Empress*— notable as the only film in which John, Ethel and Lionel Barrymore appeared together. Of his direction *Variety* opined, "It is the latter portion of the Kyne story that director Boleslawski really hits his stride. Has focused most of the interest on the regeneration of Chester Morris, showing the transition from the swashbuckling braggart into a human being eager to save a baby's life at the sacrifice of his own and his gold."

In 1948 MGM and John Ford again remade the film, this time starring a Ford favorite, John Wayne. Ford called upon his talented stable of regular actors such as Ward Bond as Perley Sweet (the sheriff who pursues the bankrobbers), Ben Johnson, Hank Worden, Jane Darwell and Fred Libby as the comic relief, deputy Curly.

Screenwriters Laurence Stallings and Frank S. Nugent basically stuck with the original story although they softened the character of Bob Hightower and gave the film a happy ending, a move which makes this film the recommended version for Christmas viewing.

John Wayne as Robert Marmaduke Hightower is not the hardened killer portrayed by Charles Bickford and Chester Morris. Wayne's Bob Hightower is a tough guy with a heart of gold—making sure there is no killing involved in the robbery in Welcome, Arizona and riding back to pick up the injured Abilene Kid (Harry Carey, Jr.). Even before the robbery he tries to talk his partners out of going with him.

When the trio find the dynamited waterhole and the stranded wagon, Bob, shaken, tells Pete (Pedro Armendariz) and the Kid about the poor woman (Mildred Natwick) soon to give birth and the snake

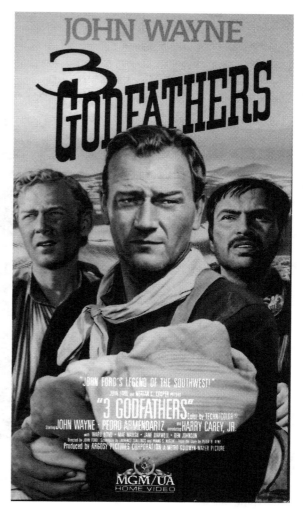

husband that left her there. Panic is in his voice as he rants, "I'm a tough bird, a awful tough old bird, but I'm not going back in there!" Later Ford uses the size of John Wayne to comic advantage as the giant of a man sits in a small chair on the desert sands and holds a tiny blue bundle. Wayne's reactions range from sheer terror to absolute delight as he holds the small miracle. The trio find a book on baby care and debate the merits of a bath but eventually decide to smear the baby with oil. Bob and the others laugh with delight as the infant squirms under the huge hand of Bob.

Bob loses his companions; but their spirits urge him onward, the Kid singing "Streets of Larado" as they both encourage him. Bob throws the Bible and reads the section it opened to, which tells of two donkeys who helped deliver the Christ child to Jerusalem. As Bob exits a canyon, Perley and posse close behind, he spies the donkeys, just like the Bible said he would. He places the baby onto the larger one and heads toward New Jerusalem. It is Christmas Eve as Bob staggers into the saloon carrying the child. "Merry Christmas everybody! Merry Christmas to all. Set 'em up bartender. Milk for the infant and a

Bob (John Wayne) looks to the heavens after finding the donkeys predicted by the Bible in *3 Godfathers*.

cool, cool beer for me!" The piano player plays "Silent Night."

Pedro "Pete," the second outlaw, delivers the baby and, when they bury the mother, prays to himself in Spanish as the Kid sings, "Shall We Gather at the River," a song John Ford used in many of his films. Pete carries the baby but stumbles and falls, breaking his leg. He orders Bob to go on to New Jerusalem and asks him to leave his gun, for the coyotes. But we know it is not for protection. "Merry Christmas," he tells Bob. "Merry Christmas, Pete." Bob sadly answers.

As the film opens a silhouetted cowboy sits atop a horse (reportedly the favorite horse of Harry Carey) and we see the words "To the memory of Harry Carey. Bright star of the early Western sky." Carey was a much loved Western star who worked often with John Ford and John Wayne and had also appeared in another Christmas film covered in this book, *Beyond Tomorrow*. Carey's son Harry Carey, Jr. would make his film debut in *3 Godfathers* as the Abilene Kid, the third member of the outlaws. The Abilene Kid was the innocent of the group and immediately connected their odyssey to that of the Three Wise Men. As the men argue about their next move, Bob, in a rage, throws a Bible. The Kid picks up it and reads where

it opened. "It says right here where we're to go. Just like it's told everything about all this. You fellas don't understand. Ya think this is all just chance? Us coming here this way. Finding the mother, helping her, the infant in the manger, the star so bright last night... it tells where we're going to next... They lifted up the child and brought him to Jerusalem to present him to the Lord." The Kid, weak from his gunshot wound, insists that he be the first to carry the baby. "That's in the book, too. There was three wise men come from the East wasn't there?... I'm one of them."

Sheriff Perley "Buck" Sweet, a name that Bob finds hilarious, is a fair man who respects the men they are chasing. "They ain't payin' me to kill folks," he says as the outlaws ride out of sight. But Perley has a plan and hastens his posse to the railroad station where they mount a flatbed car and ride to the next water tower, forcing the outlaws to move on. Perley leaves guards at the first tower and rides to the next in line where he meets up with Miss Florie (Jane Darwell), a cousin of his wife. Miss Florie is delighted with her unexpected guests and cracks merrily, "If this ain't a Christmas present for me. A whole passel of men!" When Perley figures out the trio eluded him by backtracking, he remarks, "Yes sir, the more I think of that big fella in the Texas hat, the more I admire him." Ford sets up the classic conflict of two men engaged in a duel of wits, both good men, both smart men and one man must lose.

But Bob Hightower doesn't lose, for not only has he discovered a strength and love within himself, he also wins the respect and admiration of an entire town as the folks of Welcome turn out in droves for his trial. The judge (Guy Kibbee) offers to reduce Bob's sentence if he agrees to sign papers allowing Perley and his wife to adopt the baby (whom the mother named Robert William Pedro Hightower) and never set foot in Welcome again. But Bob never hesitates, "You can throw the book at me judge. I ain't breakin' a promise to a dyin' woman." "That's just what I've been waiting for to hear you say son. I hereby give you the minimum sentence under the law. One year and one day. Court's closed, bar's open!" Bob is cheered by the town as he heads to prison; Perley's wife Carrie Lou (Mae Marsh) tearfully sees Bob off; he lovingly glances at the baby as he leaves, kissing Carrie on the cheek. The town ladies sing "Shall We Gather at the River," and the men wave their hats. Perley asks Bob to look after his deputy Curly and make sure he gets on the right train home, and the banker's daughter Ruby Latham (Dorothy Ford) asks if she can write to Bob. We just know there is romance in their future.

John Ford, a master filmmaker, once again made the most of his location filming using the stark and beautiful deserts of Death Valley and the Mojave as the pallet for his first Technicolor film. Ford's char-acters always were multi-dimensional, neither all good nor all bad, and Bob Hightower and Perley Sweet are no exception. The stellar teaming of John Ford and John Wayne would create some of the greatest films ever made including *The Quiet Man, The Man Who Shot Liberty Valance* and, of course, *The Searchers.* They would also team on another film that takes place during Christmas, *Donovan's Reef.* Ward Bond, a character actor of incredible talent and range, has the distinction of appearing in more of the AFI's Hundred Greatest Film List released in the summer of 1998 than any other actor. Also appearing in the film was Jane Darwell (Nellie Thursday in *The Lemon Drop Kid*) who won an Academy Award for her performance as Ma Joad in John Ford's *The Grapes of Wrath.* Ford would also win an Academy Award for his direction of that film.

I must confess, on a purely emotional level, this is my favorite version. It has John Wayne, the genius of John Ford and a happy ending. What more could you ask for?

As much a tear-jerker as a Western, *Three Godfathers* is a touching holiday film So get out the hankies and watch a triple-bill of the 1929, 1936 and the 1948 versions. The story would be adapted one more time, this version for television in 1974 as *The Godchild.* It starred Keith Carradine and Jack Palance. I'm sure there will eventually be another remake to add to the list, but for my money, nothing can replace the John Wayne version.

—SS

Bob stumbles into the New Jersulum saloon on Christmas Eve carrying the infant named Robert William Pedro Hightower in *3 Godfathers*.

Star in the Night

Warner Bros. Short Subject, 1945

J. Carroll Naish (right) stars in the touching Warner Bros. Academy Award-winning short *Star in the Night*.

Warner Bros. had their own version of the story of the Wise Men, *Star in the Night*, an Academy Award-winning short starring J. Carrol Naish and directed by Don Siegel who is best known for *Invasion of the Body Snatchers* (1956) and *Dirty Harry*. Naish as Nick, owner of the Star Auto Court at the edge of a desert, has lost the spirit of Christmas. The residents of the court do nothing but complain and bicker on this Christmas Eve.

As the film begins, three cowboys ride along under a star-filled sky. The scene is shot to resemble the indelible image of the Wise Men riding toward Bethlehem. The cowboys are loaded down with gifts and a small decorated Christmas tree bought to impress a pretty salesclerk. They see a bright star in the distance and decide to follow it.

A stranger approaches Nick as he finally gets a giant star atop a watertower to stay lit. They exchange words and Nick rants and raves about the holiday. "Merry Christmas. Huh. I hate Christmas. All year everybody is stingy, is mean, squeeze the money. All of a sudden comes Christmas. Why everybody got to change because it's Christmas?"

The stranger replies, "Because we can't get away from it. Because the true meaning of Christmas is peace and brotherhood and love. Seems to me that's the remedy for all the world's troubles."

Nick is not convinced, but allows the stranger to come inside the diner to get warm. A demanding couple rents the last cabin, a man complains about his laundered shirts, a woman complains about men singing Christmas carols next to her cabin and Nick looks at the stranger as if to say, "I told you so." But when a young couple enter the diner, the woman obviously in need of rest, things begin to happen. Nick's kindly wife gives them a little shed to stay in and escorts the young couple, Maria and Jose Santos, outside. She sends Jose for blankets, but she comes in soon afterward and tells him to stay there Maria is having a baby. (Due to the censors of the time, it is not even mentioned that Maria is having a baby; Nick's wife whispers the news to each person. The audience is left to their own conclusions.)

The plight of the young couple softens the hearts of everyone in the diner; the demanding wife and complaining woman offer their help, and the man offers his shirts for bandages. Nick is amazed at the change in people and his faith in humanity is restored.

The cowboys have followed Nick's star to the Auto Court and decided to give their gifts to the baby.

The stranger's words echo in our memory at the close of this charming tale:

On this night the goodness that people have in them will still be warm in the heart of the world 1,000 years from now, 10,000 years from now. People have songs in their hearts and renew their patience and courage for what may come. That's the real meaning of Christmas.

As the stranger prepares to leave, Nick offers his overcoat to keep out the cold. The stranger takes it gratefully. Is the stranger an angel, like Clarence from *It's a Wonderful Life,* sent to help Nick realize the goodness of mankind? Or is he just a wanderer who happened to stumble upon this Christmas miracle? Either way, this short from Warner Bros. packs as much emotional ammunition as any feature-length heart-tugger.
—SS

Trail of Robin Hood

1950

The B Western was about to ride off into the sunset and become a thing of the past in 1950. Even with King of the Cowboys, Roy Rogers, riding high in the saddle, television was looming in the near future (Roy Rogers' television show would make the transition easier for Rogers and his fans).

Even the theme of this superior B entry, *Trail of Robin Hood*, alludes to the end of one era and the beginning of another. One of the pivotal characters, retired Western star Jack Holt (playing himself), talks to young upstart Sis McGonigle telling her, "I was a movie star long before you were born." To which the wisecracking kid responds, "But we have television." And Holt glumly replies, "Yes, I know!"

Nearing the end of an era, taking full advantages of TruColor photography, and utilizing the talents of ace Republic serial director William Witney, this Roy Rogers entry attempted to not reinvent the wheel, but to disguise "the wheel" under Christmas ornaments with plenty of good cheer thrown in for good measure.

A common staple of the B Western storybook included the rival cattle ranchers, one comprising the hero and the struggling community, the other involving rich, profit-minded villains, who battle it out to see who gets his herd to market first.

In this holiday variation, we have—seriously—rival Christmas tree growers battling it out to get their trees to market first. And the fun and action starts right away.

Jack Holt, the retired Western star, has been growing Christmas trees for six years, to sell them at cost to families of poor children when rival growers cut and steal a wagon-load of trees from his land. Fortunately, Roy Rogers is in hot pursuit and follows the tree thieves to their camp: "J.C. Aldridge Xmas Cutting Camp #1, Mitch McCall Foreman." When Roy confronts the drivers at camp and asks, "Hey, you're cutting your Christmas trees a little early, aren't you?," he is greeted with a cold, "Any law against it!" To which the hero states, "There is when you steal them off of somebody else's property." Then the classic B Western brawl erupts as the entire camp takes on Roy, one man at a time, none of the camp ganging up on Roy. And, of course, Rogers righteously pounds each and every pursuer into the ground. Only when one

The entire town turns out to help Roy Rogers and Jack Holt get the Christmas trees to market in *Trail of Robin Hood*.

Sis (Carol Nugent) and Splinters (Gordon Jones) cut the turkey (not Sir Galahad) at a pre-Christmas feast at Jack Holt's ranch in *Trail of Robin Hood*.

camper picks up an ax does Roy's dog Bullet growl and hold the man at bay.

By this time Christmas tree tycoon Jack Holt has arrived, having followed Roy after seeing many of his trees cut down and stolen. With pride Holt introduces Rogers to foreman Mitch McCall, making sure McCall realizes that Rogers is the local head of the U.S. Soil Conservation Service. McCall with equal pride announces to Holt he makes the contracts with the Aldridge company, to which Holt mumbles, "King of the Christmas trees," recognizing the name. But when McCall offers to cut Holt in and buy all his trees for 50% of the profits, Holt gives an immediate refusal. "Sorry Mitch, but I'm gonna do my own cutting and hauling."

Roy adds, "Jack doesn't want a profit. He's selling his trees for what it cost him to raise them." Holt intends to sell his trees for 75-80 cents apiece instead of the going rate of $8 to $10 each. This underselling would put the Aldridge syndicate out of the tree business. Jack gives his reasons for selling trees at cost. "I made a little money in pictures, that's why I'm ranching. Every family that wants a tree is gonna get one. I'm not interested in making a profit—if there is one, then I'll give it to the Children's Home. Kids like that made it possible for me to become a star!"

Thus, the basic conflict is immediately established in the plot. Now, let's examine the B Western ingredients that catapult this mixture into motion. First, we have the hero's right hand man, usually a dolt with the heart of gold. As an added treat, throw in an adorable child actress whose purpose is to bounce one-liners and visual gags off the sidekick. Thus we have Splinters McGonigle (Gordon Jones), "The Fix-It Man," whose motto painted on the side of his wagon reads: "If your banjo's busted and you can't plinker, bring it to me, I'm the town's biggest tinker." His counterpoint is provided by spunky but wise Sis McGonigle (Carol Nugent), the tomboy who always takes charge with Splinters and is usually right. For instance, Splinters' shots miss at the turkey shoot, but hiding up high in a tree, Sis hits the target with her slingshot. Coming down out of the tree to compete fairly, her dead-on shot with a huge rifle wins her first prize: a live turkey that she affectionately names Sir Galahad (since, as Splinters declares, the bird would look grand on their round table). Also, after Sis comments on Splinters' lack of understanding even simple words, he retorts with the hilarious, "What I lack in brains, I make up for in ignorance." But basically, Splinters is the gadget king, the man who can fix anything (except maybe that big radio that pops out toast that is always too brown). And Sis, even though she generally takes charge, is loving and supportive to the big galloot. Bottom line: They supply comic relief and do it well.

While foreman Mitch McCall turns out to be the major villain (he hires cowboys to join Holt's gang to sabotage the operation, murders one of his own men to frame Rogers and, as we've observed, is not afraid to hire men to literally steal Christmas trees from Holt's land), his boss, J.C. Aldridge, the owner of the operation and the New York big city loudmouth (we first see him on the phone barking "All I get are alibis, alibis!"), becomes heroic and likable by movie's end (when he takes his doctor's advice of a vacation and secretly goes out West to infiltrate McCall's gang to see what exactly that rascal is pulling off). His equally aggressive daughter Toby (whom Aldridge tells "at least there's some satisfaction from having a daughter with a business head on her shoulders"), wearing all the latest New York fashions, goes out West to get Holt to sign a contract with her father stating: "I'll have a contract for those trees before he knows what happened." She is big city savvy and isn't above using her womanly wiles to get what she wants. Arriving on the scene during the Turkey Shoot, she parades down the steps wearing her Sunday finest, which puts her directly in the line of the skeets,

which someone lets loose simply to frighten the Easterner. After she picks herself up from the dirt and dusts herself off, Roy smiles and walks up declaring, "Looks like you had your tail feathers clipped." After briefly meeting McCall and seeing children ask Jack Holt for his autograph, she quickly borrows paper from McCall and walks up to the ex-film star asking for his autograph. "It isn't often I'm asked for an autograph by such a big girl." To which she coos, "Mr. Holt, you were wonderful in all of them." Soon Roy blows her scheme by announcing to Holt that this is Miss Aldridge, and all the pieces in her puzzle suddenly fall apart as Holt understands her motives. But true to form, this hard-as-nails businesswoman soon melts to Rogers' charms by the last quarter of the movie and even volunteers to cook and serve the Christmas meal, near the movie's end. Also, by this time the now domesticated citygal even wears cowgirl outfits and hat (although she stills dresses like a fashion plate).

And Jack Holt himself becomes the titular town leader, the man who inspires the whole town to close down to help him bundle and tie his trees to get them to market (even the telegraph operator closes the office, horrible for Toby who awaits a message from her father). As the merry workers tie the trees, Splinters, in typical form, falls off a tall ladder while trying

All the B Western heroes ride to the aid of Jack Holt and Roy Rogers in *Trail of Robin*

to decorate the gigantic Christmas tree inside the saloon, as Roy and friends sing "Get a Christmas tree for Johnny, Santa's on his way... and the world will smile at you." In the movie's most affectionate sequence, McCall attempts to burn down the livery stable and torch the saloon housing all of Holt's trees. Miraculously, the volunteer workers manage to carry all the trees to safety. Even Toby joins in. Sis remembers that her turkey is still inside and runs back into the inferno. Sis and Sir Galahad run to freedom, but the concerned Holt, rushing in to save Sis, is overcome by smoke. Roy uses Bullet to sniff Holt out, and carries the old codger to safety. The town doctor announces that Holt might not make it. Semiconscious, Holt mumbles that Christmas has arrived, so the entire town pretends to celebrate Christmas Day at his house, his bedroom door being opened wide to observe all the festivities in the dining room. Toby cooks the turkey dinner (the audience being allowed to think that Splinters slaughtered Sir Galahad, causing all the assembled town folk to lose its appetite, when in reality, Galahad's "brother or cousin" was slaughtered), Roy carries in the presents and the looming Christmas tree bathes the sequence in quaint nostalgia. Roy and the fellows sing "Every day is Christmas in the West." As they all gather around Holt, the very conscious man asks, "Tell me, did you get the trees to the city on time?" The honest Roy momentarily hesitates when Splinters bursts right in: "You should have seen it. Sold out almost before we could get them off the wagons!" To which Holt responds excitedly, "That's what I've been waiting to hear! That makes Christmas perfect. You kids better get into the dining room... I'll open my presents later." Holt reveals to Sis that he knows that it's not Christmas and that he knows the trees have not been delivered, but he didn't want to ruin all the fun for everyone.

However, word gets back to the party that all the Christmas tree drivers are quitting because one of them was beat up and the others were frightened by the town fire and the seriousness of the threats. But the imaginative Sis notices the framed pictures around Holt's bed of all his Western star cronies, people waiting to be called away from their homes on Christmas Day to help a friend in need. Unbeknownst to all assembled, Sis has managed to contact every one of them. Toby reluctantly offers to buy all of Holt's trees, since Roy has failed to assemble enough drivers, but in the movie's standout sequence, all the major B Western heroes suddenly ride into town. All eyes look down Main Street at the approaching strangers who yell "howdy Roy, remember me, I'm... Allan 'Rocky' Lane, Monte Hale, William Farnum, Tom Tyler, Ray Corrigan, Kermit Maynard, Tom Keene, Rex Allen." For all the youngsters of the time, this sequence must have been akin to seeing an all-star lineup of horror

veterans parading into the Gothic castle. The wonderful sequence even sports a joke. When George Chesebro approaches, Sis frowns and states, "You're the meanie," to which Chesebro utters, "But having made 20 pictures with Jack Holt, he reformed me."

Soon all the heroes are following in a procession of wagons filled to the top with Christmas trees when Roy gets word that McCall and his men are burning the Red River Bridge, preventing Holt's trees from reaching market. Rogers races to warn the caravan to "whip 'em up" as he rides ahead, reaching the bridge before the wagons arrive. Unfortunately, McCall and party have already started the fire, but instead of attending to the blaze, Rogers jumps on top of the two villains present, McCall included. While the fighting goes on, the wagons race across the bridge, each driver ducking to avoid the raging flames that lick at the horses' heels. Sis is the last driver to cross the bridge, coaxed on by Splinters, and after she passes safely, the entire structure collapses. Rogers still pursues McCall who rides to a scenic watermill where he falls to his death trying to climb over the mill.

"Jack, you cost me a quarter of a million dollars, but it was worth it," the now compassionate J.C. Aldridge utters. "From now on, we're partners, and we'll be selling them so cheap they'll think we're giving them away." The crowd begins singing again as the snow starts falling harder and faster. The always conscientious Roy Rogers announces he has to check the fences as he rides off into the snowset, framed by the strums of Christmas tunes.

B Westerns during the 1940s were probably more popular than B horror movies, for most childhood heroes of the era were Western stars, Roy Rogers and Gene Autry (and perhaps Hopalong Cassidy) being the favorites. And what a coup to have all the runners-up make a brief but thrilling cameo appearance in a film that exudes warmth, charm and nostalgia for an era of moviemaking about to end with the advent of television.

In this crazy B world of Rogers, the old West era exists side-by-side with all the glories of the modern world. Thus, we have the very important sequence where we first meet Aldridge and his daughter Toby, wearing modern clothes, barking at each other in a modern office building, using the telephone. Even when Toby makes her appearance at the Turkey Shoot, her introduction to Roy's world, she drives up in a car wearing Eastern clothes. The juxtaposition of horses and autos makes the Roy Rogers universe just as unreal as Universal's Vasaria or Transylvania. While citizens in this version of the old West ride horses, gather around storefronts to sing Western tunes and drop everything at a heartbeat to band together and help one another, this world seems strangely real and alive. In every little boy's heart, he can believe in a

The Christmas story of the birth of Jesus as seen through the eyes of the Blackfeet Indians in *Miracle in the Wilderness*.

real place out West where people truly care about their neighbors and pull together to help one another. The concept of "selling at cost" does not seem ridiculous, just decent. Villains are not slain, as much as they are challenged, pursued and then accidentally fall to their death. Aldridge might be an old codger, but one rough and tumble week in the old West cures all his ills and transforms him into an equal partner with the Western spirit. Even Toby loses her aggression and joins the team.

Today, movies such as *Trail of Robin Hood* don't seem dated as much as stylized, anachronisms of a more innocent, bygone era. The Christmas motif married to the B Western formula works only too well because the warm and fuzzy holiday spirit blends perfectly with the soul of the Hollywood Old West. By movie's end, we definitely believe that "every day is Christmas in the West."
—GJS

The following films occur during or have scenes pertaining to Christmas in the West:

Cowboy and the Indians
Cast: Gene Autry, Sheila Ryan, Frank Richards, Jay Silverheels

Credits: Producer: Armand Schaefer; Director: John English; Writers: Dwight Cummins and Dorothy Yost; Columbia; 1949

Gene Autry helps Jay Silverheels and his people fight a dishonest Indian Agent. Autry goes all the way to Washington to help the Indians. The only Christmas theme is at the very end of the film when Autry and crew show up to deliver presents on the reservation and Autry sings his famous "Here Comes Santa Claus."

Miracle in the Wilderness
Cast: Kris Kristofferson, Kim Cattrall
Credits: Producer: Wayne Morris; Director: Kevin James Dobson; Writers: Jim Byrnes and Michael Michaelian (Based on the Novel by Paul Gallico); Turner; 1992

Beautifully filmed story of Jericho Adams (Kristofferson) and his wife (Cattrall) and baby son. Jericho has given up hunting and tracking and settled down to ranching with his wife and child. A Blackfoot chief burns their house and captures the family. Jericho had killed the chief's son four years ago in self-defense. The chief has waited until Jericho had a son and plans to raise the baby as his own, give his wife to a brave and kill Jericho—but there is a grudging

KRIS KRISTOFFERSON KIM CATTRALL

MIRACLE IN THE WILDERNESS

Out of Love
and Beyond
Fear Came a
Miracle of
Goodness
from a Story
as Old as
Time.

TURNER PICTURES presents a RUDDY & MORGAN PRODUCTION of "MIRACLE IN THE WILDERNESS" KRIS KRISTOFFERSON KIM CATTRALL composer VLADIMIR HORUNZHY casting by MIKE FENTON, C.S.A. JUDY TAYLOR, C.S.A. edited by SUSAN B. BROWDY, A.C.E. production designer SHARON SEYMOUR director of photography DAN BURSTALL executive producers ALBERT RUDDY & ANDRE MORGAN produced by WAYNE MORRIS based on the novella by PAUL GALLICO teleplay by MICHAEL MICHAELIAN and JIM BYRNES directed by KEVIN JAMES DOBSON © 1991 Turner Pictures, Inc. All Rights Reserved Artwork © 1992 Turner Pictures, Inc. All Rights Reserved

TURNER PICTURES CLOSED CAPTIONED TURNER HOME ENTERTAINMENT M MATURE

wise chiefs follow a new star and give gifts to the baby.

The chief and Jericho go head-to-head since Jericho knows he will die one way or another. He bests the chief but cannot bring himself to kill him. The chief leaves the family behind and heads his tribe toward Canada and the realization that the wilderness is disappearing and one day perhaps all men will truly be brothers as Cattrall has told them. The scenery is stunning and the Native American scenes are gorgeously and respectfully filmed.

Troublemakers
Cast: Bud Spencer, Terence Hill, Anne Kasprik, Ruth Buzzi
Credits: Producer: Matthias Wendlandt; Director: Terence Hill; Triboro; 1995

Travis (Hill) goes to great lengths to get his brother Moses (Spencer) home to see their mother (Buzzi) in this comic Western.

Credits:

Hell's Heroes
Cast: Charles Bickford, Raymond Hatton, Fred Kohler, Fritzi Ridgeway
Credits: Producer: Carl Laemmle; Director: William Wyler; Writer: Tom Reed (Based on Peter B. Kyne's *The Three Godfathers*); Universal; 1930

The Three Godfathers
Cast: Chester Morris, Lewis Stone, Walter Brennan
Credits: Producer: Joseph L. Mankiewicz; Director: Richard Boleslawski; Writers: Edward E. Paramore and Manuel Seff (Based on Peter B. Kyne's *The Three Godfathers*); MGM; 1936

respect between the chief and Jericho: He plans to give him the death of a great warrior.

When storm clouds darken the sky, the tribe is astounded to find a family of deer, the female giving birth. Fawns are never born in the winter. Cattrall explains it is a sign from God and begins to tell the tribe the story of the Christ child and the first Christmas. This is where the film shines as the story is seen through the eyes of the tribe. Joseph is a strong brave and Mary a pure maiden. A message is brought to Mary by an eagle and Joseph sees a white stallion that assures him Mary is carrying the Son of God. They travel to a great meeting of the tribes where three

3 Godfathers
Cast: John Wayne, Pedro Armendariz, Harry Carey, Jr., Ward Bond, Mildred Natwick
Credits: Producers: John Ford and Merian C. Cooper; Director: John Ford; Writers: Laurence Stallings and Frank S. Nugent (Based on Peter B. Kyne's *The Three Godfathers*); MGM; 1948

Trail of Robin Hood
Cast: Roy Rogers, Penny Edwards, Gordon Jones, Jack Holt, Rex Allen, Tom Tyler, Ray Corrigan, Rocky Lane
Credits: Producer: Edward J. White; Director: William Witney; Writer: Gerald Geraghty; Republic; 1950

You Better Watch Out...

Many filmmakers, rather than making warm, fuzzy holiday films opt instead to use the Christmas season as a backdrop that makes their horrific visions all the more frightening. This chapter covers films that fall into the horror, science fiction or fantasy genres.

Gremlins

1984

Gremlins has been called "*It's a Wonderful Life* turned inside out, stood on its head and pickled in brine"; "*A Christmas Carol* visited by *The Birds*"; "*The Muppet Movie* run amok."

It is, to be sure, a veritable Frankenstein's Monster of used movie parts. Yet they have been stitched together so neatly by director Joe Dante and his crew that multitudes of viewers turned out during the summer of 1984 to make this movie the third largest box office draw of the year.

In our tale's beginning, failed inventor Rand Peltzer finds the perfect Christmas gift for his son Billy in a Chinatown junk shop: a little furry creature called a mogwai, which sings and mimics human speech. Though the junk shop owner (played by Keye Luke) refuses to sell the animal and warns that "with mogwai comes much responsibility," Peltzer disregards the admonition, and acquires the mogwai through stealth.

Before secretly selling the creature to Peltzer, the junk shop owner's grandson recites three basic rules for mogwai maintenance: 1) Keep him away from bright lights, and especially sunlight—which will kill him; 2) don't get water on him (or in him); and 3) never *never* feed him after midnight.

The remainder of the plot, of course, hinges on these rules' violation. The mogwai, it turns out, multiplies with water—but second-generation mogwai are less sweet-tempered than first. Even worse, the mogwai mutates into a vicious monster when fed after midnight—and this monster (the eponymous "gremlin") in turn multiplies with water. The best recourse against the thousands of resulting gremlins is to use the monsters' intolerance for bright lights and sunlight to destroy them, and hence save civilization as we know it.

During the ensuing havoc, the second-generation mogwai string Billy's dog Barney up in the outdoor Christmas lights, nearly turning him into a "dogcicle." The gremlins themselves attack Billy's mom (who resourcefully defends her home by using an array of kitchen appliances). They bite townspeople, sabotage street lights, cut through brake cables, try to throttle the town Santa, boobytrap the evil Mrs. Deagle's mechanical chair, and even sing Christmas carols, get drunk in the local bar and watch *Snow White and the Seven Dwarfs* at the local cinema (where Billy incinerates them all, except for gremlin leader Stripe, who escapes).

Billy (Zach Galligan) receives a special Christmas gift from his dad (Hoyt Axton) as his mother (Frances Lee McCain) looks on in *Gremlins*.

Your worst nightmare, *Gremlins'* Christmas carolers!

In the final, early-Christmas-morning showdown, Stripe shoots Billy with a *Road Warrior*-style crossbow and attacks him with a chainsaw. When the original (and still-cute) mogwai, Gizmo, arrives just in time to fling open a window sash and let early morning sunlight shine directly on the gremlin (who is now multiplying in the department store fountain), Stripe crumbles in the sunlight and then melts into a pool of ooze—a scene reminiscent of the villains' deaths in both *Horror of Dracula* and *The Wizard of Oz*.

Were the makers of *The Nightmare Before Christmas* to tell the story of how this thing got made, they might perhaps recount that a Pumpkin King in Hollywood town, derailed from his jubilant celebration of wry horror, filled a movie full of dazzling Christmas sights and sounds. But (since Halloween ran through his veins) his tale's cuddly Christmas gift spawned thousands of vicious, scaly monsters, bent on playing havoc with a picturesque small town.

And *Gremlins* began, in fact, not as a Christmas story, but as a rather straight horror fable. Writer Chris Columbus first encountered the gremlins as a film student. He met them in his own anxieties and nightmares, in fears of getting his hand chomped by the rodents that scurried across the floor of his loft each night (anxieties which survive in some of the film's first encounters with the gremlins, as several charac-

ters, including Billy, all get bit or scratched viciously on the hand). In the "incredibly gruesome" earliest versions of the script, director Dante recounts that the gremlins actually "ate the kid's dog."

During production, though—and largely as a byproduct of the clash in sensibilities between Dante, Columbus and Executive Producer Steven Spielberg—the film mutated like its gremlins into the acid-sweet story that runs on cable during Christmas season. Spielberg asked for "more charm," and so Columbus and Dante changed the script to have the original mogwai *remain* a cute little mogwai and not undergo the transformation into gremlin. Dante thought of the end result as essentially two movies existing in the same cinematic space: "a horror movie *and* this other movie—Spielbergian, with the family and the nice people and happiness and joy and Christmas."

But how much Christmas does it have *really*?

Well, it invokes the sights and sounds of Christmas, right from the film's first moments. The anthemic centerpiece of Phil Spector's Christmas album, "Christmas (Baby Please Come Home)," plays over the opening credits as we get our first view of the snow-covered town. Pete, a young friend of Billy's, dresses as a tree to help sell Christmas trees at his father's lot, and *It's a Wonderful Life* plays on TV at the Peltzers'. Christmas tradition floods the Peltzer house, complete with tree, lights, stuffed stockings, gingerbread men and even the compulsory Johnny Mathis Christmas record (all later used to horrific/comical effect by the gremlins). Not surprisingly, when Gizmo becomes Billy's gift, our hero quickly finds a little Santa cap lying around to stick on the mogwai's head.

Christmas, though, doesn't just go away once the gremlins arrive. Immediately before becoming victim to the first gremlin attack, Science teacher Mr. Hanson jokes that he'll gladly accept Super Bowl tickets for a stocking stuffer. And once the gremlins threaten to overrun the town, exasperated local DJ Rockin' Ricky tells his callers to stop feeding him this "Orson Welles crap" about "little green men." It's Christmas, after all, not Halloween!

Gremlins abounds in Christmas references, but not in what is often termed the "Christmas Spirit." Unlike Christmas classics such as *A Christmas Carol* (1951) or *It's a Wonderful Life*, *Gremlins* engages us in no serious self-appraisal, and reveals very little about traditional meanings of Christmas or the holiday's implications. Instead, it toys with Christmas, fascinated with the glossy surface of the season, but then undercutting any coherent meaning to it. Hence, Billy's girlfriend Kate tells how her father died playing Santa to his family on Christmas Eve, when he slipped inside the chimney and broke his neck.

Director Joe Dante, at least, probably had no serious urge to infuse this film with Christmas meaning. As a graduate of Roger Corman's New World Pictures, Dante just simply loved movies—all kinds of movies—from (the original) *Attack of the 50 Foot Woman* to *The Sadist*. Dante loved movies so much that he had worked for next to nothing to make them for Corman. And he even remarked in a 1982 interview that unless he found "something to say about the real world," his films could "always fall back on an interpretation of movies." He had "always cared most about" this sort of interpretation, anyway. In *Gremlins*, Dante apparently found nothing to say about Christmas or "the real world," but he sure had found a lot of movies to interpret.

Gremlins, then, is not really about Christmas at all. It's about Christmas *movies*, a reinterpretation of Christmas *cinema* (and of *It's a Wonderful Life*, in particular)… not to mention a reinterpretation of horror cinema, and every other type of movie it presents. It is, as Dante once called it, "its own triple-bill."

This film does, in fact, make several extended allusions to other movies—to *The Wizard of Oz*, *The Blob* (1958), *Invasion of the Body Snatchers* (1956) and (of course) *It's a Wonderful Life*. Mrs. Deagle, the story's villainess, blurs together Scrooge and Capra's Potter (through their mutual contempt for the poor), with Elvira Gulch and Oz's witches thrown in for good measure (through her obsession with destroy-

Billy, Kate (Phoebe Cates) and mom and dad watch as Gizmo is returned to his home in *Gremlins*.

ing Billy's dog, and her death in red slippers). Our young hero, in the spirit of *The Blob* and *Invasion of the Body Snatchers*, tries to alert local authorities to the presence of monsters; but when the cops prove less than helpful, Billy and Kate (the kids) tackle the town's salvation by themselves—even discovering a gremlin invasion at the movie house. Meanwhile, *It's a Wonderful Life* provides much of the Christmas and small-town setting for this action.

But in addition to film references (including passing references to *Psycho*, *Alien* and *E.T.*), even the casting, in some cases, points toward the cinematic past. Veteran Corman character actor Dick Miller plays the xenophobic Murray Futterman, while '50s sci-fi veteran Kenneth Tobey plays the uncredited gas station attendant. Apparently, a heavily made-up William Schallert (Patti Duke's TV dad, among a legion of other roles) also makes an uncredited appearance as the priest at the mailbox. Using, and then not crediting, the owners of such familiar faces is just another of Dante's film reference in-jokes.

Joe Dante's playfulness characterizes a specific artistic trend, one which makes movies about other movies and emphasizes pastiche rather than individual uniqueness. This trend has been labeled "post-modernism." But whatever we call it, *Gremlins* obviously lives, moves and has its being within it.

Though pastiche generally incorporates elements from other movies or alludes to their plots, it can also (as critic Fredric Jameson points out) mix several earlier time periods together within the present, as *Gremlins* does.

In addition to its direct references, the film's action seems to take place both in and out of the 1980s. The characters may wear '80s clothing and hairstyles, but the town looks like something straight out of an old Frank Capra movie, and possesses several *It's a Wonderful Life* landmarks: an Emporium, a "Savings and Trust" (where, of course, the hero works) and even an old-time movie house. Its name, "Kingston Falls," alludes directly to Bedford Falls, and the film even begins in a Chinatown apparently out of the 1940s.

All this pastiche and playfulness, of course, drew praise from many critics, but was savaged by others. In a particularly exasperated and impassioned review, David Denby complained of feeling "trapped in a pop-culture Maytag, spinning endlessly round and round"—a description which is not off-target. Denby wants *Gremlins* to conform to movies of an earlier era. He wants movies with sophisticated characterization and some meaning relevant to the real world. But this simply is not that kind of film.

Instead, *Gremlins* just wants to have fun. It is a horror comedy that serves up Christmas as window dressing, a convenience to move forward a facetiously horrific plot, a pseudo-center surrounded by anarchic chaos. And, though it may perhaps be about the dark side of Christmas (or the dark side of small towns, or the dark side of our society's relationship with nature, or what have you), this summer movie about Christmas (and other) movies is most likely just a self-enclosed world of cinema, full of sound and fury and signifying nothing.

But what more must it signify in order to entertain?

—CRC

The Nightmare Before Christmas delivers presents we wouldn't want in our stockings!

The Nightmare Before Christmas
1993

Tim Burton is one of the few contemporary directors who makes films that are both commercially successful and richly thematic. Even Burton's most blatantly "commercial" projects, such as the *Batman* films and *Mars Attacks!* (1997), have really been more art-house fare than action films or big-budget comedies. That Burton has found such a wide and appreciative audience in the current climate of empty blockbusters is astonishing, and a testament to his visionary prowess as a filmmaker.

The theme Burton returns to time and again in his films is that of the artist's place in society. Films as disparate as *Batman* (1989), *Edward Scissorhands* (1990) and *Ed Wood* (1994) all deal with the artist-as-outsider, and the ways in which creative sensibilities try to blend into a larger, more philistine society.

Batman is really about two artists, Batman and the Joker, vying for artistic supremacy over Gotham City. The Joker seeks to remake the city in his own

Santa checks his list in *The Nightmare Before Christmas*.

image: his poison, Smylex, leaves corpses with his own signature clown's grin, dollar bills will bear his likeness, and, in Gotham's art museum, the deranged artist actually believes he is *improving* the art by refashioning it in shades of purple and green.

Batman, on the other hand, has no such artistic aspirations. He seeks to remake himself and his own private world, rather than all of Gotham City. Creating his own Bat-persona, establishing his own studio with the Batcave, and further accessorizing his vision with a Batmobile, Batplane and Bat-boomerangs, he works with all the zeal of an artist held by a single, thematic obsession.

That Batman wins the fight for aesthetic supremacy (as well as the physical confrontation) is best exemplified by the closing shots of the film, where Gotham City is lit up by the Batsignal. Batman has not only claimed the city, he has signed his work as well.

Edward Scissorhands, a gentler and more accessible film than *Batman*, addresses the formative years of the artist. While it's easy to see the film as an exploration of teenage angst, Edward is first and foremost an artist. With his abilities in topiary and sculpture (and, to exaggerate the sculptor metaphor, hairstyling), it is clearly the creative urge that defines Edward. Burton uses his Gothic obsessions to great effect to underscore just how far removed Edward is from society as a whole. Not only does Edward look

different, he *is* different. Burton uses flashbacks to reveal the artificially created (by magician-inventor Vincent Price) Edward's upbringing in an atmosphere of Gothic gentility. This education leaves Edward more civilized, more sensitive than contemporary men, and enables and empowers him to explore his emotional, artistic side.

Edward Scissorhands explores Burton's personal emotional landscape more effectively than any of his films to date. With his white-face makeup, thick patch of unruly black hair and gaunt face, it's easy to see Edward (Johnny Depp) as a cartoon version of the director himself. Burton's identification with Edward seems complete. That Vincent Price is Edward's "father" is significant, given Burton's long-standing devotion to Price's cinematic identity. The snatches of autobiography that Burton has revealed concerning his own boyhood make mention of feelings of isolation and dislocation; he sought refuge in images of darkly romantic gentility found in Roger Corman's series of Edgar Allan Poe adaptations starring Price. *Vincent*, a short film Burton made in 1985 for Disney, is a slightly altered riff on this same autobiographical theme: Lonely, artistic 12-year-old Vincent Malloy seeks aesthetic harmony in identifying with the cinematic Price persona.

Burton's most conspicuous box-office failure, *Ed Wood*, also dealt with the artist and his place in society. That Wood was an aesthetic failure in his many endeavors is immaterial: It's the passion to create, to mold the world according to a set of artistic mannerisms, that allies Burton's *Ed Wood* to little Vincent, Batman, The Joker and Edward Scissorhands.

This strain of autobiography is also patently obvious in Burton's Christmas extravaganza, *The Nightmare Before Christmas* (1993).

Given Burton's obsession with Gothic themes, it's only natural that his animated Christmas musical also deals with Halloween. Christmas may be the focus of the title (and the main obsession of Burton's artist-stand-in, Jack Skellington), but the film is really Burton's tribute to all things October rather than December tinsel.

The Nightmare Before Christmas details the mid-career slump of "Pumpkin King" Jack Skellington, the master of both the holiday Halloween and its kingdom, Halloweentown. Jack's leadership of the holiday has nothing to do with heredity or lineage: This natty living skeleton is simply the master of fright. Like all artists, Jack's accomplishments are aesthetic; at one point, he sings: "And since I am dead, I can take off my head, and recite Shakespearean quotations. No animal or man, can scream like I can, with the fury of my recitations!"

However, the artist in Jack has come to an impasse. Jack is at the top of his form, but his art has lost its ability to fulfill him. Jack discovers Christmastown quite by accident, and, his artistic passion enflamed by the potential of a new holiday, Jack plans to take over Christmas and remake it in his own image.

And Burton's, too. The production design for Halloweentown is one of the most accomplished for a stop-motion animated film. With its Gothic cemetery, rustling leaves, Expressionist buildings and cast of monsters, Halloweentown has the distinct Tim Burton look. Christmastown, on the other hand, has none of Halloweentown's atmospheric cachet. Christmas, for Burton, is a place of ugly primary colors, sticky sentiment and holiday kitsch.

Jack's mission, once he has appropriated the holiday, is to turn it from a bright Norman Rockwellesque festival to a dark Tim Burtonesque celebration. Jack remolds the holiday to include shrunken heads, bats, carnivorous snakes and malefic Jack-in-boxes.

The results, of course, are disaster. Jack is an artist whose medium is

the Gothic, and any effort to change that is doomed to failure. But, unlike *Edward Scissorhands*, Burton does not end his holiday film on a bittersweet note. Understanding that being the Pumpkin King is the best realization of his talents, Jack is filled with a new burst of aesthetic vitality. It took working in another medium—Christmas—for this holiday artist to realize that Halloween is his most honest mode of expression.

It's possible to see a great deal of Burton in Jack. Both are masters of dark fantasy, and, like Jack, Burton's aesthetic heart seems to be in the right place. While most of Burton's oeuvre seems linked to a Gothic mode of German Expressionism, his films are seldom downright bleak. *Batman* is the conspicuous exception. For all the black lace, darkened eyes and Gothic frills of a typical Burton production, most of the protagonists are more misunderstood than sinister, and are often sincerely sweet.

Jack Skellington may be a self-professed master of fright, but his malignity seems to be only bone-deep. He kidnaps Santa Claus, but is very apologetic about it all. He wants to terrify, but seems to do little real harm. His minions are gross, monstrous and "scary," but these attributes never seem to penetrate beyond image. He is capable of love (falling for the Frankensteinian ragdoll Sally), not an attribute often associated with actual villains, and functions as a true

**Lock, Shock and Barrell prepare to kidnap "Sandy Claws"
in** ***The Nightmare Before Christmas***.

Jack Skellington's heart is in the right place and is shocked to learn children don't like his Christmas presents in _The Nightmare Before Christmas_.

hero at the film's climax, defeating the genuinely evil Boogie Man and releasing Santa Claus in time for Christmas.

Following Burton's success with his _Batman_ films and _Edward Scissorhands_, it is possible to see Jack as Burton's effort to reconcile his dual nature. Jack instills terror the way graphically inclined children crayon pictures on the living room wall: There's no intent to do damage, only to decorate. Similarly, Burton is an artist who finds his best expression in a dark romanticism—but his artistic mannerisms are merely a vehicle for his message. Despite the dank look of gloom, horrific landscapes and otherworldly characters that habitually appear in Burton's work, his films are not exercises in nihilism. Burton's work may look sinister, but it is seldom nasty. Many mainstream films—_Terminator_, _Lethal Weapon_ and _First Blood_ come to mind—are darker at heart than Burton at his meanest. Burton has taken the motifs of the horror film—remote and dreary landscapes, "monstrous" outsiders and uncontrolled artists—and used them to create fables and benign fairy tales. Today, true horror pictures are the action films with their casual violence, lack of moral center and unfocused aggression.

The Nightmare Before Christmas was something of an unexpected hit for Walt Disney. The studio was nervous over what they considered to be its horrific tone, and rather than release it as a Disney animated film, they distributed it as a Touchstone picture in-stead. (Disney reserves Touchstone for its more adult films.) The film was the subject of an abortive merchandising campaign (again, Disney's cold feet and image concerns with the Mouse peddling bendable skeletons and werewolves), and _The Nightmare Before Christmas_ toys are now highly-priced collectibles. (Historically, toy marketing has been a problem with Burton's films. The toys created to tie into the promotion of _Batman Returns_ were a dismal failure as marketers forgot that the film was adult fare, unappreciated by the kiddie audience.)

Many parents kept children from the film, some simply because of the word _nightmare_, but the film still found an audience. Not surprisingly, adults especially gravitated to this story of a little ghoul lost, mirroring the recent renaissance of interest in Halloween in America. Baby boomers have wrested Halloween away from the kiddie ghetto of holiday observance, and have reclaimed it as the pagan celebration it once was. Halloween is second only to Christmas in the amount of revenue it generates annually, and Halloween merchandise of all kinds is now available in varieties undreamed of 20 years ago. Halloween has become, in effect, America's Mardi Gras, with costume parties, parades and all manner of personal indulgence.

Equally important to Halloween for adult Americans is the use of masks and disguise. Many over-worked, over-tired, over-extended boomers need the release of anonymity. Halloween provides that in spades. On October 31st, it is literally possible to become somebody else, which is perhaps the secret desire of many adults caught in the web of corporate America.

The Nightmare Before Christmas addresses this need to assume new identities directly into its story line. Taking a page, perhaps, from his own Halloween, Jack not only takes over Christmas, but becomes Santa Claus as well. He subsumes his artistic identity, hiding it behind a red Santa suit and fake beard. Even at Christmas, it seems, the need for personal reinvention asserts itself.

In addition, as boomers age into an increasingly secular society, the Christian meaning of Christmas has faded somewhat, to be replaced by a Dickensian holiday of high spirits, noble works and good fellowship. (Not, I think, a bad thing.) Halloween, however, presents no spiritual hurdle because of its very irreligious nature. Adults of wildly divergent faiths can embrace the fun of Halloween without any religious guilt. Christmas remains the holiday juggernaut, but Halloween is making significant inroads as the holiday Americans celebrate most innocently.

Burton's film wisely connects both holidays, and it can be watched with satisfaction any time from mid-October to year's end.

The Nightmare Before Christmas offers a peculiarly un-Christian Christmas: Here, December 25 is a day for candy, Santa Claus and presents. This omission presents a problem neither for Burton nor his audience; in fact, had the film addressed, however obliquely, the spiritual aspect of the Christmas festival, the results could have been thematic disaster. (How would the ghoulish delights of Halloween measure up, for instance, to the birth of a savior? Presented with Jack Skellington vs. Jesus Christ, even the most secular audiences would squirm uncomfortably.) Like the stop-motion television holiday specials that proceeded it, *Nightmare*'s Christmas is a celebration steeped in folklore and legend, and not in a fundamental religious reality that must be dealt with on a year-round basis. In fact, Halloween may be the true center-piece of this holiday film because it, unlike Christmas, demands no theological investment. Both holidays may have become community (and societal) events, indiscriminate of religious orientation, but Halloween carries no spiritual baggage.

In the end, however, Christmas films have to deliver what has become its holiday spirit to succeed as seasonal films. Not surprisingly, *The Nightmare Before Christmas* has not become a holiday "event" film, like *It's a Wonderful Life* or *The Bishop's Wife*. The Christmas it contains is not the holiday Americans have come to expect; rather, it is Christmas as seen through the filter of a highly individualized artistic

temperament. To the public at large, the film is more of a curiosity, much like people who like horror films, or Tim Burton himself. While sweet at its core, the film looks too Halloween, too *Tim Burton*, to really be ritualized with such holiday fare as *Rudolph the Red-Nosed Reindeer* or *Frosty the Snowman*. The genius of *The Nightmare Before Christmas* is that it is really a Halloween film disguised, much like Jack Skellington, in a Santa Claus suit.

Whatever its faults as a piece of holiday entertainment, *The Nightmare Before Christmas* offers further insight into director Tim Burton's quest for the artist's (and his own) place in society. To Burton, this figure will always be an outsider, largely misunderstood by the society as a whole. Like the characters of Batman, Edward Scissorhands and Ed Wood (at least at the end of Burton's film), the movie *The Nightmare Before Christmas* has achieved a measure of success and celebration. However, it, like they, remains out of the mainstream.

—BM

Slay Bells, Thistletoe, and Christmas Fears— Yuletide Horror Films

That the number of horror films which take place around October 31 does not dwarf the number whose setting is December 24 and 25 might at first seem surprising. However, the reason can be deduced by understanding the *raison d'être* of the horror film itself.

Despite extensive analysis of the genre—much of it favorable—by academicians and mainstream movie critics who focus on the nonhorrific elements, its essential ingredient has always been and will always be its ability to shock. And even though what raises the goose flesh for one person might amuse or even bore another, when horror works as horror, it is because it is shocking.

So, although Christmas has become extremely commercialized and nearly devoid of its sectarian origins, it is still held in such high regard that an almost innate reflex of horror occurs when its traditions are desecrated. One expects Halloween to offer hideous demons and blood-hungry lunatics; not so the tranquil, peace-on-Earth Noël. Any horror fable (cinematic or literary) that unfolds at Christmas time is bound to shock.

An objection to this viewpoint could be that, after all, isn't Easter a far more sacred celebration, thus

A scruffy-looking St. Nick (Oliver MacGreevy) from *Tales from the Crypt*.

making it a more appropriate candidate for the horror format?[1] Yes, to the true believer the birth of the Biblical Jesus is a less important myth than His crucifixion and resurrection. But my contention is that for the general populace—for whom these movies are made—the Nativity is the most cherished festival of the year, and so using it as the environment for horrible happenings generates more of a chill than would any other.

In Christmas' current form, its secular saint is Nicholas (derived from a real Catholic saint), aka Santa Claus. The fact that, unlike Jesus, he can represent all things to all people makes him widely appealing—from the left side of the political spectrum (munificence) all the way to the right (capitalism). Except for the fundamentalist, who finds the anagram of Santa to be more of a clue to his real function, and the rationalist, who believes confusing children about the difference between fantasy and reality is harmful, probably everyone happily accepts Mr. Claus as the most representative symbol for the season. So, to stay consistent, the horror movies examined herein do not spare him; Santa Claus is a factor in about half of them. He is presented as devil, redeemer or even victim.

What is most interesting about Yuletide horror films is that a good majority revolve around the theme of family: either the agony in being without one or the mania produced from losing a beloved relative. The Christmas backdrop just enhances this melancholy. But in the few that immediately follow, the antagonists view family as a prison; and they take murderous steps to free themselves.

In *Home for the Holidays* (1972), Eleanor Parker plays Alex, the eldest of four daughters who has summoned her sisters to the estate of their sickly father (Walter Brennan) because of his accusation that their stepmother (Julie Harris) is poisoning him to death. In reality, Alex is the unstable one, and she uses the Christmas gathering to eliminate her kin one by one, for they have become dependent on her over the years to be the rock in every crisis. Freddie (Jessica Walter) is a pill-popper; Jo (Jill Haworth) is a slattern; and Chris (the angelic Sally Field) is a university student, stable but too young to help Parker with the others. When even Dad turns to Alex with his paranoid suspicions, it pushes her over the edge.

This somewhat bland ABC-TV movie,[2] co-produced by Aaron Spelling and directed by John Llewellyn Moxey (whose best film, *Horror Hotel*, was behind him), is rescued by *Psycho*-scripter Joseph Stefano's speculations on how familial burdens can cause a kind of dementia in some people. Alex feels that if she physically escaped the family environment, she would be drawn back by her emotional ties to it—but not if the members are all dead. One oddity that piqued my curiosity is that all the daughters' names would be suitable for sons as well, which leads me to wonder if Stefano was trying to make some comment about gender within the family environment.

On the big screen the same year, Freddie Francis' omnibus *Tales from the Crypt* featured a character whose attitude toward the family ideal was just as warped as Parker's. It was also the first portrayal of a slashing Santa, which in the '80s attracted so much controversy.

In the opening tale "All Through the House," Joan Collins clouts her husband (Martin Boddey) with a fireplace poker for the insurance payoff. The carols on the radio are interrupted by an announcer warning that a "homicidal maniac" dressed like Santa Claus has escaped from the "hospital for the criminally insane." When the nut shows up at her door, she cannot phone the police because she is busy trying to configure her late husband's corpse at the foot of the cellar stairs to look like an accident. But her sweet daughter (Chloe Franks) ignorantly opens the door for the scruffy-looking St. Nick (Oliver MacGreevy). "He's here, Mommy. I let him in. It's Santa."

Most people are familiar with the HBO series *Tales from the Crypt*. In the first season (1989), a jokey and not terribly good rendition of the EC comics story (with "AND" added to the beginning of the title) was made by Fred Dekker and Robert Zemeckis, starring Larry Drake in the role of the jovial madman. But probably few are aware that a couple of guys in South Carolina did a virtual remake in 1991.

Paul Talbot's and William Cooke's *Campfire Tales* is another compilation, with a linking device involving Gunnar Hansen as a campfire raconteur. The relevant story is "The Fright Before Christmas." Steve (Paul Kaufmann) hates the concept of Xmas and thinks that waiting to be given things is wrong, but taking what one wants is good. He decides to get his inheritance early by pushing his mother down the basement stairs. A black stocking filled with coal is hung on his door and he is waylaid by the creepy "Satan Claus," who his nephew had earlier explained is Santa's alter ego, the one who disciplines the bad boys and girls (which is actual folklore from Austria). After rending the matricidal young man's heart from his chest, the demon utters, "You're a heartless bastard, Steve," a quote similar to one in the "Poetic Justice" segment of Francis' anthology.

The titular character of Curtis Harrington's *Whoever Slew Auntie Roo?* (1971) is more typical of these pictures: a person with a deep psychological disorder resultant from the death of a loved one. Shelley Winters is both sympathetic and sinister as an affluent American expatriate living in England who derives immense pleasure hosting an annual Christmas party for the local orphanage. The holiday setting is crucial here, for it is Winters' charity that allows her to get close to the children. She takes a fancy to one of the young waifs, Katy (Chloe Franks again), due to a resemblance to her late daughter, but the girl's older brother Christopher (Mark Lester) thinks that Winters is the wicked witch of *Hansel and Gretel* and wants to eat them. Heightening his macabre suspicions is his discovery of the woman talking to the desiccated corpse of her daughter, who had died accidentally from a fall off the banister.

The devilish screenplay co-written by Jimmy Sangster is the converse of his *The Nanny*. Unlike the feasible exclamations of William Dix, Mark Lester's clearly fantasy-laden mutterings prevent him from being believed. Lester, who is always smarter than the adults around him in these things (*Sudden Terror, What the Peeper Saw*), completely misinterprets the sad disposition of his hostess as malevolence, but it allows him to perceive her illicit intent to kidnap little Katy. There is also a refreshing streak of amorality written into the captured siblings' roles (they show no remorse over the fate of Winters) that is only depicted with any regularity in horror pictures. Children are usually "innocent," hence incapable of malice.

A 1974 Italian movie features another study of the terrible effects a child's death can have, but it's a straightforward revenge piece. Copying the formula of *Last House on the Left, The Night Train Murders* (*L'Ultimo Treno Della Notte*) revolves around two girls traveling by rail from Germany to Italy to spend Christmas with the family of one of them. During the trip, they are tormented by two male thugs and a sadistic female accomplice. After fatally torturing one and inducing the other to jump to her death from the speeding train, the delinquents wind up at the pair's intended destination. When he realizes their identity, the surgeon father exacts gory vengeance, substituting the healing hand of his profession for a hurting one as he extinguishes the two males. The female escapes punishment by placing all the blame on her two cohorts.

Also, allegedly released as *The New House on the Left* to capitalize on the infamy of the Wes Craven vehicle, *Night Train* is, much like its model, likely too sick for the average viewer. Director Aldo Lado is in the middle of the hierarchy of Italian filmmakers, with such engaging credits as the *Don't Look Now*–inspired *Who Saw Her Die?* and the wholly unique *Malastrana*. The English language print, which is shorn of 10 minutes of footage (some of it nasty violence) has completely bastardized all the names (Aldo Lado is Evans Isle, etc.), but recognizable in the cast are many alumni of Dario Argento movies: Flavio

Bucci (*Suspiria*) is one of the male miscreants; Macha Meril (*Deep Red*) is the woman with the Sadean tastes; Irene Miracle (*Inferno*) is one of the teenage victims; and Enrico Maria Salerno (*Bird with the Crystal Plumage*) is the vigilante patriarch. The crooner of the theme song during the opening credits (under which a *Babbo Natale* gets rolled by the two male hoodlums in the Italian print only) sounds a lot like Feargal Sharkey.

The emotional damage from the massacre of one's family is the centerpiece of the most notorious Yuletide movie of all time, the one that invoked the ire of seemingly every moralistic watchdog organization in America. In *Silent Night, Deadly Night* (1984) five-year-old Billy (Jonathon Best, who is an astonishingly adept child actor) witnesses his parents being exterminated on Christmas Eve by a crook outfitted as Santa Claus. From then on, he fears any image of the jolly one. The subsequent harsh upbringing at an orphanage run by a tyrannical Mother Superior (Lilyan Chauvin) nudges him to the perimeter of sanity. When he becomes an adult, he is forced to be the Santa at the toy store where he works, which makes him totally snap and assume the identity of Father Christmas. Primarily, he adopts the retribution aspect he believes is part of the gig, exclaiming, "Punish!" as he uses various devices to do just that: arrow, hammer claw, Christmas lights (for garroting), utility knife, even a pair of antlers. In the end, he is brought down by police firearms.

Notwithstanding the unlikely assumption of the Santa persona by the adult Billy (Robert Brian Wilson), Michael Hickey's script provides a nice comparison between the myth of Santa Claus and the myths promulgated by the Church, each of which acts as an apparatus for discipline. After the young Billy spies a teenage couple having sex and the Mother Superior flogging them, she explains "...when we do something naughty, we are always caught. And then we are punished. Punishment is absolute. Punishment is necessary. Punishment is good." Still, the best bit remains the eerie interchange between Best and his grandfather (Will Hare), who is catatonic to everyone else but talks to Billy and starts him down the path of Santa phobia.

By comparison with its two immediate successors, *Silent Night, Deadly Night* is a classic. In the first sequel (1987), which just adds a "2" to the title, Billy's brother Ricky (Eric Freeman) is traumatized from seeing his sibling shot in the first movie and decides to continue "punishing." The first half of the film is all the bloodshed from Part 1 replayed as Ricky describes to a psychiatrist what drove him to his own murder spree, which in turn fills out the second, shoddy half. The murders are innovative, though. A battery charger, umbrella and audio tape are amongst the death instruments. Ricky has added "Naughty" to his assassin's vocabulary, and because of its link to the dreaded holiday, the color red sets him off. He even has a confrontation with the now-scarred Mother Superior (scarred to make the viewer forget that it is a different actress, Jean Miller); but, like his brother, he succumbs to the guns of police. Compared to the mesomorphic Eric Freeman, Robert Brian Wilson is a real thespian.

The second sequel isn't any good, either. *Silent Night, Deadly Night 3: Better Watch Out!* (1989) features a blind girl (Samantha Scully) whose psychic powers are employed to communicate with coma victims. Of course, Ricky did not die from his gunshot wounds in the last film; his brain has been reassembled and is visible through the Ed Wood–worthy transparent mechanism he wears. Laura's telepathic connections have revived Ricky (now played by the ectomorphic Bill Moseley, best remembered as Chop Top in *The Texas Chainsaw Massacre Part 2*). Naturally, his first victim is a drunken Santa making his rounds in the hospital. From that point on, the shambling Ricky stalks the blind girl. His vocabulary is even more limited than Wilson's or Freeman's. He recites the psychic's name—"Laura"—endlessly. An embarrassed Robert Culp is the cop in pursuit, but even more ignominious is that the director of this opprobrium is Corman protégé Monte Hellman.

Perhaps because Brian Yuzna took over the series, things got better with the next two. In the tradition of *Halloween 3*, the really peculiar and senseless *Silent Night, Deadly Night 4: Initiation* (1990), which Yuzna directed, has nothing to do with its predecessors. It also has nothing to do with Christmas. A society of man-hating, goddess devotees—led by Maud Adams, who describes men as possessing a "parasitic quality"—has devised a way to transform an ordinary woman into a lesbian just by inserting into her a strange caterpillar creature that purges any heterosexual cravings. The only (only!) catch is that someone must be sacrificed periodically by the subject in order to preclude her from spontaneously combusting.

More relevant, and by far the best of the group (although it is also unrelated to any of its predecessors), is *Silent Night, Deadly Night 5: The Toy Maker* (1991), which Yuzna only co-produced and co-wrote. There are similarities to *Whoever Slew Auntie Roo?* like the blending of a popular fairy tale into the holiday framework. Mickey Rooney is Joe Petto, a toy maker who fashions a boy for himself out of synthetic components. Petto's wife had died years ago while pregnant, and so he had wanted a son to fill the abyss in his heart (another homage to the Harrington film). When the mechanical lad he calls Pino (Brian Bremer) does not quite measure up, Petto seeks a human son. And like Frankenstein's creation, Pino lashes out at this rejection, building deadly presents to get back at all "real" children.

There are some great, twisted toys that would never get past the Product Safety Commission in this film, designed by Screaming Mad George (who also did the effects for Part 4), like Larry the Larvae and the *Phantasm*-inspired Santa ball. Directed by Martin Kitrosser, this is an accomplished work, and I am confident if it were just called *The Toy Maker*, it would have been better received.

The psychotic Santa motif started by *Tales from the Crypt* may have been popularized by *Silent Night, Deadly Night*, but in 1980 two pictures were released that incorporated this (to some people) disturbing element. *To All a Goodnight* begins with a girl at a finishing school unintentionally falling over a balcony to her death during a Christmastide sorority prank. This might have sparked some contemplation about the way many people feel an angry need to retaliate when a loved one dies randomly, but it is just an excuse for the Santa-suited lunatic to knife one girl in the chest, decapitate another, strangle a guy with piano wire and dispose of a couple with the tried-and-true airplane propeller to the face method. In the dumb denouement, it is revealed that there are two killer Kriss Kringles, because the slaughter has been the united effort of both the father and mother of the accident victim.

Billy (Robert Brian Wilson) is one scary Santa in *Silent Night, Deadly Night*.

Although it is not the worst of its kind, this slasher show contains possibly the least interesting characters, spouting some of the most imbecilic dialogue. One co-ed utters this bewildering gem when trying to seduce a nerdy guy: "C'mon, Einstein, it's time for your advanced course in relativity." It is doubly disappointing when you learn the director is David Hess (of *Last House on the Left*, Ruggero Deodato's *The House on the Edge of the Park* and Pasquale Festa Campanile's *Hitch-Hike*) and that Alex Rebar (*The Incredible Melting Man*) wrote the screenplay.

The other evil Santa picture that year is also the best of them all. In Lewis Jackson's *Christmas Evil* (aka *You Better Watch Out*), Harry Stadling (Brandon Maggart), an employee of the Jolly Dream toy fac-

tory, is obsessed with Christmas and detests anyone who does not display enough respect for it. Each year he dresses up as St. Nicholas, and this season, after he affixes the white beard to his face with a particularly adhesive glue, he has confirmation that he has become the fat fellow incarnate. His identification with the figure stems from an incident in his pubescence, when he caught Mommy doing more than kissing Santa Claus (his father). That, combined with the fiery frustration over his inability to start a family of his own—and fueled by jealousy and resentment observing his brother Philip's normal wife-and-two-kids' home life—pushes Harry over the edge. As Santa, he doles out rewards... but also severe punishment.

Although it might not occur to liberal-hating ideologues, this New Jersey-lensed film should appeal to

In *Silent Night, Deadly Night 5*, a toy maker fashions a son for himself out of synthetic components.

them. For example, while shielded by adoring kids from the parents who suspect he is the murderer, Harry/Santa says, "These children know things that obviously you don't understand anymore. They love me... they want someone to notice who's good and who's bad. Someone to guide them, someone to take responsibility so they don't have to make those decisions themselves." And later, to his brother Philip (Jeffrey DeMunn), "You never did believe in me. You're one of them, you're one of those people out there who don't believe in anything."

Christmas Evil does not use the trappings of the season to denounce religion's oppressive principles, the way *Silent Night, Deadly Night* does; in fact, when Santa kills worshippers filing out of a church, the message seems to be that the secular version of the holiday has killed the sectarian one, something conservatives have been decrying for a long time. What makes the movie most enjoyable is Maggart's bravura performance as the deranged, sexually repressed—and borderline pedophiliac—Harry

Stadling. His sad, painful loneliness is palpable. To top it all off, the picture ends with a revelation that is evocative of the last shot of *Being There*. It's a revelation that makes a lot of viewers groan but always brings a smile to my lips.

Although it is often called a rip-off of *Silent Night, Deadly Night* because it was released in the same year, the British *Don't Open Till Christmas* has more in common with *Christmas Evil* yet adds its own distinct spin. When he was young, Giles Harrison witnessed Santa Claus having sex with a woman during a Yule party, and although the man in the red suit was his Dad, the woman was not his Mom. Indeed, after also catching a glimpse of this scene, his mother falls down the stairs and breaks her neck. Consequently, the little boy blossoms into a crazy (Alan Lake) that offs in grisly fashion those wearing the holiday outfit: incineration, spear through the head, gunshot in the face at point blank range, dagger in the stomach and eye-gouging. The most infamous is a latrine emasculation.

There is not much to recommend this flick, which is directed by and stars Edmund Purdom (as one of the Scotland Yard detectives working on the case). Even a stage act of Caroline Munro as herself in Piccadilly Theatre is much too brief to be of any enticement to see the whole product.

A finalist in any worst slasher derby is the 1996 abomination *Santa Claws*. Debbie Rochon (who is better than most scream queens) plays Raven Quinn, a sexploitation actress simultaneously shooting a holiday video and trying to keep her marriage from crumbling. Quinn, who is supposed to have a Masters in zoology yet cannot even pronounce the term correctly, lives next door to Wayne (Grant Kramer), an obsessed fan who happens to have his own familial hang-ups. Specifically, when he was 14 he shot to death his mother and uncle because they were sleeping together just three months after the Dad died. (The sight of the uncle, naked except for a Santa cap, would drive anyone to homicide.) After donning a Father Christmas outfit spray-painted black and sporting a spade claw, Wayne begins executing anyone who mistreats the sexy star.

John Russo, most famous as the writer of *Night of the Living Dead* as well as the competent *Midnight* in the early '80s, wrote and directed this putrescence.

Even with the low-budget constraints, the burning agony suffered by someone who is unloved—rendered with delirious perfection by Maggart—could have been explored with more invention. As it stands, *Santa Claws* makes *Midnight* seem like a very long time in the past... and *NOLD* about a century ago.

I suppose it was inevitable that filmmakers would get tired of Santa and go after another revered icon. In *Jack Frost* (also 1996), a truck marked "genetic research" collides with another transporting the titular serial killer (Scott MacDonald) to his execution. Jack gets sprayed with a special acid developed by the government to somehow combine human DNA with inert materials for future resurrection in the event of a "global holocaust." He melts in a pile of snow, and after his chromosomes and the white stuff bond, the snowman starts a chilly reign of terror. He can shoot icicle projectiles and chomp down on flesh with pointed ice teeth, but he is not averse to using a sled blade to behead one troublemaking kid or shove an ax handle down a man's throat. The fearsome Frosty targets the sheriff (Chris Allport) who had captured him (Jack had vowed he would "find a way" to get back at him and his family) but is destroyed in a bath of antifreeze.

A slight spoof at best (it's no *Killer Klowns from Outer Space*), *Jack Frost* does have some charming touches: the hair dryers used to repel the transformed Jack, the somewhat askew versions of seasonal songs on the soundtrack. I especially found clever the way the producers almost contemptuously exclude any Claus images, as if trying to one-up the *Silent Night Deadly Night* movies. I could have done without the snowman's Freddy Krueger-like wisecracks while dealing out death. Screaming Mad George was in charge of the (mostly uninspired) makeup effects again. My favorite part of the film is the goofy opening credits, during which we hear the voices of a child and the uncle he/she (actually, an adult impersonating a kid) insists recount a "happy, scary" story on Christmas Eve, getting more than he/she bargained for.

A couple of pictures dispense with any grieving over domestic problems and serve up really dysfunctional clans. In the Lloyd Kaufman-produced *Silent Night, Bloody Night* (1973), Jeffrey Butler (James Patterson) is the inheritor come to claim some property in upstate New York on the night before Noël. The town council (including a mute John Carradine) wants to buy him out to hide a secret, but instead each gets eliminated. A complex flashback shows that the estate had once existed as a sanitarium for a period of time in the '30s, and that Butler's grandfather Wilfred (Phillip Bruns) was also his father, having impregnated his own daughter just before committing her. One Christmas Eve, during a party for the doctors, the inmates were let loose by the guilt-ridden grandfather, and they had commenced bloody retribution on their custodians using common garden implements and shards of champagne glasses.

John Carpenter must have been influenced by this film, because variations of some elements show up later in *Halloween*, such as the POV shots of the killer, his escape from the state hospital and his warning to the telephone operator that "I have come back." Directed by Theodore Gershuny and starring his then-wife Mary Woronov as the narrator, this movie's biggest claim to fame is that its unsettling sepia flashback headlines many contemporary stars of Warhol's New York underground as asylum inmates, like Ondine, Candy Darling and Jack (*Flaming Creatures*) Smith. The script's dearth of humor contributes to the suffocating atmosphere, though the uninformed comment by one character about the former residents of the house that "they must have had a wonderful life" is a cute swipe at Capra. Furthermore, the disclosure of the council members' identities at the end took me completely by surprise.

The tribe in Jeff Mandel's *Elves* (1989) makes the Butlers look like the Waltons. Kirsten (Julie Austin) is a high school girl whose grandfather (Borah Silver) was involved as a Nazi in genetically altering the title creatures to mate on Christmas Eve with a virgin from a "pure genetic line"...which of course is Kirsten. Her mother (Deanna Lund) divulges how this unsullied strain was achieved: "The man in the study is your grandfather... AND your father" (yes, that again). In a plot contrivance that tries to cover all bases, the coupling of monster and maiden is supposed to produce the Antichrist, as well as the master race!

Obviously trying to ape the much more light-hearted Christmas-themed *Gremlins*, this movie has so much schlock it nearly succeeds as a bad cinema classic. To start with, the title is a misnomer, since there really is only one elf (infrequently) shown. Dan Haggerty as a department store St. Nick (the guy he replaced was castrated by a knife-wielding elf) gives one of the poorest performances in a campy flick I have ever seen. He does not even smoke a cigarette believably. The highlight of Lund's hysterical role is the drowning of her daughter's cat in the toilet. Shamelessly, one Nazi plagiarizes George Romero when he states, "When there is no more room in Hell, the elves will walk the Earth." And the idea that inbreeding could produce a "pure genetic line" would have made even Mengele's eyes roll.

The Dorm that Dripped Blood (aka *Pranks*, 1981) has no connection to the familial leitmotif I have discussed; it is just a slasher film, pure and simple, and not a very good one. A bunch of college students are cleaning out a condemned dormitory while their peers

Shelley Winters takes a fancy to Katy (Chloe Franks) in *Whoever Slew Auntie Roo?*

are away on Christmas vacation. Slowly, they begin getting picked off: drill in the back of the neck, car running over the head, etc. The motivation for the killer (Stephen Sachs) has got to be one of the most moronic of all time. You see, no one ever took him seriously. There is a tiny dose of originality in the finale, when Sachs tricks the police into thinking the last potential victim is the real murderer.

The basic premise of *Dorm* is similar to Bob Clark's *Black Christmas³* (as is the use of a downbeat ending), though I almost should be shot for writing those two titles in the same sentence. Seeing Daphne Zuniga in this as one of the students who manage to get eradicated would be startling if she did not also appear in another slasher, *The Initiation*, two years later. The directing/writing team of Jeffrey Obrow and Stephen Carpenter went on to make better though not great movies (*The Power*, *The Kindred* and *Servants of Twilight*). The music by Chris Young is an imitation of Herrman's *Psycho* at a slower tempo.

One movie that is hard to put in any category brings us full circle with its backdrop of a calamitous family gathering at Christmas. In the abstruse *Bloodbeat* (1982), the visiting son's girlfriend Sarah (Claudia Peyton) inexplicably triggers the materialization of a murderous samurai every time she experiences orgasm and eventually transmogrifies into the Asian warrior herself. Only the young man and his sister survive the hormonally manifesting samurai's rampage through the conjoining of some supernatural energy the two share.

The sequence in which the house endures a quake from the hostile spiritual onslaught is staged well. In addition, there is a stab at irony: Sarah's sexually generated homicides follow an earlier revulsion at the hunting of a deer. However, this weird amateur effort from Fabrice-Ange Zaphiratos has a muddled, recondite screenplay, with everyone talking around any explanations of the plot. Generic lines are delivered as though they provide valuable data: "Mom was right," "You don't mean..." Even a revelatory exchange between Sarah and the mother toward the end is obscured by a loud soundtrack. I cannot help imagining that the cryptic surrealism is due to the fact that some of the post-production work on this Midwestern offering was done in France!

There are a handful of shockers with tangential links to Christmas. The most significant is *Curse of the Werewolf* (1960). After being raped by a beggar imprisoned at the behest of a cruel marquis, a young mute girl gives birth to a boy who later transforms into a werewolf. The reason is based on a superstition that says an unwanted child born on the Lord's birthday is an insult to Heaven. Such a malediction seems unjust, yet it neatly parallels the contradictory notion that abortion and illegitimacy are equally immoral. It also reminds me of the similarly conservative creation of the bloodsuckers in Jose Larraz's *Vampyres* (lesbians slain in the act of lovemaking).

Dario Argento's *Deep Red* (*Profondo Rosso*, 1975) has an important murder committed in front of an impressionable child during *Natale*. In fact, it is the boy's mother who embeds the carving knife in his father's back. It is another broken marriage, although this time it is not over an insurance policy... it is because Dad wanted to institutionalize Mom (I wonder why). Nearly half of Oliver Stone's *The Hand* (1981) takes place during the holiday, and it contains the false shot—derived from Michael Caine's delusions—of the title appendage springing out of a gift package and mortally assaulting its opener, Caine's mistress (Annie McEnroe). The deed is really carried out by Caine, driven to madness by his own broken marriage.

Trancers (1985) is about a megalomaniac who uses controlled humans (the title term) to do his bidding. One of them is a jaundiced mall Kriss Kringle (Pete Schrum) who attacks Tim Thomerson, the time-traveling cop hunting the megalomaniac. The funniest use of Christmas iconography has to be in Aristide Massaccesi's *Crawlers* (1990), which involves a nuclear power plant disposing of their waste in a surrounding forest and turning the roots radioactive. When they are cut off from the rest of the tree—which dies due to lack of nutrients—the tendril roots go around crushing people but are eventually defeated by being bulldozed under. The last shot is one of those "I hope there's a sequel" aspirations: a Christmas tree shimmying to life!

Other borderline horror films have their seasonal elements. *The Unholy Three* (1925/1930) has a great sequence in both the silent and sound versions of midget Harry Earles pretending to be a toddler and playing with a toy elephant (which he calls a cow) under a Christmas tree. Due to the German Earles' accent, some infants are probably easier to comprehend, so the silent version is preferred. In *Curse of the Cat People* (1944), a Christmas present figures prominently in the aggravation of an estrangement between a mother and daughter, and it jeopardizes a little girl the mother is closer to than her own child.

The wonderful Mexican *Santa Claus* (1960) involves Lucifer's plans to destroy *Navidad* by sending one of his minions, the standard red devil with horns and tail named Pitch, to Earth to prevent *Papá Noël* from getting back home after his Christmas Eve deliveries. The scenes in Hell, extended by a couple of minutes in the Spanish language print, are straight out of Dante.

Finally, *The Silent Partner* (1979), written and produced by Curtis Hanson, stars Christopher Plummer as a bank robber attired as Santa and Elliot Gould as the teller who reports a much larger take to the insurance company and media, pocketing the dif-ference. Although really more an action thriller, there is one truly horrific moment. When Plummer's female accomplice falls in love with Gould, her severed head winds up in the bank teller's exotic fishtank.

It is rather astounding how so many genre critics loathe Yuletide horror movies; to them, the genre has boundaries, past which no filmmaker should roam. These critics should be comforted by the knowledge that the spate of Noël nasties ran out of plum pudding almost a decade ago. Perhaps the *Silent Night, Deadly Night* series was the death knell. Regardless, these movies should not be singled out for special condemnation, because, like the best horror films, they trade in one cinematic truism: Horror films work best when they shock. For that they should be celebrated.

Have a scary Christmas.

—LM

Footnotes:
1) Two pictures that could be put in such a category are *The Eerie Midnight Horror Show* (*L'Ossesa*, 1974), with its statue of one of the crucified thieves at Calvary becoming animated and first ravishing and then possessing a female artist; and *Fear No Evil* (1980), whose Passion Play begins Armageddon.
2) I will not be discussing TV shows in this essay, and in fact *Home for the Holidays* is the only TV movie. One title that was too rare for me to obtain, *The Thirteenth Day of Christmas* (1985), is reportedly about a young boy who has psychopathic urges over the holiday period (which sounds a lot like a 1980 novel by Sandra Scoppettone, *Such Nice People*). It appears this is an episode in a series of one-hour made-for-TV programs from England's Granada Studios released on tape by Prism Video, and as such is not a "film."
3) *Black Christmas*, which along with *Christmas Evil* is the best Christmas-themed horror movie ever made—and after *Psycho* and maybe *Halloween* the best North American slasher film—follows.

Black Christmas
1974

Black Christmas is a difficult film to assess. It is the best Christmas horror film ever made, yet it is a "slasher" horror film that doesn't play by the rules. The time is the Christmas season—the celebration of the Christ child's birth. Yet, the most sympathetic character is demanding an abortion, the killing of her unborn child. The plot is slick enough to hold the audience in suspense, and the deranged killer theme is enough to clash pointedly with "Silent Night, Holy Night." Yet, that same plot appears to be full of holes. But is it really? So let's pour a cup of wassail and take a look at *Black Christmas*, one of the most intriguing and enigmatic horror films of the 1970s.

As "Silent Night" plays inside a college sorority house decorated for Christmas, the camera assumes the perspective of a heavy-breathing stranger outside. Thanks to camera perspective, the audience is seeing what the stranger sees as he approaches the house, climbs a trellis and enters an unused attic.

We are soon introduced to the principals. One is sorority sister Barb (Margot Kidder), a foul-mouthed, boozy, sexually promiscuous '70s girl who treats the season with cynicism. Her early scenes establish the major contrast of the film—that of the sacred vs. the profane. Barb's attitude reflects the "mature" or jaded view of Christmas and spirituality that many young people felt in the '70s and still feel today. Having become a more secular than sacred holiday, Christmas is somewhat a festive occasion and somewhat a pain in the ass for young people growing up in an era of free love and shattered ideals.

Unease settles over the sorority sisters when they receive an obscene phone call. But this is no ordinary obscene call. First, the caller appears to be speaking in two voices. "Can that be one voice?" a disturbed sorority sister gasps. Second, after being challenged by outgoing Barb, the caller concludes with a death threat. Clare (Lynne Griffin), apparently a young woman of higher moral virtue than Barb, criticizes Barb for her foul mouth and attitude, to which Barb replies, "This is a sorority house, not a convent." Again the contrasts are clear: Clare's vs. Barb's moral stance and the sorority house vs. the convent. Both are extreme contrasts (as is the sacred vs. the profane), but this is a film of extremes. It is obvious, however, that the audience is to identify with Barb more than with Clare, and we are to embrace the values of the sorority house over those of the convent. After all, the film was made in the mid-1970s before free sex became equated with death.

The obscene caller soon makes good on his death threat. The first to die is virginal Clare, who ends up in a rocking chair in the attic with a plastic bag slapped over her head. As the killer rocks her corpse, he (or she?) chants "Little Baby Bunting, Daddy's gone a-hunting," thereby reinforcing the "baby" theme first raised by the Christmas setting itself and telling us, since the voice is that of the obscene caller, that the killer in the attic and the caller are one and the same. In addition, since the killer is indeed going hunting, the song foreshadows another murder. But it isn't just the Christmas season that puts a baby on the killer's mind, as we will soon see. Later, police find the body of a murdered 13-year-old (and presumably virgin) girl in the city park. Is this another victim of the obscene caller?

We are soon introduced to Clare's father, Mr. Harrison (James Edmond), who goes to the sorority house when his daughter fails to meet him in town for Christmas break. The soft-spoken gentleman is shocked by foul-mouthed Barb and comical Mrs. Mac (Marian Waldman), the alcoholic house mother who not only assumes sexual activity on the part of her girls but also encourages it.

Producer/director Bob Clark (who would go on to direct the classic and traditional *A Christmas Story*) clearly intends that audiences sympathize with foul-mouthed Barb and hard-drinking, good-hearted Mrs. Mac, both of whom are "hip" to the contemporary scene of the mid-70s. Mr. Harrison, with his Victorian morality, is a comic foil for Barb and Mrs. Mac. Yet, all the man has done to elicit derision is exhibit a receding hairline, rear a morally virtuous daughter and express shock at lewd decorations in his daughter's sorority house at Christmas.

The scene now shifts to a personal drama involving sorority sister Jess (Olivia Hussey) and her boyfriend Peter (Keir Dullea), a graduate student in music preparing for a major recital before his faculty committee. The tempestuous affair between Peter and Jess has left Jess pregnant, and she has decided to have an abortion regardless of Peter's feelings. "Don't you ever think of anyone but yourself?" Peter angrily asks. Ironically, he soon dismisses Jess because he has to practice for his upcoming recital. The unborn life hangs in the balance between a young man who wants it to live but who must continue his piano practice and a young woman who is willing to see it die rather than marry the father or discontinue her future plans. Though Peter implores Jess to change her mind, the audience is obviously supposed to identify with Jess' "liberated" decision, just as it is supposed to identify with the "liberated" Barb and Mrs. Mac rather than with the morally conventional Clare and her milquetoast father. Still, unlike Barb and Mrs. Mac, Jess is apparently a sensitive, considerate, thoughtful young woman. If such a person could choose abortion, then abortion must be a moral option, right? It must not be the barbaric act that pro-life advocates portray it to be. At least that is the attitude Clark implies.

The threatening phone calls continue, and soon only Mrs. Mac, Barb and sorority sister Phyl (Andrea Martin) are left in the house. The killer soon dispatches Mrs. Mac after she makes a tipsy climb to the attic in search of her cat.

Later, during the piano recital, Peter leaves his faculty committee cold as he bangs discordant notes on the piano. The recital is obviously a failure, and Peter later destroys his piano in a fit of frustration and rage. Is this the work of a young man frustrated by the imminent death of his baby? Is this the frustration of a deranged serial killer? Or is it both?

Bob Clark is clearly making what we would now label a "slasher" film, but he isn't playing by the rules

Oliva Hussey and Keir Dullea star in *Black Christmas*.

later established. While later slasher films would initially sacrifice sexually promiscuous girls to the killer, saving the virgin as the last intended victim (who escapes), Clark arranges apparent virgins as the first two victims. Why?

Peter later tells the shaken Jess that he is "leaving the conservatory, and we're getting married." But Jess doesn't want to give up her ambitions just because Peter's plans have changed. "All right," he replies. "but what about the baby? You selfish bitch! You're talking about killing our baby like you'd have a wart removed... If you try to get an abortion, you're going to be very sorry." In the face of Peter's anger, Jess remains unmoved.

In an effort to find the killer, the police tap the sorority house phone. As everyone waits in fear, Peter stands outside the sorority house. A short time later, the killer in the attic moans sadly as he rocks Clare, who holds a doll in her cold arms.

Shortly after the killer has murdered foulmouthed Barb and Phyl in the upstairs of the sorority house, the phone rings and Jess answers. This time one of the raving voices says, "Just like having a wart removed," to which Jess gasps "Oh, my God!"

After another cryptic call, the police discover that the calls are coming from within the sorority house and warn Jess accordingly. The killer immediately goes after Jess, and she evades him by locking herself in the basement. The killer is soon revealed to be Peter, who dies while struggling to kill his sweetheart. Ironically, had he killed her, he would also have killed the baby he apparently wanted to save. Anyway, Daddy's hunt is over.

After the authorities arrive and sedate Jess, the spirit of Christmas and peace appears to descend on the house. But as the police work outside the house and Jess lies asleep within, vague, mad babbling begins, followed by the ominous ringing of the telephone.

So who is the killer? Well, Peter is certainly the killer. We saw him attack Jess and we heard the obscene caller repeat the "wart" analogy. The pressbook itself makes clear that the killer is a deranged student, and the only character in the film fitting that description is Peter. Unfortunately, the ending doesn't work unless we seriously entertain the idea that two killers were collaborating. One killer was killed, and the other (a woman?) remained in the house. But this is a cheat ending. It just doesn't work. And what were those cryptic phone messages all about? Still, these are the only artistic flaws in *Black Christmas*. The screenwriter's temptation to get too clever with the "surprise" ending damages our final response to the film. Nevertheless, *Black Christmas* generally delivers the goods—at least enough to influence other horror films of the '70s and beyond. We see the most direct influence in *When a Stranger Calls* (1979). But, for better or for worse, it was the plot and moral ambiguities of *Black Christmas* that led the way.

Despite the fumbled ending, *Black Christmas* works on most levels. It is suspenseful, the characters are engaging and the terrifying murders contrast effectively with the general aura of Christmas celebration sustained throughout the film. It is a jarring picture buttressed by strong performances on the part of all concerned and by the sure hand of producer/director Bob Clark. My problem with the film is its implicit message—that pro-life people are hypocritical psychotic murderers while pro-choice people are caring, life-embracing individuals. Choosing a Christmas setting for such a message is creative, maybe even brilliant, but nevertheless in poor taste.
—DGS

The following genre films all occur or have scenes pertaining to Christmas:

Batman Returns
Cast: Michael Keaton, Danny DeVito; Michelle Pfeiffer; Christopher Walken; Michael Gough
Credits: Producers: Denise DiNovi and Tim Burton; Director: Tim Burton; Writers: Daniel Waters and Sam Hamm (Based on characters by Bob Kane); Warner Bros.; 1992

Holy Christmas Disaster, Batman! The Penguin (Danny DeVito) gleefully disrupts Gotham City during the Christmas season leaving few survivors in his wake. But never fear, Bruce Wayne, aka Batman (Michael Keaton), saves the day. The film is generally detested by critics but is worth watching for the stunning Michelle Pfeiffer, whose sleekly sexy Catwoman steals the show and gleefully pays back those who have wronged her in the past, including the evil Max Shreck (Christopher Walken) who tossed her from a skyscraper.

Conquest of Space
Cast: Walter Brooke, Eric Fleming, Mickey Shaughnessy, Phil Foster
Credits: Producer: George Pal; Director: Bryon Haskin; Writers: James O'Hanlon, Philip Yordan, Barre Lyndon and George Worthing Yates (Based on *The Mars Project* by Chesley Bonestell and Willy Ley); Paramount; 1955

Christmas on Mars in *Conquest of Space*.

A spaceship crew takes off for Mars against the better judgment of some of the crew members. While on Mars, Brooke goes crazy and starts to release all of the ship's water needed for the return flight. When Fleming tries to prevent him from killing them all, he is forced to shoot Brooke, who plays his father. A depression sets in over the ship, "It's going to be a long cold winter" one notes, when the strains of "God Rest Ye Merry Gentlemen" is heard. It is now December 25. The men drink a toast using precious water amidst decorations hung on the instruments. A Christmas miracle occurs as it begins to snow on Mars and the crew rushes out to gather the snow for a return trip.

Curse of the Cat People
Cast: Simone Simon, Kent Smith, Jane Randolph, Ann Carter, Elizabeth Russell, Julia Dean
Credits: Producer: Val Lewton; Director: Robert Wise; Writer: DeWitt Bodeen; RKO, 1944

Do not be put off by the title of this film, for rather than being a horror film, the story is of Amy's (Ann Carter) fantasy friend Irena (Simone Simon) and the fear her imagination sparks in her father (Kent Smith). Amy is very shy and has no friends, but finds solace in her imaginary friend Irena and Julia Farren (Dean), an old actress she has befriended. Amy learns not to talk about Irena because it upsets her father. On Christmas she brings down packages for everyone including Mrs. Farren. When her parents ask who the unmarked present is for, she hesitates but is saved by carolers at the front door. As they sing around the piano, she hears Irena singing a French carol in the garden and gives her the present. Irena covers the trees with ice and lights them up as her present for Amy.

When Amy gives her present to Mrs. Farren, the woman tells her she has not had a Christmas present in a very long time, even though an unopened present from her daughter is beside her.

A Christmas scene from the fantasy *Curse of the Cat People*.

When the family is taking down the Christmas tree a photo falls from an album, and Amy excitedly asks her father how he knows her friend. The picture is of his first wife Irena, and he is distraught that Amy thinks his dead ex-wife is her friend. He takes her to the garden and demands she tell him Irena is not there. When Amy refuses, he takes her upstairs and spanks her. Irena comes to her in the bedroom and tells Amy she must send her away and fades from the room. Amy runs outside into a snowstorm searching for Irena. She is lost and frightened but manages to find Mrs. Farren's house. The actress' daughter (Russell) is jealous of the love her mother gives Amy and has threatened to kill the child the next time she visits. Irena saves Amy and, when the search party finds the child, her father decides to try to accept her imaginary friend.

Dead of Night
Cast: Mervyn Johns, Roland Culver, Mary Merrall, Sally Ann Howes
Credits: Producer: Michael Balcon; Director "The Christmas Story" Alberto Cavalcanti; Writers: John Baines, Angus Macphail and T.E.B. Clarke; Rank; 1945

A truly frightening horror film with five separate stories. "The Christmas Story" is related by Sally Ann Howes and her remembrances of attending a Christmas party as a child. While playing a game of hide-and-seek she hides upstairs behind a curtain with another child, Jimmy, who tells her about a horrible murder that occurred in the house where a young girl killed her brother in 1860. Howes goes off by herself and finds a weeping child in a nursery whom she comforts. Howes later learns that she was comforting the ghost of the murdered child.

Edward Scissorshands
Cast: Johnny Depp, Winona Ryder, Dianne Wiest, Kathy Baker, Anthony Michael Hall, Vincent Price, Alan Arkin
Credits: Producers: Tim Burton and Denise DiNovi; Director: Tim Burton; Writers: Caroline Thompson and Tim Burton; 20th Century Fox; 1990

Tim Burton's beautifully surrealistic film about an inventor (Vincent Price) who created Edward but didn't have time to finish his hands before he died. Edward (Depp) has scissors for hands and lives alone in a castle high atop a hill overlooking a pastel-washed suburban town. He is discovered by Peg Boggs (Wiest) and taken down into a much more bizarre place than the dark castle, suburbia. At first this strange creature is a novelty, and people turn out in droves to

Kim (Winona Ryder) and Edward (Johnny Depp) watch for angry suburbanites in *Edward Scissorshands*.

and becoming a menace to society.

The Boggses, happily unaware of the neighbors' feelings, prepare for their annual Christmas party; Bill applies roles of white cloth to his roof for snow, while Kim and Peg decorate the white artificial Christmas tree. Kim sees snow falling outside and finds Edward carving a glorious ice angel, the falling ice making a snow storm in the warm climate. Kim is enchanted and dances in the falling snow. Burton films this scene with slow-motion and close-up shots, making it unforgettable. As Edward is climbing down from the ladder, Kim is distracted by Jim and Edward accidentally cuts her. Jim causes a fuss and Edward must run for safety. Peg and Bill frantically search for him as he returns to their house where he finds Kim and she asks him to hold her, but he is afraid for he can only hurt her if he gets too close. She lifts his arms and places them around her, unafraid of the gentle Edward. But once again Jim arrives and the townspeople gather in the form of a Universal horror film torch-wielding mob. Kim tells Edward to run and he heads for the safety of the castle.

see him. He begins to cut the hair of the town women who adore the shy boy. But things turn ugly when he resists the advances of Joyce (Kathy Baker), a bored woman and when Wiest's daughter Kim (Ryder) takes a liking to Edward, angering her domineering boyfriend Jim (Hall). A group of teens, including Hall, use Depp to break into Hall's house and scatter when the police arrive, all that is but Depp. He is arrested and soon the gossips have him almost raping Joyce

Kim finds him there but so does Jim. The two fight and Edward stabs Jim and he falls out a window. Kim realizes there is only one thing to do and the two say good-bye as she takes a spare hand from the inventor's shop. Covered with blood, she walks outside and tells the waiting crowd the two killed each other and Edward's body was covered by a cave-in.

The subdued crowd turns and leaves behind the body of Jim and Edward, the haunted boy in the castle.

Years later an old woman tells the story to her granddaughter to explain why it now snows in the valley and why she never went back to find Edward.

Star Trek: Generations
Cast: Patrick Stewart, William Shatner, Jonathan Frakes, Brent Spiner, Malcolm McDowell
Credits: Producer: Rick Berman; Director: David Carson; Writers: Brannon Braga and Ronald D. Moore (Based on characters created by Gene Roddenberry); Paramount; 1994

When Captain Picard (Stewart) follows villain Soran (McDowell) to a planet surface, he is swept up in the Nexus, a phenomena that gives everyone trapped there their dearest wish. Picard finds himself happily settled into a cozy home complete with loving wife and adorable children who are preparing to celebrate the traditional Victorian Christmas. Beautifully filmed Christmas scenes make this essential viewing for Christmas fanatics.

Static
Cast: Keith Gordon, Amanda Plummer, Bob Gunton
Credits: Producer: Amy Ness; Director: Mark Romanek; Writers: Mark Romanek and Keith Gordon; Necessity; 1985

This independent film follows the adventures of Gordon as he tries to invent a television set that will show heaven. His parents were killed in an auto accident and he hopes to see them. On Christmas Eve he unveils his invention, but he is the only one who can see anything; everyone else sees static.

Credits:

Black Christmas
Cast: Olivia Hussey, Keir Dullea, Margot Kidder, Andrea Martin, John Saxon
Credits: Producer/Director: Bob Clark; Writer: Roy Moore; Ambassador; 1974

Christmas Evil
Cast: Brandon Maggart, Dianne Hull, Scott McKay, Joe Jamrog, Peter Friedman
Credits: Producers: Burt Kleiner and Pete Kameron; Director/Writer: Lewis Jackson; Pressman; 1980

Don't Open Till Christmas
Cast: Edmund Purdom, Alan Lake, Belinda Mayne, Gerry Sundquist, Caroline Munro
Credits: Producers: Dick Randall and Steve Minasian; Director: Edmund Purdom; Writers: Derek Ford and Al McGoohan; Spectacular; 1984

Dorm that Dripped Blood
Cast: Laurine Lapinski, Stephen Sachs, David Snow, Pamela Holland
Credits: Producer: Jeffrey Obrow; Directors: Jeffrey Obrow and Stephen Carpenter; Writers: Jeffrey Obrow, Stephen Carpenter and Stacey Giachino; New Image; 1983

Gremlins
Cast: Zach Galligan, Phoebe Cates, Hoyt Axton, Polly Holliday, Dick Miller, Keye Luke
Credits: Producer: Michael Finnell; Director: Joe Dante; Writer: Chris Columbus; Warner Bros.; 1984

The Nightmare Before Christmas
Cast: (voices) Danny Elfman, Chris Sarandon, Catherine O'Hara, William Hickey, Ed Ivory
Credits: Producers: Tim Burton, Denise DiNovi and Kathleen Gavin; Director: Henry Selick; Writer: Caroline Thompson; Buena Vista; 1993

Silent Night, Deadly Night
Cast: Lilyan Chauvin, Gilmer McCormick, Toni Nero, Robert Brian Wilson
Credits: Producer: Ira Richard Barmak; Director: Charles E. Sellier; Writer: Michael Hickey; TriStar; 1984

Silent Night, Deadly Night 2
Cast: Eric Freeman, James L. Newman, Elizabeth Clayton, Jean Miller
Credits: Producer: Lawrence Applebaum; Director/Writer: Lee Harry; Ascot; 1987

Silent Night, Deadly Night 3: Better Watch Out
Cast: Richard Beymer, Bill Moseley, Samatha Scully, Elizabeth Hoffman
Credits: Producer: Arthur H. Gorson; Director: Monte Hellman; Writer: Carlos Laszlo; Quiet; 1989

Silent Night, Deadly Night 5: the Toymaker
Cast: Mickey Rooney, William Thorne, Brian Bremer, Tracy Faun
Credits: Producers: Brian Yuzna and Richard N. Gladstein, Director: Martin Kitrosser; Writer: Martin Kitrosser and Brian Yuzna; Silent Films; 1991

Thirteenth Day of Christmas
Cast: Patrick Allen, Elizabeth Spriggs
Credits: British Television; 1985

To All a Good Night
Cast: Buck West, Sam Shamshak, Katherine Herington
Credits: Producer: Sandy Cobe; Director: David Hess; Writer: Alex Rebar; IRC; 1980

Whoever Slew Auntie Roo? (U.S. *Who Slew Auntie Roo?*)
Cast: Shelley Winters, Mark Lester, Ralph Richardson, Lionel Jeffries, Judy Cornwell
Credits: Producers: Samuel Z. Arkoff and James H. Nicholson; Director: Curtis Harrington; Writers: Robert Blees, Jimmy Sangster and Gavin Lambert; AIP; 1971

We're Happy Tonight...

Today, every holiday is celebrated on TV, including Christmas, Thanksgiving, Halloween, New Year's, and sometimes even Valentine's Day. It seems that the increasingly shorter and shorter network TV broadcasting year segues from one holiday to the next.

However, during television's early decades—the 1950s and the 1960s—Christmas episodes were out of the ordinary and felt special. Often writers cleverly developed special holiday episodes for very un-Christmas-like programs. Some Christmas episodes felt natural as if they belonged, while others seemed out-of-place and obtrusive.

The intention here is not to document every Christmas show produced for early television, but to examine a sampling of several and to draw conclusions about how the holiday season fared on network TV during the 1950s and 1960s.

Pictured above is the cover of the *I Love Lucy* and *The Honeymooners* Christmas laser disc "A TV Christmas Present."

The Burns and Allen Show (Oct. 1950-Sept. 1958)
"Holiday Show"

George Burns and Gracie Allen based their weekly television show on clever dialogue, one-liners and jokes—there never was very much plot evident. Often, to create a transition from one situation to the next, George, smoking a cigar, would conduct a monologue right in the middle of the show to move things along, or simply to offer a joke break. Even though "Holiday Show" is focused on Christmas, it is even more focused on the antics of Burns and Allen.

At the show's beginning, friend Harry (Fred Clarke) gives Gracie a Christmas present to hide for his wife Blanche (Bea Benadaret): a red alligator bag and shoes to match. Telling the concerned Gracie that the alligator died, Gracie counters by exclaiming, "I hope it did...!" Gracie is excited that family friend Mamie Kelly and her three children are coming to stay for the holidays and says George must be happy too. "Thirty million homes in this country, just my luck they're coming here," Gracie quotes her husband.

Harry is caught sneaking out of the house by Blanche and Gracie (he has to hide Blanche's present when Blanche appears suddenly on the scene). "I was inside talking to George... So help me I was... ask Gracie!" Without losing a beat, Gracie replies, "Better yet, ask George, he'll be home in a few minutes," as embarrassment is written all over Harry's face.

Then we have the first Burns monologue, puffing away on his cigar. He reminds the audience that only two days remain before Christmas, and only dopes wait this long to buy presents. "Thought I'd never get out of that store today!" He tells the audience, Gracie loves to speak to people she doesn't know, and she met a woman whose husband runs a Buffalo newspaper. Gracie asked her, "How did he ever teach him to read?" Another woman she met was buying gloves for her son to give to his teacher for Christmas. The woman feared they might be tight. Gracie tells her, "If they are, why don't you wait until they sober up."

Soon the house guests are arriving, and Gracie immediately makes the sleeping arrangements. In an almost risqué one-liner, Gracie tells Mamie that she can sleep with her in the master bedroom. Mamie states, "I don't wish to crowd George out." But Gracie mutters, "Don't worry, he won't be in it."

Gracie asks Harry to carry the luggage upstairs, but Harry looks at George standing a few feet away doing nothing. Gracie then shoves George clearing the way for Harry, but George grabs the bags anyway.

In a classic showbiz line, the kids ask if it is okay for them to go outside and play, and George deadpans, "I'll call my agent."

Mamie asks George to bring her big bag down, and after he does, she apologetically complains, it's the other large one she needs (to which George reminds her, feeling a little annoyed, that the other large one is *smaller* than the first). After bringing down the second bag, Mamie apologizes again and says, she was wrong, she still needs the first bag.

The rambling plot does not develop as much as it rolls on. Blanche is almost caught holding Harry's present, but immediately hands it over to Gracie and states it is a present for George. Harry innocently asks Gracie what it is, and in her confused state of mind, she mutters, "Guess." Harry then says, "It could be anything." Then Gracie beams brightly and declares, "That's what it is... George wanted one for a long time."

By this time the three children have found Harry's Christmas present for Blanche hidden in the closet— the alligator bag and shoes—and the kids prance around wearing the present. Blanche, to Harry's dismay, states she would never want to wear something like that!

The show ends with two major sequences. George Burns dresses up as Santa, his dark hair hanging out over the white Santa wig. After he gets advice from friend Harry Van Zell on how to win the children's confidence as Santa, the kids run down the stairs and say hello to their Uncle George.

Finally, Gracie tells the kids the story of Dickens' *A Christmas Carol*, but in her version Scrooge, Bob Cratchit and Tiny Tim go for a walk in the woods while their breakfast cools down. Even before Goldilocks makes her appearance, Gracie has moved on to Prince Charming with the glass slipper. She finishes with "She married him and guess who got all the money?" And in his unique way, George answers, "Walt Disney."

Once again, *The Burns and Allen Show* incorporated the Christmas holiday effortlessly into the plotline, but the focus wasn't on the holiday but on the annoying houseguests, the hiding of gifts, the fracturing of fairy tales and hen-pecked husband jokes. Never is a Christmas tree seen.

The Amos 'n' Andy Show (June 1951-June 1953)
"Christmas Show"

One of the more entertaining and seldom seen treasures of early television remains *The Amos 'n' Andy Show*, the first all black situation comedy. Called racist by many and said to perpetuate racial stereotypes by others, the show has never garnered the exposure it deserves, and in the early 1950s, it portrays Amos (Alvin Childress), Andy (Spencer Williams, Jr.) and the Kingfish (Tim Moore) as not being any dumber than any other characters to be found on the tube at this time, and in episodes such as this classic Christmas one, the characters reveal themselves to be multi-dimensional and caring human beings.

Andy Brown is very proud of his godchild, friend Amos' first daughter, and the two follow a ritual every Christmas Eve: They go out together and window shop at all the major downtown department stores. The child wishes it would snow tomorrow, thinking a white Christmas would be perfect. Looking at all the toys, the child asks Andy lots of questions that require Andy to make up answers. Seeing a Junior Paint Set for $5.95, the sign says easel additional. When asked what an easel is, Andy fakes it and says it is something you place on your head, with a little tassel, that keeps the head warm. Another sign offers Kiddie Furniture Set—$14.95, but the Perambulator is extra. Again asked what a Perambulator is, Andy says it is just like the easel, but there's no tassel. The girl looks admiringly at her uncle and swoons, "You know everything, don't you!"

Andy tells the child that he has to wrap some presents tonight, so there's only time to check out one more store window, and there Andy's godchild sees the present of her dreams. "That's a talking doll, Uncle Andy. It's my favorite." But her father already told her that Santa Claus couldn't afford it this year.

Returning to the Lodge, Andy and Lightning are wrapping presents and talking when the Kingfish walks on in, dropping hints about the $6.95 blue bathrobe and where it is sold in hopes Andy will buy it as a Christmas present for him. Pretending to measure the size of the Lodge door with his arms, the Kingfish lets Andy know that he will be coming up to the Lodge early tomorrow with a really big present for him. Andy, a sad look on his face, tells Kingfish he is embarrassed, that he is broke and doesn't have any money left to buy Kingfish a present. Immediately changing gears, the Kingfish tells Andy, that on second thought, he won't be arriving at the Lodge as early as expected tomorrow morning. "I have lots of packages to deliver, so I might not be here until February or March... don't wait up here for me!"

Andy is also embarrassed that all he could afford to buy for his godchild is another box of crayons, the exact same present he bought her nine years ago when she was born. So he immediately rushes to the Glove Department Store and offers to work anywhere doing anything to be able to afford that special talking doll. As fate would have it, the regular Santa Claus assistant had to leave early, so Andy is hired to be the rotund and jolly helper to Santa Claus. The man who hires him tells Andy to just call the floor walker if he runs into any problems. However, once out on the floor, the generally overwhelmed Andy calls for the floor walker at every opportunity he has. When the first child asks for a jet plane and train, and Andy asks the boy if he has been good all year, the child answers I won't drink my milk, and Andy calls for the floor walker, but the child changes his mind and says for these presents he will drink milk, letting Andy off the hook.

A tough older child approaches Santa and asks for a machine gun, and wants to know why he didn't get the skates he wanted last year. Putting Santa further on the spot, the same boy asks if there are trees up in the North Pole, to which Andy answers no, just snow. But the kids wants to know then where does Santa get all the oranges and apples he puts in stockings. In desperation Andy yells out for the floor walker again. But the day moves along and Andy speaks to his last child before closing time, feeling tired yet satisfied. The stock boy delivers Andy's doll and he exits the store a very satisfied man.

Taking the doll to Amos' home, he drops off presents for Amos and his wife and the other children, but the special package, from Santa Claus, Andy declares, is for his special godchild. Before Andy leaves to drop off other presents, Amos and the wife invite him to Christmas dinner tomorrow. Checking in on his daughter, Amos finds his daughter too excited to sleep, so she asks if he can listen to the radio for a while. Amos agrees, and the radio station is presenting a special musical choral version of *The Lord's Prayer*. Above the musical accompaniment, the loving father and taxicab driver, in his own way, explains the meaning of the prayer to his daughter. As she falls asleep, the camera closes in on her window, the snow beginning to fall, just in time for Christmas.

Too many people are afraid to rebroadcast *Amos 'n' Andy* in fear that it portrays the white man's stereotype of African-Americans, and while Lightning (Horace Stewart) is portrayed as being dumb and slow moving, and Andy is portrayed as being just a tad faster and smarter than Lightning, the sense of family and warmth that exists between friends always comes to the forefront in each episode. In this special Christmas one, we have the flashback of Amos calling up his friend Andy and waking him from a deep sleep. The disoriented friend, who at first forgets to get dressed before leaving his apartment, comes to the aid of a friend and comforts Amos in the delivery room while his wife is giving birth. We have the close rapport and camaraderie existing between Lightning and Andy, and even if the Kingfish is self-centered and only out to give a present when he can get one in return, there's still a close bond that exists between Andy and the Kingfish (shown in Andy's guilt at being broke and being unable to buy his friend a present). We have Andy's panic and guilt over only getting his goddaughter a box of crayons, and his trepidation and success at being a department store Santa helper (perhaps the only racist note of the entire show was calling a black Santa Claus Santa's helper and not the real thing), being able to earn his precious niece the present of her dreams. And when Andy arrives to deliver his Christmas Eve presents at Amos' home, he is taken into the family and accepted as an actual family member, given a present himself and reminded to be at Amos' family Christmas dinner, because Andy is a bachelor and alone for the holidays. And when Amos interprets the meaning of *The Lord's Prayer* to his daughter, the sense of family and commitment can be seen shining on the proud father's face. *Amos 'n' Andy* was always a comedy, and in comedies, the characters typically make fun of one another, and while some racial stereotypes may have been encouraged in the series, at least in this Christmas episode, a sense of family, community and caring rings through loud and strong.

Dragnet (Jan. 1952-Sept. 1959)
"The Big Baby Jesus"

Dragnet, one of television's favorite police dramas, opted for realism by focusing on the deadpan humor of the starring police officers themselves, Sergeant Joe Friday (Jack Webb) and his partner, Officer Frank Smith (Ben Alexander). Christmas season is a time of heightened emotions, and *Dragnet* tried its best to eradicate all emotion from the acting and the storylines. The challenge here is how to pull off a Christmas episode of the show without sacrificing the very qualities for which the show is known.

The opening sequence offers traditional *Dragnet* rapport, in a mock-serious tone that threatens to become parody at any second, even in the 1950s.

Joe Friday is writing his Christmas cards, licking stamps, seated at his office desk. Partner Frank enters carrying a large bundle of presents. "Would have sent them out [the cards] Monday but we had that stakeout," Friday mumbles. Frank, smiling, tells Joe, "You outta get married... The only system. Fay does all that stuff for me... laundry, mails cards." Frank then gives Joe a small present, offering the option of opening it now or later, adding that opening presents early puts you in a good mood. But Friday declines to open his now. Frank then hopes the precinct remains quiet, "I have more shopping to do." Joe states he's finished all his holiday shopping. When asked what he got Ann, he rattles off, "A stationery set, some paper and envelopes, leather binding." Frank, disturbed for his friend, says, "Joe, you'll never learn. No woman wants a stationery set—get her something personal." Deadly seriously he tells Smith, "It's got her initials on it." When Frank tells Joe he bought Fay a sewing machine for Christmas, Joe counters with, "That's romantic... why didn't you buy her a catcher's mitt?"

Then the phone rings, a desperate call from the Old Mission Church priest Father Rejas (Harry Bartell) who informs the police of a theft. Friday and Smith ride over to the old church, and the priest in-

forms them that their statue of baby Jesus was stolen from the nativity scene. He states it is not really expensive, costing only $70, but that parishioners took up a collection 31 years ago and that it is the only Jesus that they know. Being displayed during the Christmas holiday, this statue has become a tradition. The child Jesus was discovered missing after 6 a.m. mass. It was present, according to an altar boy, last night (the church was open for Confession). Simply purchasing a new statue wouldn't mean as much, and the father wishes to have the statue back by Christmas mass tomorrow.

The priest concludes by stating, "Sad, in so short a time men learn to steal." And Joe Friday, in his own sensitive style, retorts, "If some of them didn't, you and I would be out of work."

After putting watchdogs on all the local pawn shops, Friday and Smith go to the area's largest religious shop, owned by Mr. Flavin (Ralph Moody), who is asked if he stocks any statues of the child Jesus. He pulls out a small one, but Friday asks about a larger-sized one. Pulling out one that would be used by a church, Flavin shakes his head and states, "This will make your living room look off kilter." The policeman ask if anyone ever sells a statue back, and Flavin says never, such a person would have to be crazy.

Joe, the altar boy, comes down to headquarters to speak to Sgt. Friday. Joe served 6 a.m. mass and has the "feeling" that the statue was there before mass, although he is not certain. But he did see one man there, a regular to morning mass, who is described as being "pretty old... about 40, I guess." The boy remembers he was carrying a bundle the size of the baby Jesus.

This mystery man, Claude Stroup (James Griffith), becomes the red herring for the rest of the episode, as Friday and Smith track him down to his home, a derelict hotel called the Golden Dream, but he is away. The hotel clerk (Herb Vigran) states that this was the seventh year of the Christmas Program, where residents put up a tree and sing carols, and that Claude has never missed the Program yet, until now. The clerk states that Claude has a history of robbery "way far back, but he forgot all that."

Soon Claude is apprehended at the hotel and taken down to police headquarters, but says nothing. Turns out, his only crime is borrowing a friend's car and scraping another car's bumper, causing him to panic from fear of getting in trouble.

Friday and Smith return to the church to tell Father Rejas the bad news, that the statue will never will retrieved by Christmas morning, when suddenly a little boy with a red wagon appears. In that wagon is, you guessed it, the statue. It seems this poor parish child wished for a wagon for years and this year prayed to the baby Jesus for his toy, promising Jesus the first ride if he ever got his wish. The boy, in fear that the Devil will appear and take him to Hell, is returning the statue. Carefully placing the statue back into position in the Nativity scene, the young boy quietly pulls his wagon down the aisle to leave. The choral music swells as the story ends.

Surprisingly, working with a small crime with a poor parish involving an innocent child repaying his promise to Jesus, *Dragnet* takes on a poignancy rarely found in the series. Avoiding icons and stereotypes (a redeemed bank robber, an over-worked precinct on Christmas Eve, a reformed criminal who portrays Santa and who is accused of committing a crime, etc.), *Dragnet* deals with the little, neglected people and their Christmas spirit transcends the $70 missing statue. Even though Jack Webb and Ben Alexander are as deadpan as ever, their silent dedication to returning the statue by Christmas morning mass expresses more emotion than the duo would ever be allowed to do.

I Love Lucy
(Oct. 1951-Sept. 1961)
"Christmas Special"

I Love Lucy, perhaps the most popular TV situation comedy of all time, hosted a special Christmas Eve special December 24, 1956, which used the holiday to present a "Best of" reprise of some of the earlier episodes. Featuring the classic team of Desi Arnaz, Lucille Ball and Vivian Vance and William Frawley, and Keith Thibodeaux as Little Ricky, the ensemble added the warmth of Christmas to the comedic shenanigans.

Christmas ornaments based on the popular *I Love Lucy* "Christmas Special." Available from Command Performance 1-800-873-8263

Ricky is hanging stockings on the fireplace mantel, with Lucy making sure each stocking's position is properly balanced. Little Ricky, dressed in his pajamas, is excited that this is Christmas Eve and sits in his little chair directly in front of the fireplace, awaiting Santa Claus. However, the folks tell him that Santa won't bring the Christmas tree or the presents until he is fast asleep. To which Little Ricky

asks why, and Lucy turns over the explanation to Daddy. Ricky tells his son that Santa's sleigh circles around the neighborhood rooftops awaiting his signal, and Little Ricky fills in the fact that the Sandman must be the one who signals when children are all fast asleep. Then looking up the chimney and not seeing steps, Little Ricky wonders how Santa gets safely down the chimney. Daddy turns this one over to Lucy, she says Santa slides down the chimney like a fireman slides down his pole. Ricky buys it and goes off to sleep.

Immediately Fred and Ethel enter the apartment carrying a tree they just purchased from the neighborhood tree lot. Ricky asks how much it costs, and Ethel says the tree's on us, which of course causes Fred to complain, "The tree cost five bucks!" Ethel, expecting such a reaction, says, "We have our own Scrooge here... it's a present from me and Ebenezer!"

Lucy goes to the closet and brings out the ornaments and boxes of decorations. However, she notices that one branch on the right is unbalanced, so Fred will have to go down to the cellar and bring back his saw. After decorating trees with Ricky and Lucy for 15 years, he has the saw inside his coat and starts trimming. But as soon as one branch is cut on one side, Lucy sees another limb that needs to be trimmed on the other. Fred keeps trimming as the first flashback story occurs, the night that Lucy told Ricky, at the club, that she was pregnant.

At the end of the story, all four friends are crying, reflecting upon just how much better Little Ricky made their already grand Christmases. However, Fred says he's crying for a different reason, showing everyone the tree which now looks butchered and uneven. Ethel yells at Fred to go down to the lot and buy another tree, and we will pay! Soon Ricky leads the gang in a chorus of "Jingle Bells," but every time Lucy joins in, she sings so far off key that the others stop dead in their tracks. "I don't seem to sing well lately, anymore," Lucy confesses. "Lately," one person comments, "Anymore!" another adds. This brings us to flashback two, with Ethel, Fred and Ricky, at the club, singing a barbershop quarter number, with the fourth member, George Watson, in the barber chair, his face covered with a towel. However, the toweled face is soon revealed to be Lucy, who sings off key, forcing the others to silence her by shoving a brush with shaving cream into her mouth.

Fred delivers the new tree, better looking than the first, and since it was late, he was only charged half a buck, and the guy threw in some mistletoe. Beginning to decorate the tree, Lucy tries to get Ricky to offer a hint about her Christmas present, but he tells her to wait until tomorrow morning. Holding the mistletoe above her head, Lucy gets a passionate kiss and hug from Ricky. Ethel, borrowing the same mistletoe and holding it above her head, yells, "Freddy, go ahead!" Fred, looking solemnly at his wife, quips, "You're an incurable optimist," but then even he melts and kisses his wife. Soon the lights are strung on the tree, and for the first time in 15 years, they light immediately. However, suddenly the lights out go forcing the group to check each individual light, something they now consider an enjoyable ritual. This leads into flashback three, the night Lucy went into labor causing massive panic among Fred, Ricky and Ethel in getting Lucy to the hospital.

By now the tree is completely decorated, and presents line the entire living room, especially Little Ricky's new bike and drum set. Ricky begins to stir, and all four adults, now dressed in their complete Santa Claus outfits, decide to hide in the kitchen. However, a fifth Santa Claus, Fred, comes in the kitchen from outside, so how could five Santa Clauses possibly be in the kitchen? "Just a minute," someone says as they all pull down each other's beards, revealing their true identity. However, when pulling the beard of the stranger, he screams out "ooouch" letting the others know his beard is real. Then, mysteriously, he fades away amidst the tinkling of Christmas sounds. Dumbfounded, Ricky, Fred, Ethel and Lucy yell out, "Merry Christmas, everyone" as the show ends.

This Christmas motif serves as a wonderful comedic framing device for the producer to replay all the significant Little Ricky segments (including the announcement of his birth and Lucy going into labor), since the Christmas show is focused on the child and the happiness the five-year-old brought to the Ricardo household. The other flashback is merely icing on the cake, playing up Lucy's pathological urge to perform at the club and sing when she has such a horrible voice. The final surprise with Santa adds a dash of magic, and the sight of seeing the entire cast dressed as Santa is a delight. While this is not one of the classic episodes, this special episode does bring the charm of the holidays to the *I Love Lucy* cast, and for that reason alone, it becomes quite special.

The Jack Benny Show
(Oct. 1950-Aug. 1977)
"Christmas With Jack"

Comedian Jack Benny hosted a weekly television series similar to the one hosted by George Burns: Both shows revolved around the starring comedian, who interacted with an ensemble cast of characters who appeared regularly on the series. On the Benny show the star traded barbs with hefty announcer Don Wilson, milquetoast singer Dennis Day and black chauffeur Eddie "Rochester" Anderson. Benny created a TV persona of being a skin-flint cheapie, afraid to part with a dollar. This classic Christmas episode played strongly upon that persona.

The show opens in a crowded department store, with Christmas music playing in the background, as the crowds swarm around one sale table. As the women are shrieking to get closer, out crawls Jack Benny from under a woman's legs saying, "Christmas shopping gets worse every year!"

Asking Rochester for his Christmas list, Benny announces to his manservant that he wishes to buy his present today, but to avoid buying the same present as last year, he asks, "What did I get you last year?"Rochester replies, "A brand new dollar bill—and a lecture on the evils of wine, woman and song!"

Deciding to get Don Wilson's present first, he chooses to purchase a wallet. Looking at nice ones for $1.98, Rochester mentions better ones are over here, but they cost $40. "You've known him a long time, boss," Rochester quips. Surprisingly, Benny agrees and asks to have the present both wrapped and delivered, after he writes a card. "To Don: This gift is from Jackie, oh golly oh shucks, I hope that you like it, it costs 40 bucks!" The dutiful cashier (Mel Blanc, the voice of Warner Bros. cartoons) promises to specially wrap the present and get it to the mailroom immediately (my, how times have changed!).

Moving on to his wife Mary, Benny decides to look for the jewelry department and stops the floorwalker Mr. Nelson (Frank Nelson) for directions. Asking the man if he is indeed the store floorwalker, Nelson counters with a caustic, "What do you think I am with a carnation, a float in the Rose Parade!" Benny does not allow the snide employee to get the upper hand, but Nelson counters with, "My father owns the store." Benny then asks, "Working your way up?" Nelson responds, "No, I started out as president!" A robber wearing a mask directs Benny to the jewelry department where the comedian wishes aloud, "Hope they still have a nice selection."

Benny finally asks to see watches, and the salesperson asks him if he needs a watch for a man, a woman or a dog ("this is Beverly Hills, you know"), and Benny states a woman's watch. He is shown two—one that sells for $120 and another for $12. Benny cannot tell the difference between the two so he buys the cheaper one. The salesperson states it has an unbreakable crystal and encourages Benny to use the hammer provided to try to break the watch. With one slam the watch explodes into pieces, but he is refused his money back.

Dennis Day soon appears, claiming that he has to work as a singer in the department store because he cannot afford to live on Mr. Benny's salary. This allows a chance for Day to sing a Christmas song in Santa's Workshop with Santa and children present.

The primary humor occurs from Benny deciding that his first card for Don Wilson wasn't appropriate, so he gets the overworked cashier to reopen the already wrapped gift and insert a new card: "To Don: A Merry Christmas, Jack." Later, someone mentions that Benny is not the only Jack in the world, so he decides he has to change the card again. This time Mel Blanc is much more flustered, crying that the package already went down to delivery. He bemoans, "Why did the governor have to give me that pardon!!!" Fetching the box, the cashier tries to act calm, but it is apparent that he is at the end of his rope.

Meanwhile, Rochester goes to buy a present for Mr. Benny, but he doesn't know what to get. The salesperson offers advice: Is he the playboy type, the outdoors type, intellectual type, athletic type, the executive type? To which Rochester shakes his head and answers no. The clerk states, "Afraid there isn't much left!" To which Rochester snaps back, "That's him!"

Benny, of course, decides to change Wilson's card again, and when the comedian appears, Mel Blanc lets loose with a rip-snorting scream. Quickly calming down, the cashier keeps repeating, "The customer is always right," as he leaves to fetch the box. Blanc returns disheveled, stating the package already made it to the delivery truck, but that he got it back, looking like the truck dragged him for blocks. He then reminds Benny to sign the card.

Rochester reminds Benny it's the thought that counts, not the cost, that it doesn't matter if a present costs $40 or $1.98. Benny then decides he need not purchase the $40 wallet for Wilson, that the $2 one will do. Of course this means a return to cashier Mel Blanc who simply cries and moans, and when Benny states he wishes to exchange the more expensive wallet for the cheaper one, the cashier pulls out a gun and walks to the back storeroom where a shot rings out seconds later. Benny, leaning over to open the cash register, reminds himself that he is due some change, which he grabs without shame.

Very much a Christmas story, and very much a black comedy, daring for network television, "Christmas With Jack" becomes a laugh riot based upon carefully building comedic situations fueled by Jack's "cheap" persona and his interactions with gifted comics such as Frank Nelson, Eddie Anderson and Mel Blanc, whose performance is exceptional (his slow burn to rage and insanity is subtle and carefully developed). Benny had his pulse on the commercialization of Christmas and wanted to make a statement about the difference between spending money out of obligation and buying gifts because of the thought that counts—and he made such poignancy hilarious.

Racket Squad (June 1951-Sept. 1953)
"The Christmas Caper"
The hard-hitting police drama *Racket Squad*, attempting to make the public more aware by exposing con-

fidence men and their scams, seems the last program to offer a tender Christmas story. Yet, "The Christmas Caper," directed by horror veteran director Erle C. Kenton (*Island of Lost Souls, Ghost of Frankenstein*), offers an affecting story that touches the heart.

Captain John Braddock (Reed Hadley), head of the city's Racket Squad, is shown at work as the series begins, filing papers, etc. Directly facing the audience, Braddock states, "This is a real story." However, he adds that this is a different story in two ways from the ones generally shown: first: "Just because it is a Christmas story"; second: "It put me on the spot... I had to arrest Santa Claus."

The story begins in the tenements as elderly, retired Charles Dooley (Lloyd Corrigan) entertains all the neighborhood children who lovingly call him Uncle Dooley. His favorite is young Anne Marie (Jeri Lou James) who needs surgery for her legs, whom he offers to read a very special Christmas tale, "A Visit From St. Nicholas," or "'Twas the Night Before Christmas." One of the hard-boiled kids mutters, "Sounds like a lot of bunk to me." But after the story is told, the kids remain transfixed, disappointed that they seldom receive Christmas presents. Dooley states that perhaps they don't receive presents because they do not write letters to Santa. As the children's eyes light up, Dooley covers himself by stating that it may be a little too late to write this year, as Christmas is so close. Santa lives all the way up at the North Pole. One smart aleck offers, "What's the matter with air mail?" Asking the children to make a list of things they wish to have on Christmas, Dooley states that everyone will receive *something* on Christmas.

One concerned parent visits Dooley and speaks for all the worried parents. "The other parents, they send me to see you about, well, telling the children they're going to get Christmas presents. I know you mean well..." She complains that now the children expect more expensive presents, but that children forget disappointment quickly, so not to worry.

Dooley, not wishing to disillusion the children, searches the newspaper for a part-time job over the holidays, and he applies to "The Yuletide Agency," fronted by two con artists, Pennington (John "Jackie" Coogan) and Castle (Alan Dexter), who claim they hire sidewalk Santas for local charities. Dooley will make $10 per day, but he won't be paid until Christmas Eve at 7 p.m. If he raises enough money for the charity, he will also earn a bonus. However, the sign he is given stating that money will be donated to the "Society for the Deserving Poor Children" is not recognized by the passing-by city's Chairman of Organized Charities, who reports Dooley to the Racket Squad.

By the last day of collection on Christmas Eve, one of the scoundrels comes by with his briefcase to collect the money, but sensing he is being watched (which he is, by Braddock), dumps all his briefcase money into Dooley's kettle, and returns to the office. There Braddock arrests him and soon catches the other crook. But neither has any money on their person, so Braddock orders that Dooley be arrested.

After the action slows down, Dooley innocently returns to the Agency to turn in his money, but a black janitor (Willie Best) informs Dooley of the con, and Dooley decides to spend all the money on the children, buying them Christmas presents.

Braddock gets Dooley's address from the confidence men, and with his partner journeys to the apartment building to find all the neighbors celebrating in Dooley's apartment with the lovable old man dressed up as Santa and giving children and their mothers presents. For his beloved Anne Marie he starts a fund to pay for her medical needs. Braddock, who observes all this, asks Dooley to step outside and states he is under arrest. When Dooley asks if he could have a few more minutes to finish giving out gifts, Dooley tells the children that Santa and Uncle Dooley will both be returning to the North Pole, but Uncle Dooley will be returning later. Braddock, following the letter and spirit of the law, tells his partner, "Mr. Dooley didn't steal any money. The money he collected was for deserving children, to make Christmas happy for them." Braddock then releases Dooley and even gives him his own money to contribute to Anne Marie's fund. And he states his partner would also be glad to contribute. They wish Dooley a very merry Christmas and leave.

For 1950s television, the law was pretty cut and dried, black and white, few gray areas. Interestingly enough, *Racket Squad* has lead character Captain John Braddock use the phrase "spirit and letter" of the law, and seeing the kindness and charity which the naive Dooley is offering to the children, lets him go free. Of course, in the real world, the police would have to confiscate the criminal money and use it as evidence, but this is a Christmas story, and even the hard-hitting *Racket Squad* had to show a little compassion for the time of the year. While Reed Hadley is stiff as required, in a Jack Webb sort of way, the other actors, especially character actor Lloyd Corrigan, offer impassioned, emotional performances that truly touch the heart. Sometime the spirit of Santa perfectly fits in this world of devious crime and hard-boiled police action.

The Honeymooners (Oct. 1955-May 1971)
"'Twas the Night Before Christmas"
One of the defining programs of early television, without doubt, is Jackie Gleason's *The Honeymooners*, a comedic masterpiece that sang the praises of the American working-class people. The interchange be-

tween Gleason and Art Carney (as best pal Ed Norton) lies at the heart of the series' success. Also Ralph's sad-sack relationship with wife Alice (Audrey Meadows) is quite complex. Externally Ralph is all bluster, rants and raves, always threatening to send his wife to the moon with just one punch, but internally, Ralph loves Alice to death and wouldn't lift a finger to ever harm her. She realizes that (quite literally wearing the pants in that family) but gives Ralph enough elbow room to allow him to assert his mythical superiority in his own mind and among his male friends. Gleason's acting is masterful: He is wizard of verbal humor, is quite adept at physical humor—even with his bulk—and he can bring a tear to the eye, when making a fool out of himself and then admitting he was wrong, and can ask for forgiveness. So much humanity and soul exists within the person of Ralph that his performance alone catapults the show to classic status, but with his gifted cast of supporting players, the show goes even further.

Christmas is the ideal setting for *The Honeymooners*, working folks who barely have enough money to buy a Christmas present, but people who reverently uphold the idea of what Christmas means and hold it dearly in their hearts. The episode begins with both Alice and Ralph sneaking into the kitchen of their apartment, each clutching a wrapped Christmas present for the other spouse, looking to find a hiding place for the gift until Christmas morning tomorrow. Interestingly, each character goes to exactly the same hiding places (a drawer in the cabinet, the oven) before settling on underneath the ice box behind a drainage pan.

Trixie (Jane Randolph) sneaks down to tell Alice that Ed already gave her his Christmas present, an orange juice squeezer in the shape of Napoleon whereby the juice flows out of his ear. Not exactly the most romantic present, but men will be men. But soon Alice comes upon Ralph hiding her present, telling him that's where she hid his. Ralph begs to exchange presents tonight, but when Alice puts her foot down, Ralph calms down, says he's no kid and can wait. However, pretending to run out to Trixie's apartment, Alice in fact hides near the door, and after the door is slammed, Ralph runs out pulling the package from under the ice box. But as he rises, Alice is there to confront him. Alice thinks she has made the point that she has to hide his present again, that she cannot trust him to leave it alone before Christmas morning. But in a guilty pout Ralph shouts, "You're the one not to be trusted... you said you were going out!" Alice goes off and hides the package. She returns and tells Ralph that she trusts him and tells him exactly where the present has been hidden, as she finally leaves to see Trixie. As soon as she is gone, Ralph charges toward the back room, and within seconds, the audience hears the snap of a mouse trap and a loud yell of pain, as Ralph reappears in the kitchen with the trap curled around his fingers.

Soon Ed Norton appears, ready to exchange presents with Ralph. Looking at each box and noting the similarity in shape, Ralph concludes they each bought one another a tie. Norton looks perplexed and says, no, he bought Ralph spats, something for the man who has everything. At first becoming angry over such a useless present, Ralph cools down and says, "I know it came from your heart!" To which Norton deadpans, "No, it came from the fat man's shop!"

After getting his hand caught in the mouse trap one more time, Ralph retrieves his present to Alice, opens and shows it to Norton: a hair pin box made of 2,000 matchsticks. Both men are impressed and even more so when Ralph tells Norton that the salesman said this box is one of a kind and came from the home of the Emperor of Japan. Being so excited, and egged on by Norton, Ralph decides to give it to Alice tonight, but he is interrupted by the sudden appearance of a neighbor, Mrs. Stevens, who is leaving to visit her sister so she wishes to exchange presents with Alice tonight. Alice gives her a kitchen thermometer, but Stevens gives Alice the exact same one-of-a-kind hair pin box that Ralph purchased for Alice. Stevens says she feels embarrassed giving her the box after the wonderful present that Alice gave her and tells Alice she purchased the box from a little novelty shop down near the subway station.

Creating the pathos that Gleason is so wonderful at generating, Ralph feels both cheated and embarrassed by his own greed. He tells Norton he saved up $22, but instead of spending it on his wife, he went out and bought the bowling ball he wanted for some time. Ralph could kick himself in the head for not using that money to buy Alice a special gift. However, Uncle Leo quickly stops by the apartment, receiving a wrapped present from Alice and Ralph, and leaving a $25 gift certificate to Watson's Department Store for them. Stating he can replace the money next week, Ralph hurriedly leaves to buy his wife a present, but she comes in just as he is leaving. "You know who I met downstairs," Alice merrily asks. His smile quickly turning into a frown, Ralph says, yes I know, and turns over the gift certificate to Alice telling her this is what Uncle Leo left. "Uncle Leo was here?" Alice exclaims, stating she was talking about one of the neighborhood boys who just returned on leave from the service.

In desperation Ralph decides to hock his bowling ball for $10-$15 dollars and buy Alice a nice gift, and on Christmas morning he cannot even wait to eat his eggs before exchanging presents. Alice wants Ralph to open his present first, and in the best tradition of O. Henry's "Gift of the Magi," Ralph's jaw drops when he sees Alice got him a bowling ball bag. Insisting Ralph get his bowling ball to make sure it will fit in the bag, Ralph stutters out in embarrassment he cannot, and then tells her the story about hocking the ball. Smiling at the big lug, Alice opens his present, an orange juice squeezer in the form of Napoleon, and tells him it's the best present she ever received. The obvious love that exists between Alice and Ralph is amplified by Ralph's closing monologue: "Christmas is about the best time of the whole year. You walk down the streets even weeks before Christmas comes, and there's lights hanging up... sometimes there's snow. And people hustling some place. But they don't hustle around Christmas time like they usually do. They're a little more friendly, especially when it gets close to Christmas time... boy, what a pleasure it is to think that you got some place to go to, and that the place you're going to has somebody in it that you really love... someone you're nuts about... Merry Christmas," and the two kiss for an extended time, ending the show before the final curtain call.

Happy (Lyn Osborn) decorates his tree in *Space Patrol.*

Space Patrol (June 1951-June 1952)
"Christmas Show"

A panoramic shot of a futuristic city is shown, snow falls, as the camera slowly zooms in. The narrator informs us, one thing has endured over the ages, the spirit of Christmas.

And thus this children's space age adventure series, occurring far in outer space in the distant future, features a science fiction Christmas episode, occurring at Space Patrol Headquarters, as "Jingle Bells" plays over the soundtrack to introduce this theme. Commander Happy (Lyn Osborn) is smiling, carrying Christmas presents and preparing to decorate headquarters. Major Robinson (Ken Mayer) has glum news, there will be no Christmas tree this year because Commander Buzz Corry (Ed Kemmer) is on a mission and won't be back in time. The Major announces he has duty today, and that Carol has other plans. Many men are away for the holiday, so even on Christmas Day the duty of Space Patrol comes first. There will be no celebration, no party. Happy appears heartbroken and sulks away.

Happy, remaining within listening distance, hears Carol sneak back in and say something to Major Robinson about not having any trouble getting rid of Commander Happy. Happy now feels totally rejected and leaves. He fails to hear Carol continue that Happy will be overjoyed when he finds out about the Christmas surprise that Buzz has planned for him: a visit from Happy's parents!

For the rest of the show, we are offered shots of Happy still carrying around the presents, wearing a sad face, looking as if he lost his best friends.

Meanwhile, aboard the spaceship, Bill (Charles Calvert) and Bess (Jean Inness) Osborn share childhood stories of their beloved son, Happy. As a child he had a make-believe spaceship in their backyard and made make-believe visits to Venus. Meanwhile, back at Space Headquarters, Happy is attempting to phone his parents on Earth, but in a surprising look ahead to today's technology, no one answers and he hears "If you wish to leave a message, it will be recorded."

Soon venturing out to investigate the nearby toy store, Happy looks at a statue of Santa Claus and he imagines he sees Santa shed a tear.

Meanwhile, back at Space Patrol, Buzz, the Osborns, Carol and the Major are all preparing for the festivities. Unfortunately, a running gag has everyone bring in their own Christmas tree. Mr. Osborn decides to take all the extra trees and stand outside and give them away to the needy. Unfortunately, he gets his numbers crossed and gives away *all* the trees.

Happy prepares to decorate a small Christmas tree in his quarters, ("Guess it will be just you and me") but he is soon surprised by all his friends and family who invade Happy's room. Besides being surprised, Happy's Christmas spirit is renewed. "Look at the stars out there glow!" Buzz responds, "Something special that makes the stars glow a little brighter at this time of year—the spirit of Christmas. And this makes the universe a truly wonderful place to live." The characters exchange Christmas presents as the credits come up.

Space Patrol, which covers the same ground as *Rocky Jones—Space Ranger* would a few years later, is an imaginative science fiction adventure series geared toward children, where the villains are totally nasty and the heroes are always better than good. However, the rapport between the cast of characters is here exploited in this fuzzy/warm episode, showing that even in the vastness of the universe, in the undefined future, that basic human and cultural traditions carry on and remind us of the bond that must exist between all human beings. For the children and for all the fans of the series, this Christmas tribute feels just right.

Ray Bolger in *Where's Raymond*.

Where's Raymond (Oct. 1953–June 1955)
"Christmas Spirit"

The immensely talented Ray Bolger (always to be remembered as the scarecrow from *The Wizard of Oz*) starred in a quirky television series during the early 1950s, and if this Christmas episode is any indication, the series was certainly ahead of its time.

The episode begins in a snowy park where kids pull sleds and throw snowballs, as Christmas music plays. Suddenly Ray appears pushing a grocery cart filled with presents. He goes on to speak to Mike the Cop (Ray Teal) who comments upon the nice holiday spirit. "It's a wonderful spirit. I think maybe people are tired of worrying, of being scared and of not feeling happy," the jolly Bolger comments. Suddenly a sweet young girl, Ginny (Frances Karath), appears calling out for Uncle Ray. She has presents, one for Mike and one for her uncle. Surprisingly, Mike the Cop also has a shopping cart filled with presents. The first thing Ray asks Ginny is how does the Christmas spirit today compare to Christmas spirit when she was younger. "I think it's better," she beams back. But Ray states that people were less troubled back in the old days. Ginny asks him to define trouble, and he does (quite cleverly, so let's credit the writers here): "Trouble—money, if you love it too much; people, if you won't give them a chance; your worries, if you spend more time on them than on laughing."

Ginny is in her wishing mood, and Ray says that today, filled with magic, he can grant any wishes. Ginny suggests... what if you were everyone in the world! "Think of all the taxes I'd have to pay!" Ginny counters with, "Think of all the presents you'd get."

So, for the next segment of the fantasy-becomes-reality show, Ray Bolger plays every character that Ginny encounters while going Christmas shopping. Even the jolly Santa Claus with whom she accidentally collides. Picking up a taxi, the driver (Ray again) asks her where she wishes to go, and she mentions the Toy Emporium. The driver states that toys there are stuck up—"dolls there won't walk unless they get a ride." Instead he suggests Fogarty's Toy Basement—"The zenith, the pinnacle!" The set for the toy store itself is magnificent, featuring huge blocks and over-sized toy cars. Most of the dolls and soldiers are played by human beings who spring magically to life and dance for Ginny. Ray, as himself, appears with a baby doll who does everything—"Except pay for her-self!" When Ginny asks how much the doll costs, Ray evades the answer by saying, "The only thing I can say is, she isn't worth it!" However, he does rec-ommend an old standby, a Raggedy Ann doll. When Ginny asks, does she cry, Bolger answers, "If she be-longed to the right girl, what would she have to cry about?" Ray then offers her the doll free, along with the $7.30 the doll itself saved. Ginny says to keep the money, to use it to offer something special to a little girl who couldn't afford a doll. Bolger's sly com-ments about the over-selling of Christmas and mer-chants pushing newer, better toys on children (when the simple toys are always the best) smacks more of the 1990s than the more innocent 1950s. But his truth hits the target subtly with a smile and sense of humor.

Back to reality, Ray tells Ginny he is glad he is not everybody in the world because he wouldn't have anybody to talk to—"and talk about dull conversa-tions... I could put people to sleep at five paces just doing half the conversation." Then Ray imagines him-self looking over the breakfast table at his wife, and the wife turns out to be Ray wearing a curly blonde wig.

Ray sees Ginny off to catch a train for Boston in an hour, so he joins in with the Mitchell Boys Choir who allow Ray to be their choir director as they sing in a horse-drawn sled that parades around town. The show ends as the chorus sings, with Ray joining in, "Merry Christmas to you!"

Seldom has a star been better utilized in early television (Jackie Gleason comes to mind immedi-ately) than Ray Bolger was here. Creating a fantasy world where anything can happen, Ray's character-izations and one-liners seem truly inspired. The mes-sage this Christmas episode echoes is one that is just as profound today as it was when first broadcast in 1953.

Amazing Stories (Sept. 1985-May 1987)
"Santa '85"

For a few short years during the 1980s, wunderkind director Steven Spielberg turned his talents toward television to produce (and sometimes write for and direct) an anthology series that focused on the world of fantasy, a series that attempted to tell fantastic, imaginative tales that sparked the imaginations of the viewers. As predicted, the show was a hit and miss affair, but generally it fell firmly on the side of at least the adequate. However, the Christmas "Santa '85" episode was inventive, on one hand a warm and fuzzy Christmas tale that featured Santa Claus, but on the other hand, a biting satire of a modern world that throws Santa in prison with drunken, wannabe Santas.

Up at the North Pole, Christmas Eve 1985, Santa and Mrs. Claus are preparing for hubby's round-the-world journey. "What a great night this is to be," states Santa. Mrs. Claus warns him the night will be great as long as he pulls himself from all the cookies or else "I'll have to put a stretch band on these pants!" Santa remembers names of specific children from specific cities and asks Mrs. Claus if he remembered to pack their presents. Santa exclaims, "I can't wait for all those eager faces waiting for Santa to pay them a visit." While Santa has his head in the clouds, Mrs. Claus has her feet squarely on solid ground. "The world has changed," she warms her husband. "People feel they have more important things to believe in than Christmas or Santa!" However, Santa takes pride in his on-going work: "Did I ever let them down! I did the job... I delivered!" Santa states his philosophy is, the more things change, the more they stay the same!

Back down in the world of reality, two parents and their son Bobby prepare for bed on Christmas Eve. "Of course there's a Santa Claus, Bobby!" his parents argue. However, Bobby claims his friends tell him differently. But since Bobby wishes to believe, ulti-mately, he will still believe.

Back at the North Pole Santa finally prepares to leave. "Watch out for 747's! You scared those con-trollers half to death!," Mrs. Claus cautions. Santa takes pride that they thought he was a U.F.O. (uni-dentified fat object).

Bobby, now nestled in his bed, does not see rein-deer shadows cross his bedroom window. Santa, land-ing on the home's rooftop, cannot manage to move away the metal screen embedded across the top of the chimney. Climbing to the ground, he finds the living room window unlocked and goes inside. Seeing cook-ies and milk on the mantel, Santa dives for the cook-ies. Unfortunately, he trips the sensor and off goes the house alarm, loud sirens and flashing lights terri-fying the poor Santa. The recorded, amplified mes-sage bellows "Intruder alert, illegal entry" over and over again. Bobby jumps out of his bedroom chest and shoots Santa in the forehead with a rubber dart and his parents attack Santa. Running for his life Santa escapes outside only to hear police cry, "Freeze, drop that bag and raise those mittens!" Winking quickly at little Bobby, Santa is herded into the back of a paddy wagon with several other scraggly Santas. Bobby tells his parents, "They better let him go," now believing that this is the real deal Santa. On the way to the station, the police ask Santa how many houses he has hit, and he calmly mutters, "40 million."

Arriving at the station the bitter Sheriff (Pat Hingle) does not cut Santa Claus any slack. When Santa asks the Sheriff where is his holiday spirit, the Sheriff blurts out, "Right up there with armed robbery, vagrancy and drunk driving." Speaking further to the old spoil-sport, Santa learns that, as a child, the Sheriff wrote a nine-page letter to Santa, asking to receive a Buck Rogers Ray Gun. It never arrived. "Sometimes even Santa makes mistakes," the old elf admits. But the Sheriff has never recovered.

As they throw Santa into a cell with other drunken Santas, little Bobby finds and leads Santa's reindeer to the back of the prison cell and he ties a rope around the prison window bars. Just as the Sheriff checks in on his prisoners, the reindeer charge and take out half of the wall, freeing Santa, who quickly climbs aboard the sleigh, several police cars in hot pursuit. However, just at the right moment, the sleigh takes off into space sailing over the rooftops of the community. Lingering momentarily above the Sheriff's squad car, a lone Christmas present drops from above, of course

Art Carney in *Twilight Zone*'s "Night of the Meek."

containing the never-received Buck Rogers Ray Gun, causing the crusty old Sheriff to smile. The card on top says, "To Horace, With Love."

Proudly, in a world of disbelief, bitterness and disappointment, in communities where innocent citizens cannot go to sleep without setting overpowering alarm systems, in a world where even Santa Claus can be the guise of the criminal element, in such a cold and heartless world Santa Claus can still cut the mustard and bring back a sense of the child to even the most heartless and bitter adult. As this *Amazing Stories* demonstrates, the spirit of Santa still weaves his magic spell all over the world.

Twilight Zone (April 1956-July 1959)
"Night of the Meek"

For me, of all the Christmas episodes shown on network television, "Night of the Meek," from the original *Twilight Zone* series (it was remade during the 1980s when the series was briefly resurrected), is my favorite. The quality of the acting (especially the career-defining performance by Art Carney) and of the writing (the words of Rod Serling have never felt more profound) propel "Night of the Meek" into one of television's finest moments.

The story opens in a large department store, before a huge banner proclaiming "North Pole," the lo-

cale of Santa Claus' throne. The floor manager, Mr. Dundee (John Fiedler), makes apologies to the swarming crowd that the missing Santa Claus will be back by six.

However Henry Corwin (Art Carney), sloppily dressed in his Santa Claus outfit, is sprawled over the bar in a nearby tavern, drinking way too much, even trying to sneak a drink when the bartender is busy on the phone. "I'll break both arms up to the shoulder blades," the bartender threatens, telling the person on the phone, "No, it's just Santa Claus trying to heist the joint!"

Venturing outside into snow-covered urban city streets, Corwin is recognized by the neighborhood children who smile, wave and run up to him, demanding their presents. Trying to balance himself by holding onto a lamppost, Corwin falls, the children swooping around him. "Please, Santa, I want a carriage and a dolly," a young girl asks. Another child, a boy, states, "I want a gun," and they ramble on. Finally, "And please Santa Claus, a job for my daddy," can be heard. All that the drunken Corwin can do is hug the children and cry.

Corwin, now returning to the store, is playing with the toy trains, obviously drunk, when the irate Mr. Dundee tells the employee that he is over an hour late. "If you could keep from disillusioning a lot of kids that not only *isn't* there a Santa Claus but *this* one in *this* store happens to be a wino who would be more at home playing Rudolph the Red-Nosed Reindeer..." Corwin stumbles up to his Santa throne and has a child climb up on his lap. After the child leaves, Santa falls flat on his face as the amazed child yells, "Look Ma, Santa Claus is loaded!" When the shocked mother complains to Mr. Dundee about hiring Santas from the gutter, that she will never shop here again, Dundee has no choice but to fire Corwin. The disgraced man apologizes for his drunkenness, "I could either drink or I could weep, and drinking is so much more subtle." But he states he was not rude to the woman and suddenly the pathetic man's dignity begins to peek through. "As far as that woman, someone should remind her that Christmas is more than barging up and down department store aisles and pushing people out of the way... Christmas is richer, finer than that. It should come with patience, charity, love, compassion. That's what I would have told her." He carries on his impassioned message: "I am an aging, purposeless relic of another time and I live in a dirty rooming house on a street with hungry kids and shabby people where the only thing that comes down the chimney on Christmas Eve is more poverty." When Corwin drinks he can almost imagine he is actually Santa Claus distributing presents to all the neighborhood children. "I could save some of the hopeless and dreamless ones... for one Christmas I'd like to see the meek inherit the Earth. That's why I drink... weep." Perhaps derelicts in real life don't speak as eloquently as Mr. Corwin speaks, but Rod Serling's words ring true.

Returning to walking the streets, still dressed as Santa Claus, Corwin hears strange Christmas tinkling and follows the music to an abandoned back alley lined with trash cans and screeching cats. Soon, as he turns, he eyes a large bag with presents overflowing, slings it over his back, and runs out to the main streets yelling for kids and everybody to gather round. Then he assumes his real-life role as benevolent Santa, giving out presents to order from anyone who asks.

At the Dulancey Mission House, Sister Florence (Meg Wyllie) is leading the despondent people in song, as an old man (Burt Mustin) announces that Santa Claus is coming down the street, giving out presents to everyone. The old man, upon Santa's arrival, asks for a pipe and smoking jacket and gets exactly what he asks. "I'm just as much in the dark as anyone else... as long as it's putting out, I'm putting in," Corwin crows. However, the fetched-for policeman is not so festive, asking if Corwin has receipts for all this merchandise. The policeman than asks Sister Florence to collect all the stolen merchandise as Corwin is led off. Mr. Dundee, arriving at the police station to identify the missing merchandise, hopes that Corwin will get 10 years in prison. However, when Dundee

reaches inside the bag, all he pulls out is garbage and a cat. Dundee, to prove Corwin wrong, asks for a bottle of cherry brandy, vintage 1903, and Santa pulls it out immediately, disappearing with his bag off into the night.

After giving out the reminder of the presents, Corwin is greeted in the streets by the old man with the pipe and smoking jacket who asks, "Nothing for you?" Corwin smiles, "You know, I can't think of anything I want... I wanted to be the biggest gift-giver of all time. In a way, I think I had that tonight." His wish is to be able to do this every year.

Corwin, out of curiosity, again returns to the back alley when he originally found the bag of never-ending presents, and there waiting is a sleigh with reindeer and an elf. "We've been waiting quite a long time for you, Santa Claus. We have a year of hard work to get ready for next Christmas."

As the policeman and Dundee, now staggering drunk himself, wander off down the street and look overhead, they are dumfounded as they see Corwin fly overhead. Dundee mutters, "We'll thank God for miracles."

While the last sequence showing the sleigh and reindeer with the over-anxious elf does strain credibility, this becomes the only false moment in an otherwise emotionally gripping TV half-hour. Never has the spirit of yearning to give to others been this powerfully portrayed, and Art Carney's dignity, even when embarrassingly intoxicated, is never less than poignant. With all the human flaws and miseries surrounding the plight of the poor in the city, the Christmas spirit still contains the power to heal. And "Night of the Meek" manages to touch all our hearts.—GJS

Shirley Temple with her children Lori, Susan and Charles in *Shirley Temple's Storybook* broadcast December 21, 1959.

Selected Bibliography

Bergreen, Laurence: *As Thousands Cheer: The Life of Irving Berlin*, Penguin Books, New York, 1990

Bona, Damien and Wiley, Mason: *Inside Oscar*, Ballantine Books, New York, 1993

Brooks, Tim and Marsh, Earle: *The Complete Directory to Prime Time Network TV Shows 1946–Present*, Ballentine Books, New York, 1988

Connors, Martin and Furtaw, Julia: *VideoHound's Golden Movie Retriever*, Visible Ink, Detroit, MI, 1994

Edwards, Anne: *Judy Garland*, Simon and Schuster, New York, 1974

Eyman, Scott: *Ernst Lubitsch: Laughter in Paradise*, Simon and Schuster, New York, 1993

Green, Stanley: *Hollywood Musicals Year by Year*, Hal Leonard Publishing, Milwaukee, WI, 1990

Encyclopedia of the Musical Theatre, Da Capo Press, New York, 1980

Miller, Tice L. and Wilmeth, Don B.: *American Theatre*, Cambridge University Press, 1993

Minnelli, Vincente with Arce, Hector: *I Remember it Well*, Doubleday, New York, 1974

Ragan, David: *Who's Who in Hollywood*, Facts on File, New York, 1992

Magazines

Entertainment Weekly, Fall Movie Preview, August 21-28, 1998

Chute, David. "Dante's Inferno" in *Film Comment* (May/June 1984), 22-7.

Dante, Joe. "Joe Dante's Guilty Pleasures" in *Film Comment* (May/June 1983), 56-9;

Jameson, Fredric. "Postmodernism and Consumer Society" in *The Anti-Aesthetic: Essays in Postmodern Culture*. Ed. Hal Foster. Port Townsend, WA: Bay Press, 111-25.

Reviews: "Creature Comforts and Discomforts" by Richard Corliss, in *Time* (4 June 1984), 64-6; "Dante's 'Gremlins' Mixes Humor and Horror" by David Sterritt, in *Christian Science Monitor* (7 June 1984), 27-8; "Gremlins and Ghosts Attack Funny Bone" by Sheila Benson, in *Los Angeles Times* (8 June 1984), Calendar, 1, 14; "Fear of Boring" by David Denby, in *New York* (18 June 1984), 87-8; "*Midnight Marquee* Cinema Review: *Gremlins*" by Gary J. Svehla, in *Midnight Marquee* 33 (Fall 1984), 29; "Temple of Gremlins" by Armond White, in *Films in Review* 35 (August/September 1984), 411-3; "*Gremlins*" in *Magill's Cinema Annual: 1985*. Ed. Frank N. Magill. Englewood Cliffs, NJ: Salem Press, 230-5.

Internet Sources

The Motion Picture Guide (TV Guide.com)

Internet Movie Database

Authors

(Even though they are now grown-up,
they still believe in Santa and the Christmas spirit)

Cindy Ruth Collins

Leonard J. Kohl

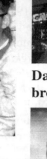

David H. Smith (right) and brother Carl

Merry Christmas Happy New Year

Don G. Smith

Robert A. Crick

Bob Madison

Joe and Jeff Indusi

Lorne Marshall

John Stell

Gary J. Svehla and Jet

Steve Kronenberg

Michael H. Price

Susan Svehla

316

Authors

Cindy Ruth Collins lives in Arlington, Virginia with her husband Brian Smith and their two cats. A writer and a college teacher, she contributes to *Midnight Marquee* magazine... and might have time to contribute elsewhere if Midnight Marquee Press weren't keeping her so swamped writing book chapters and a book of her own (on Jack the Ripper movies). Though she is Greek Orthodox, Cindy celebrates Christmas on December 25, not the more traditional January 7 ("December 25" in Caesar's day).

Robert A. Crick is a frequent contributor to Midnight Marquee Press whose work has appeared in *Cinematic Hauntings, Guilty Pleasures of the Horror Film* and *We Belong Dead: Frankenstein on Film.* He teaches high school English and journalism in Russellville, Kentucky.

Joe Indusi is a New York–based filmmaker whose interest in movies ranges from Keaton to Corman. When he's not banging out screenplays, he's usually watching (and loving) creaky old movies... the badder the better. He's also on a first name basis with Rip Taylor.

Leonard J. Kohl is a contributor to *Filmfax* and has just completed a book on the sinister serials of Boris Karloff, Bela Lugosi and Lon Chaney, Jr. for Midnight Marquee Press. He would like to thank Ed George, who proofread, and his sister-in-law, Laurie Axium Kohl, for editing suggestions.

Steve Kronenberg practices law in Florida and is co-publisher of and contributor to *Monsters from the Vault.* He also contributed to *Son of Guilty Pleasures of the Horror Film* from Midnight Marquee Press. He has never outgrown Christmas and it's still his favorite time of year.

Bob Madison is the editor of *Dracula: The First Hundred Years,* published by Midnight Marquee Press. Madison scripted an adaptation of *The Lost World* for *The Dinosaur Times,* and he is a regular contributor to such publications as *Cult Movies, Outré, Wonder,* and *Cartoonist Profiles.* His next book is *Monsters and Their Makers* published by Enslow. Bob Madison lives in New York City.

Lorne Marshall is a contributor to many film magazines including *Videooze* and *Midnight Marquee.* He is an authority on horror films and has an impressive collection of rare and obscure titles. Lorne is currently working on a book on humanism and its relation to horror films.

Michael H. Price, longtime motion-picture and jazz critic with the Fort Worth *Star-Telegram* and The New York Times News Service, is founding president of the Fort Worth Film Festival. Price's books, many of them in collaboration with the Hollywood-based filmmaker/historian George E. Turner, include the comics anthology *Southern-Fried Homicide* (Shel-Tone Publ./Cremo Studios; 1998) and the groundbreaking movie encyclopedia *Forgotten Horrors*—due soon in a revised and expanded edition from Midnight Marquee Press.

David H. Smith works for a newspaper in Southern Florida. He, wife Lynn and son Colin enjoy watching *Santa Claus Conquers the Martians* together during the holidays. A regular contributor to Midnight Marquee Press, David's work has appeared in *Son of Guilty Pleasures of the Horror Film* and *We Belong Dead: Frankenstein on Film,* as well as many other MidMar titles.

Don G. Smith is an associate professor in history, sociology and philosophy of education at Eastern Illinois University. He is the author of *Lon Chaney, Jr.* and *The Poe Cinema* from McFarland and a contributor to *Midnight Marquee.* He is currently working on a *The Cinema of H.G. Wells.*

John Stell, a CPA from Baltimore, has just seen his first book, *Psychos, Sickos and Sequels: Horror Films of the 1980s,* published. He is a frequent contributor to *Monsters from the Vault* and *Midnight Marquee.*

Gary J. Svehla began his publishing empire at the ripe old age of 13 when, inspired by *Famous Monsters of Filmland,* he began his first magazine, *Gore Creatures.* That magazine, now titled *Midnight Marquee,* is still going strong 35 years later. Gary teaches high school English in Baltimore and is looking forward to retirement so he can concentrate exclusively on Midnight Marquee Press. He has written for many magazines and books including the *Midnight Marquee Actors Series,* which featured books on Bela Lugosi, Boris Karloff and Lon Chaney, Jr. His interest has recently expanded from horror films to include film noir.

Susan Svehla has always loved film, especially musicals and light-hearted romances. To date this is her favorite book published by Midnight Marquee Press. She has contributed to the *Midnight Marquee Actors Series* as well as *Guilty Pleasures of the Horror Film.* She has also edited many of the volumes that have been published by the press in addition to designing the covers. Susan has also run FANEX, a Baltimore-based film convention, for the past 12 years.

Index